JOURNEY TO CUBEVILLE

A DILBERT™ BOOK

BY **SCOTT ADAMS**

B⧓XTREE

First published 1998 by Andrews and McMeel Publishing, Kansas City

First published in Great Britain 1998 by Boxtree
an imprint of Macmillan Publishers Ltd
25 Eccleston Place London SW1W 9NF
and Basingstoke

Associated companies throughout the world

ISBN 0 7522 2384 4

www.dilbert.com

1 3 5 7 9 8 6 4 2

A CIP catalogue record for this book is available from
the British Library.

Printed by The Bath Press

For Pam "Ah likes to read" Okasaki

Introduction

Rather than fill this page with a frivolous book introduction that you would soon forget, I thought it would be better to answer all of your questions about the nature of the universe. It's more work for me, but you're worth it. Here are the questions I get most often:

Q: I'm a student studying to be an engineer. Is it my fate to sit in a cubicle?

A: No, it's unlikely that you'll be sitting. Recent studies show that if employees are piled like firewood, up to forty can be stored in one cubicle. It's not an ideal arrangement, but you'll get used to it. One thing they don't teach you in school is that you can get used to anything if someone forces you.

Q: Do praying mantises burp?

A: Yes, if they run with their mouths open. That causes huge air pockets to form in their thoraxes, not to mention their boraxes and their pickaxes. That air has to go someplace, otherwise the praying mantis becomes bigger and bigger until eventually it buys dark glasses and becomes Howard Stern. But that only happened once.

Q: Is the planet controlled by a secret society of highly intelligent people?

A: No, we don't like to think of ourselves as a "society." It's more of a cabal. By the way, what was your home address? We'd like to send you something.

Q: Where's the rest of the moon when it's not a full moon?

A: When they landed on the moon in 1969, the astronauts shoveled most of the moon's surface into special containers and took it home. They would have taken the whole thing, but they needed to keep some dirt there to hold the flag up. If you see something that looks like a full moon, that's either a false memory or someone playing a practical joke on you.

I hope that answers all of your questions. If I missed anything, I'll handle it in the next book. In the meantime, if you would like to join the cabal of highly intelligent people, it also goes by the name of Dogbert's New Ruling Class (DNRC). After Dogbert conquers the planet, he'll make everyone outside the DNRC our personal servants. If you're tired of getting up to fetch your own beverages, this is the solution for you. To become a member, all you need to do is put your name on the list to receive the totally free DNRC newsletter, which is published according to the rigorous "whenever I feel like it" schedule. That's about three or four times a year.

To subscribe, send e-mail to listserv@listserv.unitedmedia.com in the following format:

subject: newsletter
message: Subscribe Dilbert_News Firstname Lastname

Don't include any other information—your e-mail address will be picked up automatically.

If the automatic method doesn't work for you, you can also subscribe by writing to scottadams@aol.com or via snail mail:

Dilbert Mailing List
United Media
200 Madison Avenue
New York, NY 10016

These methods are much slower than the automatic method so please be patient.

S.Adams

Scott Adams

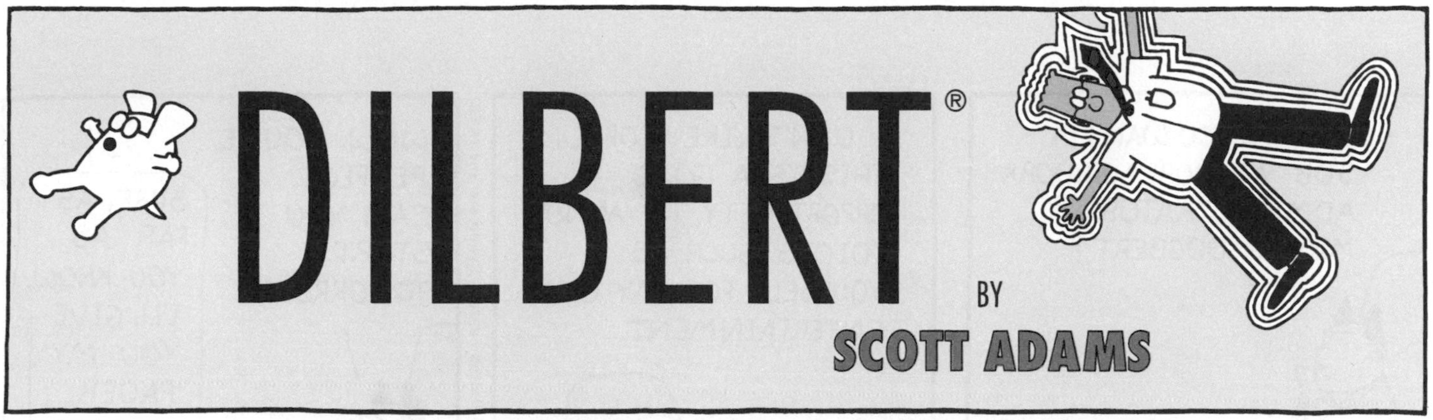
DILBERT®
BY
SCOTT ADAMS

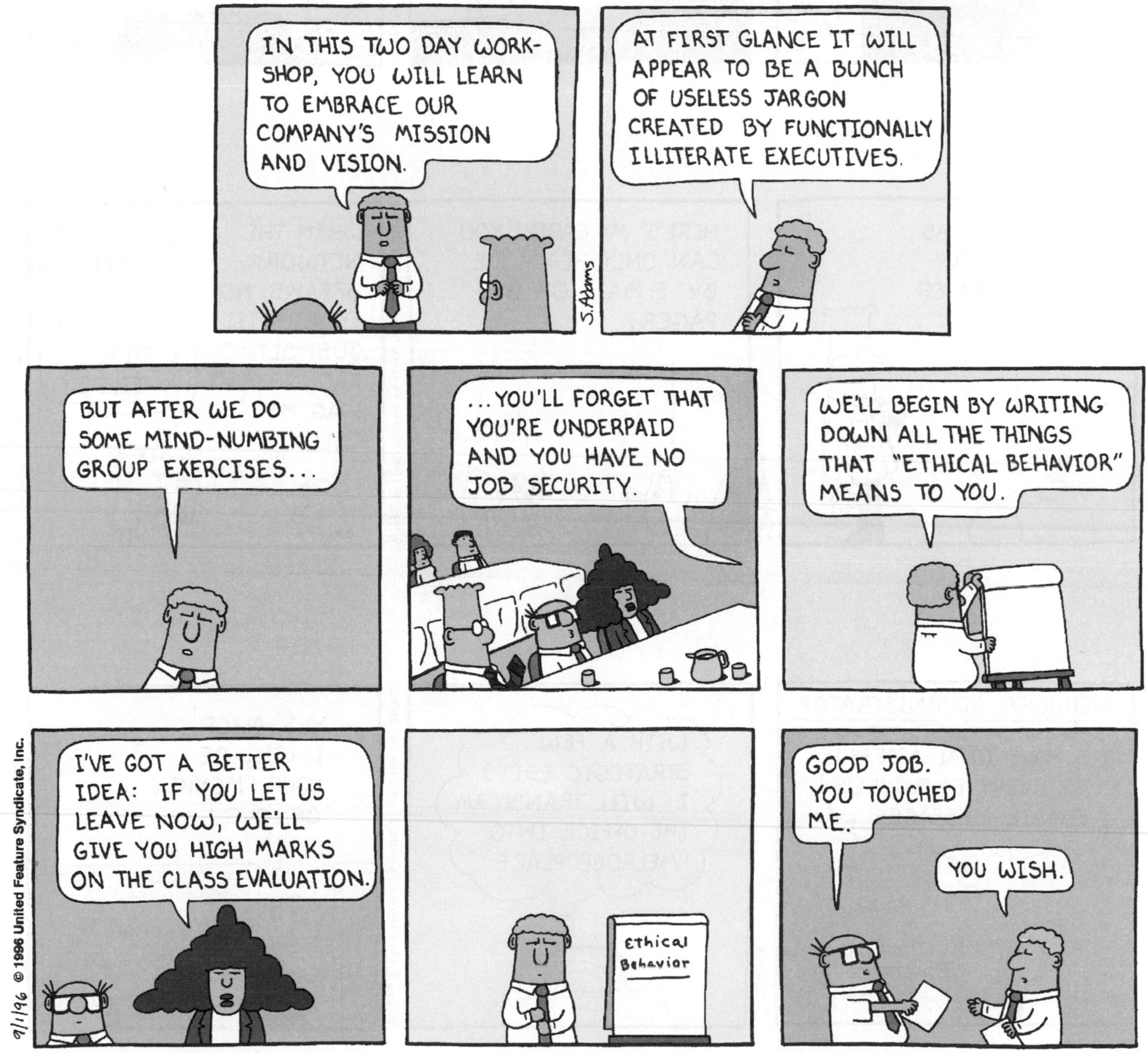
IN THIS TWO DAY WORK-SHOP, YOU WILL LEARN TO EMBRACE OUR COMPANY'S MISSION AND VISION.
S. Adams
AT FIRST GLANCE IT WILL APPEAR TO BE A BUNCH OF USELESS JARGON CREATED BY FUNCTIONALLY ILLITERATE EXECUTIVES.
BUT AFTER WE DO SOME MIND-NUMBING GROUP EXERCISES...
...YOU'LL FORGET THAT YOU'RE UNDERPAID AND YOU HAVE NO JOB SECURITY.
WE'LL BEGIN BY WRITING DOWN ALL THE THINGS THAT "ETHICAL BEHAVIOR" MEANS TO YOU.
I'VE GOT A BETTER IDEA: IF YOU LET US LEAVE NOW, WE'LL GIVE YOU HIGH MARKS ON THE CLASS EVALUATION.
Ethical Behavior
GOOD JOB. YOU TOUCHED ME.
YOU WISH.
9/1/96 © 1996 United Feature Syndicate, Inc.

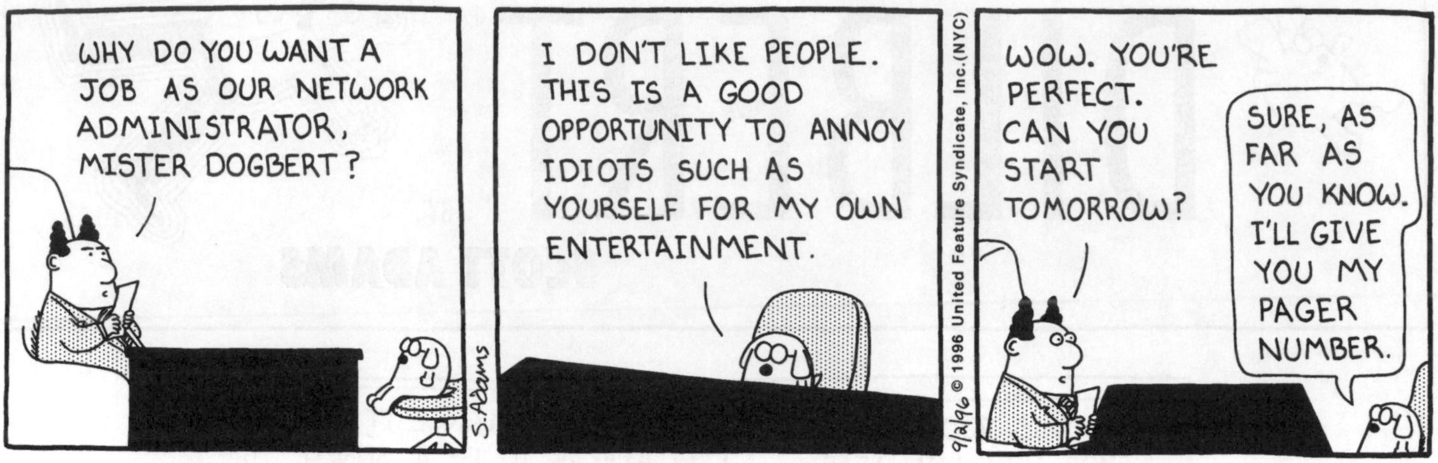
WHY DO YOU WANT A JOB AS OUR NETWORK ADMINISTRATOR, MISTER DOGBERT?
S. Adams
I DON'T LIKE PEOPLE. THIS IS A GOOD OPPORTUNITY TO ANNOY IDIOTS SUCH AS YOURSELF FOR MY OWN ENTERTAINMENT.
9/2/96 © 1996 United Feature Syndicate, Inc.(NYC)
WOW. YOU'RE PERFECT. CAN YOU START TOMORROW?
SURE, AS FAR AS YOU KNOW. I'LL GIVE YOU MY PAGER NUMBER.

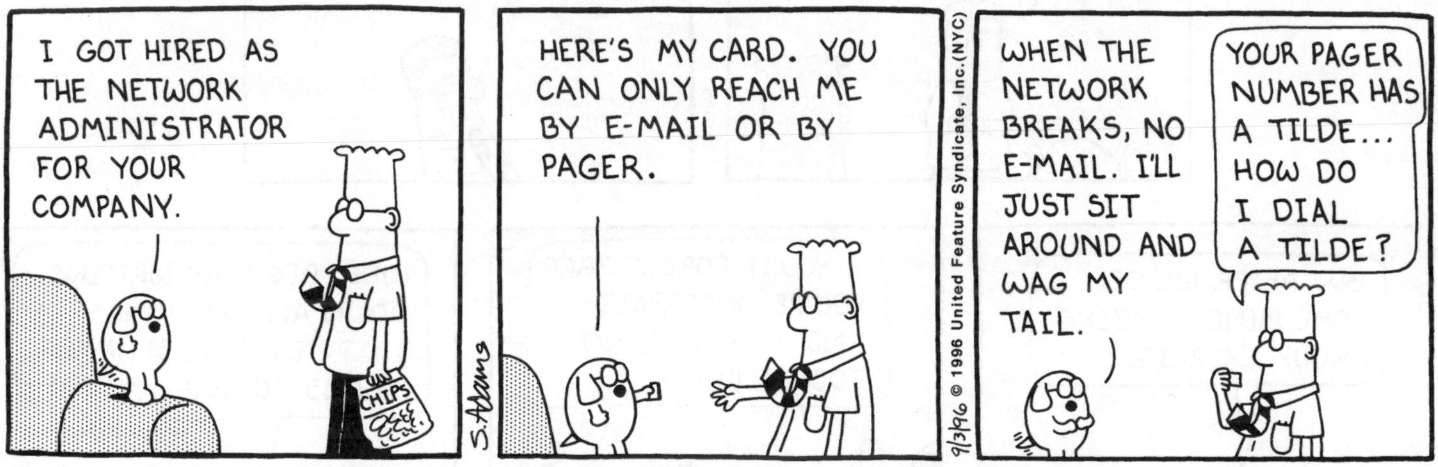
I GOT HIRED AS THE NETWORK ADMINISTRATOR FOR YOUR COMPANY.
CHIPS
S. Adams
HERE'S MY CARD. YOU CAN ONLY REACH ME BY E-MAIL OR BY PAGER.
9/3/96 © 1996 United Feature Syndicate, Inc.(NYC)
WHEN THE NETWORK BREAKS, NO E-MAIL. I'LL JUST SIT AROUND AND WAG MY TAIL.
YOUR PAGER NUMBER HAS A TILDE... HOW DO I DIAL A TILDE?

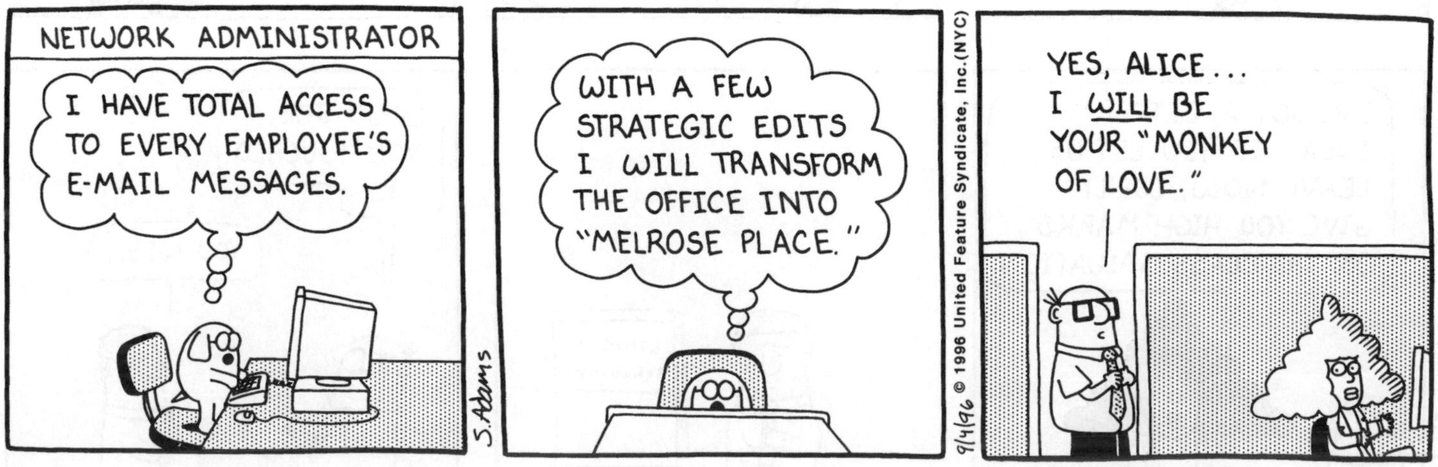
NETWORK ADMINISTRATOR
I HAVE TOTAL ACCESS TO EVERY EMPLOYEE'S E-MAIL MESSAGES.
S. Adams
WITH A FEW STRATEGIC EDITS I WILL TRANSFORM THE OFFICE INTO "MELROSE PLACE."
9/4/96 © 1996 United Feature Syndicate, Inc.(NYC)
YES, ALICE... I WILL BE YOUR "MONKEY OF LOVE."

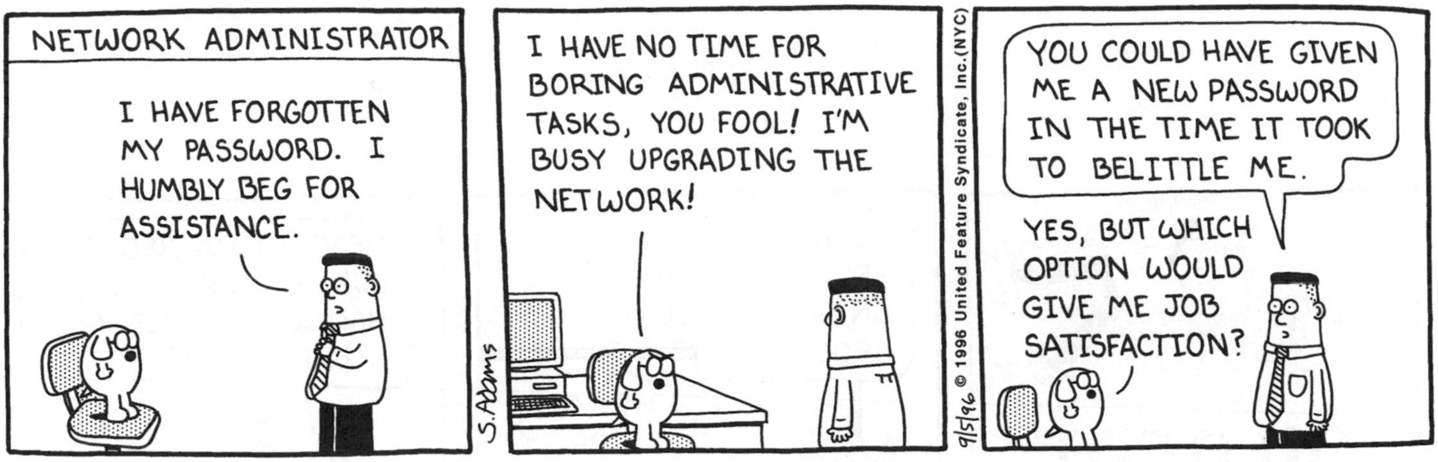
NETWORK ADMINISTRATOR
I HAVE FORGOTTEN MY PASSWORD. I HUMBLY BEG FOR ASSISTANCE.
I HAVE NO TIME FOR BORING ADMINISTRATIVE TASKS, YOU FOOL! I'M BUSY UPGRADING THE NETWORK!
S. Adams
9/5/96 © 1996 United Feature Syndicate, Inc.(NYC)
YOU COULD HAVE GIVEN ME A NEW PASSWORD IN THE TIME IT TOOK TO BELITTLE ME.
YES, BUT WHICH OPTION WOULD GIVE ME JOB SATISFACTION?

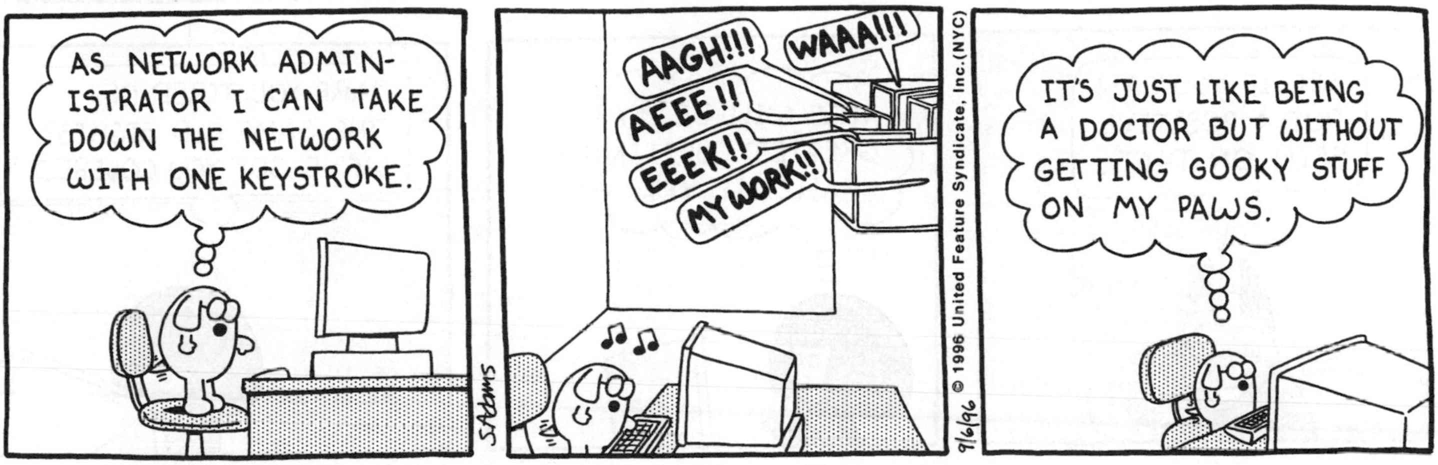
AS NETWORK ADMINISTRATOR I CAN TAKE DOWN THE NETWORK WITH ONE KEYSTROKE.
AAGH!!!
WAAA!!!
AEEE!!
EEEK!!
MY WORK!!
S. Adams
9/6/96 © 1996 United Feature Syndicate, Inc.(NYC)
IT'S JUST LIKE BEING A DOCTOR BUT WITHOUT GETTING GOOKY STUFF ON MY PAWS.

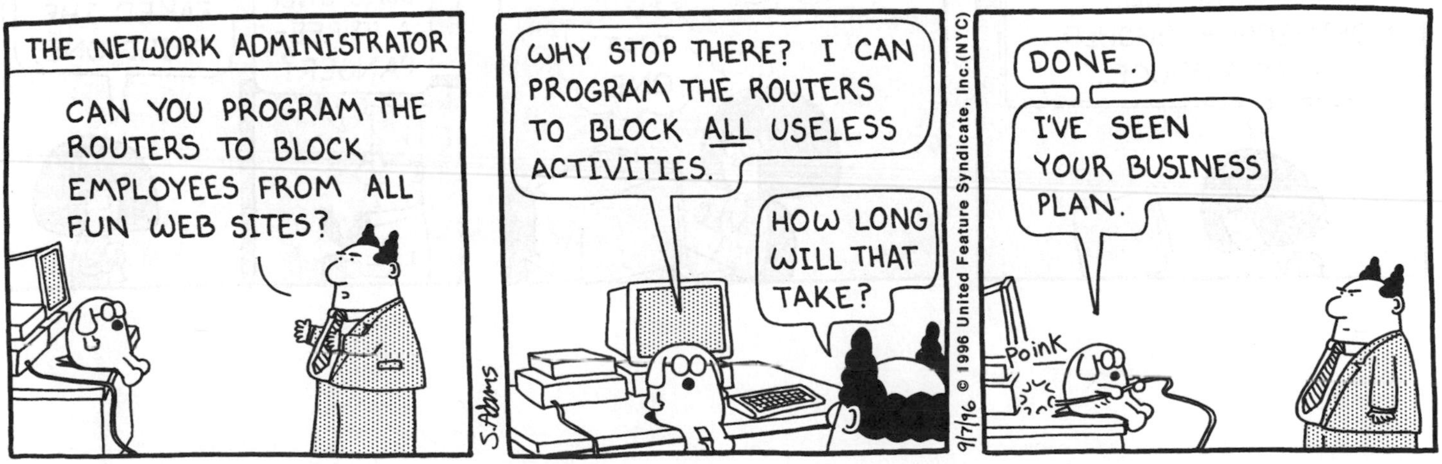
THE NETWORK ADMINISTRATOR
CAN YOU PROGRAM THE ROUTERS TO BLOCK EMPLOYEES FROM ALL FUN WEB SITES?
WHY STOP THERE? I CAN PROGRAM THE ROUTERS TO BLOCK ALL USELESS ACTIVITIES.
HOW LONG WILL THAT TAKE?
S. Adams
9/7/96 © 1996 United Feature Syndicate, Inc.(NYC)
DONE.
I'VE SEEN YOUR BUSINESS PLAN.
Poink

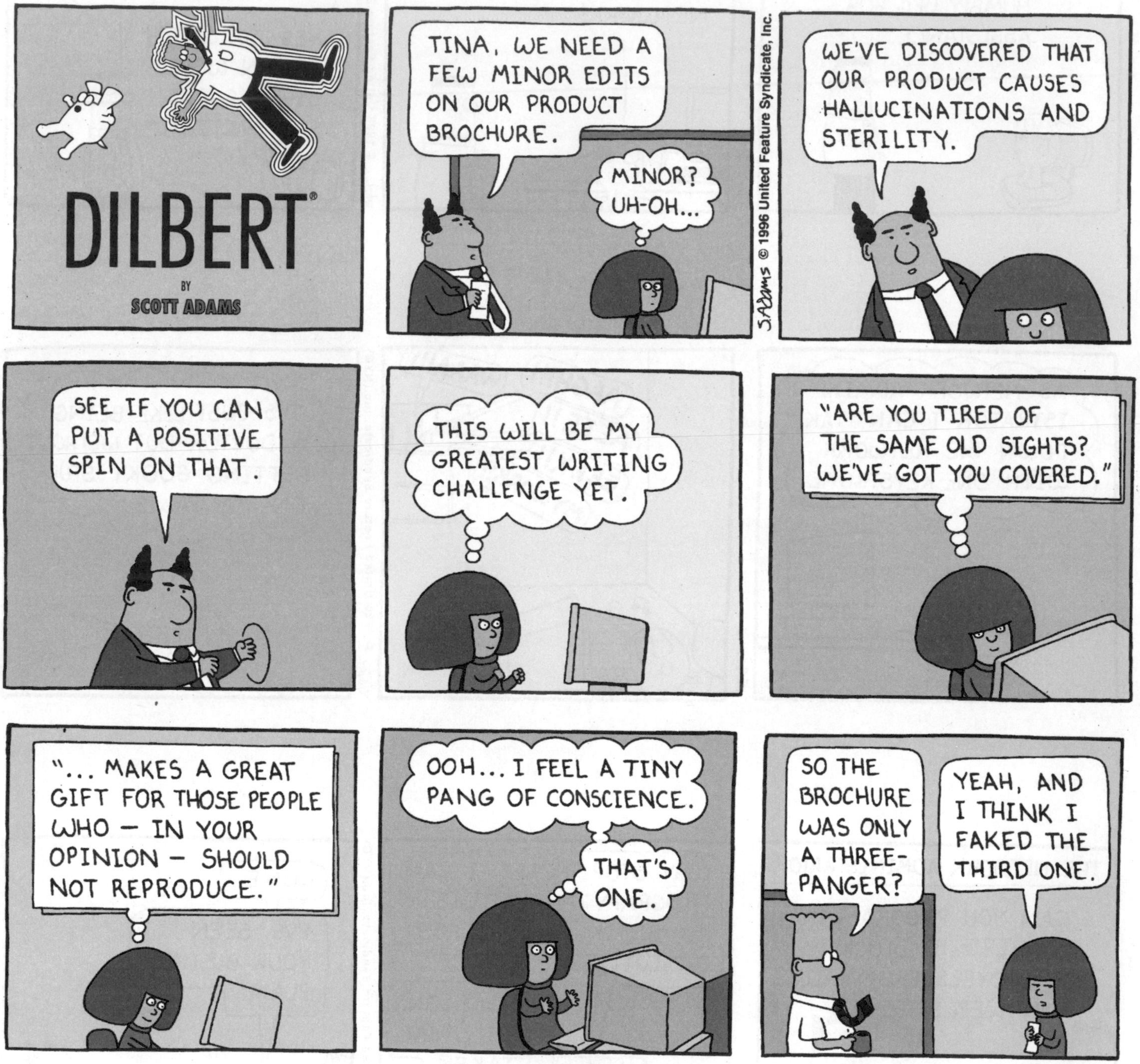
DILBERT®
BY
SCOTT ADAMS
TINA, WE NEED A FEW MINOR EDITS ON OUR PRODUCT BROCHURE.
MINOR? UH-OH...
S. Adams © 1996 United Feature Syndicate, Inc.
WE'VE DISCOVERED THAT OUR PRODUCT CAUSES HALLUCINATIONS AND STERILITY.
SEE IF YOU CAN PUT A POSITIVE SPIN ON THAT.
THIS WILL BE MY GREATEST WRITING CHALLENGE YET.
"ARE YOU TIRED OF THE SAME OLD SIGHTS? WE'VE GOT YOU COVERED."
"... MAKES A GREAT GIFT FOR THOSE PEOPLE WHO — IN YOUR OPINION — SHOULD NOT REPRODUCE."
OOH... I FEEL A TINY PANG OF CONSCIENCE.
THAT'S ONE.
SO THE BROCHURE WAS ONLY A THREE-PANGER?
YEAH, AND I THINK I FAKED THE THIRD ONE.

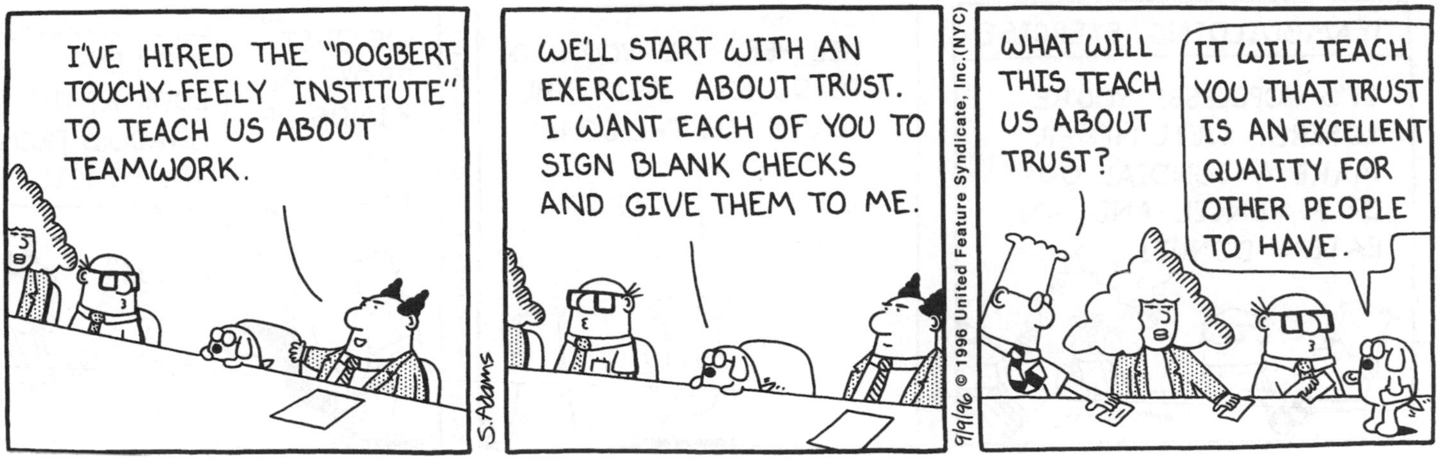
I'VE HIRED THE "DOGBERT TOUCHY-FEELY INSTITUTE" TO TEACH US ABOUT TEAMWORK.
WE'LL START WITH AN EXERCISE ABOUT TRUST. I WANT EACH OF YOU TO SIGN BLANK CHECKS AND GIVE THEM TO ME.
WHAT WILL THIS TEACH US ABOUT TRUST?
IT WILL TEACH YOU THAT TRUST IS AN EXCELLENT QUALITY FOR OTHER PEOPLE TO HAVE.
S. Adams
9/9/96 © 1996 United Feature Syndicate, Inc.(NYC)

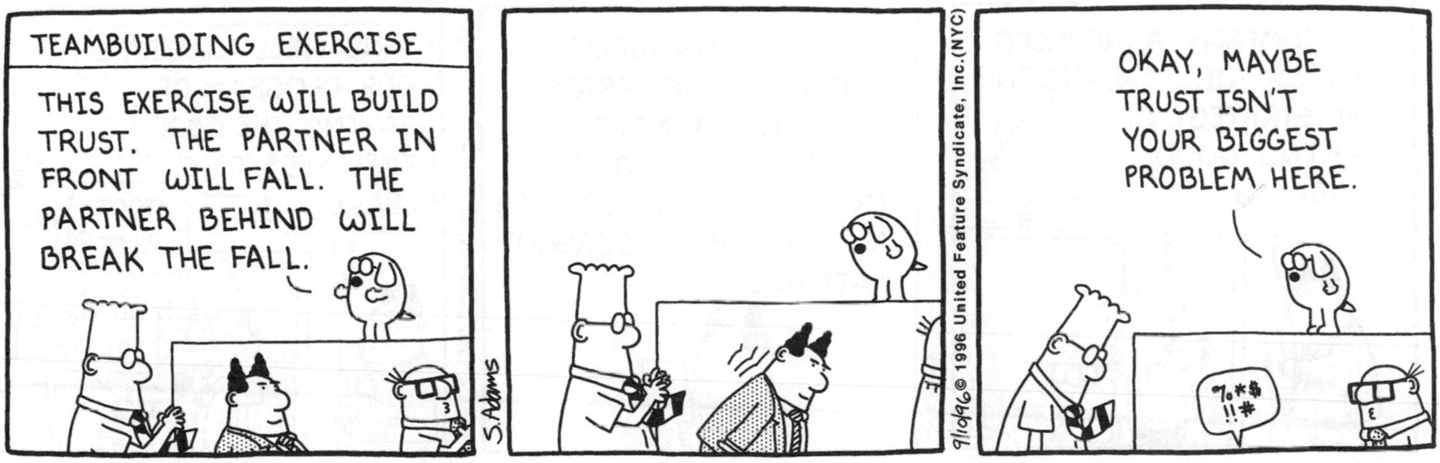
TEAMBUILDING EXERCISE
THIS EXERCISE WILL BUILD TRUST. THE PARTNER IN FRONT WILL FALL. THE PARTNER BEHIND WILL BREAK THE FALL.
OKAY, MAYBE TRUST ISN'T YOUR BIGGEST PROBLEM HERE.
%*$!!#
S. Adams
9/10/96 © 1996 United Feature Syndicate, Inc.(NYC)

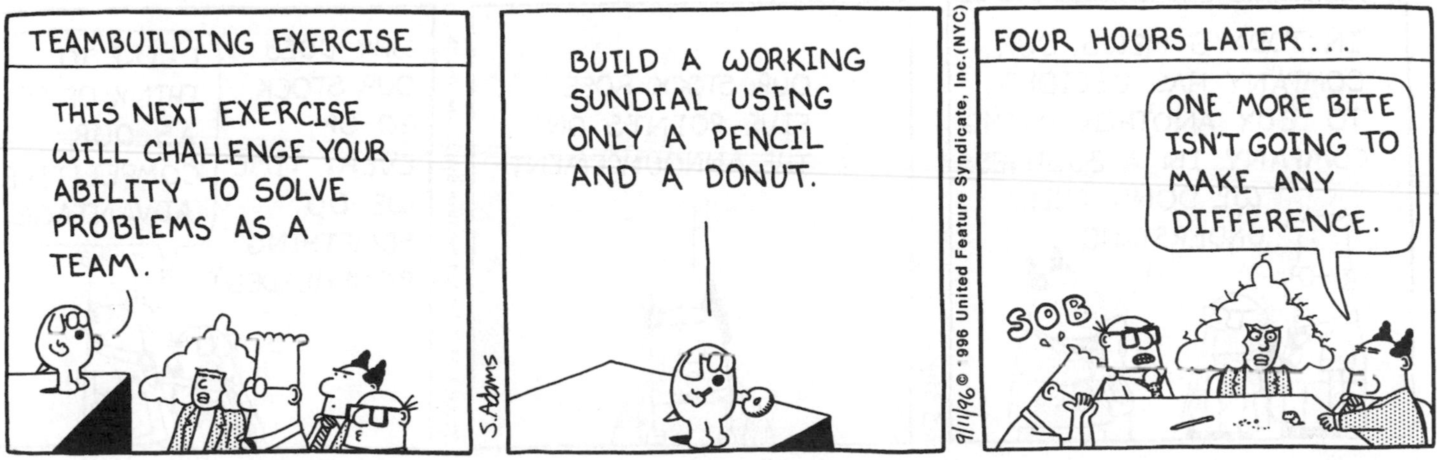
TEAMBUILDING EXERCISE
THIS NEXT EXERCISE WILL CHALLENGE YOUR ABILITY TO SOLVE PROBLEMS AS A TEAM.
BUILD A WORKING SUNDIAL USING ONLY A PENCIL AND A DONUT.
FOUR HOURS LATER...
SOB
ONE MORE BITE ISN'T GOING TO MAKE ANY DIFFERENCE.
S. Adams
9/11/96 © 1996 United Feature Syndicate, Inc.(NYC)

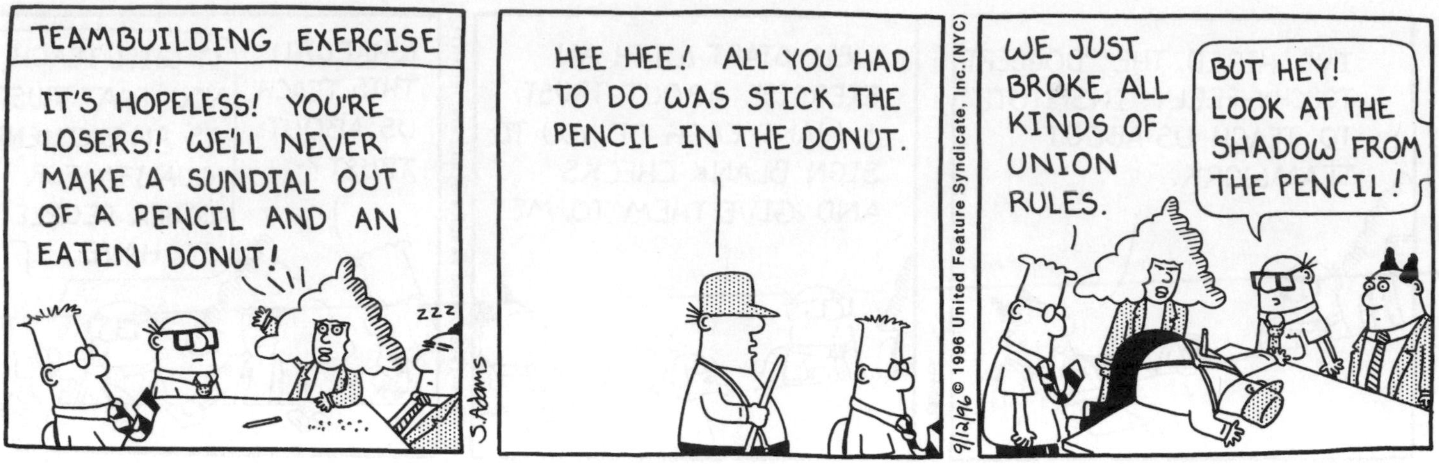
TEAMBUILDING EXERCISE
IT'S HOPELESS! YOU'RE LOSERS! WE'LL NEVER MAKE A SUNDIAL OUT OF A PENCIL AND AN EATEN DONUT!
ZZZ
S. Adams
HEE HEE! ALL YOU HAD TO DO WAS STICK THE PENCIL IN THE DONUT.
9/12/96 © 1996 United Feature Syndicate, Inc.(NYC)
WE JUST BROKE ALL KINDS OF UNION RULES.
BUT HEY! LOOK AT THE SHADOW FROM THE PENCIL!

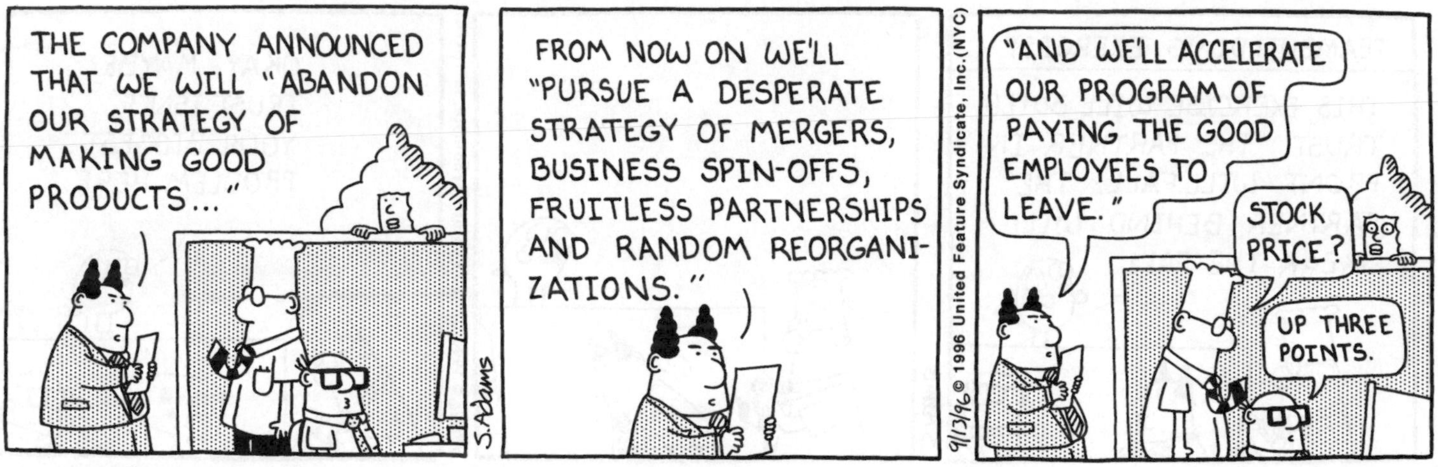
THE COMPANY ANNOUNCED THAT WE WILL "ABANDON OUR STRATEGY OF MAKING GOOD PRODUCTS..."
S. Adams
FROM NOW ON WE'LL "PURSUE A DESPERATE STRATEGY OF MERGERS, BUSINESS SPIN-OFFS, FRUITLESS PARTNERSHIPS AND RANDOM REORGANIZATIONS."
9/13/96 © 1996 United Feature Syndicate, Inc.(NYC)
"AND WE'LL ACCELERATE OUR PROGRAM OF PAYING THE GOOD EMPLOYEES TO LEAVE."
STOCK PRICE?
UP THREE POINTS.

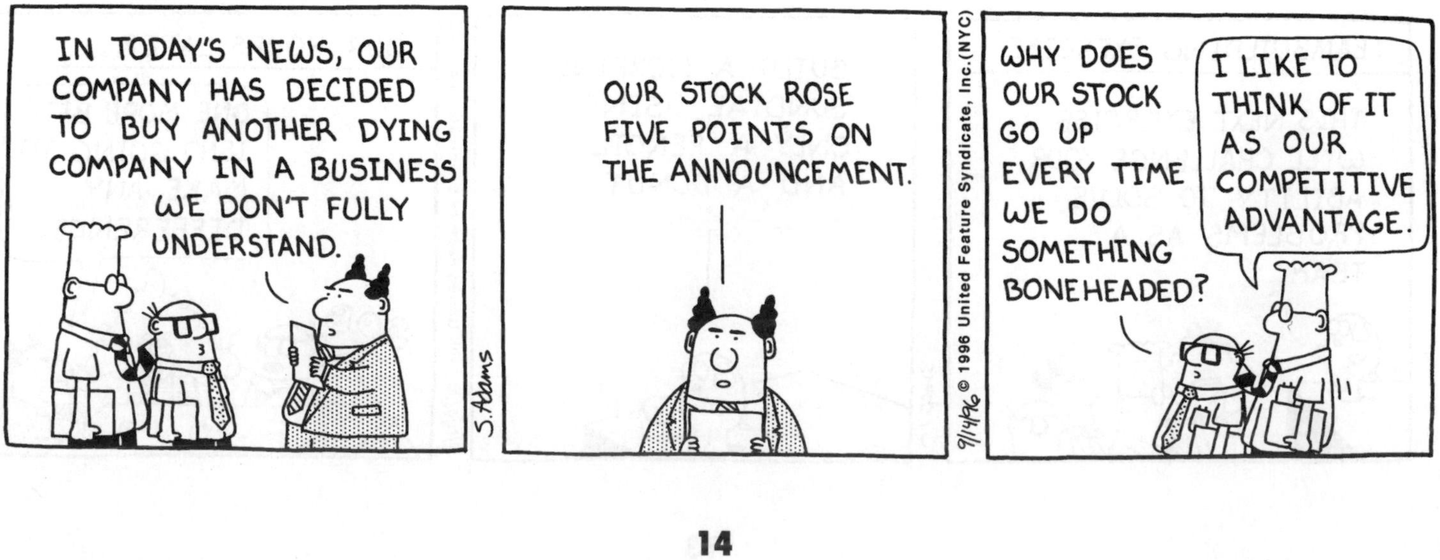
IN TODAY'S NEWS, OUR COMPANY HAS DECIDED TO BUY ANOTHER DYING COMPANY IN A BUSINESS WE DON'T FULLY UNDERSTAND.
S. Adams
OUR STOCK ROSE FIVE POINTS ON THE ANNOUNCEMENT.
9/14/96 © 1996 United Feature Syndicate, Inc.(NYC)
WHY DOES OUR STOCK GO UP EVERY TIME WE DO SOMETHING BONEHEADED?
I LIKE TO THINK OF IT AS OUR COMPETITIVE ADVANTAGE.

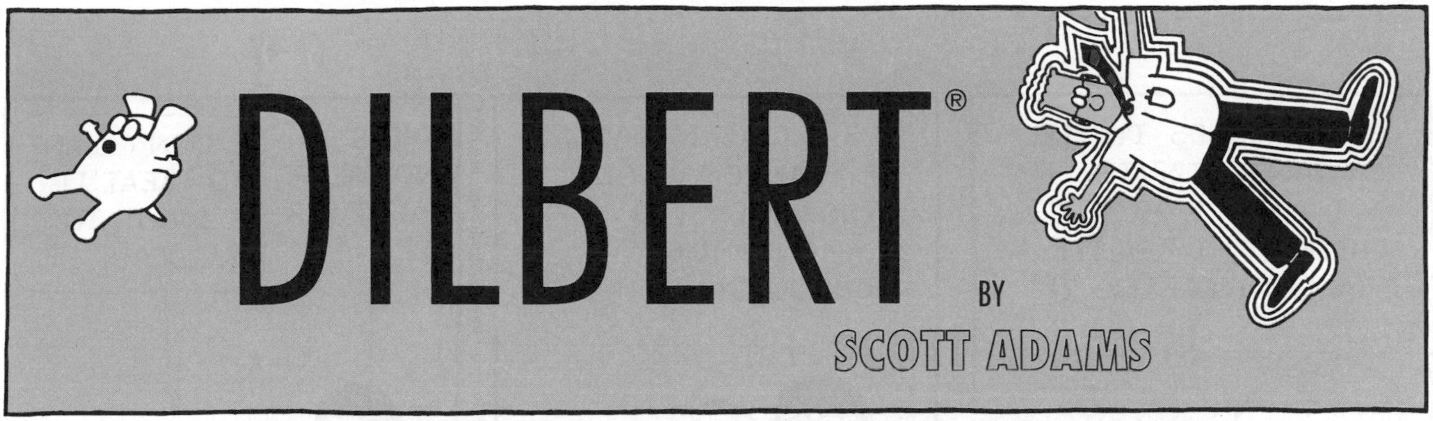
DILBERT®
BY
SCOTT ADAMS

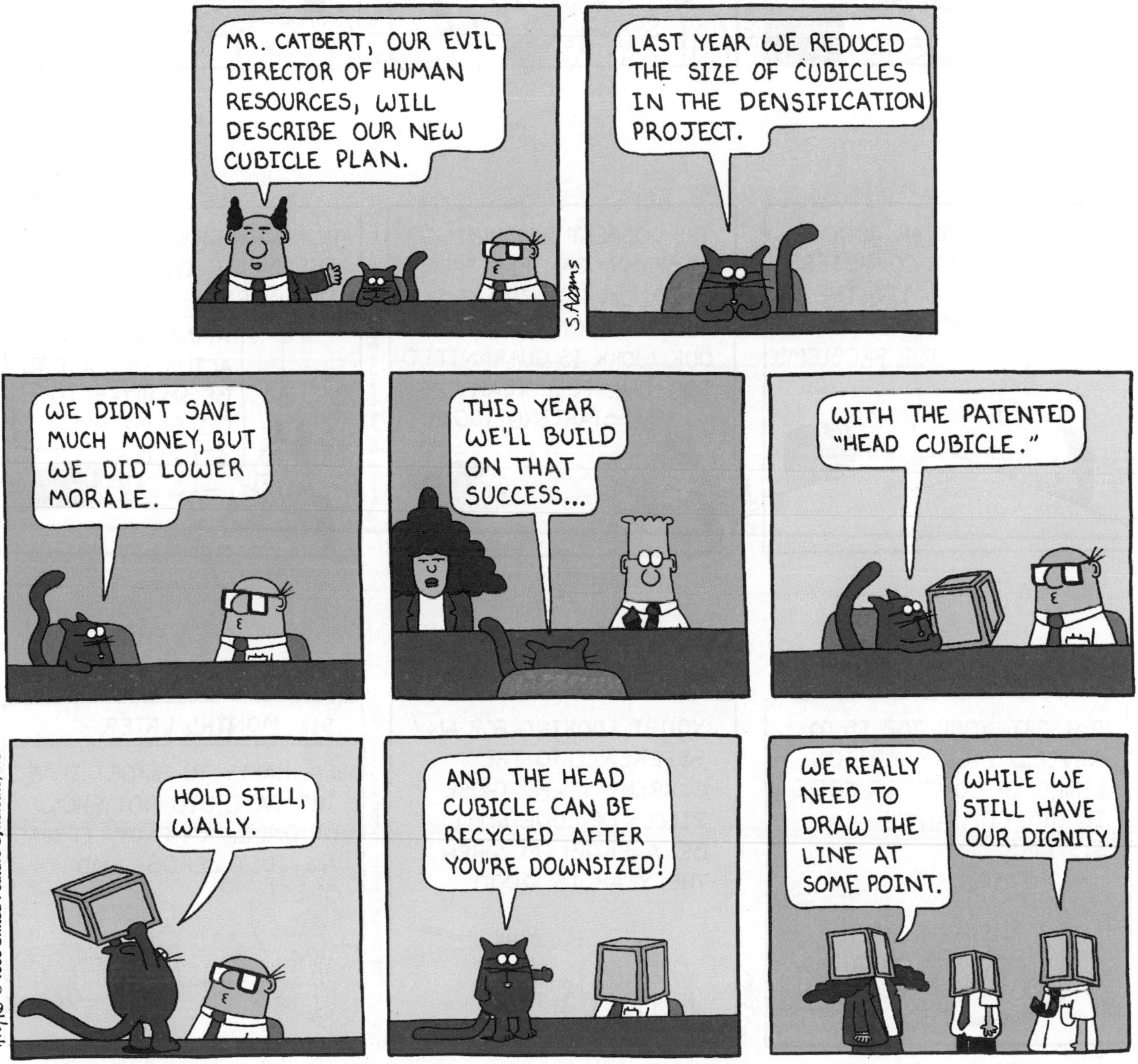
MR. CATBERT, OUR EVIL DIRECTOR OF HUMAN RESOURCES, WILL DESCRIBE OUR NEW CUBICLE PLAN.
S. Adams
LAST YEAR WE REDUCED THE SIZE OF CUBICLES IN THE DENSIFICATION PROJECT.
WE DIDN'T SAVE MUCH MONEY, BUT WE DID LOWER MORALE.
THIS YEAR WE'LL BUILD ON THAT SUCCESS...
WITH THE PATENTED "HEAD CUBICLE."
HOLD STILL, WALLY.
AND THE HEAD CUBICLE CAN BE RECYCLED AFTER YOU'RE DOWNSIZED!
WE REALLY NEED TO DRAW THE LINE AT SOME POINT.
WHILE WE STILL HAVE OUR DIGNITY.

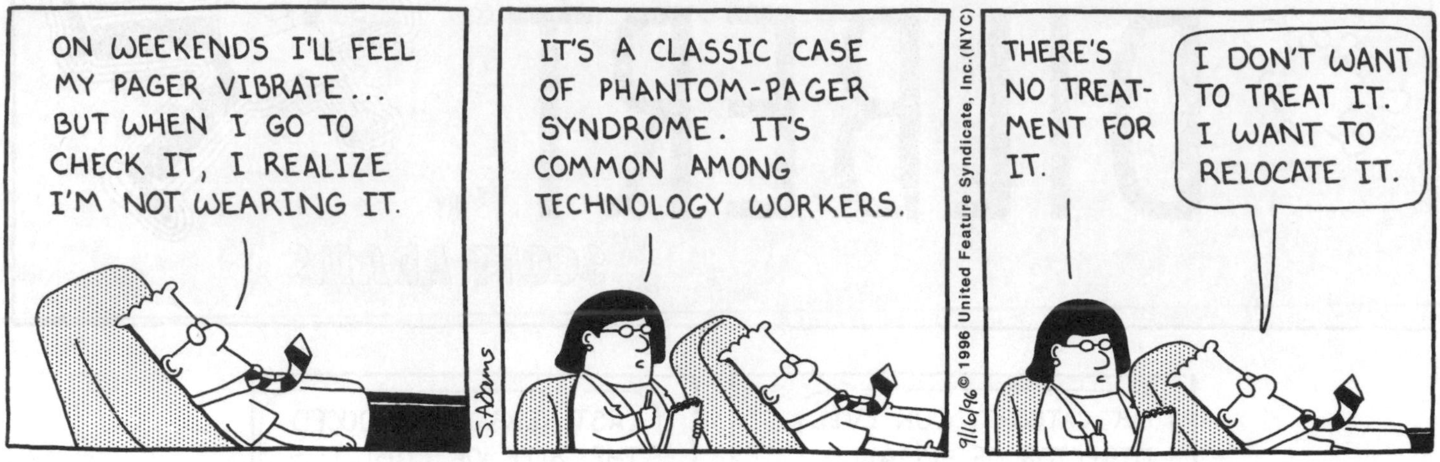

ON WEEKENDS I'LL FEEL MY PAGER VIBRATE... BUT WHEN I GO TO CHECK IT, I REALIZE I'M NOT WEARING IT.
IT'S A CLASSIC CASE OF PHANTOM-PAGER SYNDROME. IT'S COMMON AMONG TECHNOLOGY WORKERS.
THERE'S NO TREATMENT FOR IT.
I DON'T WANT TO TREAT IT. I WANT TO RELOCATE IT.
S. Adams
9/16/96 © 1996 United Feature Syndicate, Inc.(NYC)

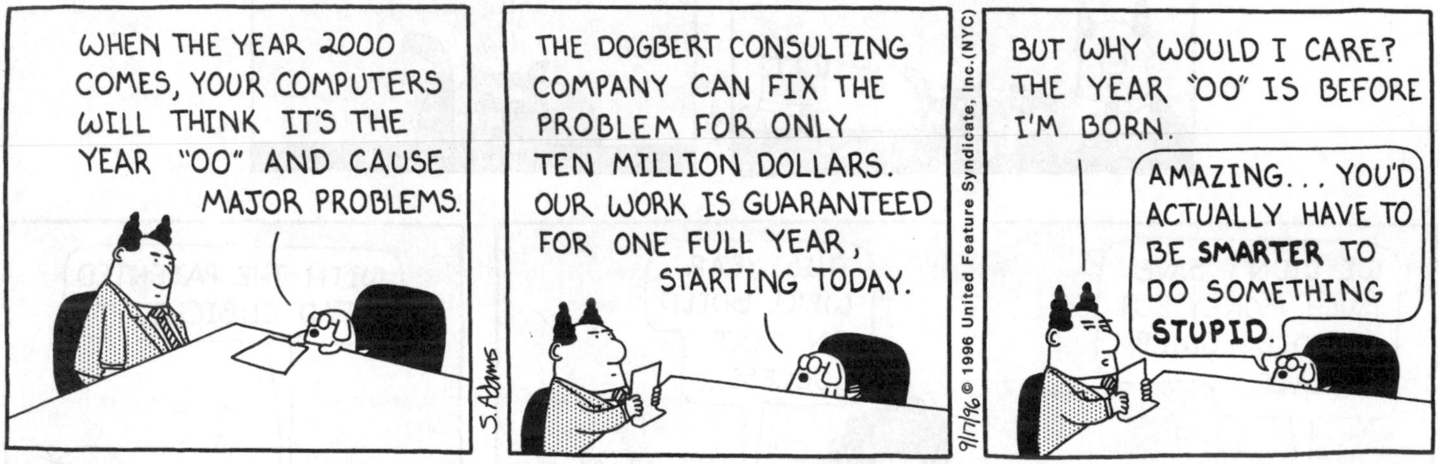

WHEN THE YEAR 2000 COMES, YOUR COMPUTERS WILL THINK IT'S THE YEAR "OO" AND CAUSE MAJOR PROBLEMS.
THE DOGBERT CONSULTING COMPANY CAN FIX THE PROBLEM FOR ONLY TEN MILLION DOLLARS. OUR WORK IS GUARANTEED FOR ONE FULL YEAR, STARTING TODAY.
BUT WHY WOULD I CARE? THE YEAR "OO" IS BEFORE I'M BORN.
AMAZING... YOU'D ACTUALLY HAVE TO BE **SMARTER** TO DO SOMETHING **STUPID**.
S. Adams
9/17/96 © 1996 United Feature Syndicate, Inc.(NYC)

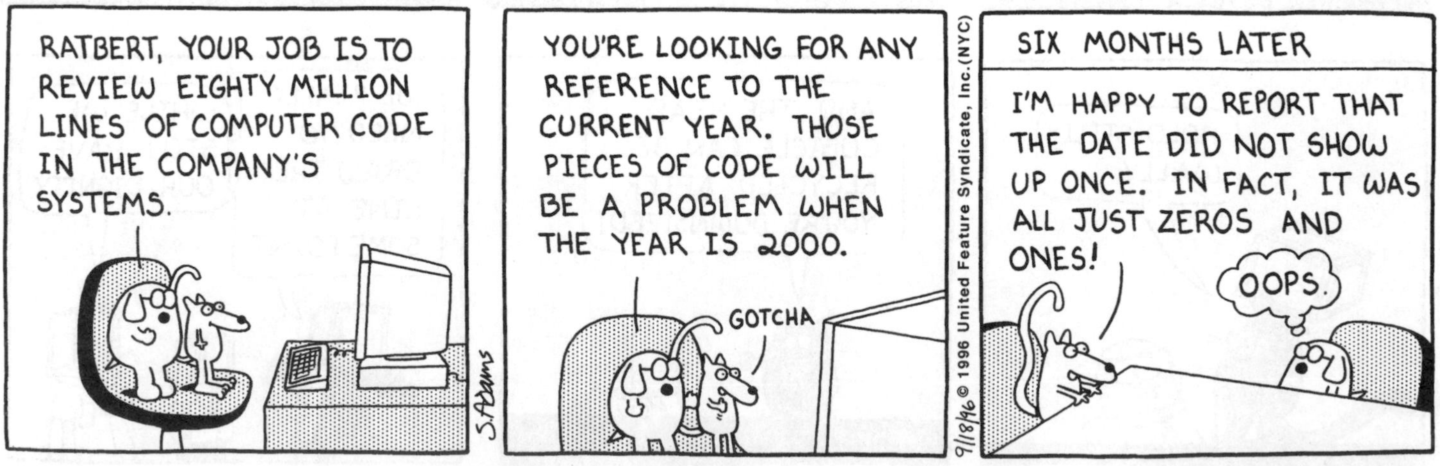

RATBERT, YOUR JOB IS TO REVIEW EIGHTY MILLION LINES OF COMPUTER CODE IN THE COMPANY'S SYSTEMS.
YOU'RE LOOKING FOR ANY REFERENCE TO THE CURRENT YEAR. THOSE PIECES OF CODE WILL BE A PROBLEM WHEN THE YEAR IS 2000.
GOTCHA
SIX MONTHS LATER
I'M HAPPY TO REPORT THAT THE DATE DID NOT SHOW UP ONCE. IN FACT, IT WAS ALL JUST ZEROS AND ONES!
OOPS.
S. Adams
9/18/96 © 1996 United Feature Syndicate, Inc.(NYC)

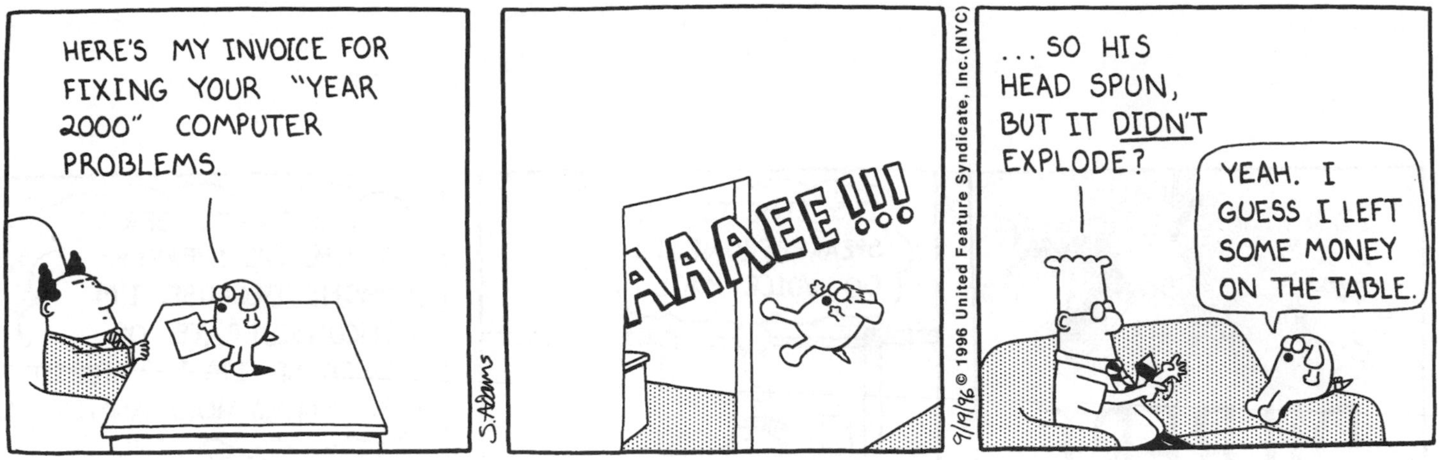
HERE'S MY INVOICE FOR FIXING YOUR "YEAR 2000" COMPUTER PROBLEMS.
AAAEE!!!
S.Adams
9/19/96 © 1996 United Feature Syndicate, Inc.(NYC)
... SO HIS HEAD SPUN, BUT IT DIDN'T EXPLODE?
YEAH. I GUESS I LEFT SOME MONEY ON THE TABLE.

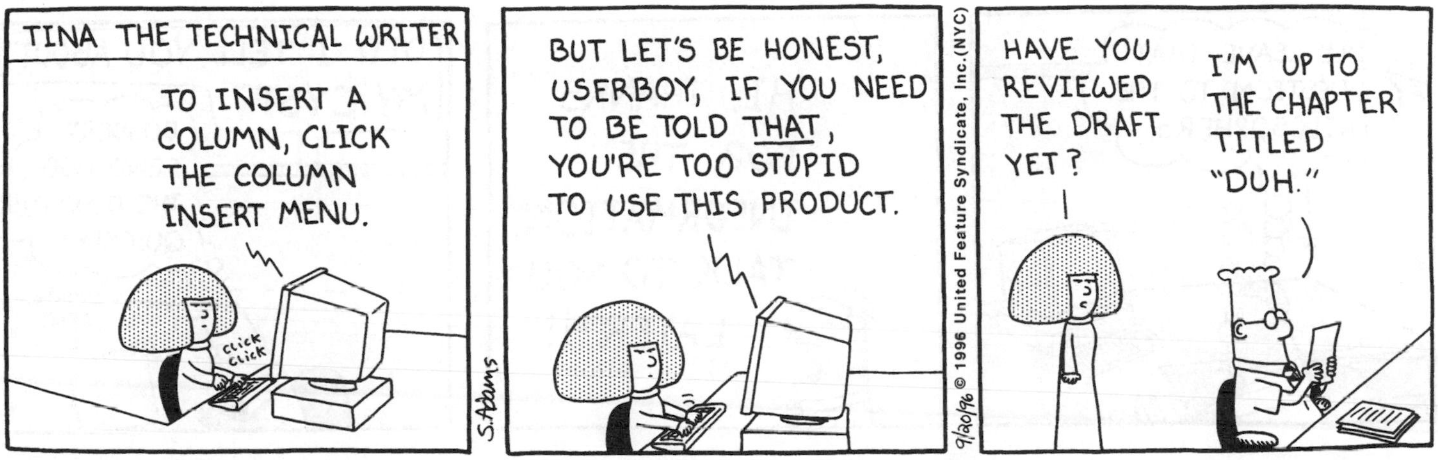
TINA THE TECHNICAL WRITER
TO INSERT A COLUMN, CLICK THE COLUMN INSERT MENU.
click click
BUT LET'S BE HONEST, USERBOY, IF YOU NEED TO BE TOLD THAT, YOU'RE TOO STUPID TO USE THIS PRODUCT.
S.Adams
9/20/96 © 1996 United Feature Syndicate, Inc.(NYC)
HAVE YOU REVIEWED THE DRAFT YET?
I'M UP TO THE CHAPTER TITLED "DUH."

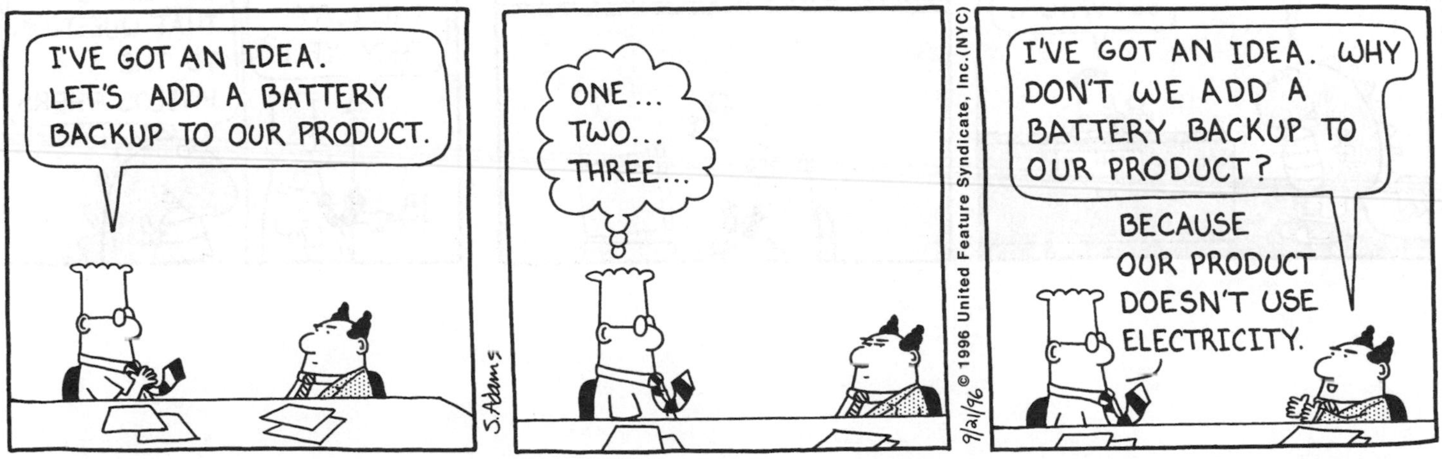
I'VE GOT AN IDEA. LET'S ADD A BATTERY BACKUP TO OUR PRODUCT.
ONE... TWO... THREE...
S.Adams
9/21/96 © 1996 United Feature Syndicate, Inc.(NYC)
I'VE GOT AN IDEA. WHY DON'T WE ADD A BATTERY BACKUP TO OUR PRODUCT?
BECAUSE OUR PRODUCT DOESN'T USE ELECTRICITY.

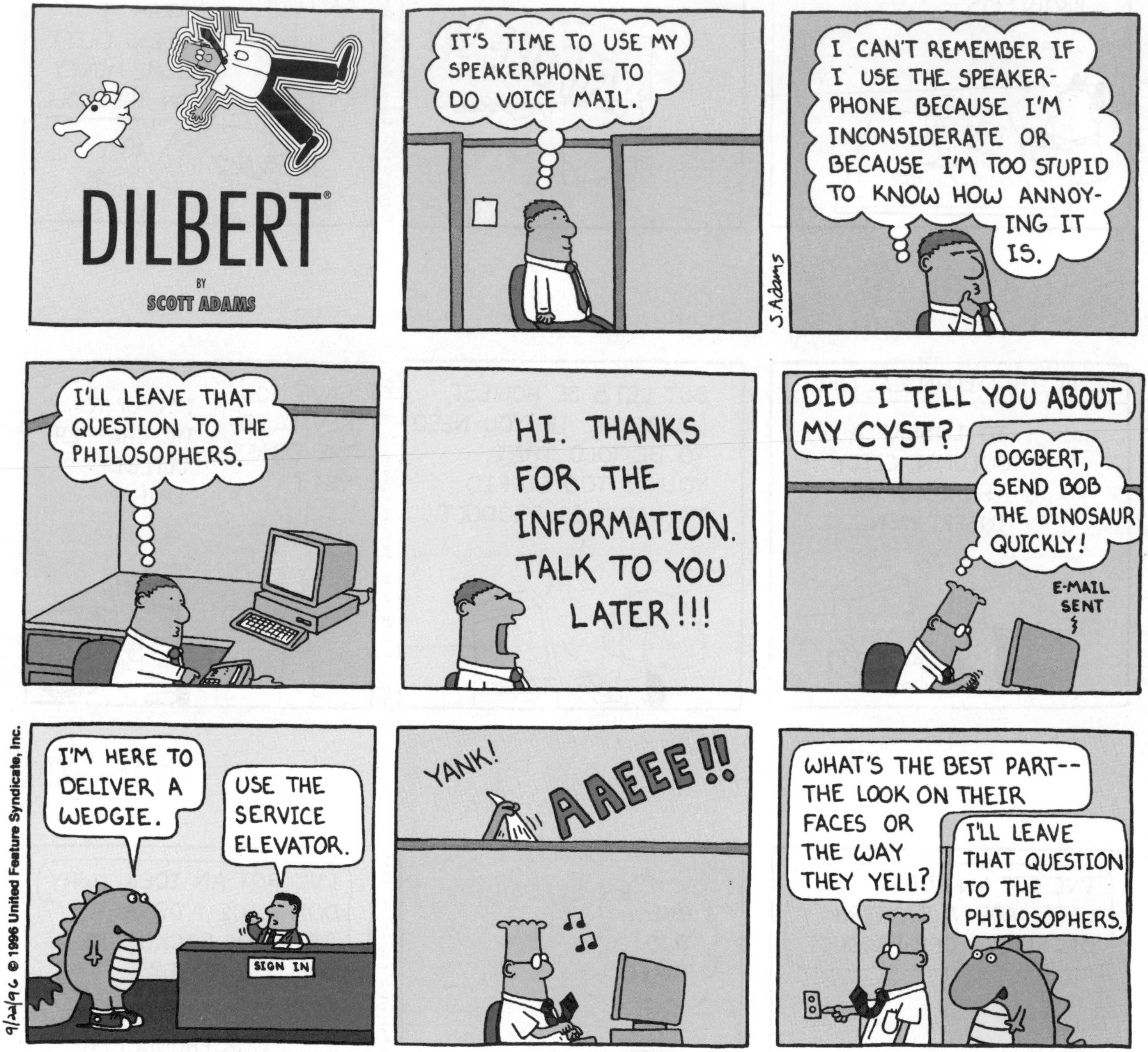
DILBERT®
BY
SCOTT ADAMS
IT'S TIME TO USE MY SPEAKERPHONE TO DO VOICE MAIL.
S. Adams
I CAN'T REMEMBER IF I USE THE SPEAKER-PHONE BECAUSE I'M INCONSIDERATE OR BECAUSE I'M TOO STUPID TO KNOW HOW ANNOY-ING IT IS.
I'LL LEAVE THAT QUESTION TO THE PHILOSOPHERS.
HI. THANKS FOR THE INFORMATION. TALK TO YOU LATER!!!
DID I TELL YOU ABOUT MY CYST?
DOGBERT, SEND BOB THE DINOSAUR QUICKLY!
E-MAIL SENT
I'M HERE TO DELIVER A WEDGIE.
USE THE SERVICE ELEVATOR.
SIGN IN
YANK!
AAEEE!!
WHAT'S THE BEST PART-- THE LOOK ON THEIR FACES OR THE WAY THEY YELL?
I'LL LEAVE THAT QUESTION TO THE PHILOSOPHERS.
9/22/96 © 1996 United Feature Syndicate, Inc.

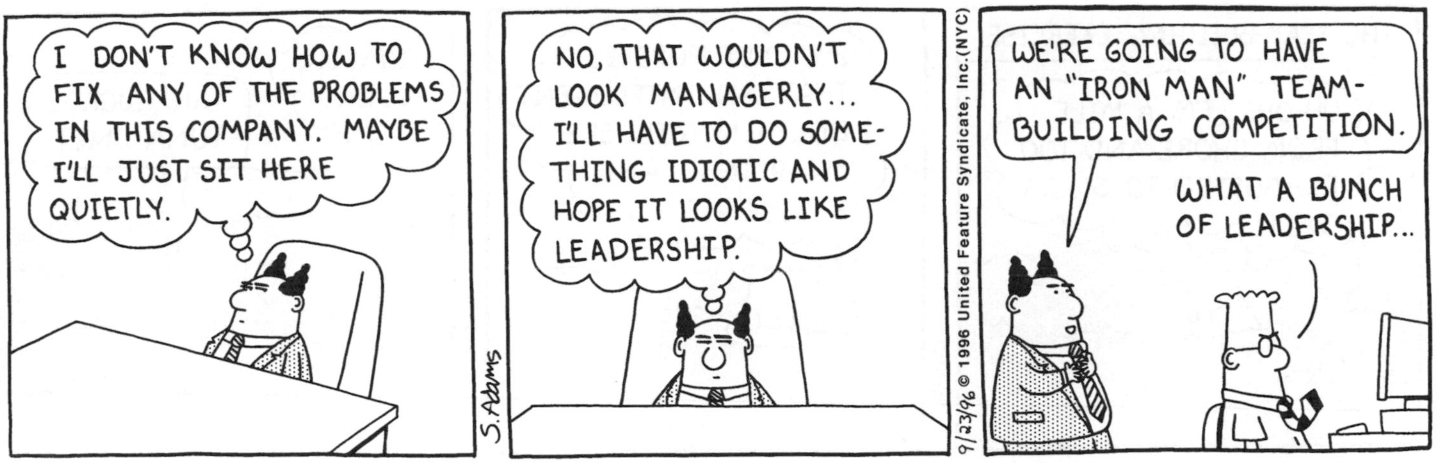
I DON'T KNOW HOW TO FIX ANY OF THE PROBLEMS IN THIS COMPANY. MAYBE I'LL JUST SIT HERE QUIETLY.
NO, THAT WOULDN'T LOOK MANAGERLY... I'LL HAVE TO DO SOMETHING IDIOTIC AND HOPE IT LOOKS LIKE LEADERSHIP.
S. Adams
9/23/96 © 1996 United Feature Syndicate, Inc.(NYC)
WE'RE GOING TO HAVE AN "IRON MAN" TEAM-BUILDING COMPETITION.
WHAT A BUNCH OF LEADERSHIP...

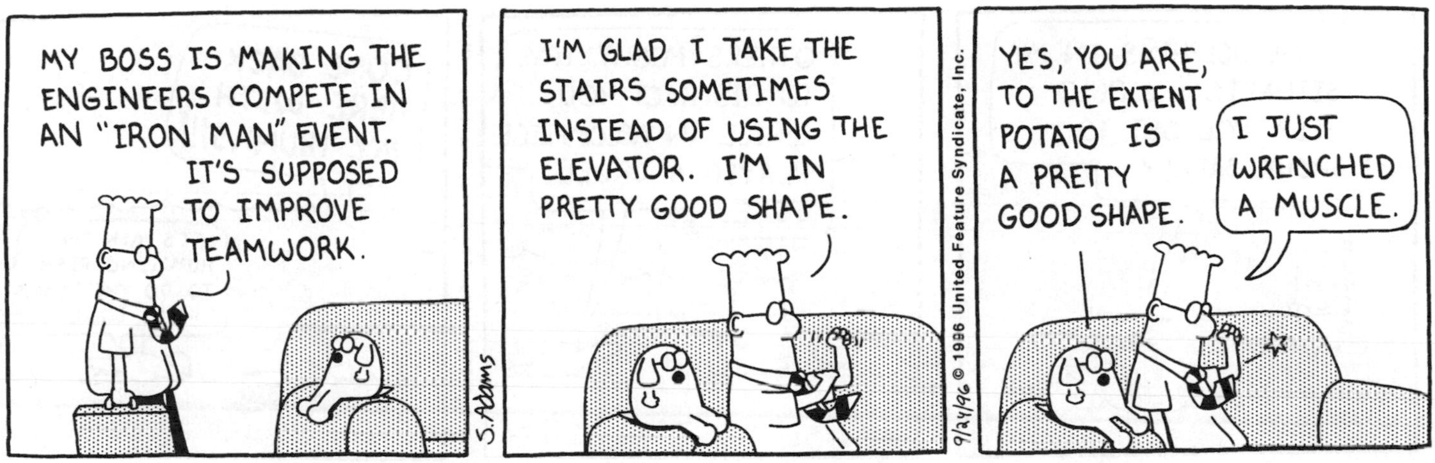
MY BOSS IS MAKING THE ENGINEERS COMPETE IN AN "IRON MAN" EVENT.
IT'S SUPPOSED TO IMPROVE TEAMWORK.
S. Adams
I'M GLAD I TAKE THE STAIRS SOMETIMES INSTEAD OF USING THE ELEVATOR. I'M IN PRETTY GOOD SHAPE.
9/24/96 © 1996 United Feature Syndicate, Inc.
YES, YOU ARE, TO THE EXTENT POTATO IS A PRETTY GOOD SHAPE.
I JUST WRENCHED A MUSCLE.

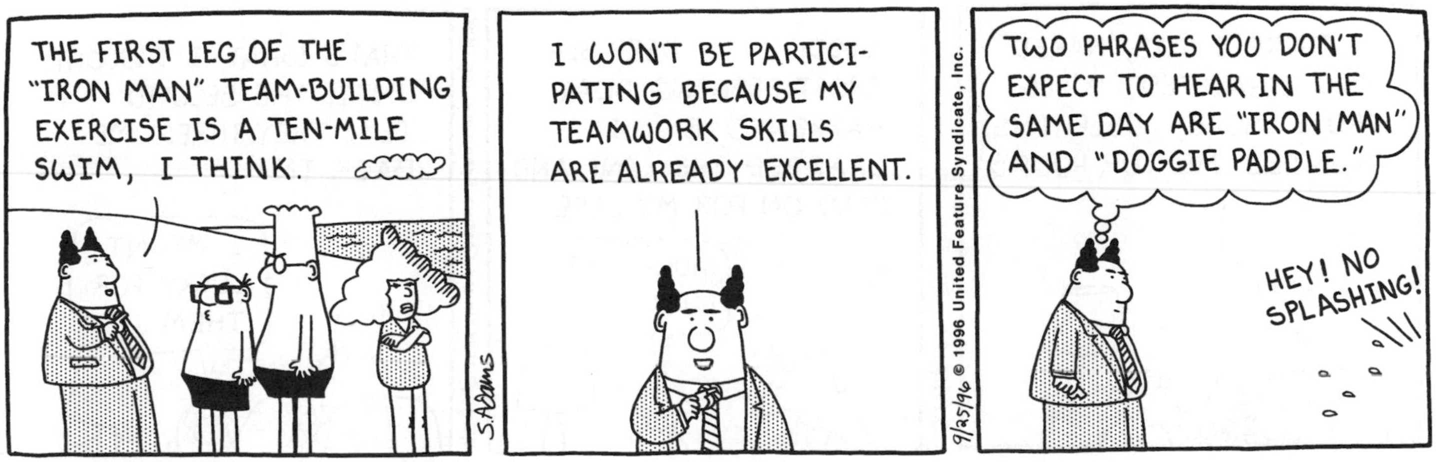
THE FIRST LEG OF THE "IRON MAN" TEAM-BUILDING EXERCISE IS A TEN-MILE SWIM, I THINK.
S. Adams
I WON'T BE PARTICIPATING BECAUSE MY TEAMWORK SKILLS ARE ALREADY EXCELLENT.
9/25/96 © 1996 United Feature Syndicate, Inc.
TWO PHRASES YOU DON'T EXPECT TO HEAR IN THE SAME DAY ARE "IRON MAN" AND "DOGGIE PADDLE."
HEY! NO SPLASHING!

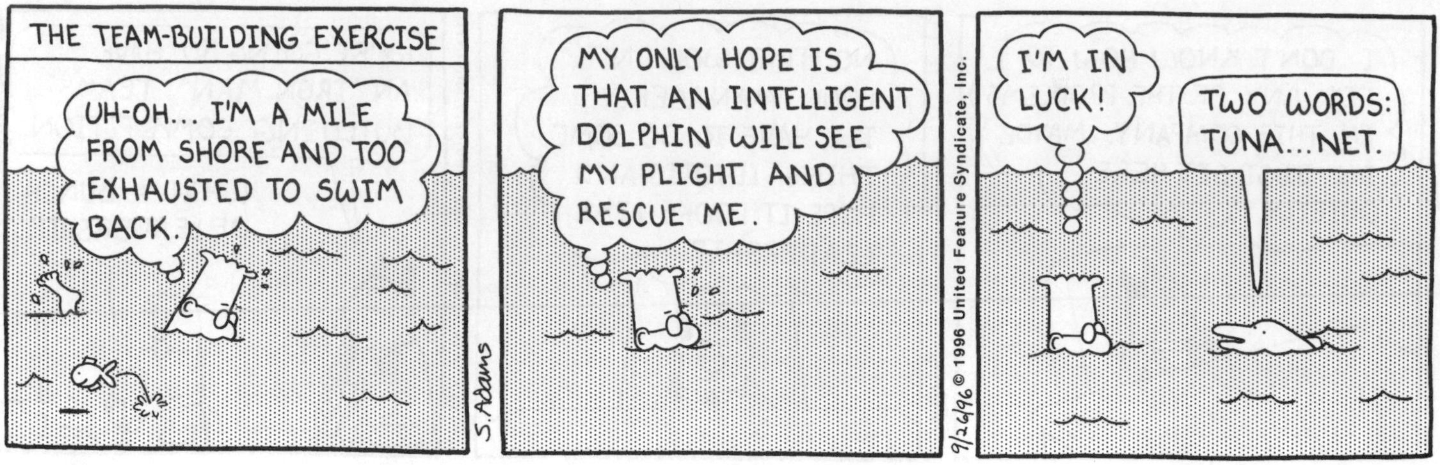
THE TEAM-BUILDING EXERCISE
UH-OH... I'M A MILE FROM SHORE AND TOO EXHAUSTED TO SWIM BACK.
S. Adams
MY ONLY HOPE IS THAT AN INTELLIGENT DOLPHIN WILL SEE MY PLIGHT AND RESCUE ME.
9/26/96 © 1996 United Feature Syndicate, Inc.
I'M IN LUCK!
TWO WORDS: TUNA...NET.

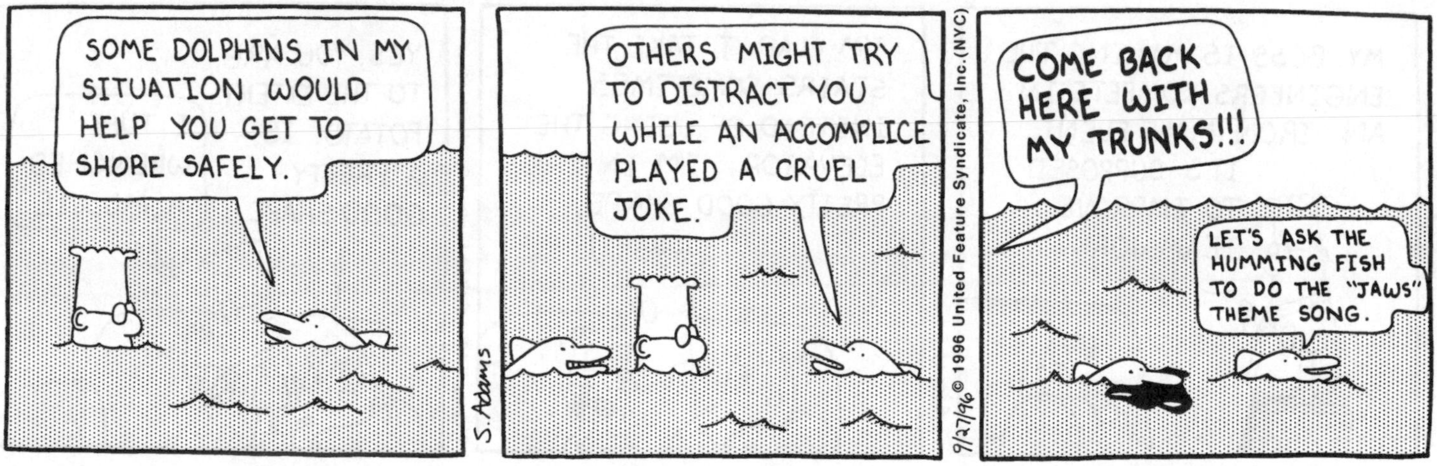
SOME DOLPHINS IN MY SITUATION WOULD HELP YOU GET TO SHORE SAFELY.
S. Adams
OTHERS MIGHT TRY TO DISTRACT YOU WHILE AN ACCOMPLICE PLAYED A CRUEL JOKE.
9/27/96 © 1996 United Feature Syndicate, Inc.(NYC)
COME BACK HERE WITH MY TRUNKS!!!
LET'S ASK THE HUMMING FISH TO DO THE "JAWS" THEME SONG.

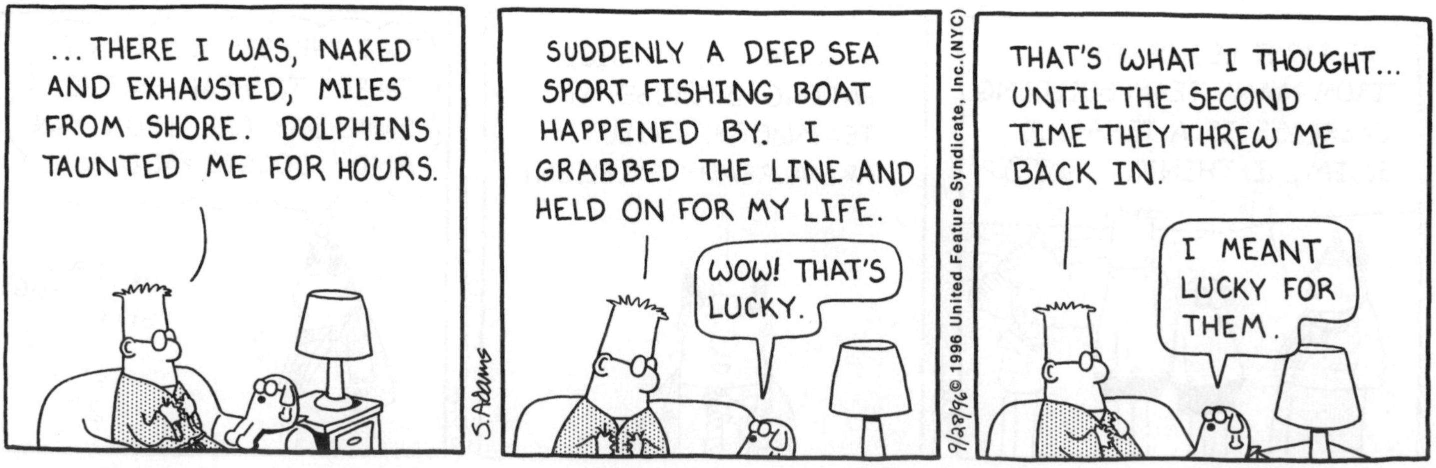
...THERE I WAS, NAKED AND EXHAUSTED, MILES FROM SHORE. DOLPHINS TAUNTED ME FOR HOURS.
S. Adams
SUDDENLY A DEEP SEA SPORT FISHING BOAT HAPPENED BY. I GRABBED THE LINE AND HELD ON FOR MY LIFE.
WOW! THAT'S LUCKY.
9/28/96 © 1996 United Feature Syndicate, Inc.(NYC)
THAT'S WHAT I THOUGHT... UNTIL THE SECOND TIME THEY THREW ME BACK IN.
I MEANT LUCKY FOR THEM.

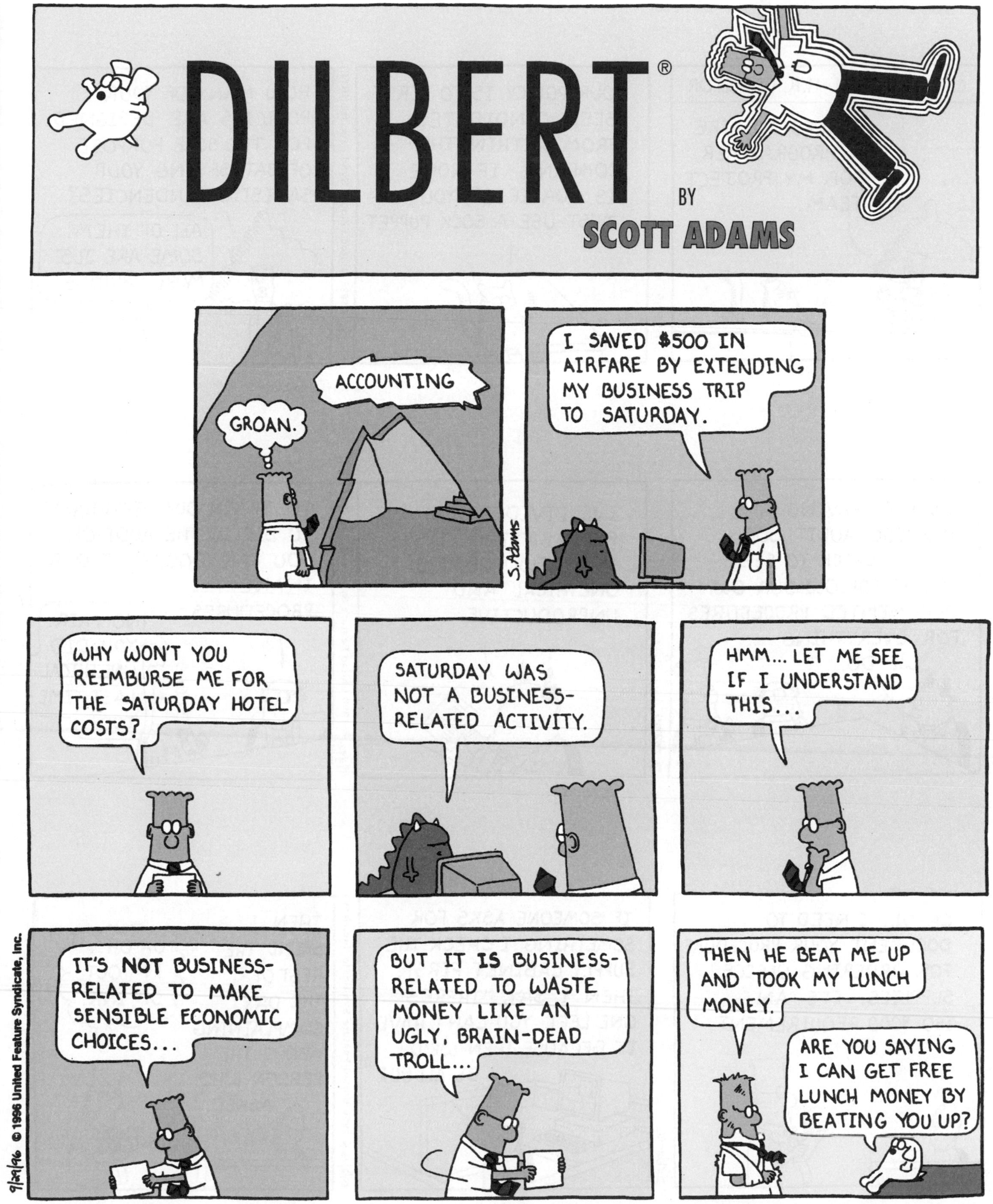

DILBERT®
BY
SCOTT ADAMS
GROAN.
ACCOUNTING
I SAVED $500 IN AIRFARE BY EXTENDING MY BUSINESS TRIP TO SATURDAY.
S. Adams
WHY WON'T YOU REIMBURSE ME FOR THE SATURDAY HOTEL COSTS?
SATURDAY WAS NOT A BUSINESS-RELATED ACTIVITY.
HMM... LET ME SEE IF I UNDERSTAND THIS...
IT'S NOT BUSINESS-RELATED TO MAKE SENSIBLE ECONOMIC CHOICES...
BUT IT IS BUSINESS-RELATED TO WASTE MONEY LIKE AN UGLY, BRAIN-DEAD TROLL...
THEN HE BEAT ME UP AND TOOK MY LUNCH MONEY.
ARE YOU SAYING I CAN GET FREE LUNCH MONEY BY BEATING YOU UP?
9/29/96 © 1996 United Feature Syndicate, Inc.

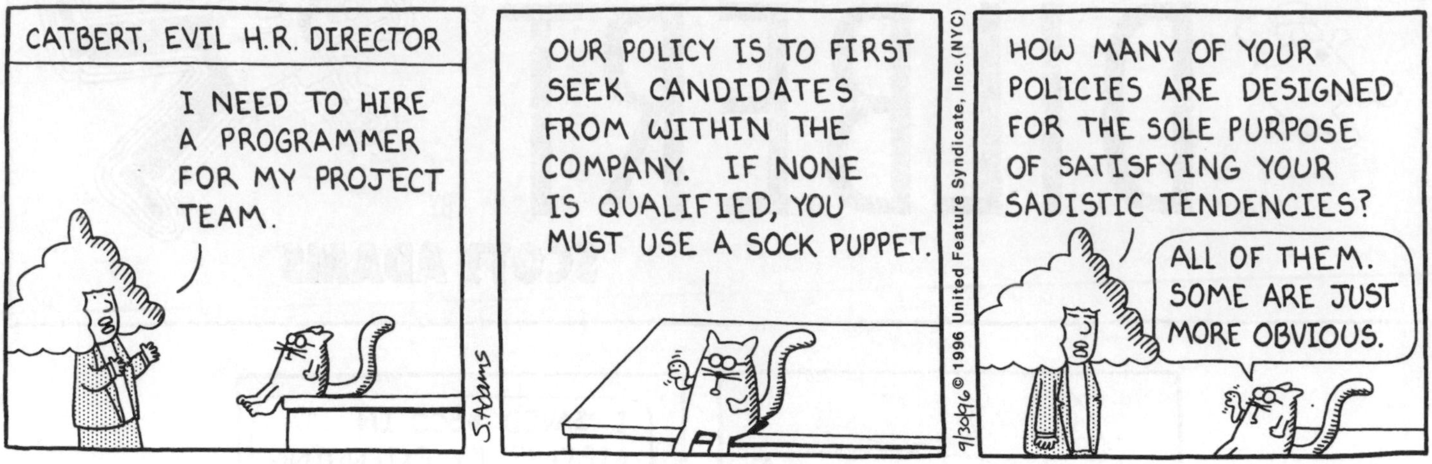
CATBERT, EVIL H.R. DIRECTOR
I NEED TO HIRE A PROGRAMMER FOR MY PROJECT TEAM.
OUR POLICY IS TO FIRST SEEK CANDIDATES FROM WITHIN THE COMPANY. IF NONE IS QUALIFIED, YOU MUST USE A SOCK PUPPET.
HOW MANY OF YOUR POLICIES ARE DESIGNED FOR THE SOLE PURPOSE OF SATISFYING YOUR SADISTIC TENDENCIES?
ALL OF THEM. SOME ARE JUST MORE OBVIOUS.
S. Adams
9/30/96 © 1996 United Feature Syndicate, Inc.(NYC)

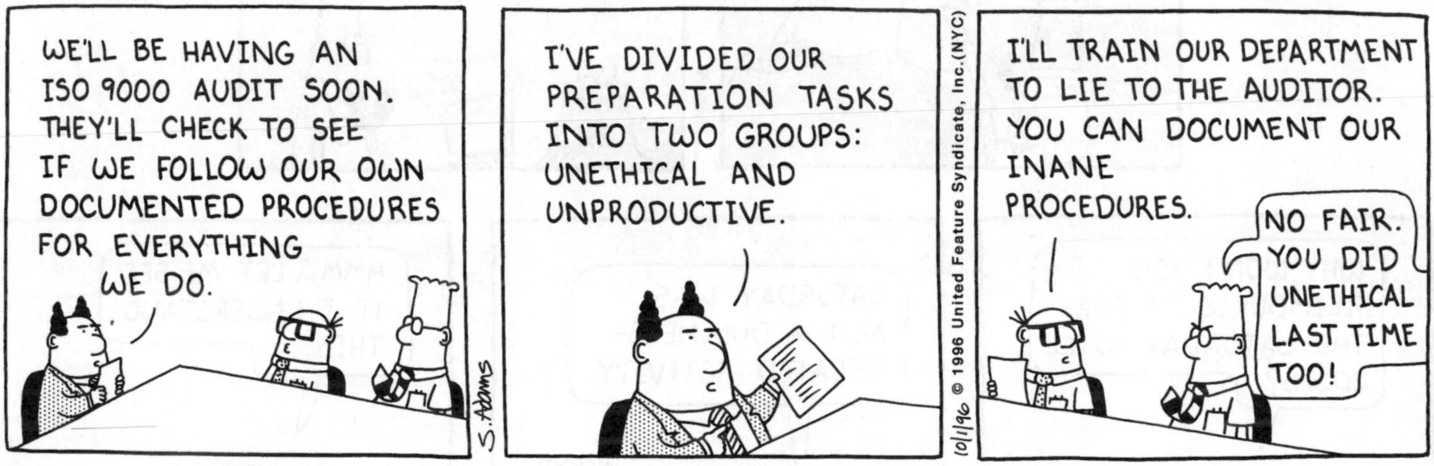
WE'LL BE HAVING AN ISO 9000 AUDIT SOON. THEY'LL CHECK TO SEE IF WE FOLLOW OUR OWN DOCUMENTED PROCEDURES FOR EVERYTHING WE DO.
I'VE DIVIDED OUR PREPARATION TASKS INTO TWO GROUPS: UNETHICAL AND UNPRODUCTIVE.
I'LL TRAIN OUR DEPARTMENT TO LIE TO THE AUDITOR. YOU CAN DOCUMENT OUR INANE PROCEDURES.
NO FAIR. YOU DID UNETHICAL LAST TIME TOO!
S. Adams
10/1/96 © 1996 United Feature Syndicate, Inc.(NYC)

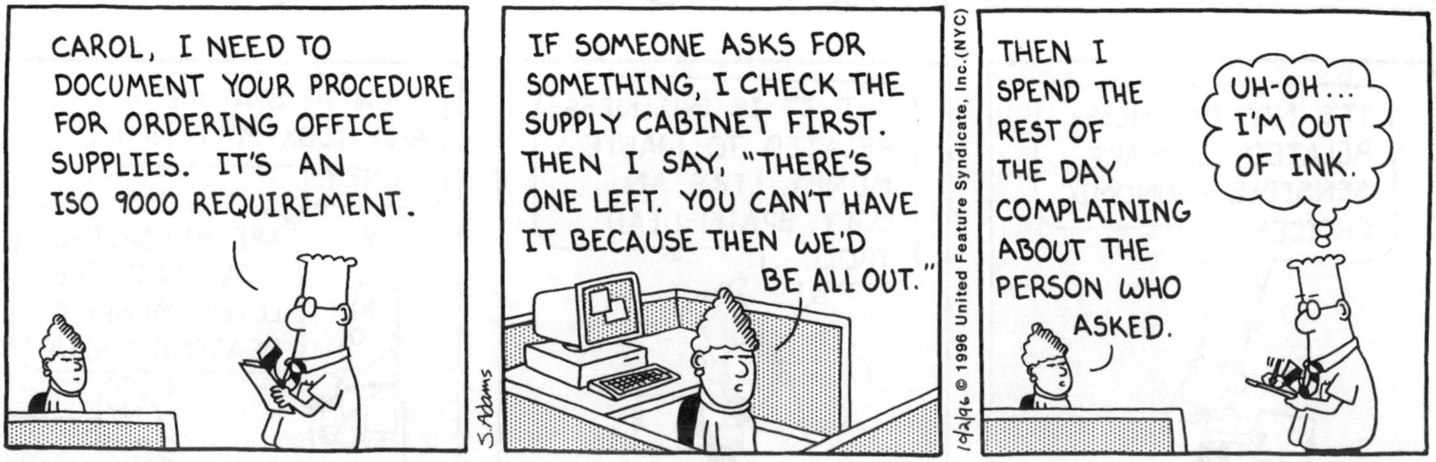
CAROL, I NEED TO DOCUMENT YOUR PROCEDURE FOR ORDERING OFFICE SUPPLIES. IT'S AN ISO 9000 REQUIREMENT.
IF SOMEONE ASKS FOR SOMETHING, I CHECK THE SUPPLY CABINET FIRST. THEN I SAY, "THERE'S ONE LEFT. YOU CAN'T HAVE IT BECAUSE THEN WE'D BE ALL OUT."
THEN I SPEND THE REST OF THE DAY COMPLAINING ABOUT THE PERSON WHO ASKED.
UH-OH... I'M OUT OF INK.
S. Adams
10/2/96 © 1996 United Feature Syndicate, Inc.(NYC)

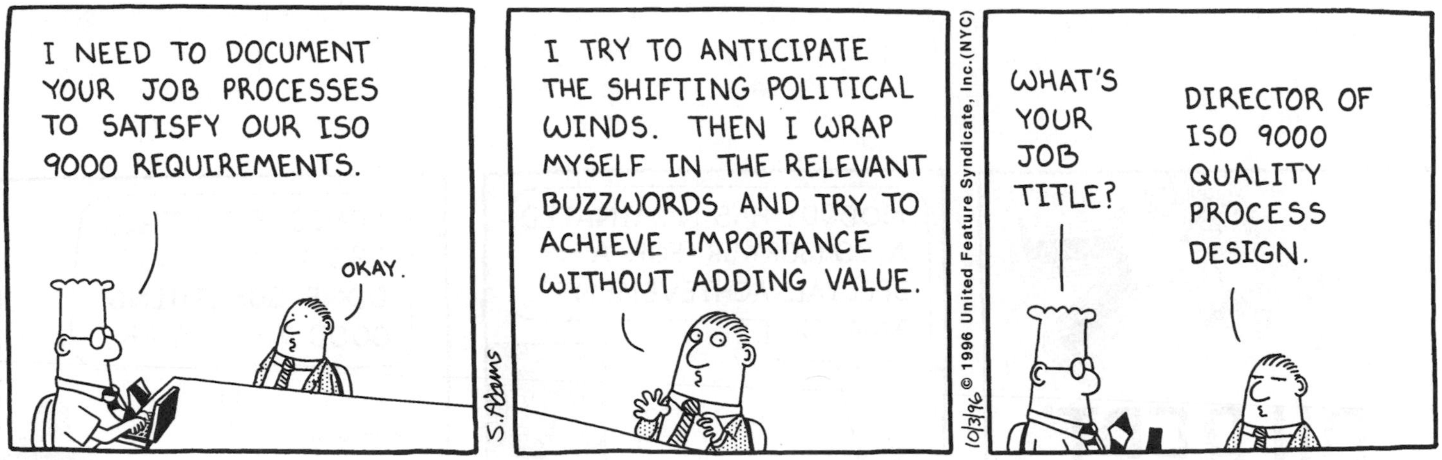
I NEED TO DOCUMENT YOUR JOB PROCESSES TO SATISFY OUR ISO 9000 REQUIREMENTS.
OKAY.
I TRY TO ANTICIPATE THE SHIFTING POLITICAL WINDS. THEN I WRAP MYSELF IN THE RELEVANT BUZZWORDS AND TRY TO ACHIEVE IMPORTANCE WITHOUT ADDING VALUE.
WHAT'S YOUR JOB TITLE?
DIRECTOR OF ISO 9000 QUALITY PROCESS DESIGN.
S. Adams
10/3/96 © 1996 United Feature Syndicate, Inc.(NYC)

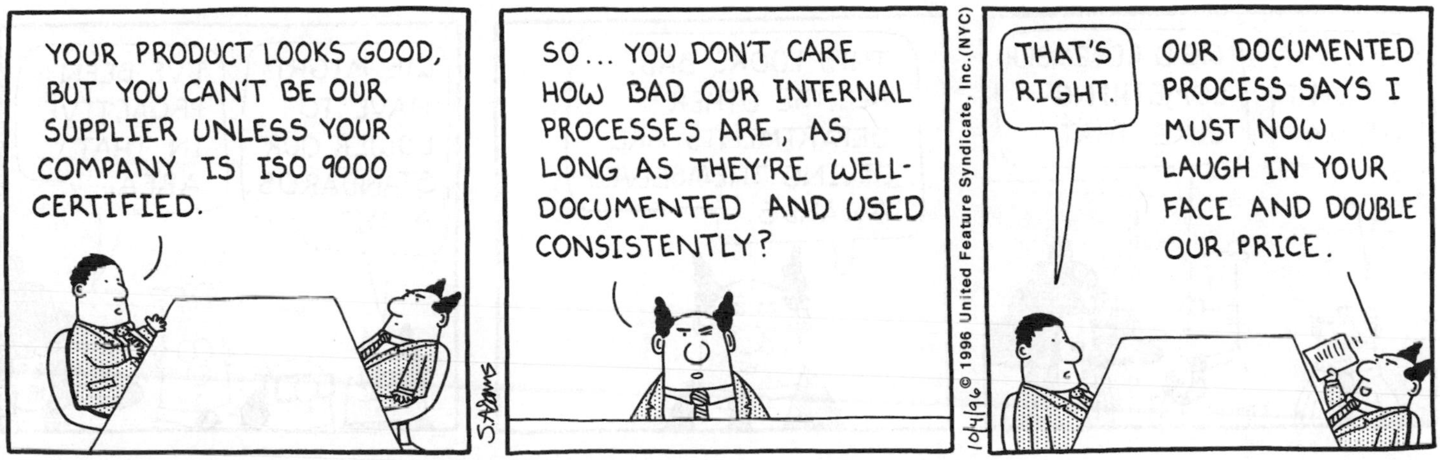
YOUR PRODUCT LOOKS GOOD, BUT YOU CAN'T BE OUR SUPPLIER UNLESS YOUR COMPANY IS ISO 9000 CERTIFIED.
SO... YOU DON'T CARE HOW BAD OUR INTERNAL PROCESSES ARE, AS LONG AS THEY'RE WELL-DOCUMENTED AND USED CONSISTENTLY?
THAT'S RIGHT.
OUR DOCUMENTED PROCESS SAYS I MUST NOW LAUGH IN YOUR FACE AND DOUBLE OUR PRICE.
S. Adams
10/4/96 © 1996 United Feature Syndicate, Inc.(NYC)

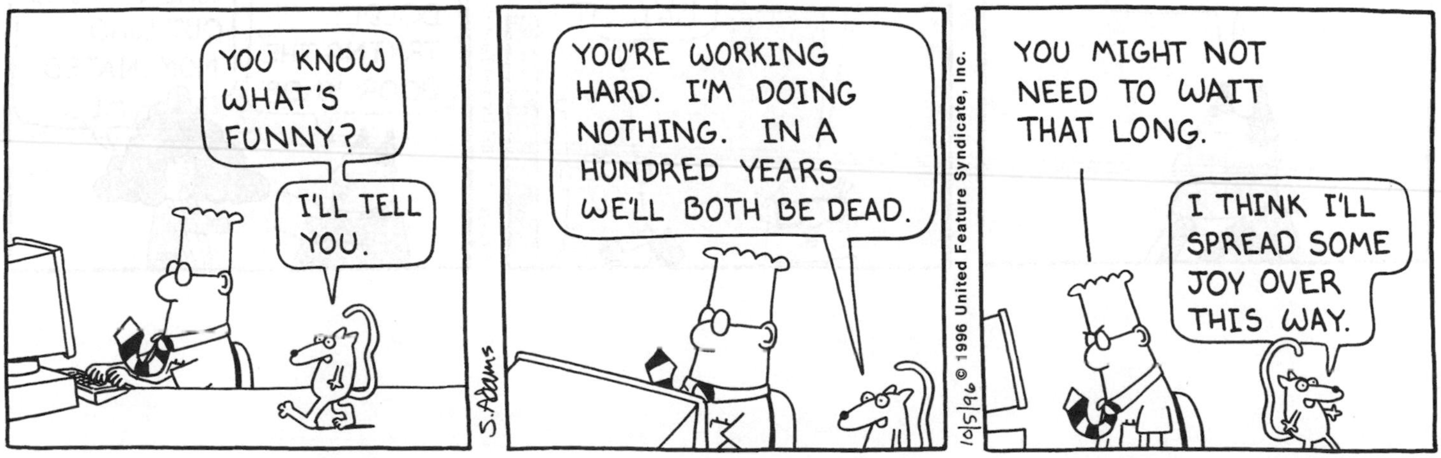
YOU KNOW WHAT'S FUNNY?
I'LL TELL YOU.
YOU'RE WORKING HARD. I'M DOING NOTHING. IN A HUNDRED YEARS WE'LL BOTH BE DEAD.
YOU MIGHT NOT NEED TO WAIT THAT LONG.
I THINK I'LL SPREAD SOME JOY OVER THIS WAY.
S. Adams
10/5/96 © 1996 United Feature Syndicate, Inc.

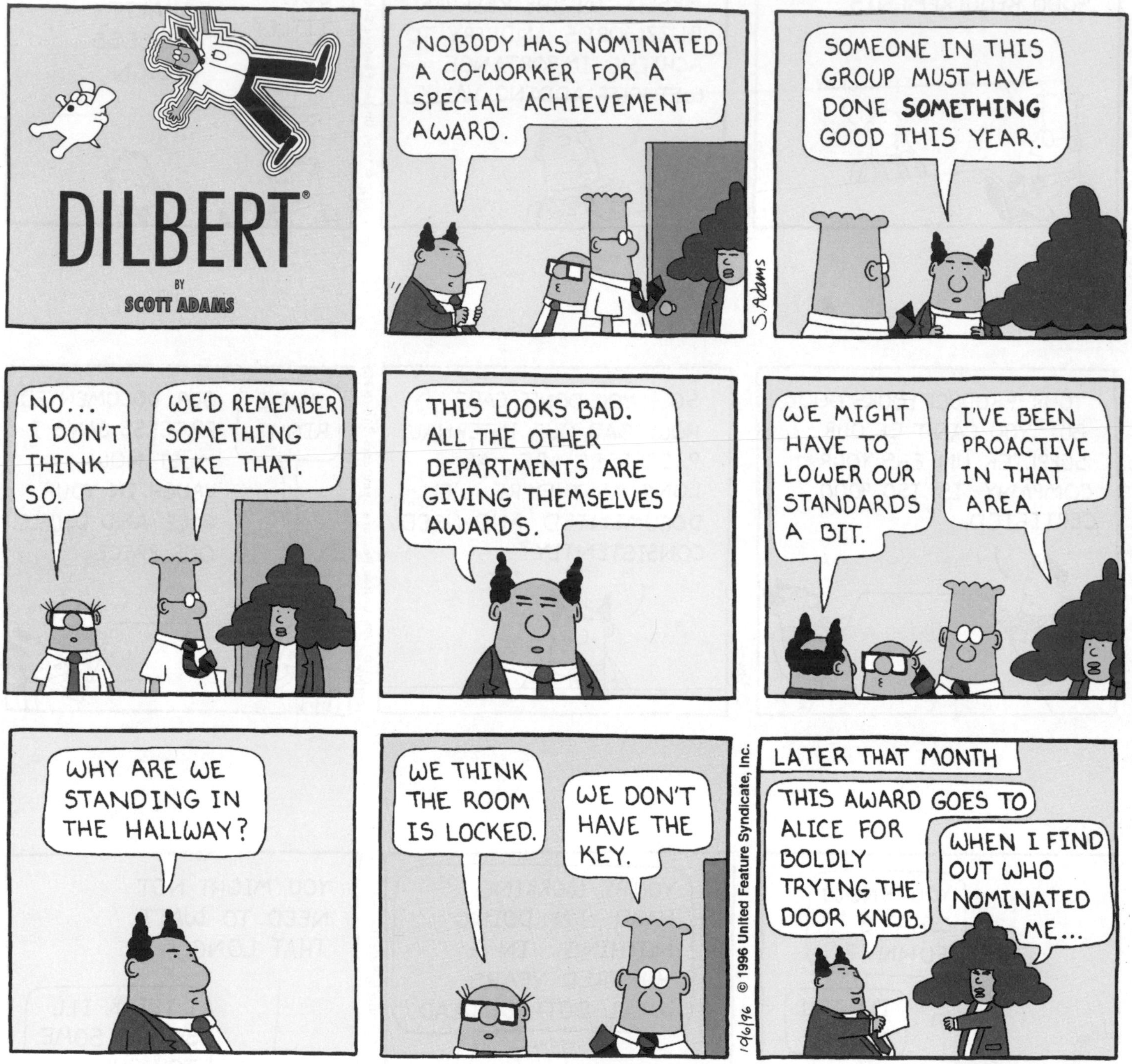
DILBERT
BY
SCOTT ADAMS
NOBODY HAS NOMINATED A CO-WORKER FOR A SPECIAL ACHIEVEMENT AWARD.
S. Adams
SOMEONE IN THIS GROUP MUST HAVE DONE SOMETHING GOOD THIS YEAR.
NO... I DON'T THINK SO.
WE'D REMEMBER SOMETHING LIKE THAT.
THIS LOOKS BAD. ALL THE OTHER DEPARTMENTS ARE GIVING THEMSELVES AWARDS.
WE MIGHT HAVE TO LOWER OUR STANDARDS A BIT.
I'VE BEEN PROACTIVE IN THAT AREA.
WHY ARE WE STANDING IN THE HALLWAY?
WE THINK THE ROOM IS LOCKED.
WE DON'T HAVE THE KEY.
10/6/96 © 1996 United Feature Syndicate, Inc.
LATER THAT MONTH
THIS AWARD GOES TO ALICE FOR BOLDLY TRYING THE DOOR KNOB.
WHEN I FIND OUT WHO NOMINATED ME...

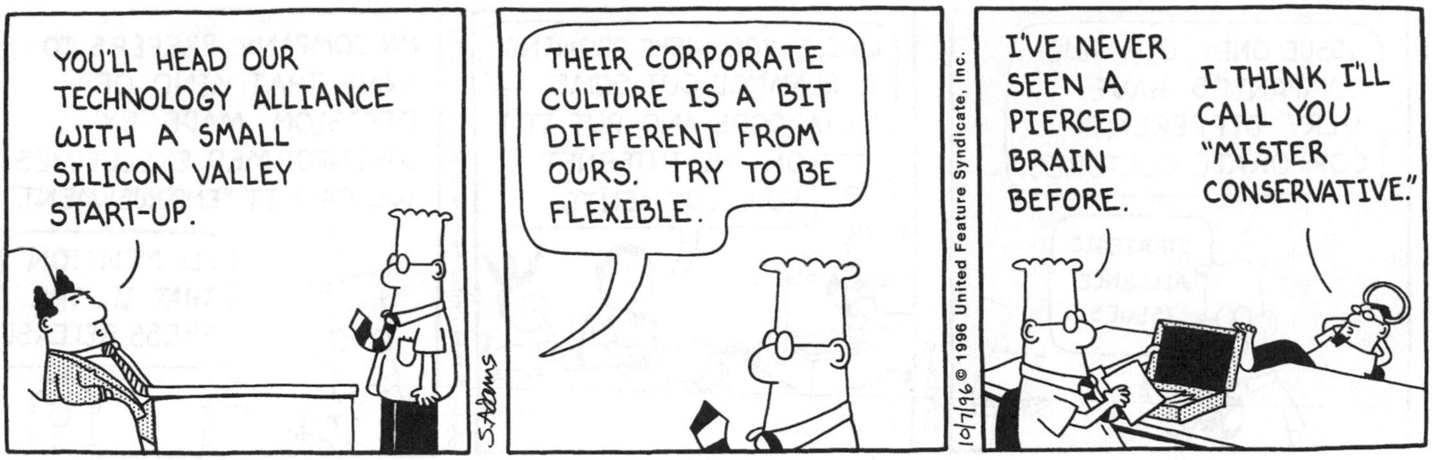
YOU'LL HEAD OUR TECHNOLOGY ALLIANCE WITH A SMALL SILICON VALLEY START-UP.
THEIR CORPORATE CULTURE IS A BIT DIFFERENT FROM OURS. TRY TO BE FLEXIBLE.
I'VE NEVER SEEN A PIERCED BRAIN BEFORE.
I THINK I'LL CALL YOU "MISTER CONSERVATIVE."
S. Adams
10/7/96 © 1996 United Feature Syndicate, Inc.

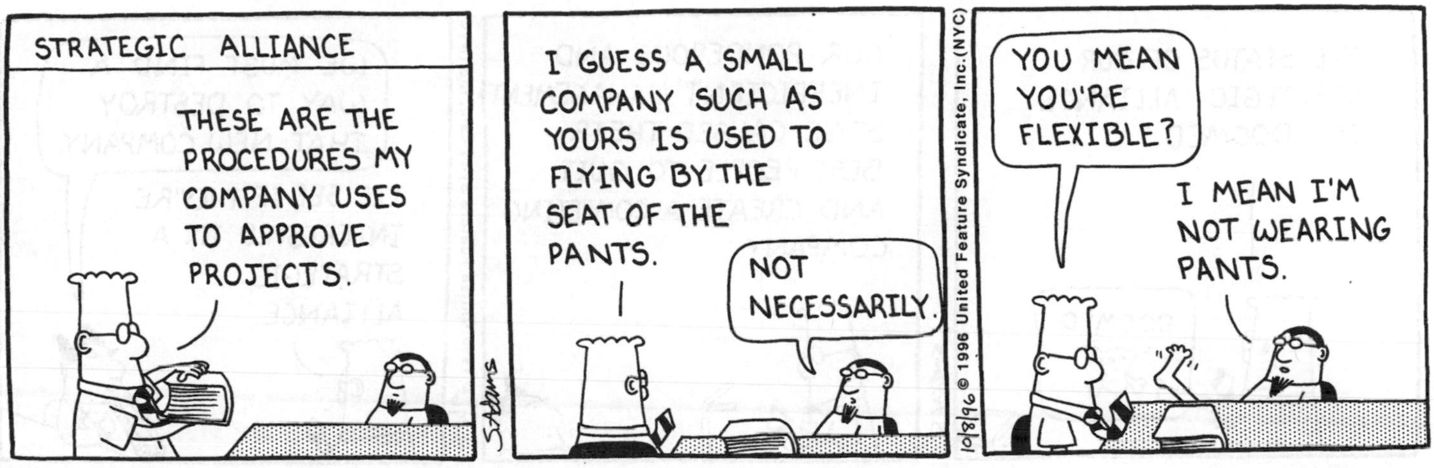
STRATEGIC ALLIANCE
THESE ARE THE PROCEDURES MY COMPANY USES TO APPROVE PROJECTS.
I GUESS A SMALL COMPANY SUCH AS YOURS IS USED TO FLYING BY THE SEAT OF THE PANTS.
NOT NECESSARILY.
YOU MEAN YOU'RE FLEXIBLE?
I MEAN I'M NOT WEARING PANTS.
S. Adams
10/8/96 © 1996 United Feature Syndicate, Inc.(NYC)

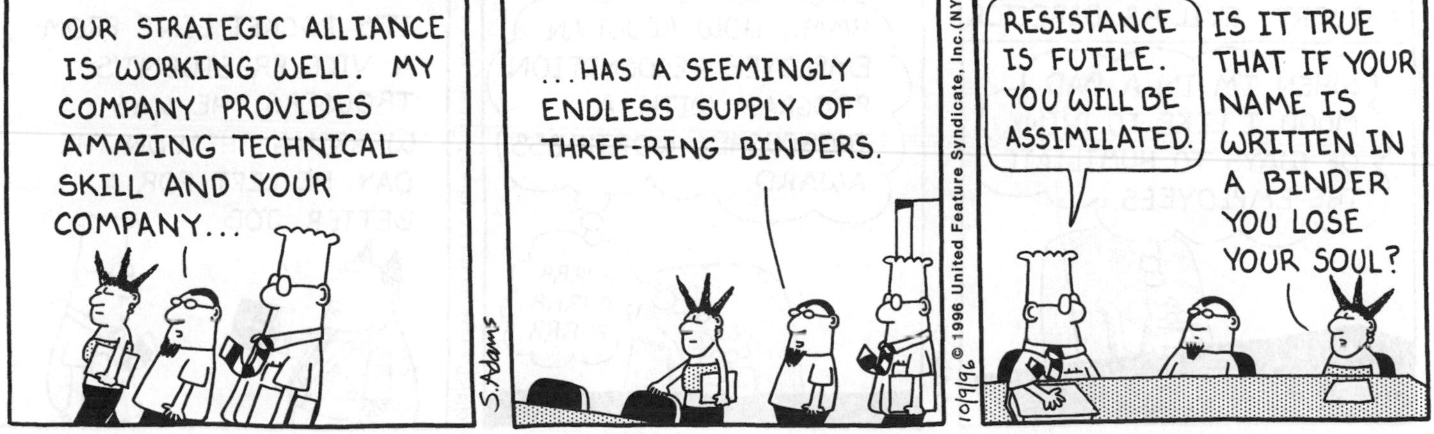
OUR STRATEGIC ALLIANCE IS WORKING WELL. MY COMPANY PROVIDES AMAZING TECHNICAL SKILL AND YOUR COMPANY...
...HAS A SEEMINGLY ENDLESS SUPPLY OF THREE-RING BINDERS.
RESISTANCE IS FUTILE. YOU WILL BE ASSIMILATED.
IS IT TRUE THAT IF YOUR NAME IS WRITTEN IN A BINDER YOU LOSE YOUR SOUL?
S. Adams
10/9/96 © 1996 United Feature Syndicate, Inc.(NYC)

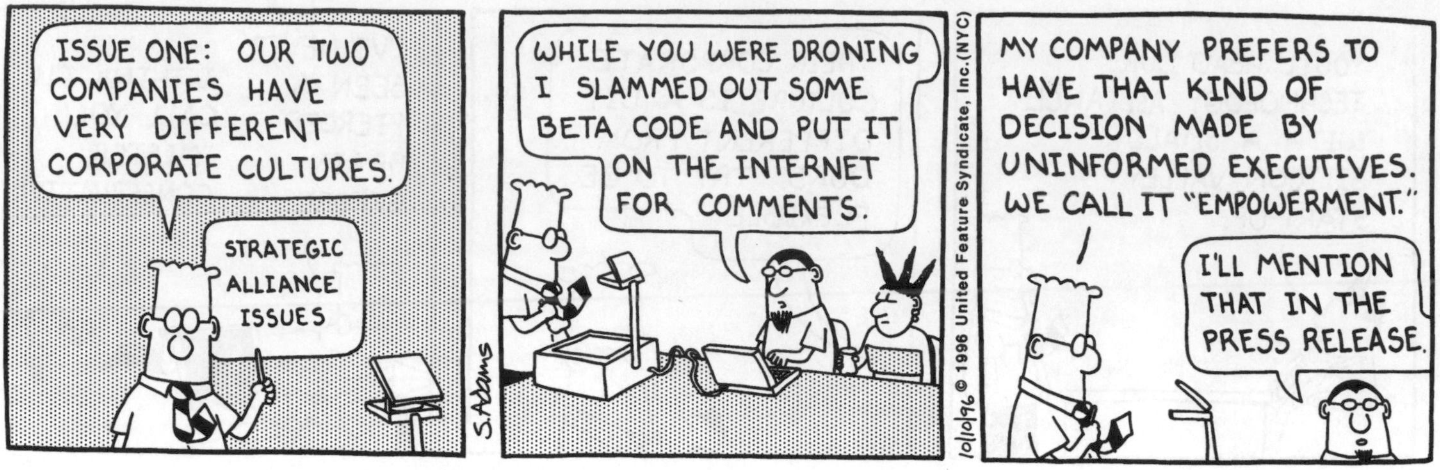
ISSUE ONE: OUR TWO COMPANIES HAVE VERY DIFFERENT CORPORATE CULTURES.
STRATEGIC ALLIANCE ISSUES
S. Adams
WHILE YOU WERE DRONING I SLAMMED OUT SOME BETA CODE AND PUT IT ON THE INTERNET FOR COMMENTS.
10/10/96 © 1996 United Feature Syndicate, Inc.(NYC)
MY COMPANY PREFERS TO HAVE THAT KIND OF DECISION MADE BY UNINFORMED EXECUTIVES. WE CALL IT "EMPOWERMENT."
I'LL MENTION THAT IN THE PRESS RELEASE.

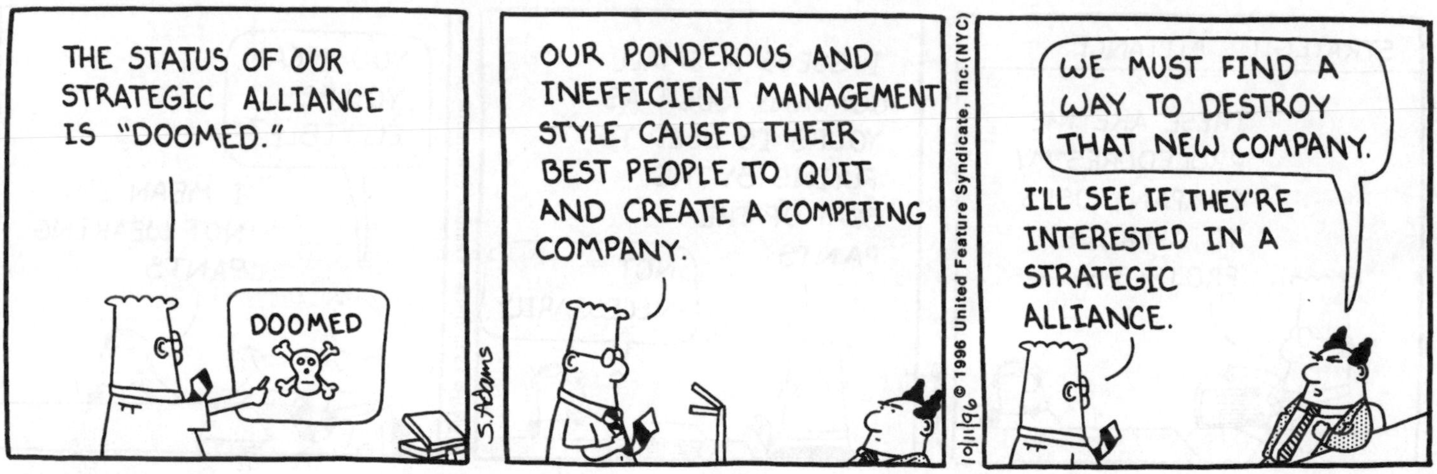
THE STATUS OF OUR STRATEGIC ALLIANCE IS "DOOMED."
DOOMED
S. Adams
OUR PONDEROUS AND INEFFICIENT MANAGEMENT STYLE CAUSED THEIR BEST PEOPLE TO QUIT AND CREATE A COMPETING COMPANY.
10/11/96 © 1996 United Feature Syndicate, Inc.(NYC)
WE MUST FIND A WAY TO DESTROY THAT NEW COMPANY.
I'LL SEE IF THEY'RE INTERESTED IN A STRATEGIC ALLIANCE.

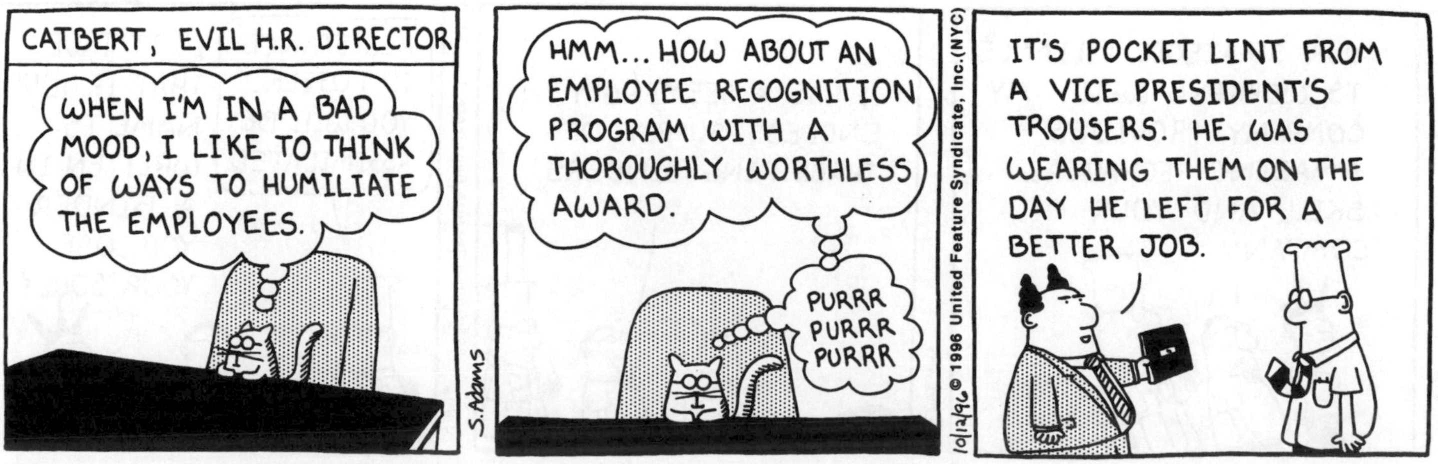
CATBERT, EVIL H.R. DIRECTOR
WHEN I'M IN A BAD MOOD, I LIKE TO THINK OF WAYS TO HUMILIATE THE EMPLOYEES.
S. Adams
HMM... HOW ABOUT AN EMPLOYEE RECOGNITION PROGRAM WITH A THOROUGHLY WORTHLESS AWARD.
PURRR PURRR PURRR
10/12/96 © 1996 United Feature Syndicate, Inc.(NYC)
IT'S POCKET LINT FROM A VICE PRESIDENT'S TROUSERS. HE WAS WEARING THEM ON THE DAY HE LEFT FOR A BETTER JOB.

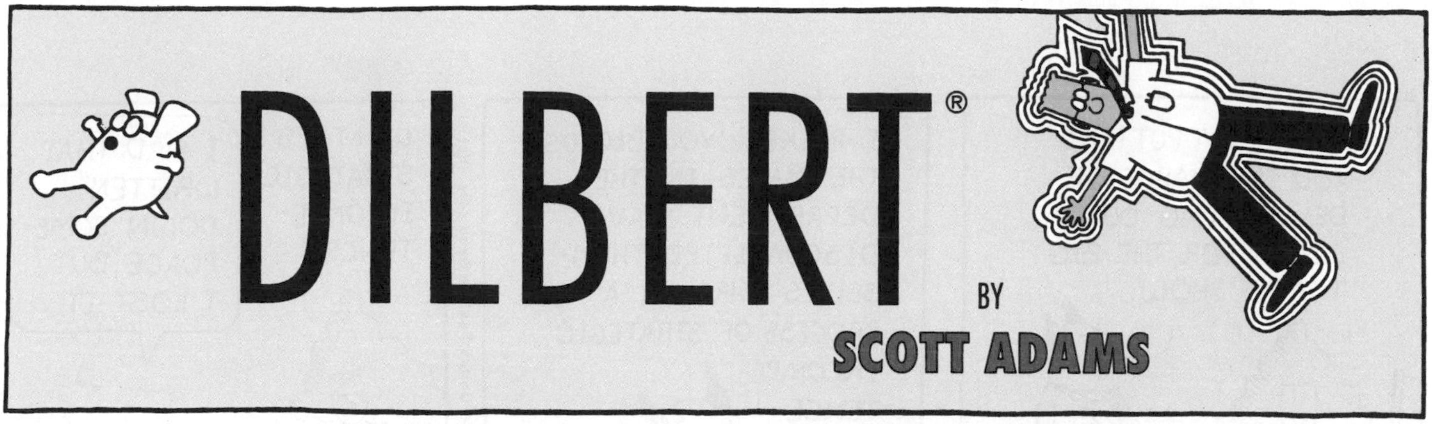

DILBERT®
BY
SCOTT ADAMS

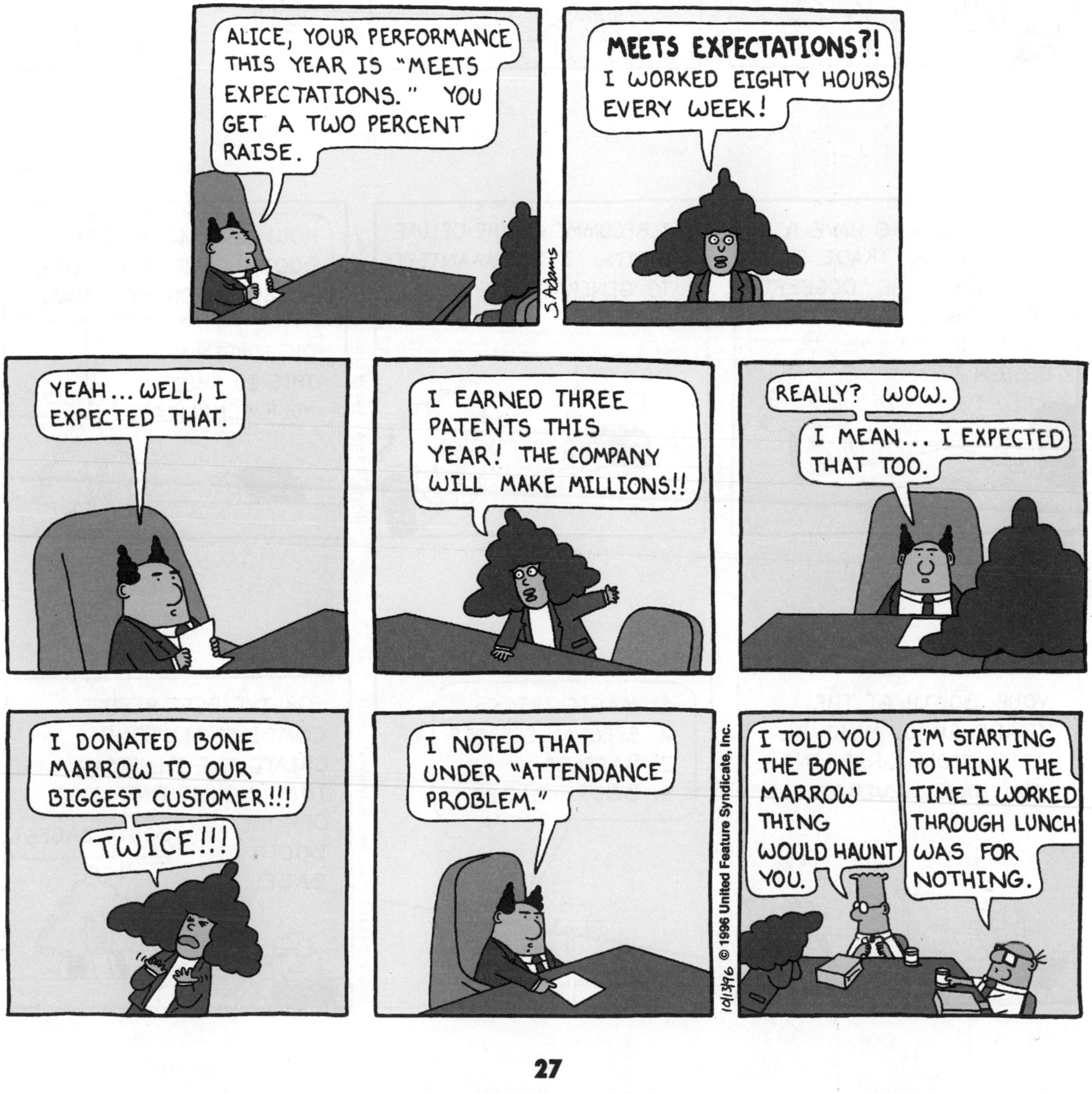

ALICE, YOUR PERFORMANCE THIS YEAR IS "MEETS EXPECTATIONS." YOU GET A TWO PERCENT RAISE.
S. Adams
MEETS EXPECTATIONS?! I WORKED EIGHTY HOURS EVERY WEEK!
YEAH... WELL, I EXPECTED THAT.
I EARNED THREE PATENTS THIS YEAR! THE COMPANY WILL MAKE MILLIONS!!
REALLY? WOW.
I MEAN... I EXPECTED THAT TOO.
I DONATED BONE MARROW TO OUR BIGGEST CUSTOMER!!!
TWICE!!!
I NOTED THAT UNDER "ATTENDANCE PROBLEM."
10/13/96 © 1996 United Feature Syndicate, Inc.
I TOLD YOU THE BONE MARROW THING WOULD HAUNT YOU.
I'M STARTING TO THINK THE TIME I WORKED THROUGH LUNCH WAS FOR NOTHING.

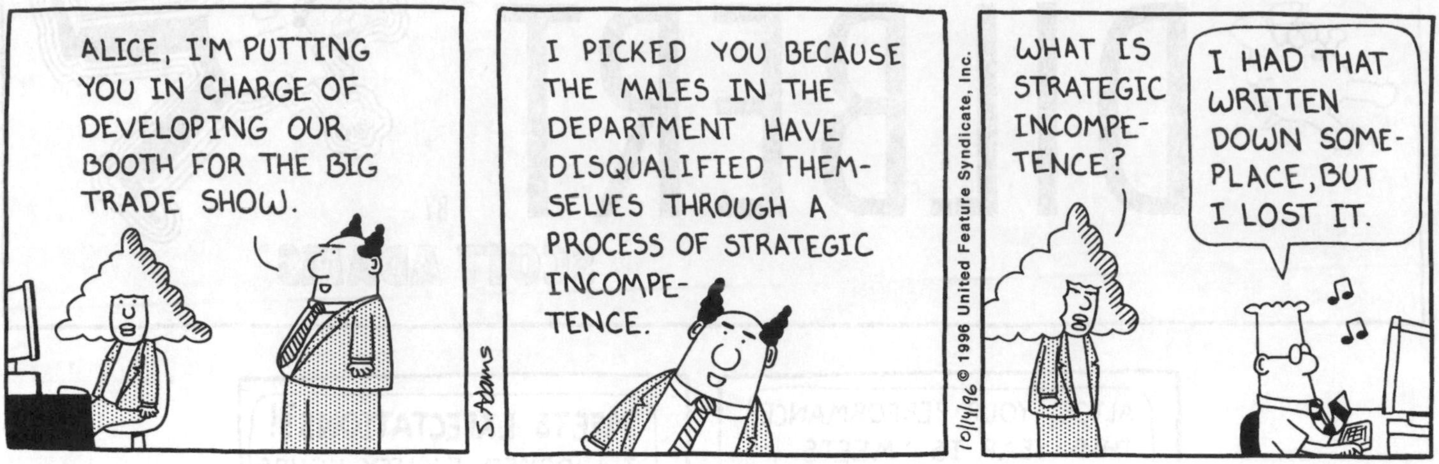
ALICE, I'M PUTTING YOU IN CHARGE OF DEVELOPING OUR BOOTH FOR THE BIG TRADE SHOW.
I PICKED YOU BECAUSE THE MALES IN THE DEPARTMENT HAVE DISQUALIFIED THEMSELVES THROUGH A PROCESS OF STRATEGIC INCOMPETENCE.
WHAT IS STRATEGIC INCOMPETENCE?
I HAD THAT WRITTEN DOWN SOMEPLACE, BUT I LOST IT.
S. Adams
10/14/96 © 1996 United Feature Syndicate, Inc.

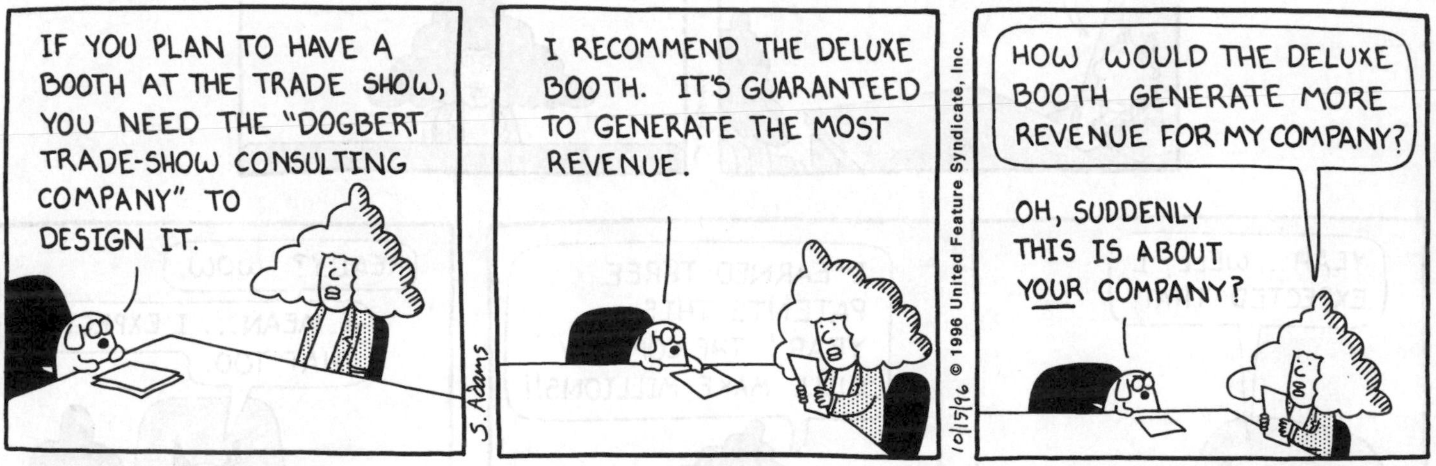
IF YOU PLAN TO HAVE A BOOTH AT THE TRADE SHOW, YOU NEED THE "DOGBERT TRADE-SHOW CONSULTING COMPANY" TO DESIGN IT.
I RECOMMEND THE DELUXE BOOTH. IT'S GUARANTEED TO GENERATE THE MOST REVENUE.
HOW WOULD THE DELUXE BOOTH GENERATE MORE REVENUE FOR MY COMPANY?
OH, SUDDENLY THIS IS ABOUT YOUR COMPANY?
S. Adams
10/15/96 © 1996 United Feature Syndicate, Inc.

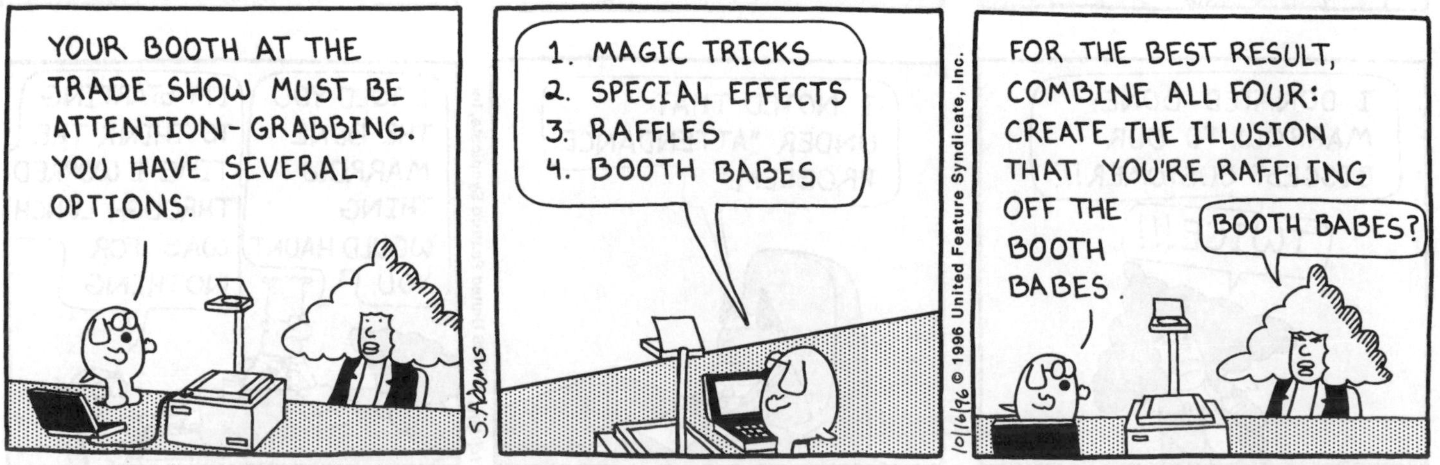
YOUR BOOTH AT THE TRADE SHOW MUST BE ATTENTION-GRABBING. YOU HAVE SEVERAL OPTIONS.
1. MAGIC TRICKS
2. SPECIAL EFFECTS
3. RAFFLES
4. BOOTH BABES
FOR THE BEST RESULT, COMBINE ALL FOUR: CREATE THE ILLUSION THAT YOU'RE RAFFLING OFF THE BOOTH BABES.
BOOTH BABES?
S. Adams
10/16/96 © 1996 United Feature Syndicate, Inc.

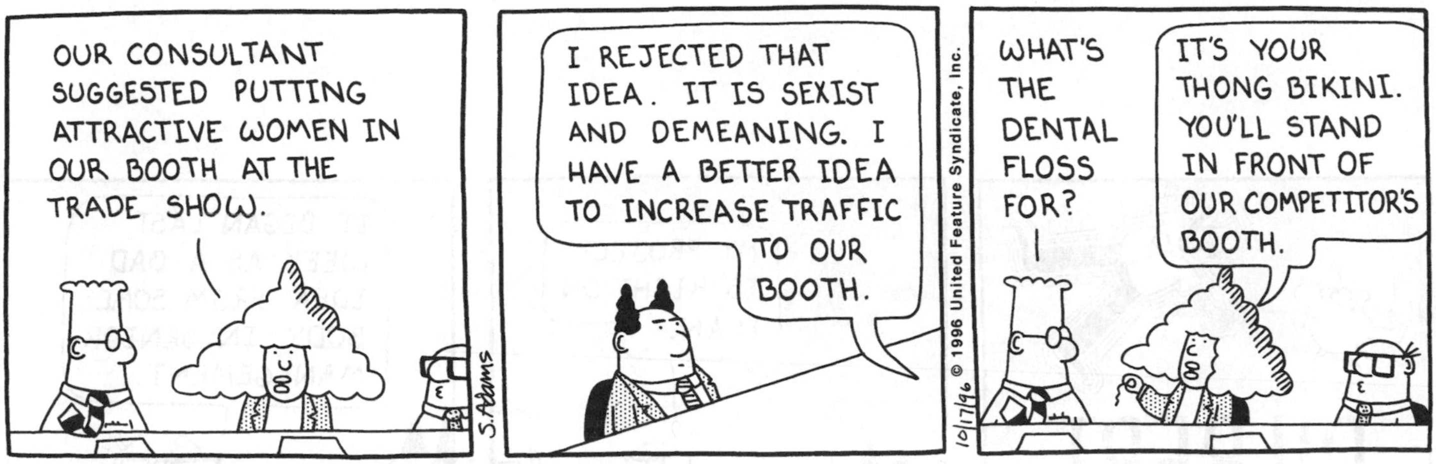
OUR CONSULTANT SUGGESTED PUTTING ATTRACTIVE WOMEN IN OUR BOOTH AT THE TRADE SHOW.
S. Adams
I REJECTED THAT IDEA. IT IS SEXIST AND DEMEANING. I HAVE A BETTER IDEA TO INCREASE TRAFFIC TO OUR BOOTH.
10/17/96 © 1996 United Feature Syndicate, Inc.
WHAT'S THE DENTAL FLOSS FOR?
IT'S YOUR THONG BIKINI. YOU'LL STAND IN FRONT OF OUR COMPETITOR'S BOOTH.

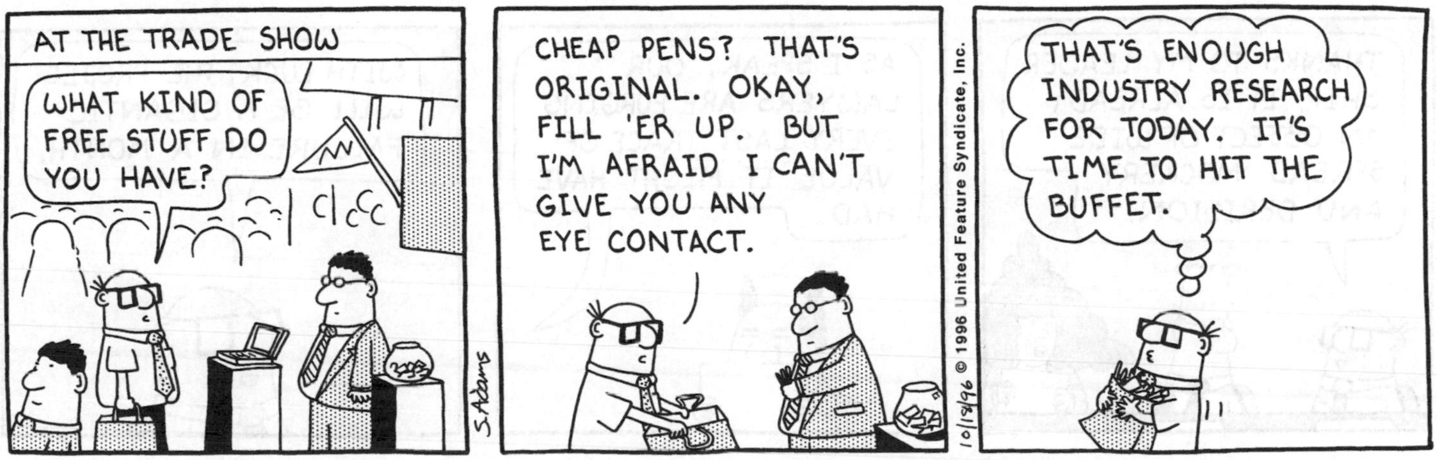
AT THE TRADE SHOW
WHAT KIND OF FREE STUFF DO YOU HAVE?
S. Adams
CHEAP PENS? THAT'S ORIGINAL. OKAY, FILL 'ER UP. BUT I'M AFRAID I CAN'T GIVE YOU ANY EYE CONTACT.
10/18/96 © 1996 United Feature Syndicate, Inc.
THAT'S ENOUGH INDUSTRY RESEARCH FOR TODAY. IT'S TIME TO HIT THE BUFFET.

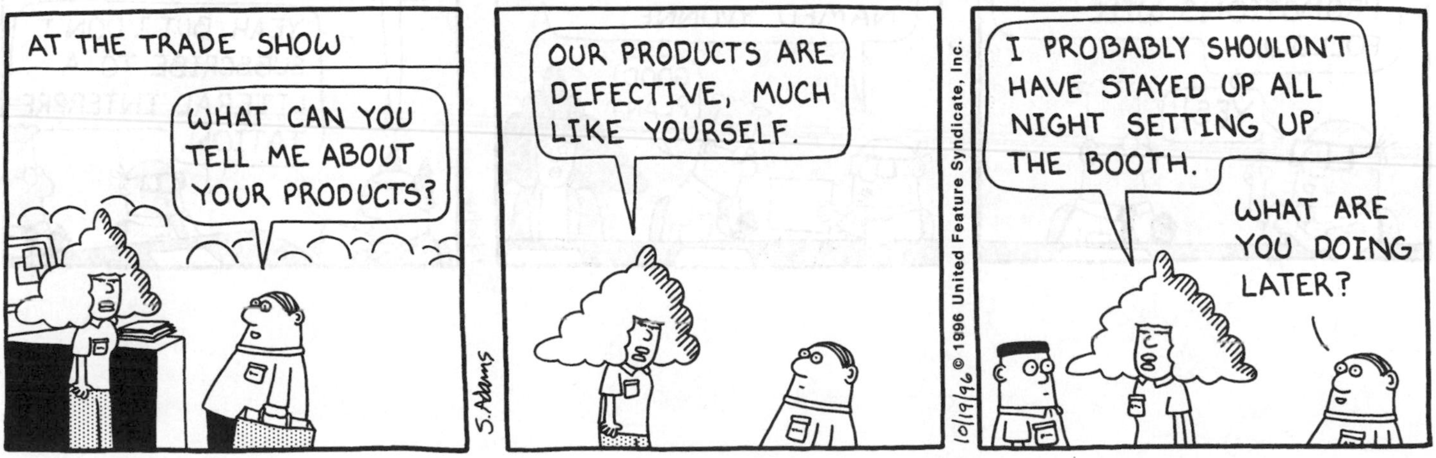
AT THE TRADE SHOW
WHAT CAN YOU TELL ME ABOUT YOUR PRODUCTS?
S. Adams
OUR PRODUCTS ARE DEFECTIVE, MUCH LIKE YOURSELF.
10/19/96 © 1996 United Feature Syndicate, Inc.
I PROBABLY SHOULDN'T HAVE STAYED UP ALL NIGHT SETTING UP THE BOOTH.
WHAT ARE YOU DOING LATER?

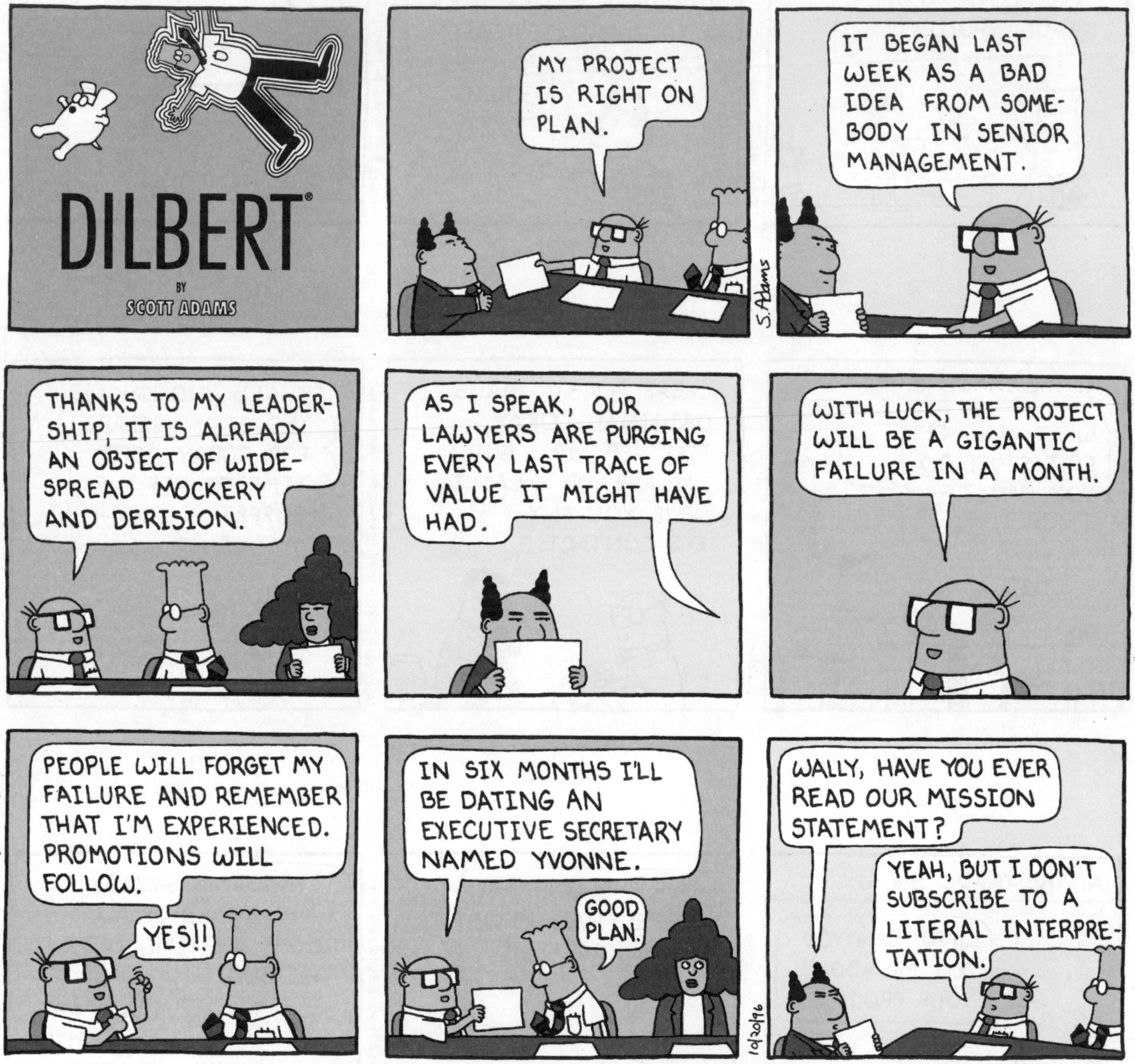
DILBERT®
BY
SCOTT ADAMS
MY PROJECT IS RIGHT ON PLAN.
S. Adams
IT BEGAN LAST WEEK AS A BAD IDEA FROM SOMEBODY IN SENIOR MANAGEMENT.
THANKS TO MY LEADERSHIP, IT IS ALREADY AN OBJECT OF WIDESPREAD MOCKERY AND DERISION.
AS I SPEAK, OUR LAWYERS ARE PURGING EVERY LAST TRACE OF VALUE IT MIGHT HAVE HAD.
WITH LUCK, THE PROJECT WILL BE A GIGANTIC FAILURE IN A MONTH.
PEOPLE WILL FORGET MY FAILURE AND REMEMBER THAT I'M EXPERIENCED. PROMOTIONS WILL FOLLOW.
YES!!
IN SIX MONTHS I'LL BE DATING AN EXECUTIVE SECRETARY NAMED YVONNE.
GOOD PLAN.
10/20/96
WALLY, HAVE YOU EVER READ OUR MISSION STATEMENT?
YEAH, BUT I DON'T SUBSCRIBE TO A LITERAL INTERPRETATION.

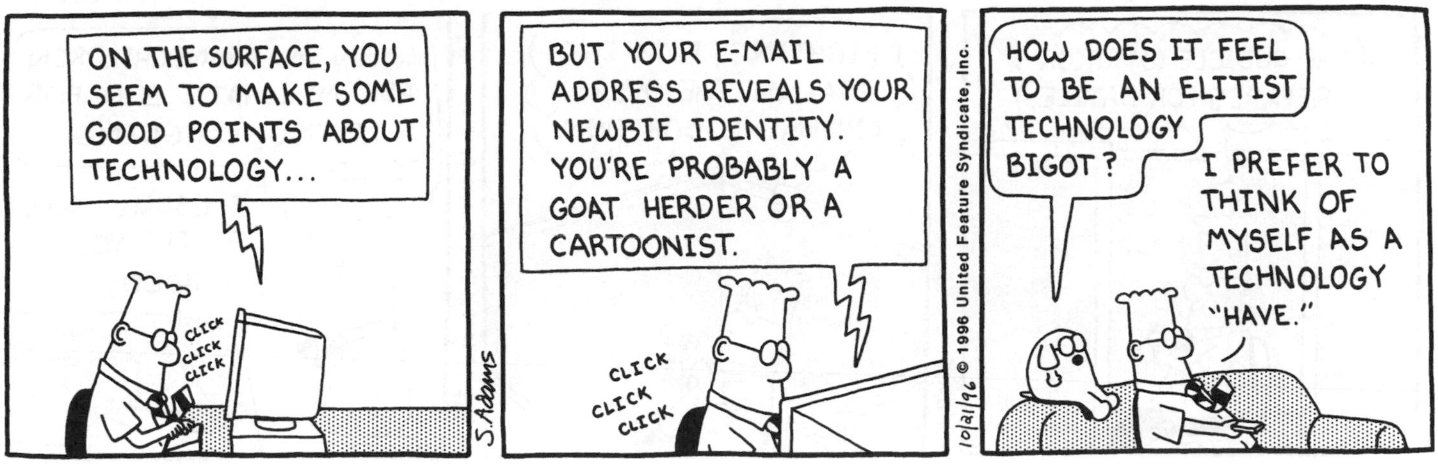

ON THE SURFACE, YOU SEEM TO MAKE SOME GOOD POINTS ABOUT TECHNOLOGY...
CLICK CLICK CLICK
S. Adams
BUT YOUR E-MAIL ADDRESS REVEALS YOUR NEWBIE IDENTITY. YOU'RE PROBABLY A GOAT HERDER OR A CARTOONIST.
CLICK CLICK CLICK
10/21/96 © 1996 United Feature Syndicate, Inc.
HOW DOES IT FEEL TO BE AN ELITIST TECHNOLOGY BIGOT?
I PREFER TO THINK OF MYSELF AS A TECHNOLOGY "HAVE."

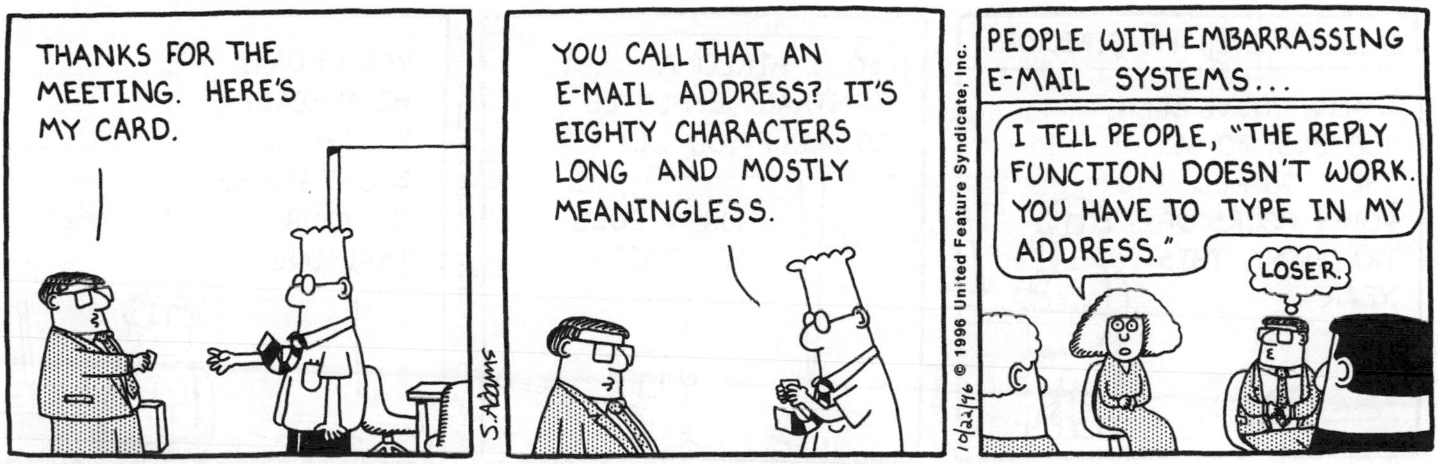

THANKS FOR THE MEETING. HERE'S MY CARD.
S. Adams
YOU CALL THAT AN E-MAIL ADDRESS? IT'S EIGHTY CHARACTERS LONG AND MOSTLY MEANINGLESS.
10/22/96 © 1996 United Feature Syndicate, Inc.
PEOPLE WITH EMBARRASSING E-MAIL SYSTEMS...
I TELL PEOPLE, "THE REPLY FUNCTION DOESN'T WORK. YOU HAVE TO TYPE IN MY ADDRESS."
LOSER.

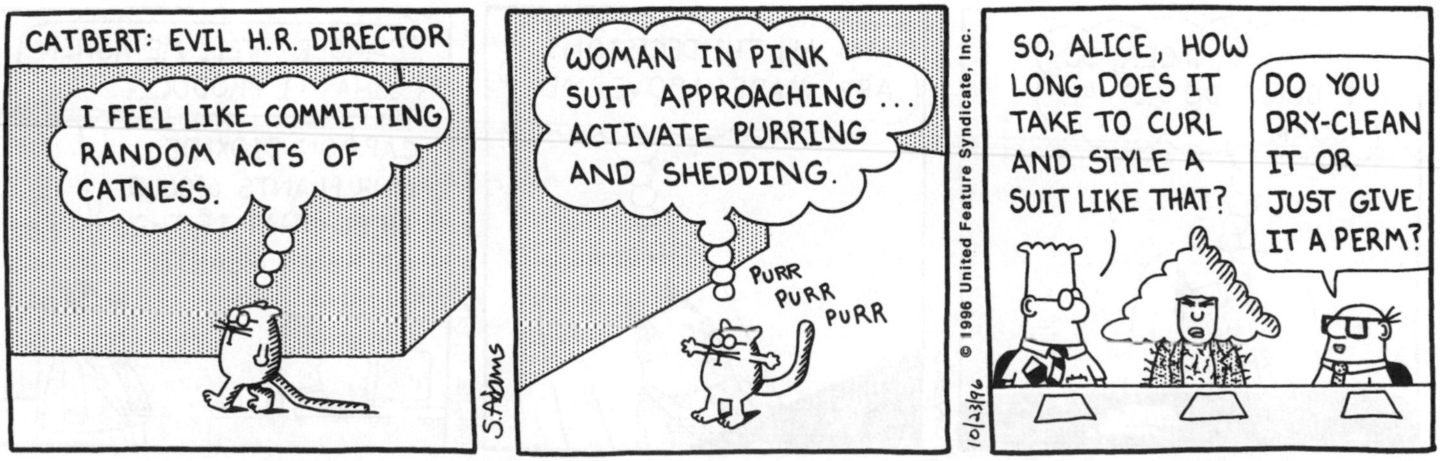

CATBERT: EVIL H.R. DIRECTOR
I FEEL LIKE COMMITTING RANDOM ACTS OF CATNESS.
S. Adams
WOMAN IN PINK SUIT APPROACHING... ACTIVATE PURRING AND SHEDDING.
PURR PURR PURR
10/23/96 © 1996 United Feature Syndicate, Inc.
SO, ALICE, HOW LONG DOES IT TAKE TO CURL AND STYLE A SUIT LIKE THAT?
DO YOU DRY-CLEAN IT OR JUST GIVE IT A PERM?

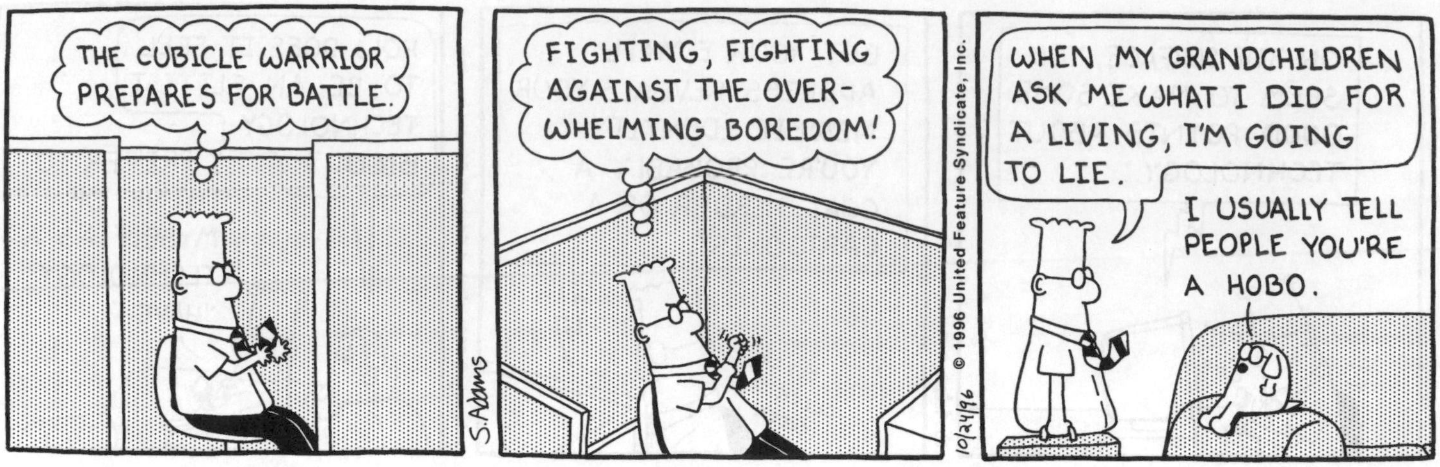
THE CUBICLE WARRIOR PREPARES FOR BATTLE.
S. Adams
FIGHTING, FIGHTING AGAINST THE OVER-WHELMING BOREDOM!
© 1996 United Feature Syndicate, Inc.
10/24/96
WHEN MY GRANDCHILDREN ASK ME WHAT I DID FOR A LIVING, I'M GOING TO LIE.
I USUALLY TELL PEOPLE YOU'RE A HOBO.

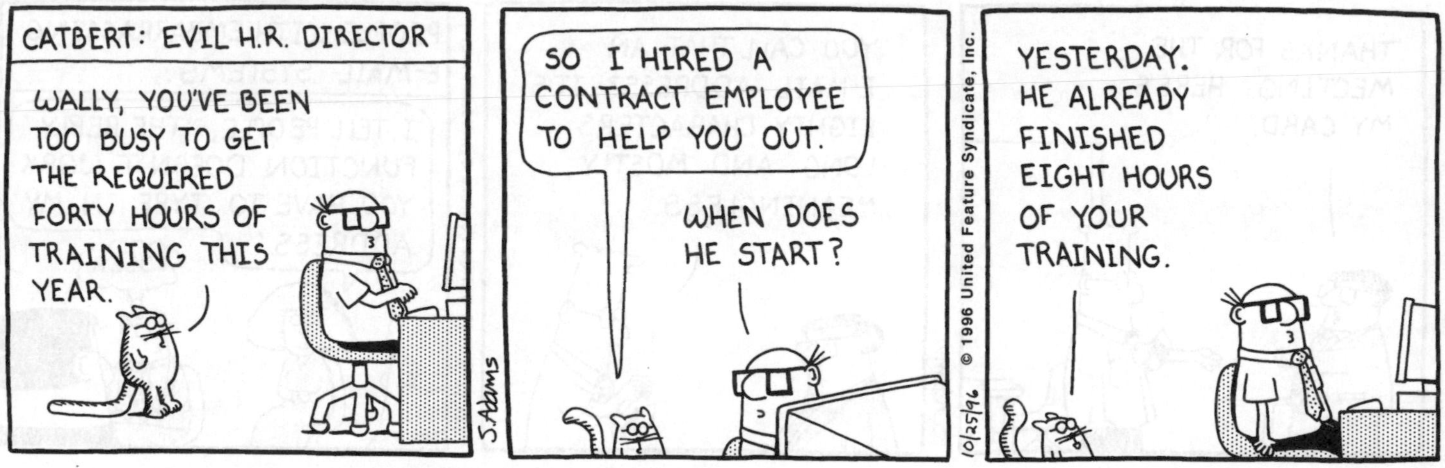
CATBERT: EVIL H.R. DIRECTOR
WALLY, YOU'VE BEEN TOO BUSY TO GET THE REQUIRED FORTY HOURS OF TRAINING THIS YEAR.
S. Adams
SO I HIRED A CONTRACT EMPLOYEE TO HELP YOU OUT.
WHEN DOES HE START?
© 1996 United Feature Syndicate, Inc.
10/25/96
YESTERDAY. HE ALREADY FINISHED EIGHT HOURS OF YOUR TRAINING.

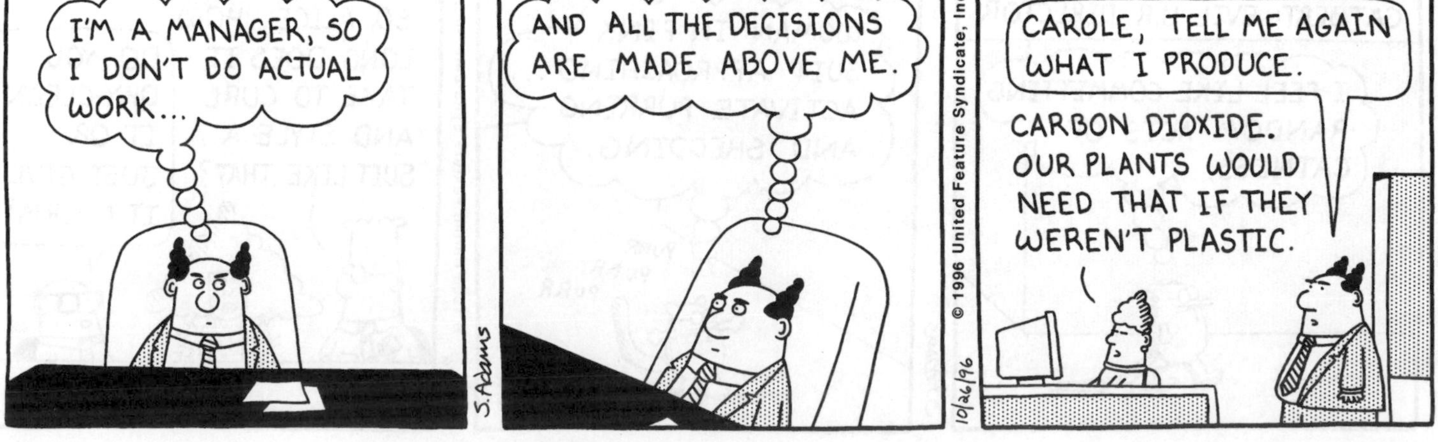
I'M A MANAGER, SO I DON'T DO ACTUAL WORK...
S. Adams
AND ALL THE DECISIONS ARE MADE ABOVE ME.
© 1996 United Feature Syndicate, Inc.
10/26/96
CAROLE, TELL ME AGAIN WHAT I PRODUCE.
CARBON DIOXIDE. OUR PLANTS WOULD NEED THAT IF THEY WEREN'T PLASTIC.

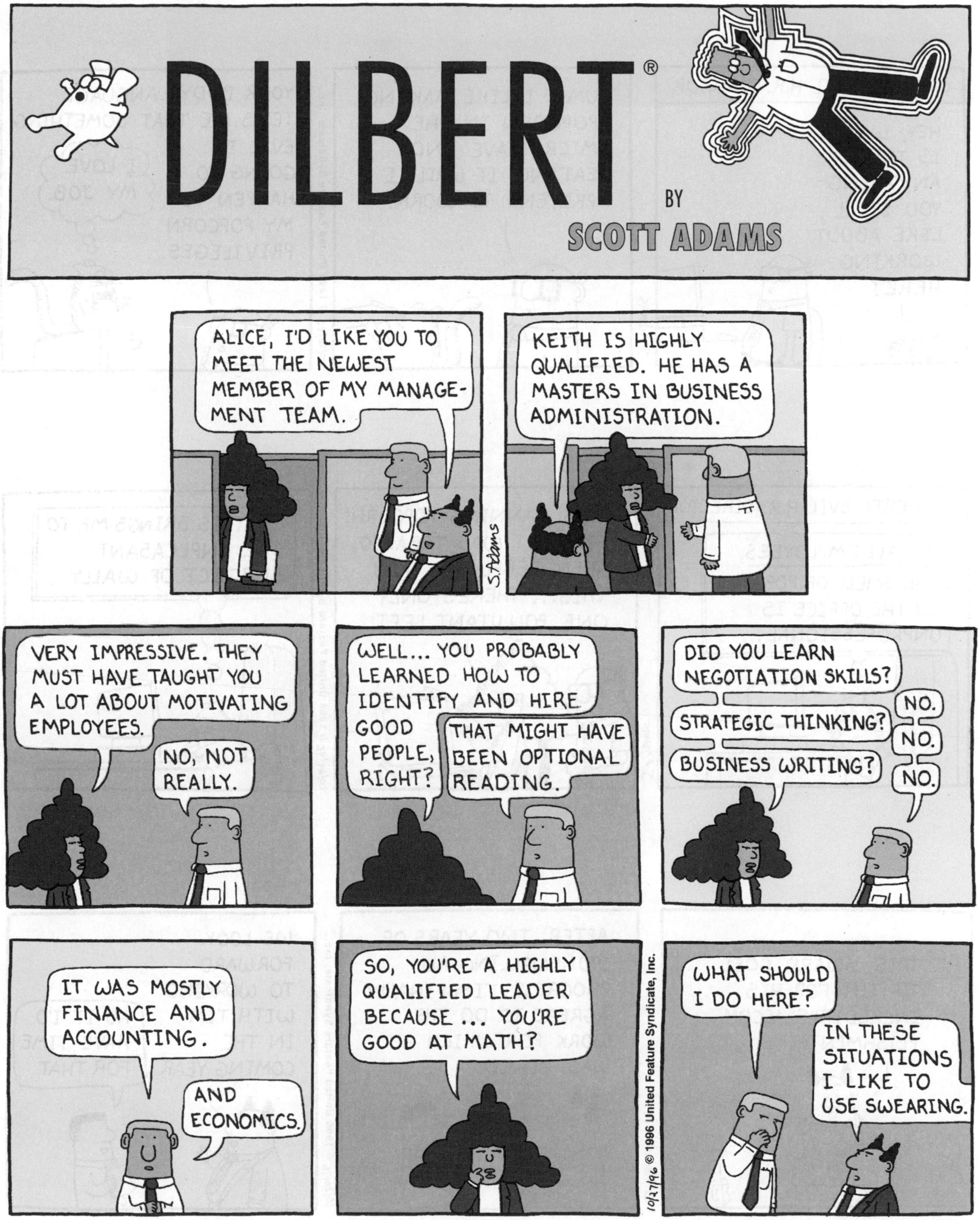
DILBERT®
BY
SCOTT ADAMS
ALICE, I'D LIKE YOU TO MEET THE NEWEST MEMBER OF MY MANAGEMENT TEAM.
S. Adams
KEITH IS HIGHLY QUALIFIED. HE HAS A MASTERS IN BUSINESS ADMINISTRATION.
VERY IMPRESSIVE. THEY MUST HAVE TAUGHT YOU A LOT ABOUT MOTIVATING EMPLOYEES.
NO, NOT REALLY.
WELL... YOU PROBABLY LEARNED HOW TO IDENTIFY AND HIRE GOOD PEOPLE, RIGHT?
THAT MIGHT HAVE BEEN OPTIONAL READING.
DID YOU LEARN NEGOTIATION SKILLS?
NO.
STRATEGIC THINKING?
NO.
BUSINESS WRITING?
NO.
IT WAS MOSTLY FINANCE AND ACCOUNTING.
AND ECONOMICS.
SO, YOU'RE A HIGHLY QUALIFIED LEADER BECAUSE ... YOU'RE GOOD AT MATH?
10/27/96 © 1996 United Feature Syndicate, Inc.
WHAT SHOULD I DO HERE?
IN THESE SITUATIONS I LIKE TO USE SWEARING.

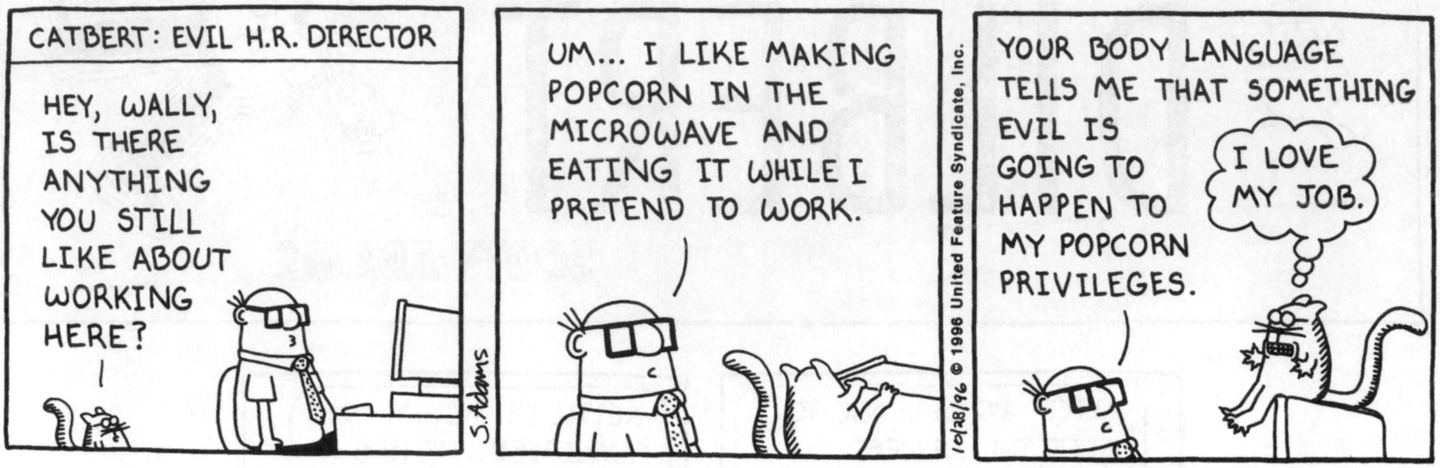
CATBERT: EVIL H.R. DIRECTOR
HEY, WALLY, IS THERE ANYTHING YOU STILL LIKE ABOUT WORKING HERE?
S. Adams
UM... I LIKE MAKING POPCORN IN THE MICROWAVE AND EATING IT WHILE I PRETEND TO WORK.
10/28/96 © 1996 United Feature Syndicate, Inc.
YOUR BODY LANGUAGE TELLS ME THAT SOMETHING EVIL IS GOING TO HAPPEN TO MY POPCORN PRIVILEGES.
I LOVE MY JOB.

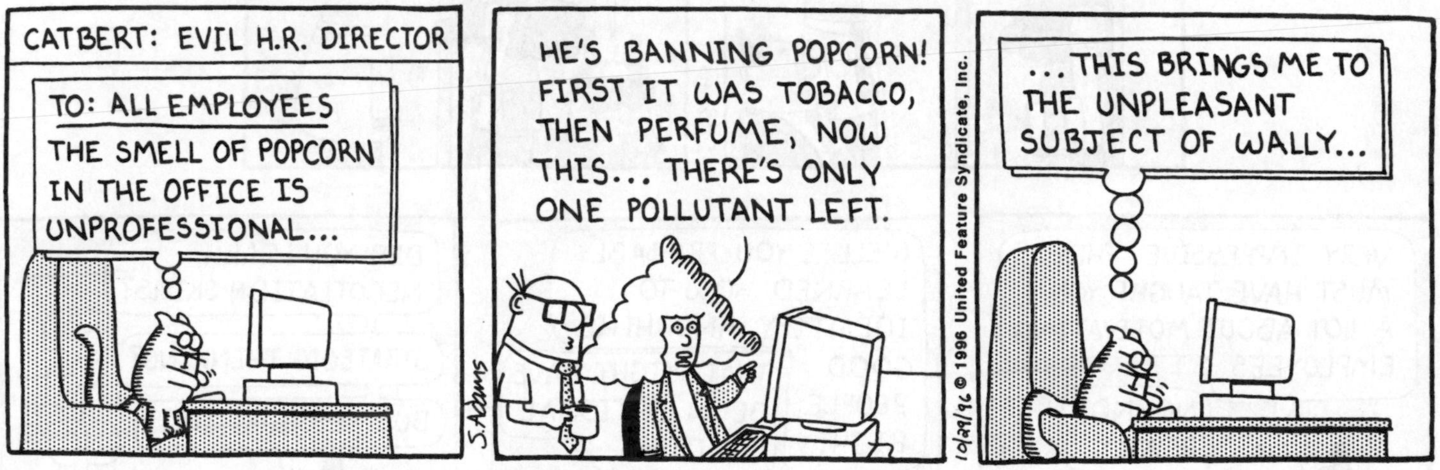
CATBERT: EVIL H.R. DIRECTOR
TO: ALL EMPLOYEES
THE SMELL OF POPCORN IN THE OFFICE IS UNPROFESSIONAL...
S. Adams
HE'S BANNING POPCORN! FIRST IT WAS TOBACCO, THEN PERFUME, NOW THIS... THERE'S ONLY ONE POLLUTANT LEFT.
10/29/96 © 1996 United Feature Syndicate, Inc.
...THIS BRINGS ME TO THE UNPLEASANT SUBJECT OF WALLY...

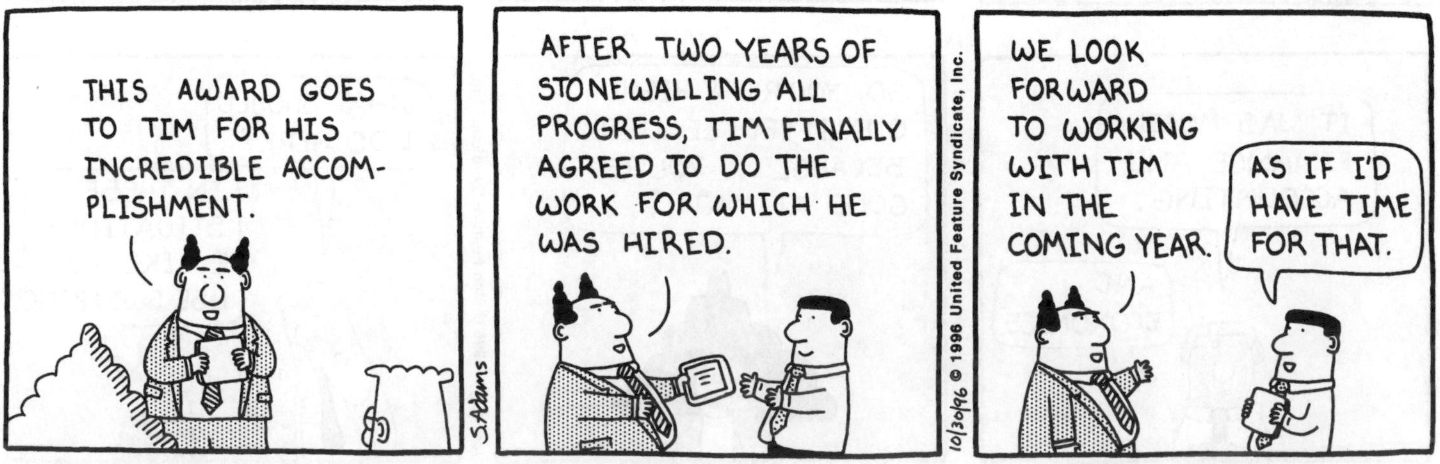
THIS AWARD GOES TO TIM FOR HIS INCREDIBLE ACCOM-PLISHMENT.
S. Adams
AFTER TWO YEARS OF STONEWALLING ALL PROGRESS, TIM FINALLY AGREED TO DO THE WORK FOR WHICH HE WAS HIRED.
10/30/96 © 1996 United Feature Syndicate, Inc.
WE LOOK FORWARD TO WORKING WITH TIM IN THE COMING YEAR.
AS IF I'D HAVE TIME FOR THAT.

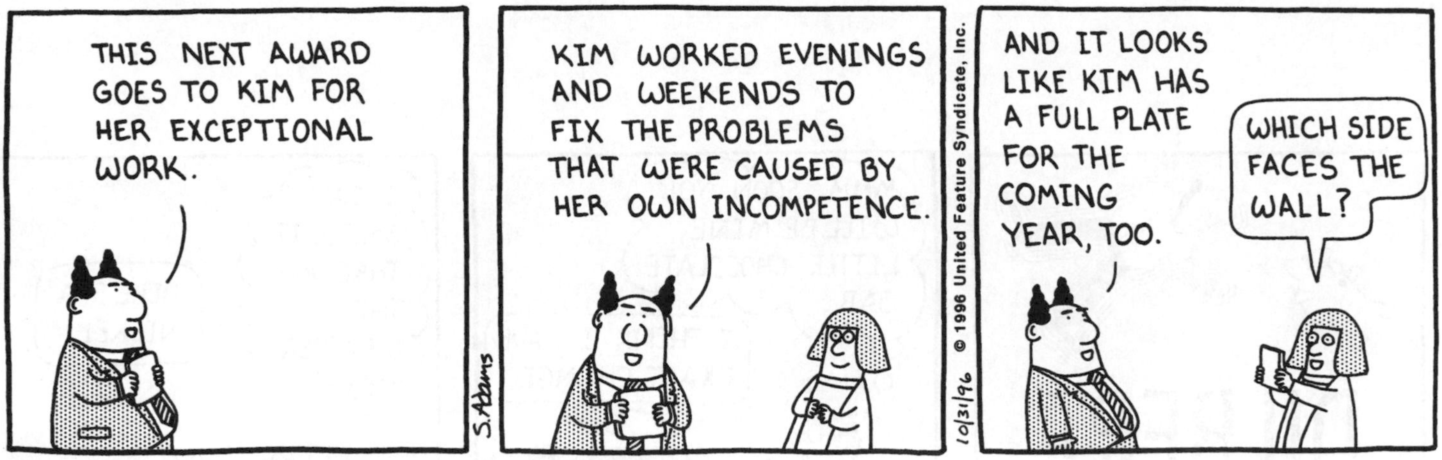
THIS NEXT AWARD GOES TO KIM FOR HER EXCEPTIONAL WORK.
KIM WORKED EVENINGS AND WEEKENDS TO FIX THE PROBLEMS THAT WERE CAUSED BY HER OWN INCOMPETENCE.
S. Adams
10/31/96 © 1996 United Feature Syndicate, Inc.
AND IT LOOKS LIKE KIM HAS A FULL PLATE FOR THE COMING YEAR, TOO.
WHICH SIDE FACES THE WALL?

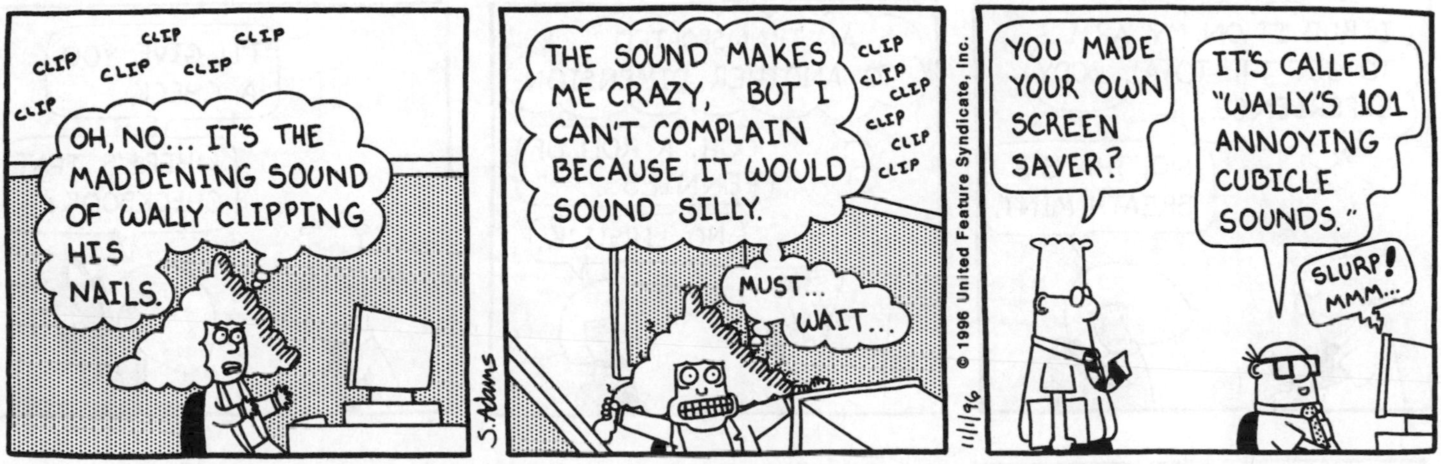
CLIP CLIP CLIP CLIP CLIP CLIP
OH, NO... IT'S THE MADDENING SOUND OF WALLY CLIPPING HIS NAILS.
S. Adams
THE SOUND MAKES ME CRAZY, BUT I CAN'T COMPLAIN BECAUSE IT WOULD SOUND SILLY.
CLIP CLIP CLIP CLIP CLIP CLIP
MUST... WAIT...
11/1/96 © 1996 United Feature Syndicate, Inc.
YOU MADE YOUR OWN SCREEN SAVER?
IT'S CALLED "WALLY'S 101 ANNOYING CUBICLE SOUNDS."
SLURP! MMM...

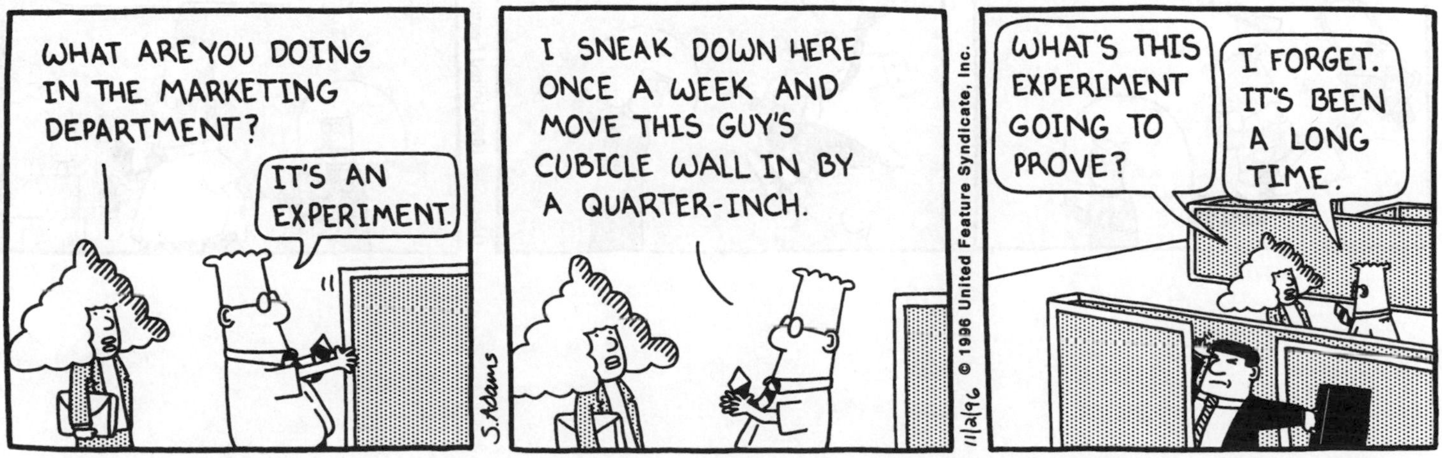
WHAT ARE YOU DOING IN THE MARKETING DEPARTMENT?
IT'S AN EXPERIMENT.
S. Adams
I SNEAK DOWN HERE ONCE A WEEK AND MOVE THIS GUY'S CUBICLE WALL IN BY A QUARTER-INCH.
11/2/96 © 1996 United Feature Syndicate, Inc.
WHAT'S THIS EXPERIMENT GOING TO PROVE?
I FORGET. IT'S BEEN A LONG TIME.

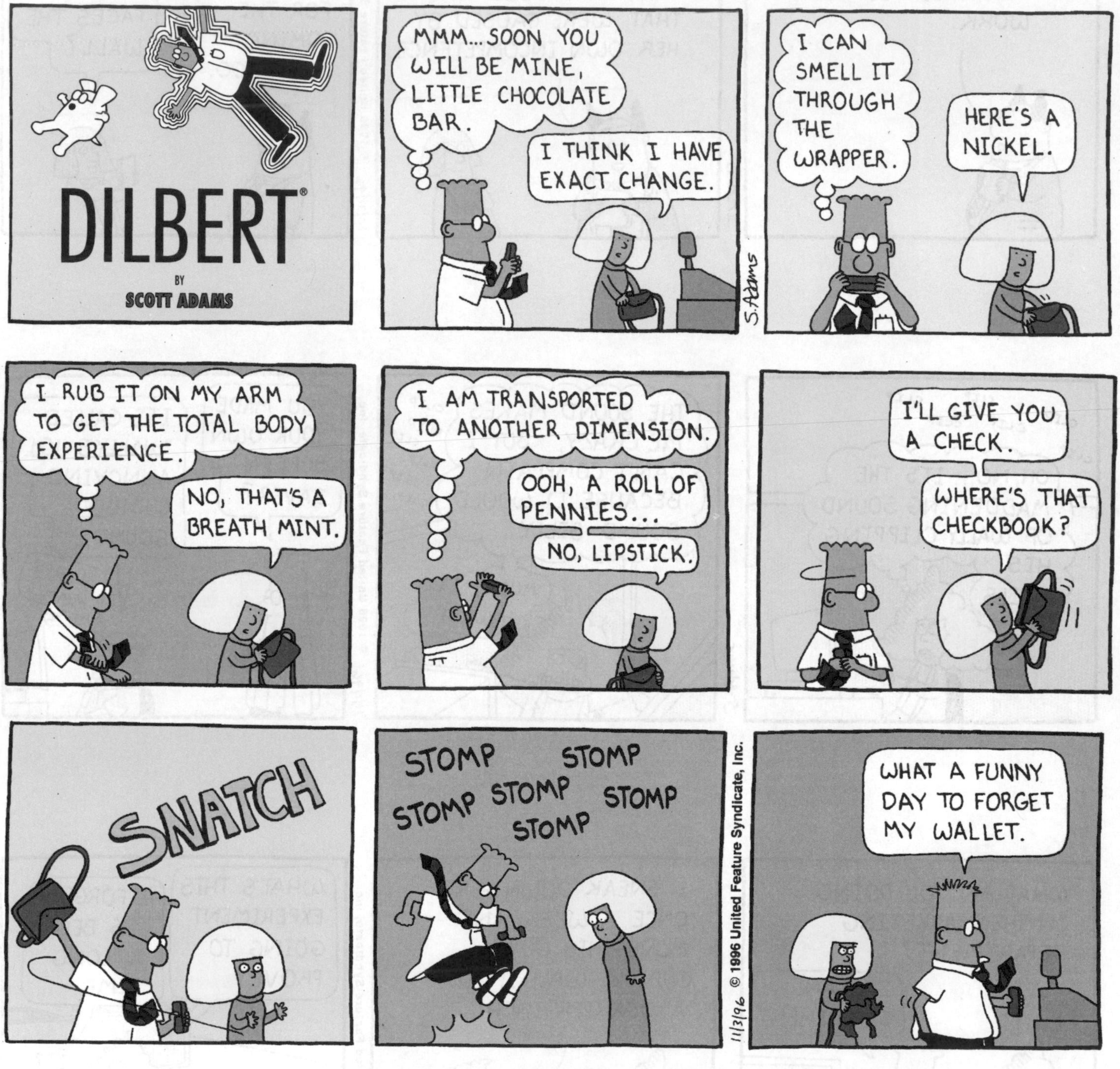

DILBERT®
BY
SCOTT ADAMS
MMM... SOON YOU WILL BE MINE, LITTLE CHOCOLATE BAR.
I THINK I HAVE EXACT CHANGE.
S. Adams
I CAN SMELL IT THROUGH THE WRAPPER.
HERE'S A NICKEL.
I RUB IT ON MY ARM TO GET THE TOTAL BODY EXPERIENCE.
NO, THAT'S A BREATH MINT.
I AM TRANSPORTED TO ANOTHER DIMENSION.
OOH, A ROLL OF PENNIES...
NO, LIPSTICK.
I'LL GIVE YOU A CHECK.
WHERE'S THAT CHECKBOOK?
SNATCH
STOMP STOMP
STOMP STOMP STOMP
STOMP
11/3/96 © 1996 United Feature Syndicate, Inc.
WHAT A FUNNY DAY TO FORGET MY WALLET.

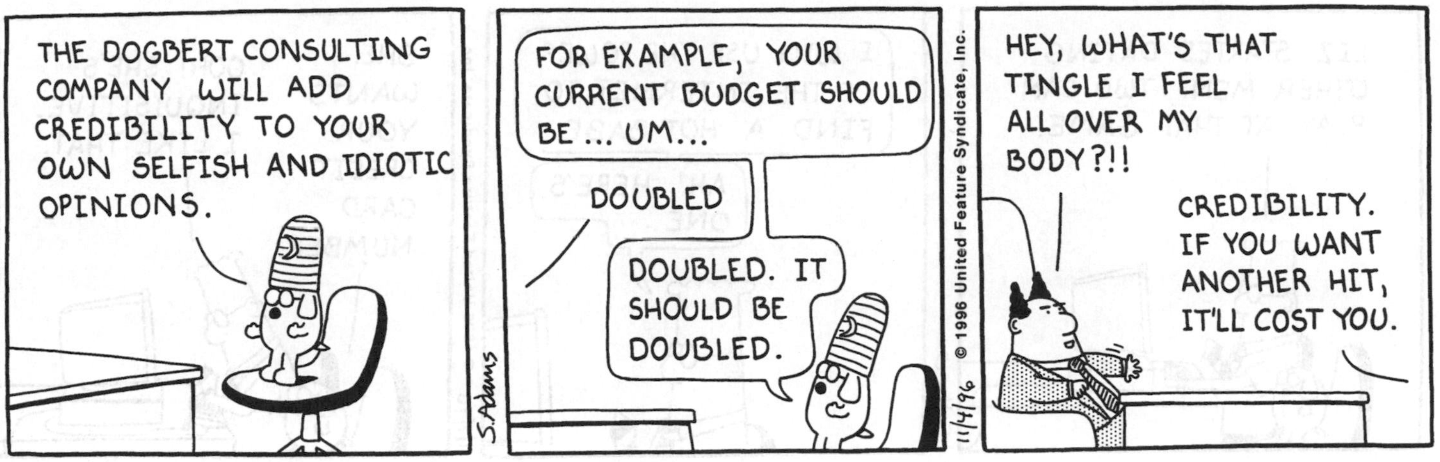
THE DOGBERT CONSULTING COMPANY WILL ADD CREDIBILITY TO YOUR OWN SELFISH AND IDIOTIC OPINIONS.
S. Adams
FOR EXAMPLE, YOUR CURRENT BUDGET SHOULD BE ... UM ...
DOUBLED
DOUBLED. IT SHOULD BE DOUBLED.
11/4/96
© 1996 United Feature Syndicate, Inc.
HEY, WHAT'S THAT TINGLE I FEEL ALL OVER MY BODY?!!
CREDIBILITY. IF YOU WANT ANOTHER HIT, IT'LL COST YOU.

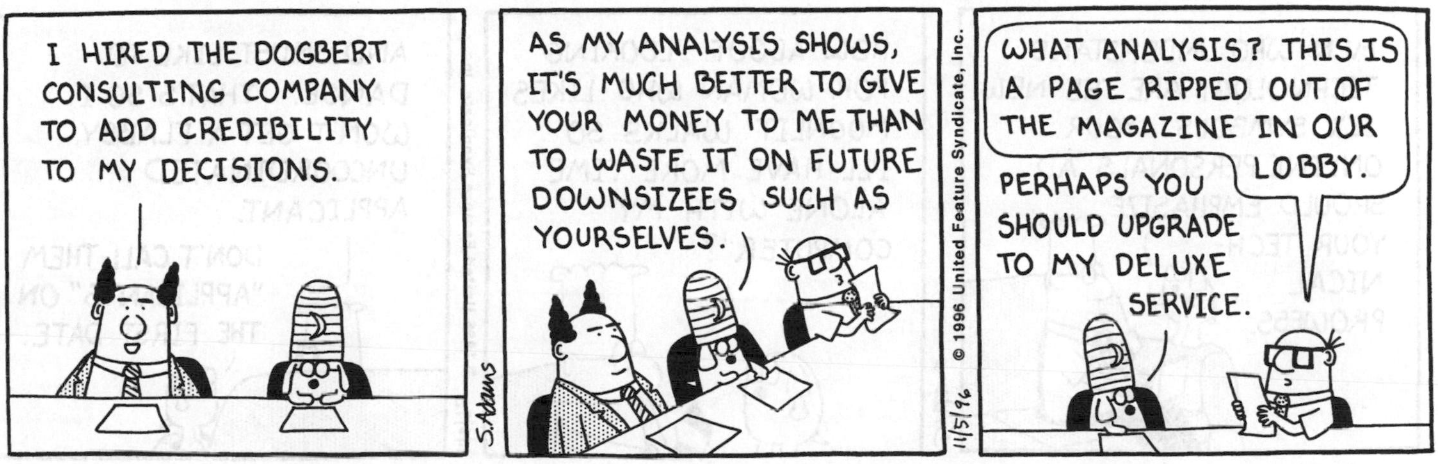
I HIRED THE DOGBERT CONSULTING COMPANY TO ADD CREDIBILITY TO MY DECISIONS.
S. Adams
AS MY ANALYSIS SHOWS, IT'S MUCH BETTER TO GIVE YOUR MONEY TO ME THAN TO WASTE IT ON FUTURE DOWNSIZEES SUCH AS YOURSELVES.
11/5/96
© 1996 United Feature Syndicate, Inc.
WHAT ANALYSIS? THIS IS A PAGE RIPPED OUT OF THE MAGAZINE IN OUR LOBBY.
PERHAPS YOU SHOULD UPGRADE TO MY DELUXE SERVICE.

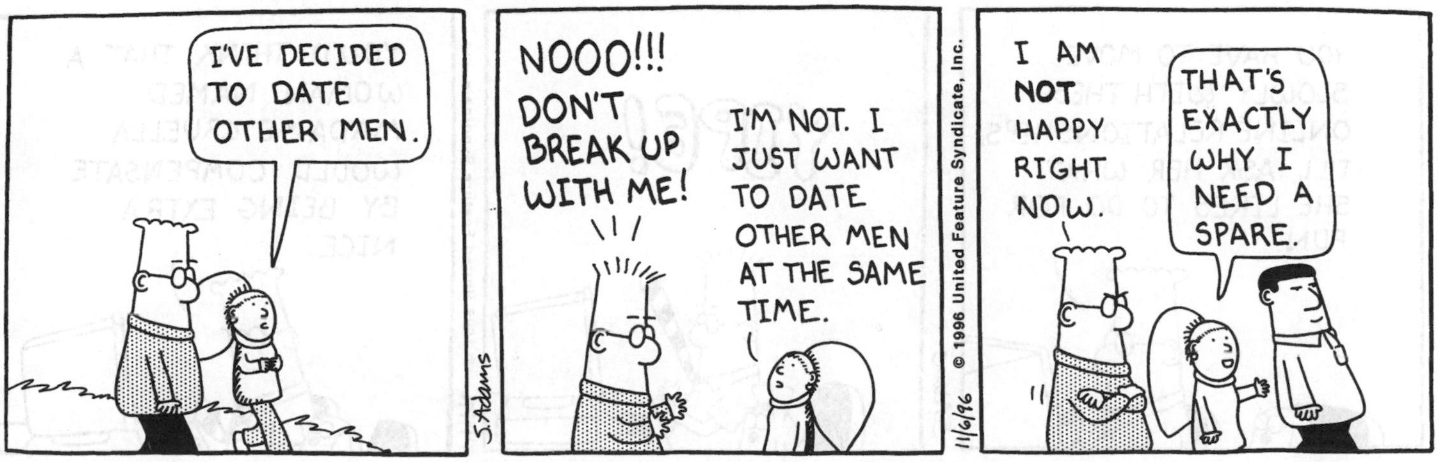
I'VE DECIDED TO DATE OTHER MEN.
S. Adams
NOOO!!! DON'T BREAK UP WITH ME!
I'M NOT. I JUST WANT TO DATE OTHER MEN AT THE SAME TIME.
11/6/96
© 1996 United Feature Syndicate, Inc.
I AM **NOT** HAPPY RIGHT NOW.
THAT'S EXACTLY WHY I NEED A SPARE.

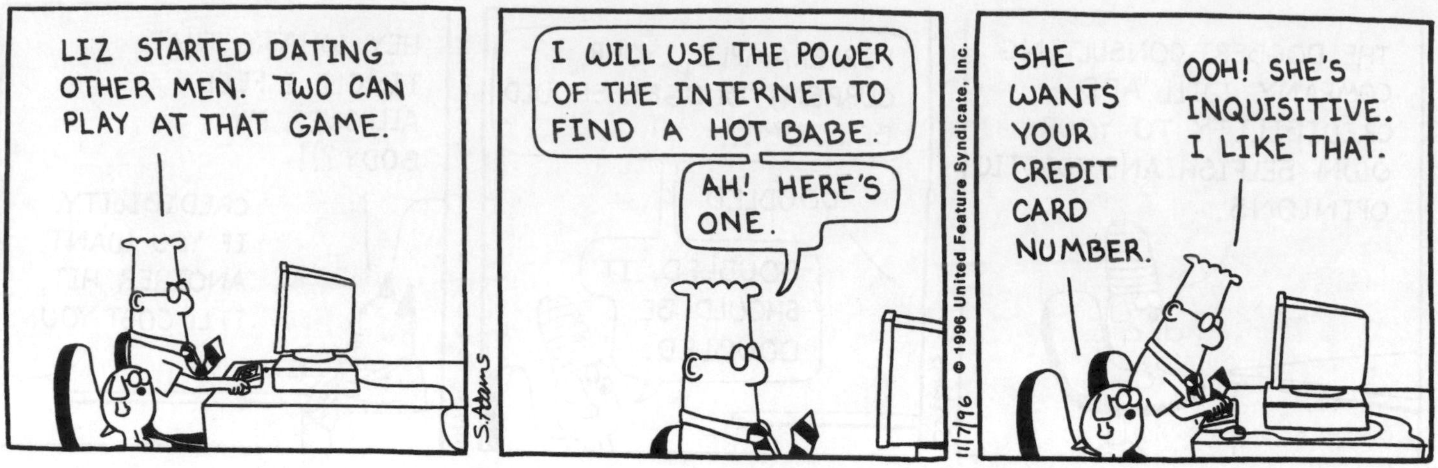
LIZ STARTED DATING OTHER MEN. TWO CAN PLAY AT THAT GAME.
S.Adams
I WILL USE THE POWER OF THE INTERNET TO FIND A HOT BABE.
AH! HERE'S ONE.
11/7/96 © 1996 United Feature Syndicate, Inc.
SHE WANTS YOUR CREDIT CARD NUMBER.
OOH! SHE'S INQUISITIVE. I LIKE THAT.

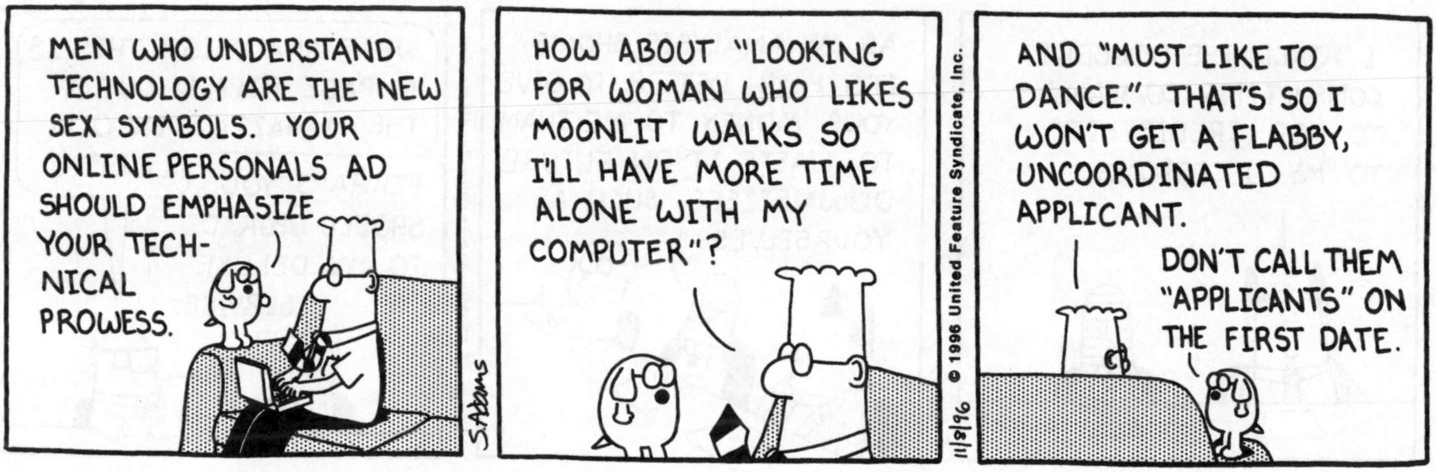
MEN WHO UNDERSTAND TECHNOLOGY ARE THE NEW SEX SYMBOLS. YOUR ONLINE PERSONALS AD SHOULD EMPHASIZE YOUR TECHNICAL PROWESS.
S.Adams
HOW ABOUT "LOOKING FOR WOMAN WHO LIKES MOONLIT WALKS SO I'LL HAVE MORE TIME ALONE WITH MY COMPUTER"?
11/8/96 © 1996 United Feature Syndicate, Inc.
AND "MUST LIKE TO DANCE." THAT'S SO I WON'T GET A FLABBY, UNCOORDINATED APPLICANT.
DON'T CALL THEM "APPLICANTS" ON THE FIRST DATE.

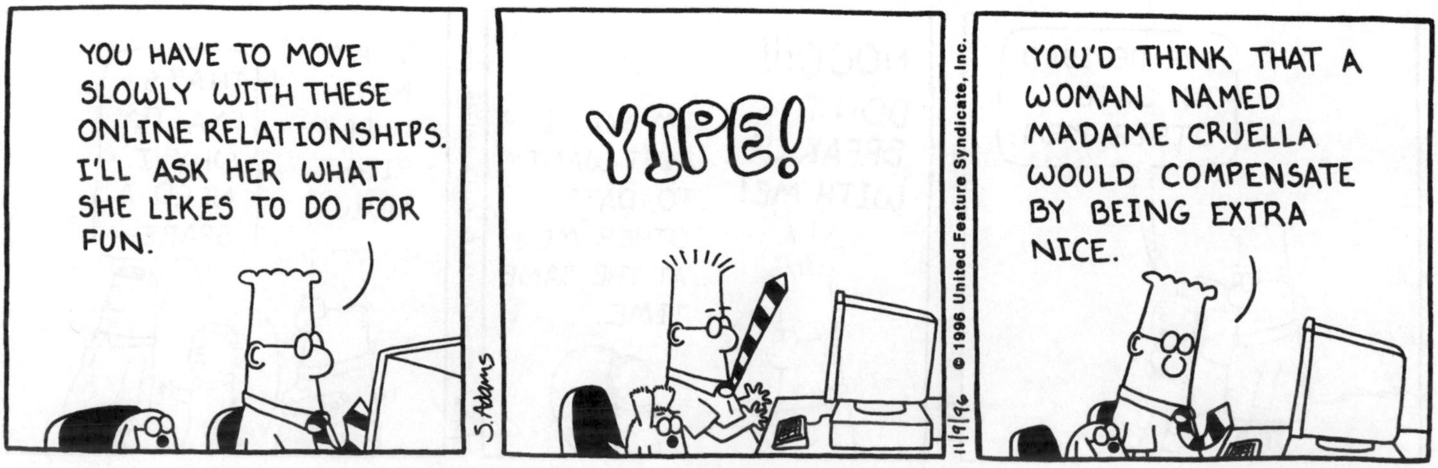
YOU HAVE TO MOVE SLOWLY WITH THESE ONLINE RELATIONSHIPS. I'LL ASK HER WHAT SHE LIKES TO DO FOR FUN.
S.Adams
YIPE!
11/9/96 © 1996 United Feature Syndicate, Inc.
YOU'D THINK THAT A WOMAN NAMED MADAME CRUELLA WOULD COMPENSATE BY BEING EXTRA NICE.

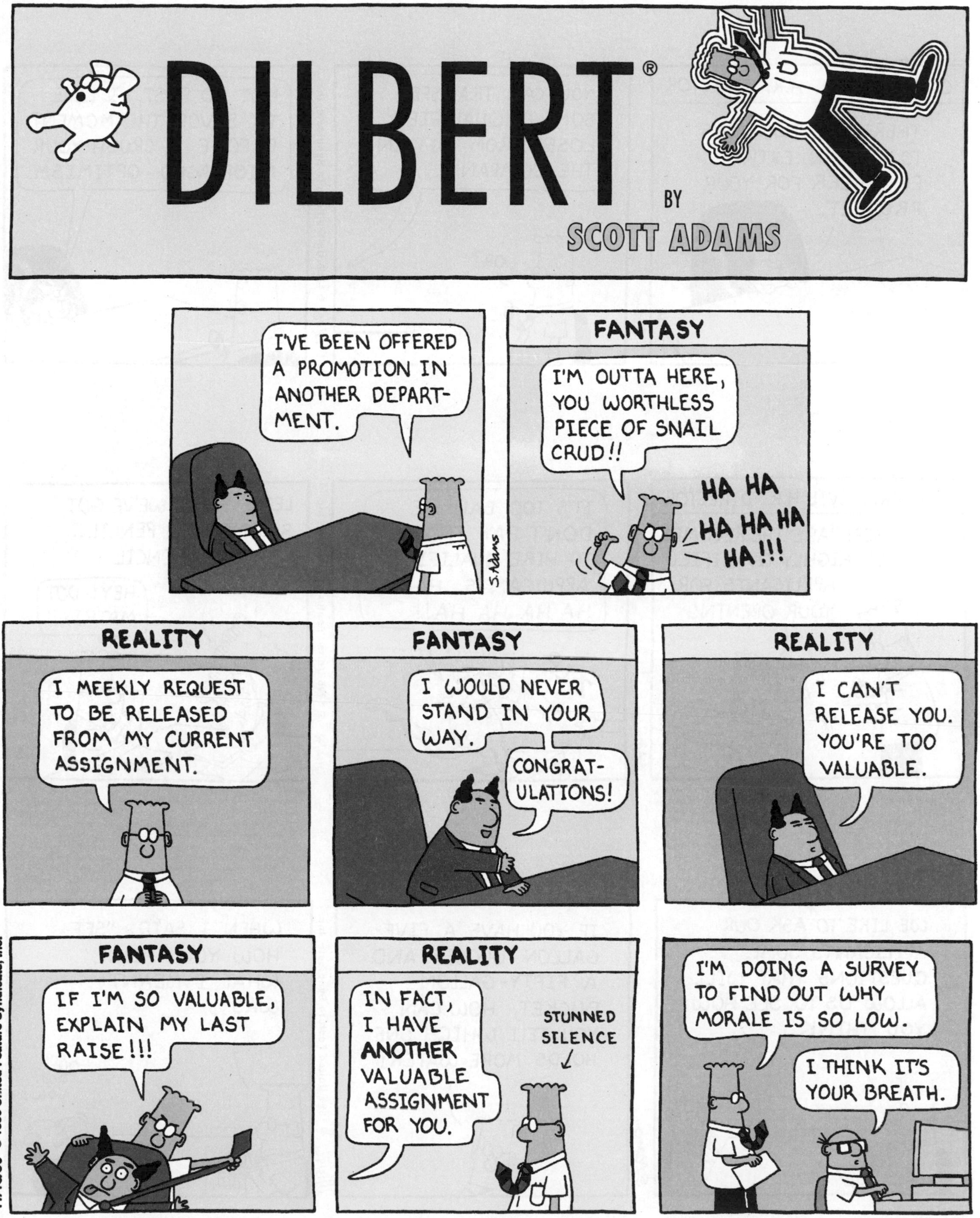
DILBERT®
BY
SCOTT ADAMS
I'VE BEEN OFFERED A PROMOTION IN ANOTHER DEPART-MENT.
S. Adams
FANTASY
I'M OUTTA HERE, YOU WORTHLESS PIECE OF SNAIL CRUD!!
HA HA HA HA HA HA!!!
REALITY
I MEEKLY REQUEST TO BE RELEASED FROM MY CURRENT ASSIGNMENT.
FANTASY
I WOULD NEVER STAND IN YOUR WAY.
CONGRAT-ULATIONS!
REALITY
I CAN'T RELEASE YOU. YOU'RE TOO VALUABLE.
FANTASY
IF I'M SO VALUABLE, EXPLAIN MY LAST RAISE!!!
REALITY
IN FACT, I HAVE ANOTHER VALUABLE ASSIGNMENT FOR YOU.
STUNNED SILENCE
I'M DOING A SURVEY TO FIND OUT WHY MORALE IS SO LOW.
I THINK IT'S YOUR BREATH.

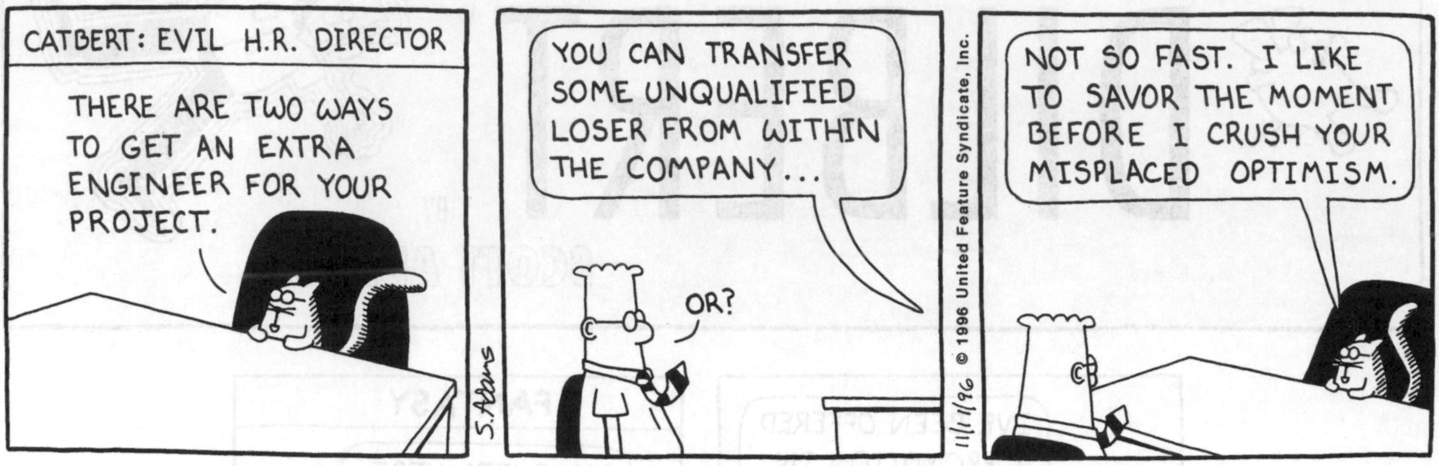
CATBERT: EVIL H.R. DIRECTOR
THERE ARE TWO WAYS TO GET AN EXTRA ENGINEER FOR YOUR PROJECT.
YOU CAN TRANSFER SOME UNQUALIFIED LOSER FROM WITHIN THE COMPANY...
OR?
NOT SO FAST. I LIKE TO SAVOR THE MOMENT BEFORE I CRUSH YOUR MISPLACED OPTIMISM.
S. Adams
11/1/96 © 1996 United Feature Syndicate, Inc.

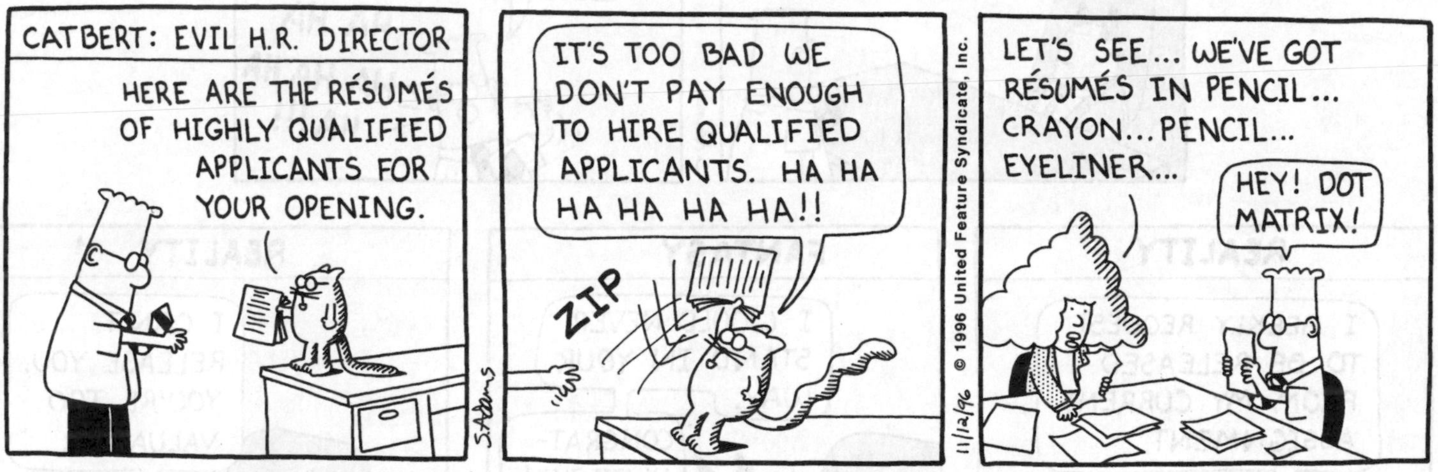
CATBERT: EVIL H.R. DIRECTOR
HERE ARE THE RÉSUMÉS OF HIGHLY QUALIFIED APPLICANTS FOR YOUR OPENING.
IT'S TOO BAD WE DON'T PAY ENOUGH TO HIRE QUALIFIED APPLICANTS. HA HA HA HA HA HA!!
ZIP
LET'S SEE... WE'VE GOT RÉSUMÉS IN PENCIL... CRAYON... PENCIL... EYELINER...
HEY! DOT MATRIX!
S. Adams
11/12/96 © 1996 United Feature Syndicate, Inc.

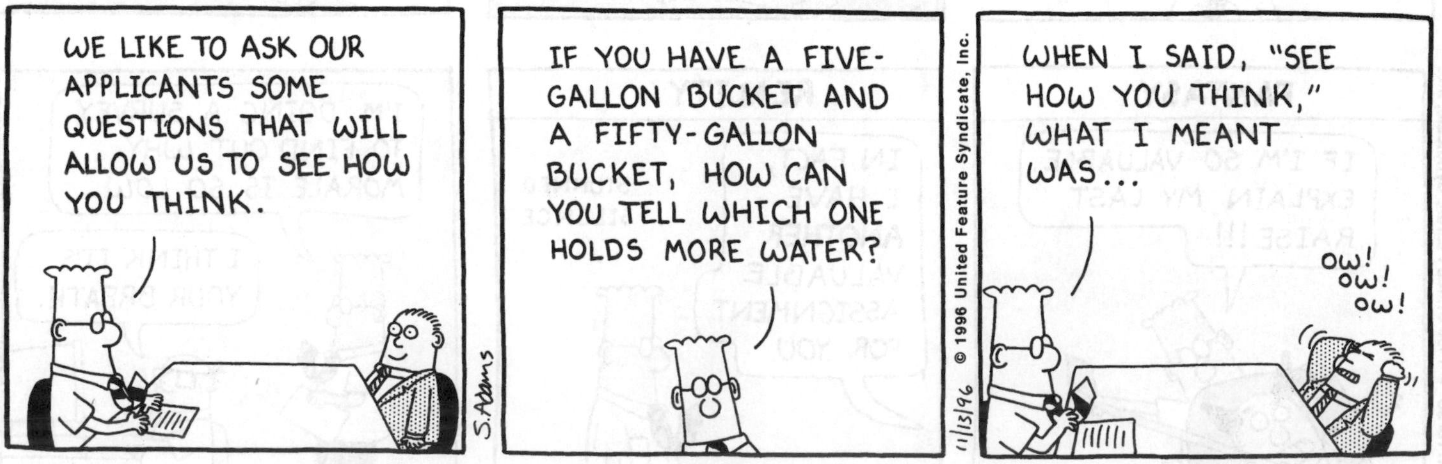
WE LIKE TO ASK OUR APPLICANTS SOME QUESTIONS THAT WILL ALLOW US TO SEE HOW YOU THINK.
IF YOU HAVE A FIVE-GALLON BUCKET AND A FIFTY-GALLON BUCKET, HOW CAN YOU TELL WHICH ONE HOLDS MORE WATER?
WHEN I SAID, "SEE HOW YOU THINK," WHAT I MEANT WAS...
OW! OW! OW!
S. Adams
11/13/96 © 1996 United Feature Syndicate, Inc.

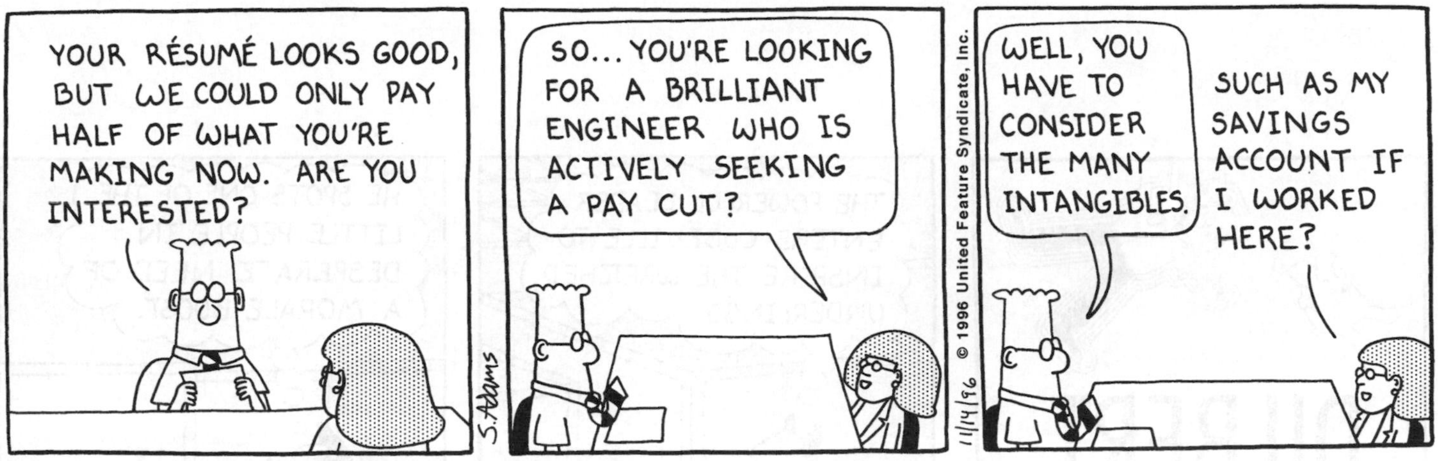
YOUR RÉSUMÉ LOOKS GOOD, BUT WE COULD ONLY PAY HALF OF WHAT YOU'RE MAKING NOW. ARE YOU INTERESTED?
SO... YOU'RE LOOKING FOR A BRILLIANT ENGINEER WHO IS ACTIVELY SEEKING A PAY CUT?
WELL, YOU HAVE TO CONSIDER THE MANY INTANGIBLES.
SUCH AS MY SAVINGS ACCOUNT IF I WORKED HERE?
S. Adams
11/14/96 © 1996 United Feature Syndicate, Inc.

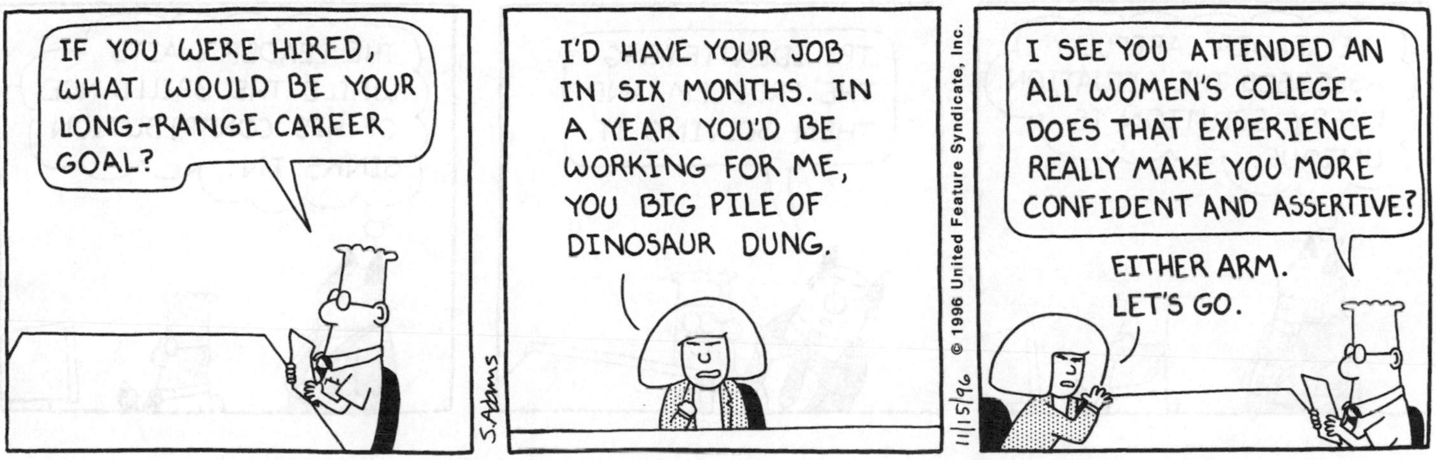
IF YOU WERE HIRED, WHAT WOULD BE YOUR LONG-RANGE CAREER GOAL?
I'D HAVE YOUR JOB IN SIX MONTHS. IN A YEAR YOU'D BE WORKING FOR ME, YOU BIG PILE OF DINOSAUR DUNG.
I SEE YOU ATTENDED AN ALL WOMEN'S COLLEGE. DOES THAT EXPERIENCE REALLY MAKE YOU MORE CONFIDENT AND ASSERTIVE?
EITHER ARM. LET'S GO.
S. Adams
11/15/96 © 1996 United Feature Syndicate, Inc.

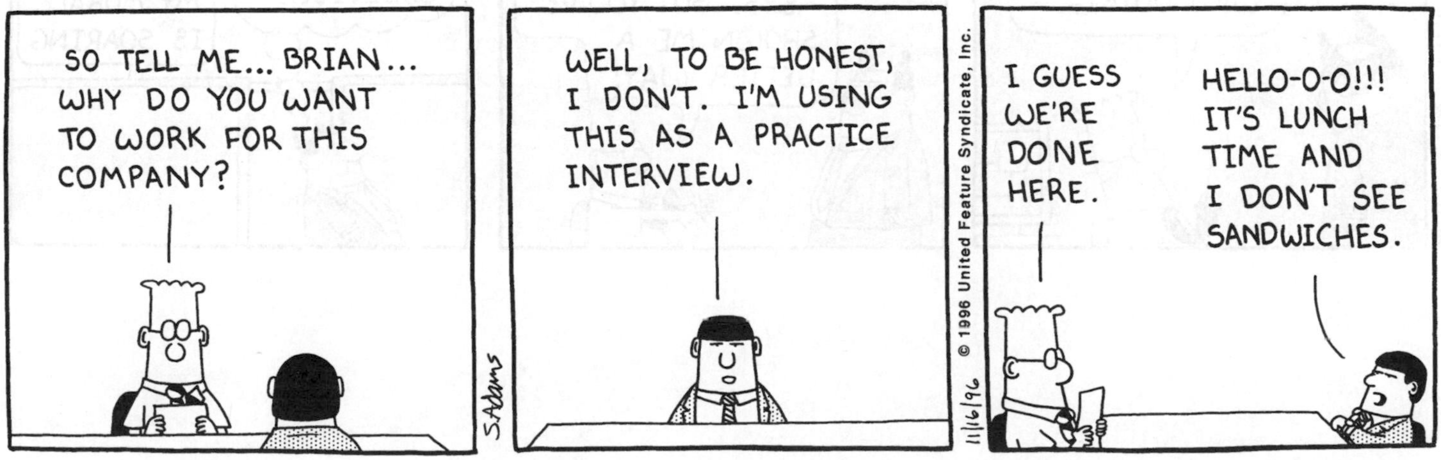
SO TELL ME... BRIAN... WHY DO YOU WANT TO WORK FOR THIS COMPANY?
WELL, TO BE HONEST, I DON'T. I'M USING THIS AS A PRACTICE INTERVIEW.
I GUESS WE'RE DONE HERE.
HELLO-O-O!!! IT'S LUNCH TIME AND I DON'T SEE SANDWICHES.
S. Adams
11/16/96 © 1996 United Feature Syndicate, Inc.

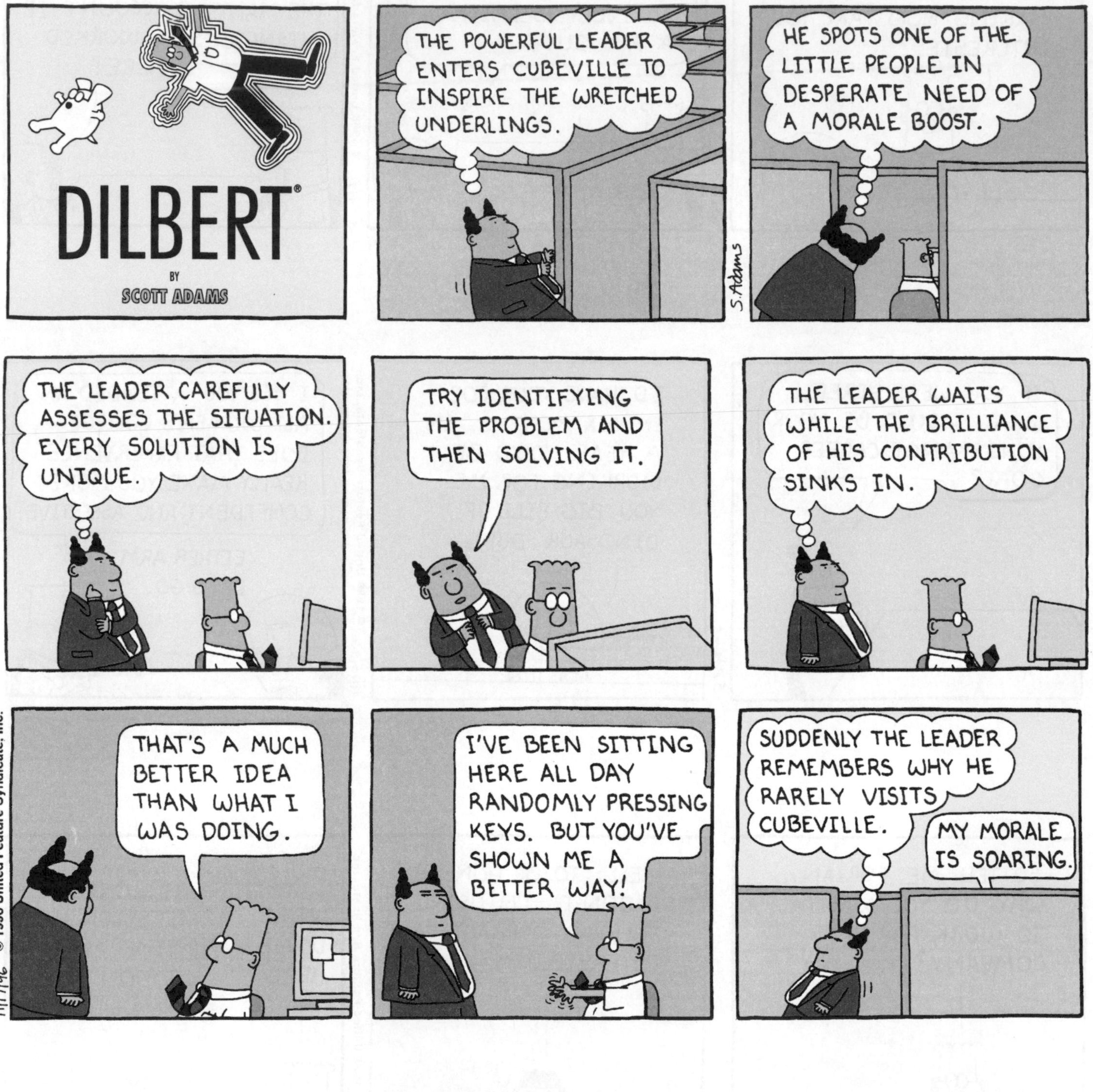
DILBERT®
BY
SCOTT ADAMS
THE POWERFUL LEADER ENTERS CUBEVILLE TO INSPIRE THE WRETCHED UNDERLINGS.
S. Adams
HE SPOTS ONE OF THE LITTLE PEOPLE IN DESPERATE NEED OF A MORALE BOOST.
THE LEADER CAREFULLY ASSESSES THE SITUATION. EVERY SOLUTION IS UNIQUE.
TRY IDENTIFYING THE PROBLEM AND THEN SOLVING IT.
THE LEADER WAITS WHILE THE BRILLIANCE OF HIS CONTRIBUTION SINKS IN.
11/17/96 © 1996 United Feature Syndicate, Inc.
THAT'S A MUCH BETTER IDEA THAN WHAT I WAS DOING.
I'VE BEEN SITTING HERE ALL DAY RANDOMLY PRESSING KEYS. BUT YOU'VE SHOWN ME A BETTER WAY!
SUDDENLY THE LEADER REMEMBERS WHY HE RARELY VISITS CUBEVILLE.
MY MORALE IS SOARING.

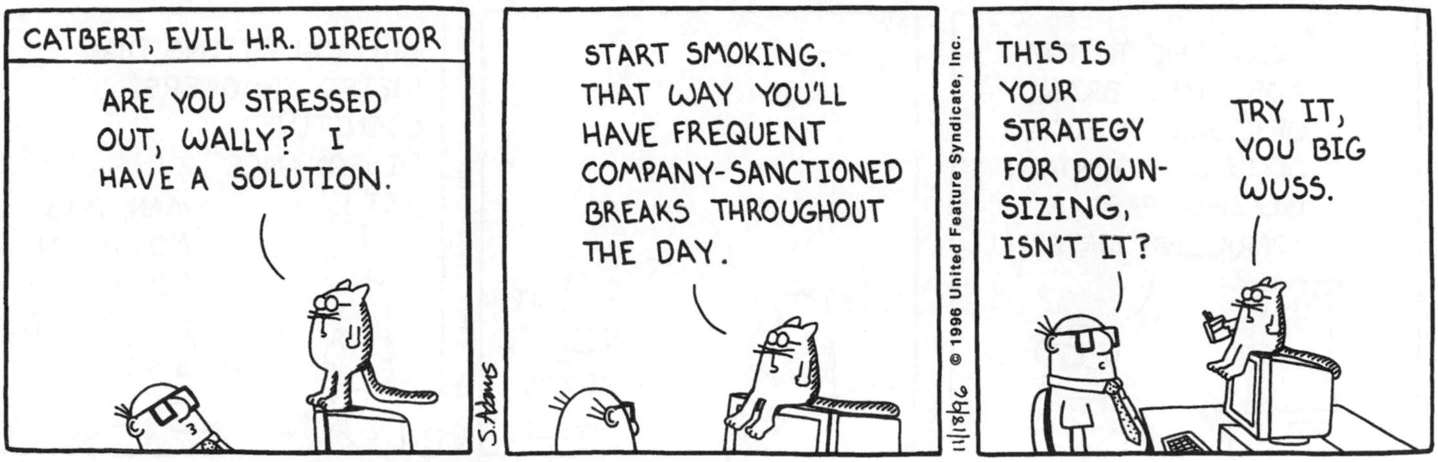
CATBERT, EVIL H.R. DIRECTOR
ARE YOU STRESSED OUT, WALLY? I HAVE A SOLUTION.
START SMOKING. THAT WAY YOU'LL HAVE FREQUENT COMPANY-SANCTIONED BREAKS THROUGHOUT THE DAY.
THIS IS YOUR STRATEGY FOR DOWN-SIZING, ISN'T IT?
TRY IT, YOU BIG WUSS.
S. Adams
11/18/96
© 1996 United Feature Syndicate, Inc.

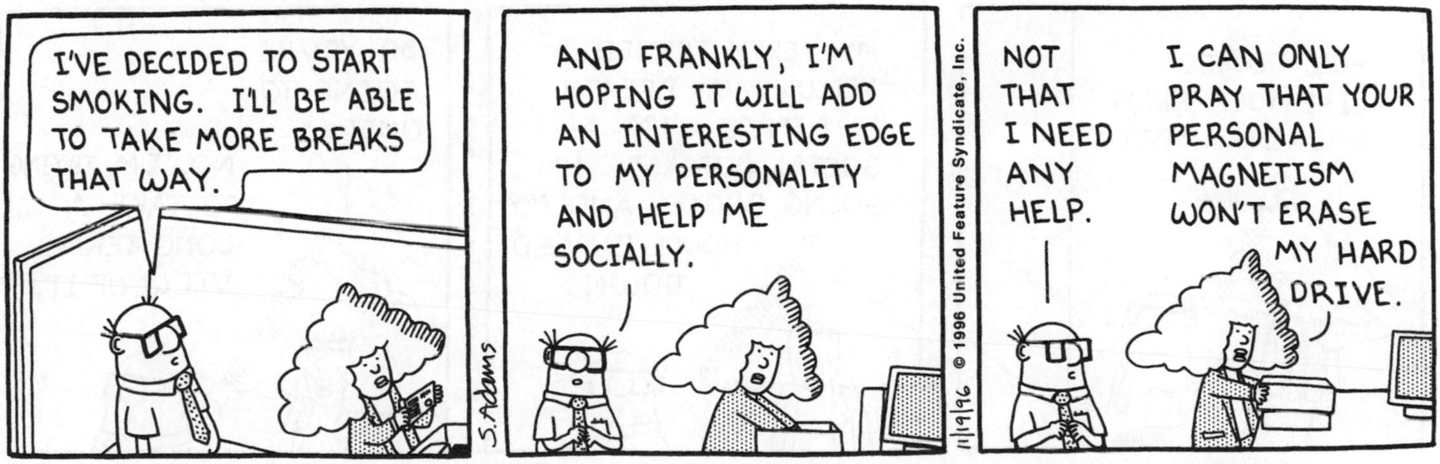
I'VE DECIDED TO START SMOKING. I'LL BE ABLE TO TAKE MORE BREAKS THAT WAY.
AND FRANKLY, I'M HOPING IT WILL ADD AN INTERESTING EDGE TO MY PERSONALITY AND HELP ME SOCIALLY.
NOT THAT I NEED ANY HELP.
I CAN ONLY PRAY THAT YOUR PERSONAL MAGNETISM WON'T ERASE MY HARD DRIVE.
S. Adams
11/19/96
© 1996 United Feature Syndicate, Inc.

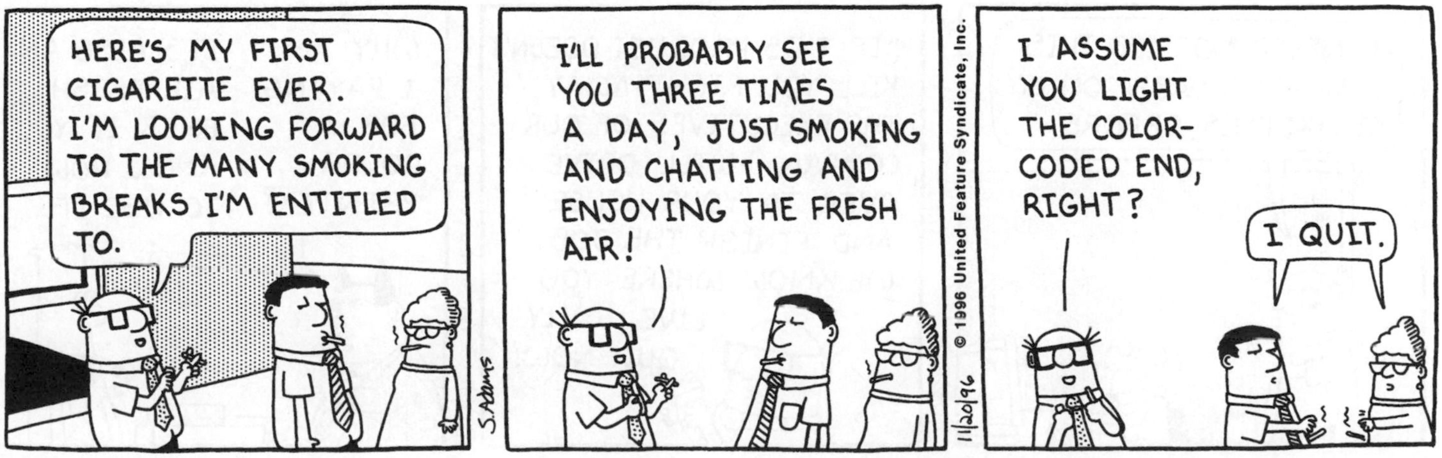
HERE'S MY FIRST CIGARETTE EVER. I'M LOOKING FORWARD TO THE MANY SMOKING BREAKS I'M ENTITLED TO.
I'LL PROBABLY SEE YOU THREE TIMES A DAY, JUST SMOKING AND CHATTING AND ENJOYING THE FRESH AIR!
I ASSUME YOU LIGHT THE COLOR-CODED END, RIGHT?
I QUIT.
S. Adams
11/20/96
© 1996 United Feature Syndicate, Inc.

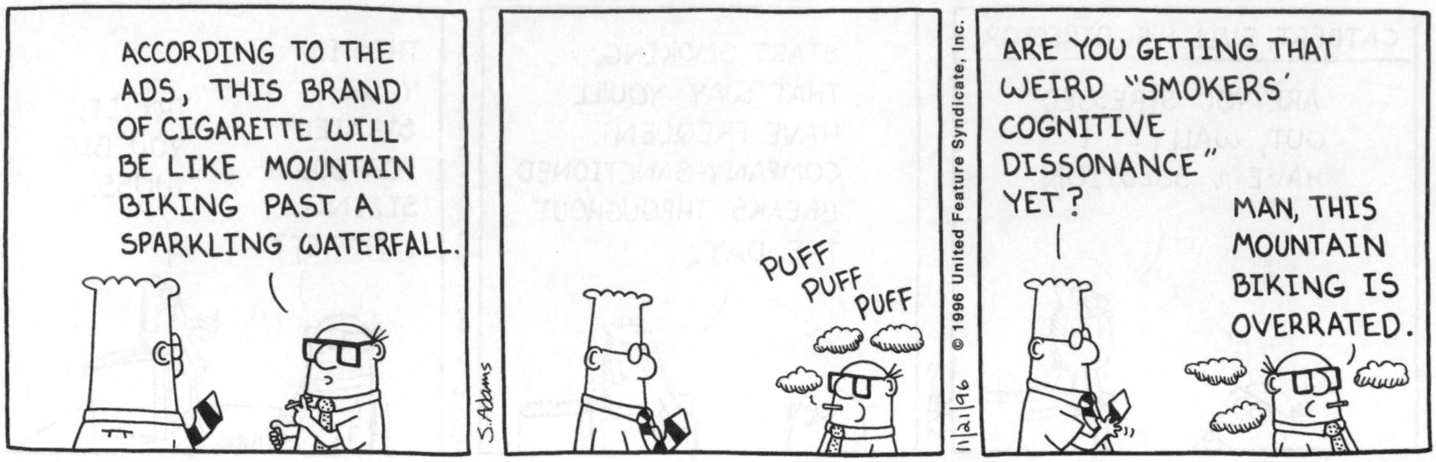
ACCORDING TO THE ADS, THIS BRAND OF CIGARETTE WILL BE LIKE MOUNTAIN BIKING PAST A SPARKLING WATERFALL.
S. Adams
PUFF PUFF PUFF
11/21/96 © 1996 United Feature Syndicate, Inc.
ARE YOU GETTING THAT WEIRD "SMOKERS' COGNITIVE DISSONANCE" YET?
MAN, THIS MOUNTAIN BIKING IS OVERRATED.

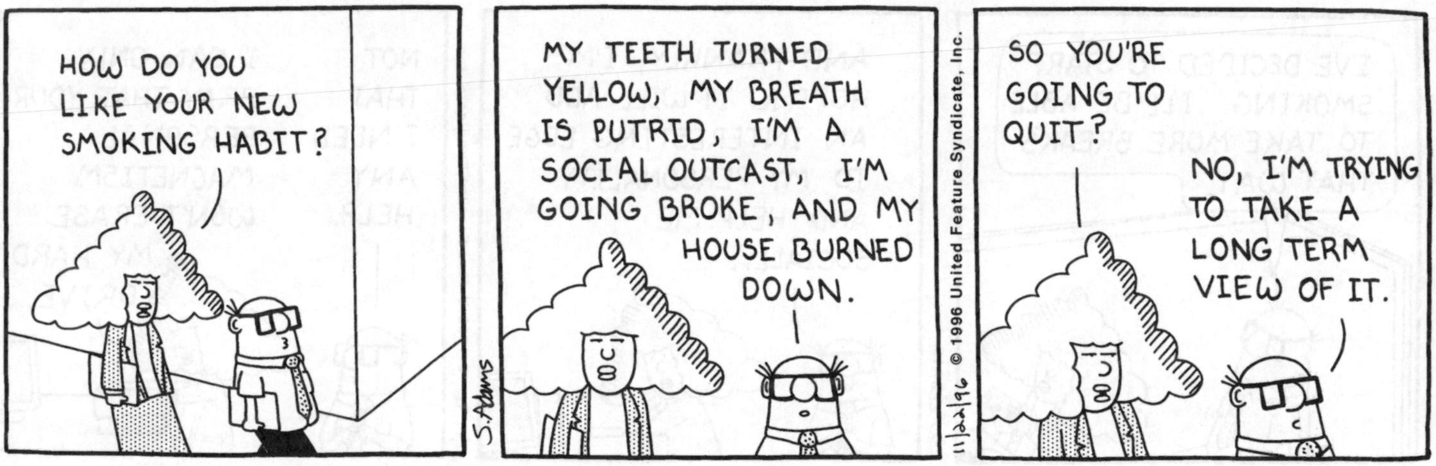
HOW DO YOU LIKE YOUR NEW SMOKING HABIT?
S. Adams
MY TEETH TURNED YELLOW, MY BREATH IS PUTRID, I'M A SOCIAL OUTCAST, I'M GOING BROKE, AND MY HOUSE BURNED DOWN.
11/22/96 © 1996 United Feature Syndicate, Inc.
SO YOU'RE GOING TO QUIT?
NO, I'M TRYING TO TAKE A LONG TERM VIEW OF IT.

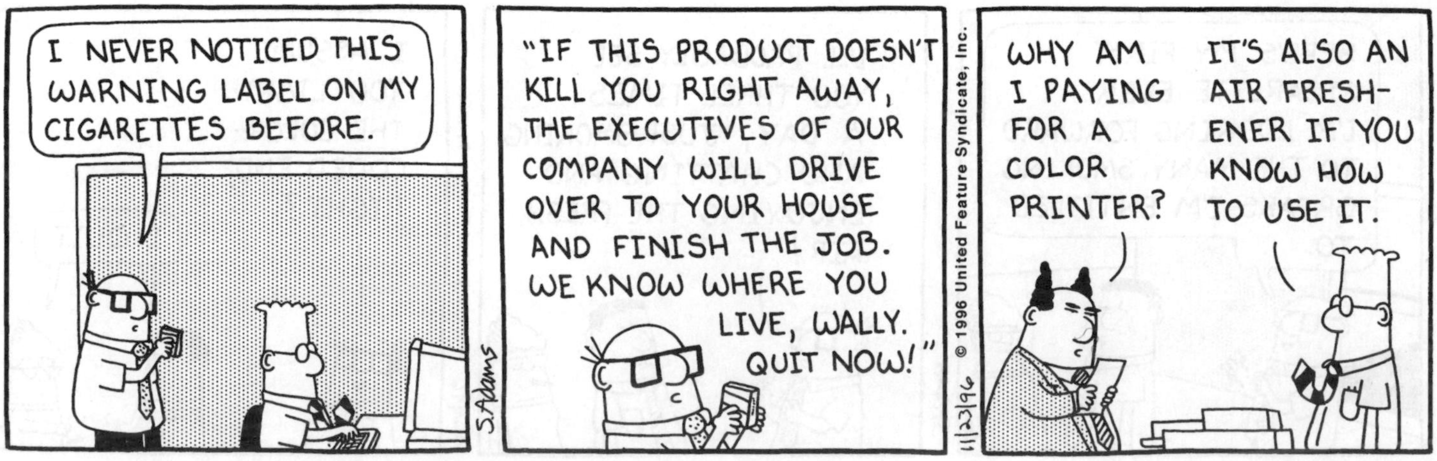
I NEVER NOTICED THIS WARNING LABEL ON MY CIGARETTES BEFORE.
S. Adams
"IF THIS PRODUCT DOESN'T KILL YOU RIGHT AWAY, THE EXECUTIVES OF OUR COMPANY WILL DRIVE OVER TO YOUR HOUSE AND FINISH THE JOB. WE KNOW WHERE YOU LIVE, WALLY. QUIT NOW!"
11/23/96 © 1996 United Feature Syndicate, Inc.
WHY AM I PAYING FOR A COLOR PRINTER?
IT'S ALSO AN AIR FRESHENER IF YOU KNOW HOW TO USE IT.

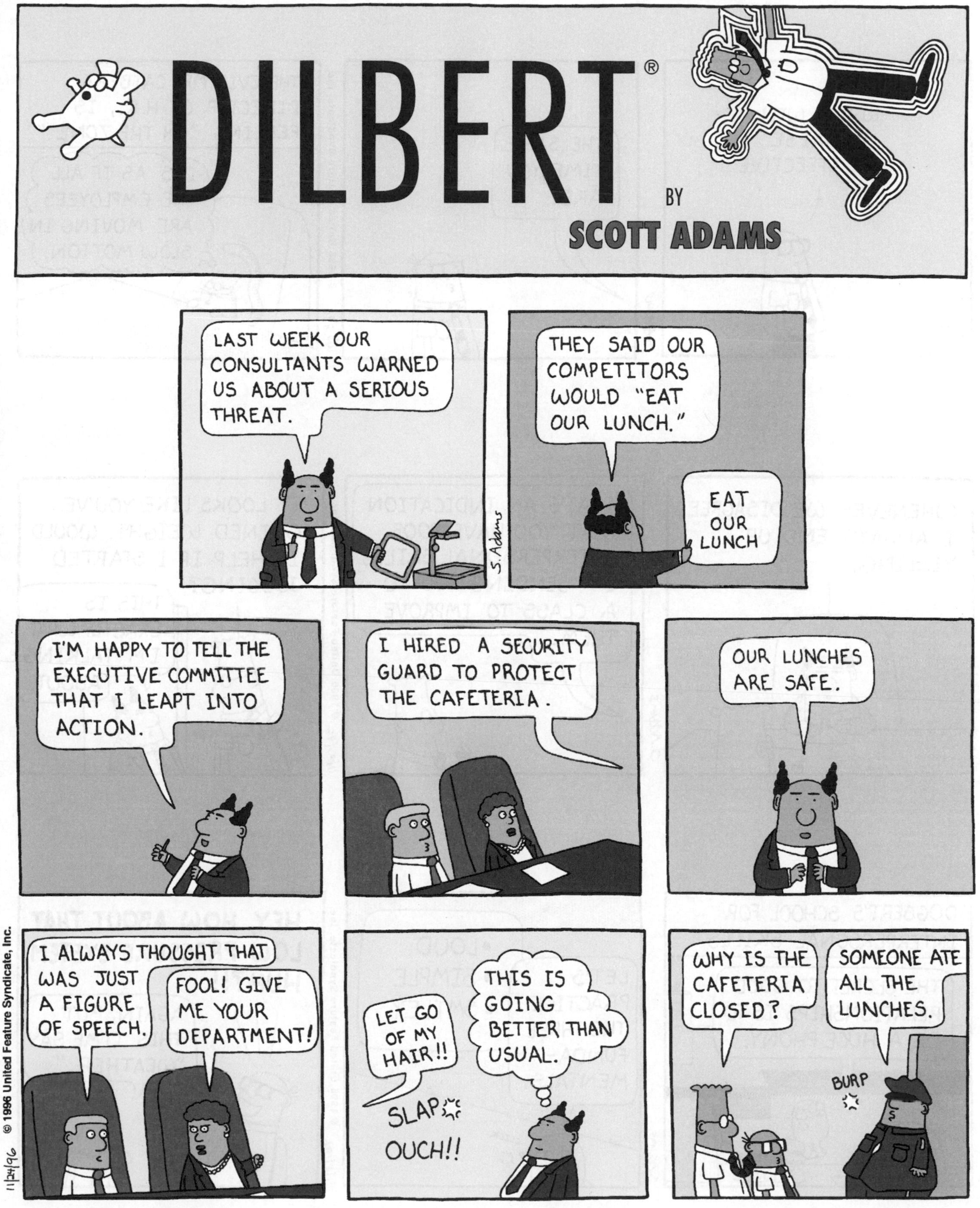
DILBERT®
BY
SCOTT ADAMS
LAST WEEK OUR CONSULTANTS WARNED US ABOUT A SERIOUS THREAT.
S. Adams
THEY SAID OUR COMPETITORS WOULD "EAT OUR LUNCH."
EAT OUR LUNCH
I'M HAPPY TO TELL THE EXECUTIVE COMMITTEE THAT I LEAPT INTO ACTION.
I HIRED A SECURITY GUARD TO PROTECT THE CAFETERIA.
OUR LUNCHES ARE SAFE.
I ALWAYS THOUGHT THAT WAS JUST A FIGURE OF SPEECH.
FOOL! GIVE ME YOUR DEPARTMENT!
LET GO OF MY HAIR!!
SLAP
OUCH!!
THIS IS GOING BETTER THAN USUAL.
WHY IS THE CAFETERIA CLOSED?
SOMEONE ATE ALL THE LUNCHES.
BURP
11/24/96 © 1996 United Feature Syndicate, Inc.

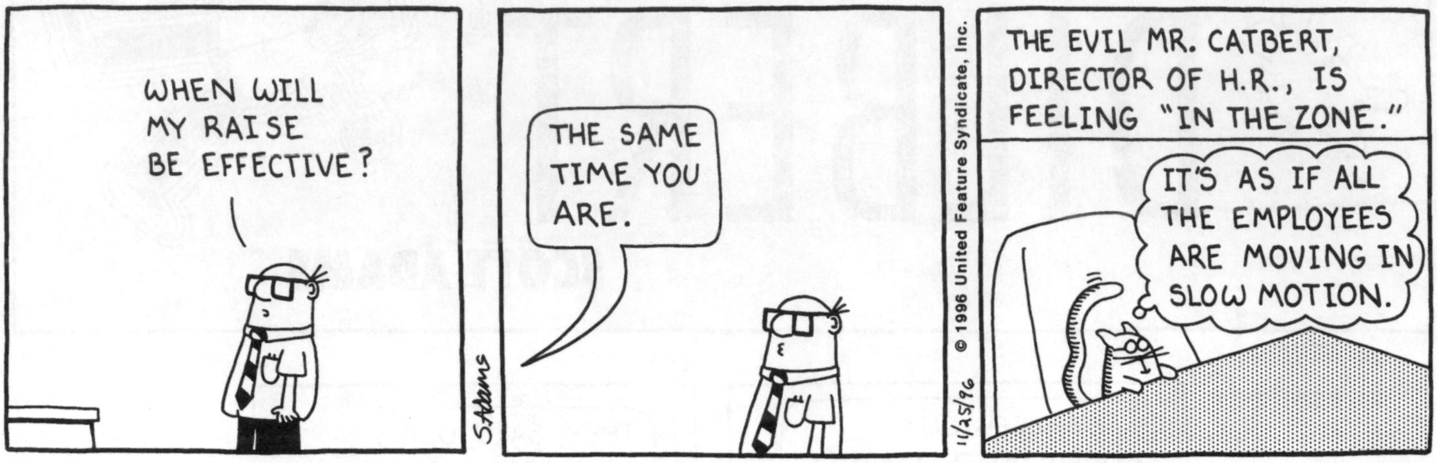
WHEN WILL MY RAISE BE EFFECTIVE?
THE SAME TIME YOU ARE.
THE EVIL MR. CATBERT, DIRECTOR OF H.R., IS FEELING "IN THE ZONE."
IT'S AS IF ALL THE EMPLOYEES ARE MOVING IN SLOW MOTION.
S. Adams
11/25/96 © 1996 United Feature Syndicate, Inc.

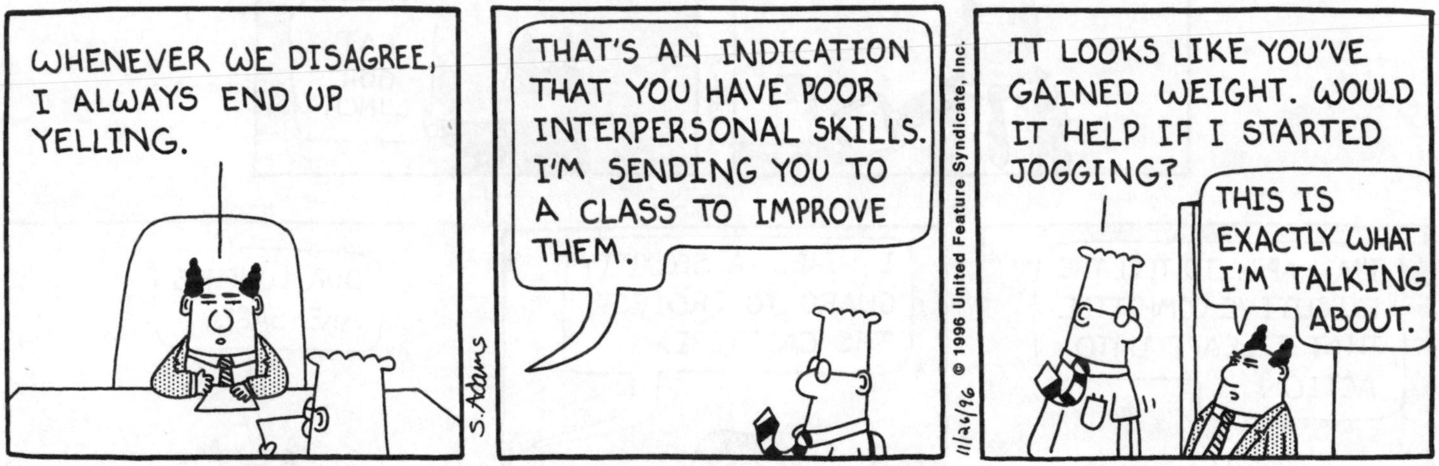
WHENEVER WE DISAGREE, I ALWAYS END UP YELLING.
THAT'S AN INDICATION THAT YOU HAVE POOR INTERPERSONAL SKILLS. I'M SENDING YOU TO A CLASS TO IMPROVE THEM.
IT LOOKS LIKE YOU'VE GAINED WEIGHT. WOULD IT HELP IF I STARTED JOGGING?
THIS IS EXACTLY WHAT I'M TALKING ABOUT.
S. Adams
11/26/96 © 1996 United Feature Syndicate, Inc.

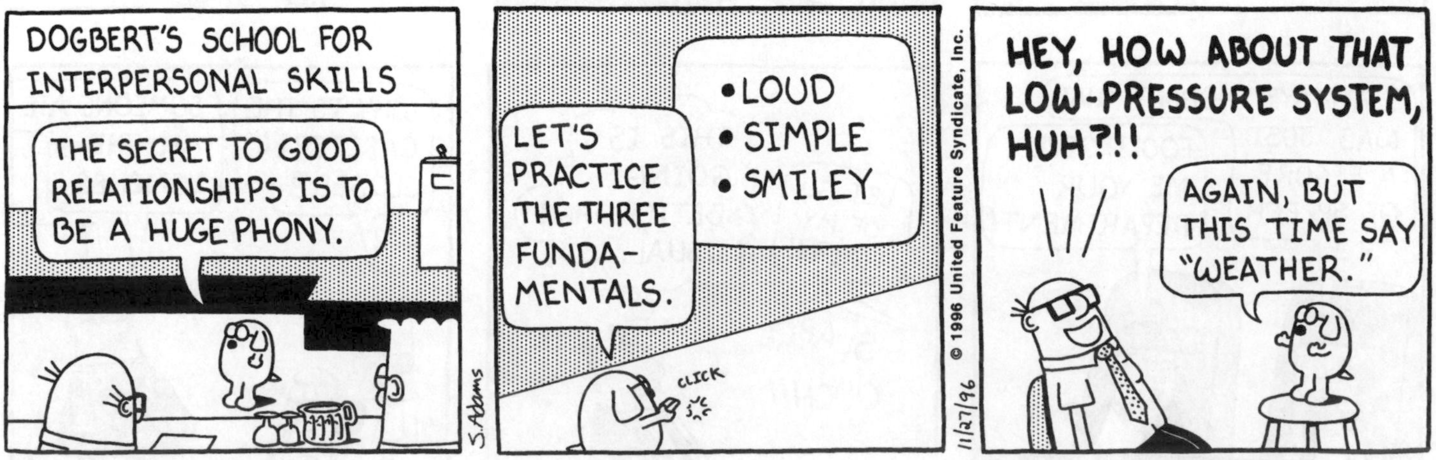
DOGBERT'S SCHOOL FOR INTERPERSONAL SKILLS
THE SECRET TO GOOD RELATIONSHIPS IS TO BE A HUGE PHONY.
LET'S PRACTICE THE THREE FUNDA-MENTALS.
• LOUD
• SIMPLE
• SMILEY
CLICK
HEY, HOW ABOUT THAT LOW-PRESSURE SYSTEM, HUH?!!
AGAIN, BUT THIS TIME SAY "WEATHER."
S. Adams
11/27/96 © 1996 United Feature Syndicate, Inc.

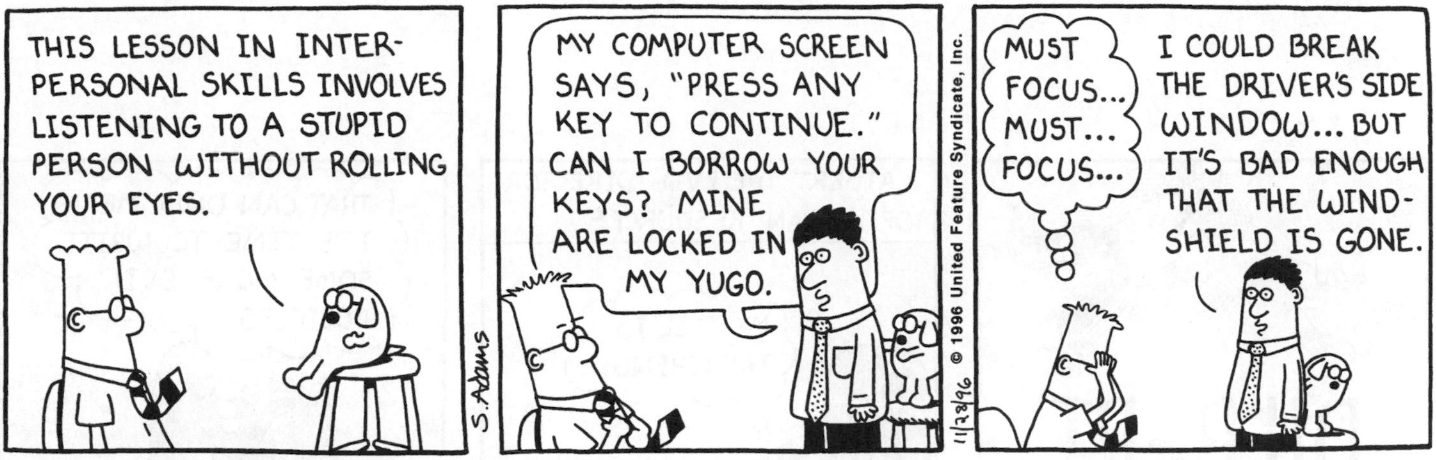
THIS LESSON IN INTER-PERSONAL SKILLS INVOLVES LISTENING TO A STUPID PERSON WITHOUT ROLLING YOUR EYES.
MY COMPUTER SCREEN SAYS, "PRESS ANY KEY TO CONTINUE." CAN I BORROW YOUR KEYS? MINE ARE LOCKED IN MY YUGO.
MUST FOCUS... MUST... FOCUS...
I COULD BREAK THE DRIVER'S SIDE WINDOW... BUT IT'S BAD ENOUGH THAT THE WIND-SHIELD IS GONE.
S. Adams
11/28/96 © 1996 United Feature Syndicate, Inc.

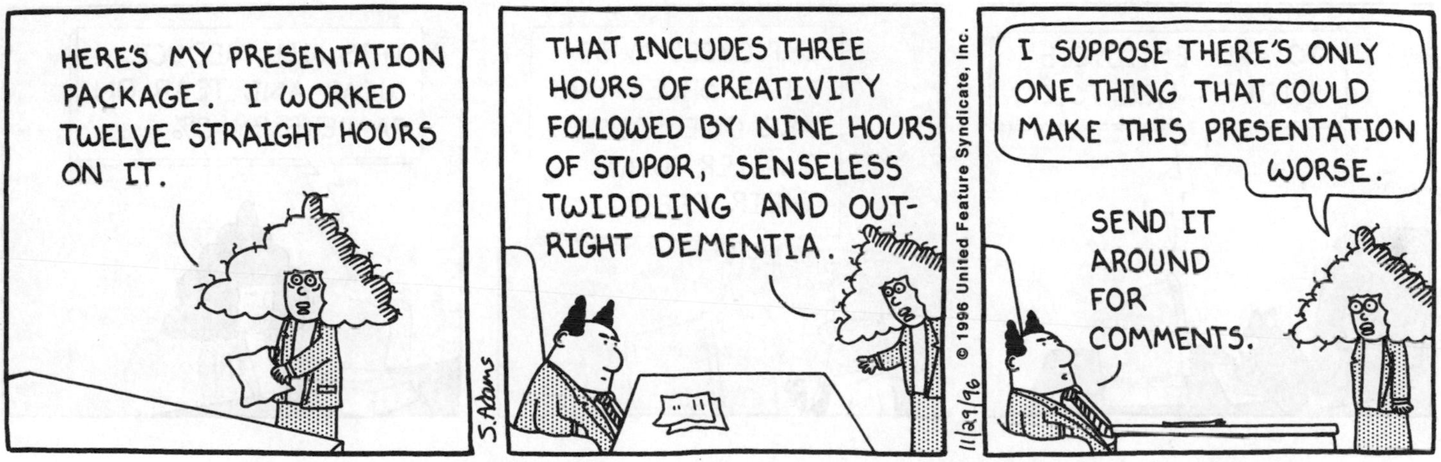
HERE'S MY PRESENTATION PACKAGE. I WORKED TWELVE STRAIGHT HOURS ON IT.
THAT INCLUDES THREE HOURS OF CREATIVITY FOLLOWED BY NINE HOURS OF STUPOR, SENSELESS TWIDDLING AND OUT-RIGHT DEMENTIA.
SEND IT AROUND FOR COMMENTS.
I SUPPOSE THERE'S ONLY ONE THING THAT COULD MAKE THIS PRESENTATION WORSE.
S. Adams
11/29/96 © 1996 United Feature Syndicate, Inc.

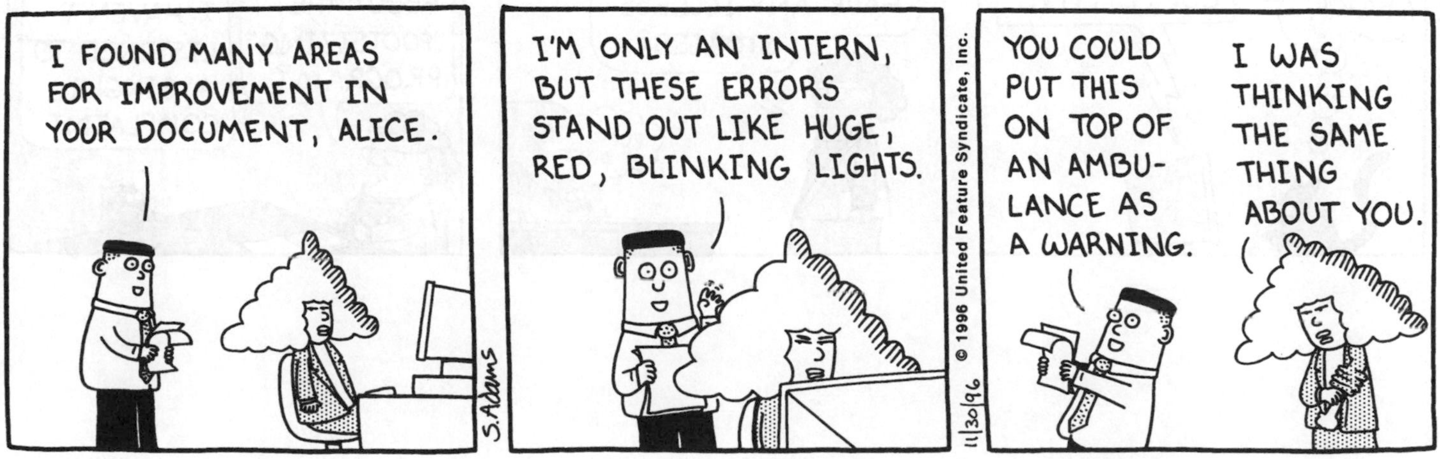
I FOUND MANY AREAS FOR IMPROVEMENT IN YOUR DOCUMENT, ALICE.
I'M ONLY AN INTERN, BUT THESE ERRORS STAND OUT LIKE HUGE, RED, BLINKING LIGHTS.
YOU COULD PUT THIS ON TOP OF AN AMBU-LANCE AS A WARNING.
I WAS THINKING THE SAME THING ABOUT YOU.
S. Adams
11/30/96 © 1996 United Feature Syndicate, Inc.

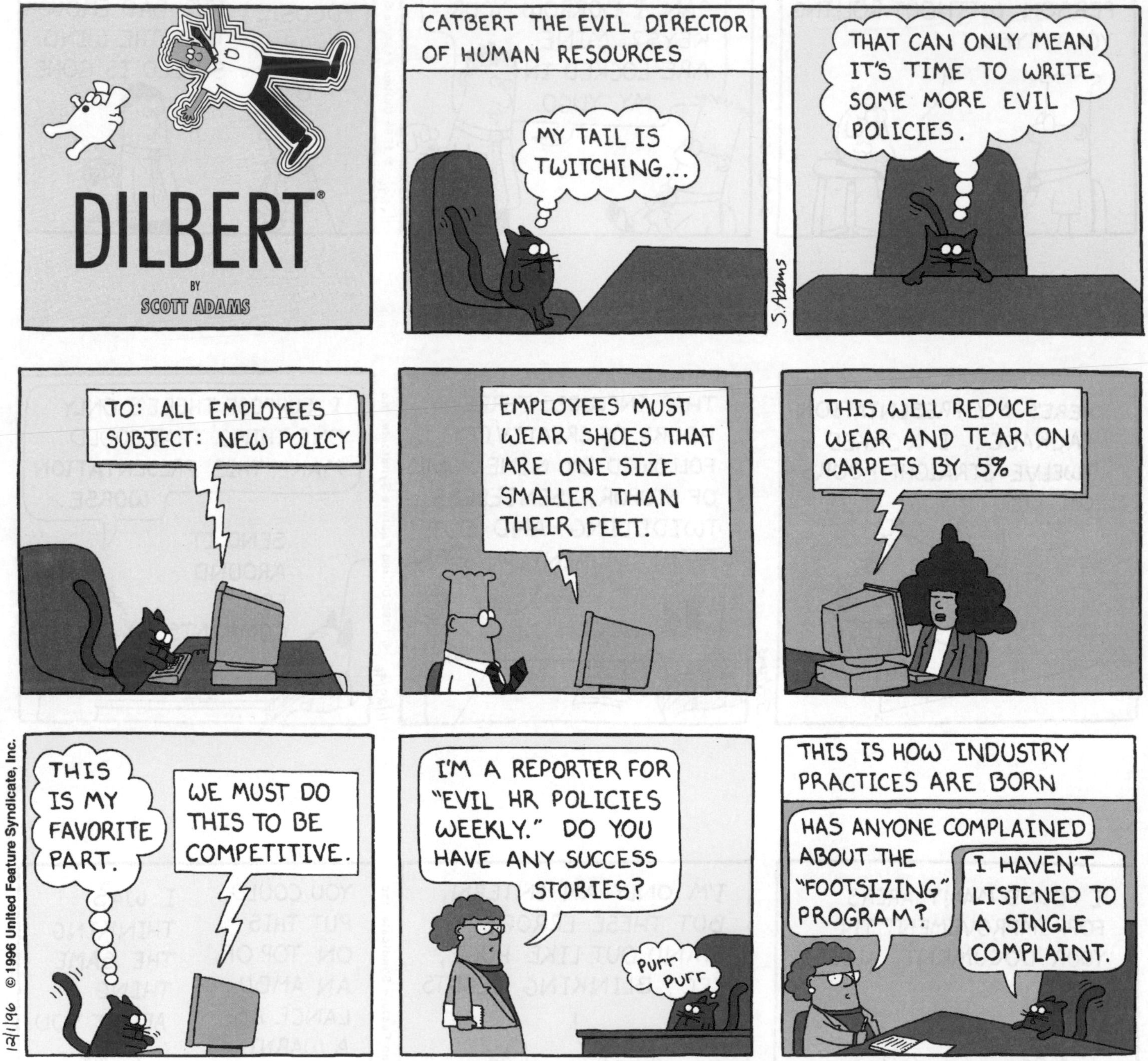
DILBERT®
BY
SCOTT ADAMS
CATBERT THE EVIL DIRECTOR OF HUMAN RESOURCES
MY TAIL IS TWITCHING...
S. Adams
THAT CAN ONLY MEAN IT'S TIME TO WRITE SOME MORE EVIL POLICIES.
TO: ALL EMPLOYEES
SUBJECT: NEW POLICY
EMPLOYEES MUST WEAR SHOES THAT ARE ONE SIZE SMALLER THAN THEIR FEET.
THIS WILL REDUCE WEAR AND TEAR ON CARPETS BY 5%
THIS IS MY FAVORITE PART.
WE MUST DO THIS TO BE COMPETITIVE.
I'M A REPORTER FOR "EVIL HR POLICIES WEEKLY." DO YOU HAVE ANY SUCCESS STORIES?
Purr Purr
THIS IS HOW INDUSTRY PRACTICES ARE BORN
HAS ANYONE COMPLAINED ABOUT THE "FOOTSIZING" PROGRAM?
I HAVEN'T LISTENED TO A SINGLE COMPLAINT.
12/1/96 © 1996 United Feature Syndicate, Inc.

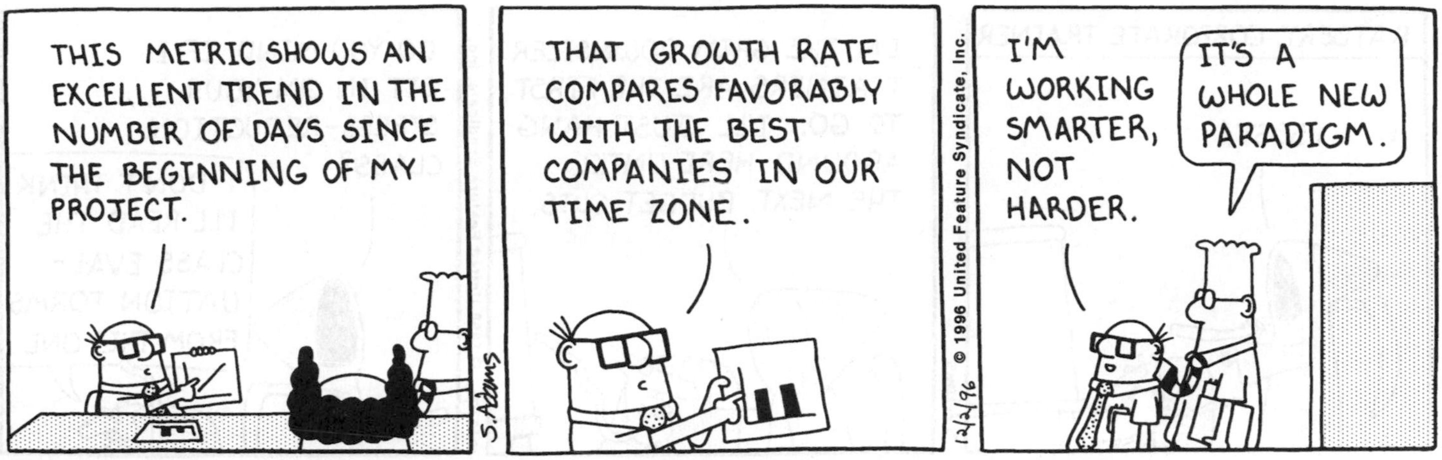
THIS METRIC SHOWS AN EXCELLENT TREND IN THE NUMBER OF DAYS SINCE THE BEGINNING OF MY PROJECT.
S. Adams
THAT GROWTH RATE COMPARES FAVORABLY WITH THE BEST COMPANIES IN OUR TIME ZONE.
12/2/96
© 1996 United Feature Syndicate, Inc.
I'M WORKING SMARTER, NOT HARDER.
IT'S A WHOLE NEW PARADIGM.

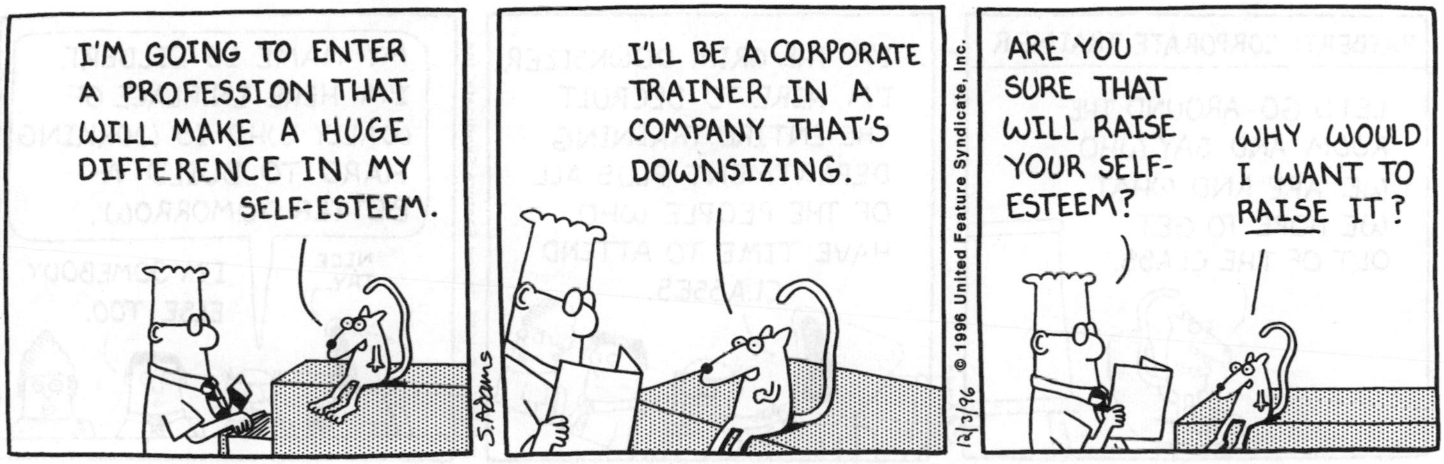
I'M GOING TO ENTER A PROFESSION THAT WILL MAKE A HUGE DIFFERENCE IN MY SELF-ESTEEM.
S. Adams
I'LL BE A CORPORATE TRAINER IN A COMPANY THAT'S DOWNSIZING.
12/3/96
© 1996 United Feature Syndicate, Inc.
ARE YOU SURE THAT WILL RAISE YOUR SELF-ESTEEM?
WHY WOULD I WANT TO RAISE IT?

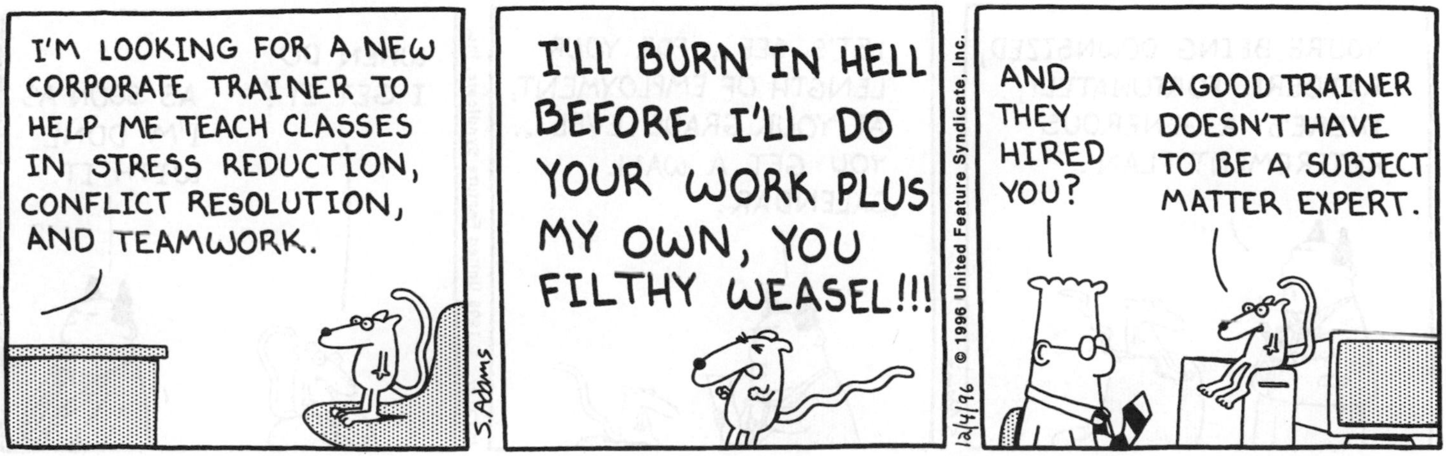
I'M LOOKING FOR A NEW CORPORATE TRAINER TO HELP ME TEACH CLASSES IN STRESS REDUCTION, CONFLICT RESOLUTION, AND TEAMWORK.
S. Adams
I'LL BURN IN HELL BEFORE I'LL DO YOUR WORK PLUS MY OWN, YOU FILTHY WEASEL!!!
12/4/96
© 1996 United Feature Syndicate, Inc.
AND THEY HIRED YOU?
A GOOD TRAINER DOESN'T HAVE TO BE A SUBJECT MATTER EXPERT.

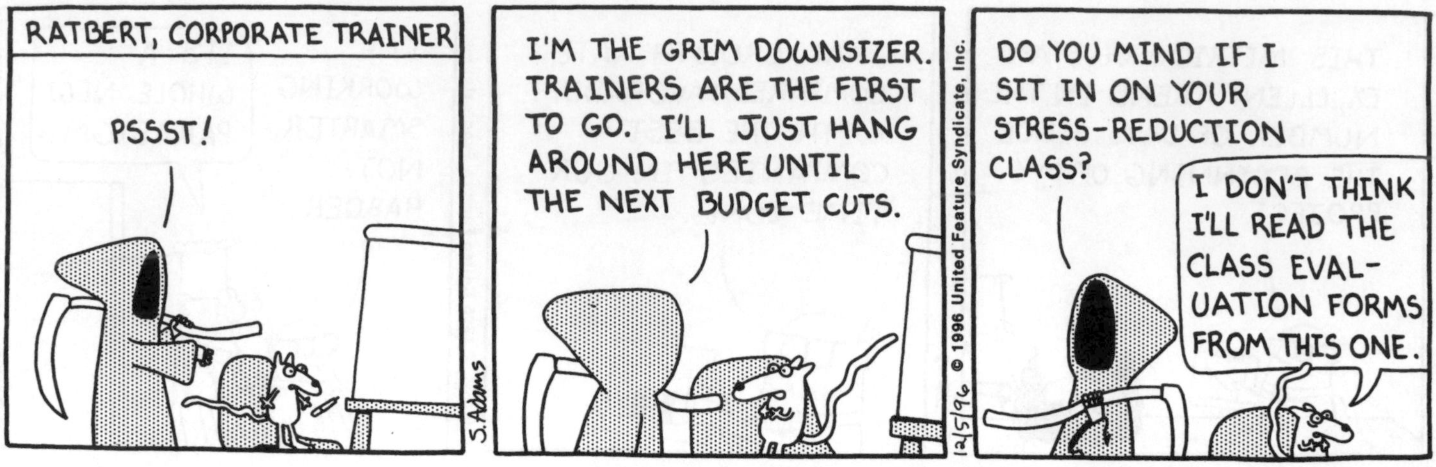
RATBERT, CORPORATE TRAINER
PSSST!
I'M THE GRIM DOWNSIZER. TRAINERS ARE THE FIRST TO GO. I'LL JUST HANG AROUND HERE UNTIL THE NEXT BUDGET CUTS.
DO YOU MIND IF I SIT IN ON YOUR STRESS-REDUCTION CLASS?
I DON'T THINK I'LL READ THE CLASS EVAL-UATION FORMS FROM THIS ONE.
S. Adams
12/5/96 © 1996 United Feature Syndicate, Inc.

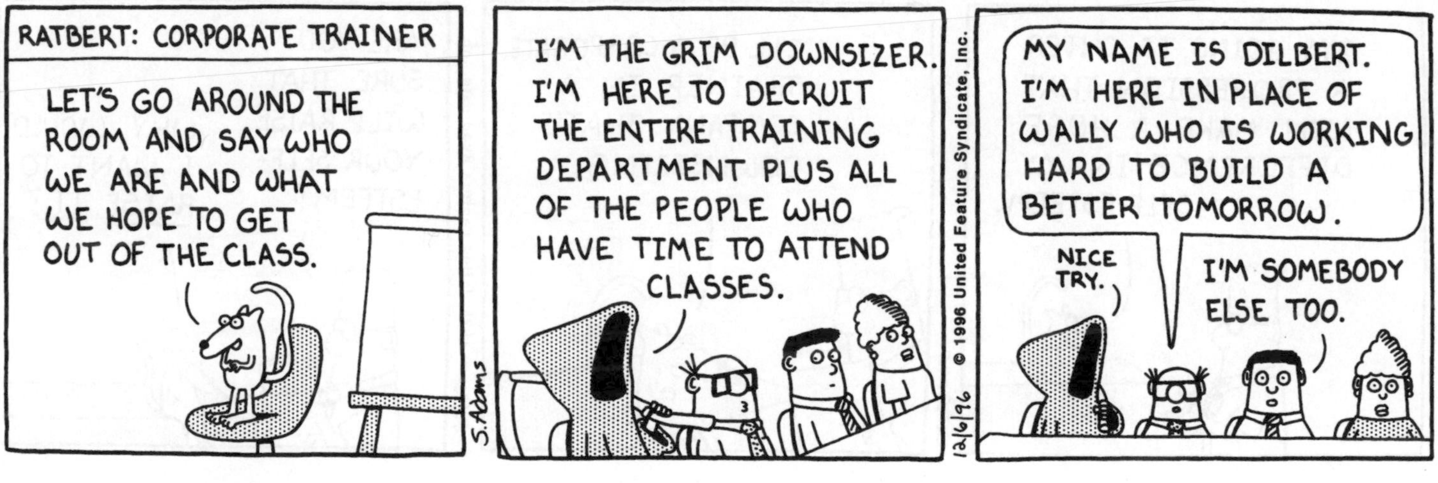
RATBERT: CORPORATE TRAINER
LET'S GO AROUND THE ROOM AND SAY WHO WE ARE AND WHAT WE HOPE TO GET OUT OF THE CLASS.
I'M THE GRIM DOWNSIZER. I'M HERE TO DECRUIT THE ENTIRE TRAINING DEPARTMENT PLUS ALL OF THE PEOPLE WHO HAVE TIME TO ATTEND CLASSES.
MY NAME IS DILBERT. I'M HERE IN PLACE OF WALLY WHO IS WORKING HARD TO BUILD A BETTER TOMORROW.
NICE TRY.
I'M SOMEBODY ELSE TOO.
S. Adams
12/6/96 © 1996 United Feature Syndicate, Inc.

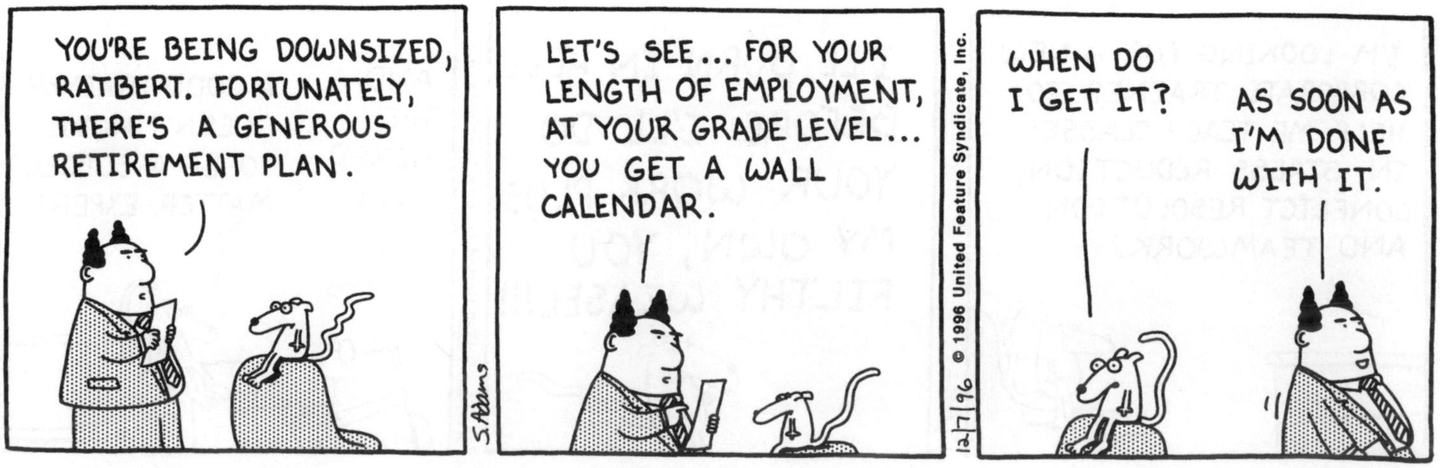
YOU'RE BEING DOWNSIZED, RATBERT. FORTUNATELY, THERE'S A GENEROUS RETIREMENT PLAN.
LET'S SEE... FOR YOUR LENGTH OF EMPLOYMENT, AT YOUR GRADE LEVEL... YOU GET A WALL CALENDAR.
WHEN DO I GET IT?
AS SOON AS I'M DONE WITH IT.
S. Adams
12/7/96 © 1996 United Feature Syndicate, Inc.

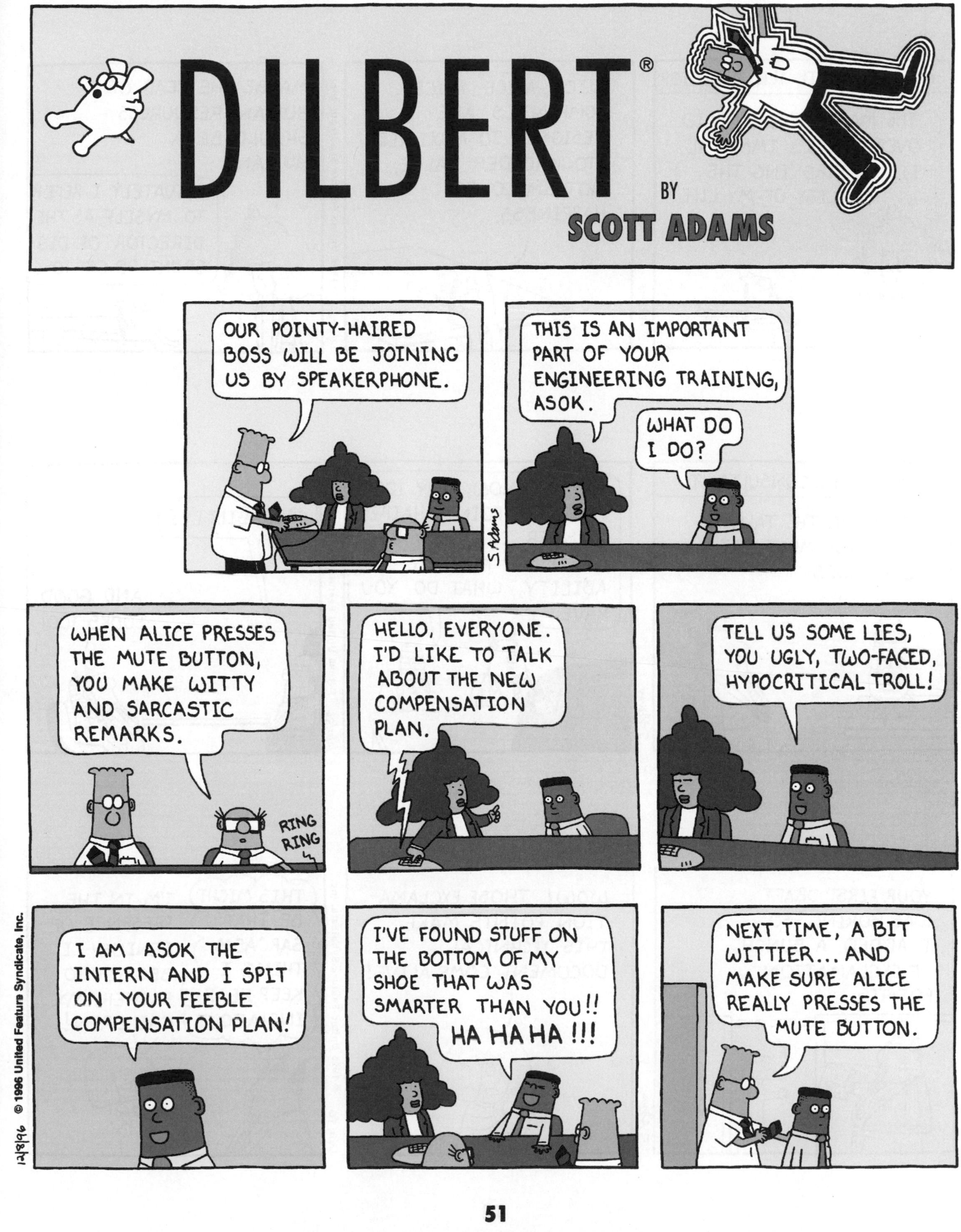
DILBERT®
BY SCOTT ADAMS
OUR POINTY-HAIRED BOSS WILL BE JOINING US BY SPEAKERPHONE.
S. Adams
THIS IS AN IMPORTANT PART OF YOUR ENGINEERING TRAINING, ASOK.
WHAT DO I DO?
WHEN ALICE PRESSES THE MUTE BUTTON, YOU MAKE WITTY AND SARCASTIC REMARKS.
RING RING
HELLO, EVERYONE. I'D LIKE TO TALK ABOUT THE NEW COMPENSATION PLAN.
TELL US SOME LIES, YOU UGLY, TWO-FACED, HYPOCRITICAL TROLL!
I AM ASOK THE INTERN AND I SPIT ON YOUR FEEBLE COMPENSATION PLAN!
I'VE FOUND STUFF ON THE BOTTOM OF MY SHOE THAT WAS SMARTER THAN YOU!!
HA HA HA!!!
NEXT TIME, A BIT WITTIER... AND MAKE SURE ALICE REALLY PRESSES THE MUTE BUTTON.
12/8/96 © 1996 United Feature Syndicate, Inc.

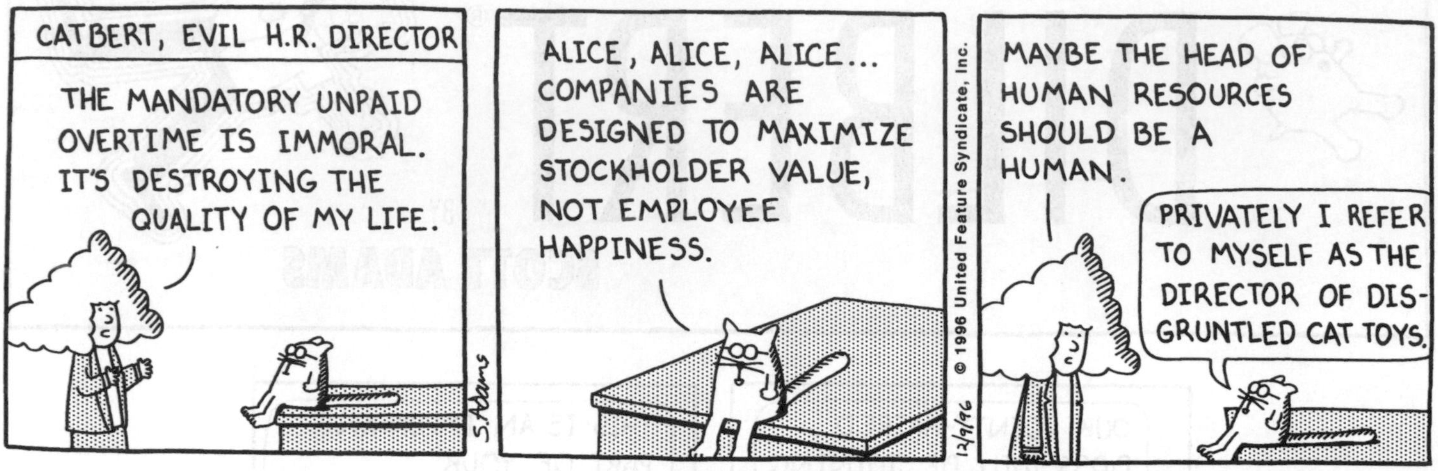
CATBERT, EVIL H.R. DIRECTOR
THE MANDATORY UNPAID OVERTIME IS IMMORAL. IT'S DESTROYING THE QUALITY OF MY LIFE.
S. Adams
ALICE, ALICE, ALICE... COMPANIES ARE DESIGNED TO MAXIMIZE STOCKHOLDER VALUE, NOT EMPLOYEE HAPPINESS.
12/9/96
© 1996 United Feature Syndicate, Inc.
MAYBE THE HEAD OF HUMAN RESOURCES SHOULD BE A HUMAN.
PRIVATELY I REFER TO MYSELF AS THE DIRECTOR OF DIS-GRUNTLED CAT TOYS.

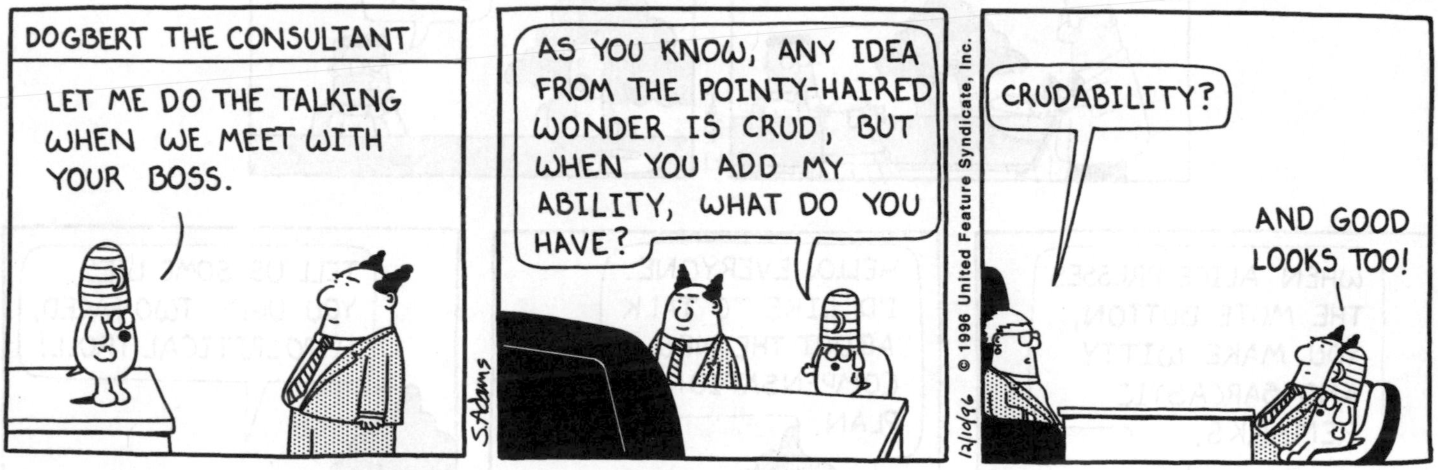
DOGBERT THE CONSULTANT
LET ME DO THE TALKING WHEN WE MEET WITH YOUR BOSS.
S. Adams
AS YOU KNOW, ANY IDEA FROM THE POINTY-HAIRED WONDER IS CRUD, BUT WHEN YOU ADD MY ABILITY, WHAT DO YOU HAVE?
12/10/96
© 1996 United Feature Syndicate, Inc.
CRUDABILITY?
AND GOOD LOOKS TOO!

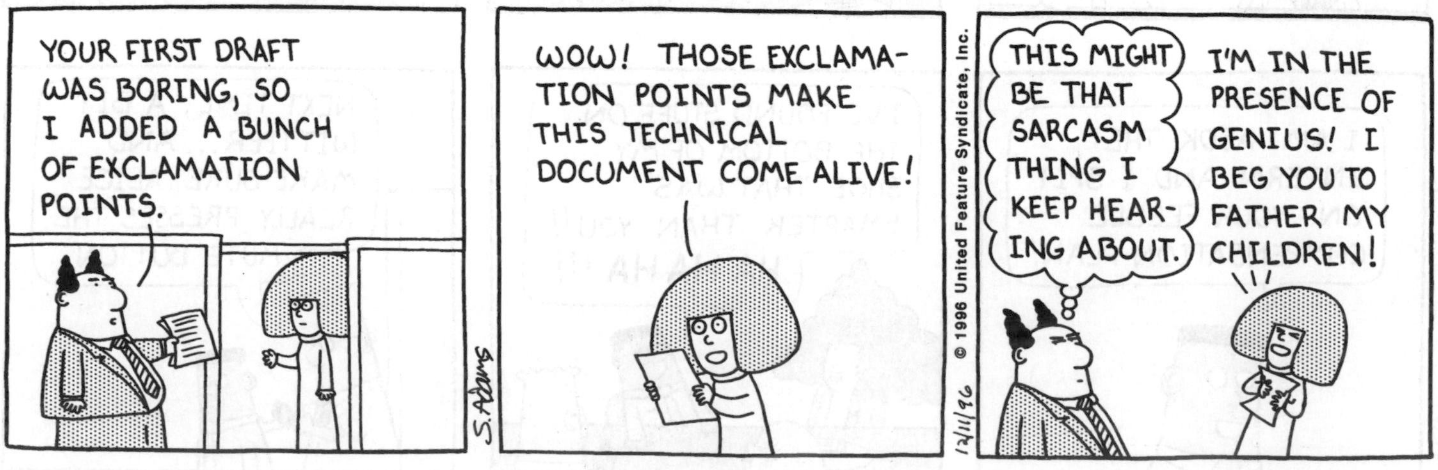
YOUR FIRST DRAFT WAS BORING, SO I ADDED A BUNCH OF EXCLAMATION POINTS.
S. Adams
WOW! THOSE EXCLAMA-TION POINTS MAKE THIS TECHNICAL DOCUMENT COME ALIVE!
12/11/96
© 1996 United Feature Syndicate, Inc.
THIS MIGHT BE THAT SARCASM THING I KEEP HEAR-ING ABOUT.
I'M IN THE PRESENCE OF GENIUS! I BEG YOU TO FATHER MY CHILDREN!

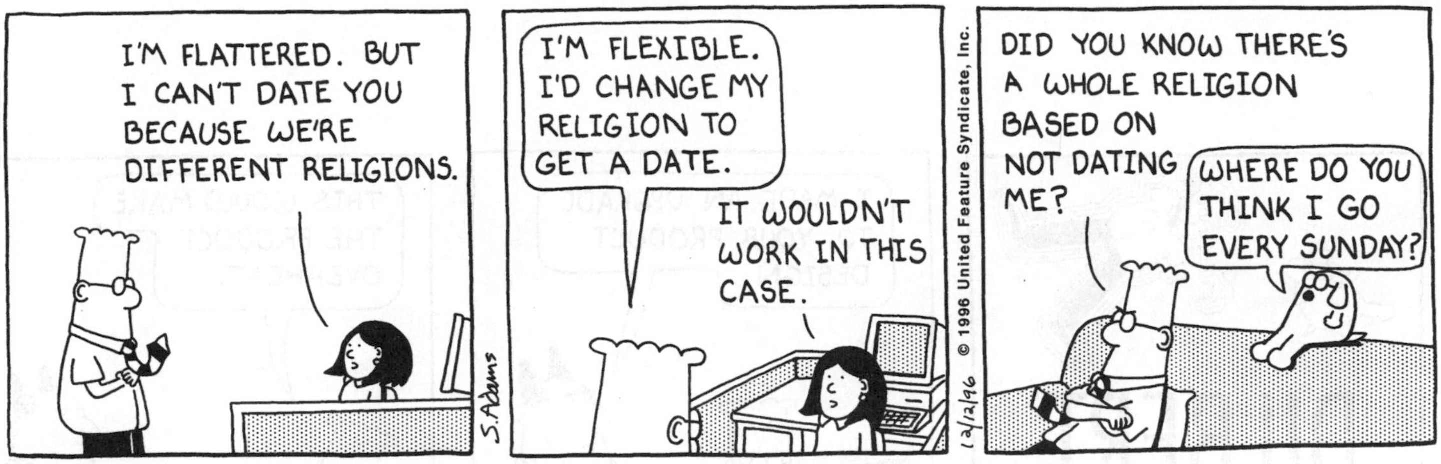
I'M FLATTERED. BUT I CAN'T DATE YOU BECAUSE WE'RE DIFFERENT RELIGIONS.
I'M FLEXIBLE. I'D CHANGE MY RELIGION TO GET A DATE.
IT WOULDN'T WORK IN THIS CASE.
DID YOU KNOW THERE'S A WHOLE RELIGION BASED ON NOT DATING ME?
WHERE DO YOU THINK I GO EVERY SUNDAY?
S. Adams
12/12/96
© 1996 United Feature Syndicate, Inc.

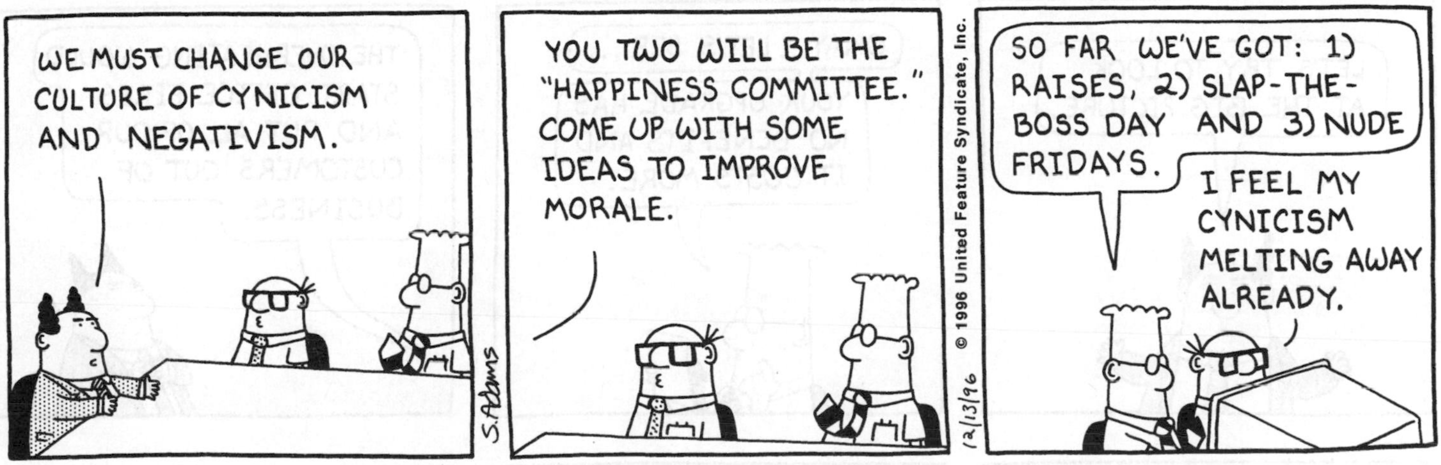
WE MUST CHANGE OUR CULTURE OF CYNICISM AND NEGATIVISM.
YOU TWO WILL BE THE "HAPPINESS COMMITTEE." COME UP WITH SOME IDEAS TO IMPROVE MORALE.
SO FAR WE'VE GOT: 1) RAISES, 2) SLAP-THE-BOSS DAY AND 3) NUDE FRIDAYS.
I FEEL MY CYNICISM MELTING AWAY ALREADY.
S. Adams
12/13/96
© 1996 United Feature Syndicate, Inc.

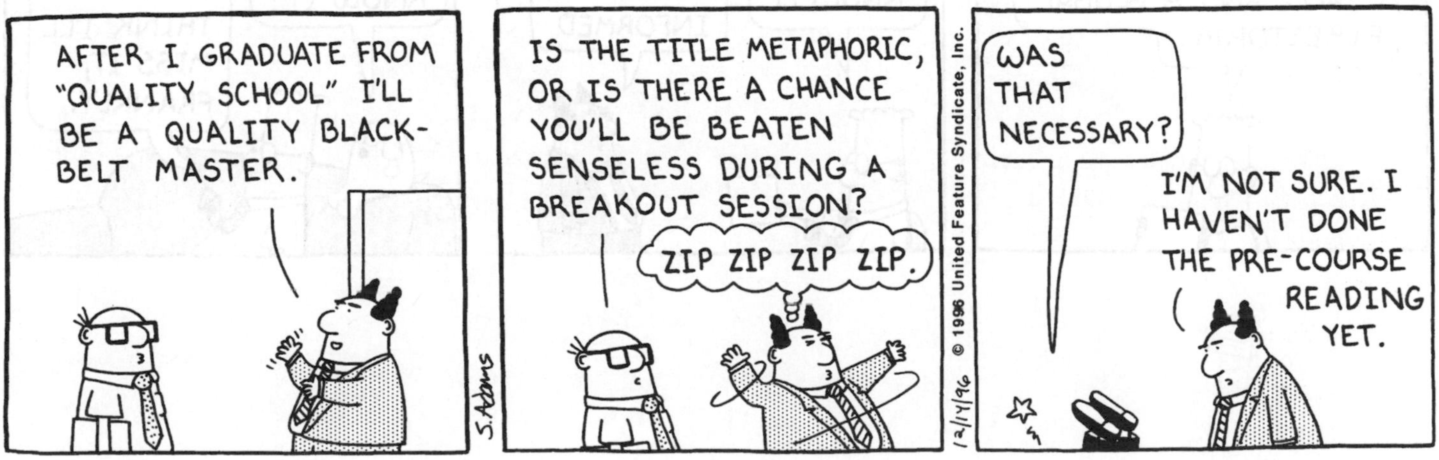
AFTER I GRADUATE FROM "QUALITY SCHOOL" I'LL BE A QUALITY BLACK-BELT MASTER.
IS THE TITLE METAPHORIC, OR IS THERE A CHANCE YOU'LL BE BEATEN SENSELESS DURING A BREAKOUT SESSION?
ZIP ZIP ZIP ZIP.
WAS THAT NECESSARY?
I'M NOT SURE. I HAVEN'T DONE THE PRE-COURSE READING YET.
S. Adams
12/14/96
© 1996 United Feature Syndicate, Inc.

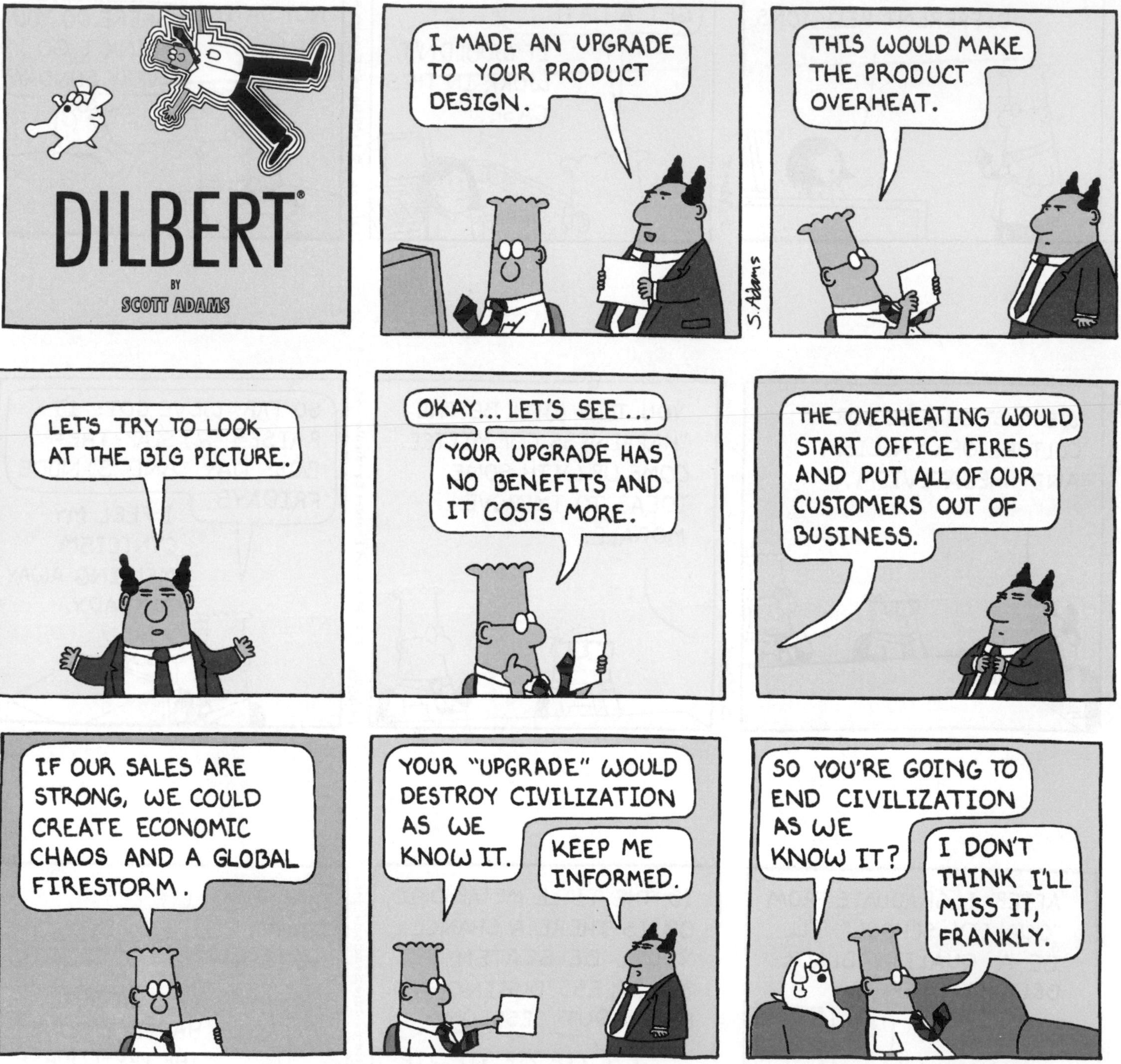
DILBERT®
BY
SCOTT ADAMS
I MADE AN UPGRADE TO YOUR PRODUCT DESIGN.
S. Adams
THIS WOULD MAKE THE PRODUCT OVERHEAT.
LET'S TRY TO LOOK AT THE BIG PICTURE.
OKAY... LET'S SEE...
YOUR UPGRADE HAS NO BENEFITS AND IT COSTS MORE.
THE OVERHEATING WOULD START OFFICE FIRES AND PUT ALL OF OUR CUSTOMERS OUT OF BUSINESS.
IF OUR SALES ARE STRONG, WE COULD CREATE ECONOMIC CHAOS AND A GLOBAL FIRESTORM.
YOUR "UPGRADE" WOULD DESTROY CIVILIZATION AS WE KNOW IT.
KEEP ME INFORMED.
SO YOU'RE GOING TO END CIVILIZATION AS WE KNOW IT?
I DON'T THINK I'LL MISS IT, FRANKLY.

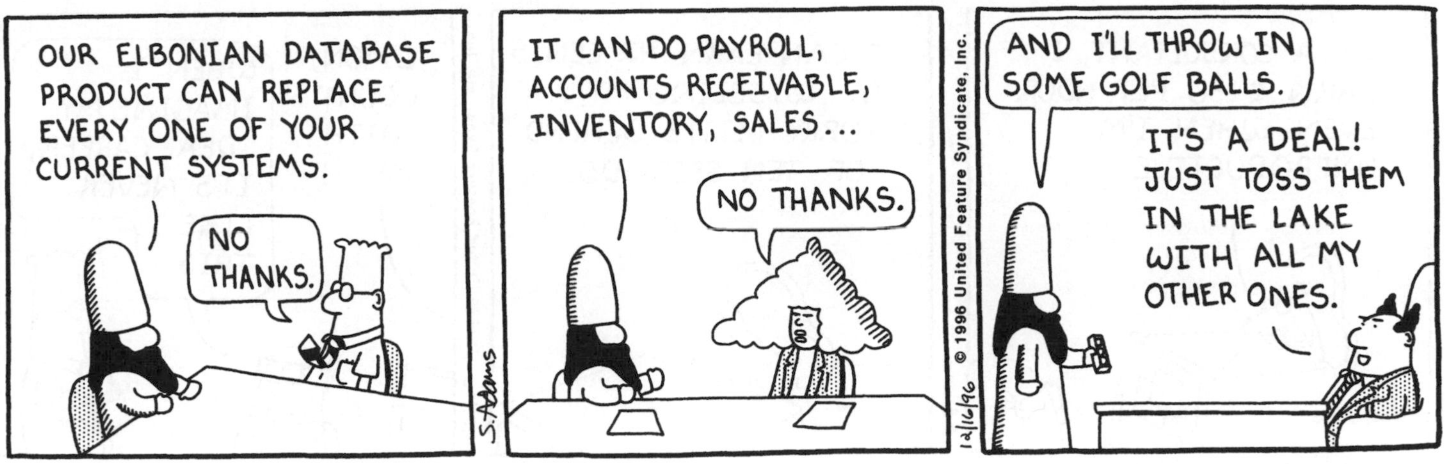
OUR ELBONIAN DATABASE PRODUCT CAN REPLACE EVERY ONE OF YOUR CURRENT SYSTEMS.
NO THANKS.
IT CAN DO PAYROLL, ACCOUNTS RECEIVABLE, INVENTORY, SALES...
NO THANKS.
AND I'LL THROW IN SOME GOLF BALLS.
IT'S A DEAL! JUST TOSS THEM IN THE LAKE WITH ALL MY OTHER ONES.
S. Adams
12/16/96
© 1996 United Feature Syndicate, Inc.

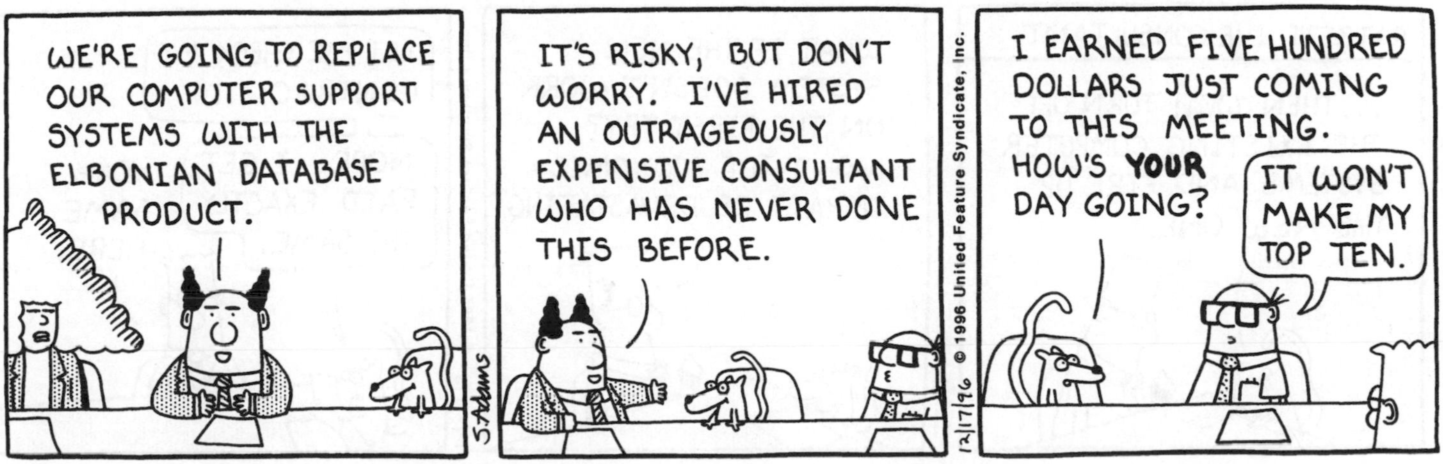
WE'RE GOING TO REPLACE OUR COMPUTER SUPPORT SYSTEMS WITH THE ELBONIAN DATABASE PRODUCT.
IT'S RISKY, BUT DON'T WORRY. I'VE HIRED AN OUTRAGEOUSLY EXPENSIVE CONSULTANT WHO HAS NEVER DONE THIS BEFORE.
I EARNED FIVE HUNDRED DOLLARS JUST COMING TO THIS MEETING. HOW'S **YOUR** DAY GOING?
IT WON'T MAKE MY TOP TEN.
S. Adams
12/17/96
© 1996 United Feature Syndicate, Inc.

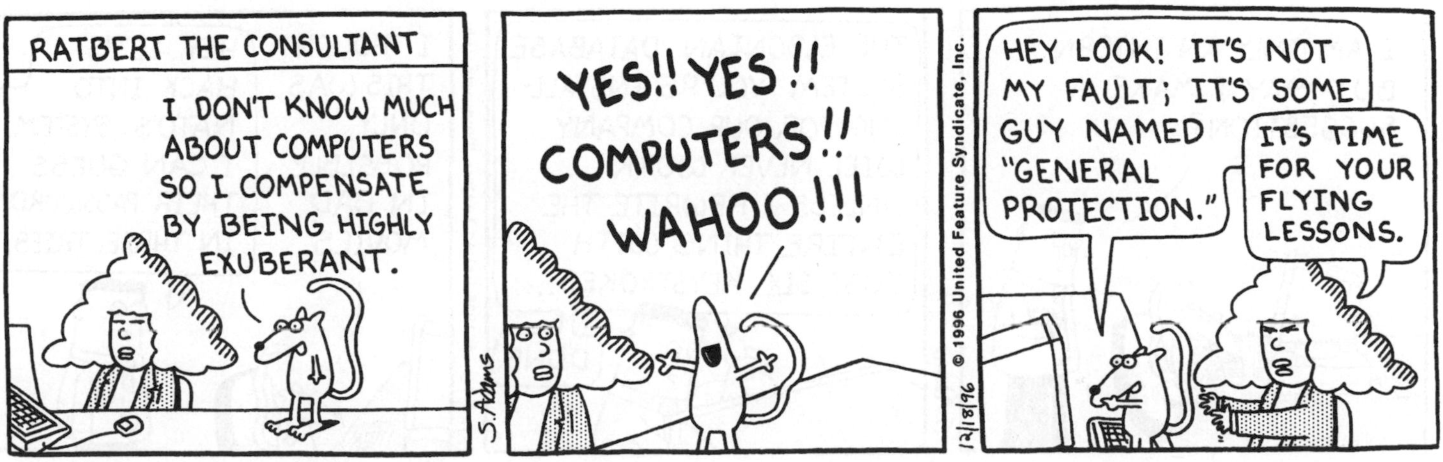
RATBERT THE CONSULTANT
I DON'T KNOW MUCH ABOUT COMPUTERS SO I COMPENSATE BY BEING HIGHLY EXUBERANT.
YES!! YES!! COMPUTERS!! WAHOO!!!
HEY LOOK! IT'S NOT MY FAULT; IT'S SOME GUY NAMED "GENERAL PROTECTION."
IT'S TIME FOR YOUR FLYING LESSONS.
S. Adams
12/18/96
© 1996 United Feature Syndicate, Inc.

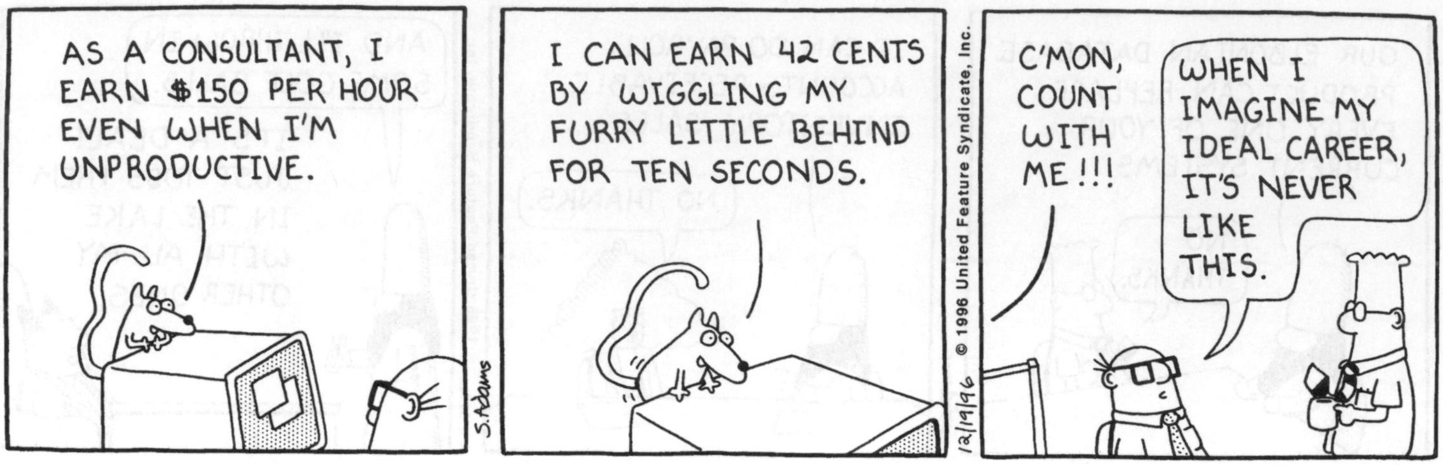
AS A CONSULTANT, I EARN $150 PER HOUR EVEN WHEN I'M UNPRODUCTIVE.
S. Adams
I CAN EARN 42 CENTS BY WIGGLING MY FURRY LITTLE BEHIND FOR TEN SECONDS.
12/19/96 © 1996 United Feature Syndicate, Inc.
C'MON, COUNT WITH ME!!!
WHEN I IMAGINE MY IDEAL CAREER, IT'S NEVER LIKE THIS.

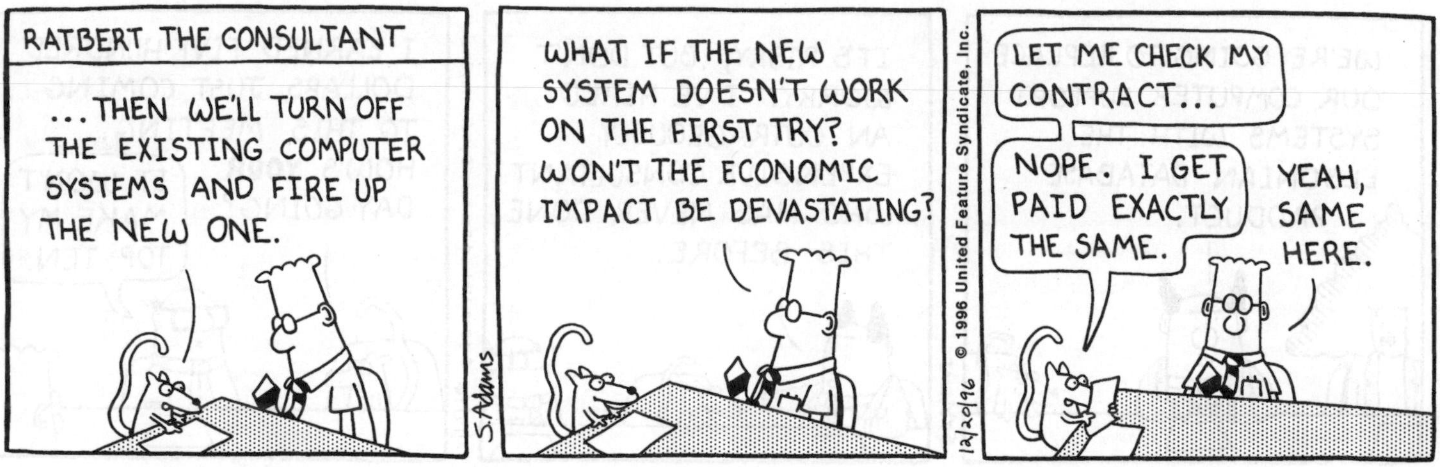
RATBERT THE CONSULTANT
...THEN WE'LL TURN OFF THE EXISTING COMPUTER SYSTEMS AND FIRE UP THE NEW ONE.
S. Adams
WHAT IF THE NEW SYSTEM DOESN'T WORK ON THE FIRST TRY? WON'T THE ECONOMIC IMPACT BE DEVASTATING?
12/20/96 © 1996 United Feature Syndicate, Inc.
LET ME CHECK MY CONTRACT...
NOPE. I GET PAID EXACTLY THE SAME.
YEAH, SAME HERE.

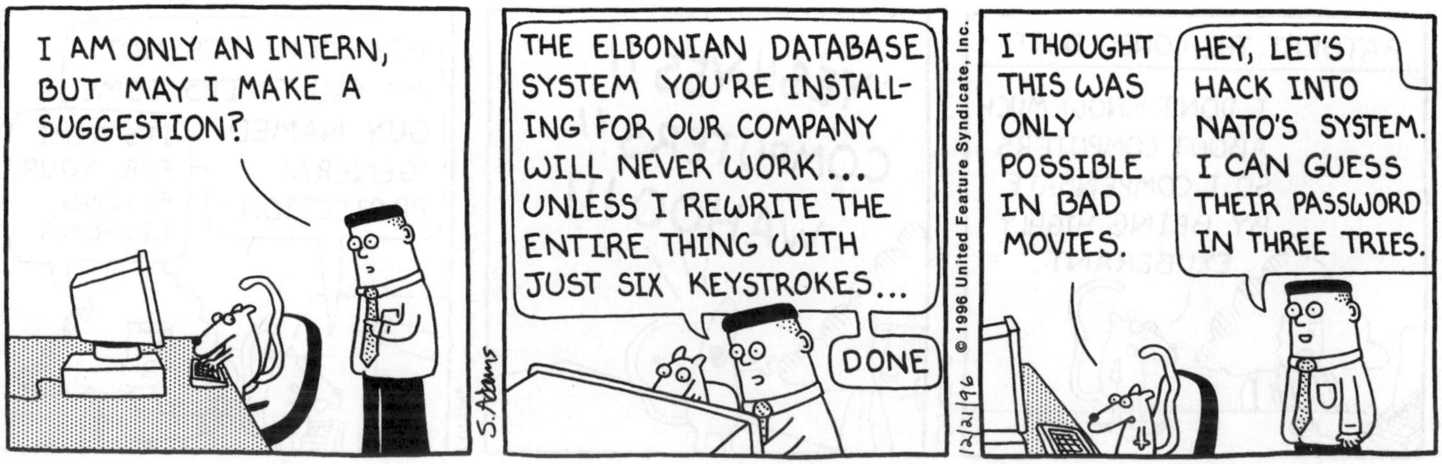
I AM ONLY AN INTERN, BUT MAY I MAKE A SUGGESTION?
S. Adams
THE ELBONIAN DATABASE SYSTEM YOU'RE INSTALLING FOR OUR COMPANY WILL NEVER WORK... UNLESS I REWRITE THE ENTIRE THING WITH JUST SIX KEYSTROKES...
DONE
12/21/96 © 1996 United Feature Syndicate, Inc.
I THOUGHT THIS WAS ONLY POSSIBLE IN BAD MOVIES.
HEY, LET'S HACK INTO NATO'S SYSTEM. I CAN GUESS THEIR PASSWORD IN THREE TRIES.

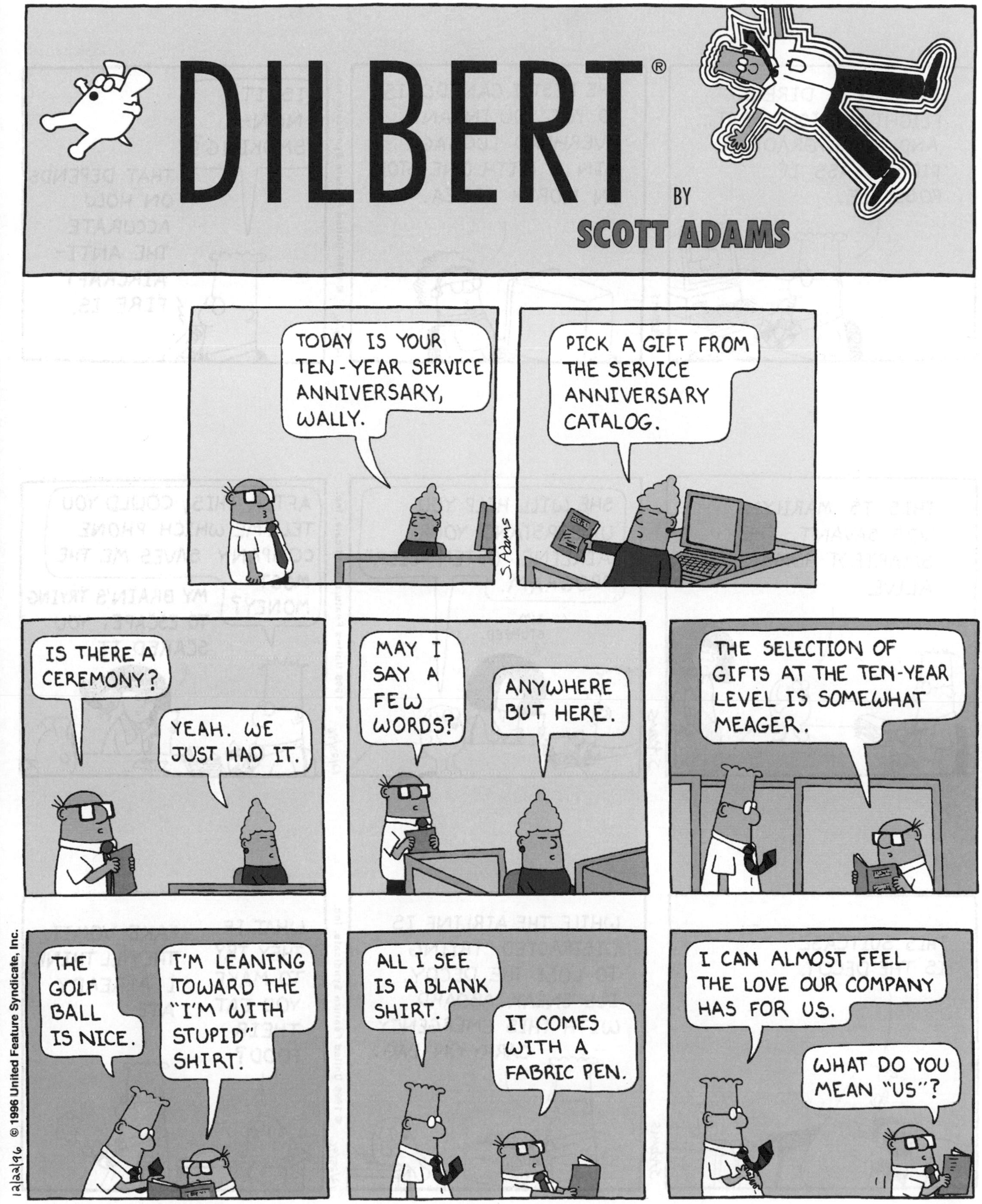
DILBERT®
BY
SCOTT ADAMS
TODAY IS YOUR TEN-YEAR SERVICE ANNIVERSARY, WALLY.
PICK A GIFT FROM THE SERVICE ANNIVERSARY CATALOG.
S. Adams
IS THERE A CEREMONY?
YEAH. WE JUST HAD IT.
MAY I SAY A FEW WORDS?
ANYWHERE BUT HERE.
THE SELECTION OF GIFTS AT THE TEN-YEAR LEVEL IS SOMEWHAT MEAGER.
THE GOLF BALL IS NICE.
I'M LEANING TOWARD THE "I'M WITH STUPID" SHIRT.
ALL I SEE IS A BLANK SHIRT.
IT COMES WITH A FABRIC PEN.
I CAN ALMOST FEEL THE LOVE OUR COMPANY HAS FOR US.
WHAT DO YOU MEAN "US"?
12/22/96 © 1996 United Feature Syndicate, Inc.

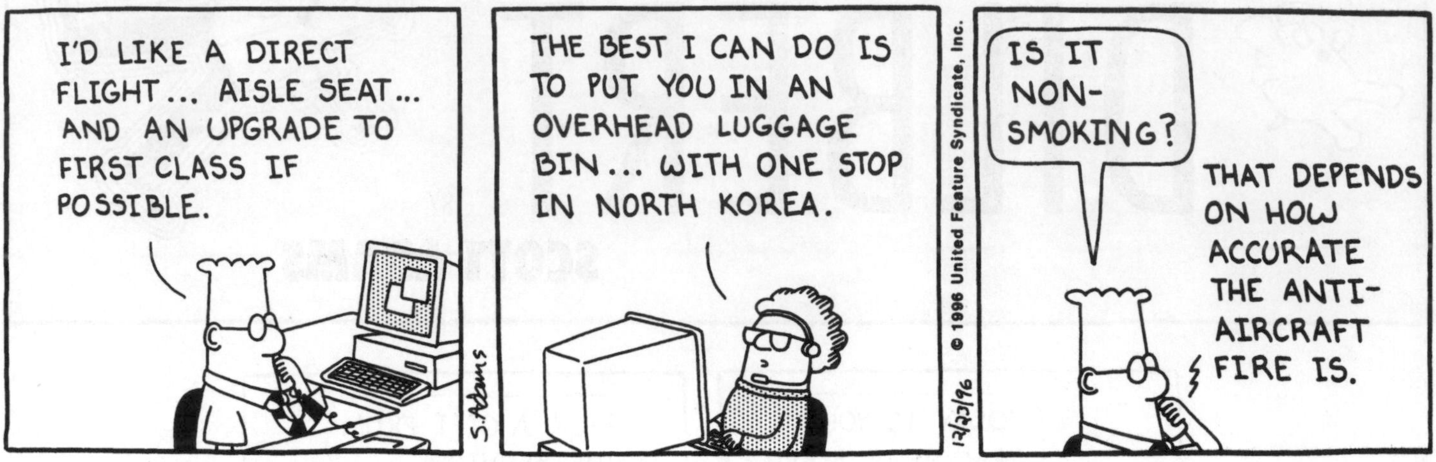
I'D LIKE A DIRECT FLIGHT... AISLE SEAT... AND AN UPGRADE TO FIRST CLASS IF POSSIBLE.
THE BEST I CAN DO IS TO PUT YOU IN AN OVERHEAD LUGGAGE BIN... WITH ONE STOP IN NORTH KOREA.
IS IT NON-SMOKING?
THAT DEPENDS ON HOW ACCURATE THE ANTI-AIRCRAFT FIRE IS.
S. Adams
12/23/96
© 1996 United Feature Syndicate, Inc.

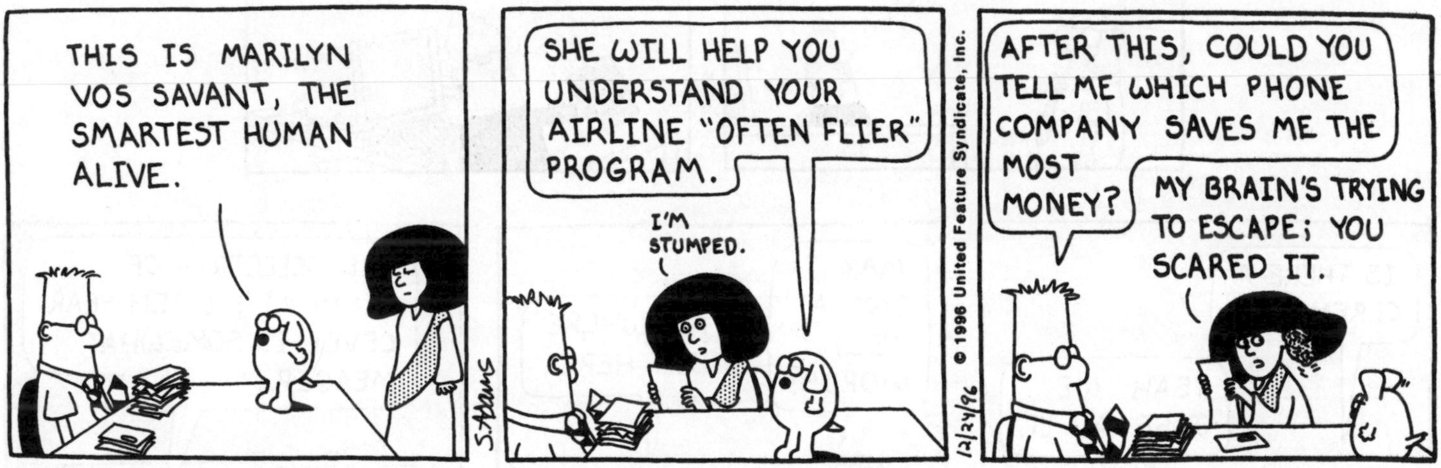
THIS IS MARILYN VOS SAVANT, THE SMARTEST HUMAN ALIVE.
SHE WILL HELP YOU UNDERSTAND YOUR AIRLINE "OFTEN FLIER" PROGRAM.
I'M STUMPED.
AFTER THIS, COULD YOU TELL ME WHICH PHONE COMPANY SAVES ME THE MOST MONEY?
MY BRAIN'S TRYING TO ESCAPE; YOU SCARED IT.
S. Adams
12/24/96
© 1996 United Feature Syndicate, Inc.

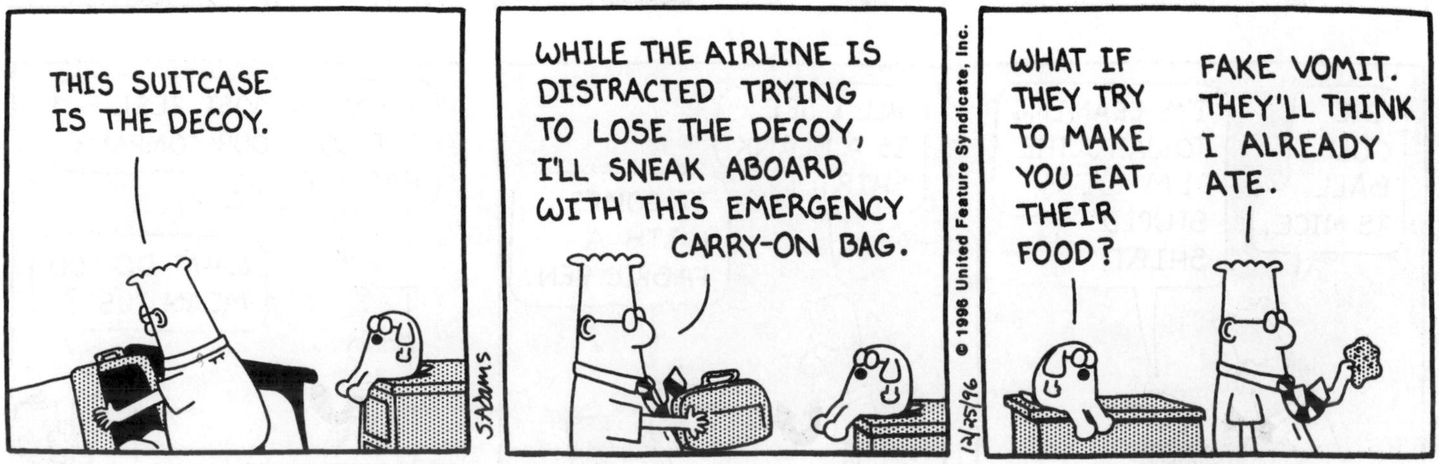
THIS SUITCASE IS THE DECOY.
WHILE THE AIRLINE IS DISTRACTED TRYING TO LOSE THE DECOY, I'LL SNEAK ABOARD WITH THIS EMERGENCY CARRY-ON BAG.
WHAT IF THEY TRY TO MAKE YOU EAT THEIR FOOD?
FAKE VOMIT. THEY'LL THINK I ALREADY ATE.
S. Adams
12/25/96
© 1996 United Feature Syndicate, Inc.

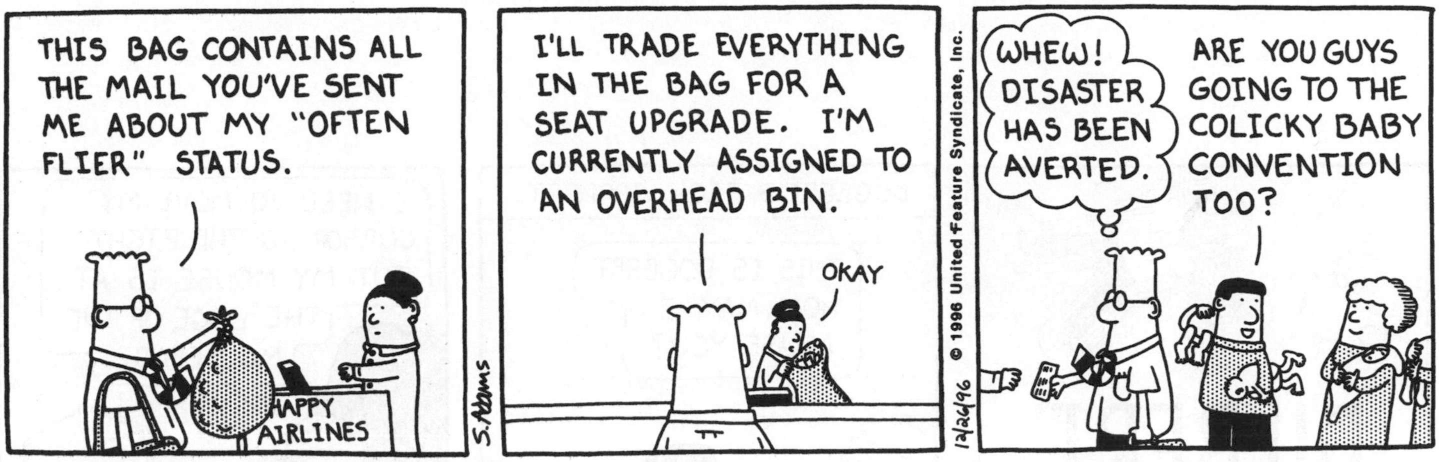
THIS BAG CONTAINS ALL THE MAIL YOU'VE SENT ME ABOUT MY "OFTEN FLIER" STATUS.
HAPPY AIRLINES
S. Adams
I'LL TRADE EVERYTHING IN THE BAG FOR A SEAT UPGRADE. I'M CURRENTLY ASSIGNED TO AN OVERHEAD BIN.
OKAY
12/26/96
© 1996 United Feature Syndicate, Inc.
WHEW! DISASTER HAS BEEN AVERTED.
ARE YOU GUYS GOING TO THE COLICKY BABY CONVENTION TOO?

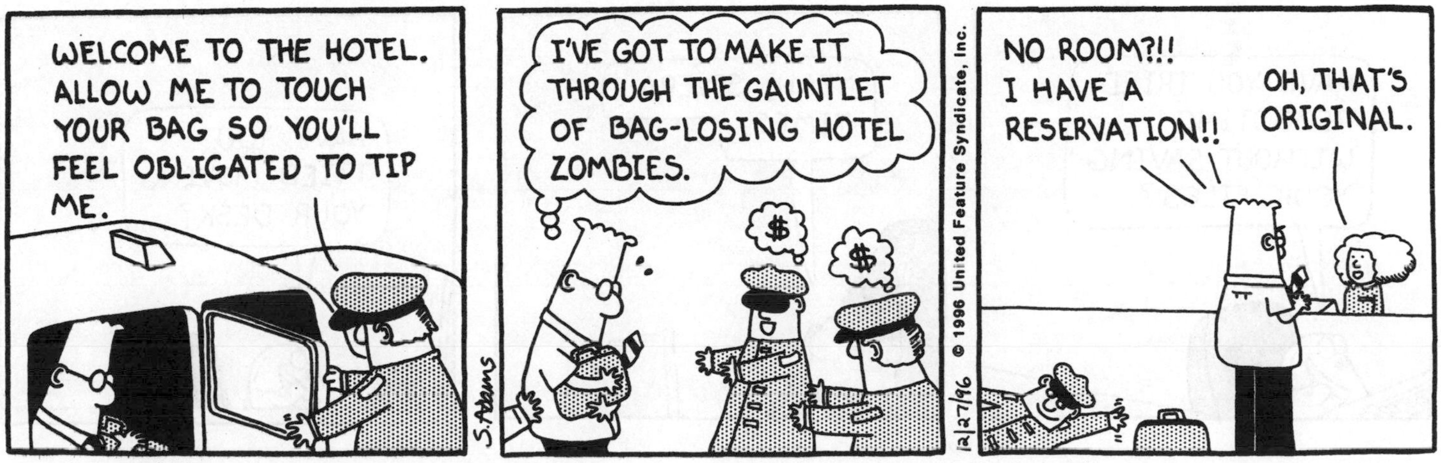
WELCOME TO THE HOTEL. ALLOW ME TO TOUCH YOUR BAG SO YOU'LL FEEL OBLIGATED TO TIP ME.
S. Adams
I'VE GOT TO MAKE IT THROUGH THE GAUNTLET OF BAG-LOSING HOTEL ZOMBIES.
$
$
12/27/96
© 1996 United Feature Syndicate, Inc.
NO ROOM?!! I HAVE A RESERVATION!!
OH, THAT'S ORIGINAL.

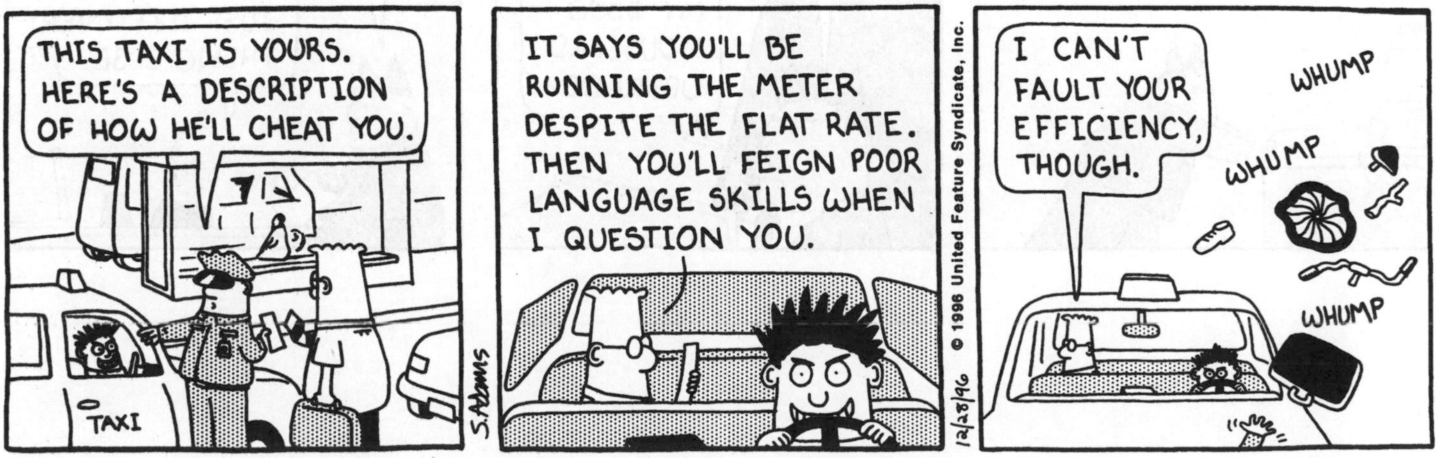
THIS TAXI IS YOURS. HERE'S A DESCRIPTION OF HOW HE'LL CHEAT YOU.
TAXI
S. Adams
IT SAYS YOU'LL BE RUNNING THE METER DESPITE THE FLAT RATE. THEN YOU'LL FEIGN POOR LANGUAGE SKILLS WHEN I QUESTION YOU.
12/28/96
© 1996 United Feature Syndicate, Inc.
I CAN'T FAULT YOUR EFFICIENCY, THOUGH.
WHUMP
WHUMP
WHUMP

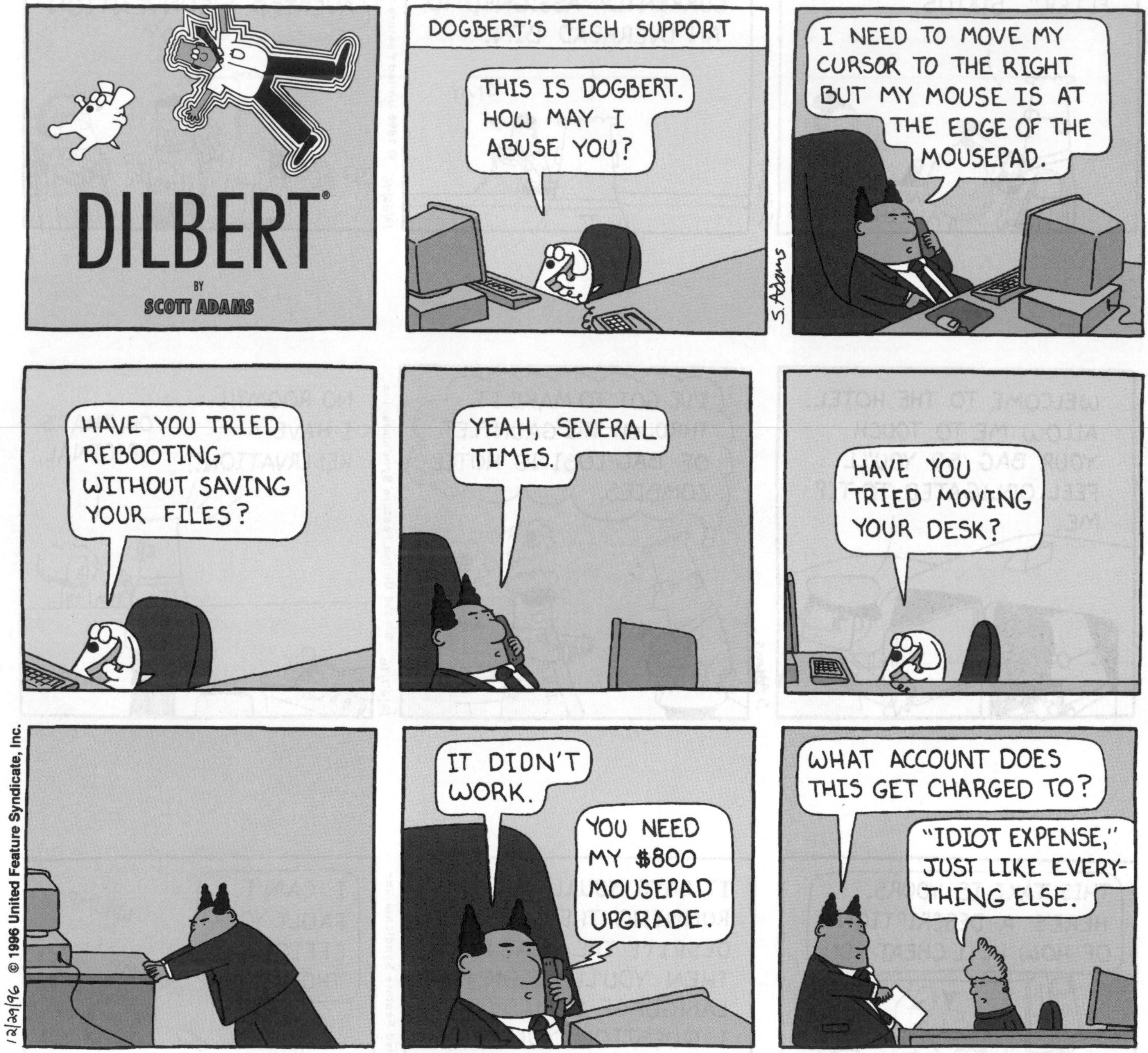
DILBERT®
BY
SCOTT ADAMS
DOGBERT'S TECH SUPPORT
THIS IS DOGBERT. HOW MAY I ABUSE YOU?
S. Adams
I NEED TO MOVE MY CURSOR TO THE RIGHT BUT MY MOUSE IS AT THE EDGE OF THE MOUSEPAD.
HAVE YOU TRIED REBOOTING WITHOUT SAVING YOUR FILES?
YEAH, SEVERAL TIMES.
HAVE YOU TRIED MOVING YOUR DESK?
12/29/96 © 1996 United Feature Syndicate, Inc.
IT DIDN'T WORK.
YOU NEED MY $800 MOUSEPAD UPGRADE.
WHAT ACCOUNT DOES THIS GET CHARGED TO?
"IDIOT EXPENSE," JUST LIKE EVERYTHING ELSE.

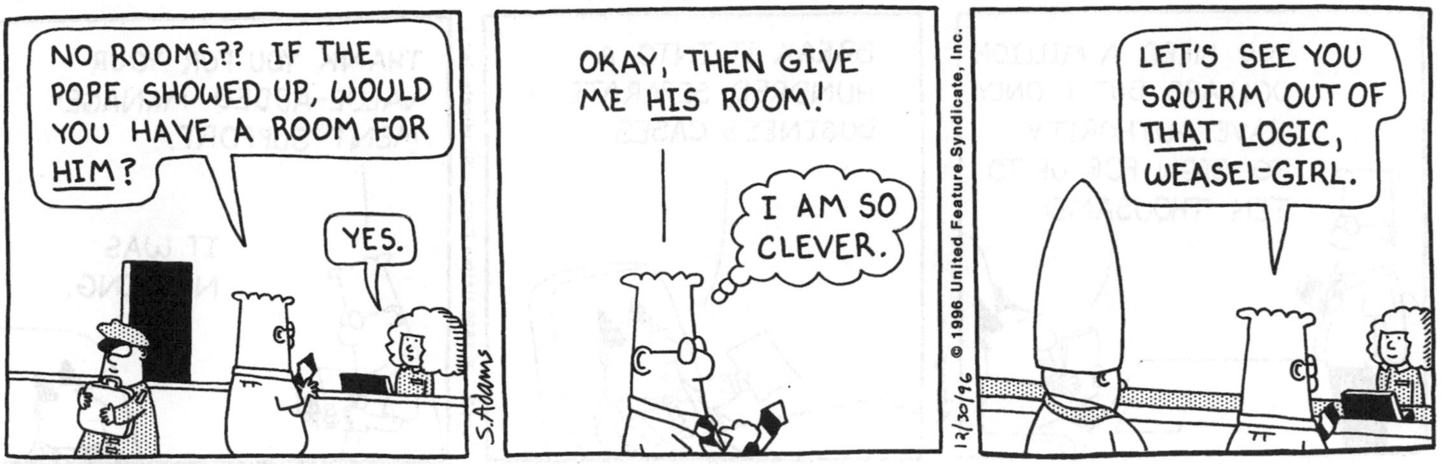
NO ROOMS?? IF THE POPE SHOWED UP, WOULD YOU HAVE A ROOM FOR HIM?
YES.
S.Adams
OKAY, THEN GIVE ME HIS ROOM!
I AM SO CLEVER.
12/30/96 © 1996 United Feature Syndicate, Inc.
LET'S SEE YOU SQUIRM OUT OF THAT LOGIC, WEASEL-GIRL.

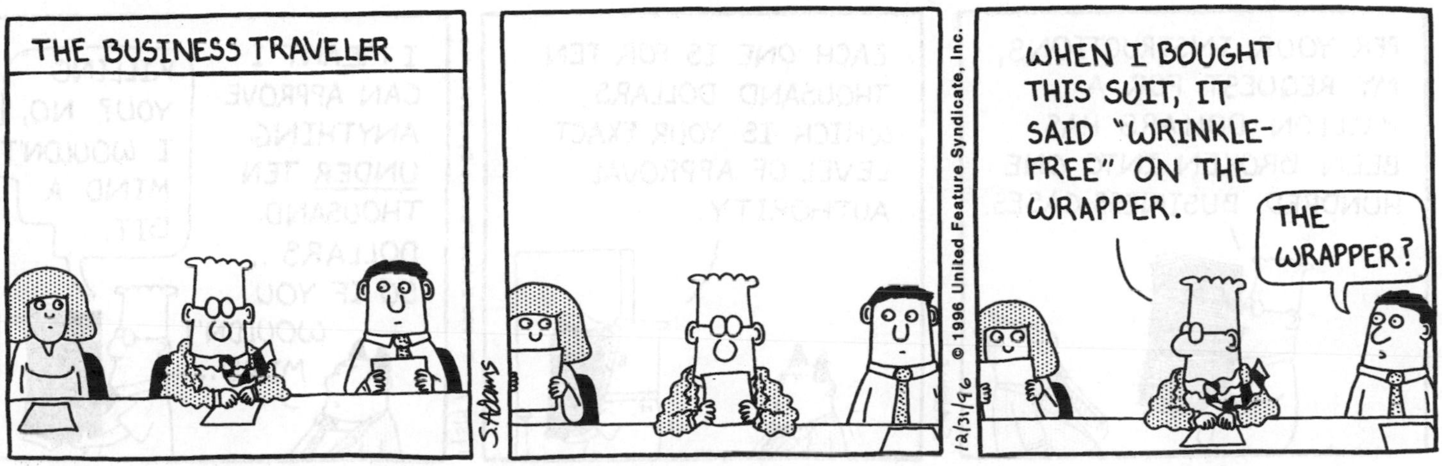
THE BUSINESS TRAVELER
S.Adams
12/31/96 © 1996 United Feature Syndicate, Inc.
WHEN I BOUGHT THIS SUIT, IT SAID "WRINKLE-FREE" ON THE WRAPPER.
THE WRAPPER?

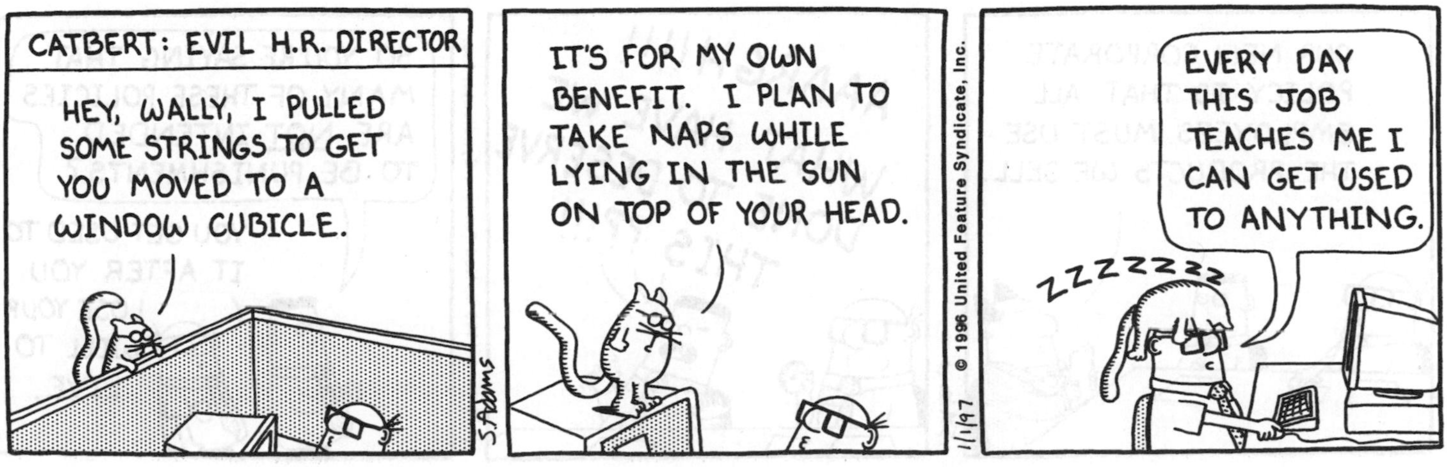
CATBERT: EVIL H.R. DIRECTOR
HEY, WALLY, I PULLED SOME STRINGS TO GET YOU MOVED TO A WINDOW CUBICLE.
S.Adams
IT'S FOR MY OWN BENEFIT. I PLAN TO TAKE NAPS WHILE LYING IN THE SUN ON TOP OF YOUR HEAD.
1/1/97 © 1996 United Feature Syndicate, Inc.
EVERY DAY THIS JOB TEACHES ME I CAN GET USED TO ANYTHING.
ZZZZZZZ

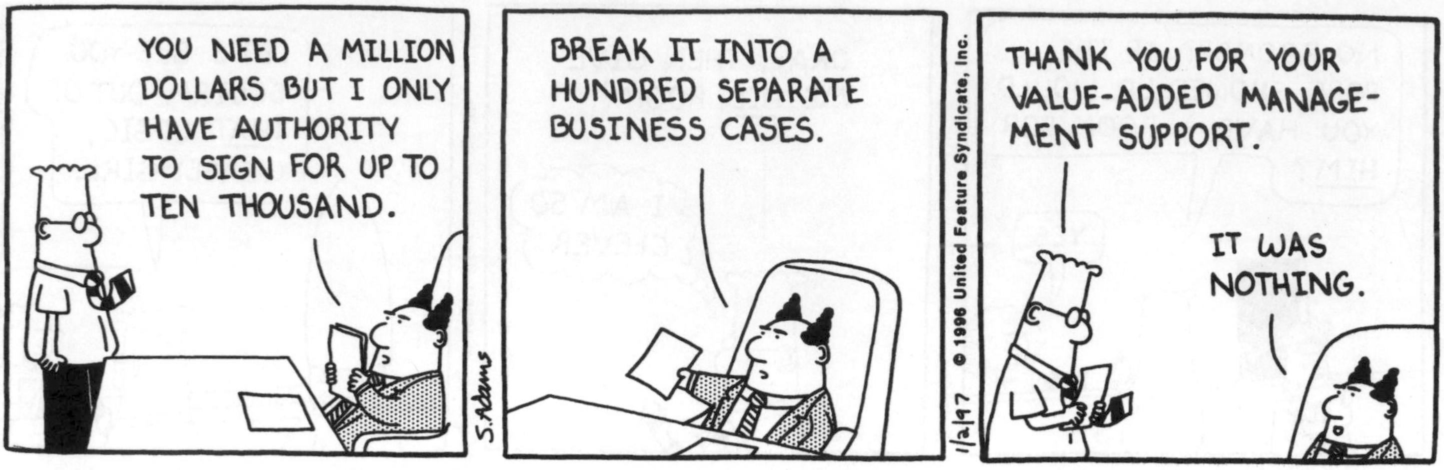
YOU NEED A MILLION DOLLARS BUT I ONLY HAVE AUTHORITY TO SIGN FOR UP TO TEN THOUSAND.
BREAK IT INTO A HUNDRED SEPARATE BUSINESS CASES.
THANK YOU FOR YOUR VALUE-ADDED MANAGE-MENT SUPPORT.
IT WAS NOTHING.
S.Adams
1/2/97 © 1996 United Feature Syndicate, Inc.

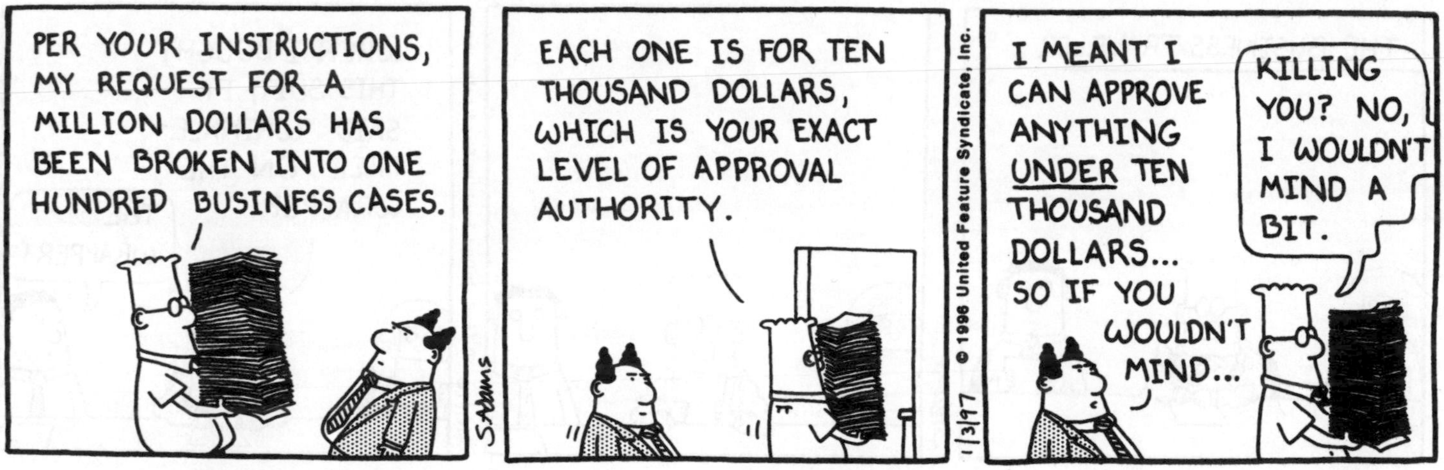
PER YOUR INSTRUCTIONS, MY REQUEST FOR A MILLION DOLLARS HAS BEEN BROKEN INTO ONE HUNDRED BUSINESS CASES.
EACH ONE IS FOR TEN THOUSAND DOLLARS, WHICH IS YOUR EXACT LEVEL OF APPROVAL AUTHORITY.
I MEANT I CAN APPROVE ANYTHING UNDER TEN THOUSAND DOLLARS... SO IF YOU WOULDN'T MIND...
KILLING YOU? NO, I WOULDN'T MIND A BIT.
S.Adams
1/3/97 © 1996 United Feature Syndicate, Inc.

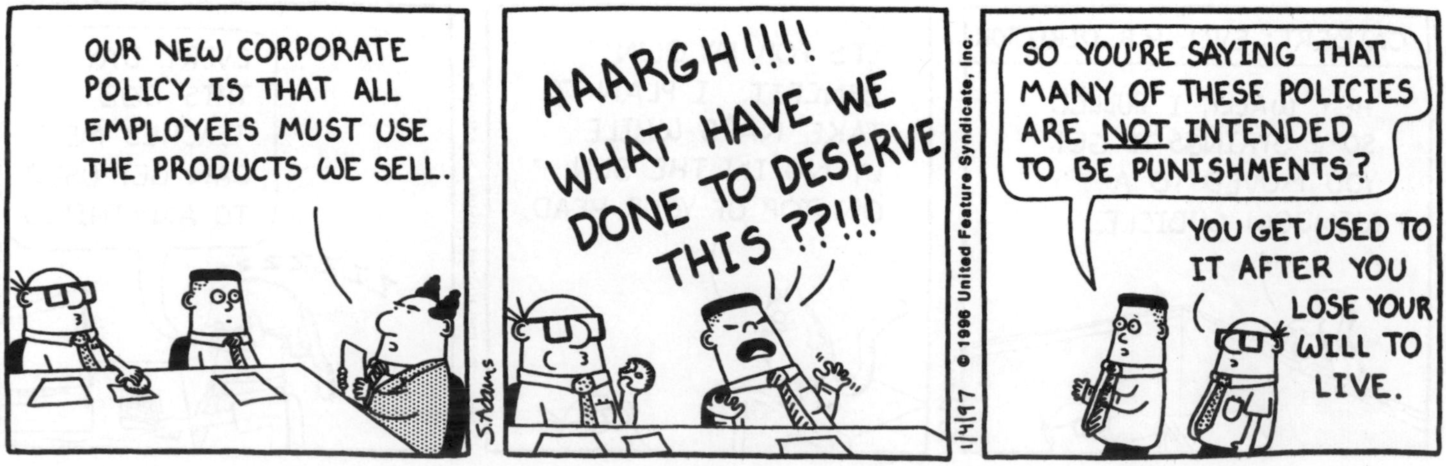
OUR NEW CORPORATE POLICY IS THAT ALL EMPLOYEES MUST USE THE PRODUCTS WE SELL.
AAARGH!!!! WHAT HAVE WE DONE TO DESERVE THIS ??!!!
SO YOU'RE SAYING THAT MANY OF THESE POLICIES ARE NOT INTENDED TO BE PUNISHMENTS?
YOU GET USED TO IT AFTER YOU LOSE YOUR WILL TO LIVE.
S.Adams
1/4/97 © 1996 United Feature Syndicate, Inc.

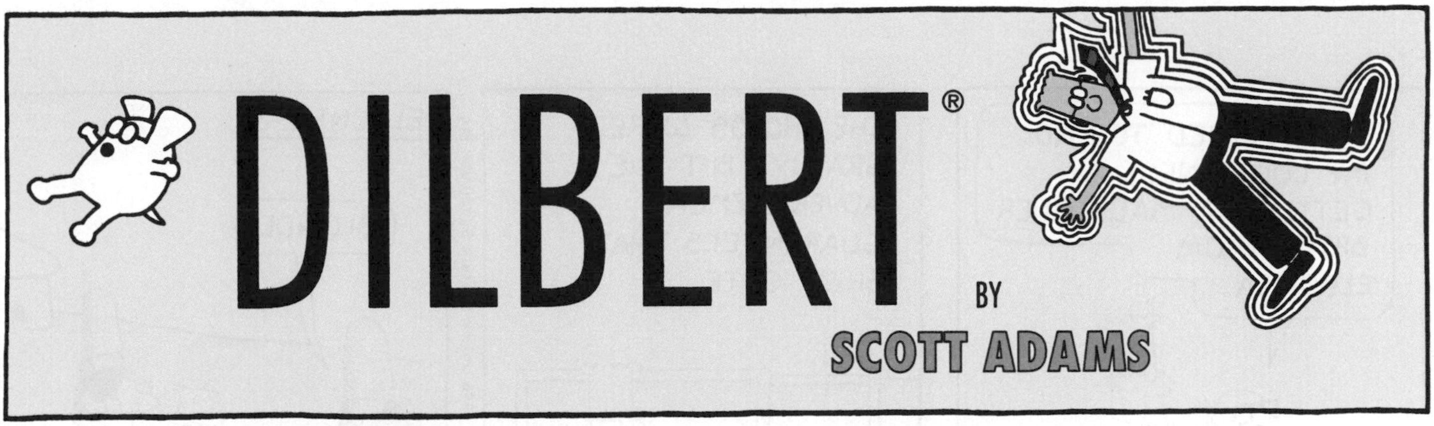
DILBERT®
BY
SCOTT ADAMS

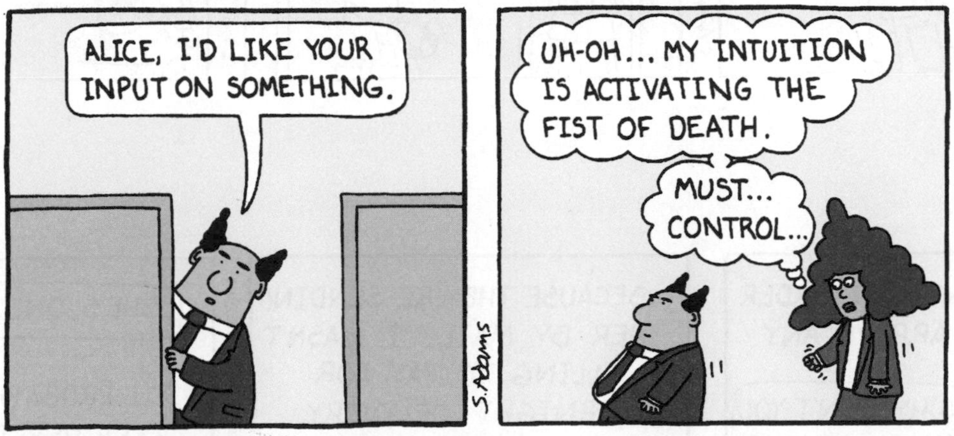
ALICE, I'D LIKE YOUR INPUT ON SOMETHING.
S. Adams
UH-OH... MY INTUITION IS ACTIVATING THE FIST OF DEATH.
MUST... CONTROL...

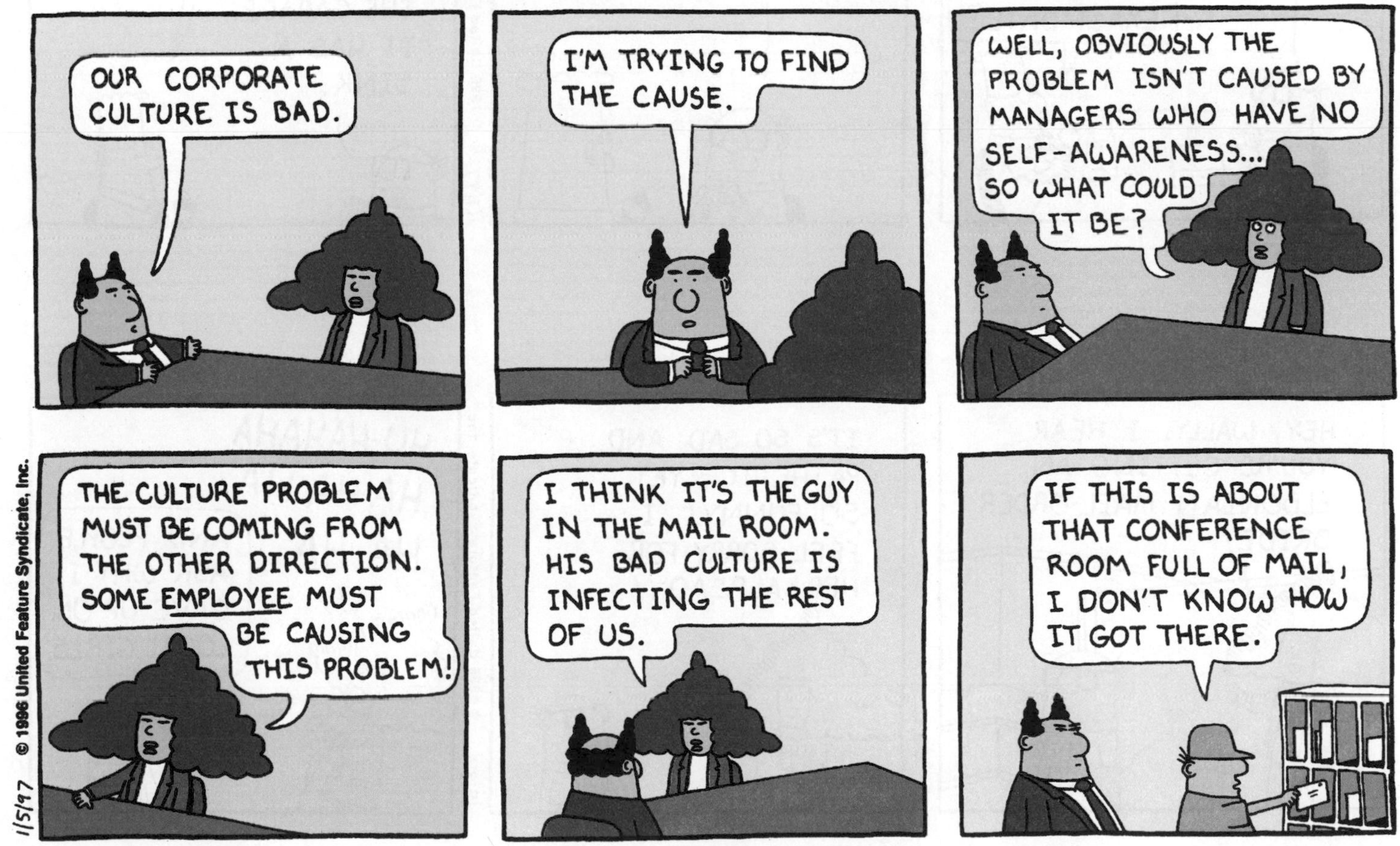
OUR CORPORATE CULTURE IS BAD.
I'M TRYING TO FIND THE CAUSE.
WELL, OBVIOUSLY THE PROBLEM ISN'T CAUSED BY MANAGERS WHO HAVE NO SELF-AWARENESS... SO WHAT COULD IT BE?
THE CULTURE PROBLEM MUST BE COMING FROM THE OTHER DIRECTION. SOME EMPLOYEE MUST BE CAUSING THIS PROBLEM!
I THINK IT'S THE GUY IN THE MAIL ROOM. HIS BAD CULTURE IS INFECTING THE REST OF US.
IF THIS IS ABOUT THAT CONFERENCE ROOM FULL OF MAIL, I DON'T KNOW HOW IT GOT THERE.
1/5/97
© 1996 United Feature Syndicate, Inc.

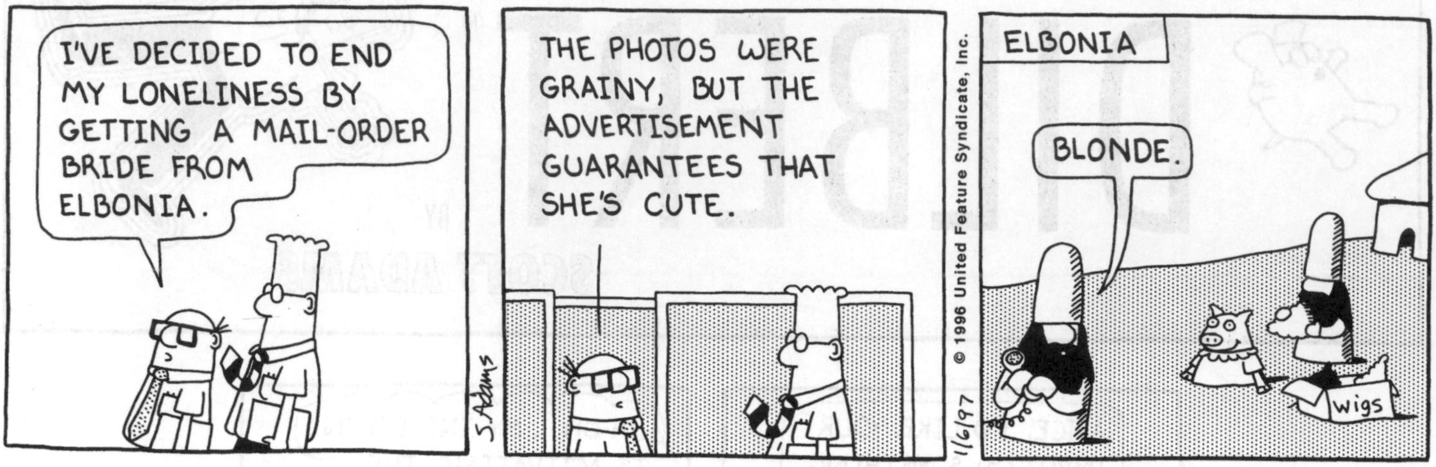
I'VE DECIDED TO END MY LONELINESS BY GETTING A MAIL-ORDER BRIDE FROM ELBONIA.
S. Adams
THE PHOTOS WERE GRAINY, BUT THE ADVERTISEMENT GUARANTEES THAT SHE'S CUTE.
1/6/97
© 1996 United Feature Syndicate, Inc.
ELBONIA
BLONDE.
wigs

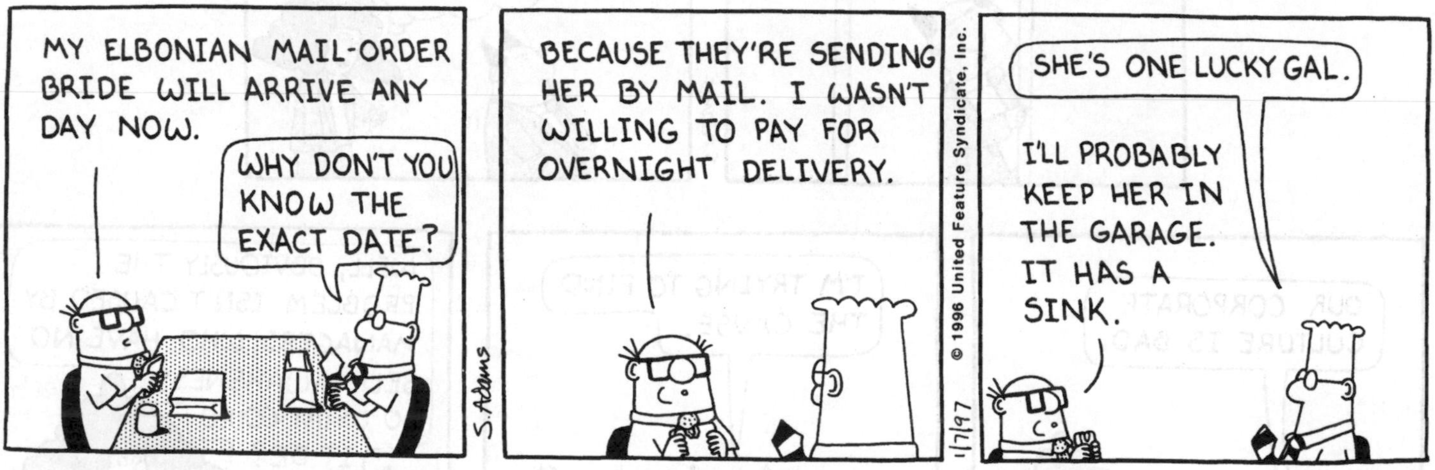
MY ELBONIAN MAIL-ORDER BRIDE WILL ARRIVE ANY DAY NOW.
WHY DON'T YOU KNOW THE EXACT DATE?
S. Adams
BECAUSE THEY'RE SENDING HER BY MAIL. I WASN'T WILLING TO PAY FOR OVERNIGHT DELIVERY.
1/7/97
© 1996 United Feature Syndicate, Inc.
SHE'S ONE LUCKY GAL.
I'LL PROBABLY KEEP HER IN THE GARAGE. IT HAS A SINK.

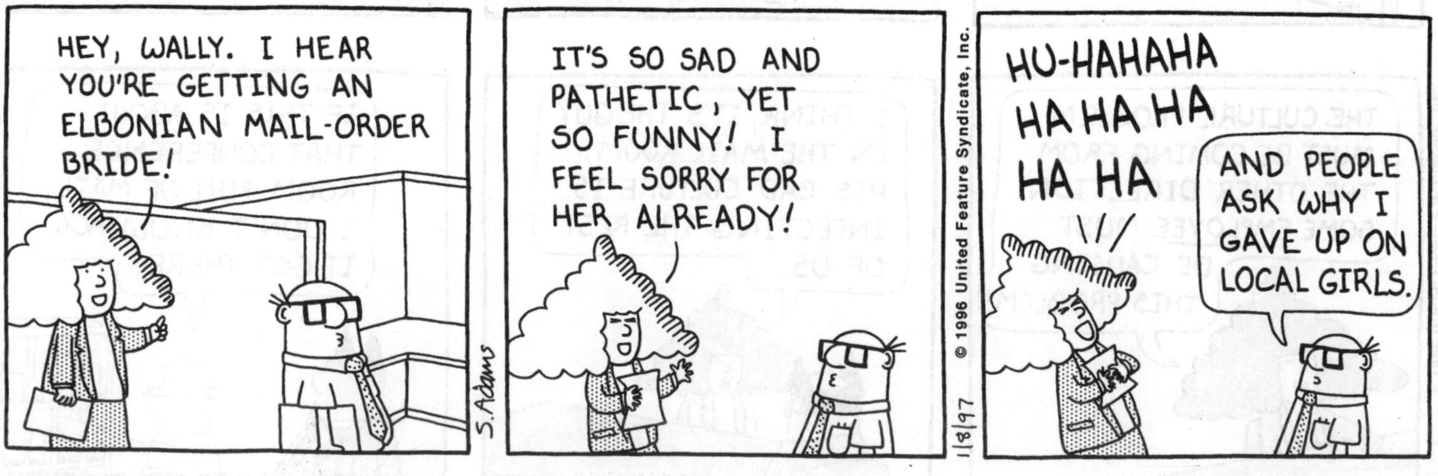
HEY, WALLY. I HEAR YOU'RE GETTING AN ELBONIAN MAIL-ORDER BRIDE!
S. Adams
IT'S SO SAD AND PATHETIC, YET SO FUNNY! I FEEL SORRY FOR HER ALREADY!
1/8/97
© 1996 United Feature Syndicate, Inc.
HU-HAHAHA HA HA HA HA HA
AND PEOPLE ASK WHY I GAVE UP ON LOCAL GIRLS.

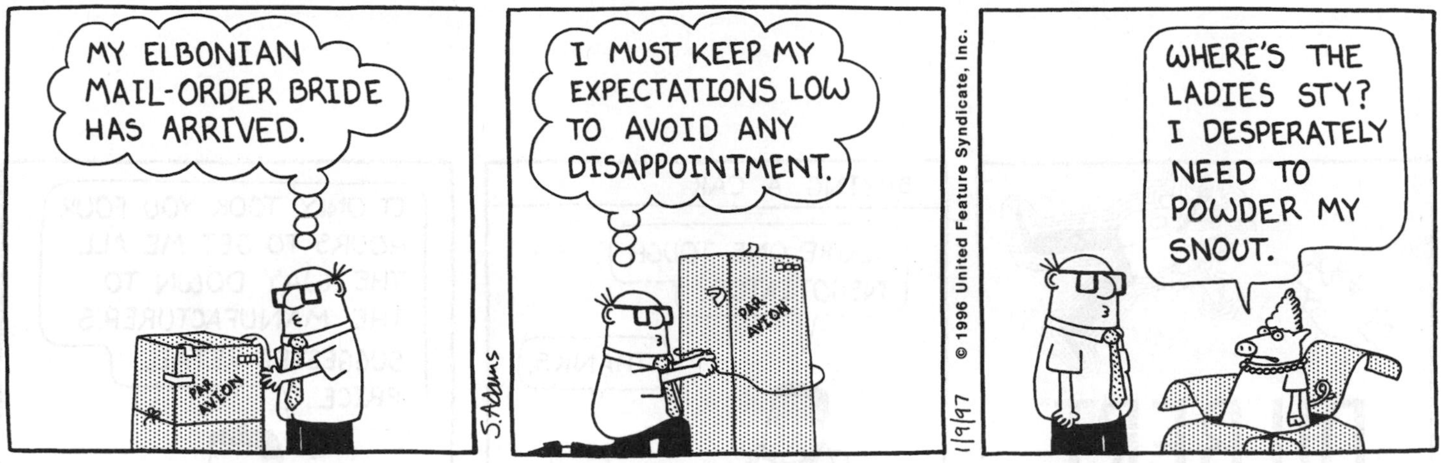
MY ELBONIAN MAIL-ORDER BRIDE HAS ARRIVED.
I MUST KEEP MY EXPECTATIONS LOW TO AVOID ANY DISAPPOINTMENT.
WHERE'S THE LADIES STY? I DESPERATELY NEED TO POWDER MY SNOUT.
S.Adams
1/9/97 © 1996 United Feature Syndicate, Inc.

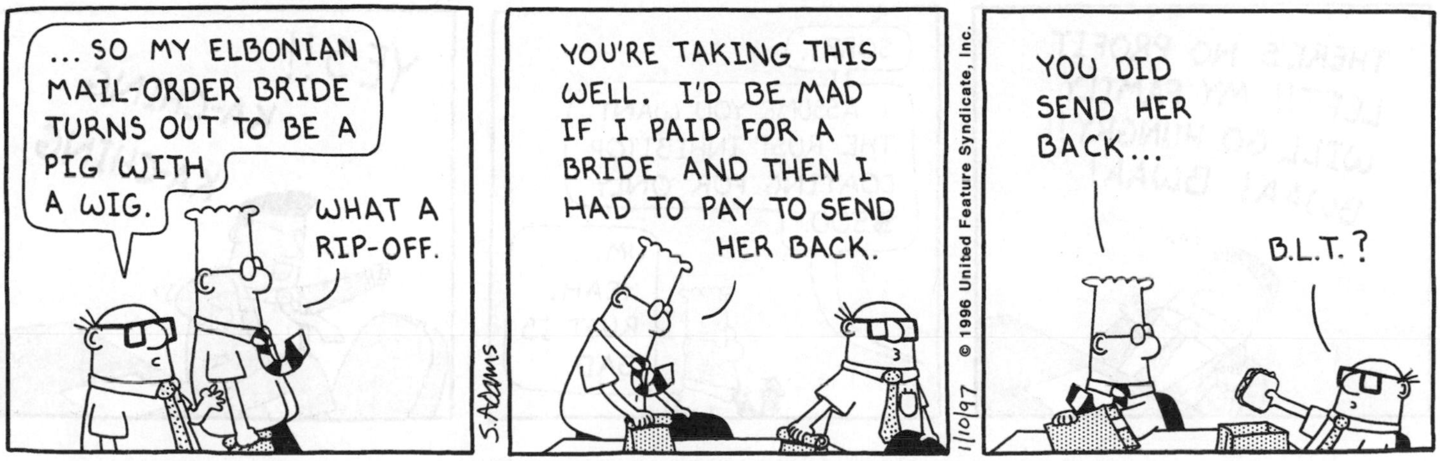
... SO MY ELBONIAN MAIL-ORDER BRIDE TURNS OUT TO BE A PIG WITH A WIG.
WHAT A RIP-OFF.
YOU'RE TAKING THIS WELL. I'D BE MAD IF I PAID FOR A BRIDE AND THEN I HAD TO PAY TO SEND HER BACK.
YOU DID SEND HER BACK...
B.L.T.?
S.Adams
1/10/97 © 1996 United Feature Syndicate, Inc.

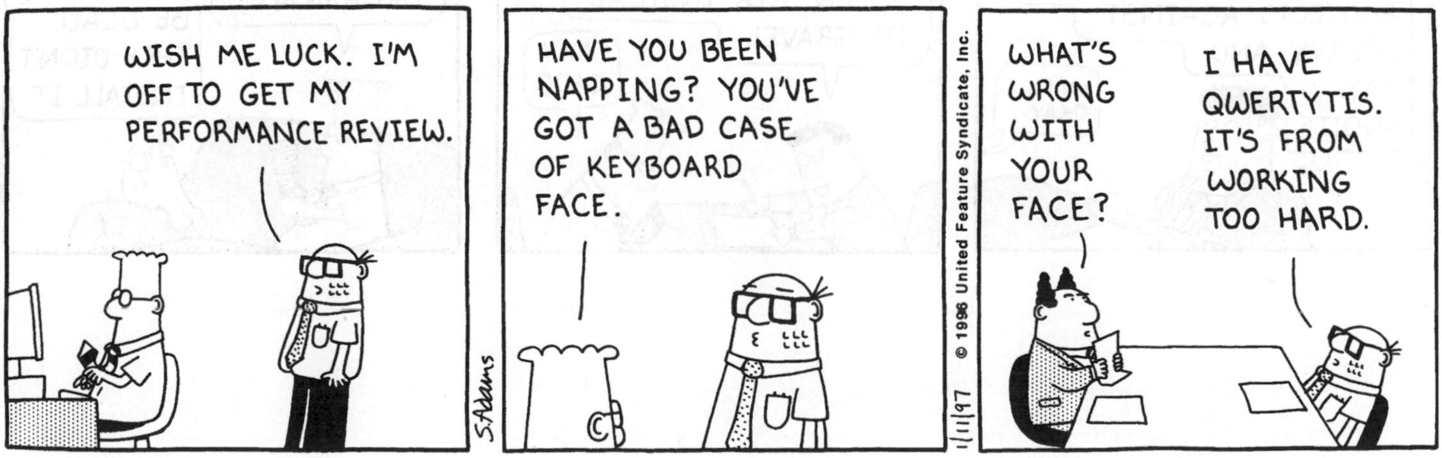
WISH ME LUCK. I'M OFF TO GET MY PERFORMANCE REVIEW.
HAVE YOU BEEN NAPPING? YOU'VE GOT A BAD CASE OF KEYBOARD FACE.
WHAT'S WRONG WITH YOUR FACE?
I HAVE QWERTYTIS. IT'S FROM WORKING TOO HARD.
S.Adams
1/11/97 © 1996 United Feature Syndicate, Inc.

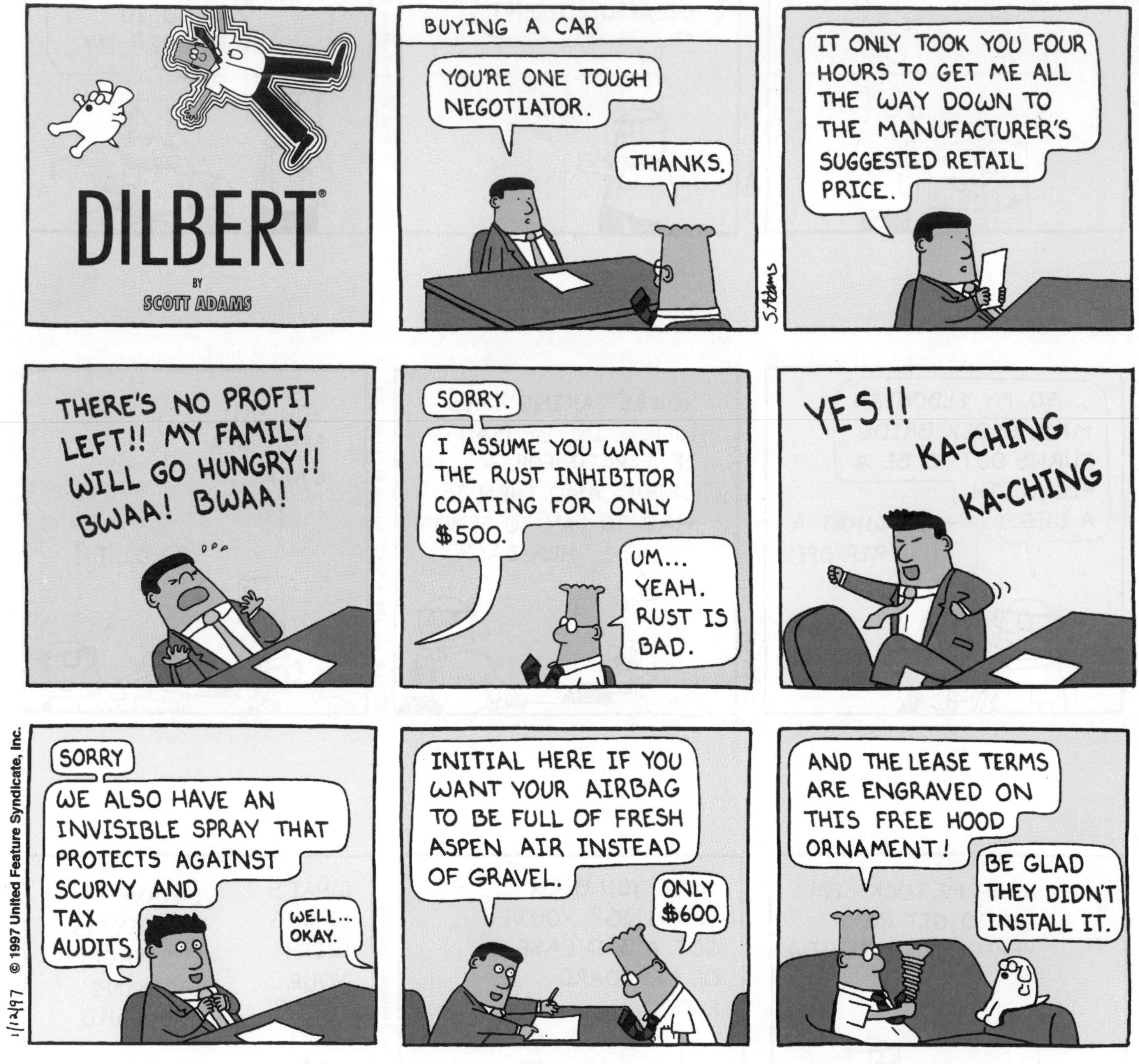
DILBERT®
BY
SCOTT ADAMS
BUYING A CAR
YOU'RE ONE TOUGH NEGOTIATOR.
THANKS.
S.Adams
IT ONLY TOOK YOU FOUR HOURS TO GET ME ALL THE WAY DOWN TO THE MANUFACTURER'S SUGGESTED RETAIL PRICE.
THERE'S NO PROFIT LEFT!! MY FAMILY WILL GO HUNGRY!! BWAA! BWAA!
SORRY.
I ASSUME YOU WANT THE RUST INHIBITOR COATING FOR ONLY $500.
UM... YEAH. RUST IS BAD.
YES!!
KA-CHING
KA-CHING
SORRY
WE ALSO HAVE AN INVISIBLE SPRAY THAT PROTECTS AGAINST SCURVY AND TAX AUDITS.
WELL... OKAY.
INITIAL HERE IF YOU WANT YOUR AIRBAG TO BE FULL OF FRESH ASPEN AIR INSTEAD OF GRAVEL.
ONLY $600.
AND THE LEASE TERMS ARE ENGRAVED ON THIS FREE HOOD ORNAMENT!
BE GLAD THEY DIDN'T INSTALL IT.
1/12/97

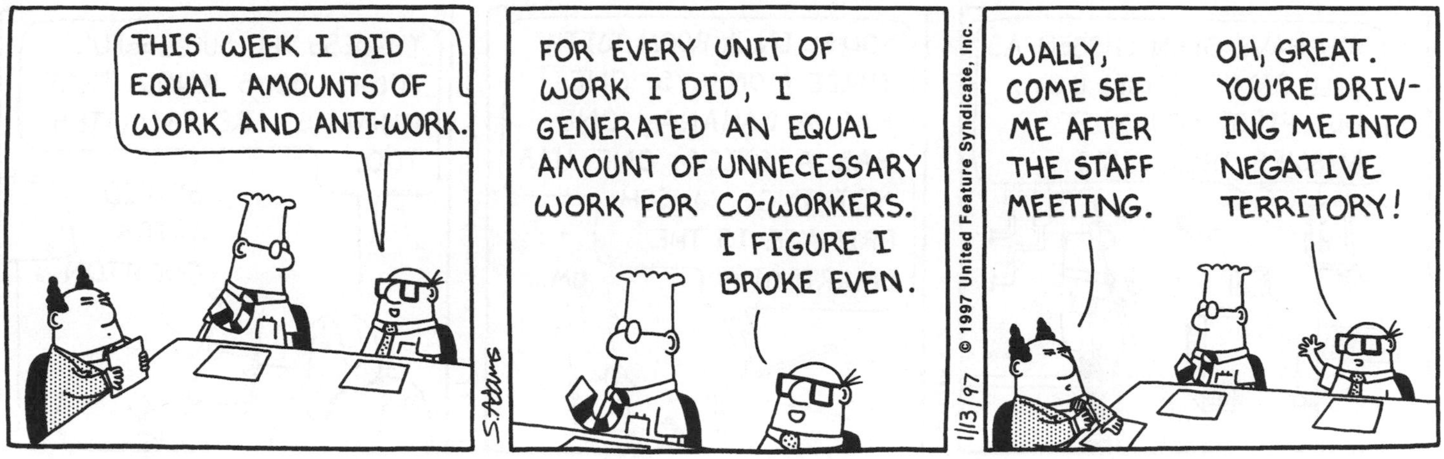
THIS WEEK I DID EQUAL AMOUNTS OF WORK AND ANTI-WORK.
FOR EVERY UNIT OF WORK I DID, I GENERATED AN EQUAL AMOUNT OF UNNECESSARY WORK FOR CO-WORKERS.
I FIGURE I BROKE EVEN.
S. Adams
1/13/97 © 1997 United Feature Syndicate, Inc.
WALLY, COME SEE ME AFTER THE STAFF MEETING.
OH, GREAT. YOU'RE DRIV-ING ME INTO NEGATIVE TERRITORY!

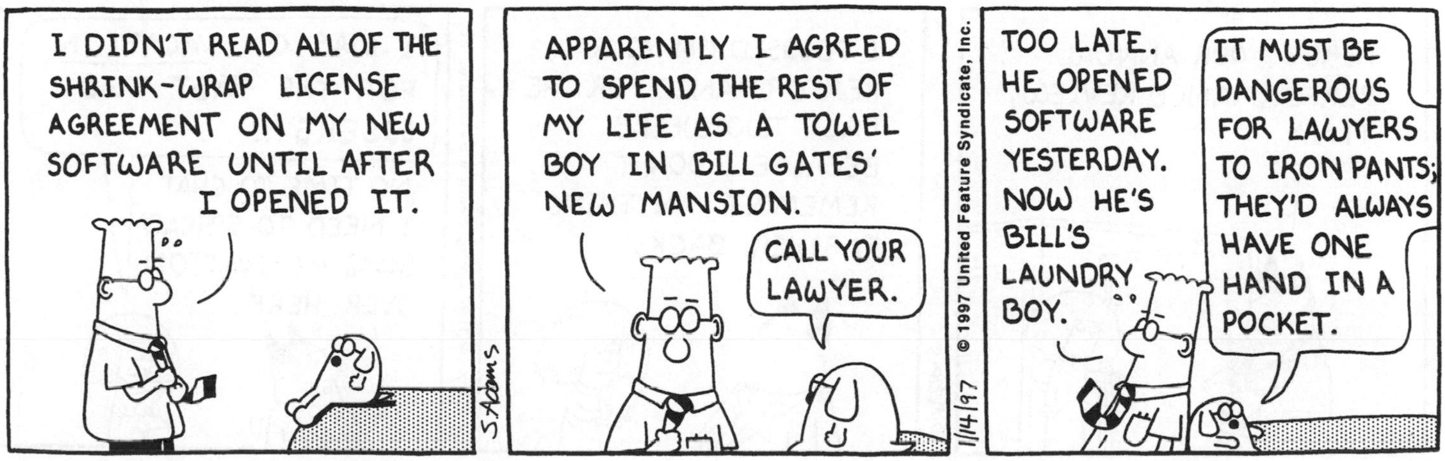
I DIDN'T READ ALL OF THE SHRINK-WRAP LICENSE AGREEMENT ON MY NEW SOFTWARE UNTIL AFTER I OPENED IT.
S. Adams
APPARENTLY I AGREED TO SPEND THE REST OF MY LIFE AS A TOWEL BOY IN BILL GATES' NEW MANSION.
CALL YOUR LAWYER.
1/14/97 © 1997 United Feature Syndicate, Inc.
TOO LATE. HE OPENED SOFTWARE YESTERDAY. NOW HE'S BILL'S LAUNDRY BOY.
IT MUST BE DANGEROUS FOR LAWYERS TO IRON PANTS; THEY'D ALWAYS HAVE ONE HAND IN A POCKET.

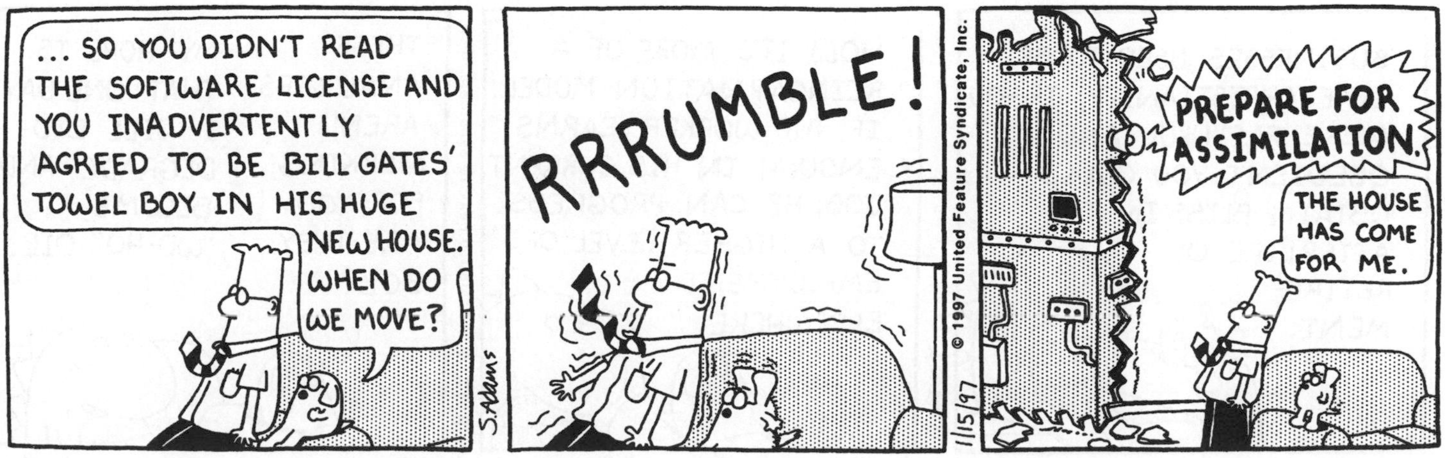
... SO YOU DIDN'T READ THE SOFTWARE LICENSE AND YOU INADVERTENTLY AGREED TO BE BILL GATES' TOWEL BOY IN HIS HUGE NEW HOUSE.
WHEN DO WE MOVE?
S. Adams
RRRUMBLE!
1/15/97 © 1997 United Feature Syndicate, Inc.
PREPARE FOR ASSIMILATION.
THE HOUSE HAS COME FOR ME.

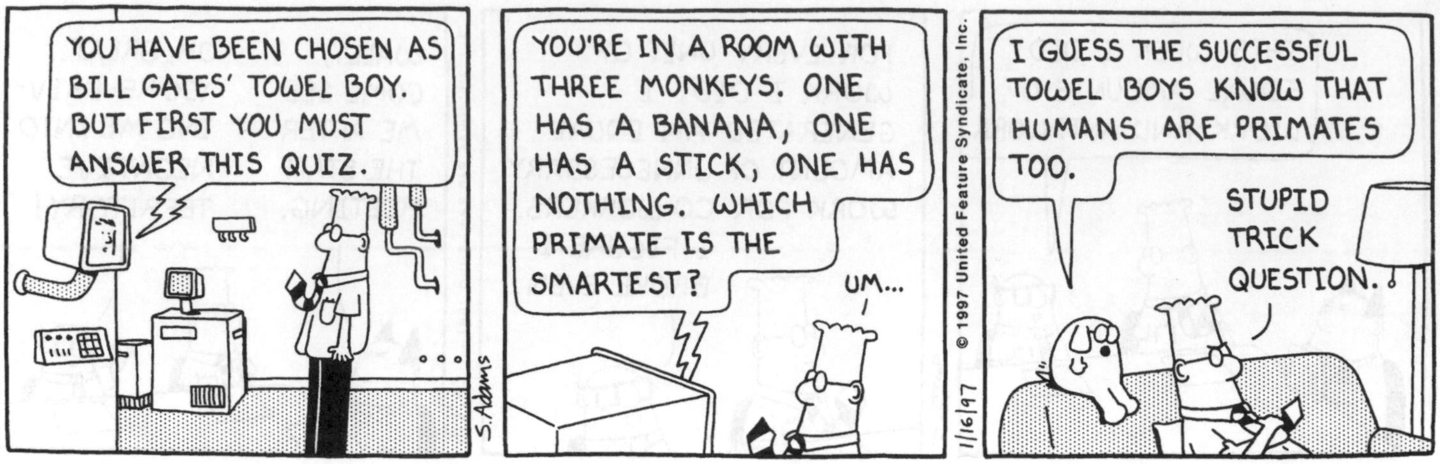
YOU HAVE BEEN CHOSEN AS BILL GATES' TOWEL BOY. BUT FIRST YOU MUST ANSWER THIS QUIZ.
...
S. Adams
YOU'RE IN A ROOM WITH THREE MONKEYS. ONE HAS A BANANA, ONE HAS A STICK, ONE HAS NOTHING. WHICH PRIMATE IS THE SMARTEST?
UM...
1/16/97
© 1997 United Feature Syndicate, Inc.
I GUESS THE SUCCESSFUL TOWEL BOYS KNOW THAT HUMANS ARE PRIMATES TOO.
STUPID TRICK QUESTION.

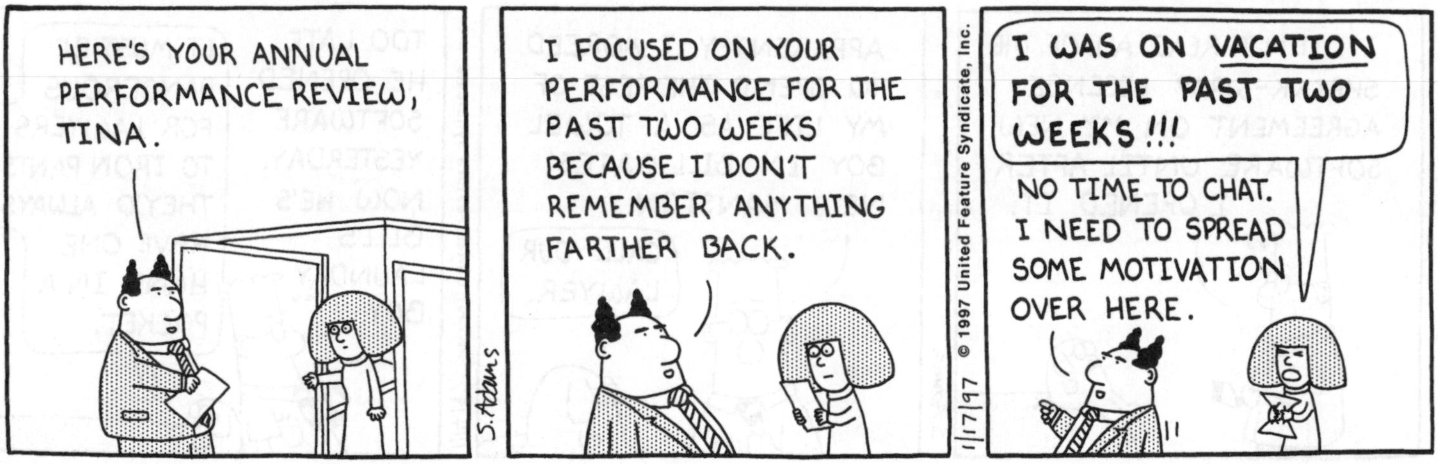
HERE'S YOUR ANNUAL PERFORMANCE REVIEW, TINA.
S. Adams
I FOCUSED ON YOUR PERFORMANCE FOR THE PAST TWO WEEKS BECAUSE I DON'T REMEMBER ANYTHING FARTHER BACK.
1/17/97
© 1997 United Feature Syndicate, Inc.
I WAS ON VACATION FOR THE PAST TWO WEEKS!!!
NO TIME TO CHAT. I NEED TO SPREAD SOME MOTIVATION OVER HERE.

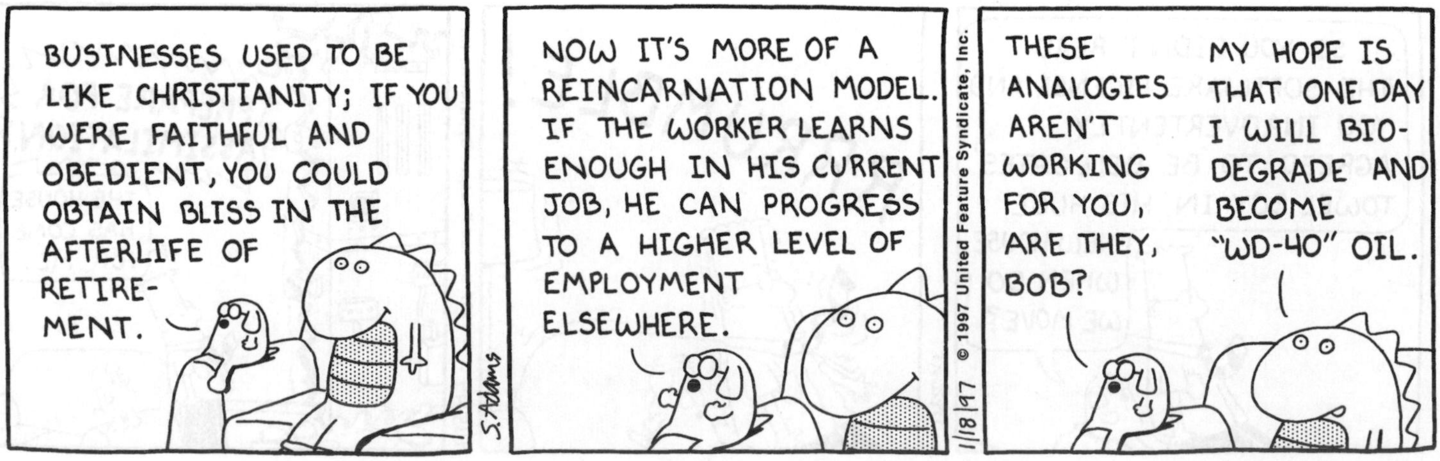
BUSINESSES USED TO BE LIKE CHRISTIANITY; IF YOU WERE FAITHFUL AND OBEDIENT, YOU COULD OBTAIN BLISS IN THE AFTERLIFE OF RETIREMENT.
S. Adams
NOW IT'S MORE OF A REINCARNATION MODEL. IF THE WORKER LEARNS ENOUGH IN HIS CURRENT JOB, HE CAN PROGRESS TO A HIGHER LEVEL OF EMPLOYMENT ELSEWHERE.
1/18/97
© 1997 United Feature Syndicate, Inc.
THESE ANALOGIES AREN'T WORKING FOR YOU, ARE THEY, BOB?
MY HOPE IS THAT ONE DAY I WILL BIODEGRADE AND BECOME "WD-40" OIL.

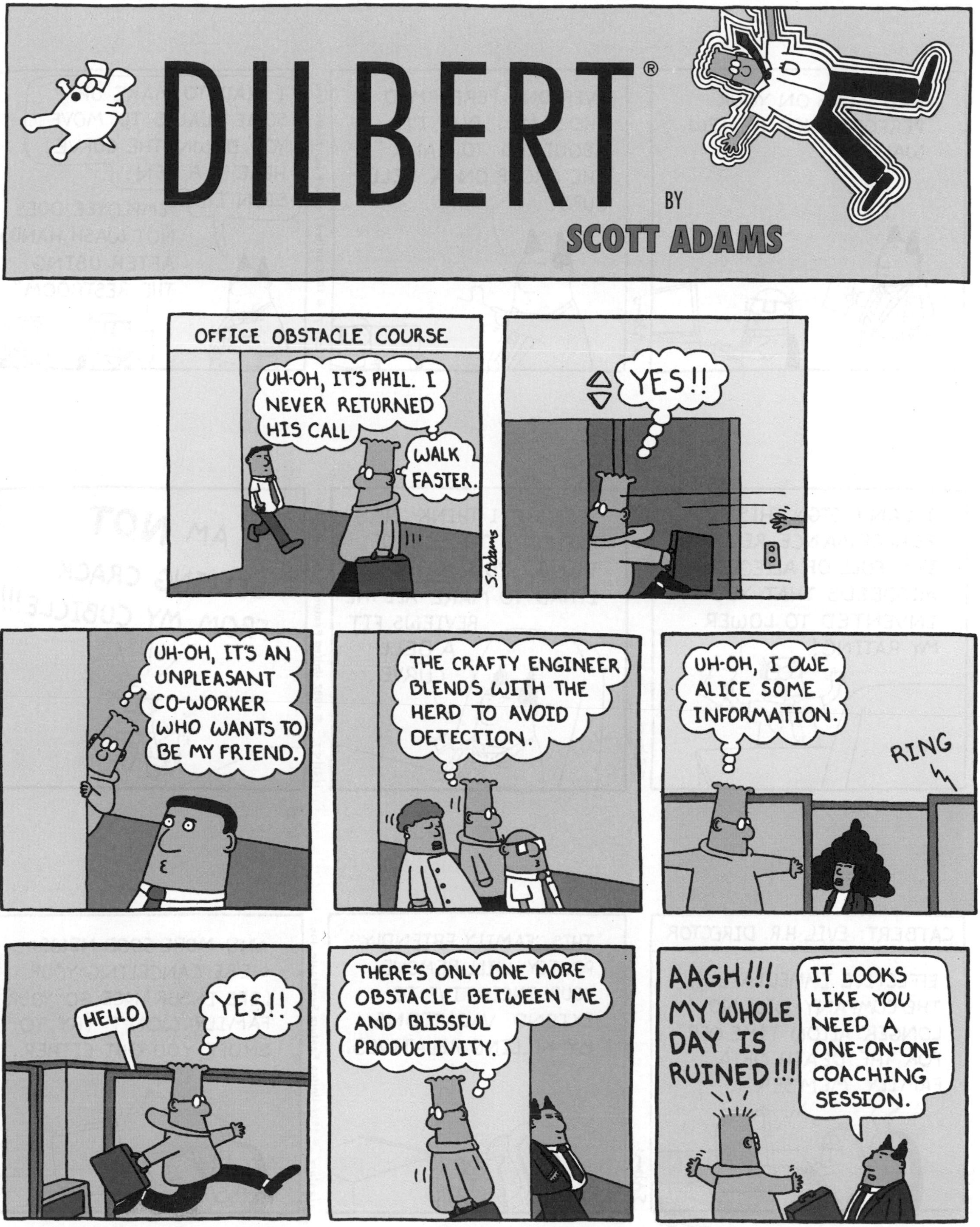
DILBERT®
BY
SCOTT ADAMS
OFFICE OBSTACLE COURSE
UH-OH, IT'S PHIL. I NEVER RETURNED HIS CALL
WALK FASTER.
S. Adams
YES!!
UH-OH, IT'S AN UNPLEASANT CO-WORKER WHO WANTS TO BE MY FRIEND.
THE CRAFTY ENGINEER BLENDS WITH THE HERD TO AVOID DETECTION.
UH-OH, I OWE ALICE SOME INFORMATION.
RING
HELLO
YES!!
THERE'S ONLY ONE MORE OBSTACLE BETWEEN ME AND BLISSFUL PRODUCTIVITY.
AAGH!!! MY WHOLE DAY IS RUINED!!!
IT LOOKS LIKE YOU NEED A ONE-ON-ONE COACHING SESSION.

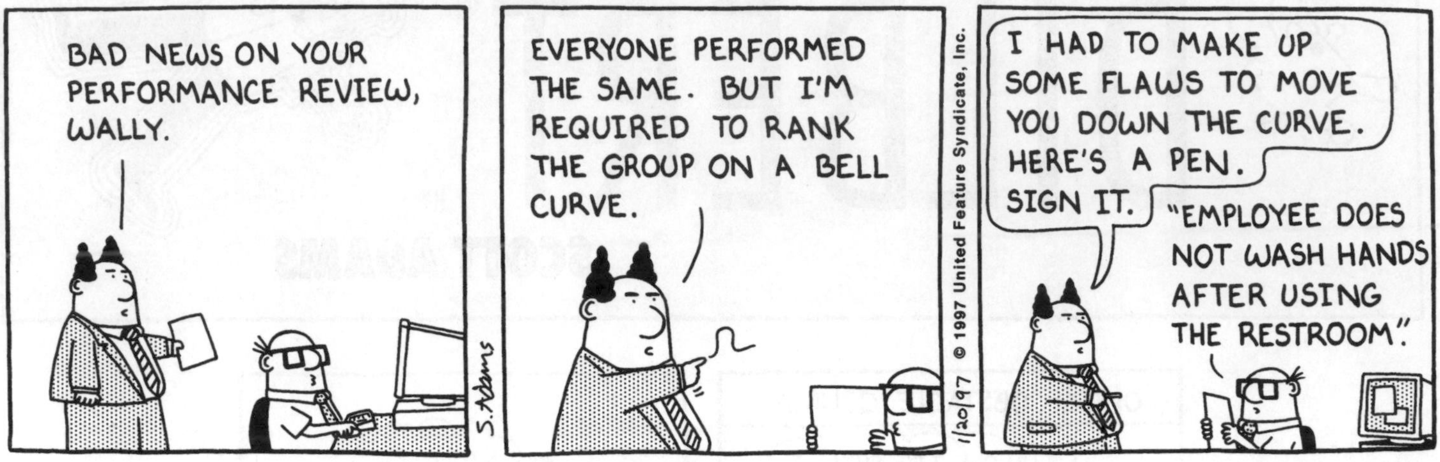
BAD NEWS ON YOUR PERFORMANCE REVIEW, WALLY.
S. Adams
EVERYONE PERFORMED THE SAME. BUT I'M REQUIRED TO RANK THE GROUP ON A BELL CURVE.
1/20/97 © 1997 United Feature Syndicate, Inc.
I HAD TO MAKE UP SOME FLAWS TO MOVE YOU DOWN THE CURVE. HERE'S A PEN. SIGN IT.
"EMPLOYEE DOES NOT WASH HANDS AFTER USING THE RESTROOM".

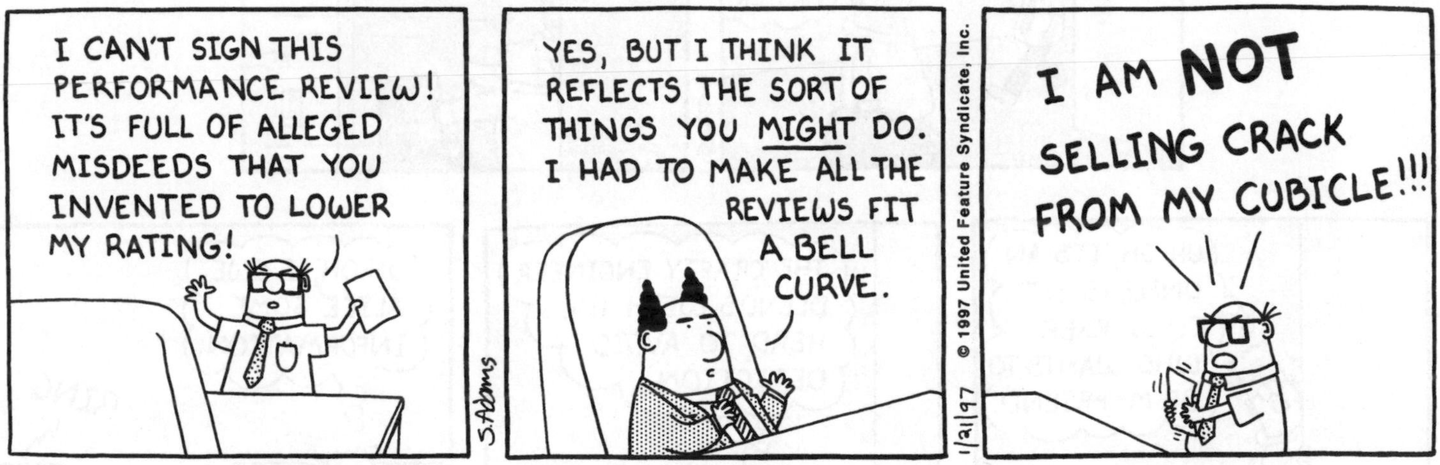
I CAN'T SIGN THIS PERFORMANCE REVIEW! IT'S FULL OF ALLEGED MISDEEDS THAT YOU INVENTED TO LOWER MY RATING!
S. Adams
YES, BUT I THINK IT REFLECTS THE SORT OF THINGS YOU MIGHT DO. I HAD TO MAKE ALL THE REVIEWS FIT A BELL CURVE.
1/21/97 © 1997 United Feature Syndicate, Inc.
I AM NOT SELLING CRACK FROM MY CUBICLE!!!

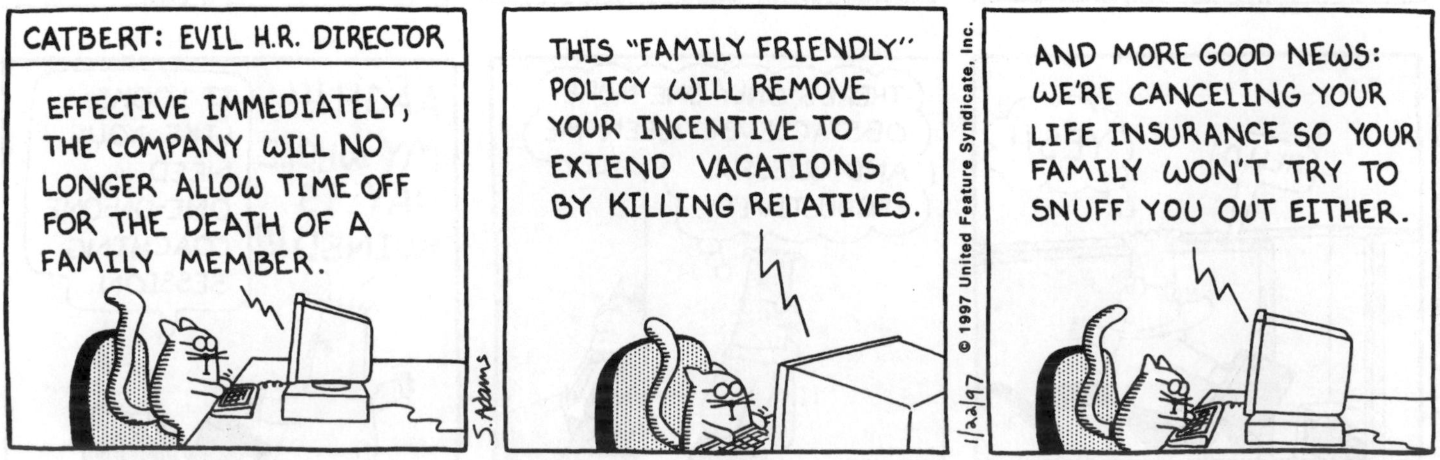
CATBERT: EVIL H.R. DIRECTOR
EFFECTIVE IMMEDIATELY, THE COMPANY WILL NO LONGER ALLOW TIME OFF FOR THE DEATH OF A FAMILY MEMBER.
S. Adams
THIS "FAMILY FRIENDLY" POLICY WILL REMOVE YOUR INCENTIVE TO EXTEND VACATIONS BY KILLING RELATIVES.
1/22/97 © 1997 United Feature Syndicate, Inc.
AND MORE GOOD NEWS: WE'RE CANCELING YOUR LIFE INSURANCE SO YOUR FAMILY WON'T TRY TO SNUFF YOU OUT EITHER.

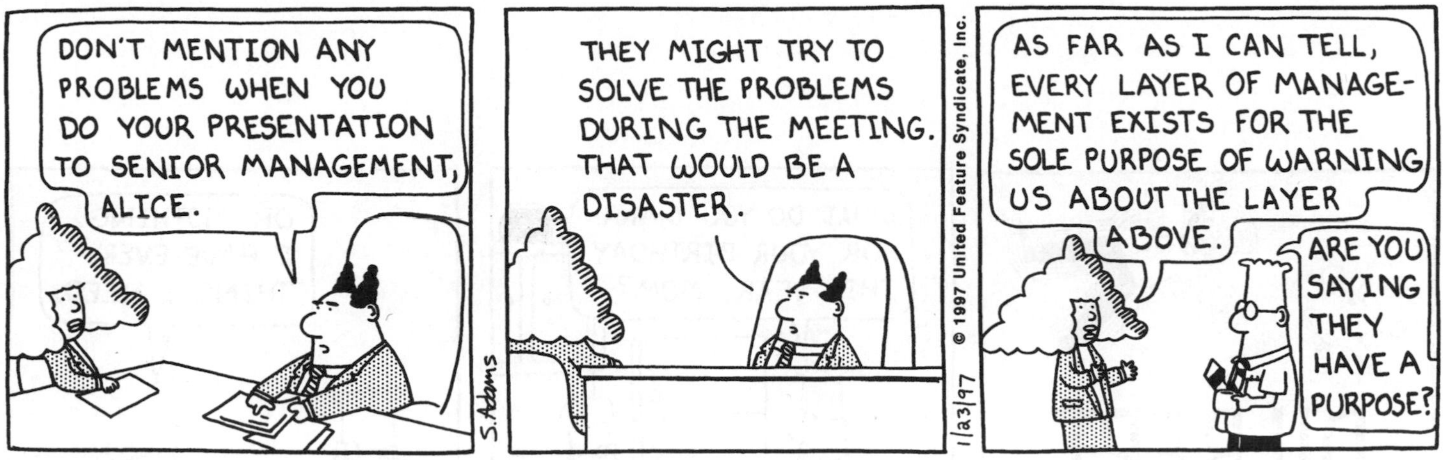
DON'T MENTION ANY PROBLEMS WHEN YOU DO YOUR PRESENTATION TO SENIOR MANAGEMENT, ALICE.
THEY MIGHT TRY TO SOLVE THE PROBLEMS DURING THE MEETING. THAT WOULD BE A DISASTER.
S. Adams
1/23/97
© 1997 United Feature Syndicate, Inc.
AS FAR AS I CAN TELL, EVERY LAYER OF MANAGEMENT EXISTS FOR THE SOLE PURPOSE OF WARNING US ABOUT THE LAYER ABOVE.
ARE YOU SAYING THEY HAVE A PURPOSE?

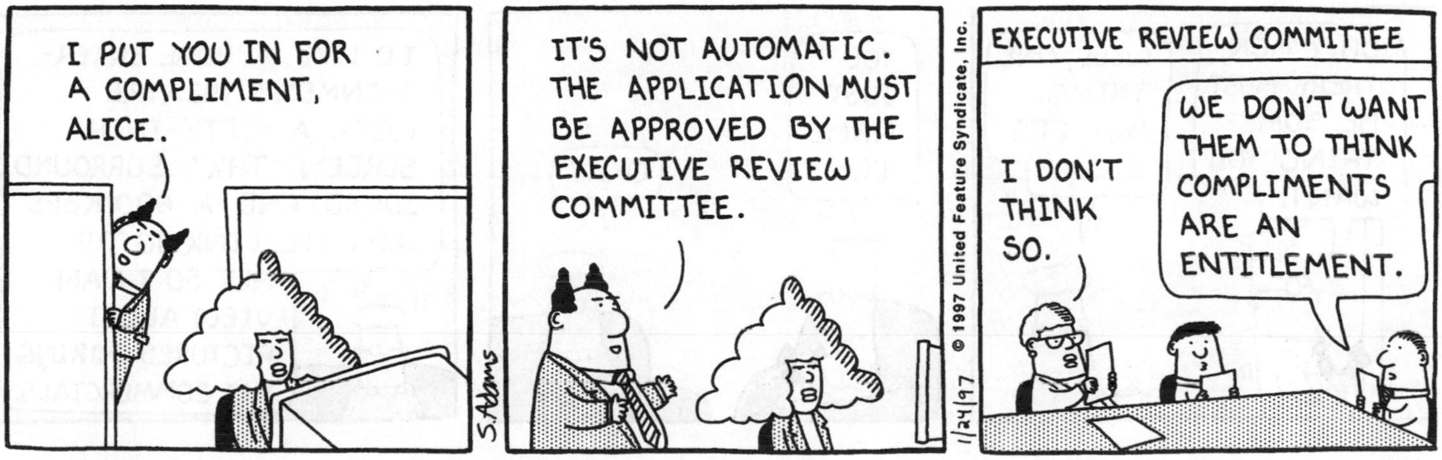
I PUT YOU IN FOR A COMPLIMENT, ALICE.
IT'S NOT AUTOMATIC. THE APPLICATION MUST BE APPROVED BY THE EXECUTIVE REVIEW COMMITTEE.
S. Adams
1/24/97
© 1997 United Feature Syndicate, Inc.
EXECUTIVE REVIEW COMMITTEE
I DON'T THINK SO.
WE DON'T WANT THEM TO THINK COMPLIMENTS ARE AN ENTITLEMENT.

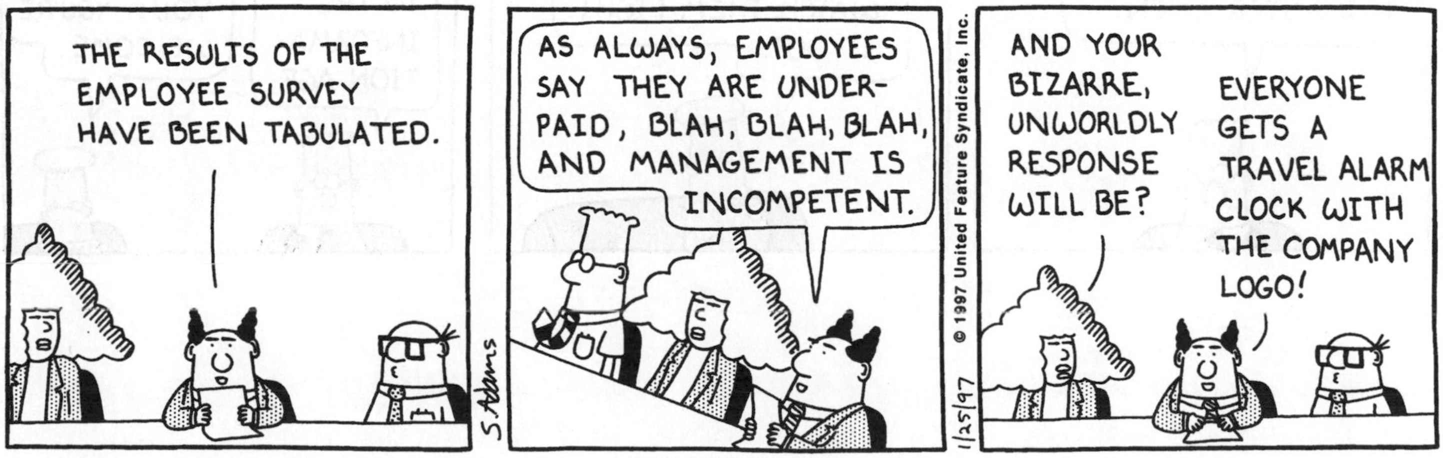
THE RESULTS OF THE EMPLOYEE SURVEY HAVE BEEN TABULATED.
AS ALWAYS, EMPLOYEES SAY THEY ARE UNDERPAID, BLAH, BLAH, BLAH, AND MANAGEMENT IS INCOMPETENT.
S. Adams
1/25/97
© 1997 United Feature Syndicate, Inc.
AND YOUR BIZARRE, UNWORLDLY RESPONSE WILL BE?
EVERYONE GETS A TRAVEL ALARM CLOCK WITH THE COMPANY LOGO!

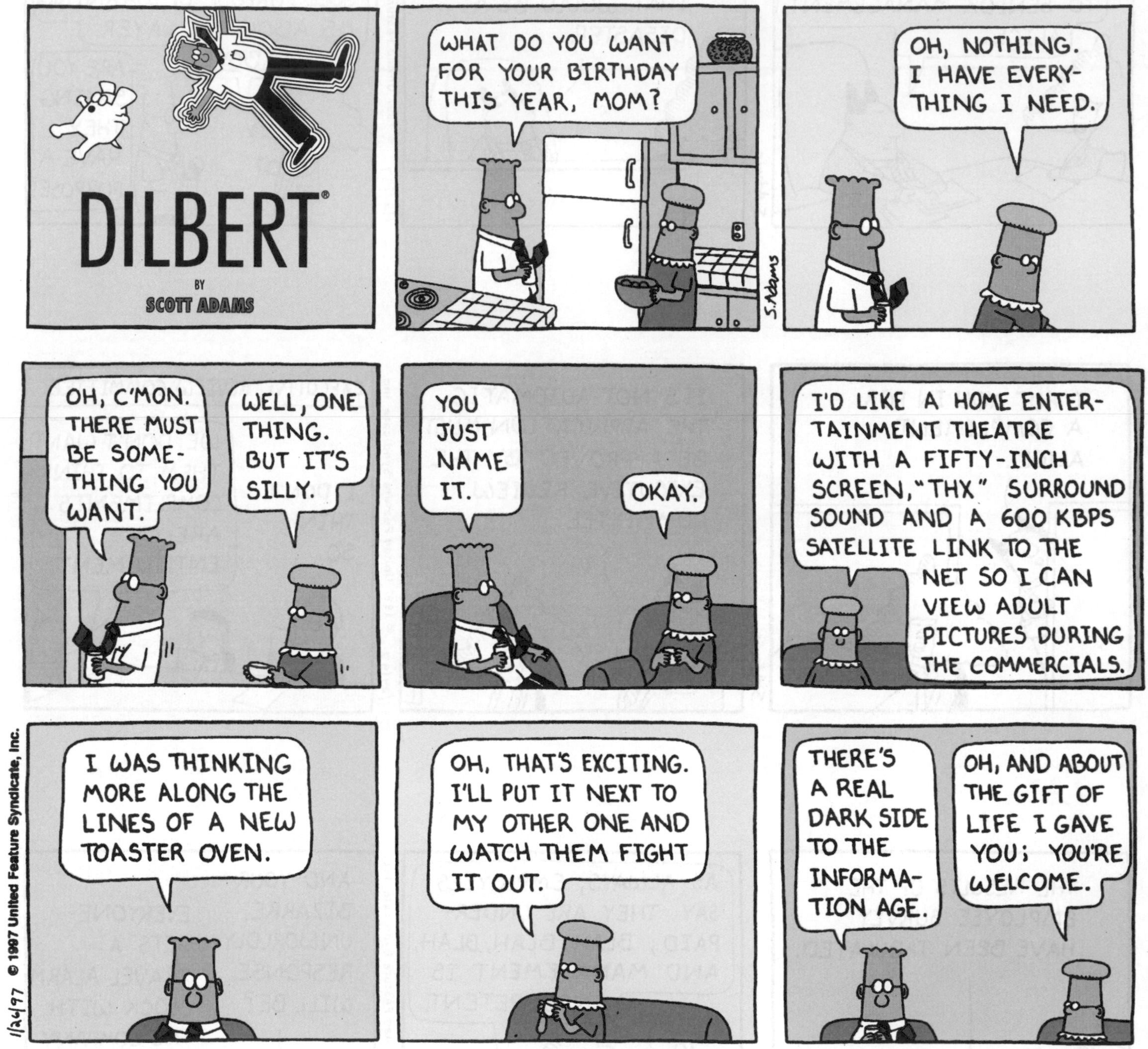
DILBERT®
BY
SCOTT ADAMS
WHAT DO YOU WANT FOR YOUR BIRTHDAY THIS YEAR, MOM?
S. Adams
OH, NOTHING. I HAVE EVERYTHING I NEED.
OH, C'MON. THERE MUST BE SOMETHING YOU WANT.
WELL, ONE THING. BUT IT'S SILLY.
YOU JUST NAME IT.
OKAY.
I'D LIKE A HOME ENTERTAINMENT THEATRE WITH A FIFTY-INCH SCREEN, "THX" SURROUND SOUND AND A 600 KBPS SATELLITE LINK TO THE NET SO I CAN VIEW ADULT PICTURES DURING THE COMMERCIALS.
I WAS THINKING MORE ALONG THE LINES OF A NEW TOASTER OVEN.
OH, THAT'S EXCITING. I'LL PUT IT NEXT TO MY OTHER ONE AND WATCH THEM FIGHT IT OUT.
THERE'S A REAL DARK SIDE TO THE INFORMATION AGE.
OH, AND ABOUT THE GIFT OF LIFE I GAVE YOU; YOU'RE WELCOME.
1/26/97 © 1997 United Feature Syndicate, Inc.

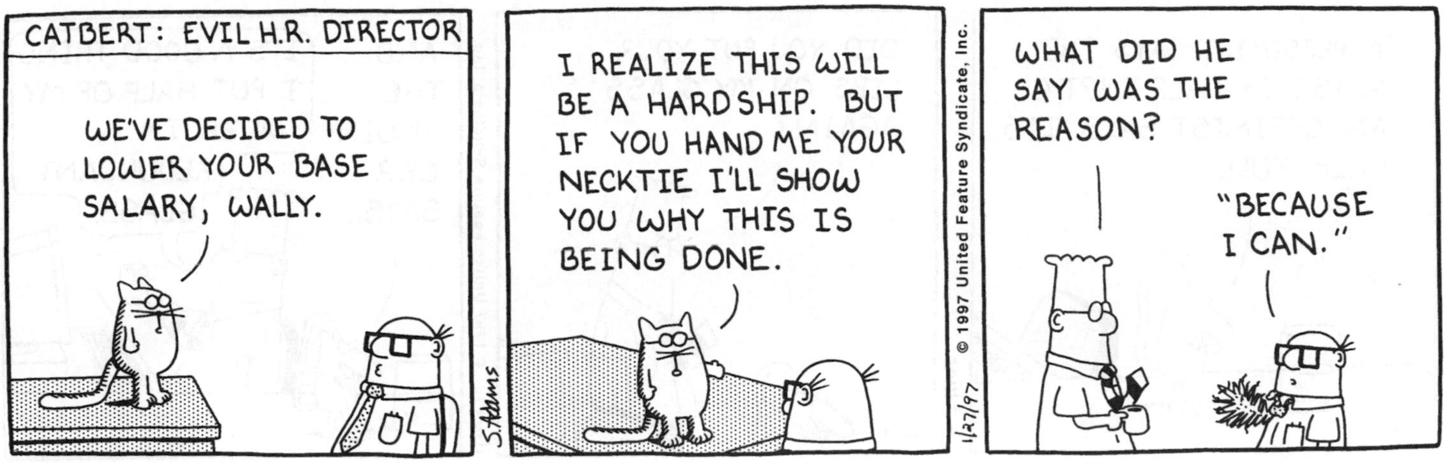
CATBERT: EVIL H.R. DIRECTOR
WE'VE DECIDED TO LOWER YOUR BASE SALARY, WALLY.
S. Adams
I REALIZE THIS WILL BE A HARDSHIP. BUT IF YOU HAND ME YOUR NECKTIE I'LL SHOW YOU WHY THIS IS BEING DONE.
1/27/97 © 1997 United Feature Syndicate, Inc.
WHAT DID HE SAY WAS THE REASON?
"BECAUSE I CAN."

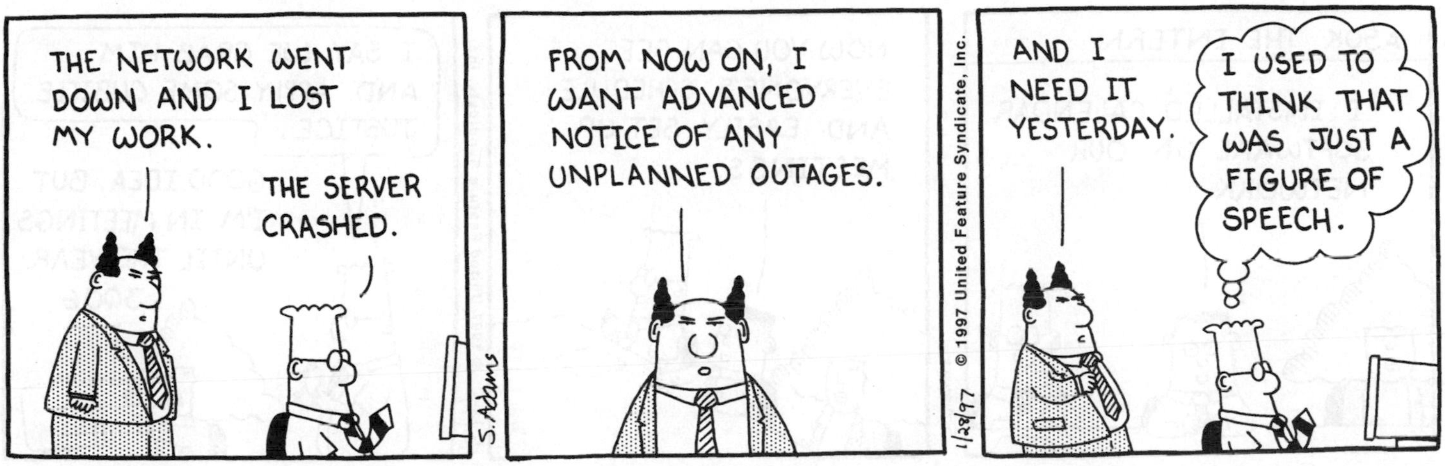
THE NETWORK WENT DOWN AND I LOST MY WORK.
THE SERVER CRASHED.
S. Adams
FROM NOW ON, I WANT ADVANCED NOTICE OF ANY UNPLANNED OUTAGES.
1/28/97 © 1997 United Feature Syndicate, Inc.
AND I NEED IT YESTERDAY.
I USED TO THINK THAT WAS JUST A FIGURE OF SPEECH.

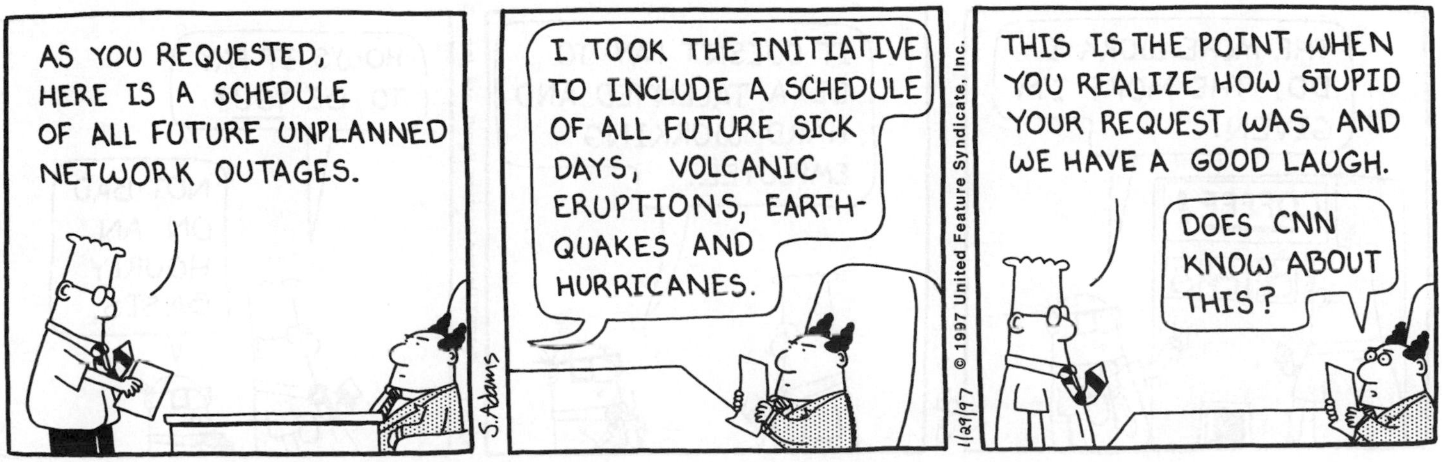
AS YOU REQUESTED, HERE IS A SCHEDULE OF ALL FUTURE UNPLANNED NETWORK OUTAGES.
S. Adams
I TOOK THE INITIATIVE TO INCLUDE A SCHEDULE OF ALL FUTURE SICK DAYS, VOLCANIC ERUPTIONS, EARTHQUAKES AND HURRICANES.
1/29/97 © 1997 United Feature Syndicate, Inc.
THIS IS THE POINT WHEN YOU REALIZE HOW STUPID YOUR REQUEST WAS AND WE HAVE A GOOD LAUGH.
DOES CNN KNOW ABOUT THIS?

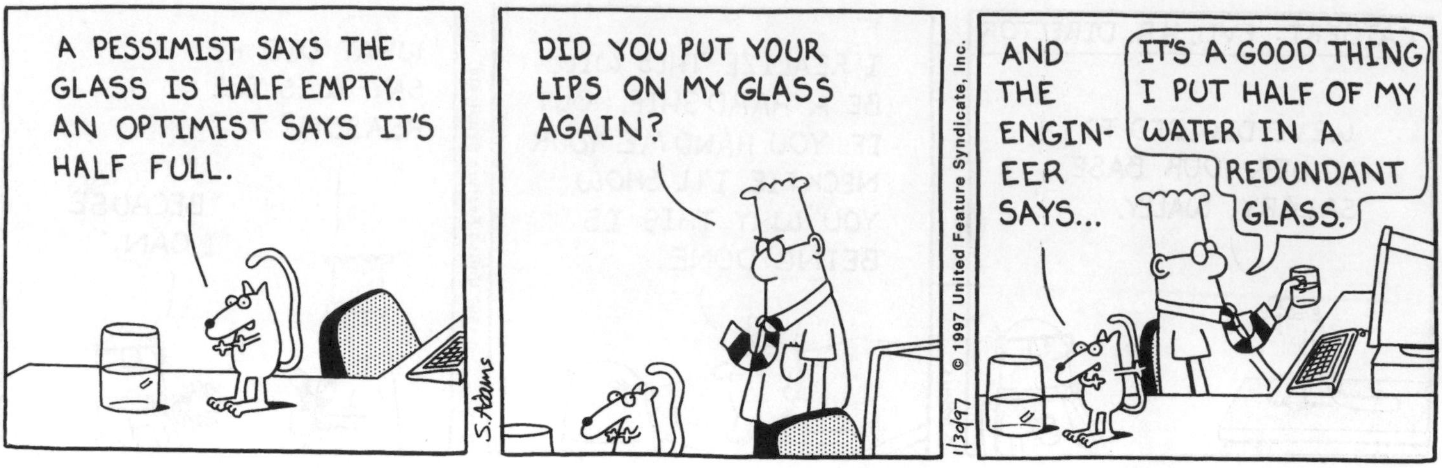
A PESSIMIST SAYS THE GLASS IS HALF EMPTY. AN OPTIMIST SAYS IT'S HALF FULL.
DID YOU PUT YOUR LIPS ON MY GLASS AGAIN?
AND THE ENGIN-EER SAYS...
IT'S A GOOD THING I PUT HALF OF MY WATER IN A REDUNDANT GLASS.
S. Adams
1/30/97
© 1997 United Feature Syndicate, Inc.

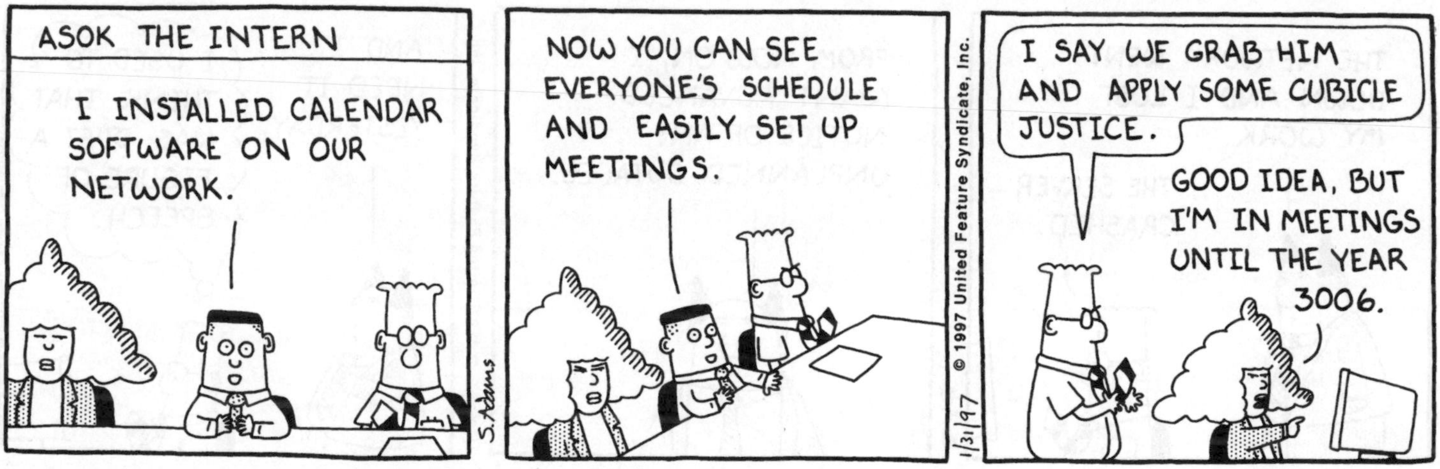
ASOK THE INTERN
I INSTALLED CALENDAR SOFTWARE ON OUR NETWORK.
NOW YOU CAN SEE EVERYONE'S SCHEDULE AND EASILY SET UP MEETINGS.
I SAY WE GRAB HIM AND APPLY SOME CUBICLE JUSTICE.
GOOD IDEA, BUT I'M IN MEETINGS UNTIL THE YEAR 3006.
S. Adams
1/31/97
© 1997 United Feature Syndicate, Inc.

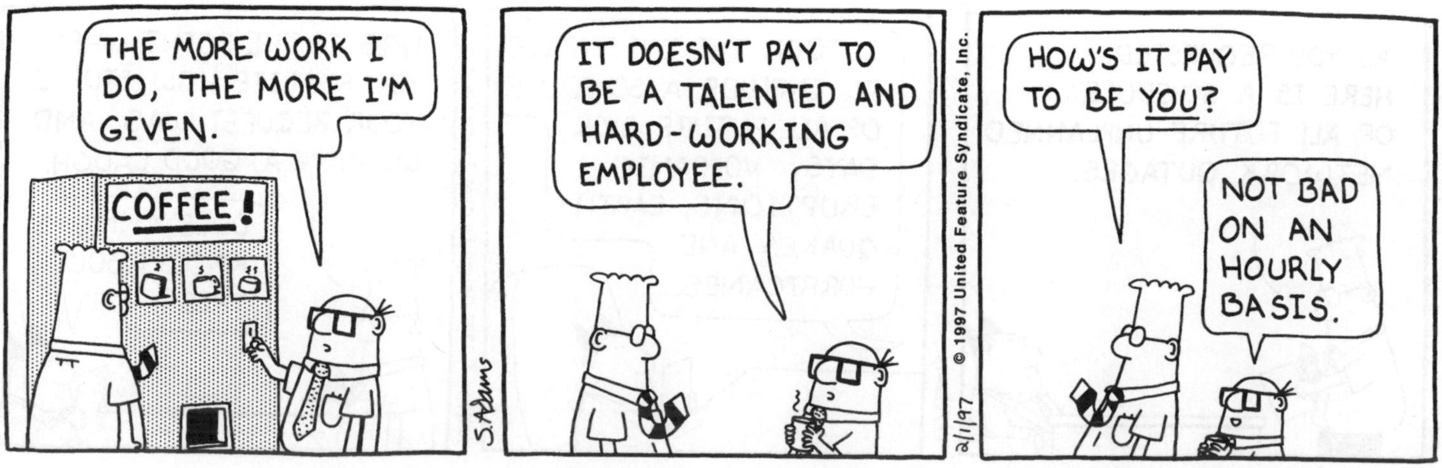
THE MORE WORK I DO, THE MORE I'M GIVEN.
COFFEE!
IT DOESN'T PAY TO BE A TALENTED AND HARD-WORKING EMPLOYEE.
HOW'S IT PAY TO BE YOU?
NOT BAD ON AN HOURLY BASIS.
S. Adams
2/1/97
© 1997 United Feature Syndicate, Inc.

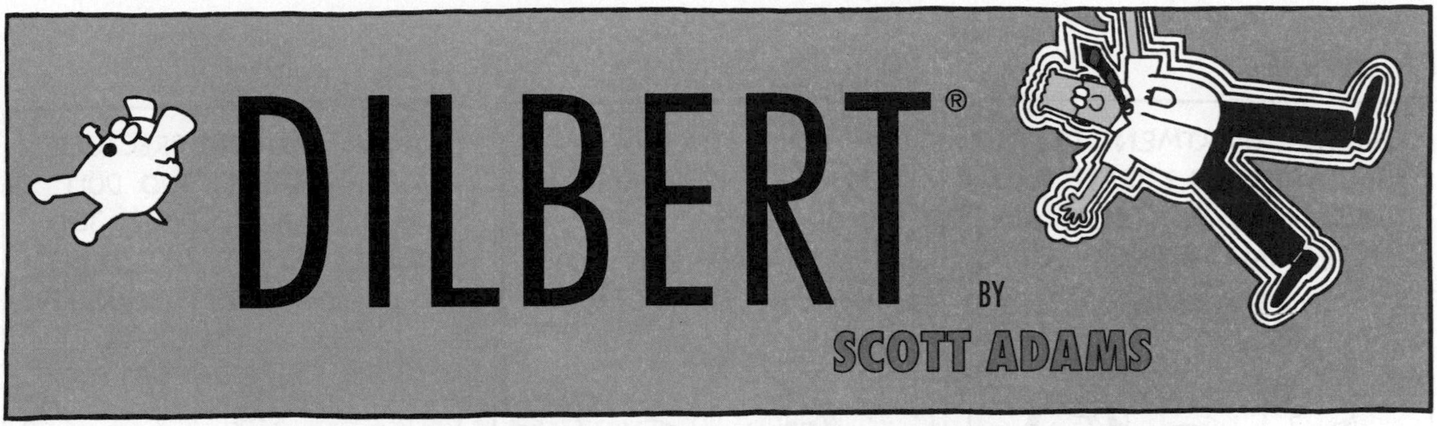
DILBERT®
BY
SCOTT ADAMS

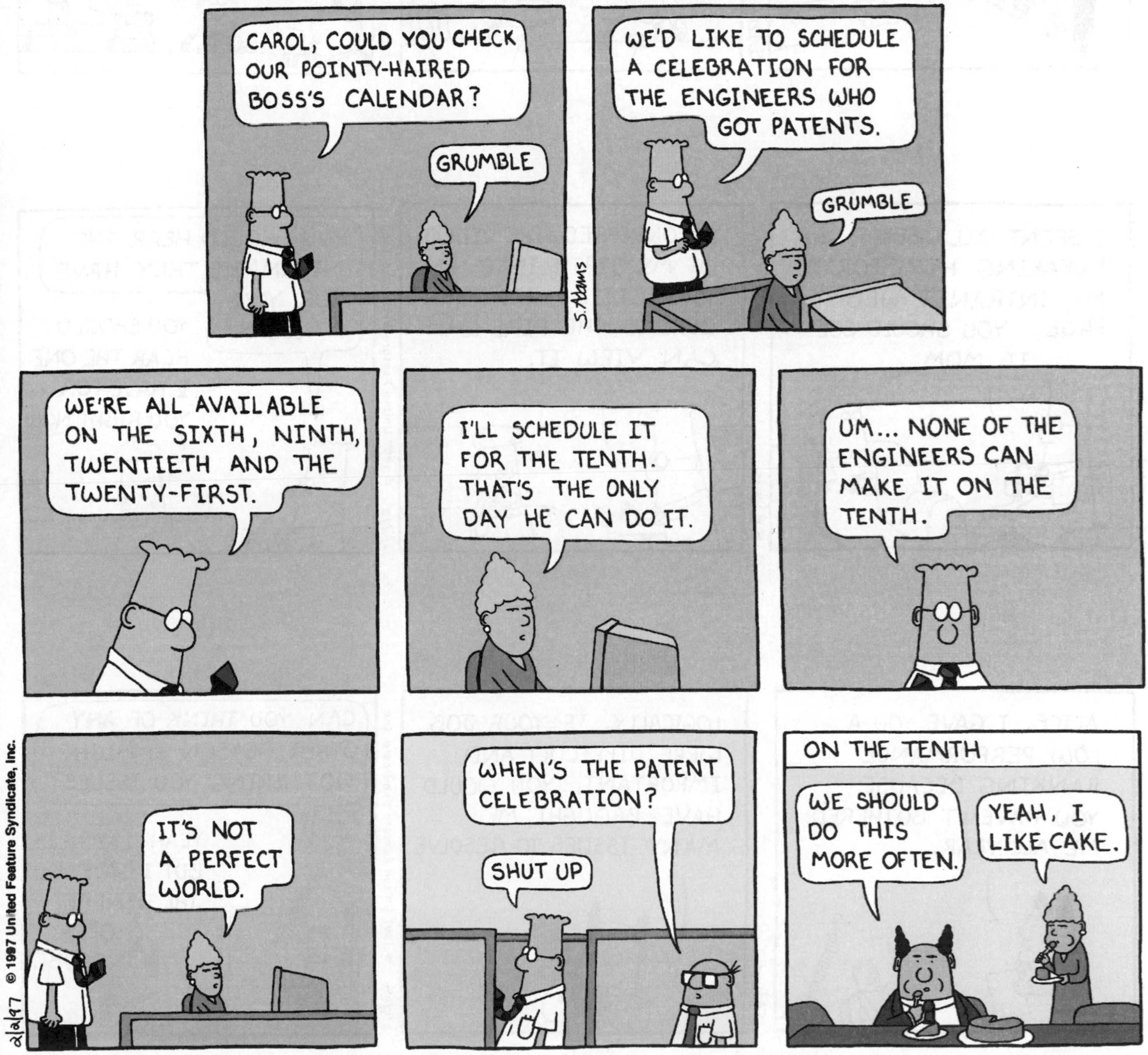
CAROL, COULD YOU CHECK OUR POINTY-HAIRED BOSS'S CALENDAR?
GRUMBLE
S. Adams
WE'D LIKE TO SCHEDULE A CELEBRATION FOR THE ENGINEERS WHO GOT PATENTS.
GRUMBLE
WE'RE ALL AVAILABLE ON THE SIXTH, NINTH, TWENTIETH AND THE TWENTY-FIRST.
I'LL SCHEDULE IT FOR THE TENTH. THAT'S THE ONLY DAY HE CAN DO IT.
UM... NONE OF THE ENGINEERS CAN MAKE IT ON THE TENTH.
IT'S NOT A PERFECT WORLD.
WHEN'S THE PATENT CELEBRATION?
SHUT UP
ON THE TENTH
WE SHOULD DO THIS MORE OFTEN.
YEAH, I LIKE CAKE.
© 1997 United Feature Syndicate, Inc.
2/2/97

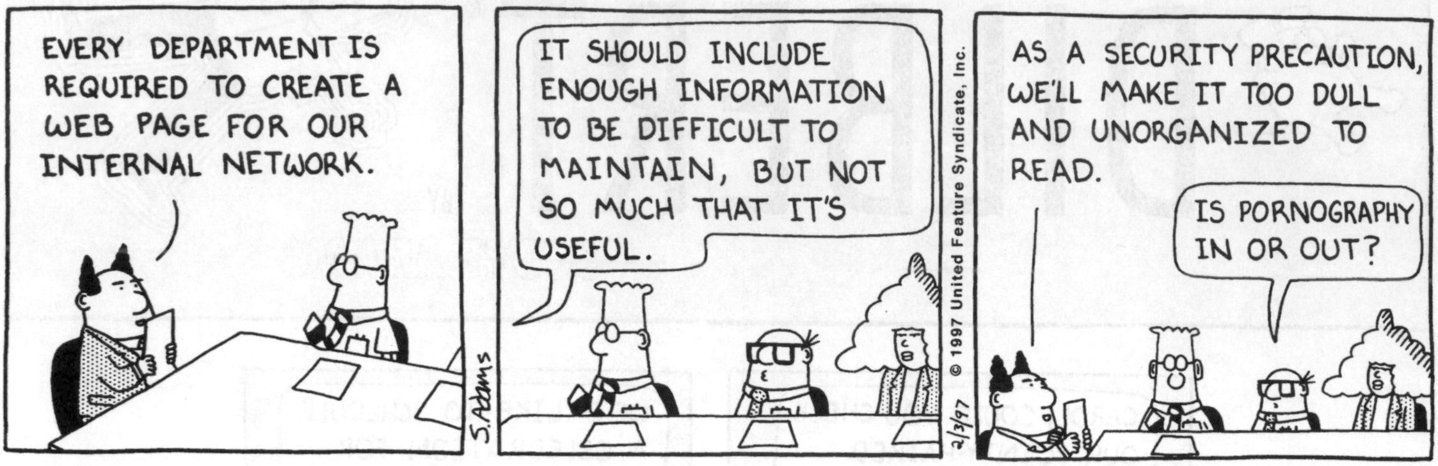
EVERY DEPARTMENT IS REQUIRED TO CREATE A WEB PAGE FOR OUR INTERNAL NETWORK.
IT SHOULD INCLUDE ENOUGH INFORMATION TO BE DIFFICULT TO MAINTAIN, BUT NOT SO MUCH THAT IT'S USEFUL.
S. Adams
2/3/97 © 1997 United Feature Syndicate, Inc.
AS A SECURITY PRECAUTION, WE'LL MAKE IT TOO DULL AND UNORGANIZED TO READ.
IS PORNOGRAPHY IN OR OUT?

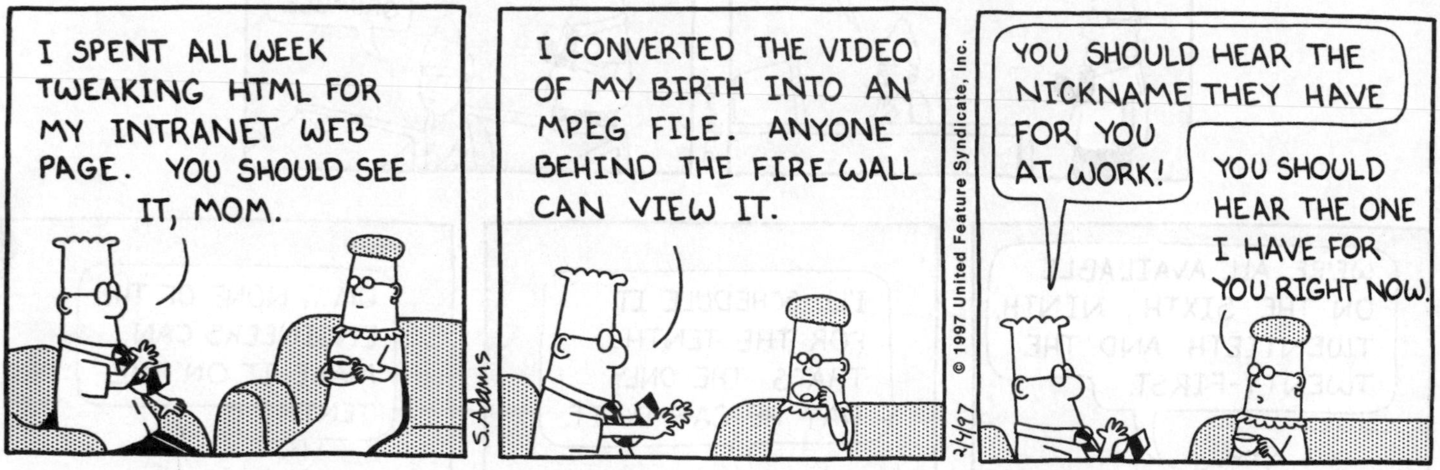
I SPENT ALL WEEK TWEAKING HTML FOR MY INTRANET WEB PAGE. YOU SHOULD SEE IT, MOM.
S. Adams
I CONVERTED THE VIDEO OF MY BIRTH INTO AN MPEG FILE. ANYONE BEHIND THE FIRE WALL CAN VIEW IT.
2/4/97 © 1997 United Feature Syndicate, Inc.
YOU SHOULD HEAR THE NICKNAME THEY HAVE FOR YOU AT WORK!
YOU SHOULD HEAR THE ONE I HAVE FOR YOU RIGHT NOW.

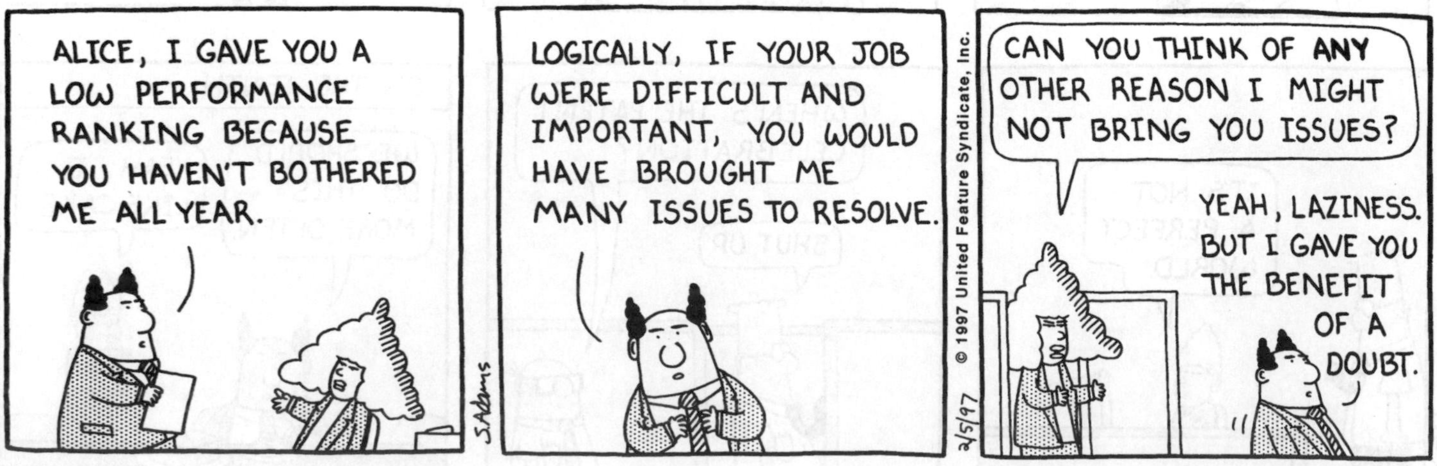
ALICE, I GAVE YOU A LOW PERFORMANCE RANKING BECAUSE YOU HAVEN'T BOTHERED ME ALL YEAR.
S. Adams
LOGICALLY, IF YOUR JOB WERE DIFFICULT AND IMPORTANT, YOU WOULD HAVE BROUGHT ME MANY ISSUES TO RESOLVE.
2/5/97 © 1997 United Feature Syndicate, Inc.
CAN YOU THINK OF ANY OTHER REASON I MIGHT NOT BRING YOU ISSUES?
YEAH, LAZINESS. BUT I GAVE YOU THE BENEFIT OF A DOUBT.

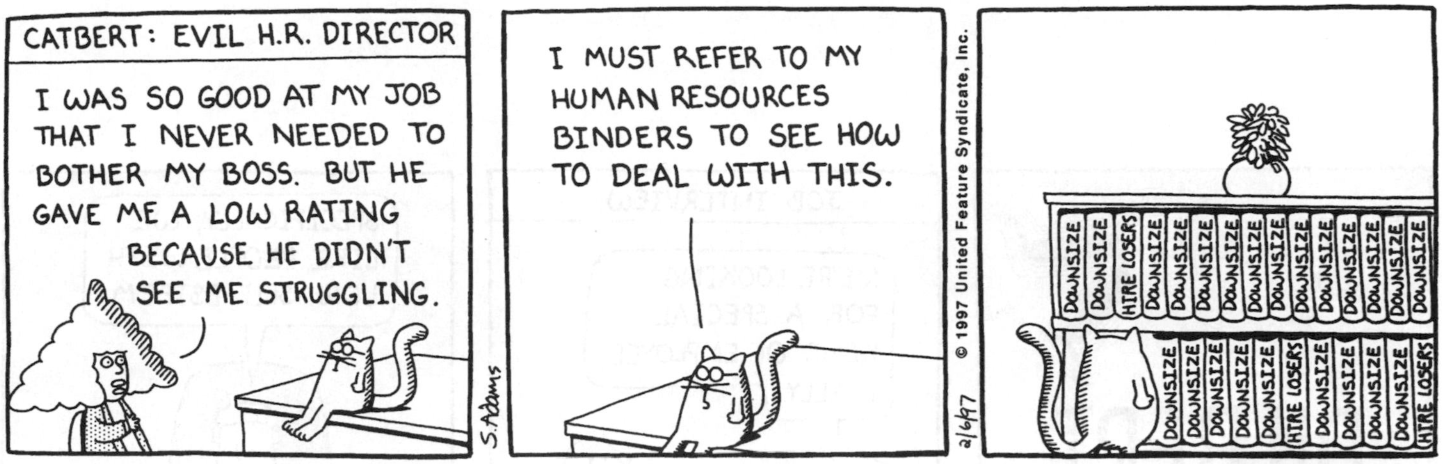
CATBERT: EVIL H.R. DIRECTOR
I WAS SO GOOD AT MY JOB THAT I NEVER NEEDED TO BOTHER MY BOSS. BUT HE GAVE ME A LOW RATING BECAUSE HE DIDN'T SEE ME STRUGGLING.
S. Adams
I MUST REFER TO MY HUMAN RESOURCES BINDERS TO SEE HOW TO DEAL WITH THIS.
2/6/97
© 1997 United Feature Syndicate, Inc.
DOWNSIZE
HIRE LOSERS

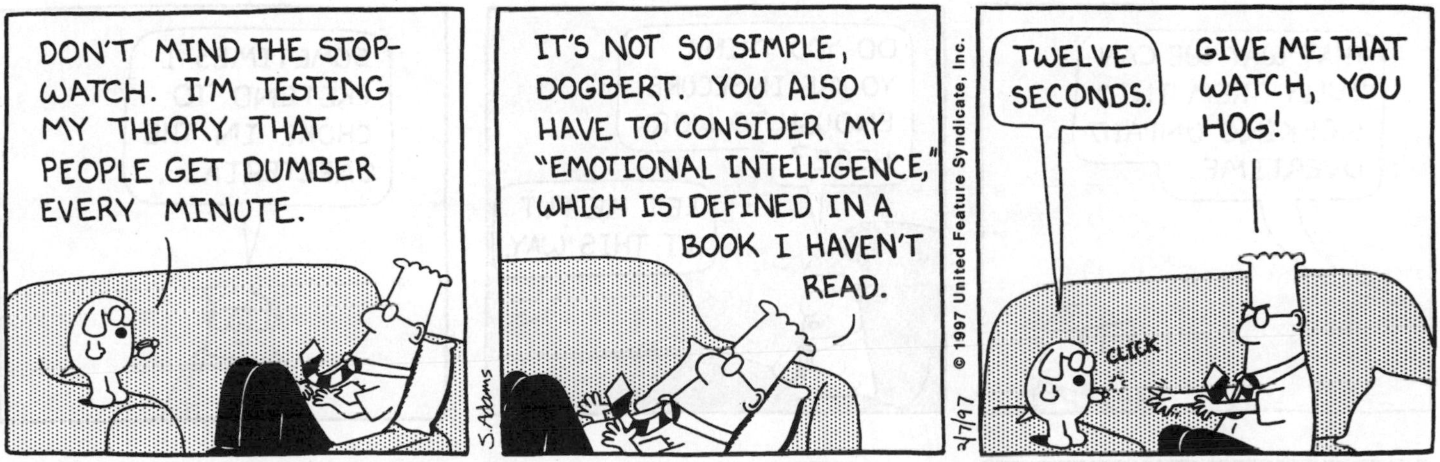
DON'T MIND THE STOP-WATCH. I'M TESTING MY THEORY THAT PEOPLE GET DUMBER EVERY MINUTE.
S. Adams
IT'S NOT SO SIMPLE, DOGBERT. YOU ALSO HAVE TO CONSIDER MY "EMOTIONAL INTELLIGENCE," WHICH IS DEFINED IN A BOOK I HAVEN'T READ.
2/7/97
© 1997 United Feature Syndicate, Inc.
TWELVE SECONDS.
CLICK
GIVE ME THAT WATCH, YOU HOG!

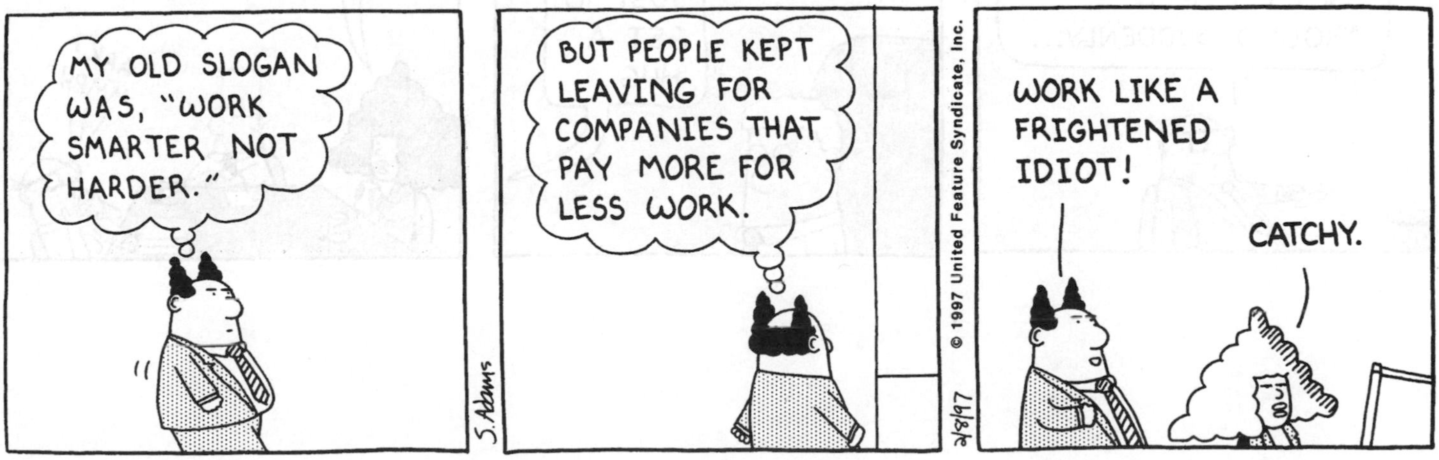
MY OLD SLOGAN WAS, "WORK SMARTER NOT HARDER."
S. Adams
BUT PEOPLE KEPT LEAVING FOR COMPANIES THAT PAY MORE FOR LESS WORK.
2/8/97
© 1997 United Feature Syndicate, Inc.
WORK LIKE A FRIGHTENED IDIOT!
CATCHY.

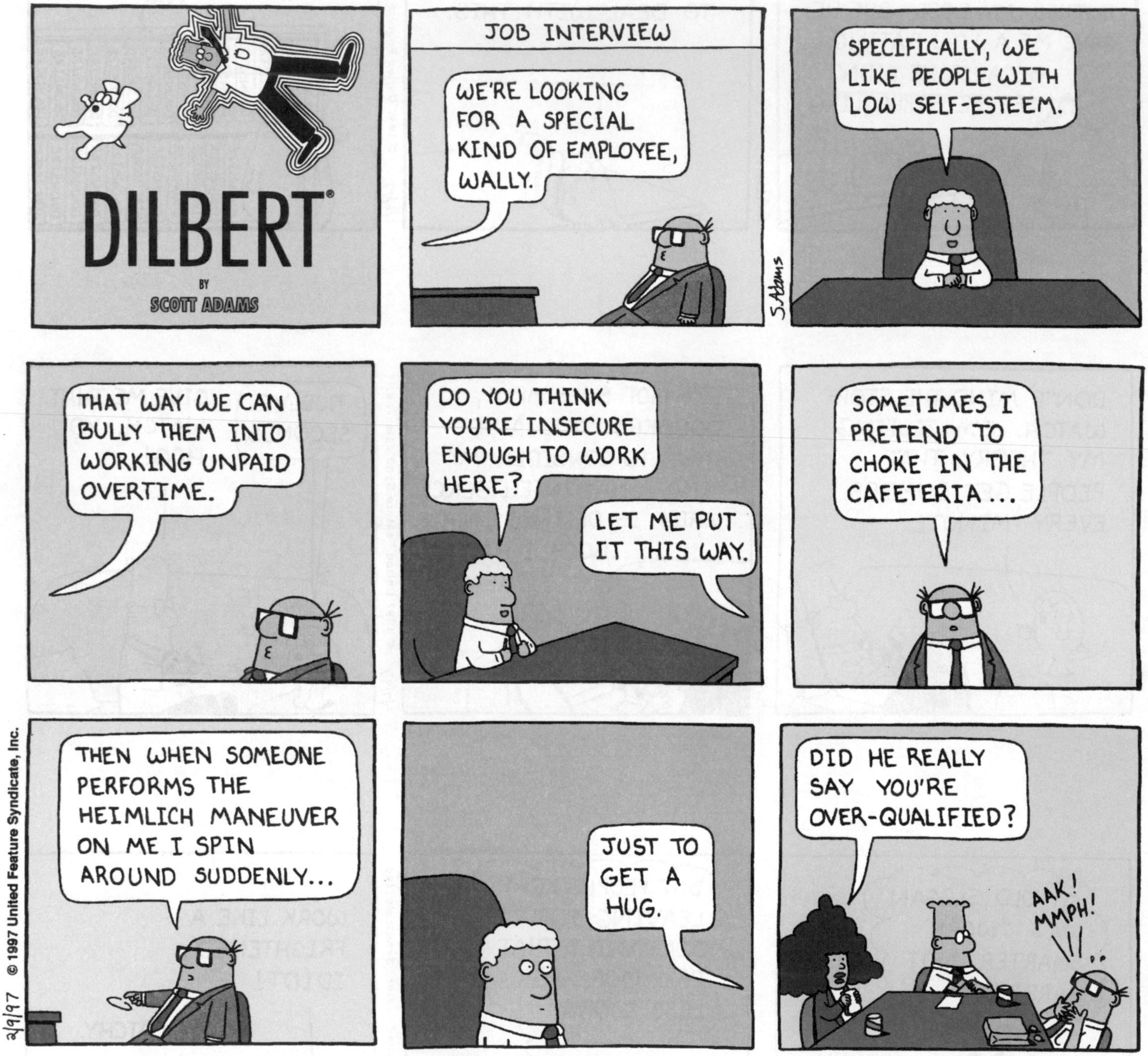
DILBERT®
BY
SCOTT ADAMS
JOB INTERVIEW
WE'RE LOOKING FOR A SPECIAL KIND OF EMPLOYEE, WALLY.
S. Adams
SPECIFICALLY, WE LIKE PEOPLE WITH LOW SELF-ESTEEM.
THAT WAY WE CAN BULLY THEM INTO WORKING UNPAID OVERTIME.
DO YOU THINK YOU'RE INSECURE ENOUGH TO WORK HERE?
LET ME PUT IT THIS WAY.
SOMETIMES I PRETEND TO CHOKE IN THE CAFETERIA...
THEN WHEN SOMEONE PERFORMS THE HEIMLICH MANEUVER ON ME I SPIN AROUND SUDDENLY...
JUST TO GET A HUG.
DID HE REALLY SAY YOU'RE OVER-QUALIFIED?
AAK! MMPH!
2/9/97 © 1997 United Feature Syndicate, Inc.

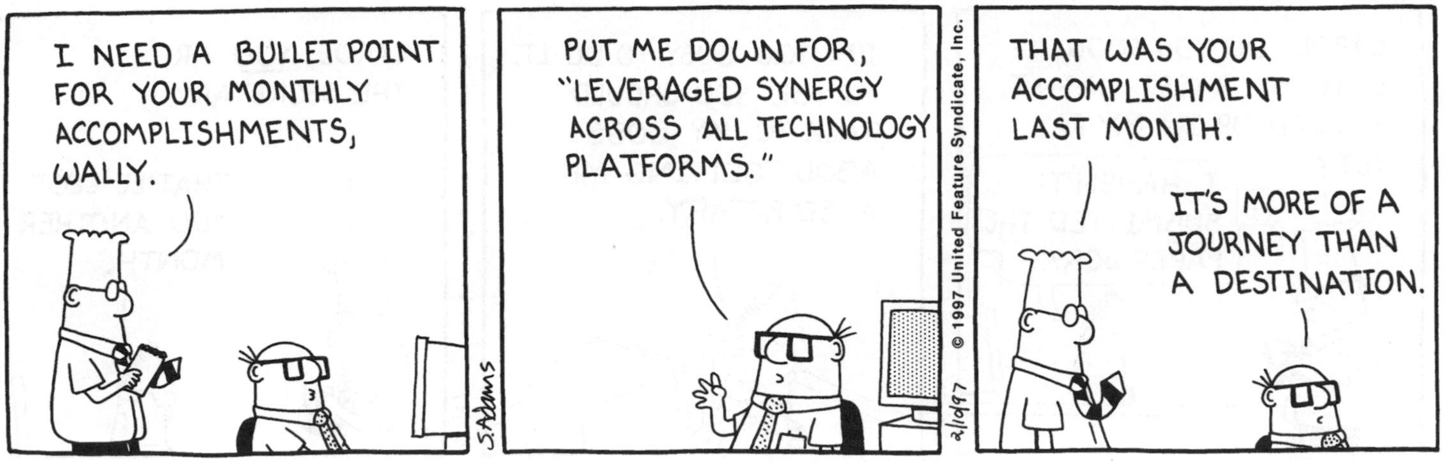
I NEED A BULLET POINT FOR YOUR MONTHLY ACCOMPLISHMENTS, WALLY.
PUT ME DOWN FOR, "LEVERAGED SYNERGY ACROSS ALL TECHNOLOGY PLATFORMS."
THAT WAS YOUR ACCOMPLISHMENT LAST MONTH.
IT'S MORE OF A JOURNEY THAN A DESTINATION.
S. Adams
2/10/97
© 1997 United Feature Syndicate, Inc.

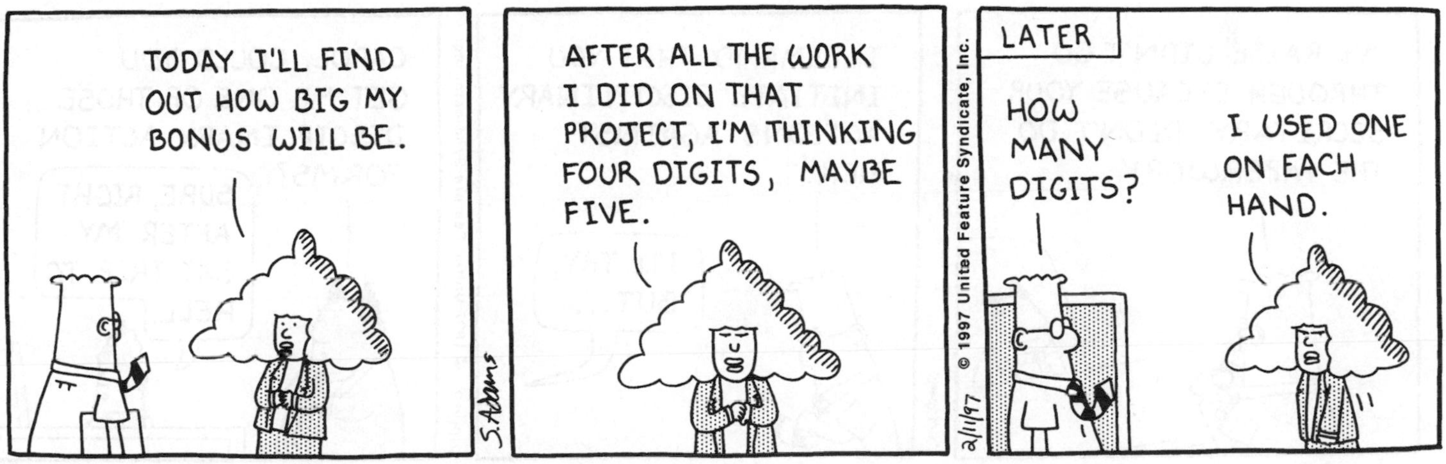
TODAY I'LL FIND OUT HOW BIG MY BONUS WILL BE.
AFTER ALL THE WORK I DID ON THAT PROJECT, I'M THINKING FOUR DIGITS, MAYBE FIVE.
LATER
HOW MANY DIGITS?
I USED ONE ON EACH HAND.
S. Adams
2/11/97
© 1997 United Feature Syndicate, Inc.

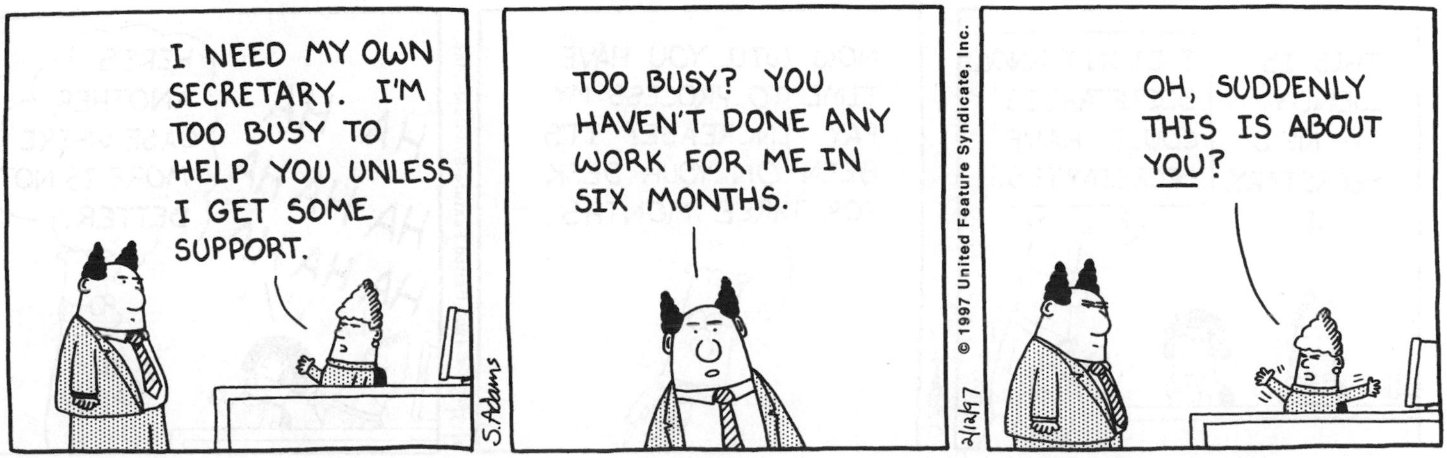
I NEED MY OWN SECRETARY. I'M TOO BUSY TO HELP YOU UNLESS I GET SOME SUPPORT.
TOO BUSY? YOU HAVEN'T DONE ANY WORK FOR ME IN SIX MONTHS.
OH, SUDDENLY THIS IS ABOUT YOU?
S. Adams
2/12/97
© 1997 United Feature Syndicate, Inc.

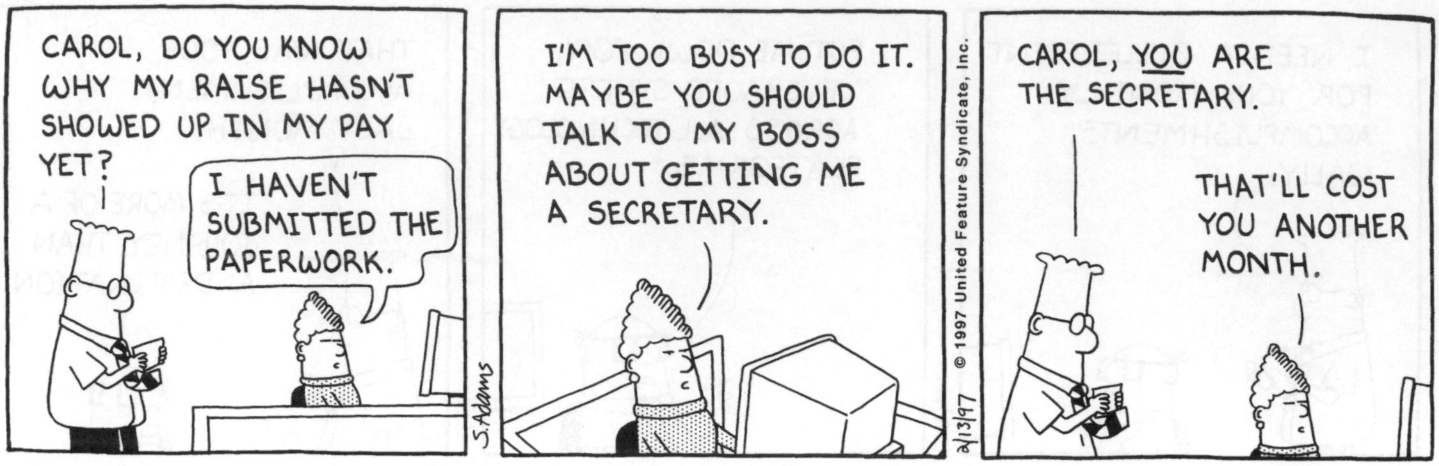
CAROL, DO YOU KNOW WHY MY RAISE HASN'T SHOWED UP IN MY PAY YET?
I HAVEN'T SUBMITTED THE PAPERWORK.
S. Adams
I'M TOO BUSY TO DO IT. MAYBE YOU SHOULD TALK TO MY BOSS ABOUT GETTING ME A SECRETARY.
2/13/97 © 1997 United Feature Syndicate, Inc.
CAROL, YOU ARE THE SECRETARY.
THAT'LL COST YOU ANOTHER MONTH.

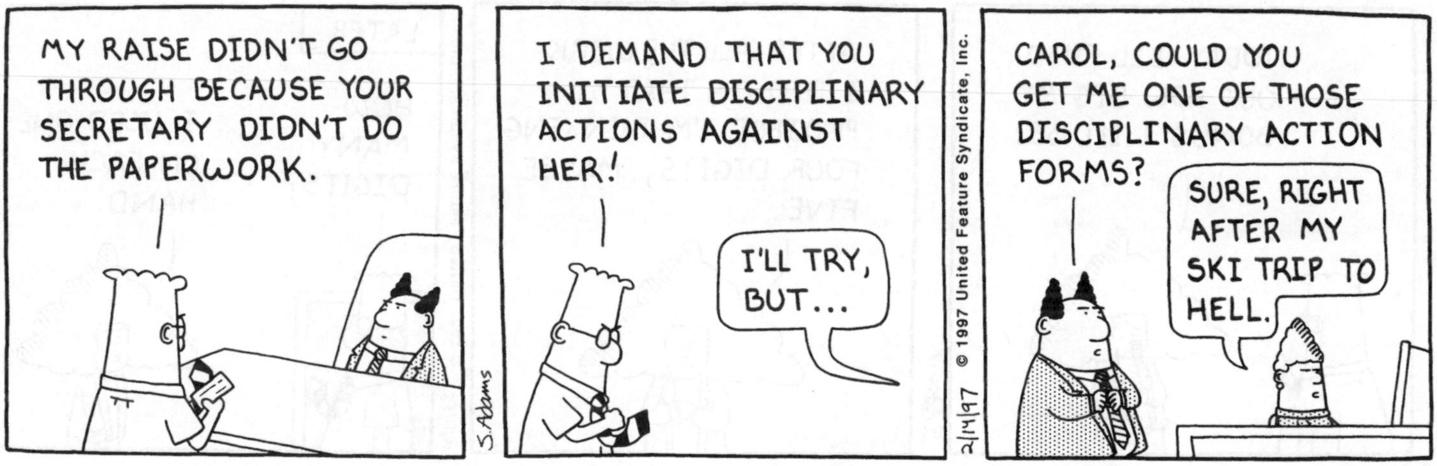
MY RAISE DIDN'T GO THROUGH BECAUSE YOUR SECRETARY DIDN'T DO THE PAPERWORK.
S. Adams
I DEMAND THAT YOU INITIATE DISCIPLINARY ACTIONS AGAINST HER!
I'LL TRY, BUT...
2/14/97 © 1997 United Feature Syndicate, Inc.
CAROL, COULD YOU GET ME ONE OF THOSE DISCIPLINARY ACTION FORMS?
SURE, RIGHT AFTER MY SKI TRIP TO HELL.

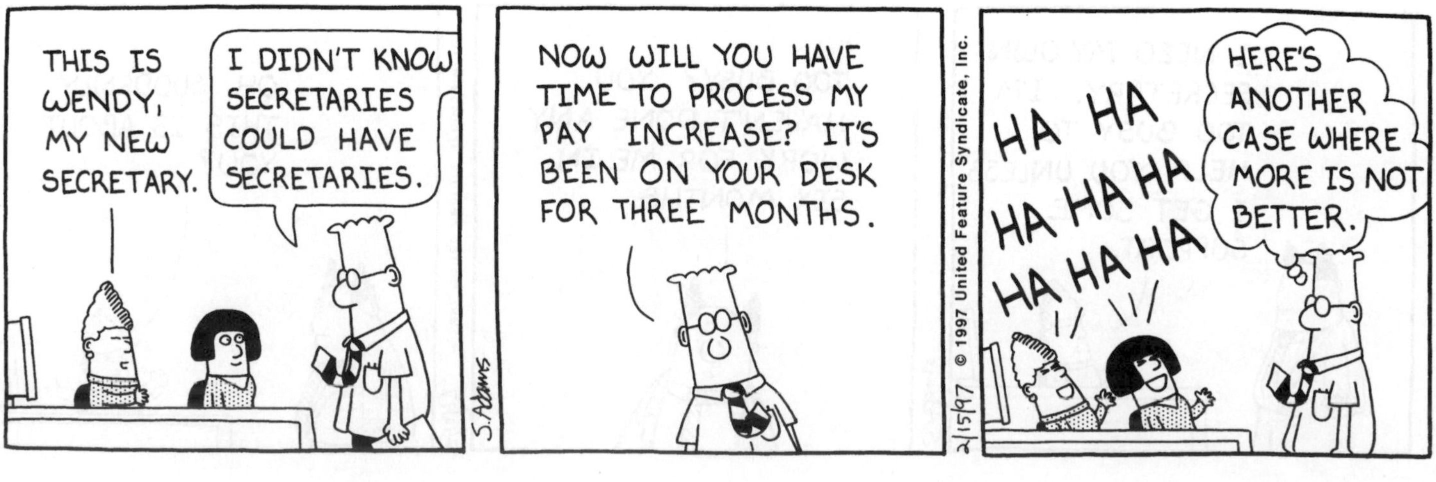
THIS IS WENDY, MY NEW SECRETARY.
I DIDN'T KNOW SECRETARIES COULD HAVE SECRETARIES.
S. Adams
NOW WILL YOU HAVE TIME TO PROCESS MY PAY INCREASE? IT'S BEEN ON YOUR DESK FOR THREE MONTHS.
2/15/97 © 1997 United Feature Syndicate, Inc.
HA HA HA HA HA HA HA HA HA
HERE'S ANOTHER CASE WHERE MORE IS NOT BETTER.

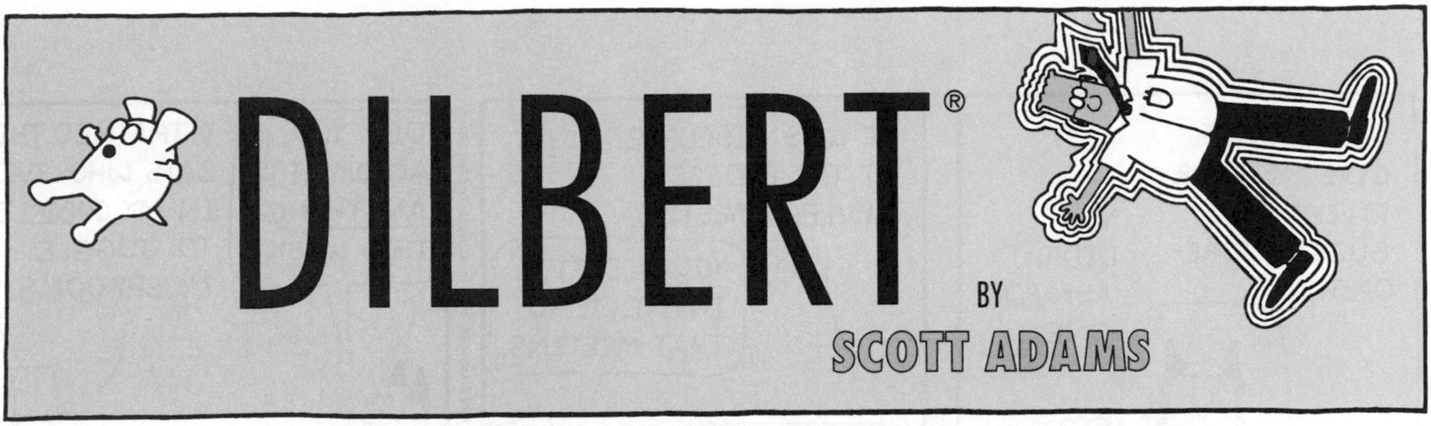
DILBERT®
BY
SCOTT ADAMS

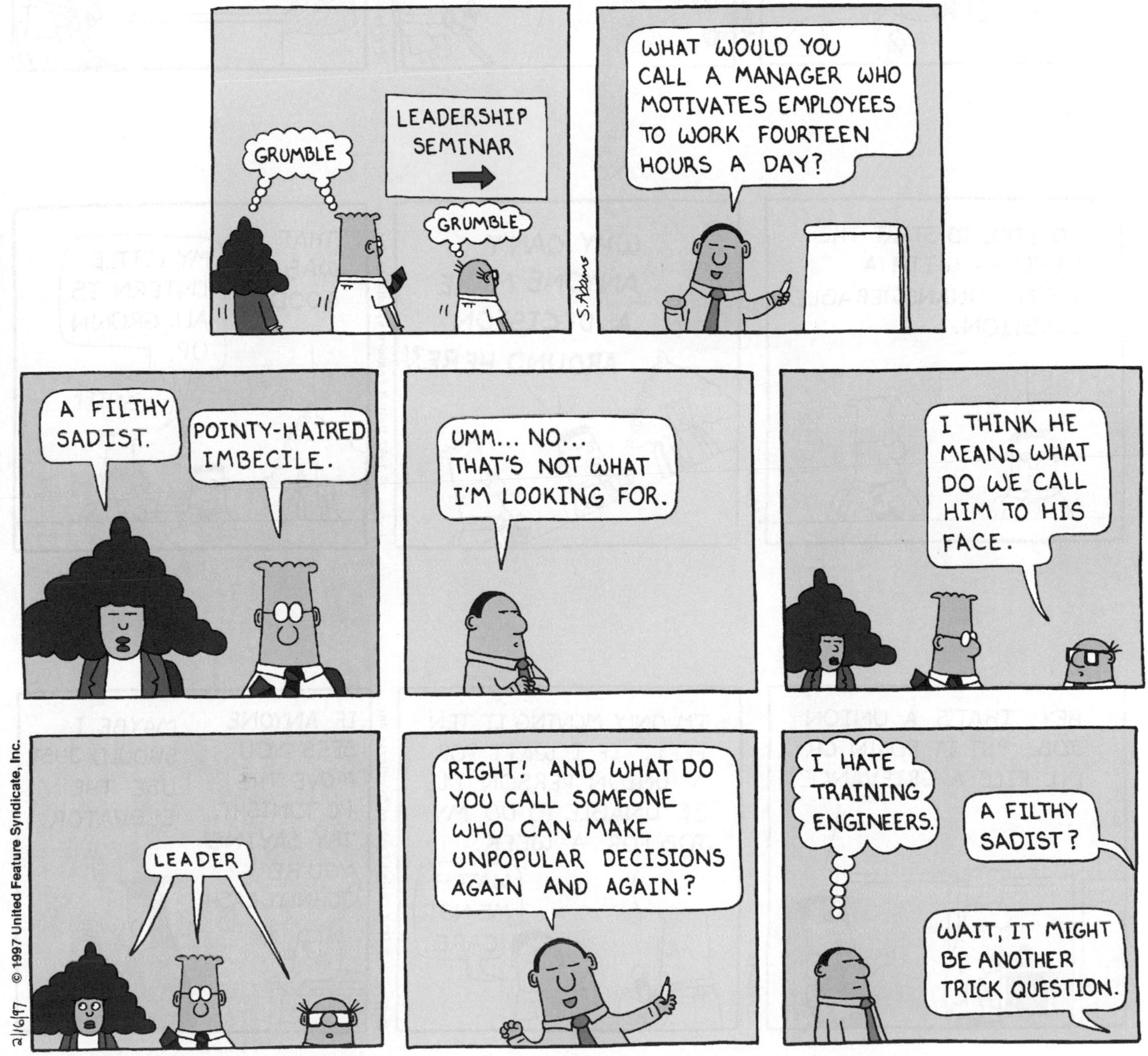
GRUMBLE
LEADERSHIP SEMINAR
GRUMBLE
S. Adams
WHAT WOULD YOU CALL A MANAGER WHO MOTIVATES EMPLOYEES TO WORK FOURTEEN HOURS A DAY?
A FILTHY SADIST.
POINTY-HAIRED IMBECILE.
UMM... NO... THAT'S NOT WHAT I'M LOOKING FOR.
I THINK HE MEANS WHAT DO WE CALL HIM TO HIS FACE.
LEADER
RIGHT! AND WHAT DO YOU CALL SOMEONE WHO CAN MAKE UNPOPULAR DECISIONS AGAIN AND AGAIN?
I HATE TRAINING ENGINEERS.
A FILTHY SADIST?
WAIT, IT MIGHT BE ANOTHER TRICK QUESTION.
2/16/97 © 1997 United Feature Syndicate, Inc.

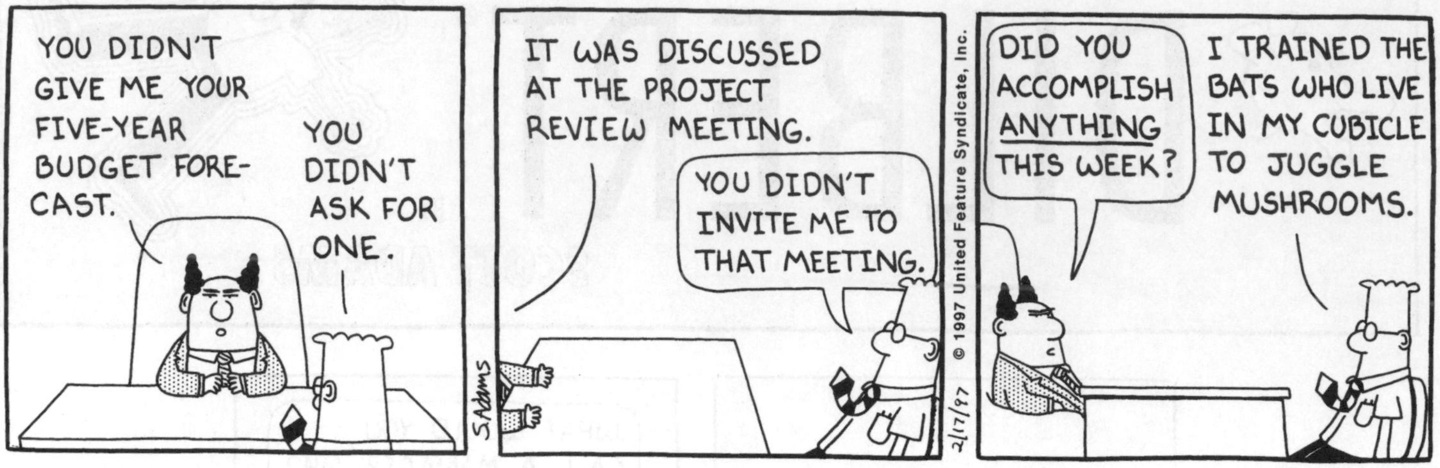
YOU DIDN'T GIVE ME YOUR FIVE-YEAR BUDGET FORECAST.
YOU DIDN'T ASK FOR ONE.
IT WAS DISCUSSED AT THE PROJECT REVIEW MEETING.
YOU DIDN'T INVITE ME TO THAT MEETING.
DID YOU ACCOMPLISH ANYTHING THIS WEEK?
I TRAINED THE BATS WHO LIVE IN MY CUBICLE TO JUGGLE MUSHROOMS.
S. Adams
2/17/97
© 1997 United Feature Syndicate, Inc.

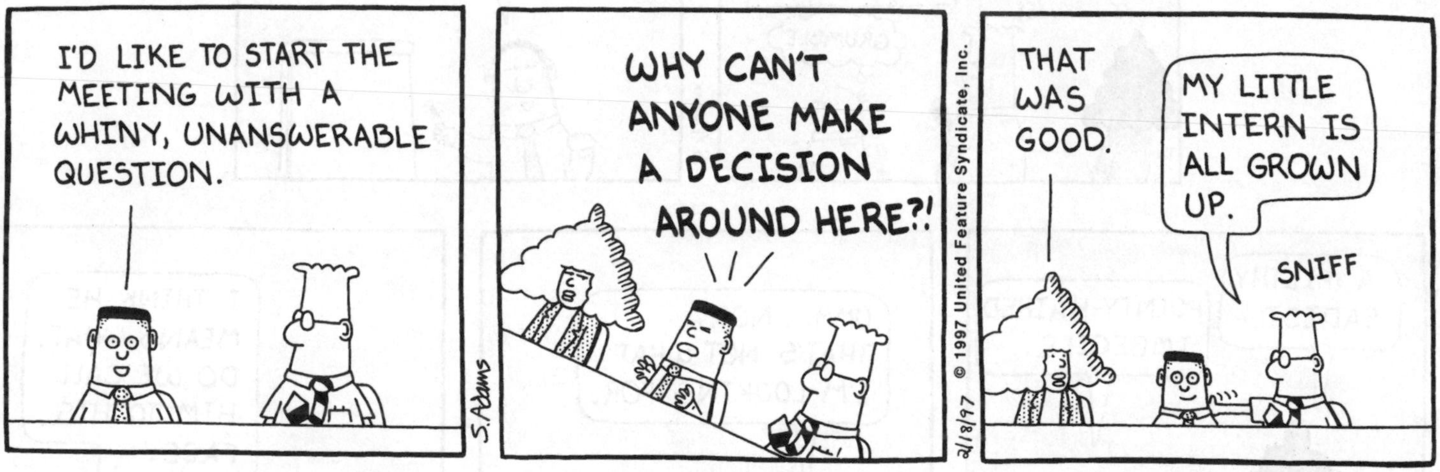
I'D LIKE TO START THE MEETING WITH A WHINY, UNANSWERABLE QUESTION.
WHY CAN'T ANYONE MAKE A DECISION AROUND HERE?!
THAT WAS GOOD.
MY LITTLE INTERN IS ALL GROWN UP.
SNIFF
S. Adams
2/18/97
© 1997 United Feature Syndicate, Inc.

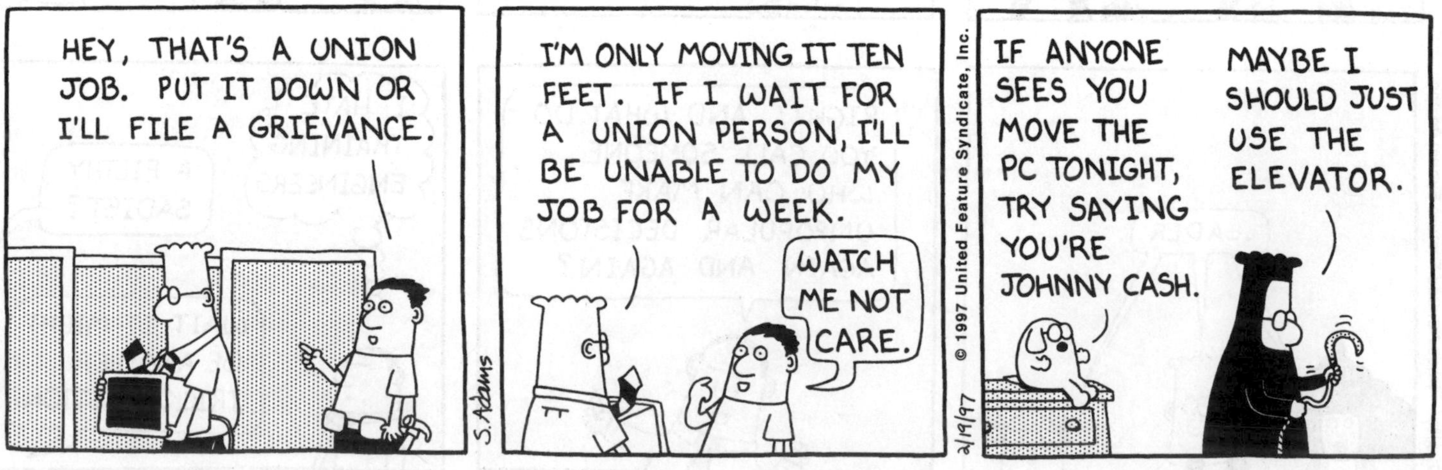
HEY, THAT'S A UNION JOB. PUT IT DOWN OR I'LL FILE A GRIEVANCE.
I'M ONLY MOVING IT TEN FEET. IF I WAIT FOR A UNION PERSON, I'LL BE UNABLE TO DO MY JOB FOR A WEEK.
WATCH ME NOT CARE.
IF ANYONE SEES YOU MOVE THE PC TONIGHT, TRY SAYING YOU'RE JOHNNY CASH.
MAYBE I SHOULD JUST USE THE ELEVATOR.
S. Adams
2/19/97
© 1997 United Feature Syndicate, Inc.

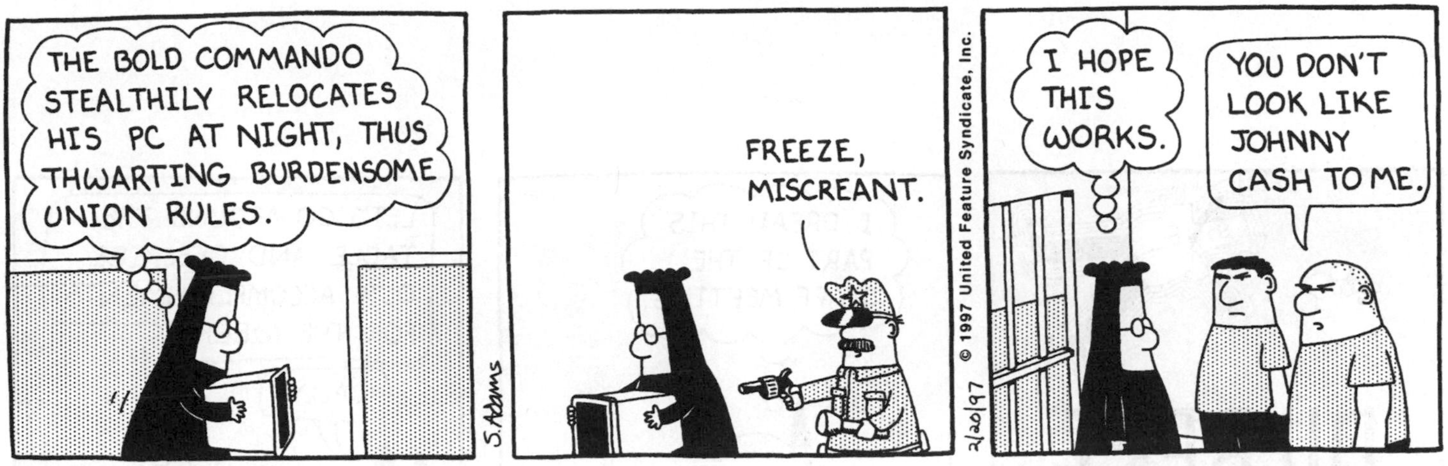
THE BOLD COMMANDO STEALTHILY RELOCATES HIS PC AT NIGHT, THUS THWARTING BURDENSOME UNION RULES.
FREEZE, MISCREANT.
S. Adams
© 1997 United Feature Syndicate, Inc.
2/20/97
I HOPE THIS WORKS.
YOU DON'T LOOK LIKE JOHNNY CASH TO ME.

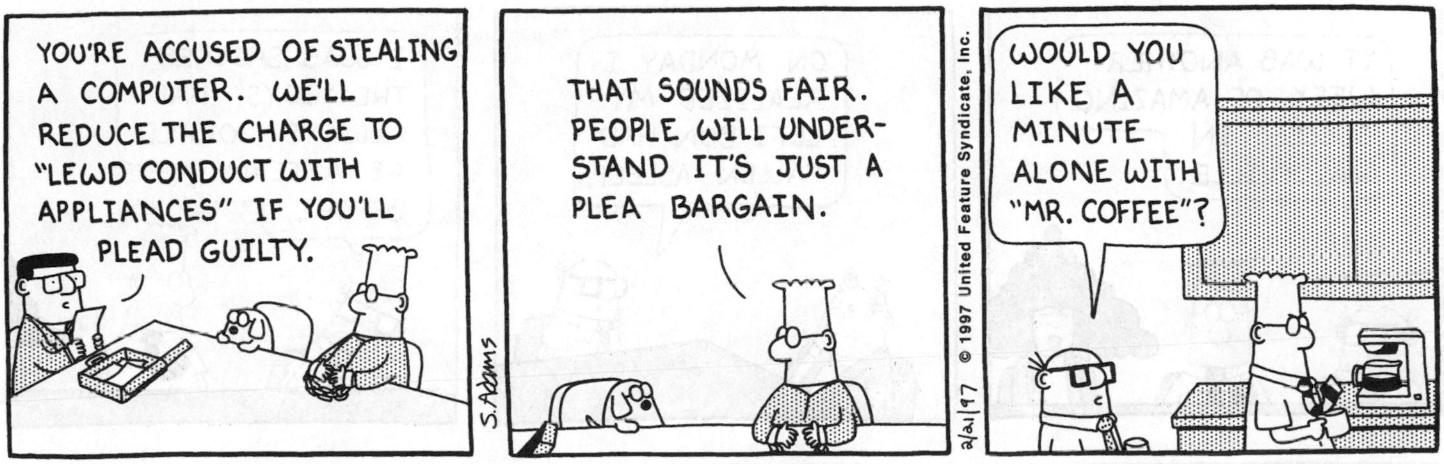
YOU'RE ACCUSED OF STEALING A COMPUTER. WE'LL REDUCE THE CHARGE TO "LEWD CONDUCT WITH APPLIANCES" IF YOU'LL PLEAD GUILTY.
THAT SOUNDS FAIR. PEOPLE WILL UNDERSTAND IT'S JUST A PLEA BARGAIN.
S. Adams
© 1997 United Feature Syndicate, Inc.
2/21/97
WOULD YOU LIKE A MINUTE ALONE WITH "MR. COFFEE"?

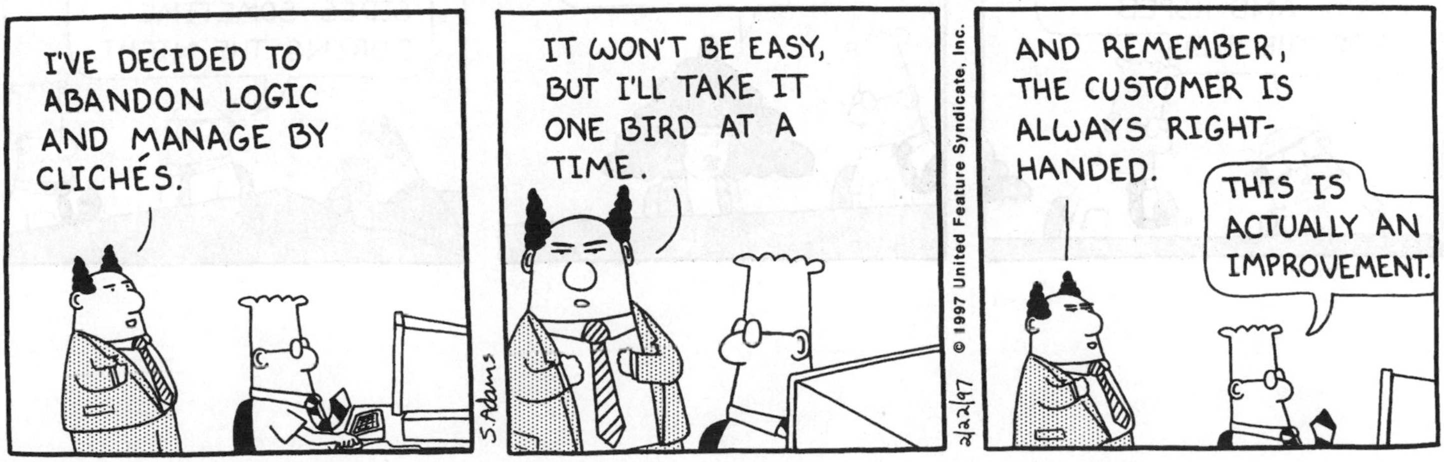
I'VE DECIDED TO ABANDON LOGIC AND MANAGE BY CLICHÉS.
IT WON'T BE EASY, BUT I'LL TAKE IT ONE BIRD AT A TIME.
S. Adams
© 1997 United Feature Syndicate, Inc.
2/22/97
AND REMEMBER, THE CUSTOMER IS ALWAYS RIGHT-HANDED.
THIS IS ACTUALLY AN IMPROVEMENT.

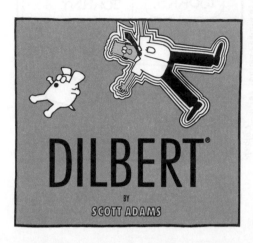

DILBERT®
BY SCOTT ADAMS
I DREAD THIS PART OF THE STAFF MEETING.
LET'S GO AROUND THE TABLE AND DESCRIBE OUR ACCOMPLISHMENTS FOR THE WEEK.
WALLY?
S. Adams
IT WAS ANOTHER WEEK OF AMAZING SUCCESS IN WALLYVILLE.
ON MONDAY I REALIZED MY LEFT BUN HAD FALLEN ASLEEP.
I WAS SHOCKED. THE "BOYS" HAD ALWAYS WORKED AS A TEAM BEFORE.
THINKING QUICKLY, I SHIFTED MY WEIGHT TO MY RIGHT BUN AND HOPED FOR THE BEST.
THAT'S YOUR LEFT SIDE, NOT YOUR RIGHT.
THAT'S THE OTHER THING; APPARENTLY THE BOYS SWITCHED SIDES SOMETIME DURING THE NIGHT.
2/23/97 © 1997 United Feature Syndicate, Inc.

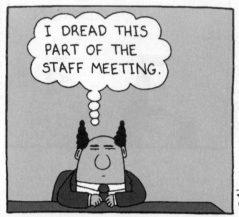

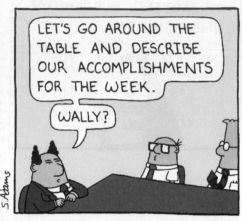

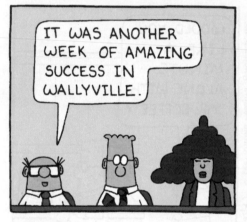

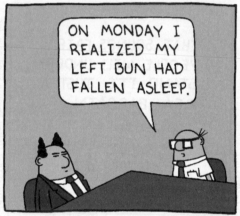

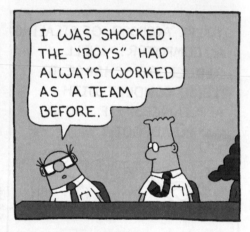

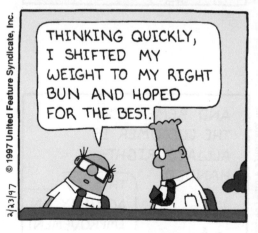

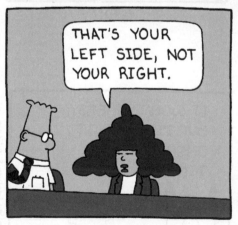

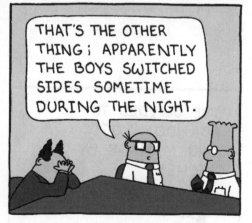

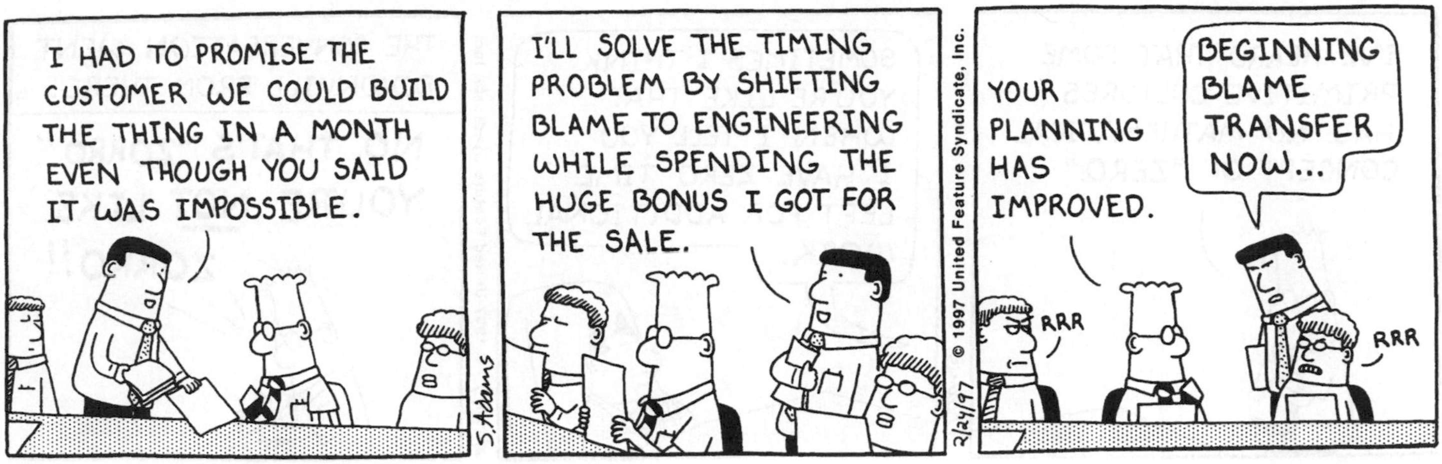
I HAD TO PROMISE THE CUSTOMER WE COULD BUILD THE THING IN A MONTH EVEN THOUGH YOU SAID IT WAS IMPOSSIBLE.
S. Adams
I'LL SOLVE THE TIMING PROBLEM BY SHIFTING BLAME TO ENGINEERING WHILE SPENDING THE HUGE BONUS I GOT FOR THE SALE.
2/24/97 © 1997 United Feature Syndicate, Inc.
YOUR PLANNING HAS IMPROVED.
BEGINNING BLAME TRANSFER NOW...
RRR
RRR

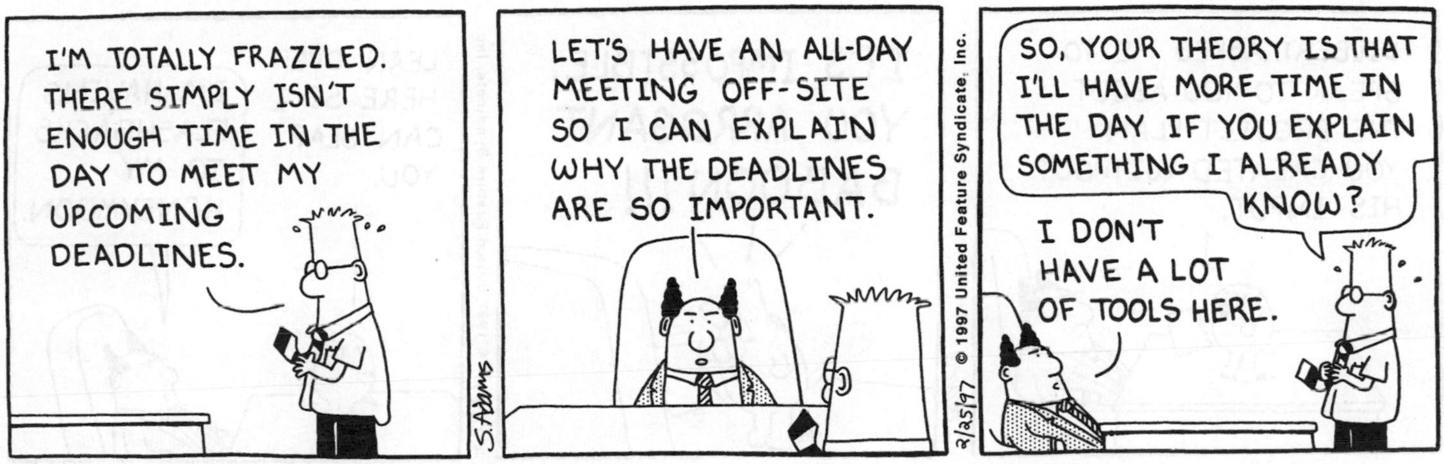
I'M TOTALLY FRAZZLED. THERE SIMPLY ISN'T ENOUGH TIME IN THE DAY TO MEET MY UPCOMING DEADLINES.
S. Adams
LET'S HAVE AN ALL-DAY MEETING OFF-SITE SO I CAN EXPLAIN WHY THE DEADLINES ARE SO IMPORTANT.
2/25/97 © 1997 United Feature Syndicate, Inc.
SO, YOUR THEORY IS THAT I'LL HAVE MORE TIME IN THE DAY IF YOU EXPLAIN SOMETHING I ALREADY KNOW?
I DON'T HAVE A LOT OF TOOLS HERE.

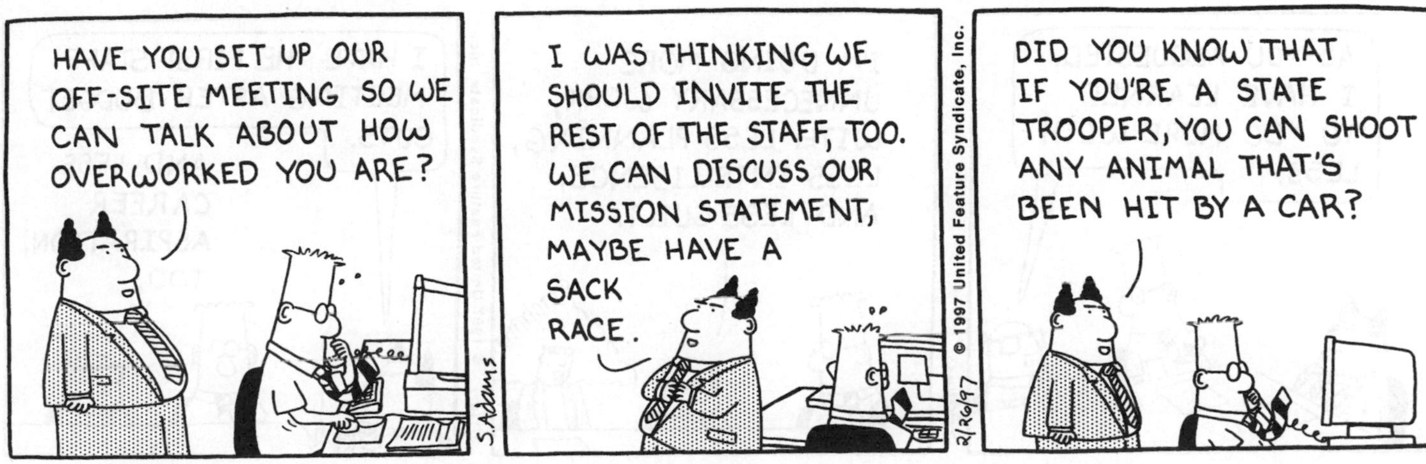
HAVE YOU SET UP OUR OFF-SITE MEETING SO WE CAN TALK ABOUT HOW OVERWORKED YOU ARE?
S. Adams
I WAS THINKING WE SHOULD INVITE THE REST OF THE STAFF, TOO. WE CAN DISCUSS OUR MISSION STATEMENT, MAYBE HAVE A SACK RACE.
2/26/97 © 1997 United Feature Syndicate, Inc.
DID YOU KNOW THAT IF YOU'RE A STATE TROOPER, YOU CAN SHOOT ANY ANIMAL THAT'S BEEN HIT BY A CAR?

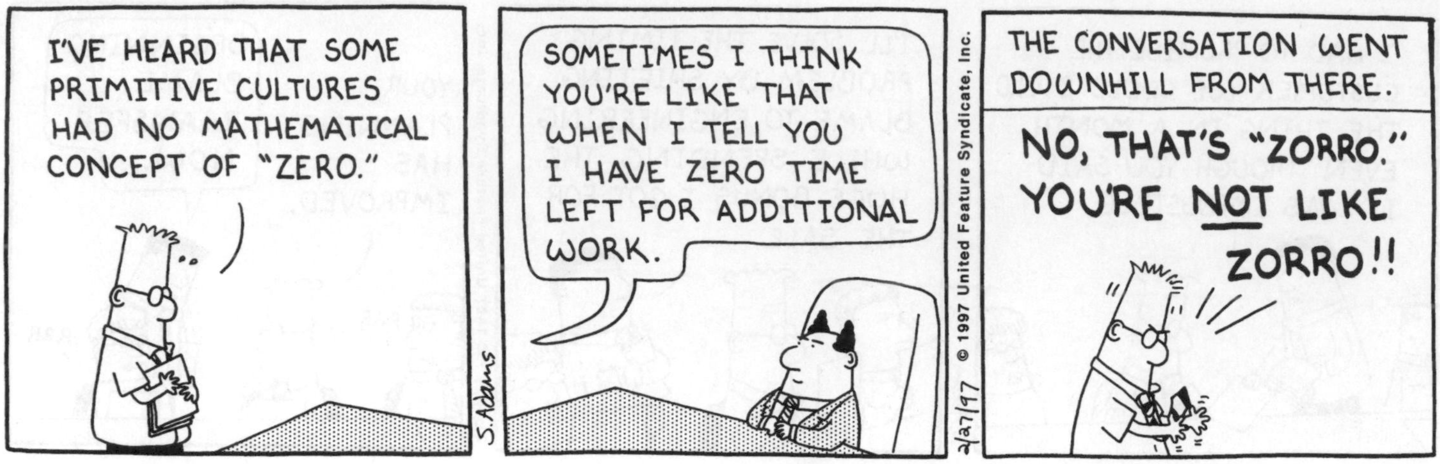
I'VE HEARD THAT SOME PRIMITIVE CULTURES HAD NO MATHEMATICAL CONCEPT OF "ZERO."
SOMETIMES I THINK YOU'RE LIKE THAT WHEN I TELL YOU I HAVE ZERO TIME LEFT FOR ADDITIONAL WORK.
S.Adams
2/27/97 © 1997 United Feature Syndicate, Inc.
THE CONVERSATION WENT DOWNHILL FROM THERE.
NO, THAT'S "ZORRO." YOU'RE NOT LIKE ZORRO!!

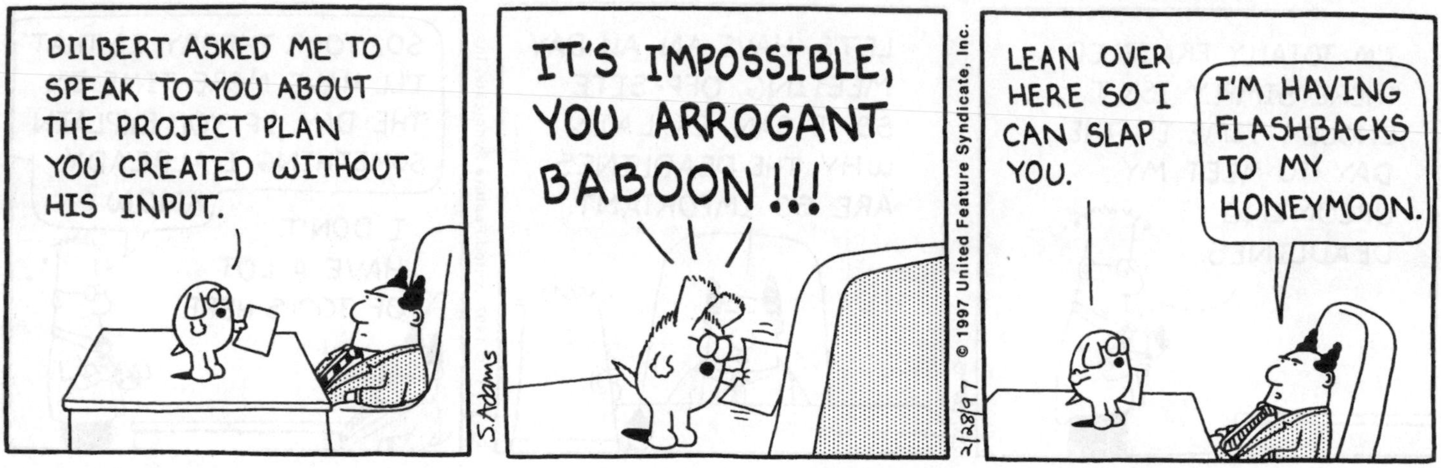
DILBERT ASKED ME TO SPEAK TO YOU ABOUT THE PROJECT PLAN YOU CREATED WITHOUT HIS INPUT.
IT'S IMPOSSIBLE, YOU ARROGANT BABOON!!!
S.Adams
2/28/97 © 1997 United Feature Syndicate, Inc.
LEAN OVER HERE SO I CAN SLAP YOU.
I'M HAVING FLASHBACKS TO MY HONEYMOON.

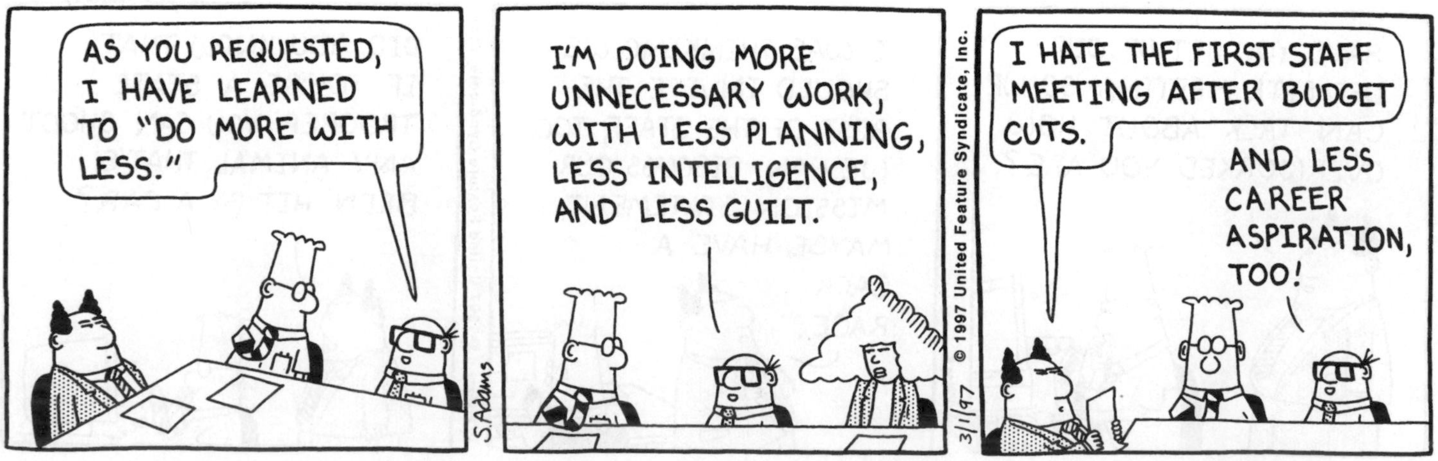
AS YOU REQUESTED, I HAVE LEARNED TO "DO MORE WITH LESS."
I'M DOING MORE UNNECESSARY WORK, WITH LESS PLANNING, LESS INTELLIGENCE, AND LESS GUILT.
S.Adams
3/1/97 © 1997 United Feature Syndicate, Inc.
I HATE THE FIRST STAFF MEETING AFTER BUDGET CUTS.
AND LESS CAREER ASPIRATION, TOO!

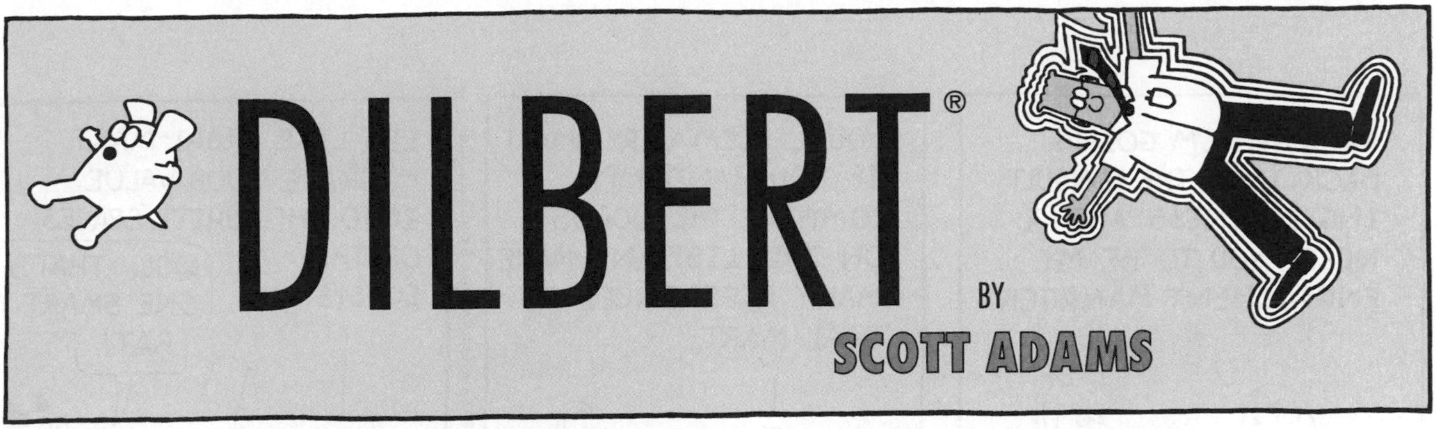
DILBERT®
BY
SCOTT ADAMS

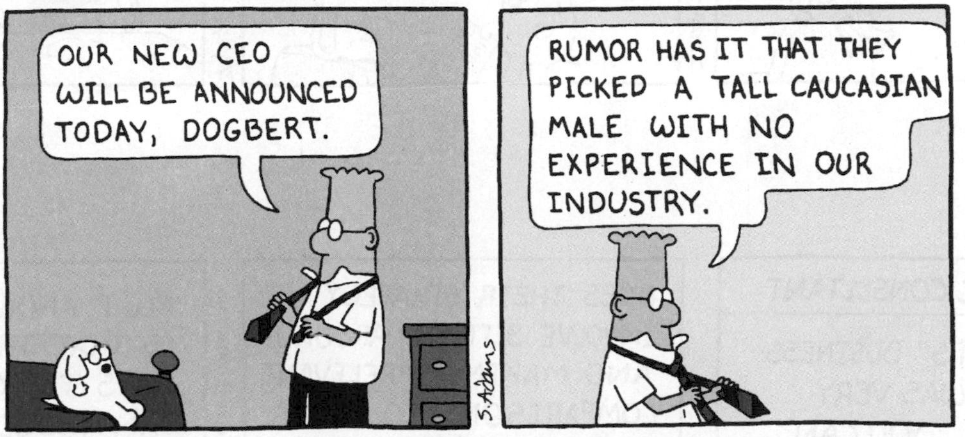
OUR NEW CEO WILL BE ANNOUNCED TODAY, DOGBERT.
RUMOR HAS IT THAT THEY PICKED A TALL CAUCASIAN MALE WITH NO EXPERIENCE IN OUR INDUSTRY.
S. Adams

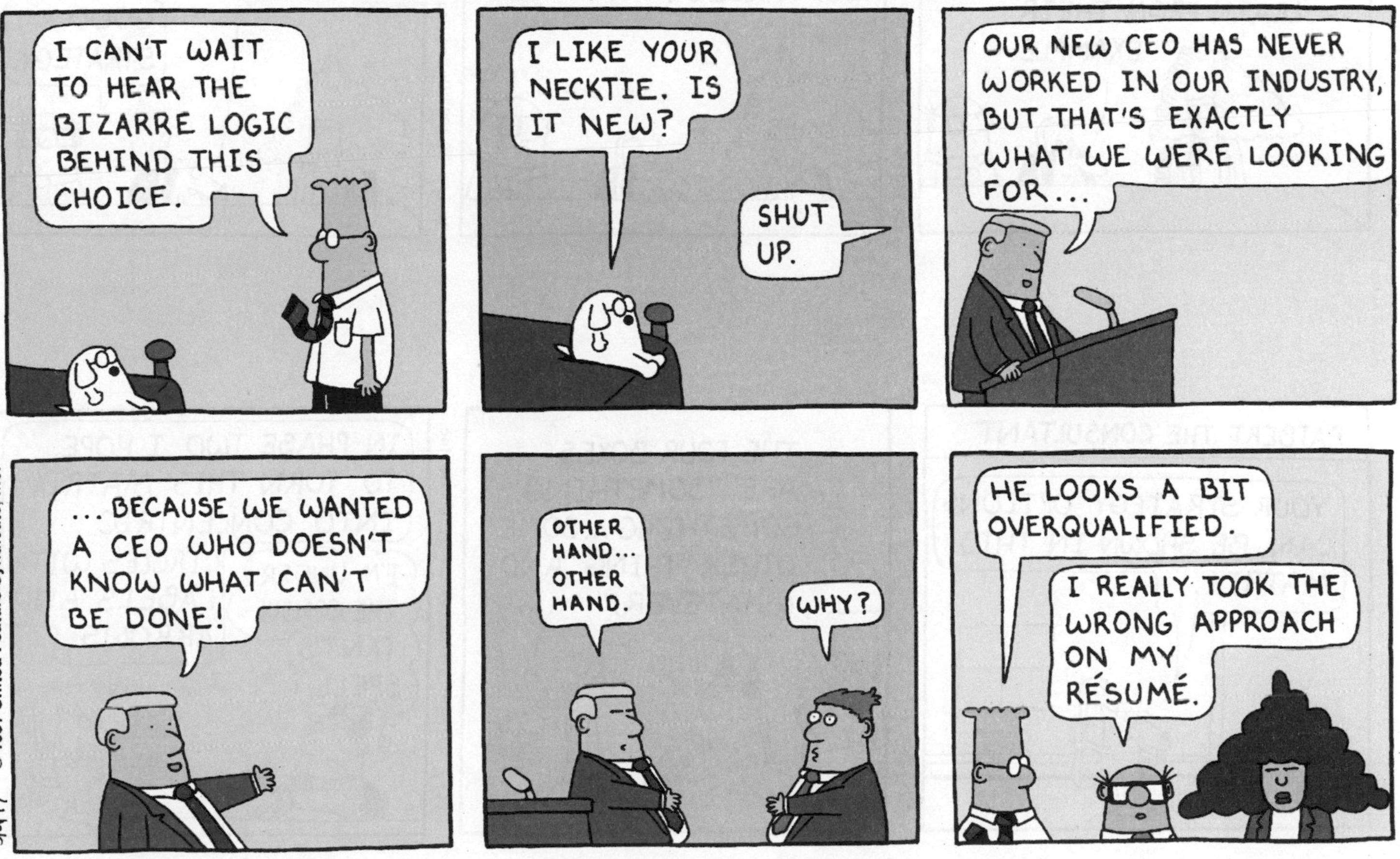
I CAN'T WAIT TO HEAR THE BIZARRE LOGIC BEHIND THIS CHOICE.
I LIKE YOUR NECKTIE. IS IT NEW?
SHUT UP.
OUR NEW CEO HAS NEVER WORKED IN OUR INDUSTRY, BUT THAT'S EXACTLY WHAT WE WERE LOOKING FOR...
... BECAUSE WE WANTED A CEO WHO DOESN'T KNOW WHAT CAN'T BE DONE!
OTHER HAND... OTHER HAND.
WHY?
HE LOOKS A BIT OVERQUALIFIED.
I REALLY TOOK THE WRONG APPROACH ON MY RÉSUMÉ.

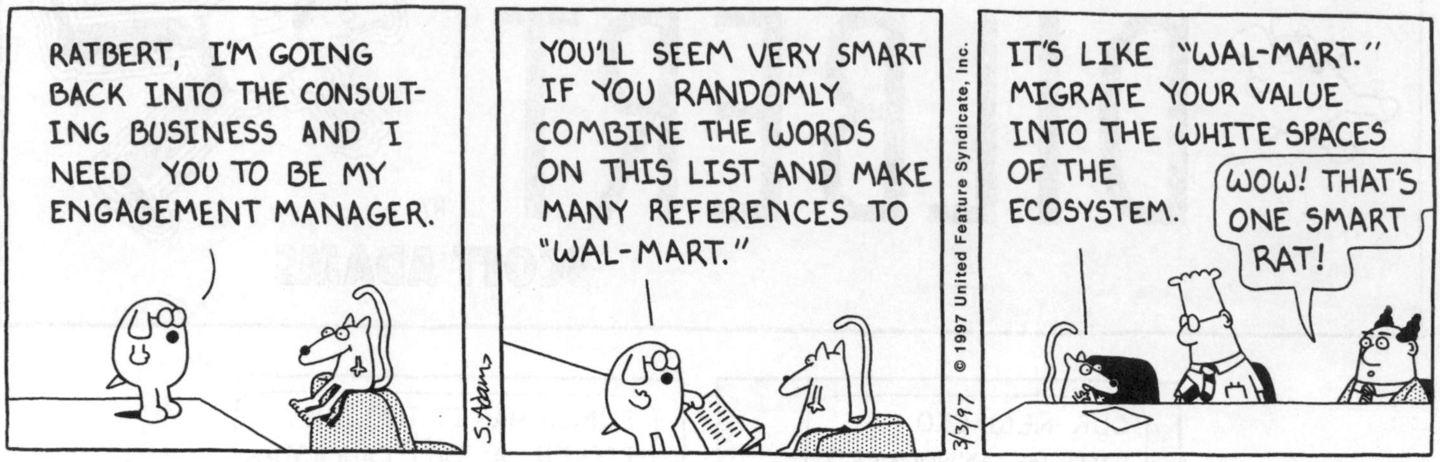
RATBERT, I'M GOING BACK INTO THE CONSULTING BUSINESS AND I NEED YOU TO BE MY ENGAGEMENT MANAGER.
YOU'LL SEEM VERY SMART IF YOU RANDOMLY COMBINE THE WORDS ON THIS LIST AND MAKE MANY REFERENCES TO "WAL-MART."
IT'S LIKE "WAL-MART." MIGRATE YOUR VALUE INTO THE WHITE SPACES OF THE ECOSYSTEM.
WOW! THAT'S ONE SMART RAT!
S. Adams
3/3/97
© 1997 United Feature Syndicate, Inc.

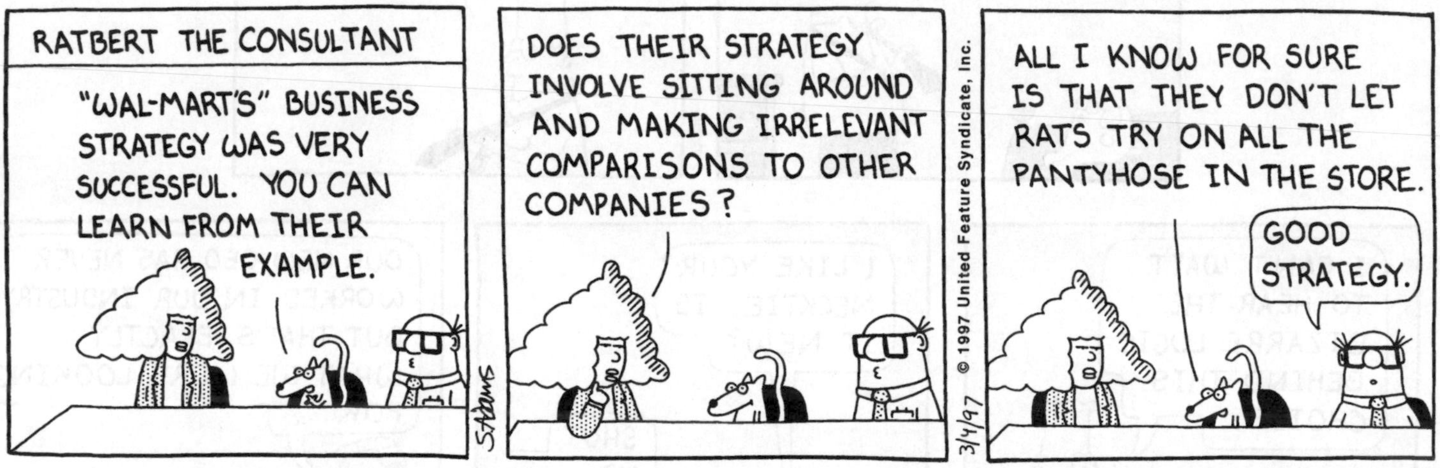
RATBERT THE CONSULTANT
"WAL-MART'S" BUSINESS STRATEGY WAS VERY SUCCESSFUL. YOU CAN LEARN FROM THEIR EXAMPLE.
DOES THEIR STRATEGY INVOLVE SITTING AROUND AND MAKING IRRELEVANT COMPARISONS TO OTHER COMPANIES?
ALL I KNOW FOR SURE IS THAT THEY DON'T LET RATS TRY ON ALL THE PANTYHOSE IN THE STORE.
GOOD STRATEGY.
S. Adams
3/4/97
© 1997 United Feature Syndicate, Inc.

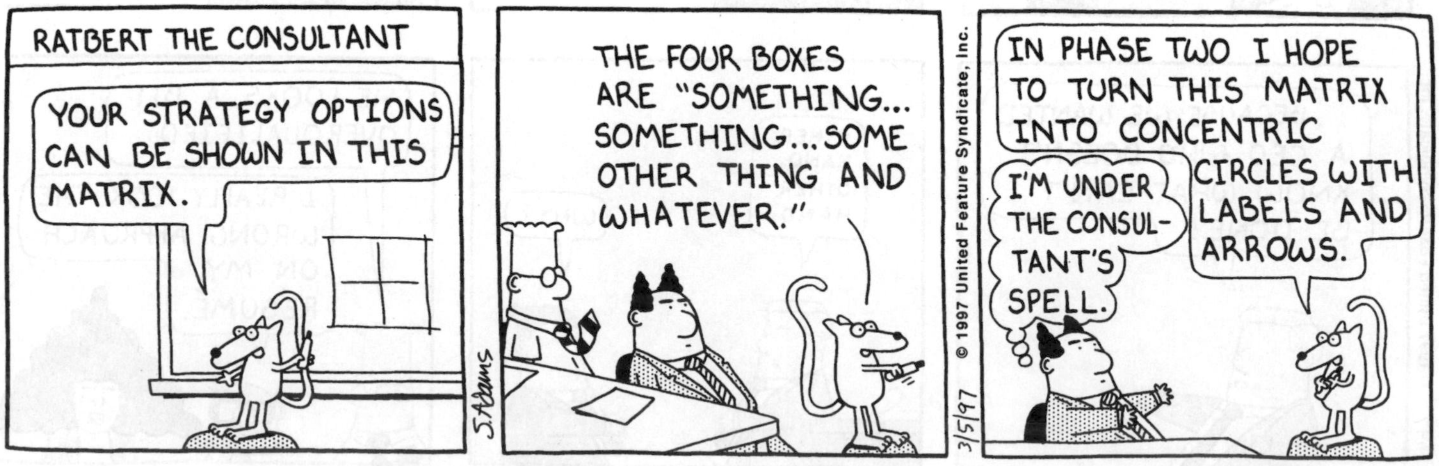
RATBERT THE CONSULTANT
YOUR STRATEGY OPTIONS CAN BE SHOWN IN THIS MATRIX.
THE FOUR BOXES ARE "SOMETHING... SOMETHING... SOME OTHER THING AND WHATEVER."
IN PHASE TWO I HOPE TO TURN THIS MATRIX INTO CONCENTRIC CIRCLES WITH LABELS AND ARROWS.
I'M UNDER THE CONSULTANT'S SPELL.
S. Adams
3/5/97
© 1997 United Feature Syndicate, Inc.

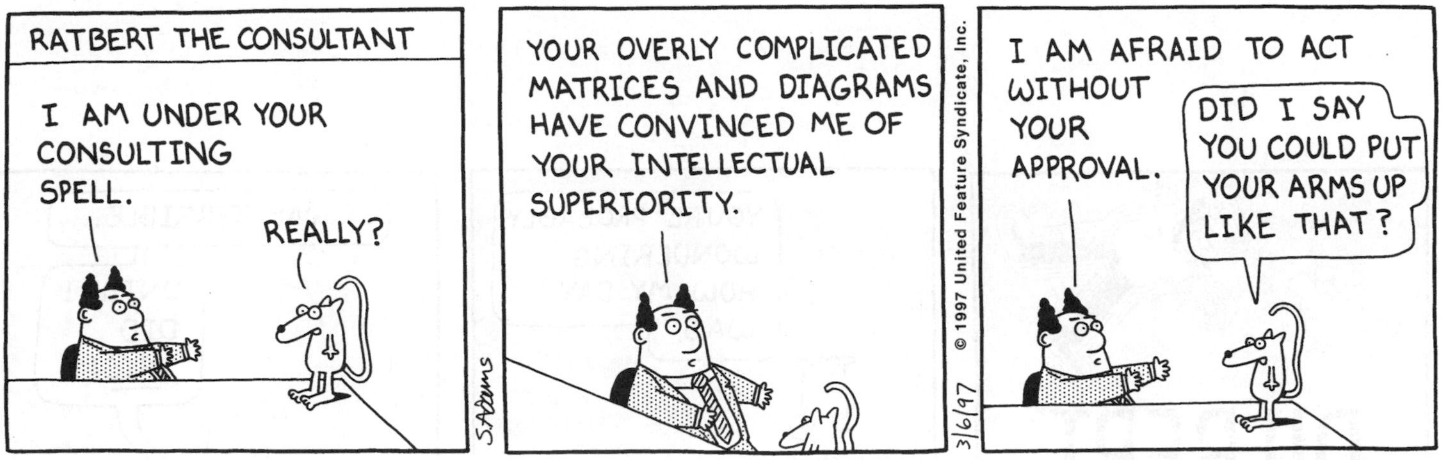
RATBERT THE CONSULTANT
I AM UNDER YOUR CONSULTING SPELL.
REALLY?
YOUR OVERLY COMPLICATED MATRICES AND DIAGRAMS HAVE CONVINCED ME OF YOUR INTELLECTUAL SUPERIORITY.
S.Adams
3/6/97 © 1997 United Feature Syndicate, Inc.
I AM AFRAID TO ACT WITHOUT YOUR APPROVAL.
DID I SAY YOU COULD PUT YOUR ARMS UP LIKE THAT?

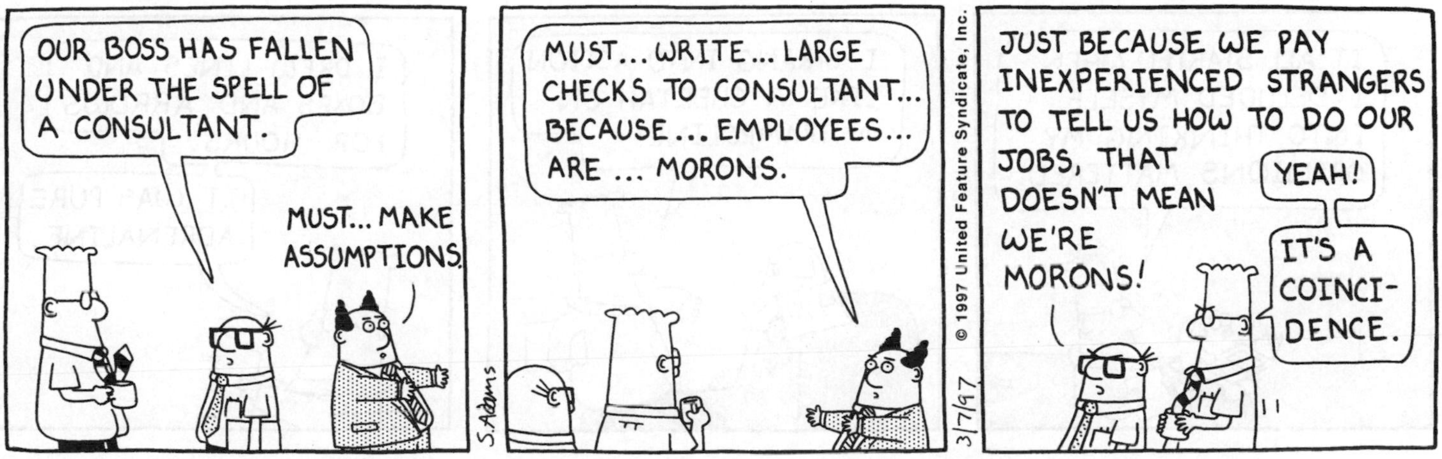
OUR BOSS HAS FALLEN UNDER THE SPELL OF A CONSULTANT.
MUST... MAKE ASSUMPTIONS.
MUST... WRITE... LARGE CHECKS TO CONSULTANT... BECAUSE... EMPLOYEES... ARE ... MORONS.
S.Adams
3/7/97 © 1997 United Feature Syndicate, Inc.
JUST BECAUSE WE PAY INEXPERIENCED STRANGERS TO TELL US HOW TO DO OUR JOBS, THAT DOESN'T MEAN WE'RE MORONS!
YEAH!
IT'S A COINCI-DENCE.

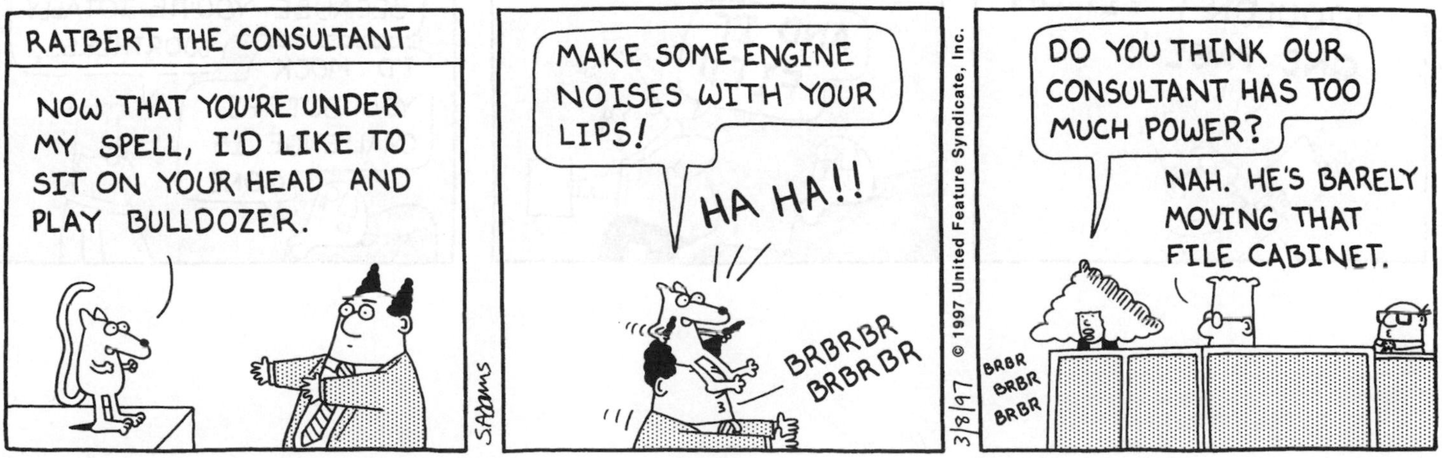
RATBERT THE CONSULTANT
NOW THAT YOU'RE UNDER MY SPELL, I'D LIKE TO SIT ON YOUR HEAD AND PLAY BULLDOZER.
MAKE SOME ENGINE NOISES WITH YOUR LIPS!
HA HA!!
BRBRBR BRBRBR
S.Adams
3/8/97 © 1997 United Feature Syndicate, Inc.
DO YOU THINK OUR CONSULTANT HAS TOO MUCH POWER?
NAH. HE'S BARELY MOVING THAT FILE CABINET.
BRBR BRBR BRBR

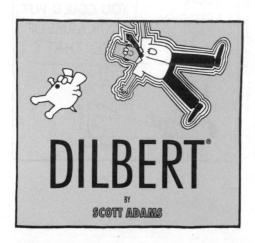

DILBERT®
BY
SCOTT ADAMS
YOU'RE PROBABLY WONDERING HOW MY DAY WAS.
S. Adams
IT WAS TERRIBLE...
UNTIL I DID THIS!
IT ALL STARTED WHEN I DELUDED MYSELF INTO THINKING MY OPINIONS MATTERED.
I SPRANG INTO ACTION LIKE A CHEETAH ON A TRAMPOLINE!
I DREW LINES AND BOXES AND ARROWS FOR HOURS.
IT WAS PURE ADRENALINE.
3/9/97 © 1997 United Feature Syndicate, Inc.
SUDDENLY, TROUBLE STRUCK! IT WOULDN'T FIT ON ONE PAGE!!
SO I SHRUNK EVERY-THING UNTIL IT WAS TOTALLY UNREADABLE.
AND IT FIT!!
THE MORAL OF THE STORY IS THAT YOU DON'T HAVE TO FEEL BAD JUST BECAUSE YOU'RE TOTALLY WORTHLESS.
I'D MOCK YOU BUT THE CHALLENGE IS GONE.

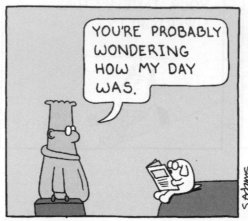

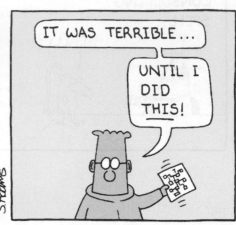

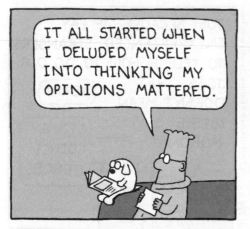

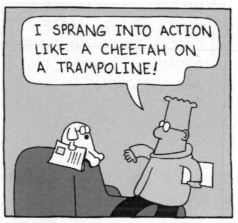

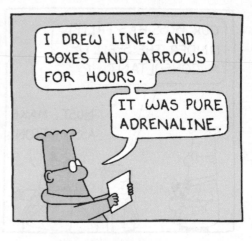

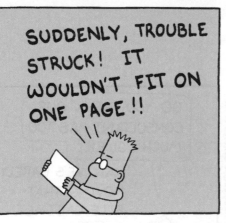

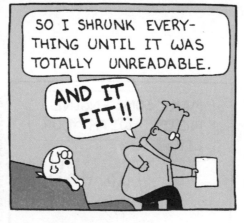

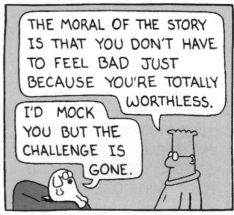

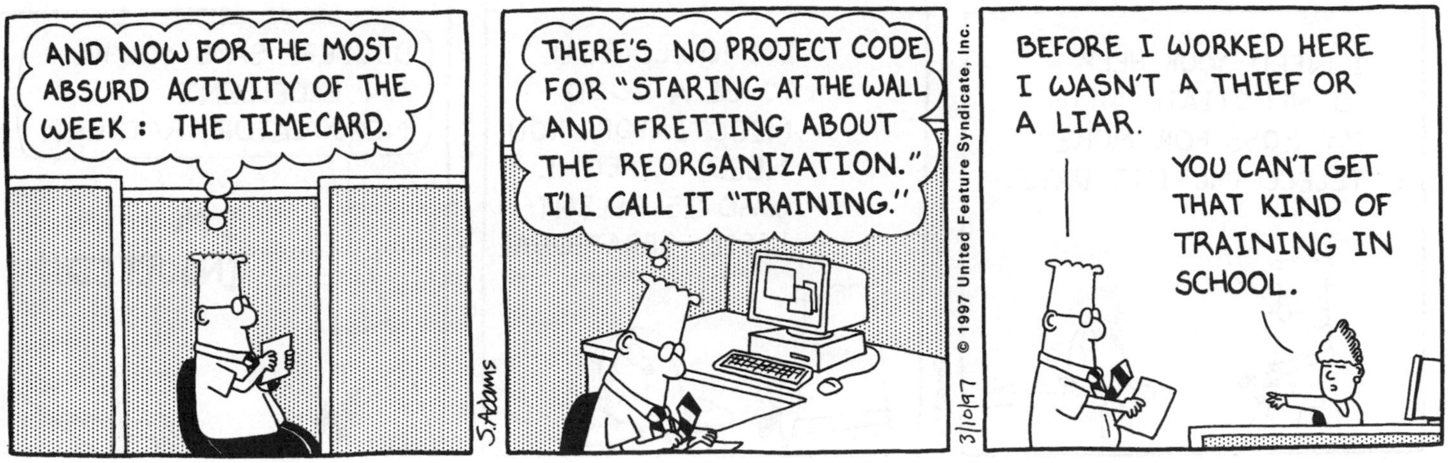
AND NOW FOR THE MOST ABSURD ACTIVITY OF THE WEEK: THE TIMECARD.
S.Adams
THERE'S NO PROJECT CODE FOR "STARING AT THE WALL AND FRETTING ABOUT THE REORGANIZATION." I'LL CALL IT "TRAINING."
3/10/97 © 1997 United Feature Syndicate, Inc.
BEFORE I WORKED HERE I WASN'T A THIEF OR A LIAR.
YOU CAN'T GET THAT KIND OF TRAINING IN SCHOOL.

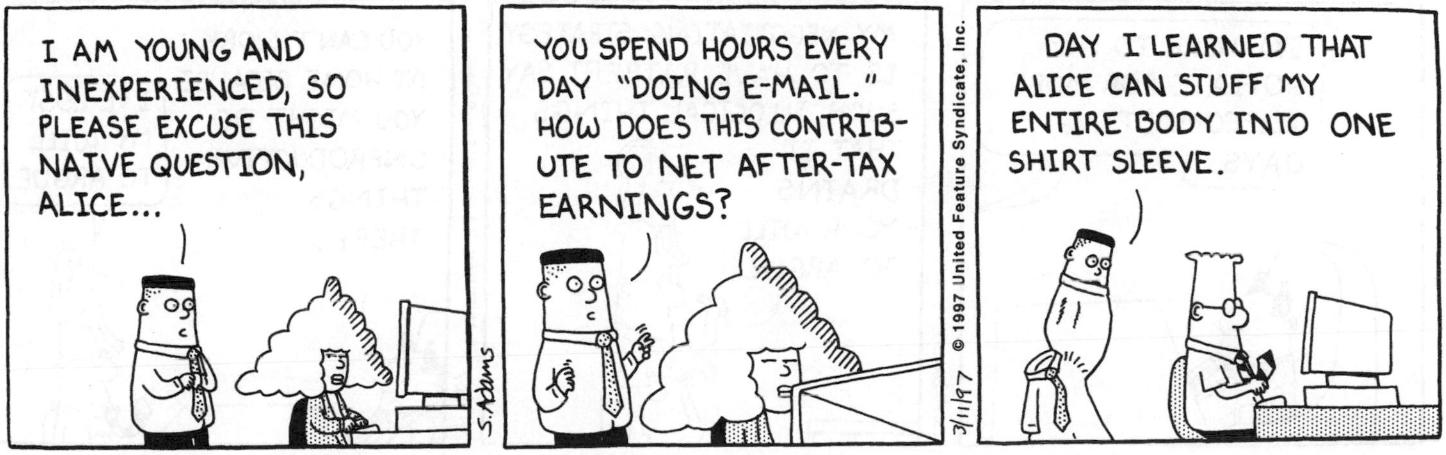
I AM YOUNG AND INEXPERIENCED, SO PLEASE EXCUSE THIS NAIVE QUESTION, ALICE...
S.Adams
YOU SPEND HOURS EVERY DAY "DOING E-MAIL." HOW DOES THIS CONTRIBUTE TO NET AFTER-TAX EARNINGS?
3/11/97 © 1997 United Feature Syndicate, Inc.
DAY I LEARNED THAT ALICE CAN STUFF MY ENTIRE BODY INTO ONE SHIRT SLEEVE.

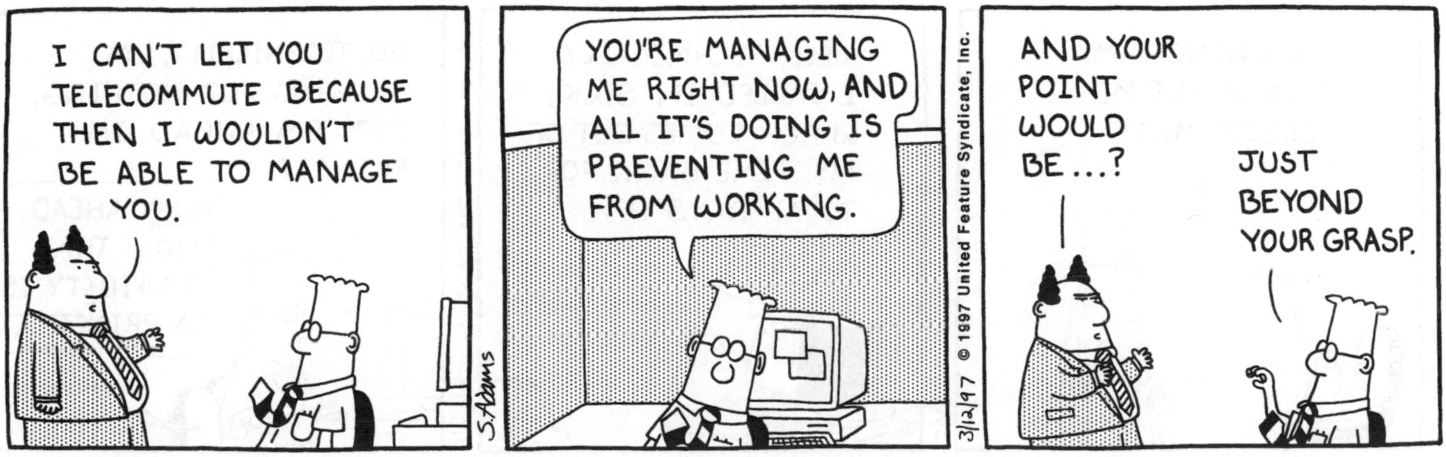
I CAN'T LET YOU TELECOMMUTE BECAUSE THEN I WOULDN'T BE ABLE TO MANAGE YOU.
S.Adams
YOU'RE MANAGING ME RIGHT NOW, AND ALL IT'S DOING IS PREVENTING ME FROM WORKING.
3/12/97 © 1997 United Feature Syndicate, Inc.
AND YOUR POINT WOULD BE...?
JUST BEYOND YOUR GRASP.

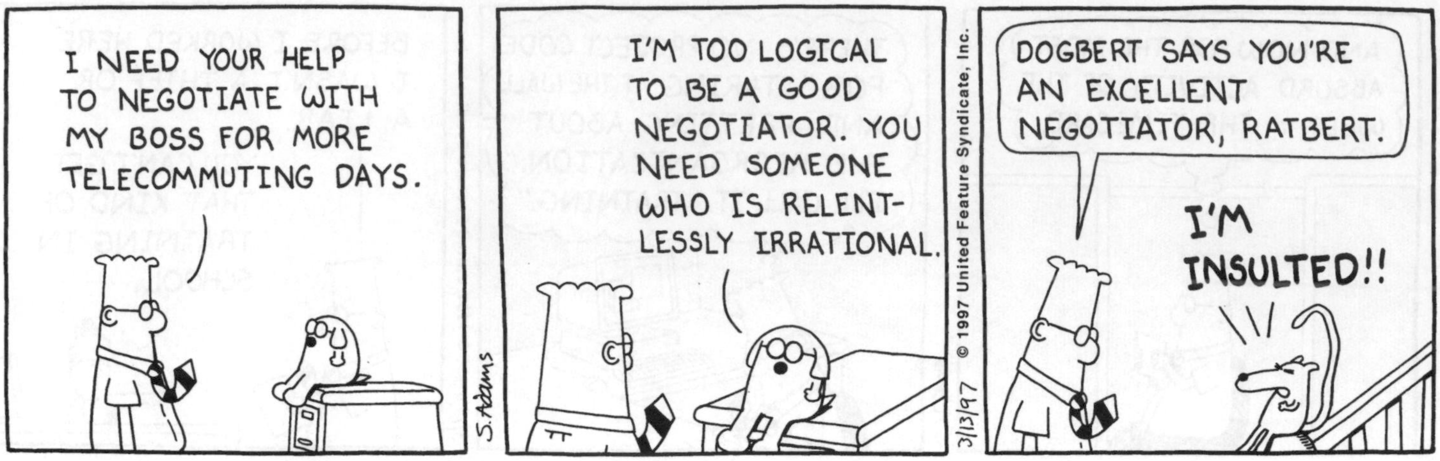
I NEED YOUR HELP TO NEGOTIATE WITH MY BOSS FOR MORE TELECOMMUTING DAYS.
I'M TOO LOGICAL TO BE A GOOD NEGOTIATOR. YOU NEED SOMEONE WHO IS RELENTLESSLY IRRATIONAL.
S. Adams
3/13/97 © 1997 United Feature Syndicate, Inc.
DOGBERT SAYS YOU'RE AN EXCELLENT NEGOTIATOR, RATBERT.
I'M INSULTED!!

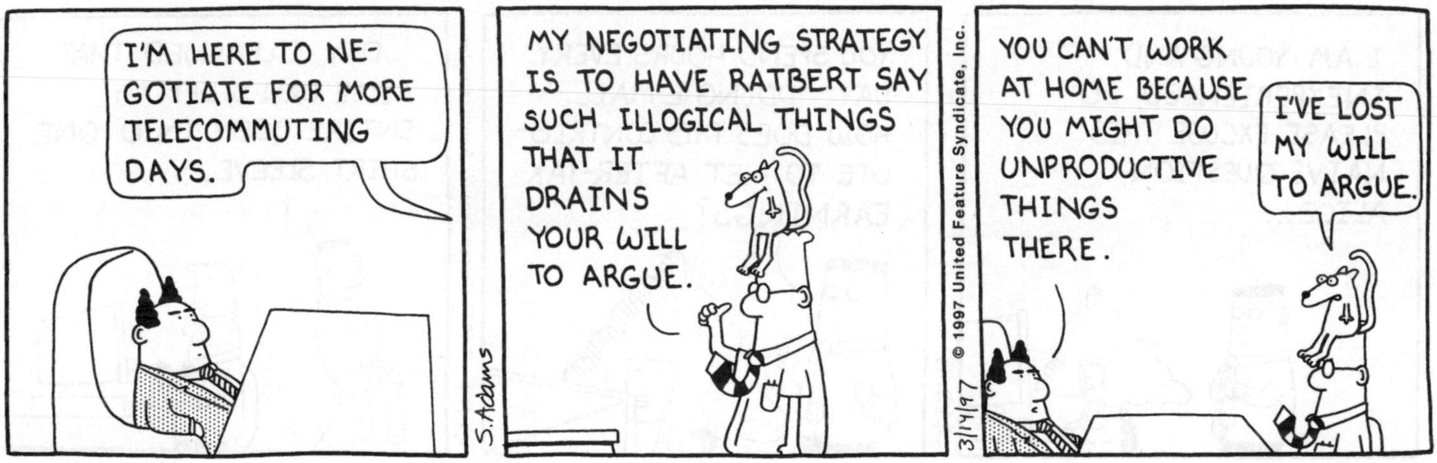
I'M HERE TO NEGOTIATE FOR MORE TELECOMMUTING DAYS.
MY NEGOTIATING STRATEGY IS TO HAVE RATBERT SAY SUCH ILLOGICAL THINGS THAT IT DRAINS YOUR WILL TO ARGUE.
S. Adams
3/14/97 © 1997 United Feature Syndicate, Inc.
YOU CAN'T WORK AT HOME BECAUSE YOU MIGHT DO UNPRODUCTIVE THINGS THERE.
I'VE LOST MY WILL TO ARGUE.

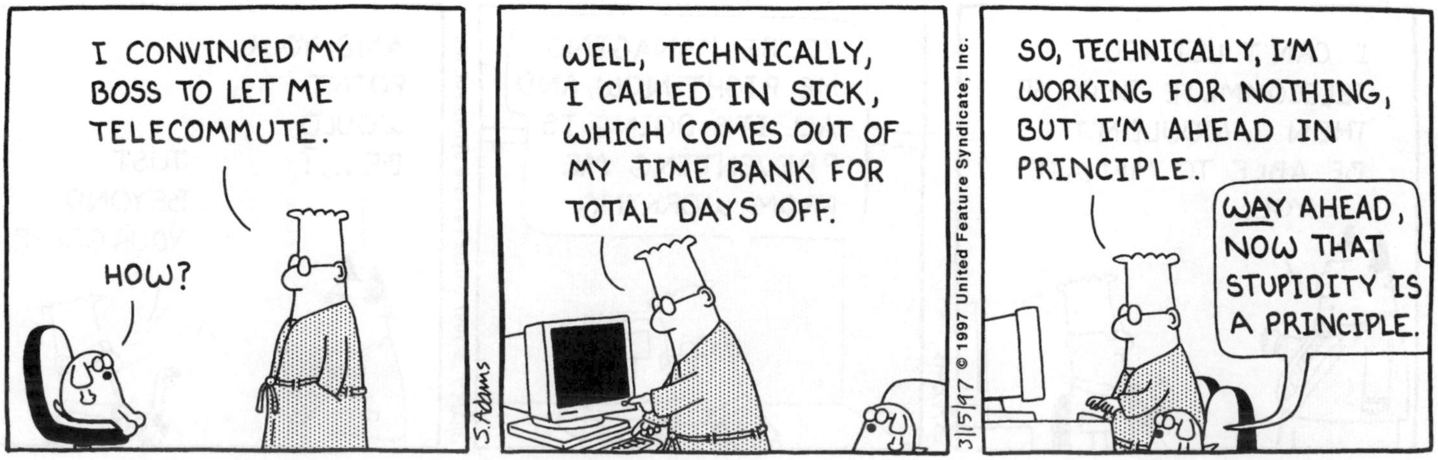
I CONVINCED MY BOSS TO LET ME TELECOMMUTE.
HOW?
WELL, TECHNICALLY, I CALLED IN SICK, WHICH COMES OUT OF MY TIME BANK FOR TOTAL DAYS OFF.
S. Adams
3/15/97 © 1997 United Feature Syndicate, Inc.
SO, TECHNICALLY, I'M WORKING FOR NOTHING, BUT I'M AHEAD IN PRINCIPLE.
WAY AHEAD, NOW THAT STUPIDITY IS A PRINCIPLE.

DILBERT

BY SCOTT ADAMS

Boss: YOU'LL LOVE YOUR NEW ASSIGNMENT, ALICE.

Alice (thought): UH-OH.

Boss: YOU'RE GOING TO REDESIGN ALL OF OUR BROCHURES!

Alice: I'M AN ELECTRICAL ENGINEER, NOT A GRAPHIC ARTIST.

Boss: WE CAN DISCUSS YOUR HUGE INADEQUACIES DURING YOUR ANNUAL REVIEW.

Alice: I'M NOT INADEQUATE. I'M A HIGHLY SKILLED ENGINEER.

Boss: AND YET YOU CAN'T MAKE BROCHURES.

Alice: OKAY, LET ME TRY TO EXPLAIN THIS IN THE SIMPLEST POSSIBLE WAY...

Alice: YOU...ARE...AN...IDIOT.

Alice (thought): THE SIMPLEST POSSIBLE EXPLANATION ISN'T ALWAYS THE BEST.

Wally: HEY, IT LOOKS LIKE A BROCHURE, ONLY UGLIER!

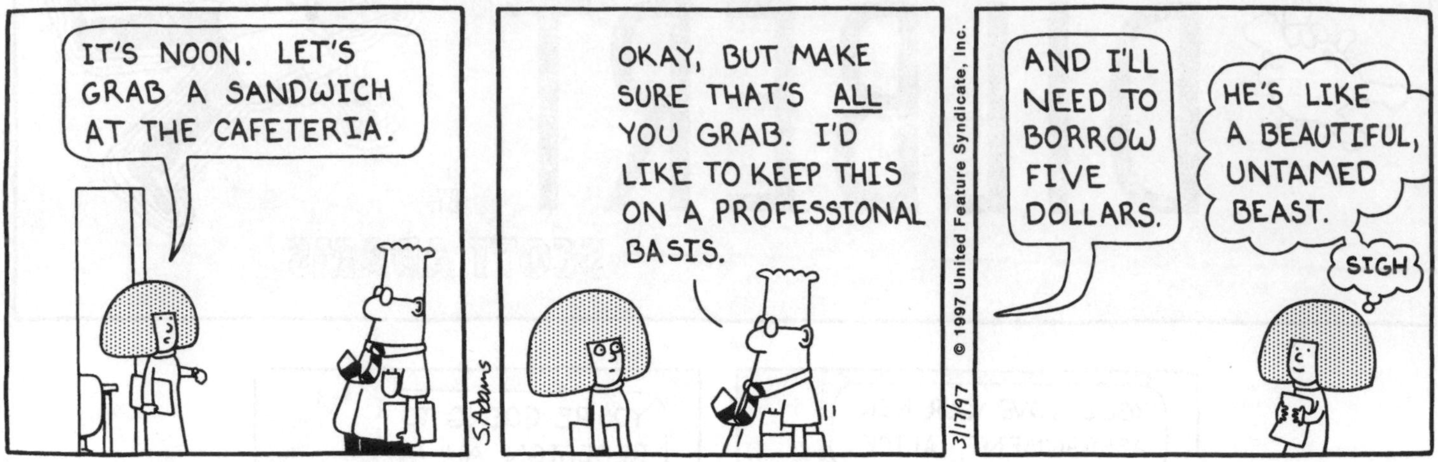
IT'S NOON. LET'S GRAB A SANDWICH AT THE CAFETERIA.
OKAY, BUT MAKE SURE THAT'S ALL YOU GRAB. I'D LIKE TO KEEP THIS ON A PROFESSIONAL BASIS.
AND I'LL NEED TO BORROW FIVE DOLLARS.
HE'S LIKE A BEAUTIFUL, UNTAMED BEAST.
SIGH
S.Adams
3/17/97
© 1997 United Feature Syndicate, Inc.

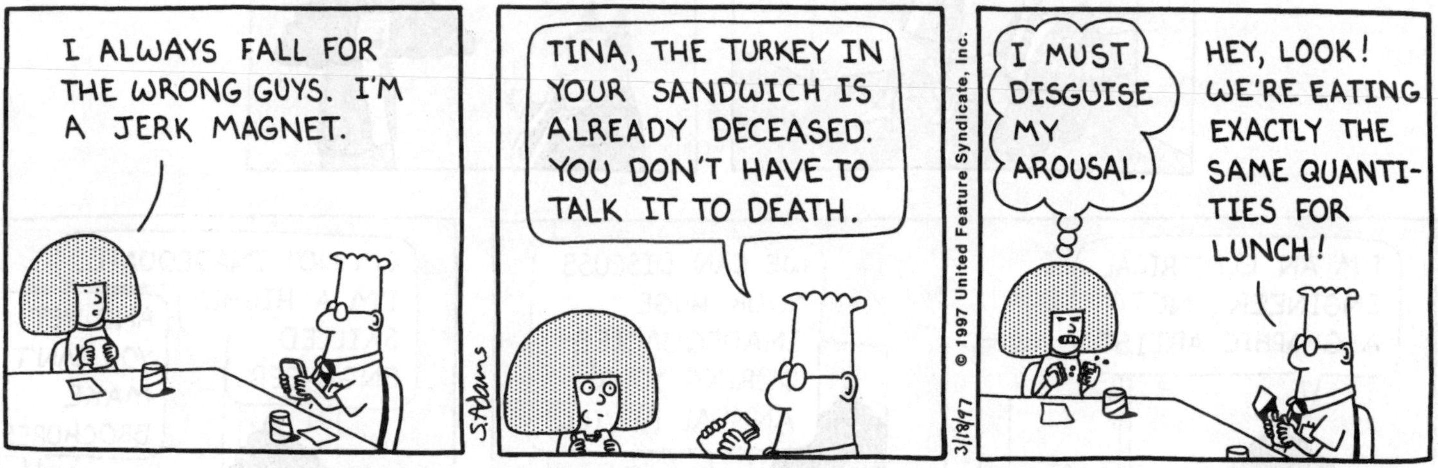
I ALWAYS FALL FOR THE WRONG GUYS. I'M A JERK MAGNET.
TINA, THE TURKEY IN YOUR SANDWICH IS ALREADY DECEASED. YOU DON'T HAVE TO TALK IT TO DEATH.
I MUST DISGUISE MY AROUSAL.
HEY, LOOK! WE'RE EATING EXACTLY THE SAME QUANTITIES FOR LUNCH!
S.Adams
3/18/97
© 1997 United Feature Syndicate, Inc.

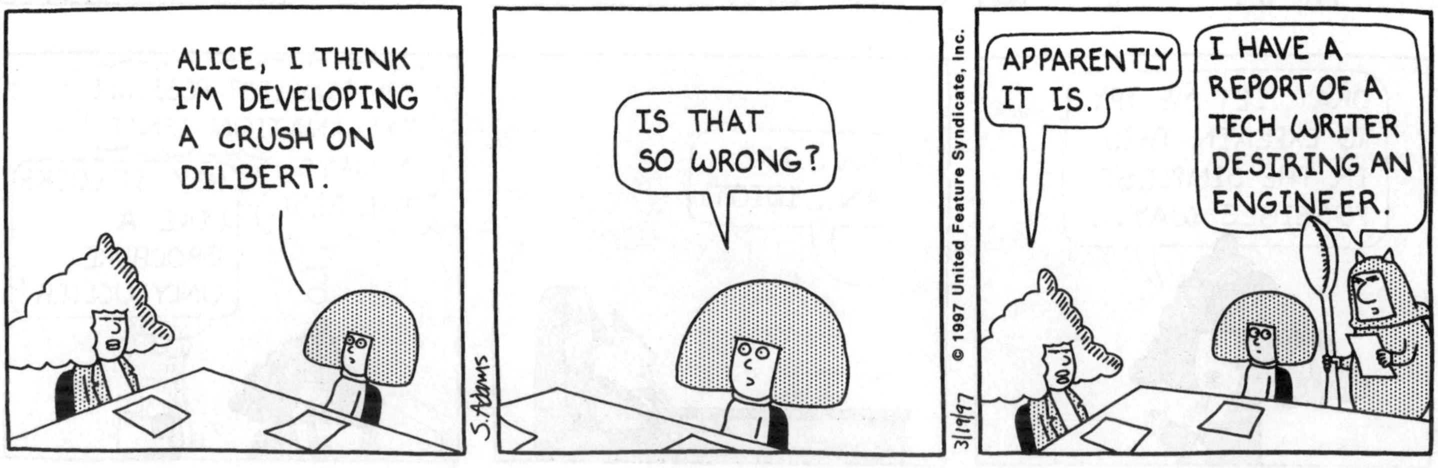
ALICE, I THINK I'M DEVELOPING A CRUSH ON DILBERT.
IS THAT SO WRONG?
APPARENTLY IT IS.
I HAVE A REPORT OF A TECH WRITER DESIRING AN ENGINEER.
S.Adams
3/19/97
© 1997 United Feature Syndicate, Inc.

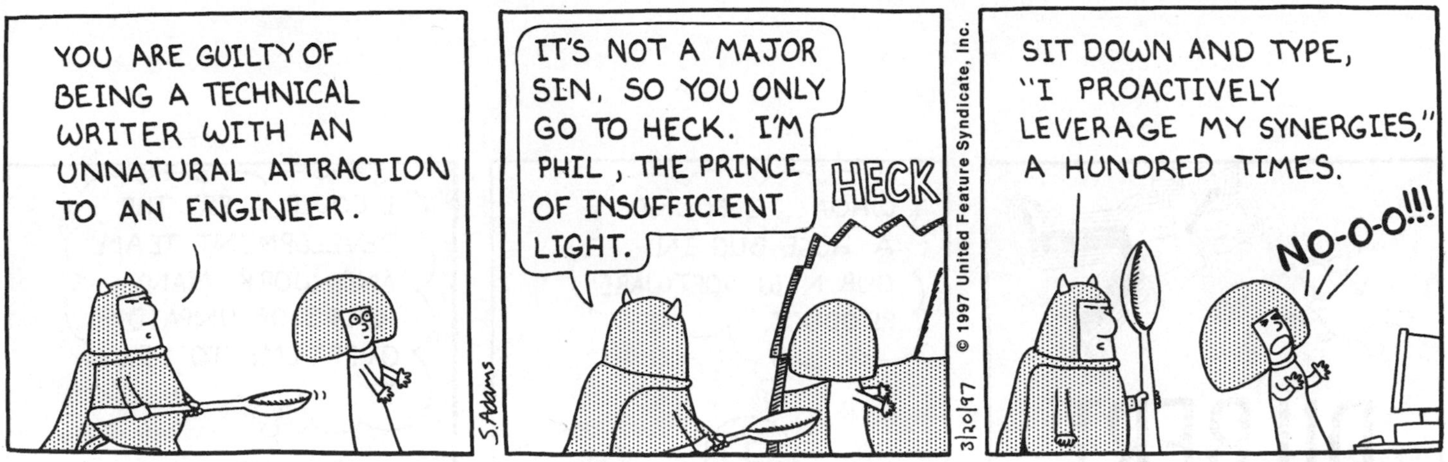
YOU ARE GUILTY OF BEING A TECHNICAL WRITER WITH AN UNNATURAL ATTRACTION TO AN ENGINEER.
S. Adams
IT'S NOT A MAJOR SIN, SO YOU ONLY GO TO HECK. I'M PHIL, THE PRINCE OF INSUFFICIENT LIGHT.
HECK
3/20/97 © 1997 United Feature Syndicate, Inc.
SIT DOWN AND TYPE, "I PROACTIVELY LEVERAGE MY SYNERGIES," A HUNDRED TIMES.
NO-O-O!!!

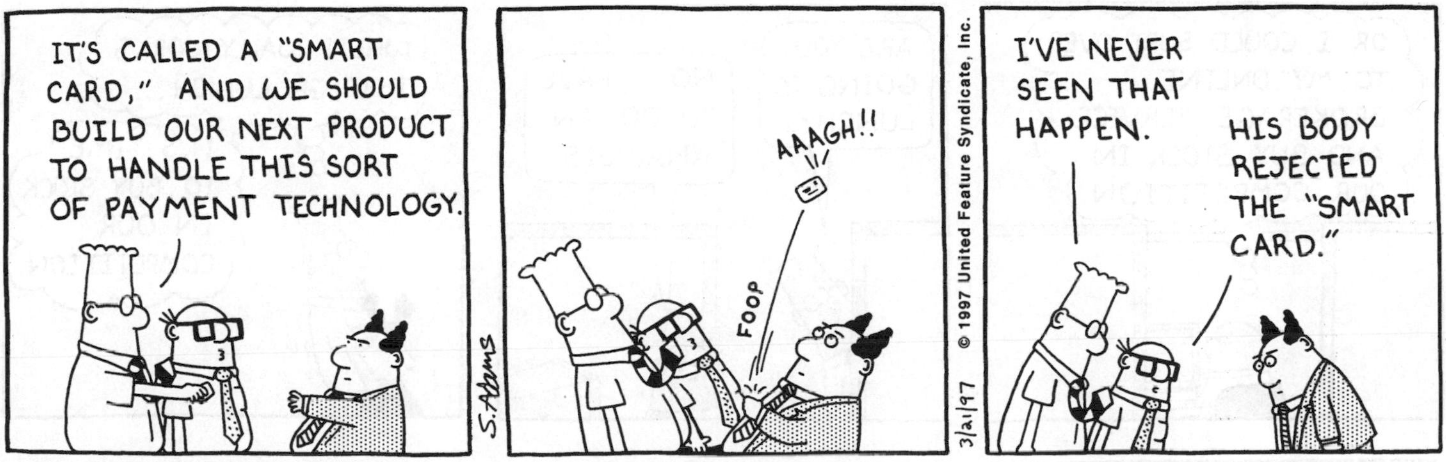
IT'S CALLED A "SMART CARD," AND WE SHOULD BUILD OUR NEXT PRODUCT TO HANDLE THIS SORT OF PAYMENT TECHNOLOGY.
S. Adams
AAAGH!!
FOOP
3/21/97 © 1997 United Feature Syndicate, Inc.
I'VE NEVER SEEN THAT HAPPEN.
HIS BODY REJECTED THE "SMART CARD."

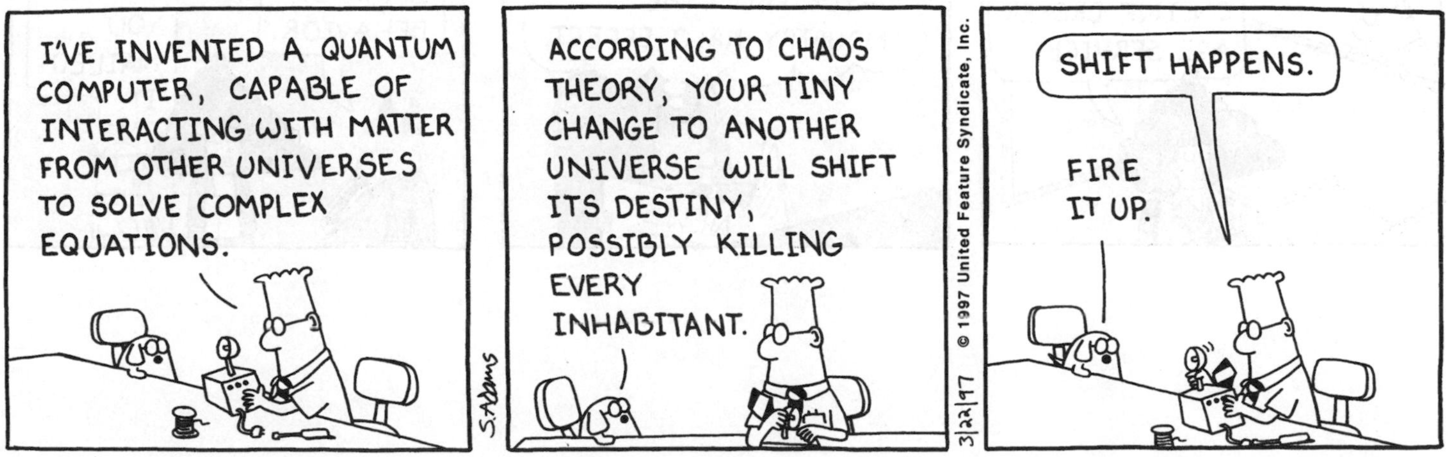
I'VE INVENTED A QUANTUM COMPUTER, CAPABLE OF INTERACTING WITH MATTER FROM OTHER UNIVERSES TO SOLVE COMPLEX EQUATIONS.
S. Adams
ACCORDING TO CHAOS THEORY, YOUR TINY CHANGE TO ANOTHER UNIVERSE WILL SHIFT ITS DESTINY, POSSIBLY KILLING EVERY INHABITANT.
3/22/97 © 1997 United Feature Syndicate, Inc.
FIRE IT UP.
SHIFT HAPPENS.

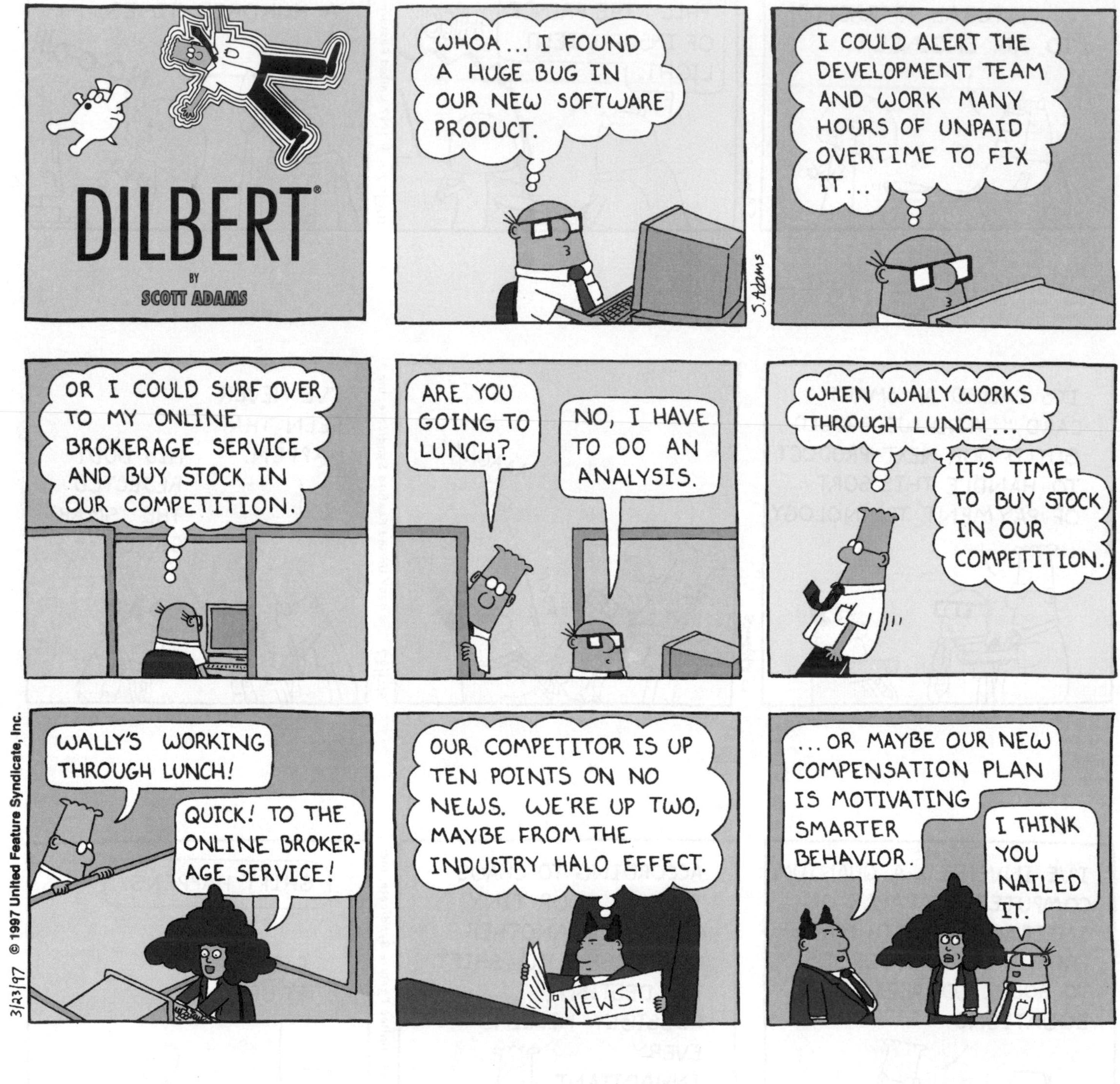
DILBERT®
BY
SCOTT ADAMS
WHOA... I FOUND A HUGE BUG IN OUR NEW SOFTWARE PRODUCT.
S. Adams
I COULD ALERT THE DEVELOPMENT TEAM AND WORK MANY HOURS OF UNPAID OVERTIME TO FIX IT...
OR I COULD SURF OVER TO MY ONLINE BROKERAGE SERVICE AND BUY STOCK IN OUR COMPETITION.
ARE YOU GOING TO LUNCH?
NO, I HAVE TO DO AN ANALYSIS.
WHEN WALLY WORKS THROUGH LUNCH...
IT'S TIME TO BUY STOCK IN OUR COMPETITION.
WALLY'S WORKING THROUGH LUNCH!
QUICK! TO THE ONLINE BROKER-AGE SERVICE!
OUR COMPETITOR IS UP TEN POINTS ON NO NEWS. WE'RE UP TWO, MAYBE FROM THE INDUSTRY HALO EFFECT.
NEWS!
...OR MAYBE OUR NEW COMPENSATION PLAN IS MOTIVATING SMARTER BEHAVIOR.
I THINK YOU NAILED IT.
3/23/97 © 1997 United Feature Syndicate, Inc.

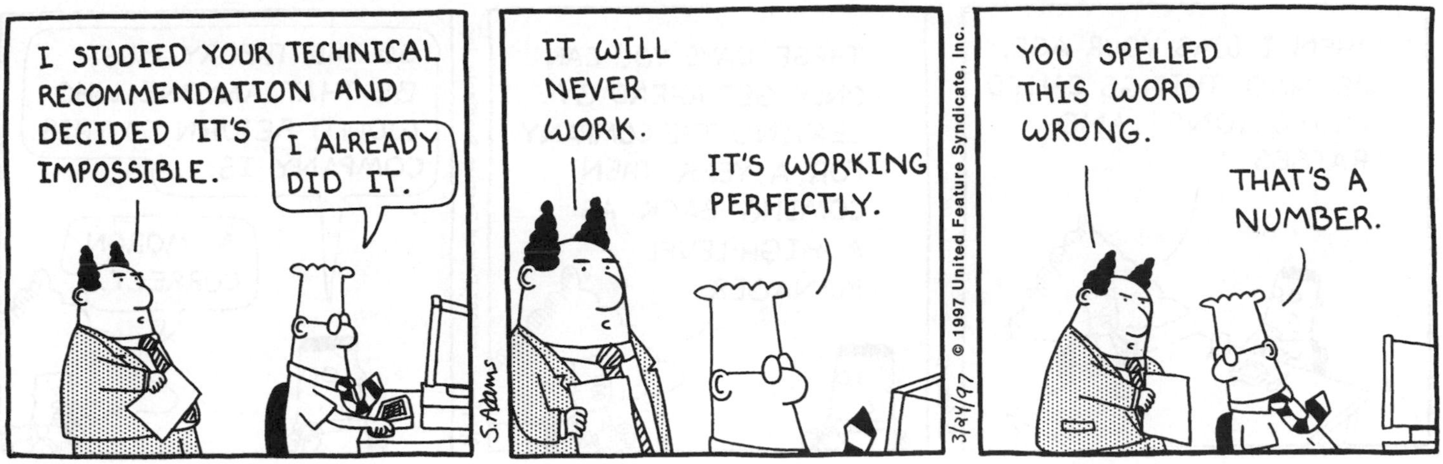
I STUDIED YOUR TECHNICAL RECOMMENDATION AND DECIDED IT'S IMPOSSIBLE.
I ALREADY DID IT.
IT WILL NEVER WORK.
IT'S WORKING PERFECTLY.
YOU SPELLED THIS WORD WRONG.
THAT'S A NUMBER.
S. Adams
3/24/97
© 1997 United Feature Syndicate, Inc.

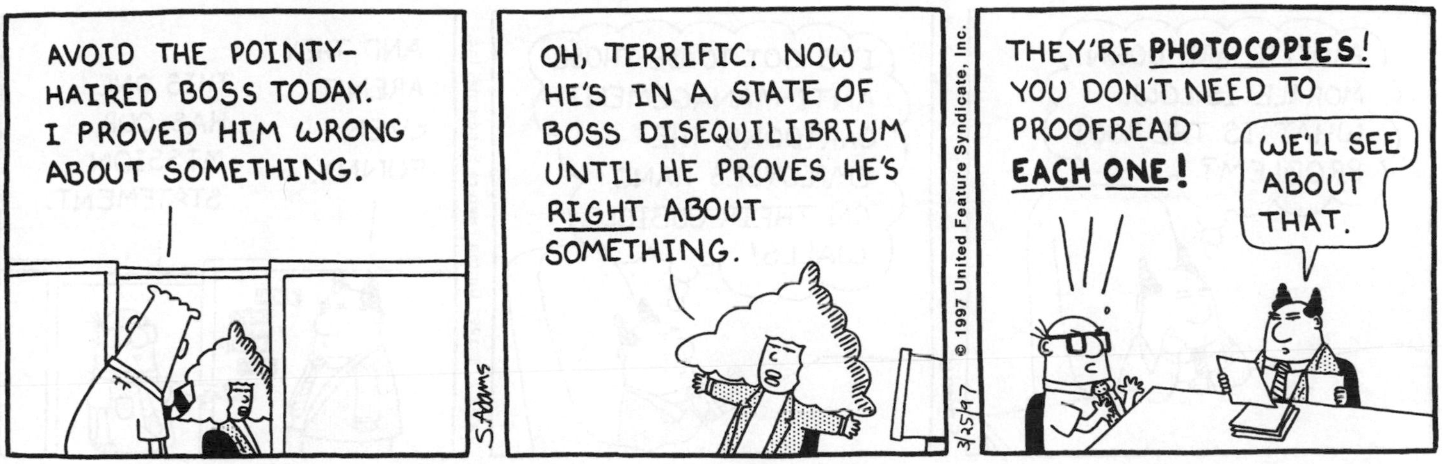
AVOID THE POINTY-HAIRED BOSS TODAY. I PROVED HIM WRONG ABOUT SOMETHING.
OH, TERRIFIC. NOW HE'S IN A STATE OF BOSS DISEQUILIBRIUM UNTIL HE PROVES HE'S RIGHT ABOUT SOMETHING.
THEY'RE PHOTOCOPIES! YOU DON'T NEED TO PROOFREAD EACH ONE!
WE'LL SEE ABOUT THAT.
S. Adams
3/25/97
© 1997 United Feature Syndicate, Inc.

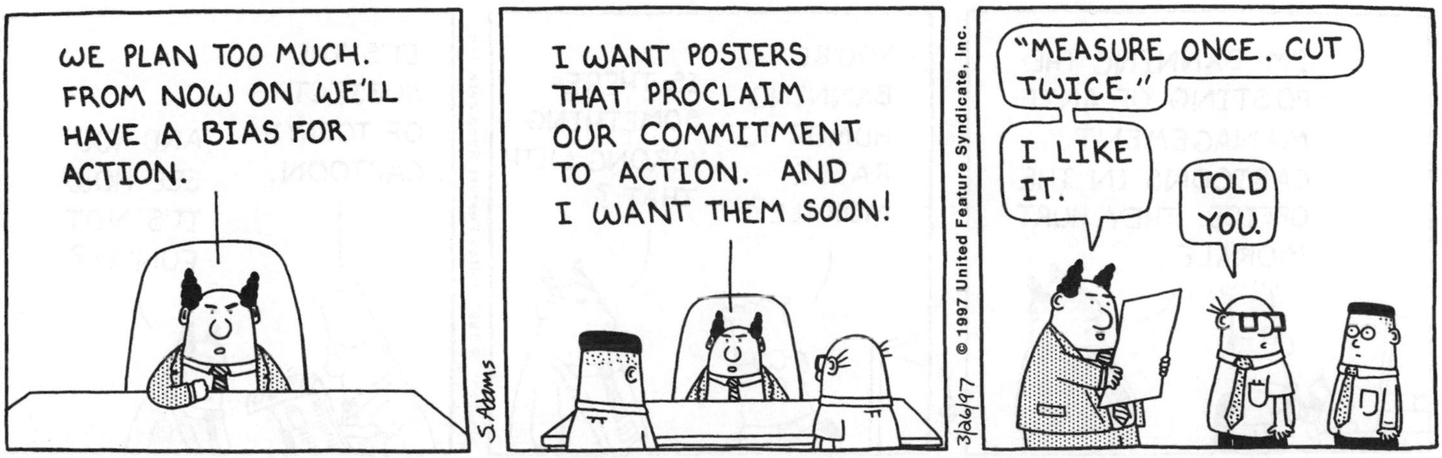
WE PLAN TOO MUCH. FROM NOW ON WE'LL HAVE A BIAS FOR ACTION.
I WANT POSTERS THAT PROCLAIM OUR COMMITMENT TO ACTION. AND I WANT THEM SOON!
"MEASURE ONCE. CUT TWICE."
I LIKE IT.
TOLD YOU.
S. Adams
3/26/97
© 1997 United Feature Syndicate, Inc.

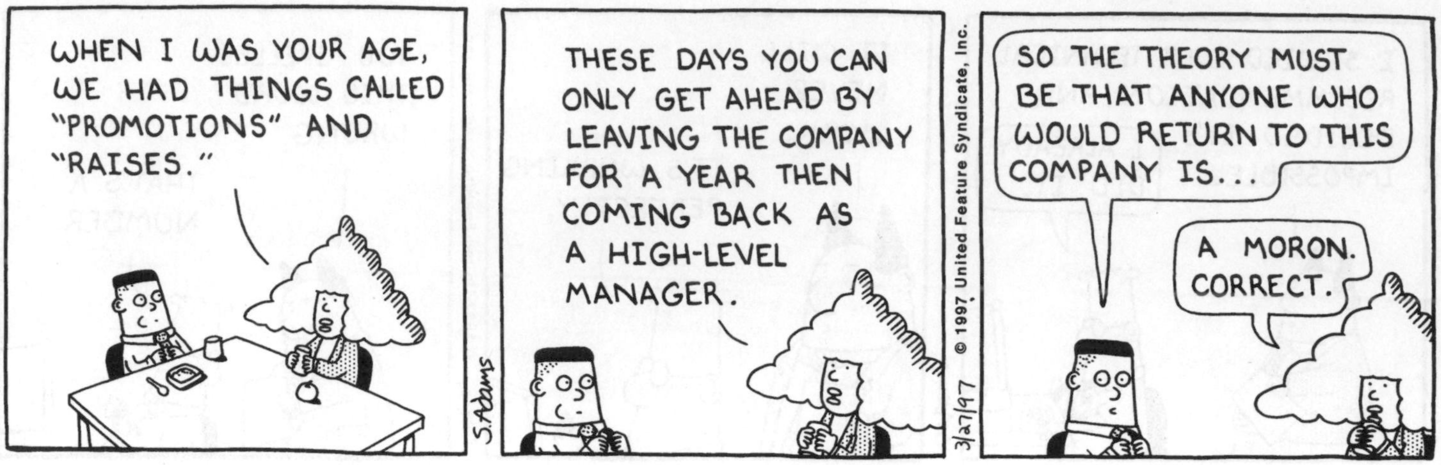
WHEN I WAS YOUR AGE, WE HAD THINGS CALLED "PROMOTIONS" AND "RAISES."
THESE DAYS YOU CAN ONLY GET AHEAD BY LEAVING THE COMPANY FOR A YEAR THEN COMING BACK AS A HIGH-LEVEL MANAGER.
SO THE THEORY MUST BE THAT ANYONE WHO WOULD RETURN TO THIS COMPANY IS...
A MORON. CORRECT.
S.Adams
3/27/97 © 1997 United Feature Syndicate, Inc.

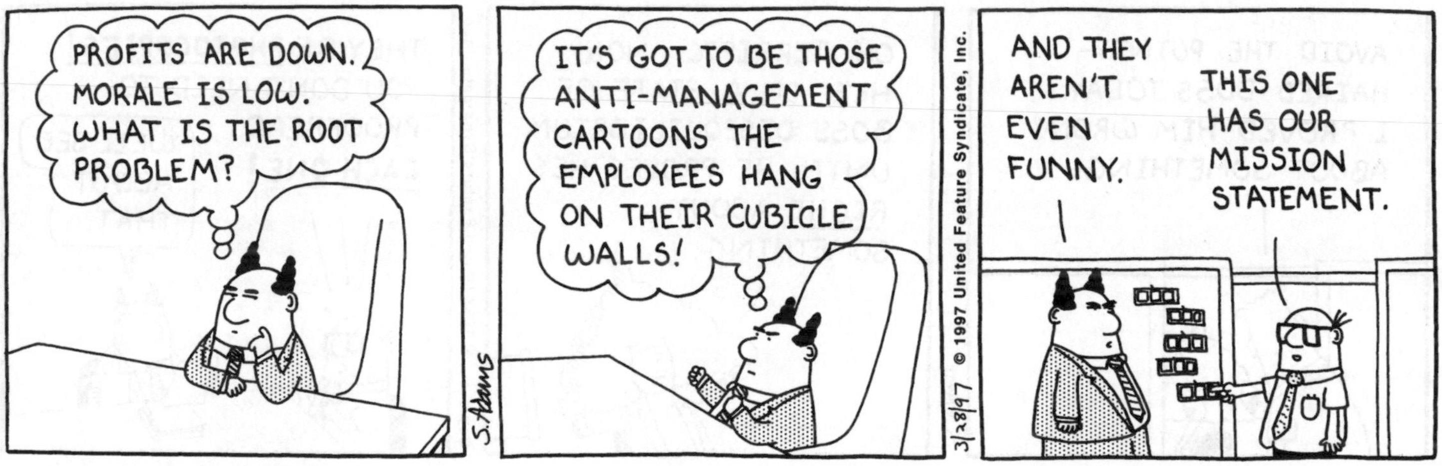
PROFITS ARE DOWN. MORALE IS LOW. WHAT IS THE ROOT PROBLEM?
IT'S GOT TO BE THOSE ANTI-MANAGEMENT CARTOONS THE EMPLOYEES HANG ON THEIR CUBICLE WALLS!
AND THEY AREN'T EVEN FUNNY.
THIS ONE HAS OUR MISSION STATEMENT.
S.Adams
3/28/97 © 1997 United Feature Syndicate, Inc.

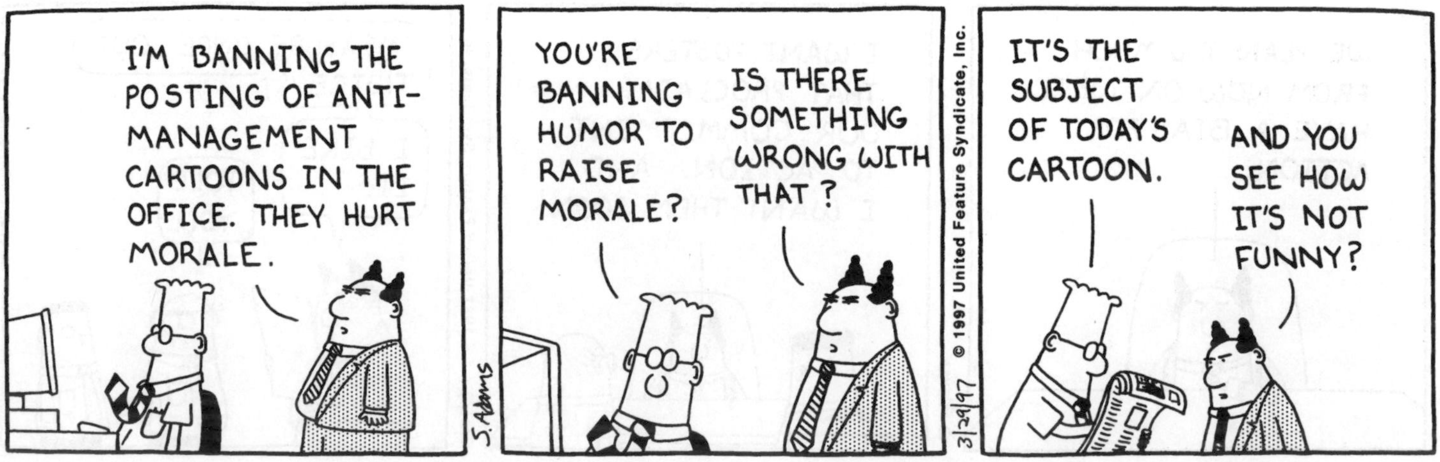
I'M BANNING THE POSTING OF ANTI-MANAGEMENT CARTOONS IN THE OFFICE. THEY HURT MORALE.
YOU'RE BANNING HUMOR TO RAISE MORALE?
IS THERE SOMETHING WRONG WITH THAT?
IT'S THE SUBJECT OF TODAY'S CARTOON.
AND YOU SEE HOW IT'S NOT FUNNY?
S.Adams
3/29/97 © 1997 United Feature Syndicate, Inc.

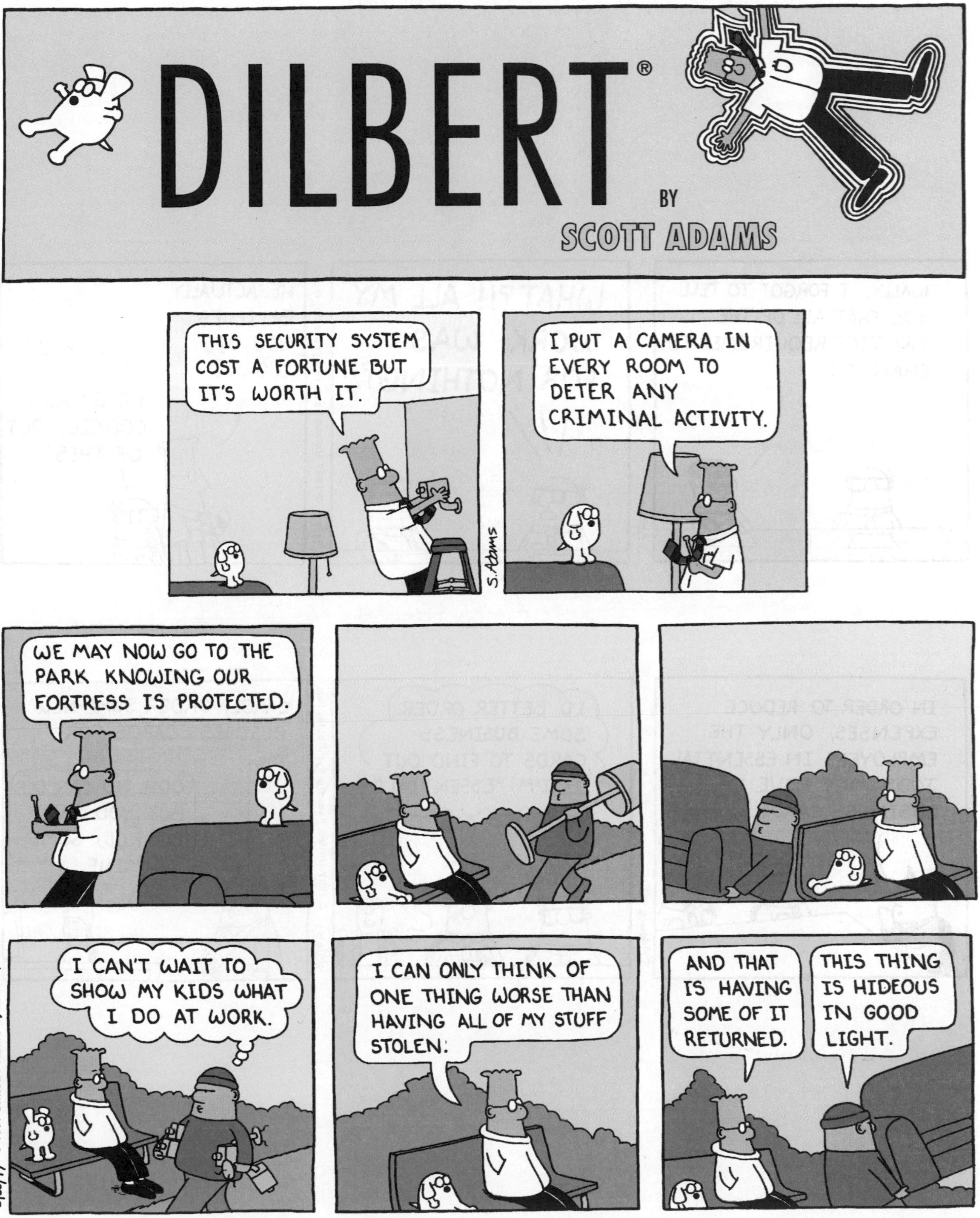
DILBERT®
BY
SCOTT ADAMS
THIS SECURITY SYSTEM COST A FORTUNE BUT IT'S WORTH IT.
S. Adams
I PUT A CAMERA IN EVERY ROOM TO DETER ANY CRIMINAL ACTIVITY.
WE MAY NOW GO TO THE PARK KNOWING OUR FORTRESS IS PROTECTED.
I CAN'T WAIT TO SHOW MY KIDS WHAT I DO AT WORK.
I CAN ONLY THINK OF ONE THING WORSE THAN HAVING ALL OF MY STUFF STOLEN:
AND THAT IS HAVING SOME OF IT RETURNED.
THIS THING IS HIDEOUS IN GOOD LIGHT.

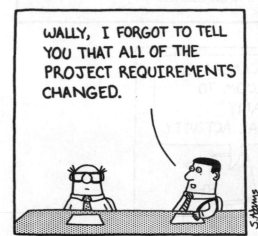

WALLY, I FORGOT TO TELL YOU THAT ALL OF THE PROJECT REQUIREMENTS CHANGED.
WHAT?!! ALL MY WORK WAS FOR NOTHING?!!
HE ACTUALLY BELIEVES YOU DID WORK?
I THINK I'LL GET SOME HOMEMADE COOKIES OUT OF THIS!
S. Adams
3/31/97
© 1997 United Feature Syndicate, Inc.

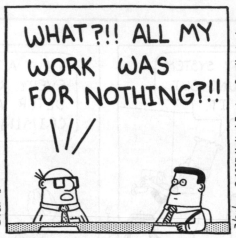

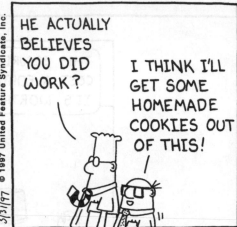

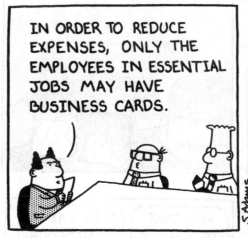

IN ORDER TO REDUCE EXPENSES, ONLY THE EMPLOYEES IN ESSENTIAL JOBS MAY HAVE BUSINESS CARDS.
I'D BETTER ORDER SOME BUSINESS CARDS TO FIND OUT IF I'M "ESSENTIAL."
CAROL, ORDER SOME NEW BUSINESS CARDS FOR ME.
OOH. NO CAN DO. BUT YOU CAN BORROW SOME OF MINE.
S. Adams
4/2/97
© 1997 United Feature Syndicate, Inc.

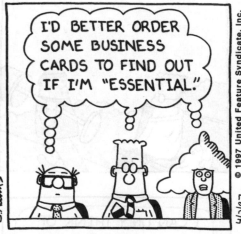

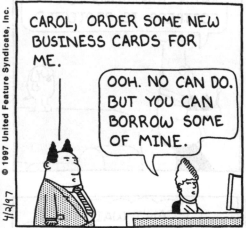

HEY, DILBERT! YOU'LL NEVER BE HUNGRY AS LONG AS YOU'RE WORKIN' IN THIS STRIP...
...'CAUSE YOU'RE SURE OF THREE SQUARES EVERY DAY!
SOME OF US HAFTA KEEP GOIN' AROUND IN CIRCLES!
-SECURITY?
© 1997 United Feature Syndicate, Inc.
4/1/97
BIL KEANE
FAMILY CIRCUS

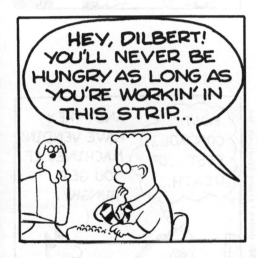

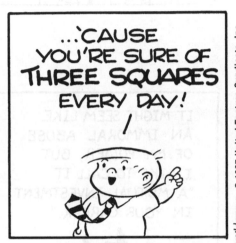

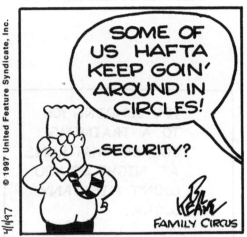

Editor's Note: On April Fool's Day, 1997, 46 syndicated cartoonists perpetrated a great hoax on newspaper comics readers by swapping strips for the day. One result was the above *Dilbert* strip. Scott Adams said of the swap-fest, "I think it was Nostradamus who predicted that when Pat Boone sings heavy metal and Bil Keane [*Family Circus*] draws *Dilbert*, it's a sign of the approaching apocalypse." (We say, "Duck!")

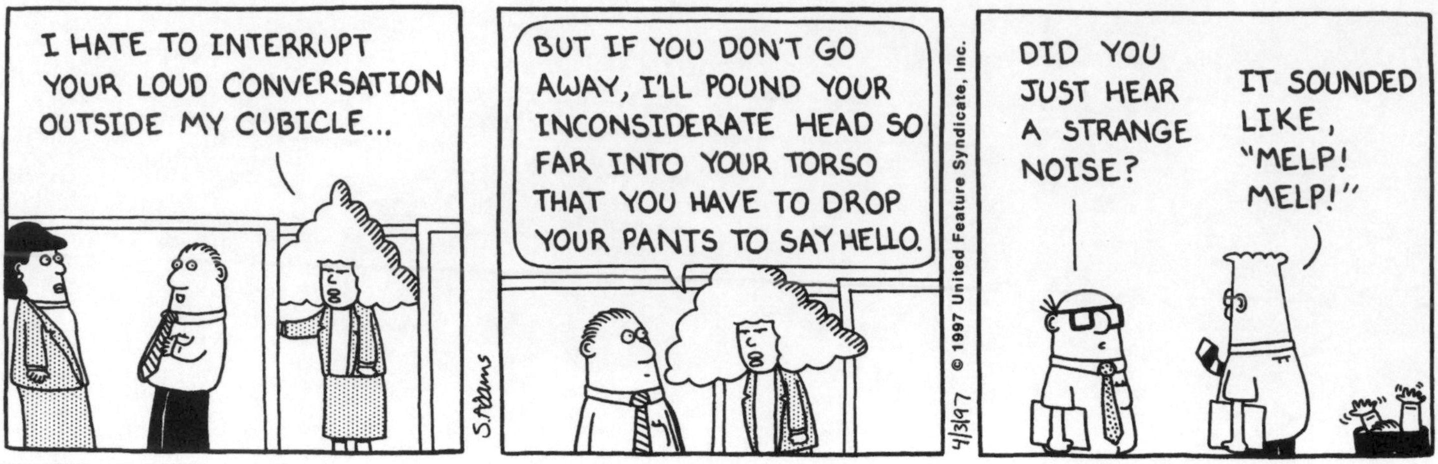
I HATE TO INTERRUPT YOUR LOUD CONVERSATION OUTSIDE MY CUBICLE...
BUT IF YOU DON'T GO AWAY, I'LL POUND YOUR INCONSIDERATE HEAD SO FAR INTO YOUR TORSO THAT YOU HAVE TO DROP YOUR PANTS TO SAY HELLO.
S.Adams
4/3/97
© 1997 United Feature Syndicate, Inc.
DID YOU JUST HEAR A STRANGE NOISE?
IT SOUNDED LIKE, "MELP! MELP!"

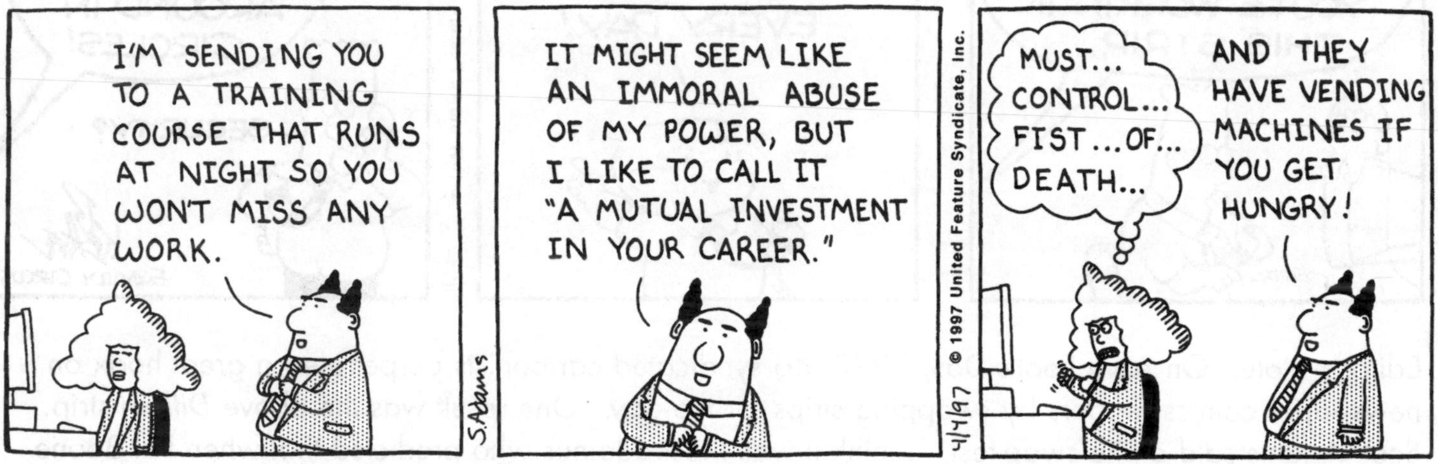
I'M SENDING YOU TO A TRAINING COURSE THAT RUNS AT NIGHT SO YOU WON'T MISS ANY WORK.
IT MIGHT SEEM LIKE AN IMMORAL ABUSE OF MY POWER, BUT I LIKE TO CALL IT "A MUTUAL INVESTMENT IN YOUR CAREER."
S.Adams
4/4/97
© 1997 United Feature Syndicate, Inc.
MUST... CONTROL... FIST... OF... DEATH...
AND THEY HAVE VENDING MACHINES IF YOU GET HUNGRY!

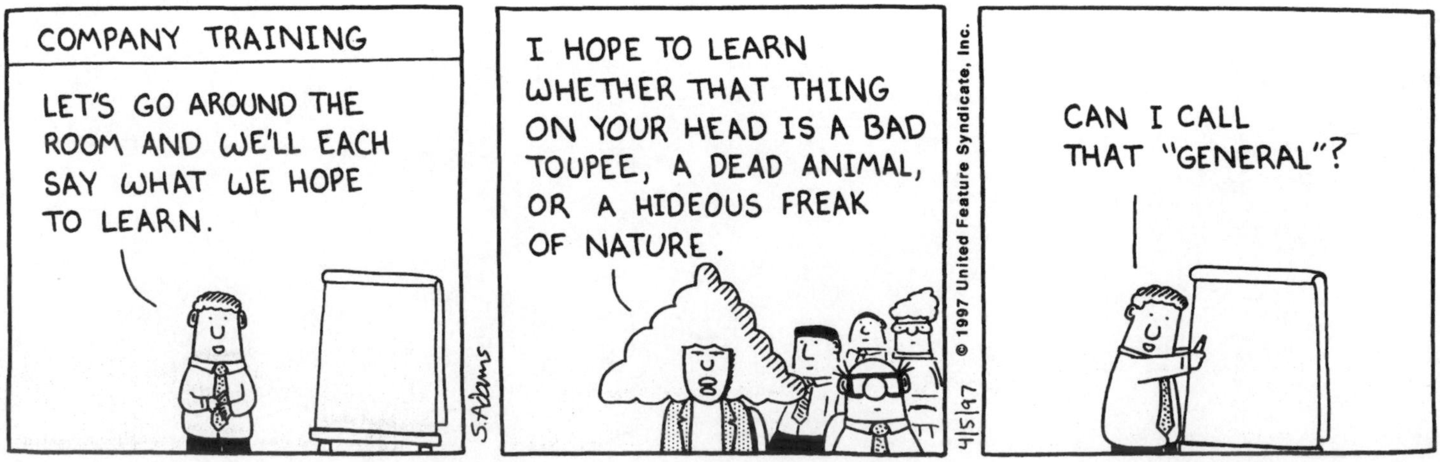
COMPANY TRAINING
LET'S GO AROUND THE ROOM AND WE'LL EACH SAY WHAT WE HOPE TO LEARN.
I HOPE TO LEARN WHETHER THAT THING ON YOUR HEAD IS A BAD TOUPEE, A DEAD ANIMAL, OR A HIDEOUS FREAK OF NATURE.
S.Adams
4/5/97
© 1997 United Feature Syndicate, Inc.
CAN I CALL THAT "GENERAL"?

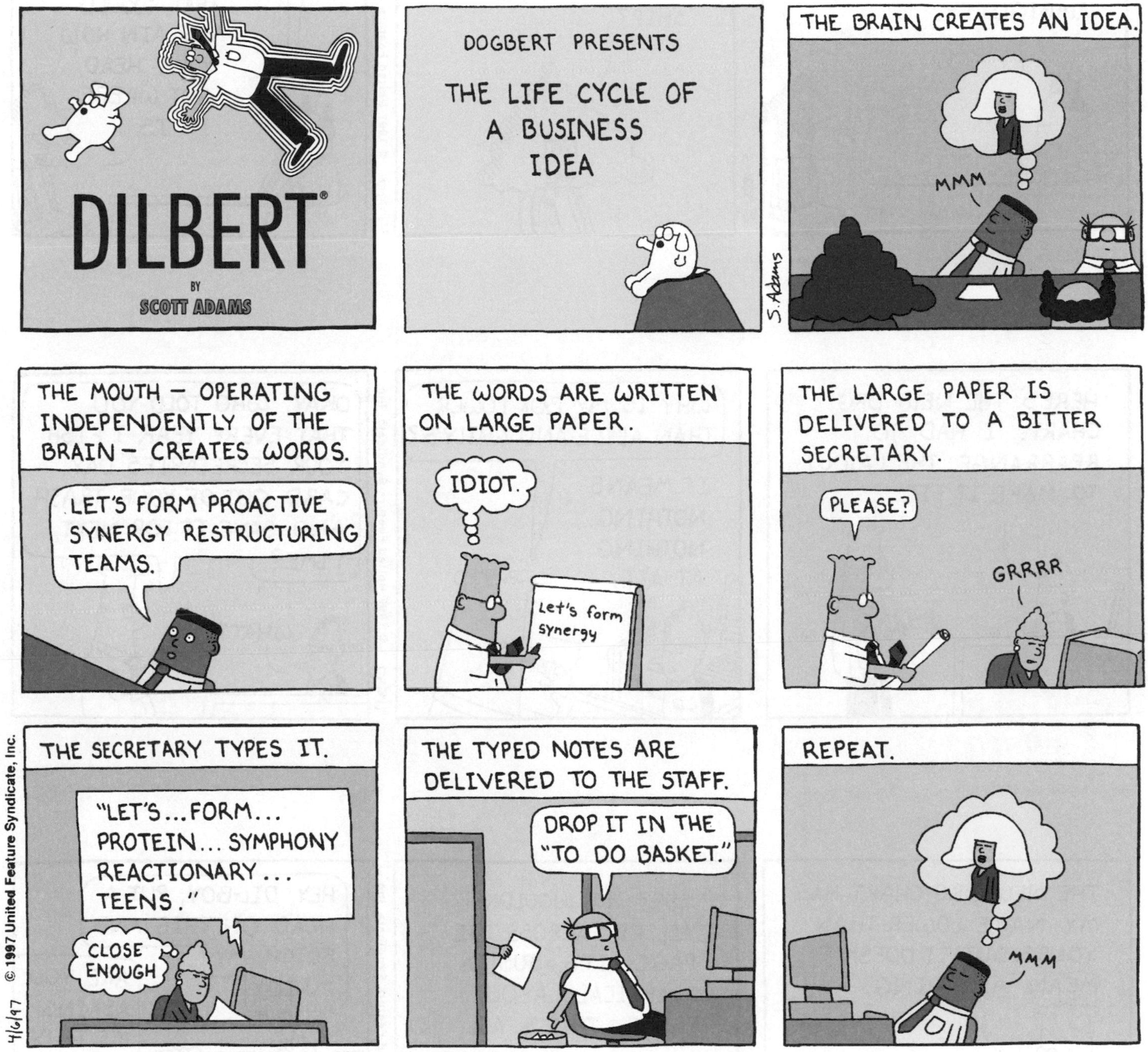
DILBERT®
BY
SCOTT ADAMS
DOGBERT PRESENTS
THE LIFE CYCLE OF A BUSINESS IDEA
THE BRAIN CREATES AN IDEA.
MMM
S. Adams
THE MOUTH — OPERATING INDEPENDENTLY OF THE BRAIN — CREATES WORDS.
LET'S FORM PROACTIVE SYNERGY RESTRUCTURING TEAMS.
THE WORDS ARE WRITTEN ON LARGE PAPER.
IDIOT.
Let's form synergy
THE LARGE PAPER IS DELIVERED TO A BITTER SECRETARY.
PLEASE?
GRRRR
THE SECRETARY TYPES IT.
"LET'S... FORM... PROTEIN... SYMPHONY REACTIONARY... TEENS."
CLOSE ENOUGH
THE TYPED NOTES ARE DELIVERED TO THE STAFF.
DROP IT IN THE "TO DO BASKET."
REPEAT.
MMM
4/6/97 © 1997 United Feature Syndicate, Inc.

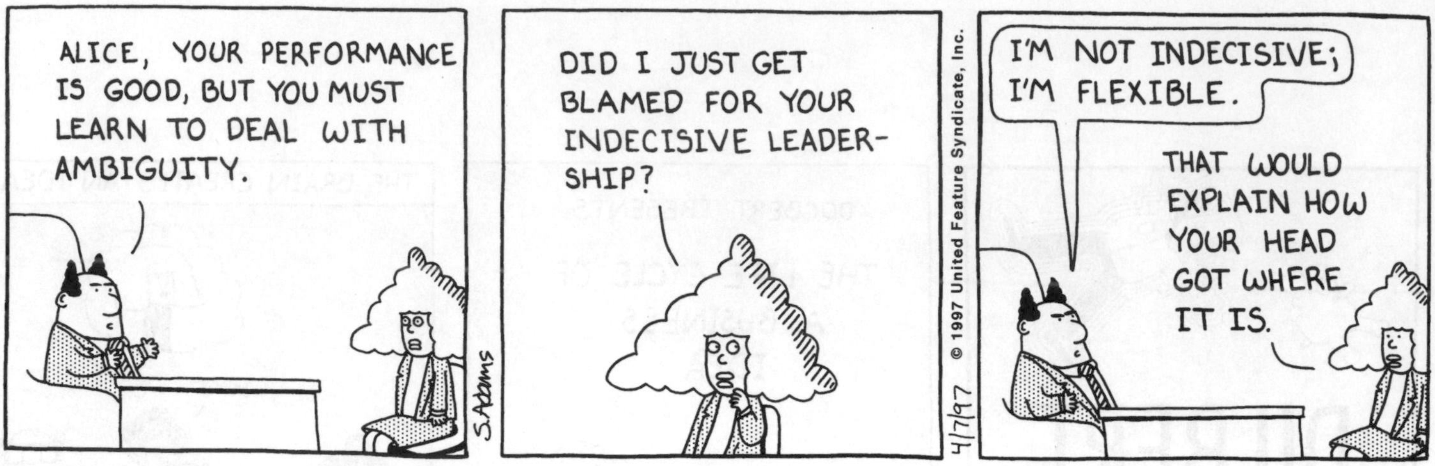
ALICE, YOUR PERFORMANCE IS GOOD, BUT YOU MUST LEARN TO DEAL WITH AMBIGUITY.
DID I JUST GET BLAMED FOR YOUR INDECISIVE LEADERSHIP?
I'M NOT INDECISIVE; I'M FLEXIBLE.
THAT WOULD EXPLAIN HOW YOUR HEAD GOT WHERE IT IS.
S. Adams
4/7/97
© 1997 United Feature Syndicate, Inc.

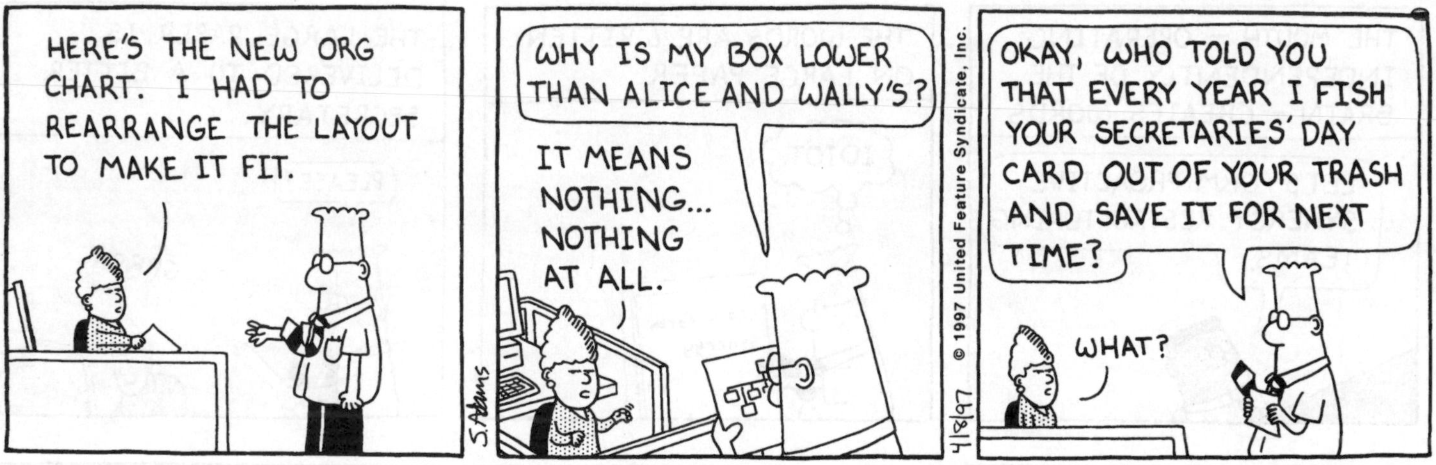
HERE'S THE NEW ORG CHART. I HAD TO REARRANGE THE LAYOUT TO MAKE IT FIT.
WHY IS MY BOX LOWER THAN ALICE AND WALLY'S?
IT MEANS NOTHING... NOTHING AT ALL.
OKAY, WHO TOLD YOU THAT EVERY YEAR I FISH YOUR SECRETARIES' DAY CARD OUT OF YOUR TRASH AND SAVE IT FOR NEXT TIME?
WHAT?
S. Adams
4/8/97
© 1997 United Feature Syndicate, Inc.

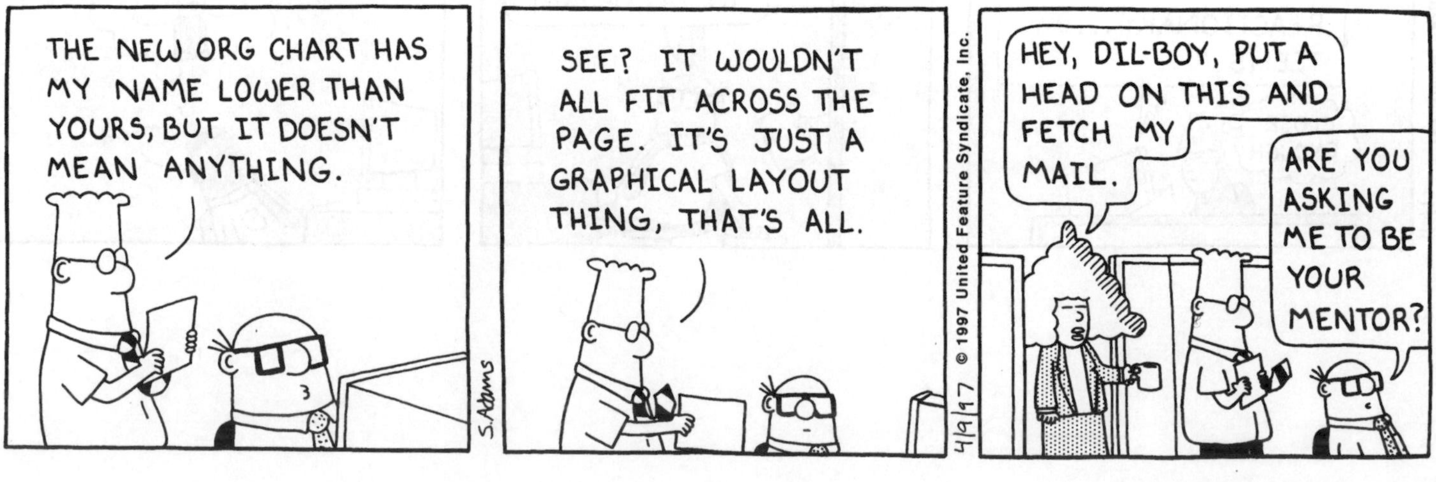
THE NEW ORG CHART HAS MY NAME LOWER THAN YOURS, BUT IT DOESN'T MEAN ANYTHING.
SEE? IT WOULDN'T ALL FIT ACROSS THE PAGE. IT'S JUST A GRAPHICAL LAYOUT THING, THAT'S ALL.
HEY, DIL-BOY, PUT A HEAD ON THIS AND FETCH MY MAIL.
ARE YOU ASKING ME TO BE YOUR MENTOR?
S. Adams
4/9/97
© 1997 United Feature Syndicate, Inc.

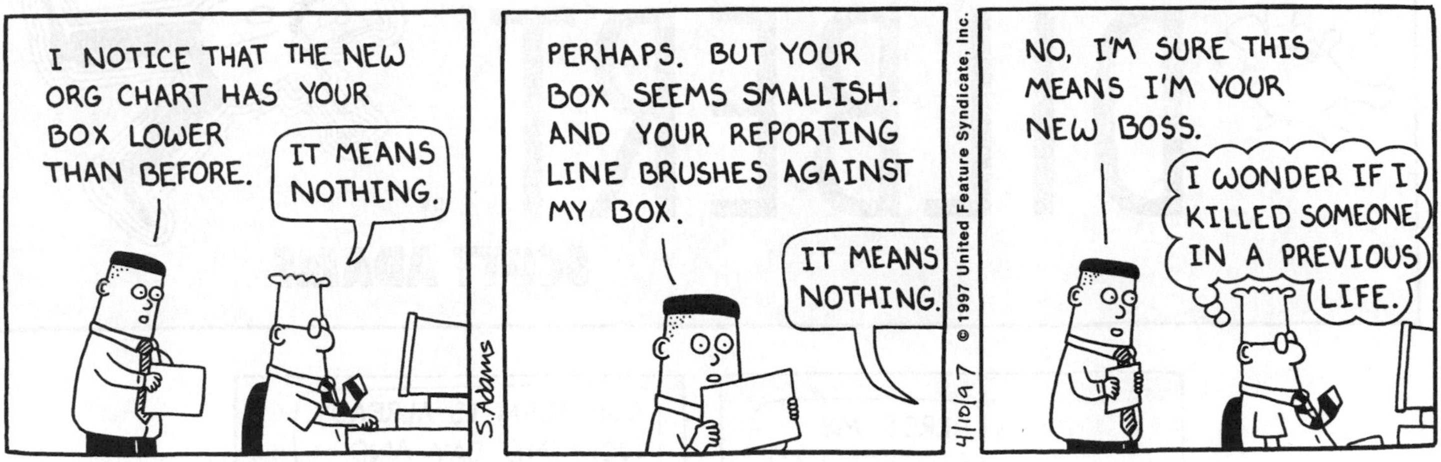
I NOTICE THAT THE NEW ORG CHART HAS YOUR BOX LOWER THAN BEFORE.
IT MEANS NOTHING.
S. Adams
PERHAPS. BUT YOUR BOX SEEMS SMALLISH. AND YOUR REPORTING LINE BRUSHES AGAINST MY BOX.
IT MEANS NOTHING.
4/10/97 © 1997 United Feature Syndicate, Inc.
NO, I'M SURE THIS MEANS I'M YOUR NEW BOSS.
I WONDER IF I KILLED SOMEONE IN A PREVIOUS LIFE.

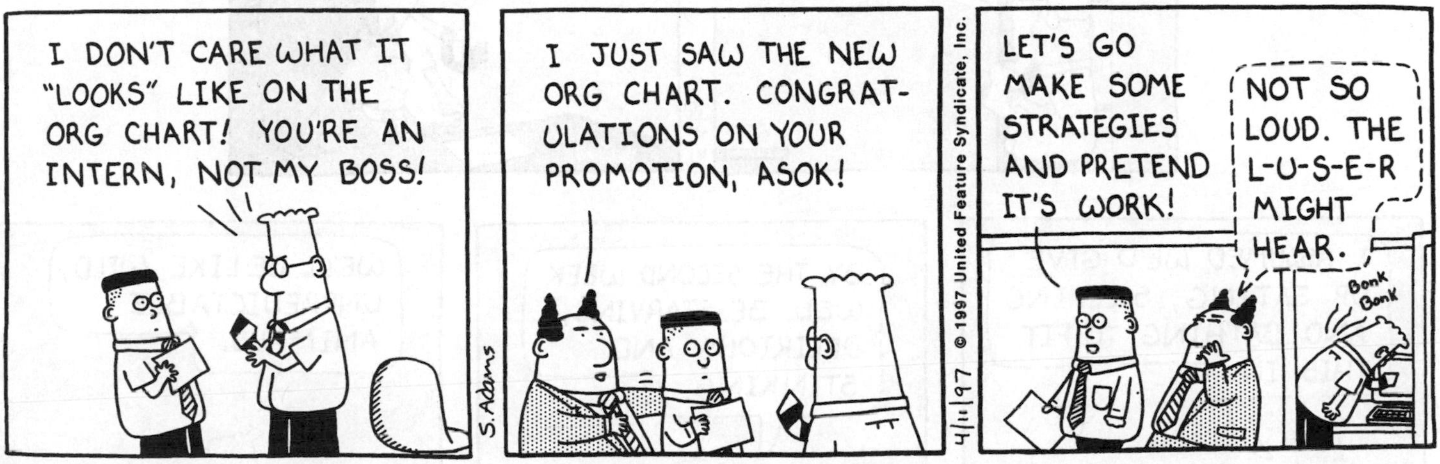
I DON'T CARE WHAT IT "LOOKS" LIKE ON THE ORG CHART! YOU'RE AN INTERN, NOT MY BOSS!
S. Adams
I JUST SAW THE NEW ORG CHART. CONGRATULATIONS ON YOUR PROMOTION, ASOK!
4/11/97 © 1997 United Feature Syndicate, Inc.
LET'S GO MAKE SOME STRATEGIES AND PRETEND IT'S WORK!
NOT SO LOUD. THE L-U-S-E-R MIGHT HEAR.
Bonk Bonk

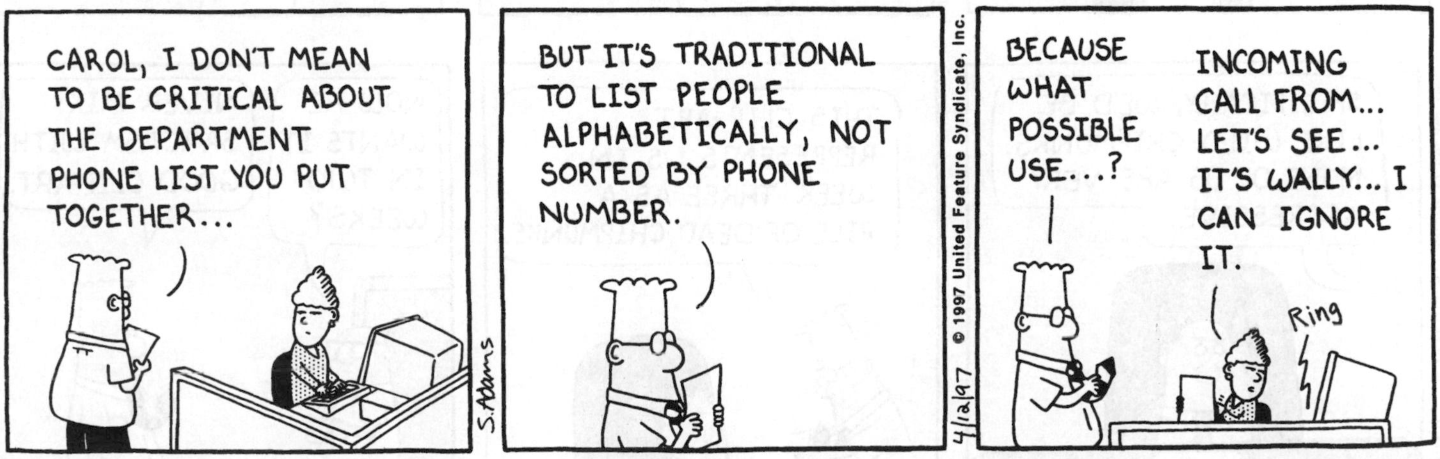
CAROL, I DON'T MEAN TO BE CRITICAL ABOUT THE DEPARTMENT PHONE LIST YOU PUT TOGETHER...
S. Adams
BUT IT'S TRADITIONAL TO LIST PEOPLE ALPHABETICALLY, NOT SORTED BY PHONE NUMBER.
4/12/97 © 1997 United Feature Syndicate, Inc.
BECAUSE WHAT POSSIBLE USE...?
INCOMING CALL FROM... LET'S SEE... IT'S WALLY... I CAN IGNORE IT.
Ring

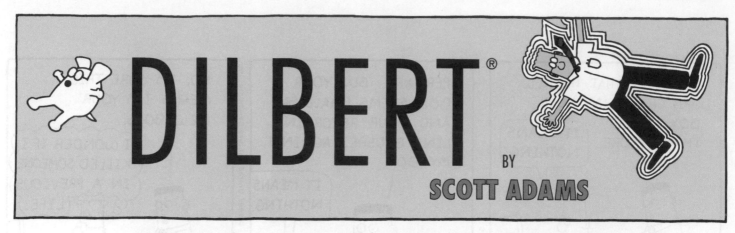

DILBERT®

BY **SCOTT ADAMS**

HERE'S MY PROJECT PLAN AS YOU REQUESTED.

OUR TEAM IS ALREADY WORKING DAY AND NIGHT ON OTHER PROJECTS.

I ASSUMED WE'D GIVE UP EATING, SLEEPING AND BATHING TO FIT THIS IN.

BY THE SECOND WEEK WE'LL BE STARVING, DELIRIOUS AND STINKING.

WE'LL BE LIKE WILD, UNPREDICTABLE ANIMALS.

SPECIFICALLY, WE'D BE LIKE WILD CHIPMUNKS. NONE OF US ARE VERY AGGRESSIVE.

THIS CLIP-ART REPRESENTS US IN WEEK THREE AS A PILE OF DEAD CHIPMUNKS.

NOW HE WANTS IT IN TWO WEEKS?

NEVER MIX SARCASM WITH GOOD CLIP-ART.

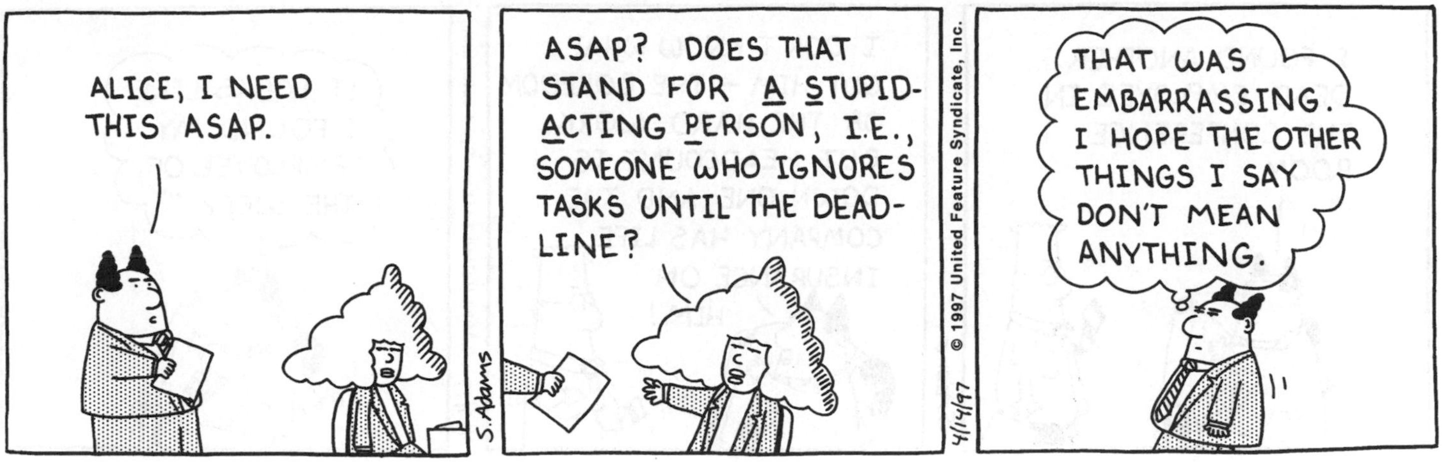
ALICE, I NEED THIS ASAP.
S. Adams
ASAP? DOES THAT STAND FOR A STUPID-ACTING PERSON, I.E., SOMEONE WHO IGNORES TASKS UNTIL THE DEAD-LINE?
4/14/97
© 1997 United Feature Syndicate, Inc.
THAT WAS EMBARRASSING. I HOPE THE OTHER THINGS I SAY DON'T MEAN ANYTHING.

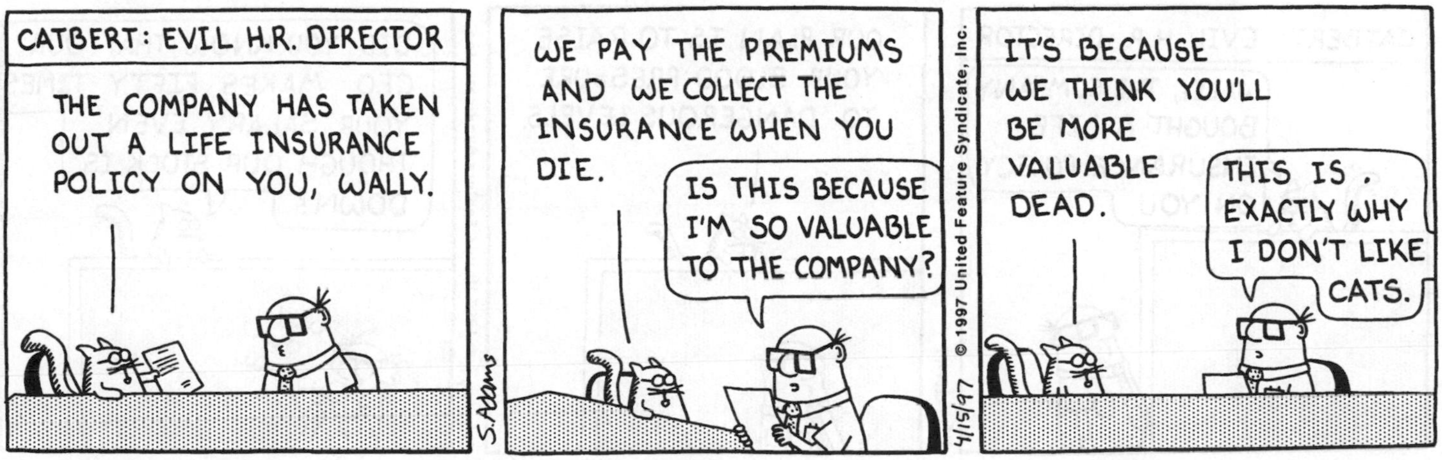
CATBERT: EVIL H.R. DIRECTOR
THE COMPANY HAS TAKEN OUT A LIFE INSURANCE POLICY ON YOU, WALLY.
S. Adams
WE PAY THE PREMIUMS AND WE COLLECT THE INSURANCE WHEN YOU DIE.
IS THIS BECAUSE I'M SO VALUABLE TO THE COMPANY?
4/15/97
© 1997 United Feature Syndicate, Inc.
IT'S BECAUSE WE THINK YOU'LL BE MORE VALUABLE DEAD.
THIS IS EXACTLY WHY I DON'T LIKE CATS.

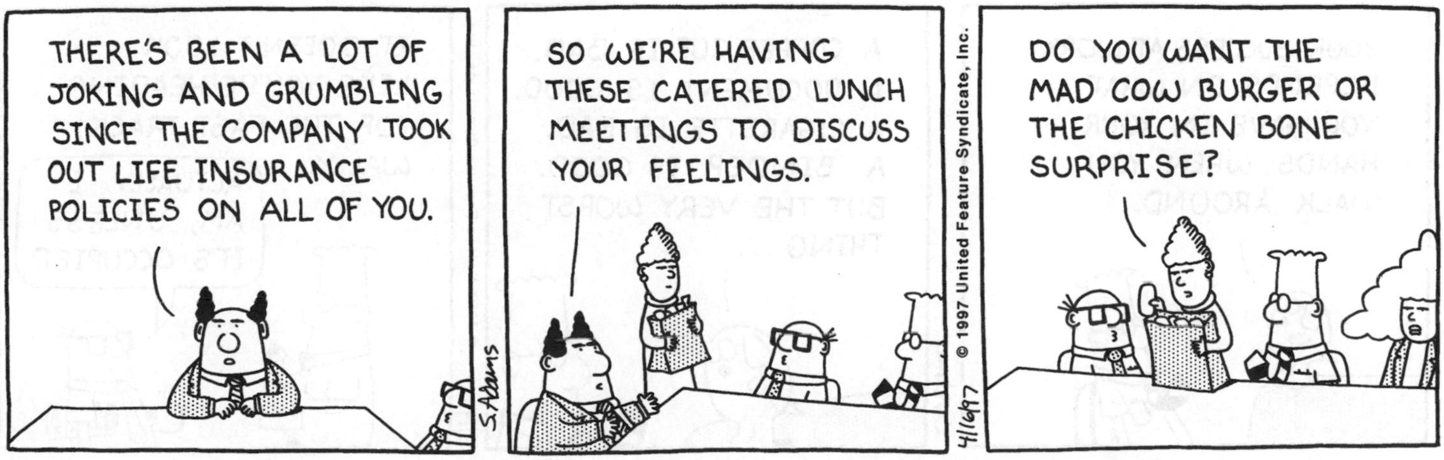
THERE'S BEEN A LOT OF JOKING AND GRUMBLING SINCE THE COMPANY TOOK OUT LIFE INSURANCE POLICIES ON ALL OF YOU.
S. Adams
SO WE'RE HAVING THESE CATERED LUNCH MEETINGS TO DISCUSS YOUR FEELINGS.
4/16/97
© 1997 United Feature Syndicate, Inc.
DO YOU WANT THE MAD COW BURGER OR THE CHICKEN BONE SURPRISE?

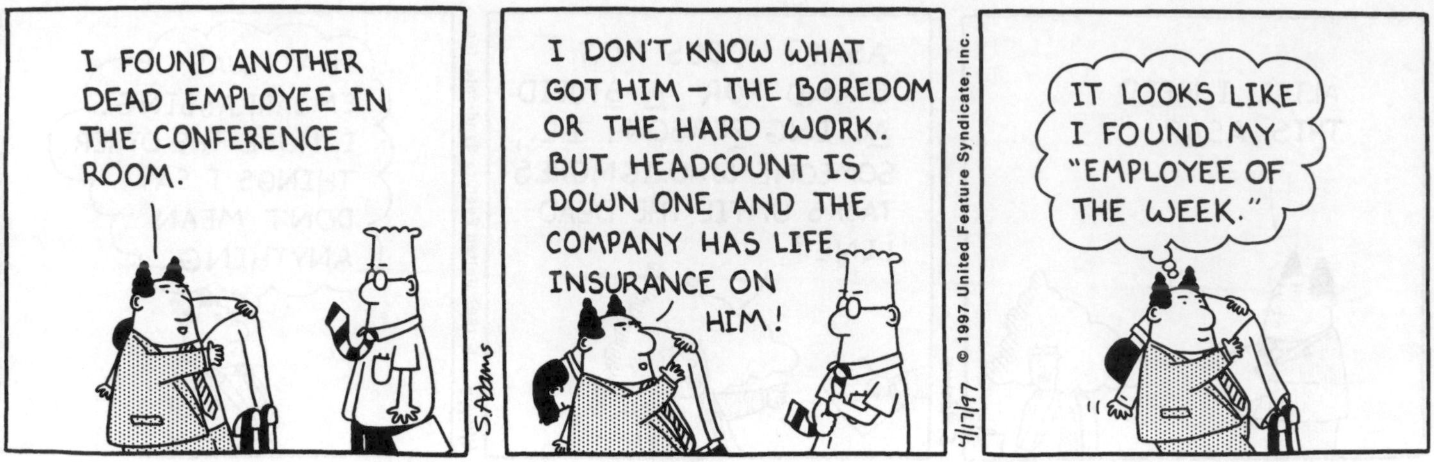
I FOUND ANOTHER DEAD EMPLOYEE IN THE CONFERENCE ROOM.
I DON'T KNOW WHAT GOT HIM – THE BOREDOM OR THE HARD WORK. BUT HEADCOUNT IS DOWN ONE AND THE COMPANY HAS LIFE INSURANCE ON HIM!
S.Adams
4/17/97
© 1997 United Feature Syndicate, Inc.
IT LOOKS LIKE I FOUND MY "EMPLOYEE OF THE WEEK."

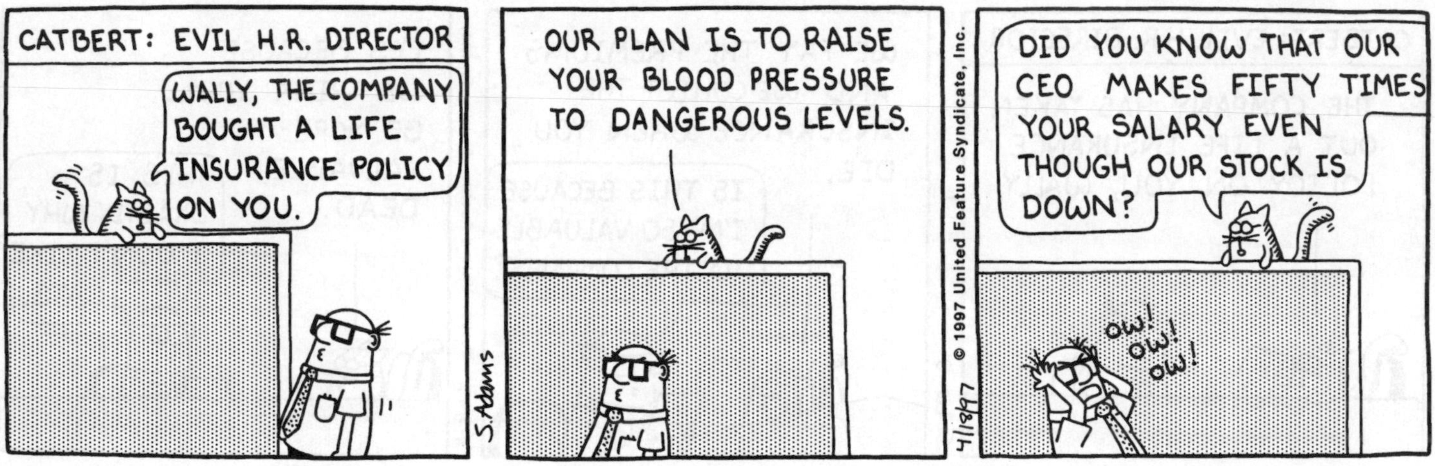
CATBERT: EVIL H.R. DIRECTOR
WALLY, THE COMPANY BOUGHT A LIFE INSURANCE POLICY ON YOU.
OUR PLAN IS TO RAISE YOUR BLOOD PRESSURE TO DANGEROUS LEVELS.
S.Adams
4/18/97
© 1997 United Feature Syndicate, Inc.
DID YOU KNOW THAT OUR CEO MAKES FIFTY TIMES YOUR SALARY EVEN THOUGH OUR STOCK IS DOWN?
OW! OW! OW!

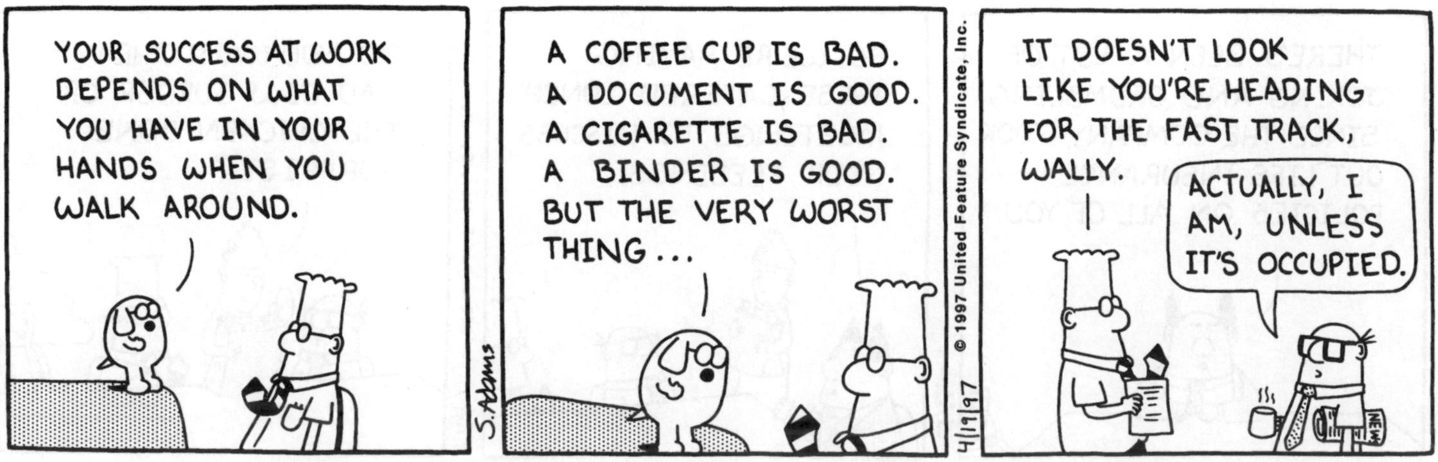
YOUR SUCCESS AT WORK DEPENDS ON WHAT YOU HAVE IN YOUR HANDS WHEN YOU WALK AROUND.
A COFFEE CUP IS BAD. A DOCUMENT IS GOOD. A CIGARETTE IS BAD. A BINDER IS GOOD. BUT THE VERY WORST THING . . .
S.Adams
4/19/97
© 1997 United Feature Syndicate, Inc.
IT DOESN'T LOOK LIKE YOU'RE HEADING FOR THE FAST TRACK, WALLY.
ACTUALLY, I AM, UNLESS IT'S OCCUPIED.
NEWS

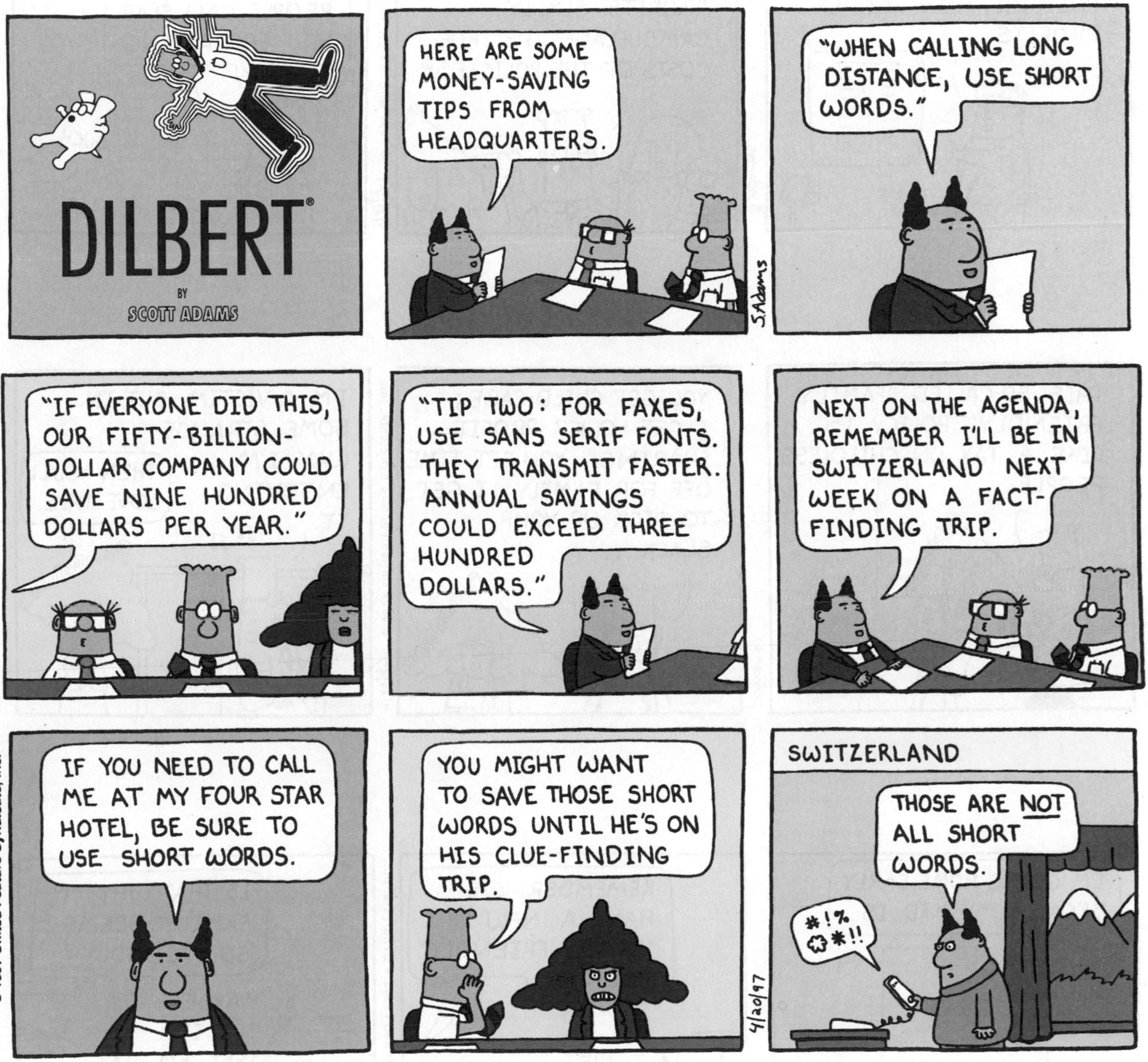
DILBERT®
BY
SCOTT ADAMS
HERE ARE SOME MONEY-SAVING TIPS FROM HEADQUARTERS.
S.Adams
"WHEN CALLING LONG DISTANCE, USE SHORT WORDS."
"IF EVERYONE DID THIS, OUR FIFTY-BILLION-DOLLAR COMPANY COULD SAVE NINE HUNDRED DOLLARS PER YEAR."
"TIP TWO: FOR FAXES, USE SANS SERIF FONTS. THEY TRANSMIT FASTER. ANNUAL SAVINGS COULD EXCEED THREE HUNDRED DOLLARS."
NEXT ON THE AGENDA, REMEMBER I'LL BE IN SWITZERLAND NEXT WEEK ON A FACT-FINDING TRIP.
IF YOU NEED TO CALL ME AT MY FOUR STAR HOTEL, BE SURE TO USE SHORT WORDS.
YOU MIGHT WANT TO SAVE THOSE SHORT WORDS UNTIL HE'S ON HIS CLUE-FINDING TRIP.
4/20/97
SWITZERLAND
THOSE ARE NOT ALL SHORT WORDS.
*!%
*!!

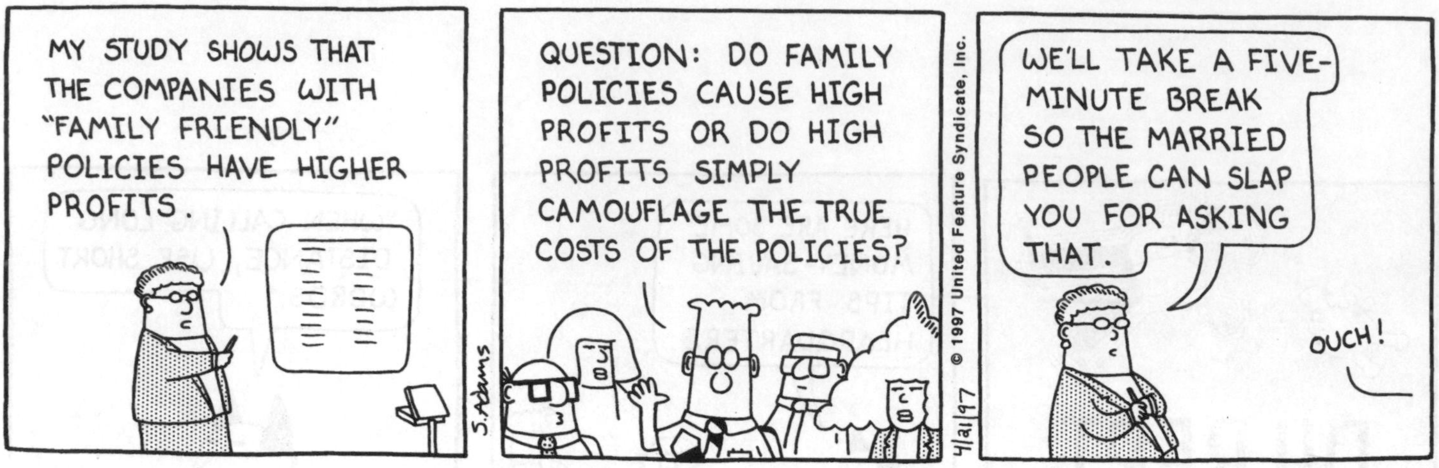
MY STUDY SHOWS THAT THE COMPANIES WITH "FAMILY FRIENDLY" POLICIES HAVE HIGHER PROFITS.
QUESTION: DO FAMILY POLICIES CAUSE HIGH PROFITS OR DO HIGH PROFITS SIMPLY CAMOUFLAGE THE TRUE COSTS OF THE POLICIES?
S.Adams
4/21/97
© 1997 United Feature Syndicate, Inc.
WE'LL TAKE A FIVE-MINUTE BREAK SO THE MARRIED PEOPLE CAN SLAP YOU FOR ASKING THAT.
OUCH!

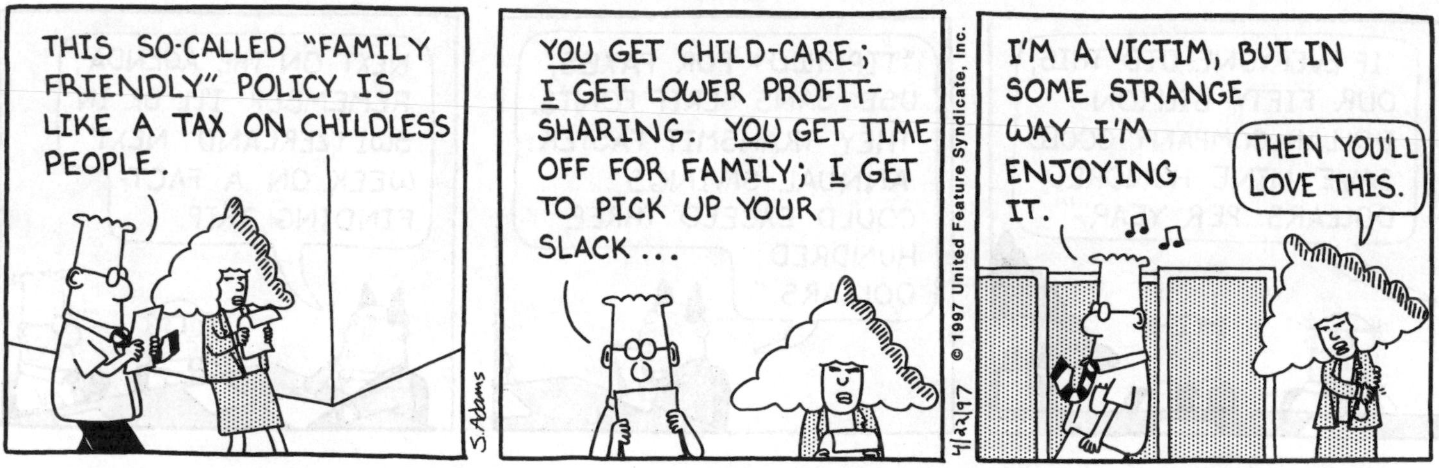
THIS SO-CALLED "FAMILY FRIENDLY" POLICY IS LIKE A TAX ON CHILDLESS PEOPLE.
S.Adams
YOU GET CHILD-CARE; I GET LOWER PROFIT-SHARING. YOU GET TIME OFF FOR FAMILY; I GET TO PICK UP YOUR SLACK...
4/22/97
© 1997 United Feature Syndicate, Inc.
I'M A VICTIM, BUT IN SOME STRANGE WAY I'M ENJOYING IT.
THEN YOU'LL LOVE THIS.

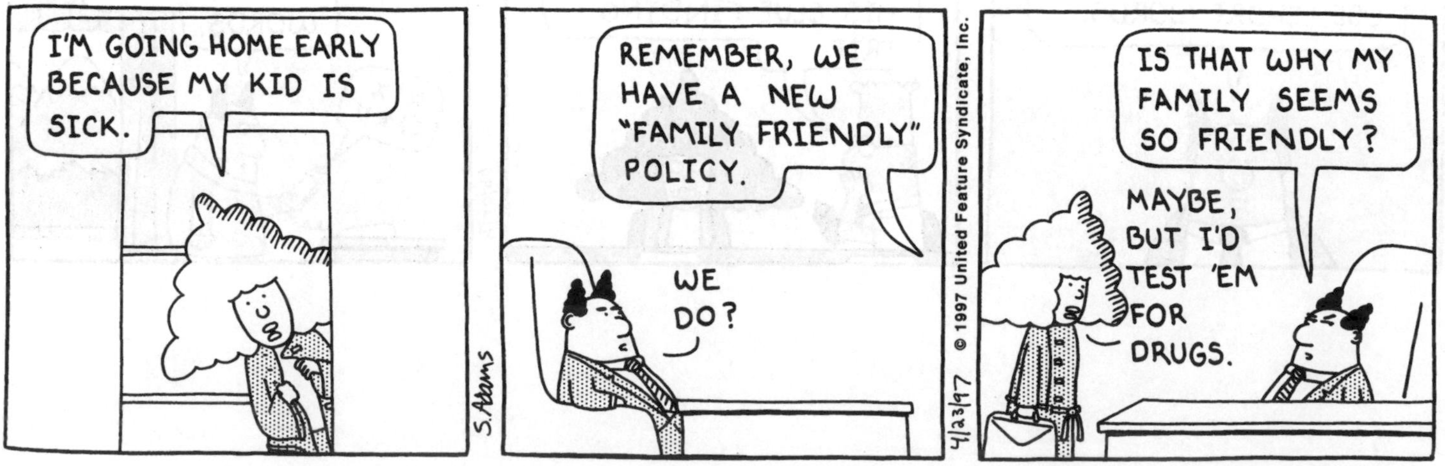
I'M GOING HOME EARLY BECAUSE MY KID IS SICK.
S.Adams
REMEMBER, WE HAVE A NEW "FAMILY FRIENDLY" POLICY.
WE DO?
4/23/97
© 1997 United Feature Syndicate, Inc.
IS THAT WHY MY FAMILY SEEMS SO FRIENDLY?
MAYBE, BUT I'D TEST 'EM FOR DRUGS.

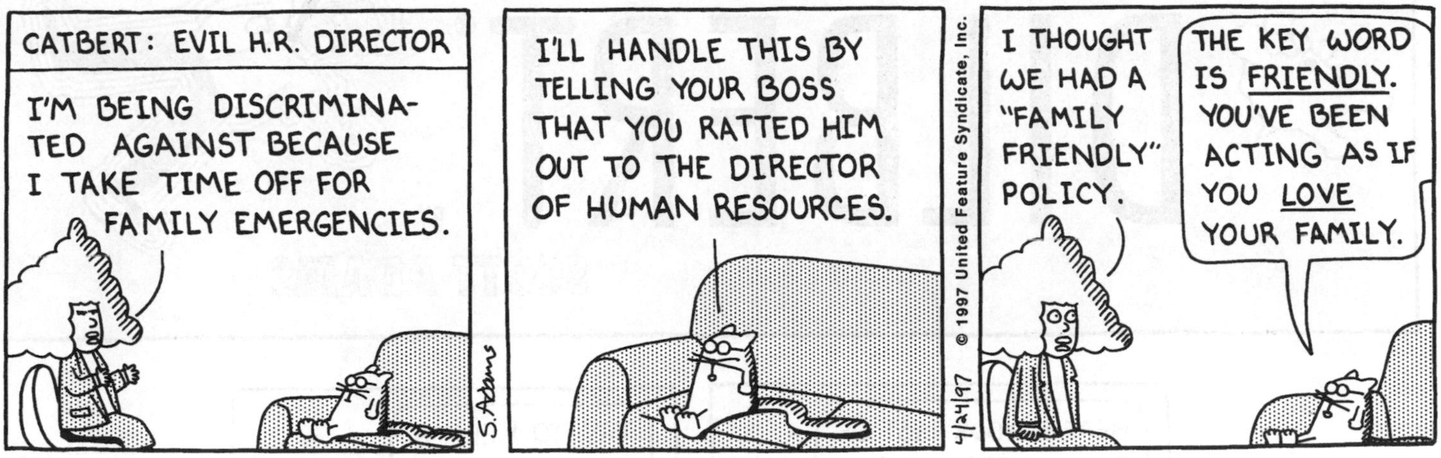

CATBERT: EVIL H.R. DIRECTOR
I'M BEING DISCRIMINATED AGAINST BECAUSE I TAKE TIME OFF FOR FAMILY EMERGENCIES.
I'LL HANDLE THIS BY TELLING YOUR BOSS THAT YOU RATTED HIM OUT TO THE DIRECTOR OF HUMAN RESOURCES.
I THOUGHT WE HAD A "FAMILY FRIENDLY" POLICY.
THE KEY WORD IS FRIENDLY. YOU'VE BEEN ACTING AS IF YOU LOVE YOUR FAMILY.
S. Adams
4/24/97
© 1997 United Feature Syndicate, Inc.

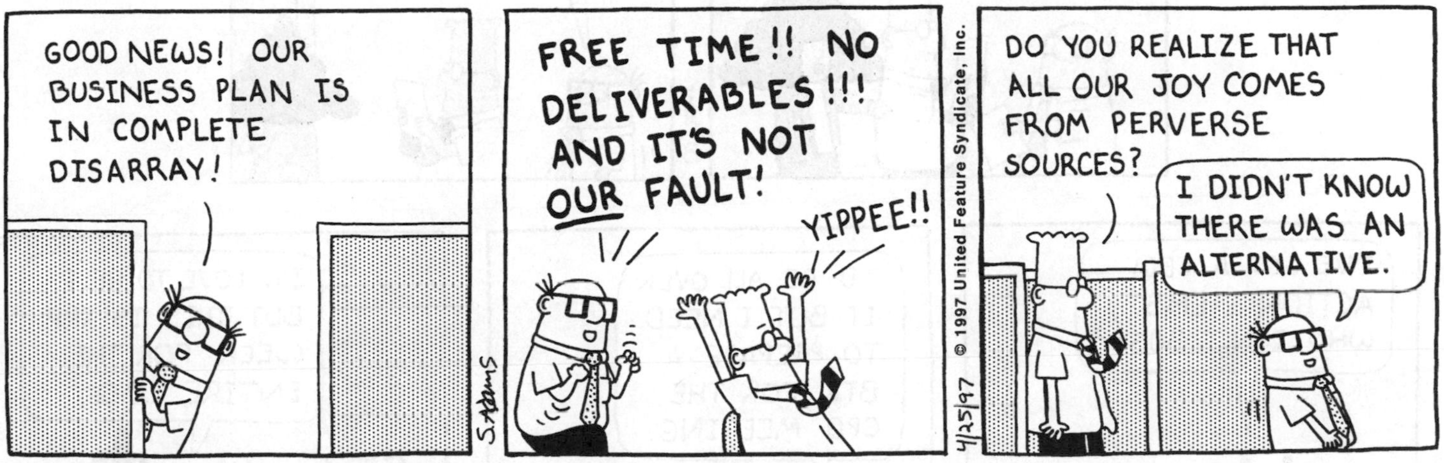

GOOD NEWS! OUR BUSINESS PLAN IS IN COMPLETE DISARRAY!
FREE TIME!! NO DELIVERABLES!!! AND IT'S NOT OUR FAULT!
YIPPEE!!
DO YOU REALIZE THAT ALL OUR JOY COMES FROM PERVERSE SOURCES?
I DIDN'T KNOW THERE WAS AN ALTERNATIVE.
S. Adams
4/25/97
© 1997 United Feature Syndicate, Inc.

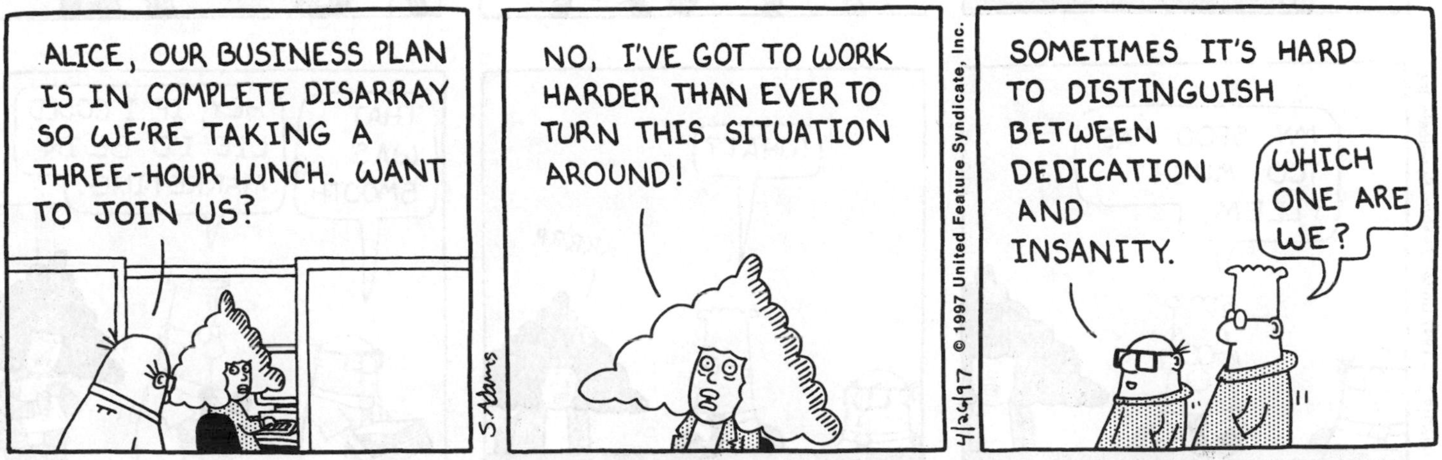

ALICE, OUR BUSINESS PLAN IS IN COMPLETE DISARRAY SO WE'RE TAKING A THREE-HOUR LUNCH. WANT TO JOIN US?
NO, I'VE GOT TO WORK HARDER THAN EVER TO TURN THIS SITUATION AROUND!
SOMETIMES IT'S HARD TO DISTINGUISH BETWEEN DEDICATION AND INSANITY.
WHICH ONE ARE WE?
S. Adams
4/26/97
© 1997 United Feature Syndicate, Inc.

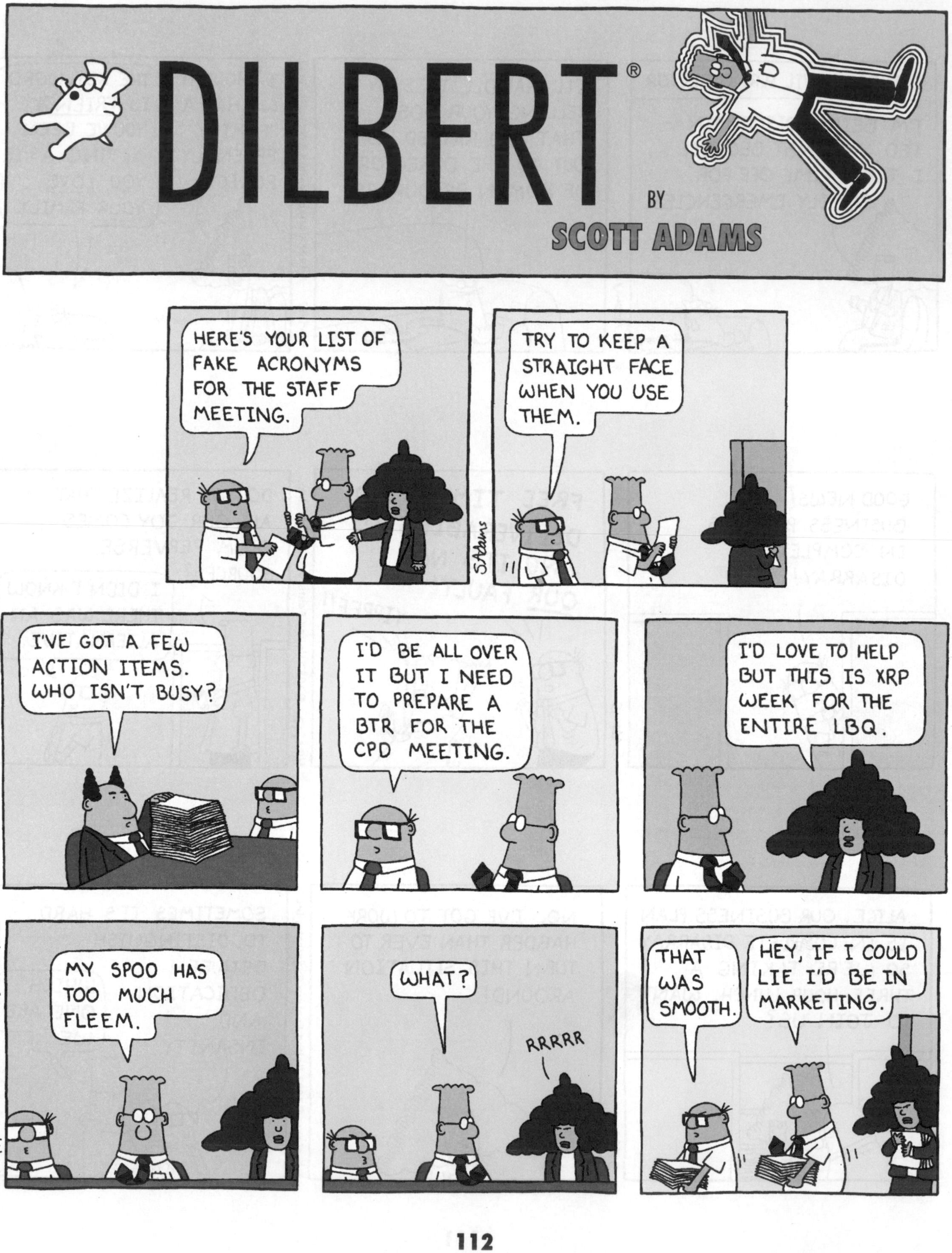
DILBERT®
BY
SCOTT ADAMS
HERE'S YOUR LIST OF FAKE ACRONYMS FOR THE STAFF MEETING.
TRY TO KEEP A STRAIGHT FACE WHEN YOU USE THEM.
SAdams
I'VE GOT A FEW ACTION ITEMS. WHO ISN'T BUSY?
I'D BE ALL OVER IT BUT I NEED TO PREPARE A BTR FOR THE CPD MEETING.
I'D LOVE TO HELP BUT THIS IS XRP WEEK FOR THE ENTIRE LBQ.
MY SPOO HAS TOO MUCH FLEEM.
WHAT?
RRRRR
THAT WAS SMOOTH.
HEY, IF I COULD LIE I'D BE IN MARKETING.
4/27/97 © 1997 United Feature Syndicate, Inc.

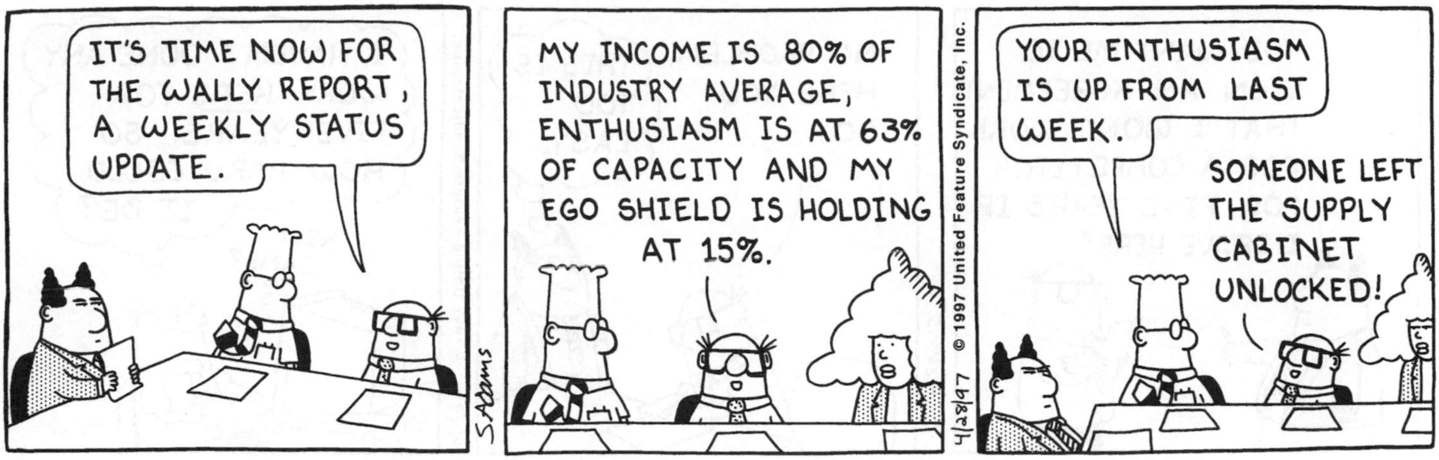
IT'S TIME NOW FOR THE WALLY REPORT, A WEEKLY STATUS UPDATE.
MY INCOME IS 80% OF INDUSTRY AVERAGE, ENTHUSIASM IS AT 63% OF CAPACITY AND MY EGO SHIELD IS HOLDING AT 15%.
YOUR ENTHUSIASM IS UP FROM LAST WEEK.
SOMEONE LEFT THE SUPPLY CABINET UNLOCKED!
S. Adams
4/28/97 © 1997 United Feature Syndicate, Inc.

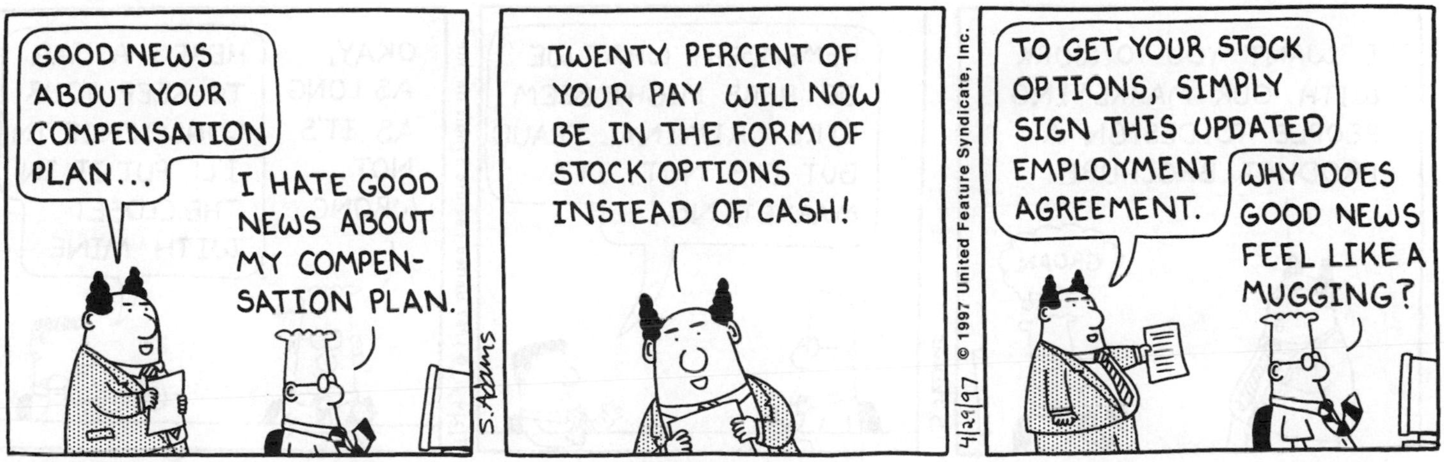
GOOD NEWS ABOUT YOUR COMPENSATION PLAN...
I HATE GOOD NEWS ABOUT MY COMPENSATION PLAN.
TWENTY PERCENT OF YOUR PAY WILL NOW BE IN THE FORM OF STOCK OPTIONS INSTEAD OF CASH!
TO GET YOUR STOCK OPTIONS, SIMPLY SIGN THIS UPDATED EMPLOYMENT AGREEMENT.
WHY DOES GOOD NEWS FEEL LIKE A MUGGING?
S. Adams
4/29/97 © 1997 United Feature Syndicate, Inc.

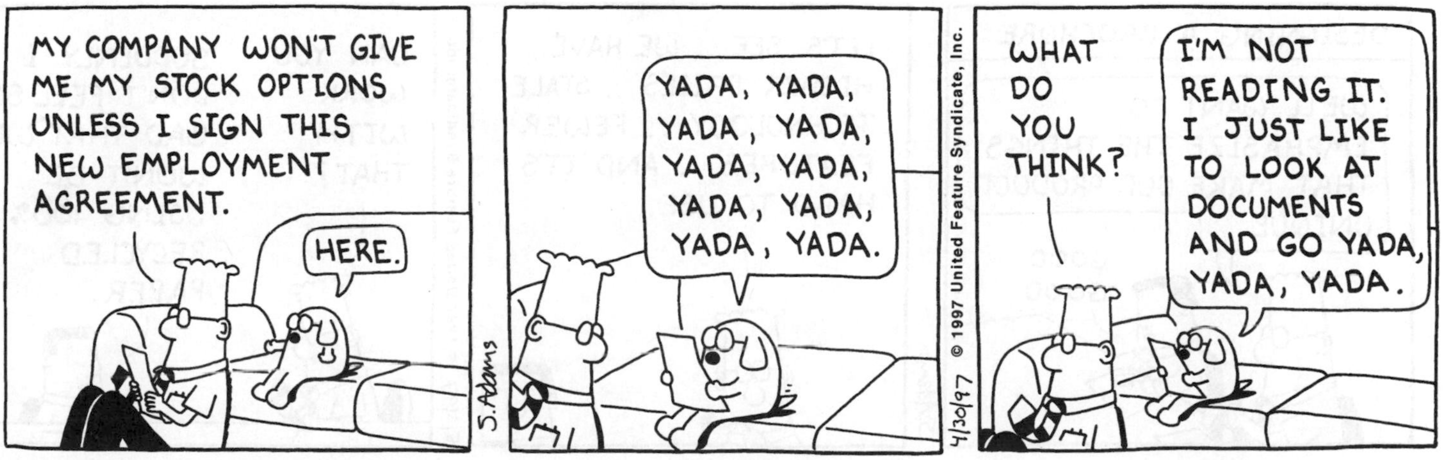
MY COMPANY WON'T GIVE ME MY STOCK OPTIONS UNLESS I SIGN THIS NEW EMPLOYMENT AGREEMENT.
HERE.
YADA, YADA, YADA, YADA, YADA, YADA, YADA, YADA, YADA, YADA.
WHAT DO YOU THINK?
I'M NOT READING IT. I JUST LIKE TO LOOK AT DOCUMENTS AND GO YADA, YADA, YADA.
S. Adams
4/30/97 © 1997 United Feature Syndicate, Inc.

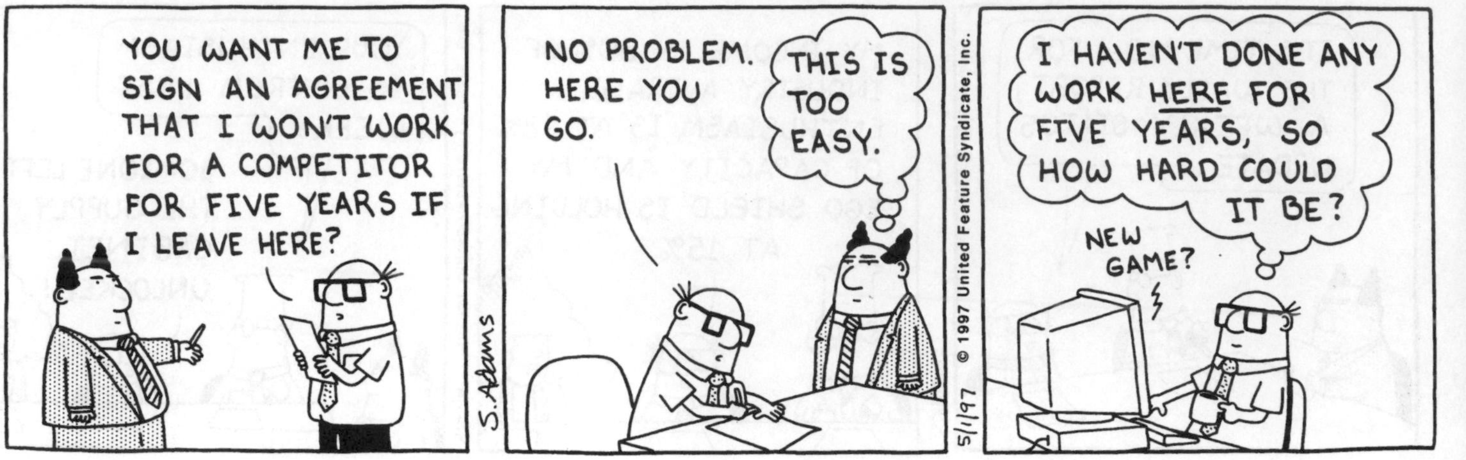
YOU WANT ME TO SIGN AN AGREEMENT THAT I WON'T WORK FOR A COMPETITOR FOR FIVE YEARS IF I LEAVE HERE?
S. Adams
NO PROBLEM. HERE YOU GO.
THIS IS TOO EASY.
5/1/97 © 1997 United Feature Syndicate, Inc.
I HAVEN'T DONE ANY WORK HERE FOR FIVE YEARS, SO HOW HARD COULD IT BE?
NEW GAME?

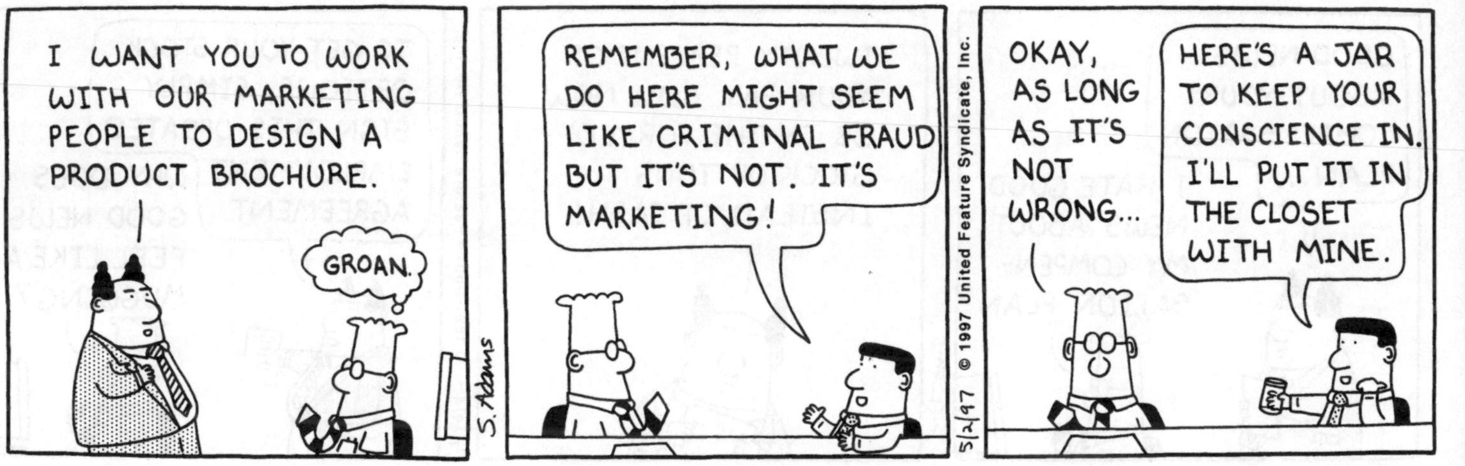
I WANT YOU TO WORK WITH OUR MARKETING PEOPLE TO DESIGN A PRODUCT BROCHURE.
GROAN.
S. Adams
REMEMBER, WHAT WE DO HERE MIGHT SEEM LIKE CRIMINAL FRAUD BUT IT'S NOT. IT'S MARKETING!
5/2/97 © 1997 United Feature Syndicate, Inc.
OKAY, AS LONG AS IT'S NOT WRONG...
HERE'S A JAR TO KEEP YOUR CONSCIENCE IN. I'LL PUT IT IN THE CLOSET WITH MINE.

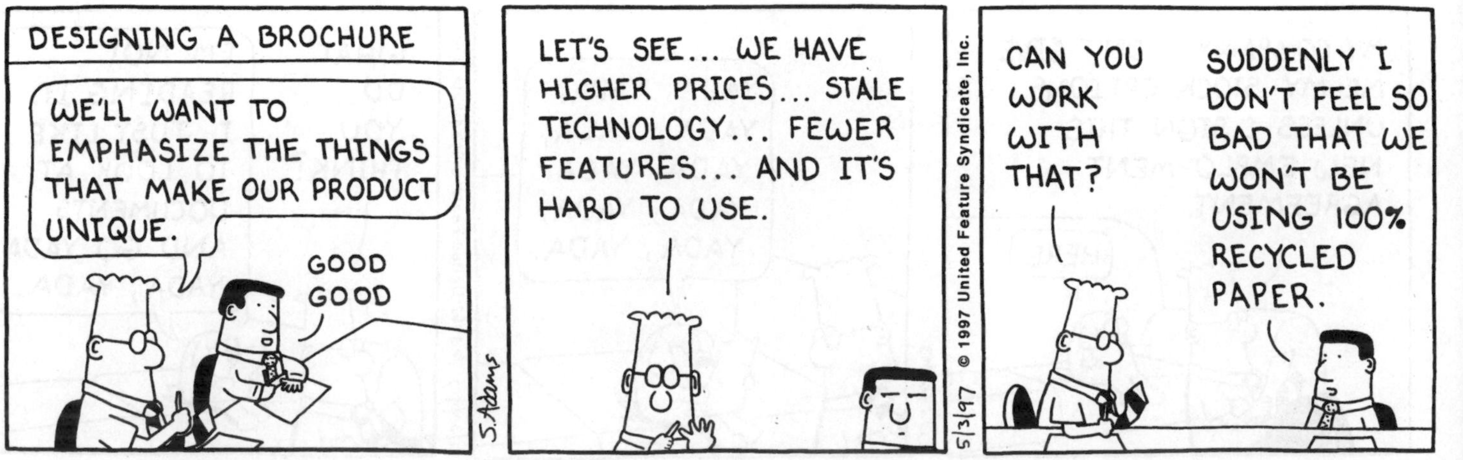
DESIGNING A BROCHURE
WE'LL WANT TO EMPHASIZE THE THINGS THAT MAKE OUR PRODUCT UNIQUE.
GOOD GOOD
S. Adams
LET'S SEE... WE HAVE HIGHER PRICES... STALE TECHNOLOGY... FEWER FEATURES... AND IT'S HARD TO USE.
5/3/97 © 1997 United Feature Syndicate, Inc.
CAN YOU WORK WITH THAT?
SUDDENLY I DON'T FEEL SO BAD THAT WE WON'T BE USING 100% RECYCLED PAPER.

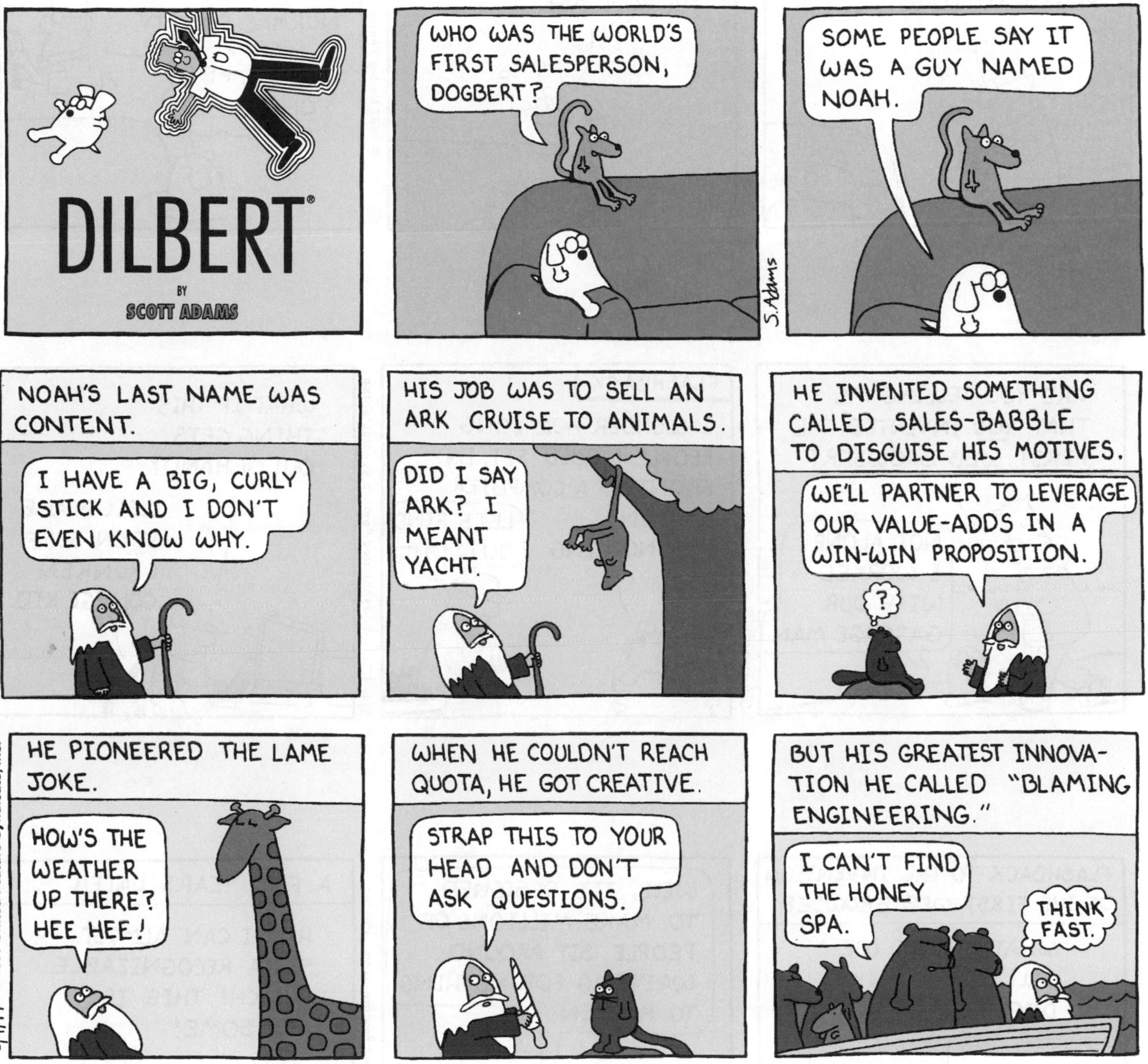
DILBERT®
BY
SCOTT ADAMS
WHO WAS THE WORLD'S FIRST SALESPERSON, DOGBERT?
SOME PEOPLE SAY IT WAS A GUY NAMED NOAH.
S. Adams
NOAH'S LAST NAME WAS CONTENT.
I HAVE A BIG, CURLY STICK AND I DON'T EVEN KNOW WHY.
HIS JOB WAS TO SELL AN ARK CRUISE TO ANIMALS.
DID I SAY ARK? I MEANT YACHT.
HE INVENTED SOMETHING CALLED SALES-BABBLE TO DISGUISE HIS MOTIVES.
WE'LL PARTNER TO LEVERAGE OUR VALUE-ADDS IN A WIN-WIN PROPOSITION.
?
HE PIONEERED THE LAME JOKE.
HOW'S THE WEATHER UP THERE? HEE HEE!
WHEN HE COULDN'T REACH QUOTA, HE GOT CREATIVE.
STRAP THIS TO YOUR HEAD AND DON'T ASK QUESTIONS.
BUT HIS GREATEST INNOVATION HE CALLED "BLAMING ENGINEERING."
I CAN'T FIND THE HONEY SPA.
THINK FAST.
5/4/97 © 1997 United Feature Syndicate, Inc.

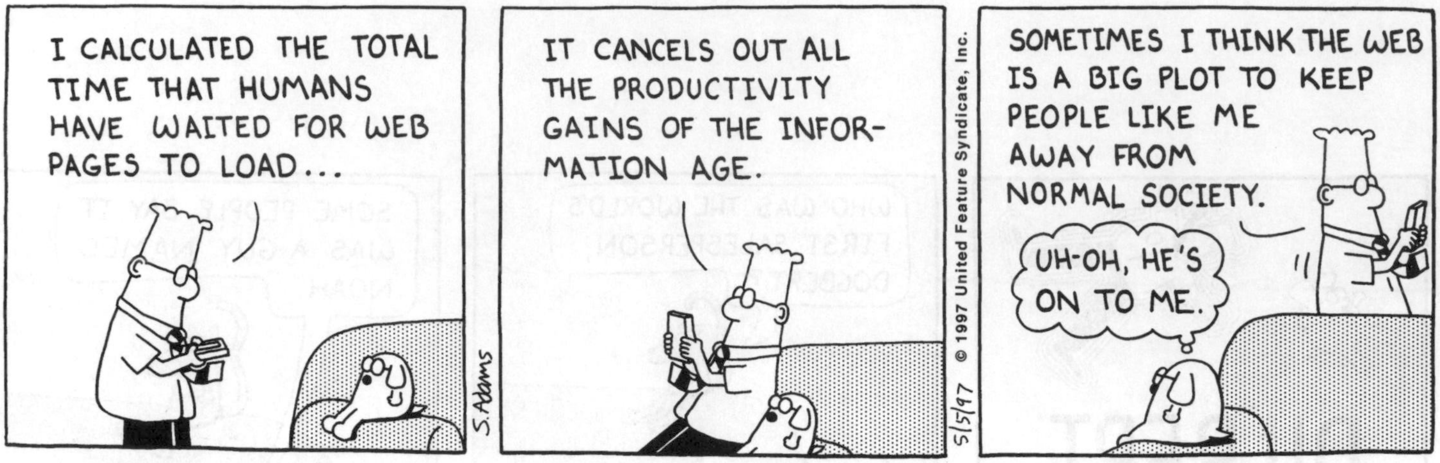
I CALCULATED THE TOTAL TIME THAT HUMANS HAVE WAITED FOR WEB PAGES TO LOAD...
S. Adams
IT CANCELS OUT ALL THE PRODUCTIVITY GAINS OF THE INFORMATION AGE.
5/5/97 © 1997 United Feature Syndicate, Inc.
SOMETIMES I THINK THE WEB IS A BIG PLOT TO KEEP PEOPLE LIKE ME AWAY FROM NORMAL SOCIETY.
UH-OH, HE'S ON TO ME.

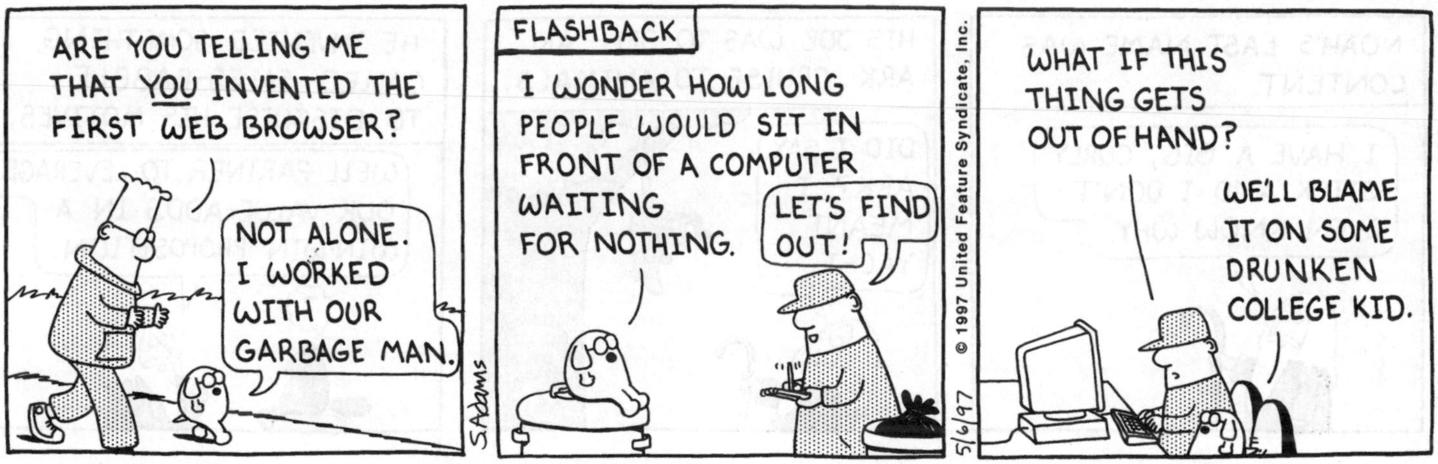
ARE YOU TELLING ME THAT YOU INVENTED THE FIRST WEB BROWSER?
NOT ALONE. I WORKED WITH OUR GARBAGE MAN.
S. Adams
FLASHBACK
I WONDER HOW LONG PEOPLE WOULD SIT IN FRONT OF A COMPUTER WAITING FOR NOTHING.
LET'S FIND OUT!
5/6/97 © 1997 United Feature Syndicate, Inc.
WHAT IF THIS THING GETS OUT OF HAND?
WE'LL BLAME IT ON SOME DRUNKEN COLLEGE KID.

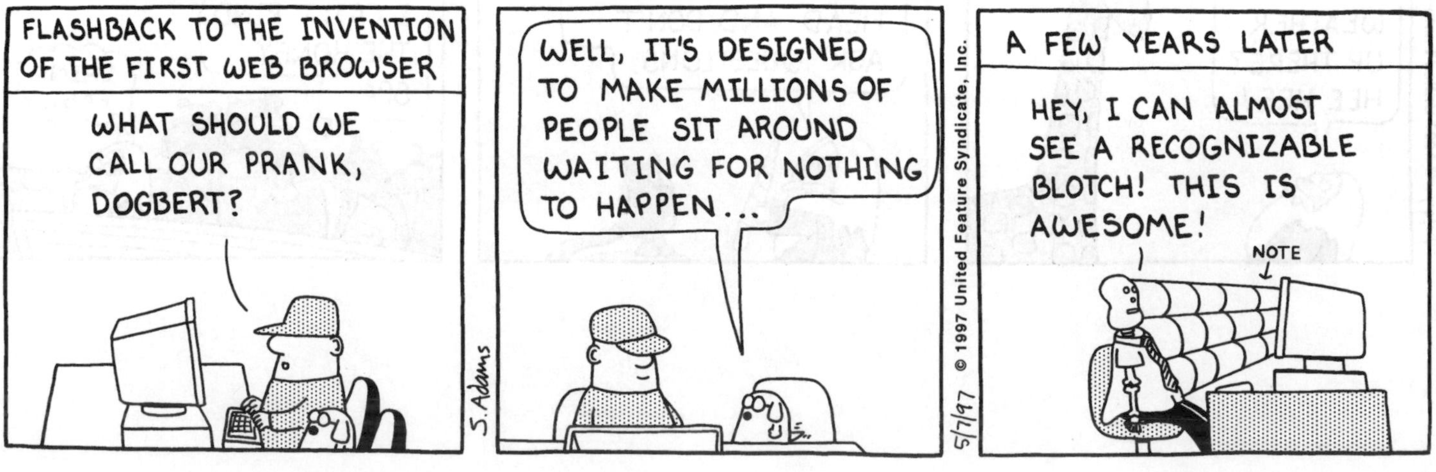
FLASHBACK TO THE INVENTION OF THE FIRST WEB BROWSER
WHAT SHOULD WE CALL OUR PRANK, DOGBERT?
S. Adams
WELL, IT'S DESIGNED TO MAKE MILLIONS OF PEOPLE SIT AROUND WAITING FOR NOTHING TO HAPPEN...
5/7/97 © 1997 United Feature Syndicate, Inc.
A FEW YEARS LATER
HEY, I CAN ALMOST SEE A RECOGNIZABLE BLOTCH! THIS IS AWESOME!
NOTE

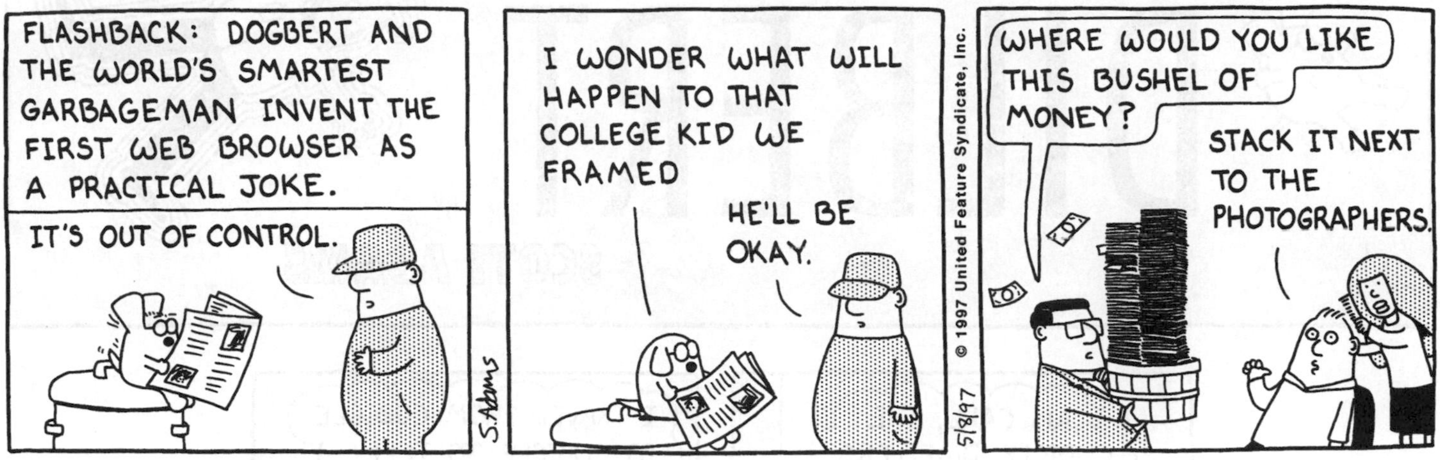
FLASHBACK: DOGBERT AND THE WORLD'S SMARTEST GARBAGEMAN INVENT THE FIRST WEB BROWSER AS A PRACTICAL JOKE.
IT'S OUT OF CONTROL.
S. Adams
I WONDER WHAT WILL HAPPEN TO THAT COLLEGE KID WE FRAMED
HE'LL BE OKAY.
5/8/97 © 1997 United Feature Syndicate, Inc.
WHERE WOULD YOU LIKE THIS BUSHEL OF MONEY?
STACK IT NEXT TO THE PHOTOGRAPHERS.

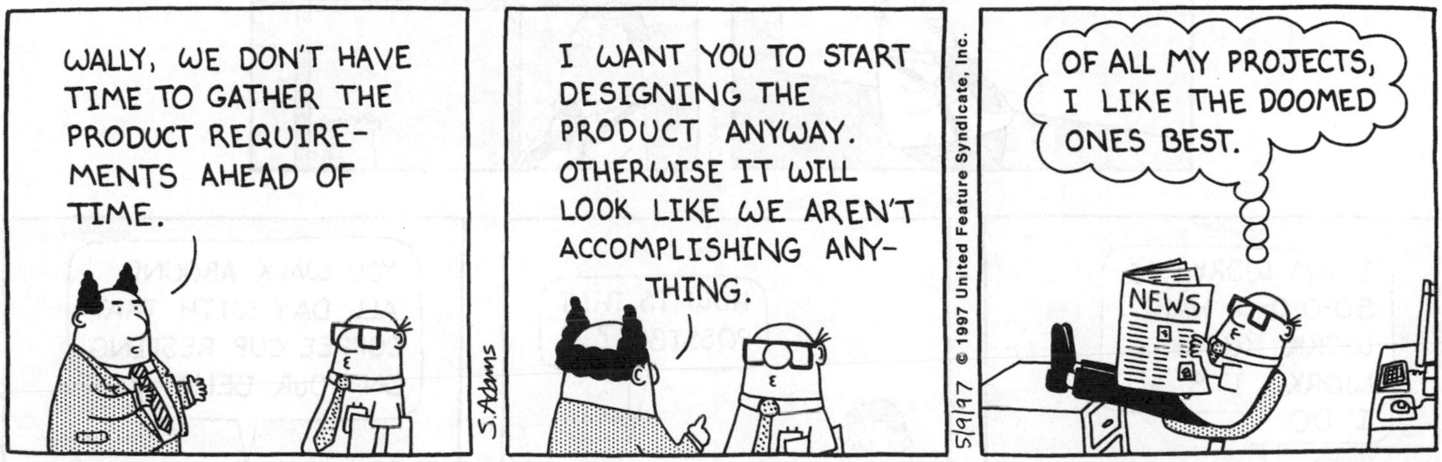
WALLY, WE DON'T HAVE TIME TO GATHER THE PRODUCT REQUIRE-MENTS AHEAD OF TIME.
S. Adams
I WANT YOU TO START DESIGNING THE PRODUCT ANYWAY. OTHERWISE IT WILL LOOK LIKE WE AREN'T ACCOMPLISHING ANY-THING.
5/9/97 © 1997 United Feature Syndicate, Inc.
OF ALL MY PROJECTS, I LIKE THE DOOMED ONES BEST.
NEWS

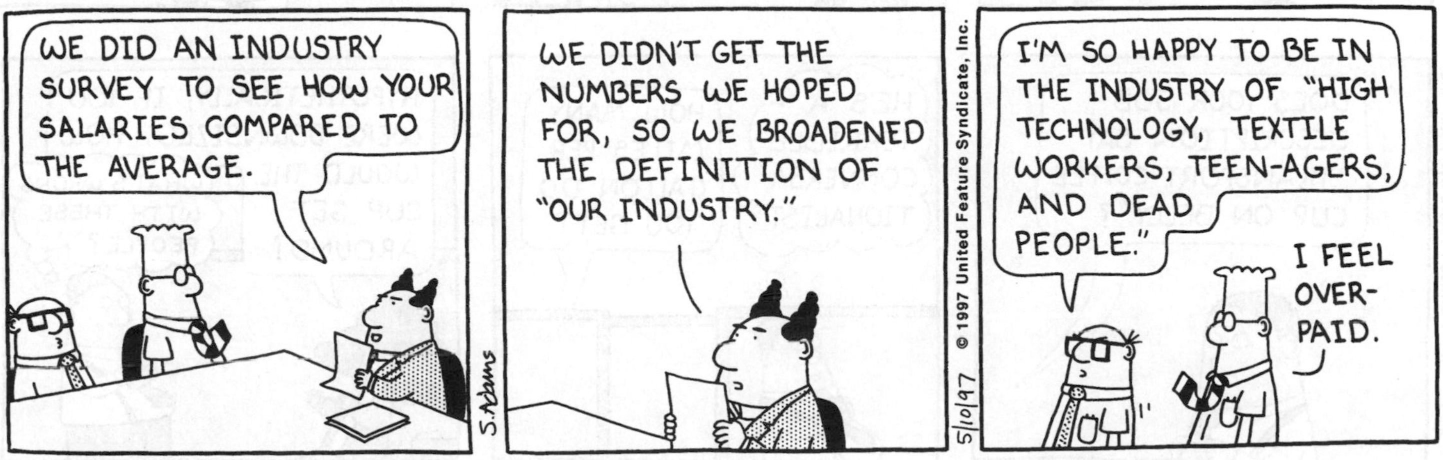
WE DID AN INDUSTRY SURVEY TO SEE HOW YOUR SALARIES COMPARED TO THE AVERAGE.
S. Adams
WE DIDN'T GET THE NUMBERS WE HOPED FOR, SO WE BROADENED THE DEFINITION OF "OUR INDUSTRY."
5/10/97 © 1997 United Feature Syndicate, Inc.
I'M SO HAPPY TO BE IN THE INDUSTRY OF "HIGH TECHNOLOGY, TEXTILE WORKERS, TEEN-AGERS, AND DEAD PEOPLE."
I FEEL OVER-PAID.

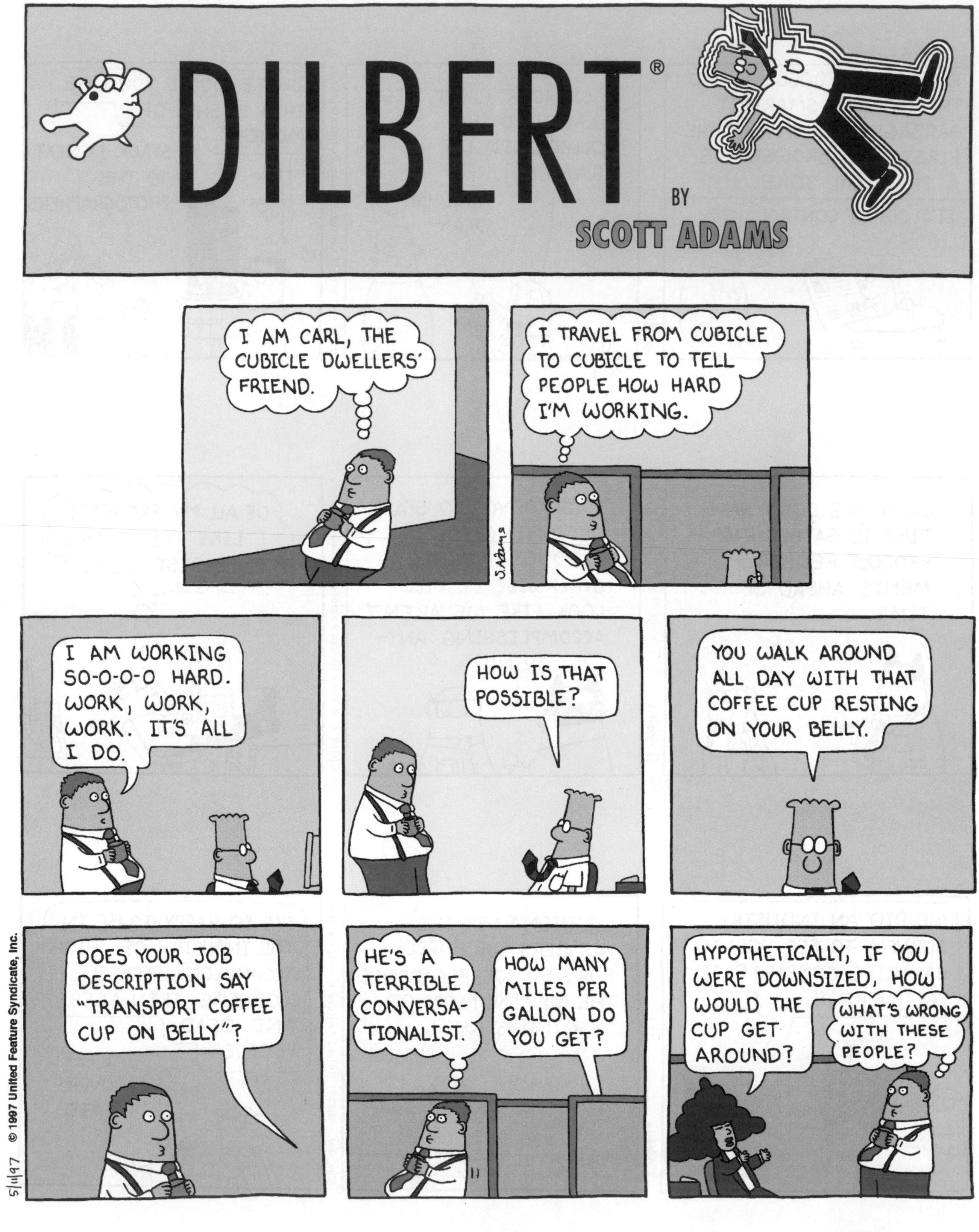
DILBERT®
BY
SCOTT ADAMS
I AM CARL, THE CUBICLE DWELLERS' FRIEND.
I TRAVEL FROM CUBICLE TO CUBICLE TO TELL PEOPLE HOW HARD I'M WORKING.
S. Adams
I AM WORKING SO-O-O-O HARD. WORK, WORK, WORK. IT'S ALL I DO.
HOW IS THAT POSSIBLE?
YOU WALK AROUND ALL DAY WITH THAT COFFEE CUP RESTING ON YOUR BELLY.
DOES YOUR JOB DESCRIPTION SAY "TRANSPORT COFFEE CUP ON BELLY"?
HE'S A TERRIBLE CONVERSA-TIONALIST.
HOW MANY MILES PER GALLON DO YOU GET?
HYPOTHETICALLY, IF YOU WERE DOWNSIZED, HOW WOULD THE CUP GET AROUND?
WHAT'S WRONG WITH THESE PEOPLE?
5/11/97 © 1997 United Feature Syndicate, Inc.

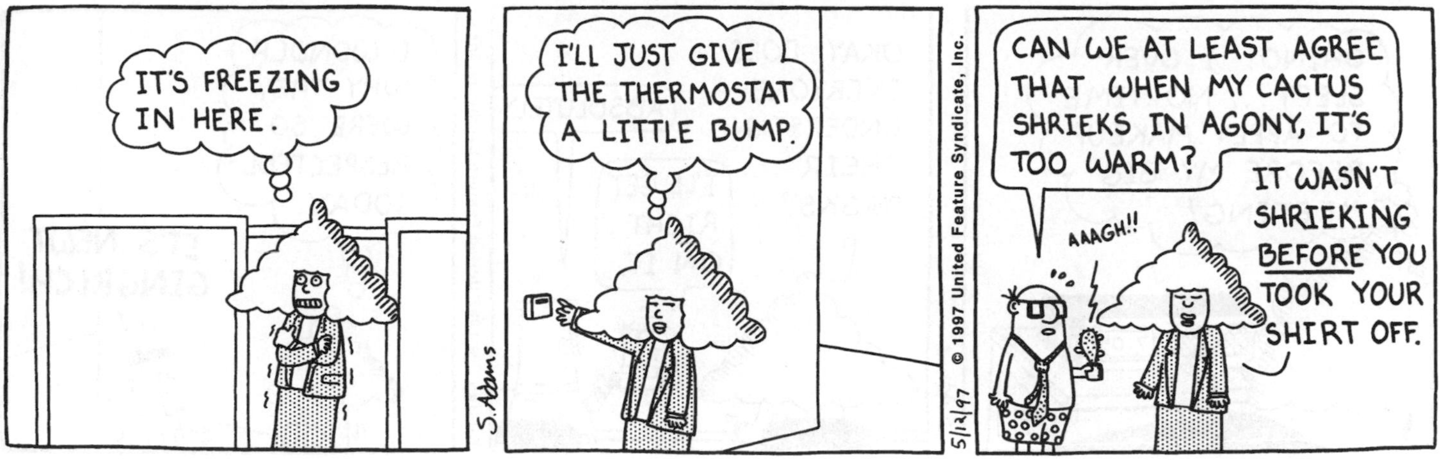
IT'S FREEZING IN HERE.
I'LL JUST GIVE THE THERMOSTAT A LITTLE BUMP.
S. Adams
5/12/97
© 1997 United Feature Syndicate, Inc.
CAN WE AT LEAST AGREE THAT WHEN MY CACTUS SHRIEKS IN AGONY, IT'S TOO WARM?
AAAGH!!
IT WASN'T SHRIEKING BEFORE YOU TOOK YOUR SHIRT OFF.

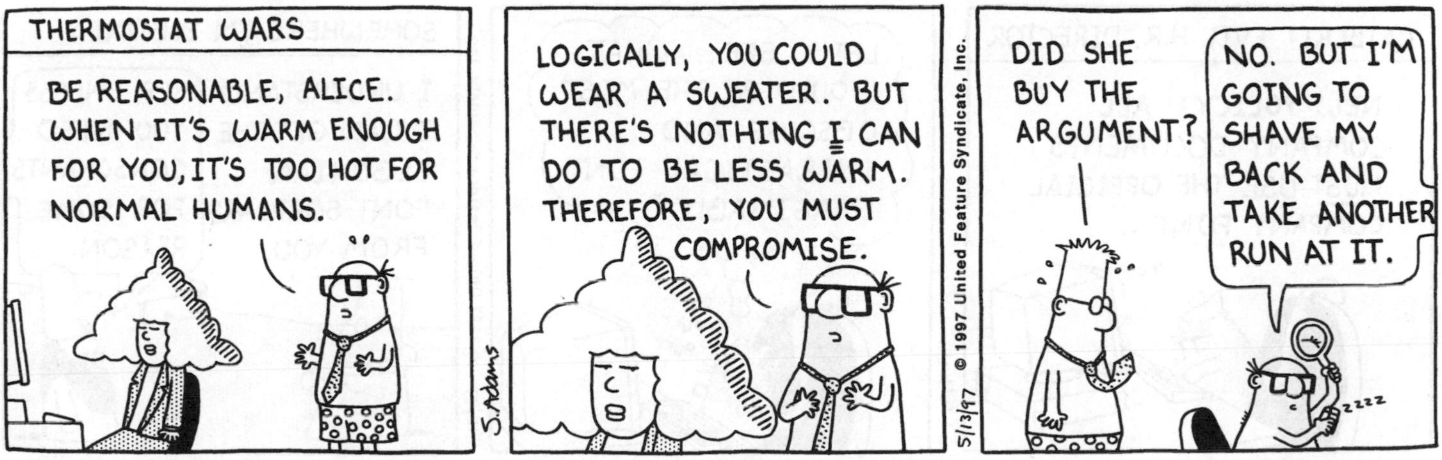
THERMOSTAT WARS
BE REASONABLE, ALICE. WHEN IT'S WARM ENOUGH FOR YOU, IT'S TOO HOT FOR NORMAL HUMANS.
LOGICALLY, YOU COULD WEAR A SWEATER. BUT THERE'S NOTHING I CAN DO TO BE LESS WARM. THEREFORE, YOU MUST COMPROMISE.
S. Adams
5/13/97
© 1997 United Feature Syndicate, Inc.
DID SHE BUY THE ARGUMENT?
NO. BUT I'M GOING TO SHAVE MY BACK AND TAKE ANOTHER RUN AT IT.
ZZZZ

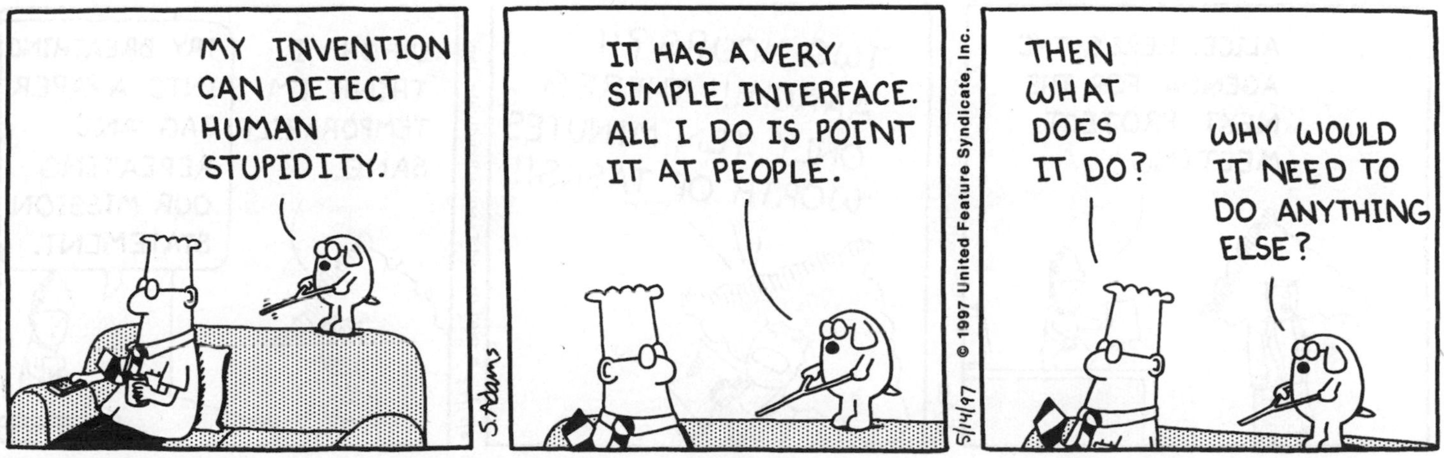
MY INVENTION CAN DETECT HUMAN STUPIDITY.
IT HAS A VERY SIMPLE INTERFACE. ALL I DO IS POINT IT AT PEOPLE.
S. Adams
5/14/97
© 1997 United Feature Syndicate, Inc.
THEN WHAT DOES IT DO?
WHY WOULD IT NEED TO DO ANYTHING ELSE?

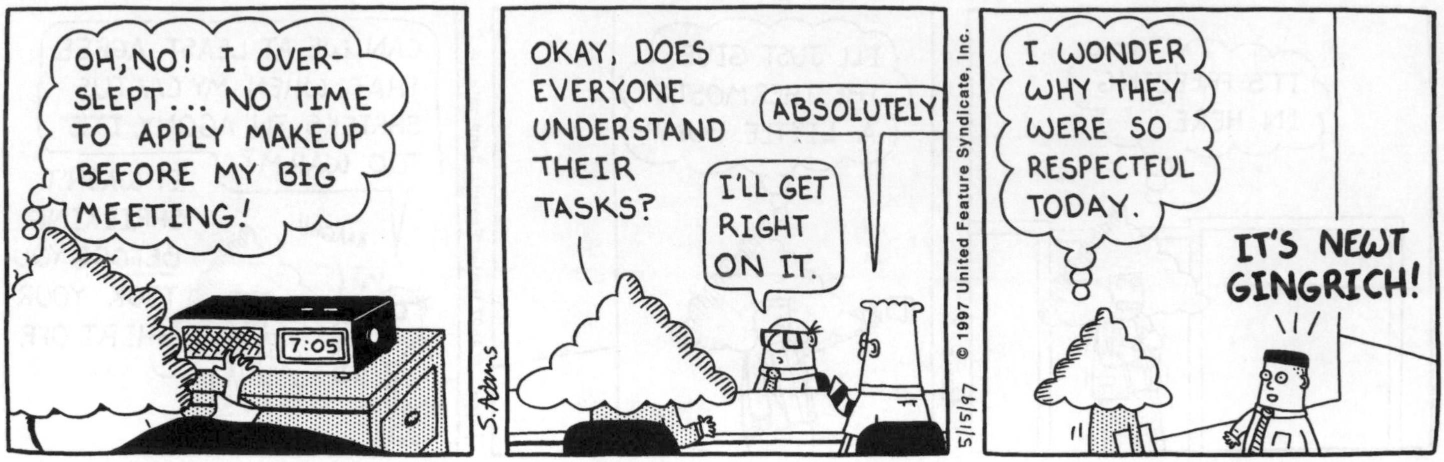
OH, NO! I OVERSLEPT... NO TIME TO APPLY MAKEUP BEFORE MY BIG MEETING!
7:05
S. Adams
OKAY, DOES EVERYONE UNDERSTAND THEIR TASKS?
ABSOLUTELY
I'LL GET RIGHT ON IT.
5/15/97
© 1997 United Feature Syndicate, Inc.
I WONDER WHY THEY WERE SO RESPECTFUL TODAY.
IT'S NEWT GINGRICH!

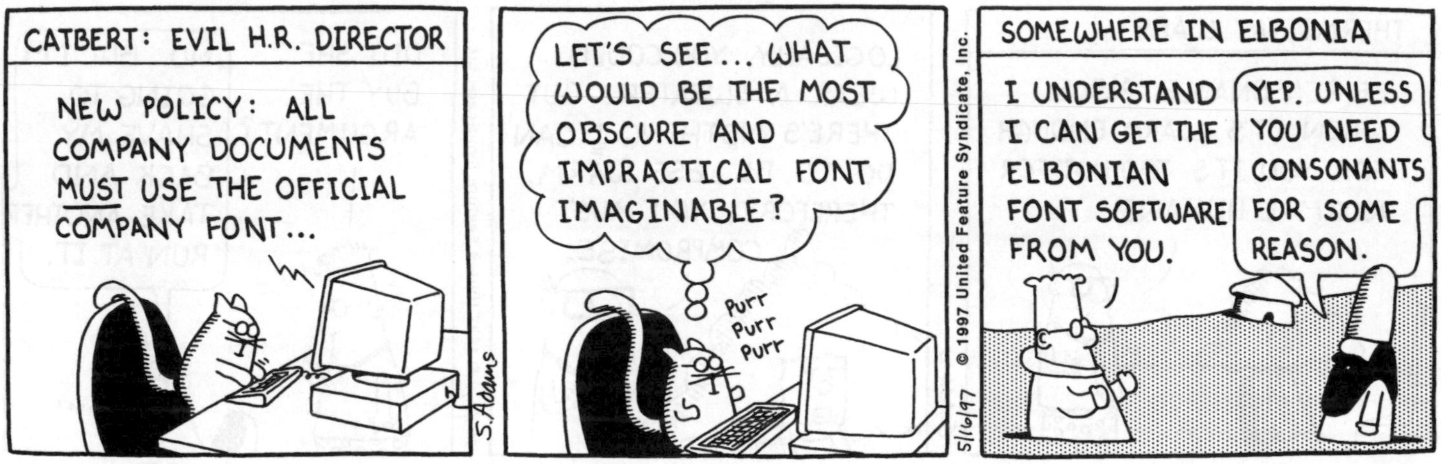
CATBERT: EVIL H.R. DIRECTOR
NEW POLICY: ALL COMPANY DOCUMENTS MUST USE THE OFFICIAL COMPANY FONT...
S. Adams
LET'S SEE... WHAT WOULD BE THE MOST OBSCURE AND IMPRACTICAL FONT IMAGINABLE?
Purr Purr Purr
5/16/97
© 1997 United Feature Syndicate, Inc.
SOMEWHERE IN ELBONIA
I UNDERSTAND I CAN GET THE ELBONIAN FONT SOFTWARE FROM YOU.
YEP. UNLESS YOU NEED CONSONANTS FOR SOME REASON.

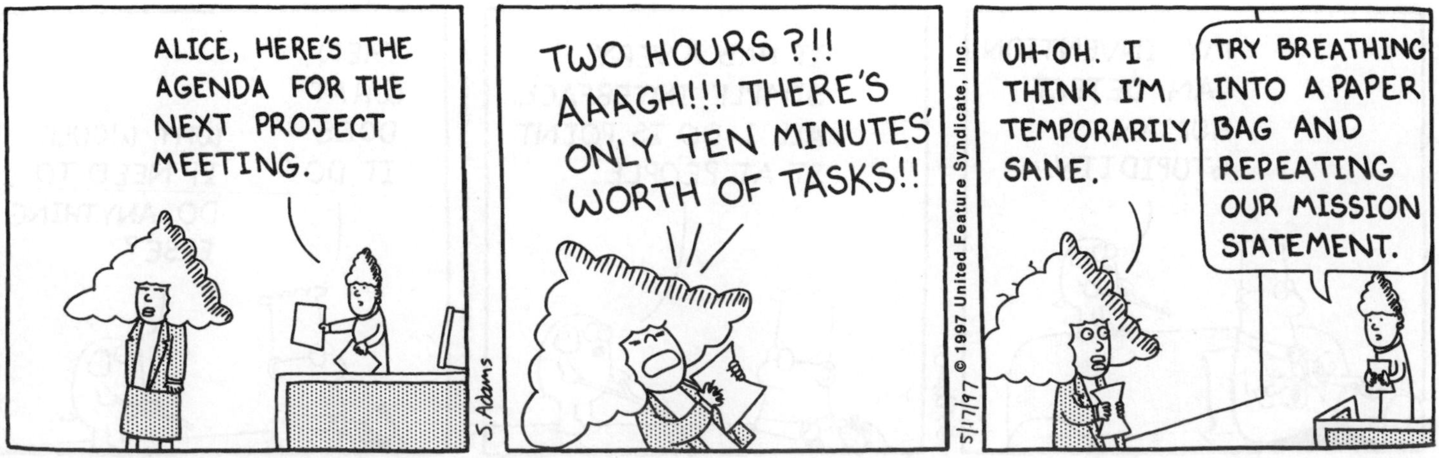
ALICE, HERE'S THE AGENDA FOR THE NEXT PROJECT MEETING.
S. Adams
TWO HOURS?!! AAAGH!!! THERE'S ONLY TEN MINUTES' WORTH OF TASKS!!
5/17/97
© 1997 United Feature Syndicate, Inc.
UH-OH. I THINK I'M TEMPORARILY SANE.
TRY BREATHING INTO A PAPER BAG AND REPEATING OUR MISSION STATEMENT.

DILBERT

BY

SCOTT ADAMS

THANK YOU. PLEASE COME AGAIN.

AFTER I'M DEAD.

IF WE EACH PUT IN TWELVE DOLLARS, THAT WILL GIVE HER A HEALTHY FOURTEEN PERCENT TIP.

THE SERVICE WAS EXCELLENT. I'LL PUT IN A LITTLE EXTRA.

ME TOO.

ME TOO.

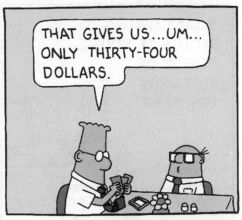

THAT GIVES US...UM... ONLY THIRTY-FOUR DOLLARS.

ONE OF US IS A CHEAP, LYING, UNSCRUPULOUS WEASEL.

OR MAYBE THE SERVICE WAS BAD.

SHE DIDN'T SMILE ENOUGH.

SAME AS LAST WEEK.

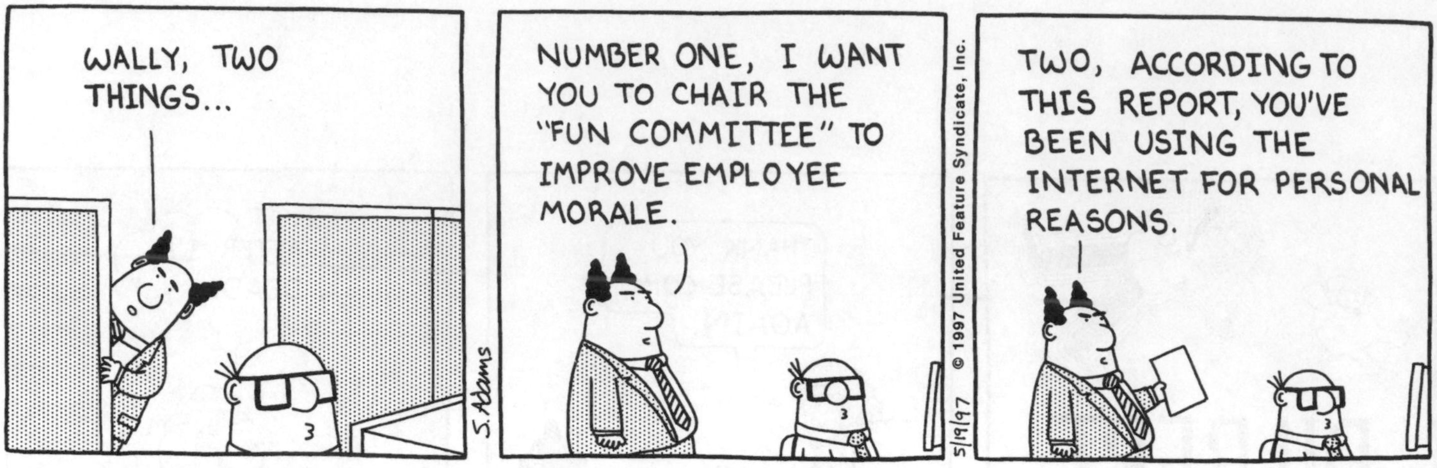
WALLY, TWO THINGS...
NUMBER ONE, I WANT YOU TO CHAIR THE "FUN COMMITTEE" TO IMPROVE EMPLOYEE MORALE.
TWO, ACCORDING TO THIS REPORT, YOU'VE BEEN USING THE INTERNET FOR PERSONAL REASONS.
S. Adams
5/19/97
© 1997 United Feature Syndicate, Inc.

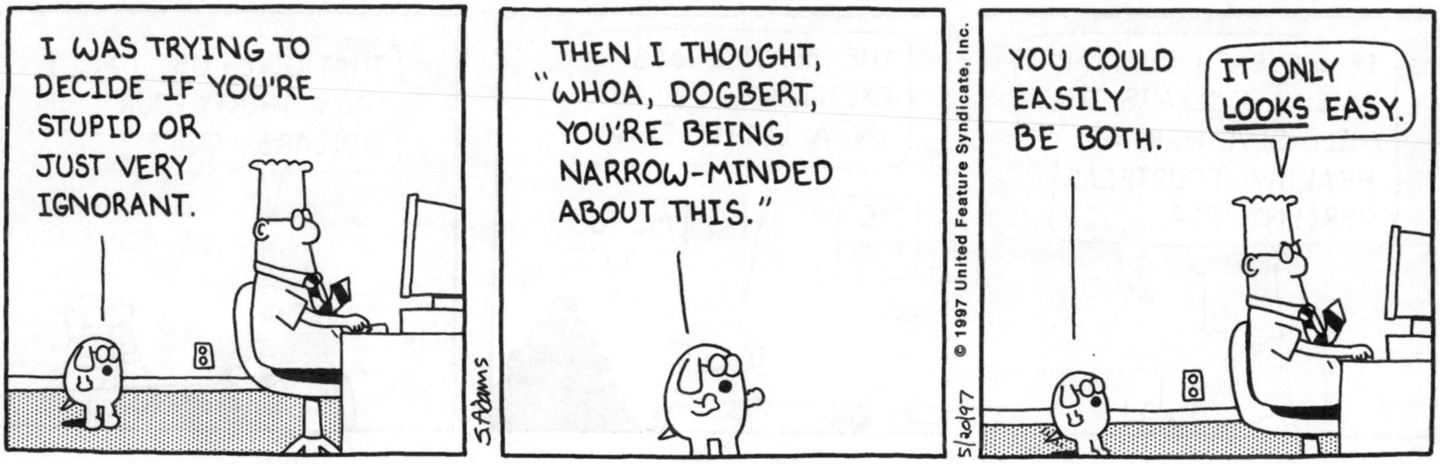
I WAS TRYING TO DECIDE IF YOU'RE STUPID OR JUST VERY IGNORANT.
THEN I THOUGHT, "WHOA, DOGBERT, YOU'RE BEING NARROW-MINDED ABOUT THIS."
YOU COULD EASILY BE BOTH.
IT ONLY LOOKS EASY.
S. Adams
5/20/97
© 1997 United Feature Syndicate, Inc.

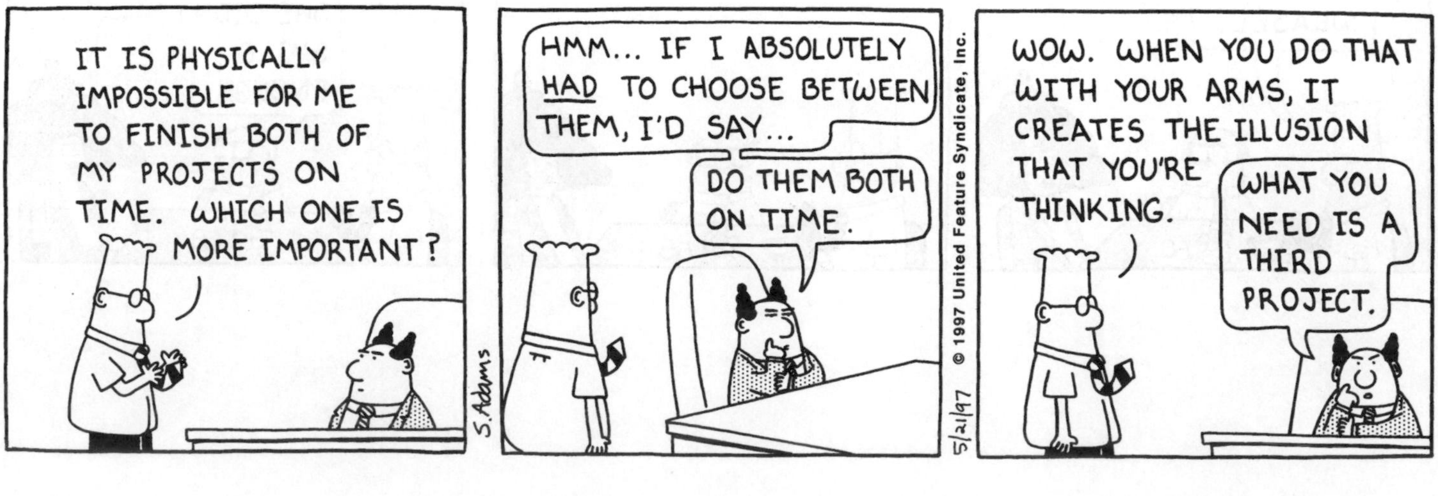
IT IS PHYSICALLY IMPOSSIBLE FOR ME TO FINISH BOTH OF MY PROJECTS ON TIME. WHICH ONE IS MORE IMPORTANT?
HMM... IF I ABSOLUTELY HAD TO CHOOSE BETWEEN THEM, I'D SAY...
DO THEM BOTH ON TIME.
WOW. WHEN YOU DO THAT WITH YOUR ARMS, IT CREATES THE ILLUSION THAT YOU'RE THINKING.
WHAT YOU NEED IS A THIRD PROJECT.
S. Adams
5/21/97
© 1997 United Feature Syndicate, Inc.

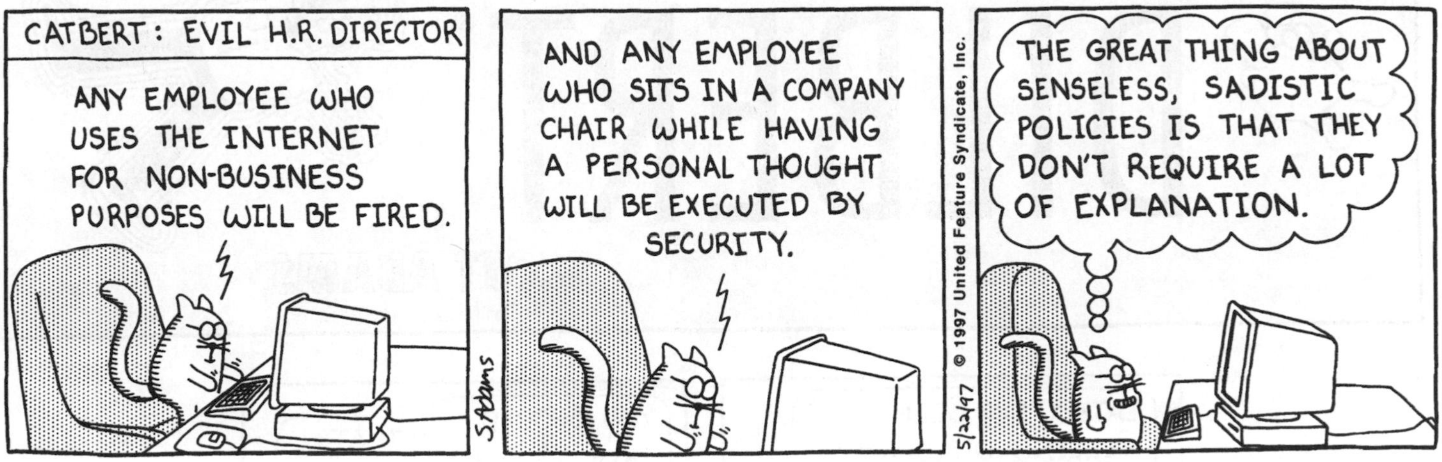
CATBERT: EVIL H.R. DIRECTOR
ANY EMPLOYEE WHO USES THE INTERNET FOR NON-BUSINESS PURPOSES WILL BE FIRED.
S. Adams
AND ANY EMPLOYEE WHO SITS IN A COMPANY CHAIR WHILE HAVING A PERSONAL THOUGHT WILL BE EXECUTED BY SECURITY.
5/22/97
© 1997 United Feature Syndicate, Inc.
THE GREAT THING ABOUT SENSELESS, SADISTIC POLICIES IS THAT THEY DON'T REQUIRE A LOT OF EXPLANATION.

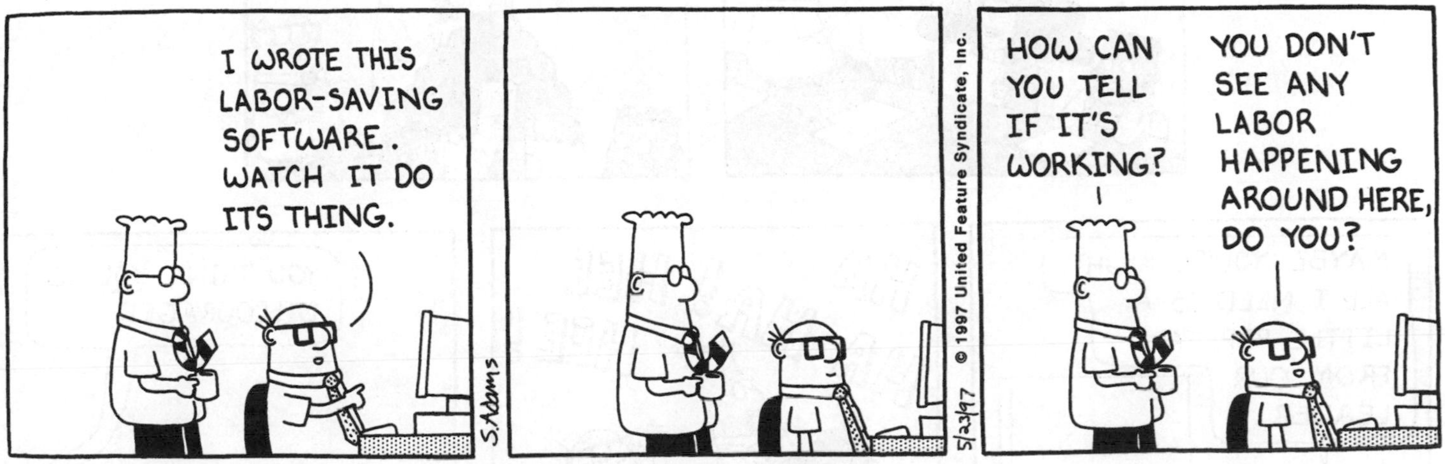
I WROTE THIS LABOR-SAVING SOFTWARE. WATCH IT DO ITS THING.
S. Adams
5/23/97
© 1997 United Feature Syndicate, Inc.
HOW CAN YOU TELL IF IT'S WORKING?
YOU DON'T SEE ANY LABOR HAPPENING AROUND HERE, DO YOU?

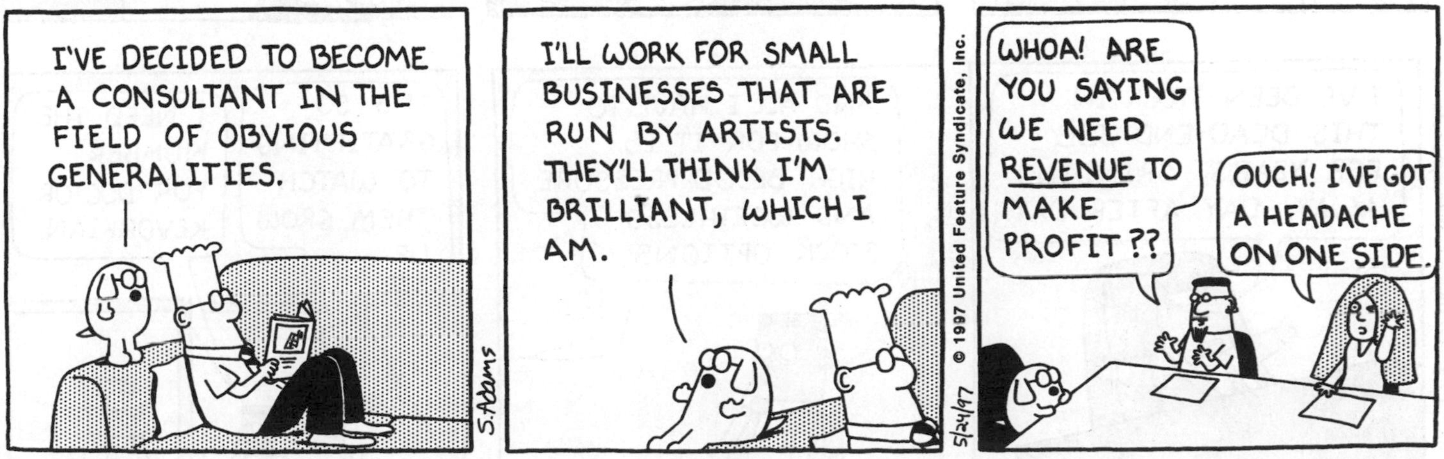
I'VE DECIDED TO BECOME A CONSULTANT IN THE FIELD OF OBVIOUS GENERALITIES.
S. Adams
I'LL WORK FOR SMALL BUSINESSES THAT ARE RUN BY ARTISTS. THEY'LL THINK I'M BRILLIANT, WHICH I AM.
5/24/97
© 1997 United Feature Syndicate, Inc.
WHOA! ARE YOU SAYING WE NEED REVENUE TO MAKE PROFIT??
OUCH! I'VE GOT A HEADACHE ON ONE SIDE.

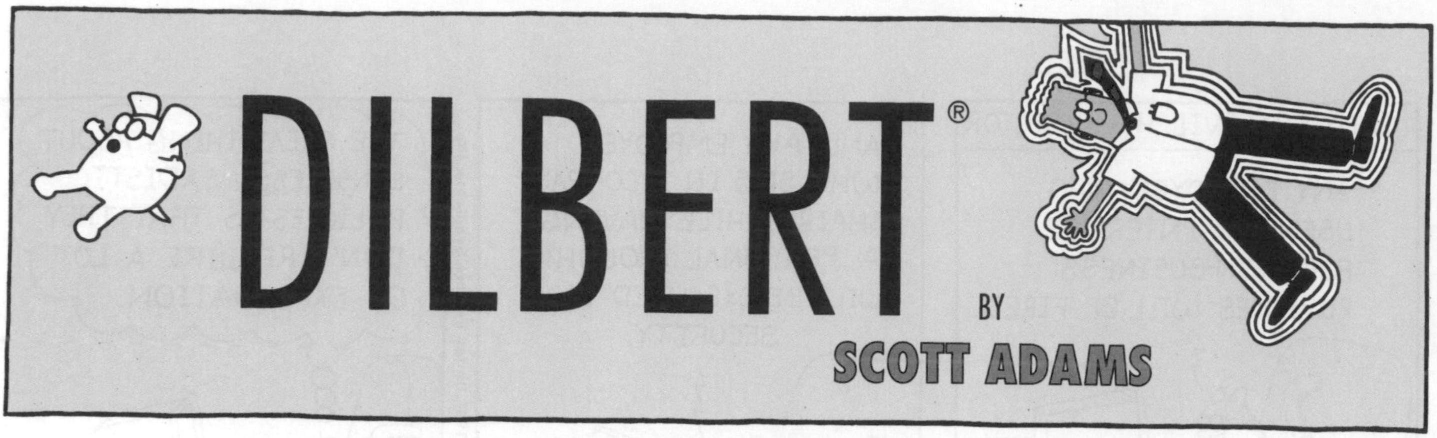
DILBERT®
BY
SCOTT ADAMS

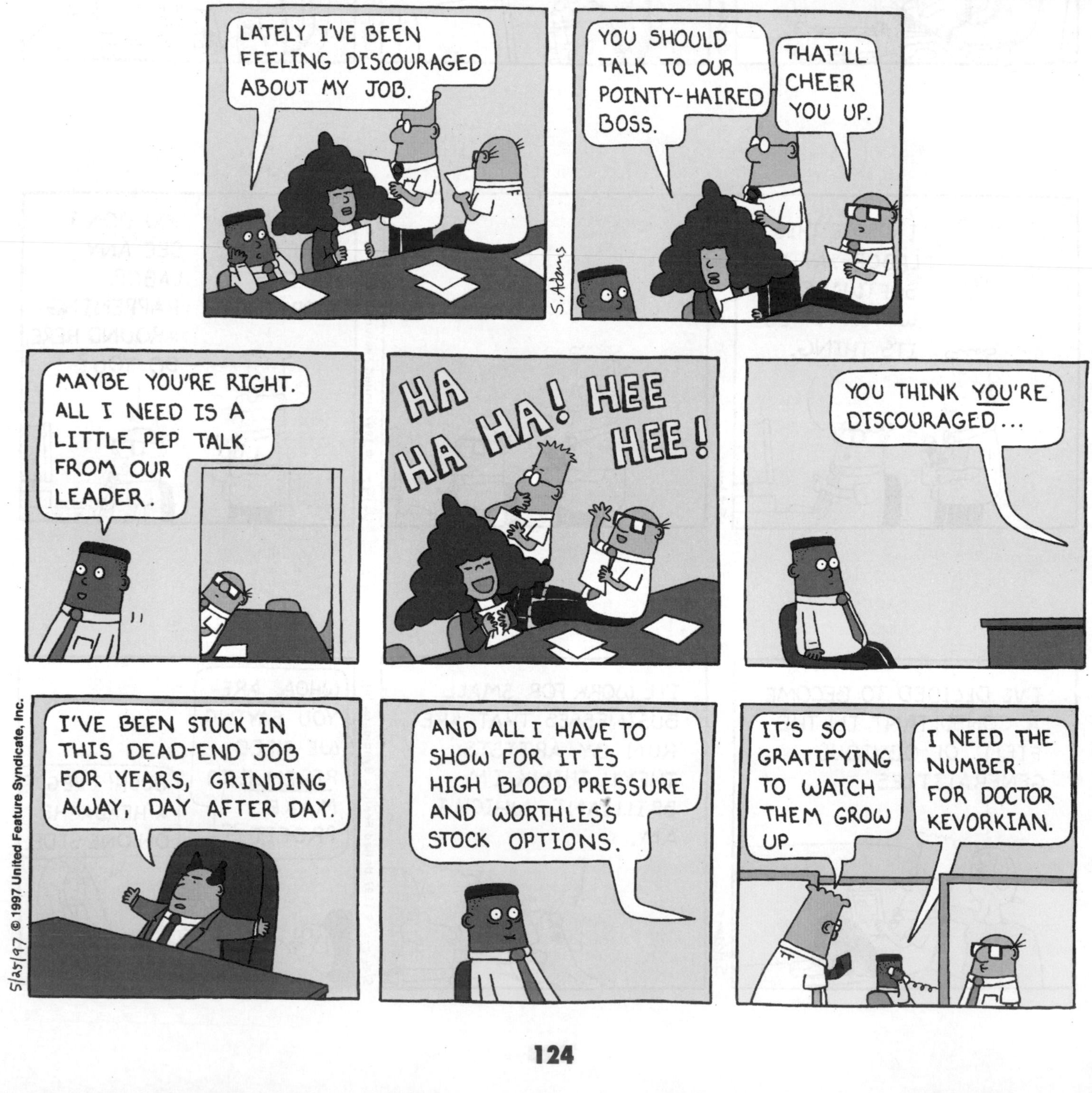
LATELY I'VE BEEN FEELING DISCOURAGED ABOUT MY JOB.
S. Adams
YOU SHOULD TALK TO OUR POINTY-HAIRED BOSS.
THAT'LL CHEER YOU UP.
MAYBE YOU'RE RIGHT. ALL I NEED IS A LITTLE PEP TALK FROM OUR LEADER.
HA HA HA! HEE HEE!
YOU THINK YOU'RE DISCOURAGED...
I'VE BEEN STUCK IN THIS DEAD-END JOB FOR YEARS, GRINDING AWAY, DAY AFTER DAY.
AND ALL I HAVE TO SHOW FOR IT IS HIGH BLOOD PRESSURE AND WORTHLESS STOCK OPTIONS.
IT'S SO GRATIFYING TO WATCH THEM GROW UP.
I NEED THE NUMBER FOR DOCTOR KEVORKIAN.
5/25/97 © 1997 United Feature Syndicate, Inc.

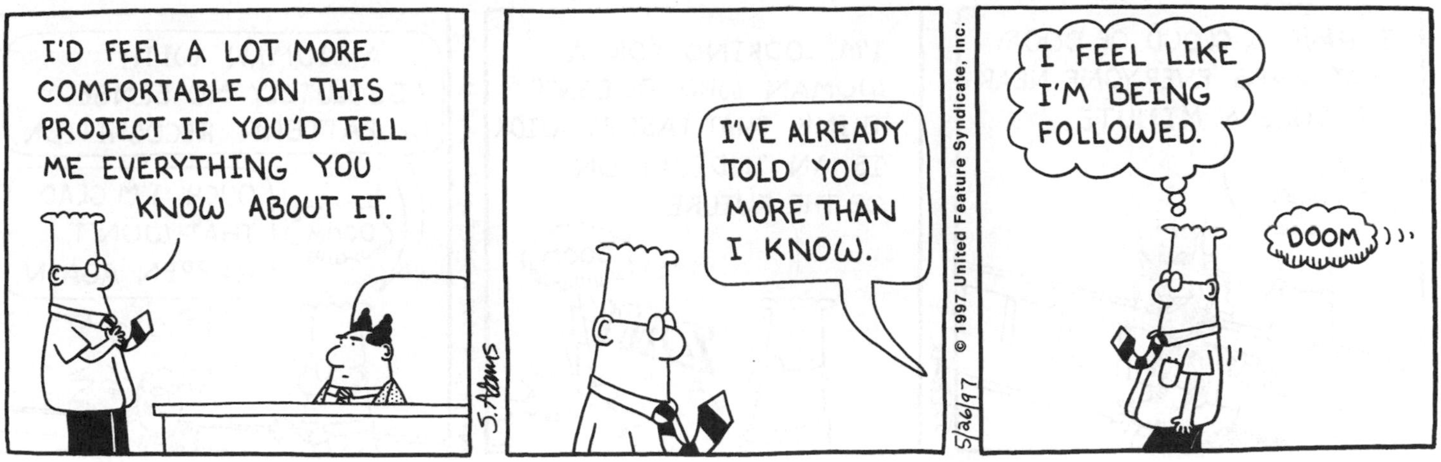

I'D FEEL A LOT MORE COMFORTABLE ON THIS PROJECT IF YOU'D TELL ME EVERYTHING YOU KNOW ABOUT IT.
I'VE ALREADY TOLD YOU MORE THAN I KNOW.
I FEEL LIKE I'M BEING FOLLOWED.
DOOM
S. Adams
5/26/97
© 1997 United Feature Syndicate, Inc.

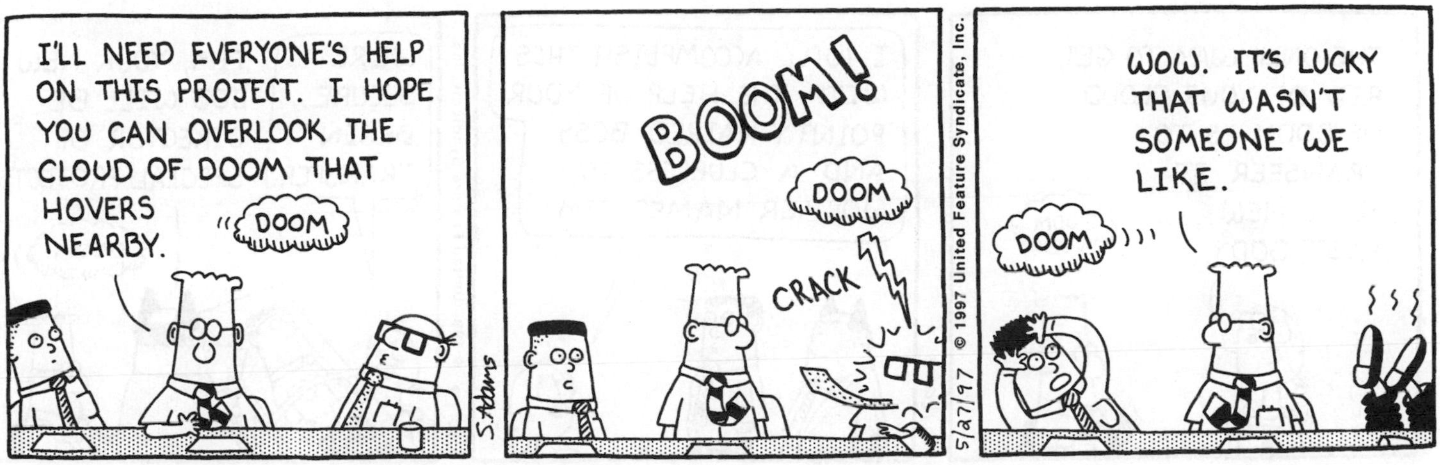

I'LL NEED EVERYONE'S HELP ON THIS PROJECT. I HOPE YOU CAN OVERLOOK THE CLOUD OF DOOM THAT HOVERS NEARBY.
DOOM
BOOM!
DOOM
CRACK
DOOM
WOW. IT'S LUCKY THAT WASN'T SOMEONE WE LIKE.
S. Adams
5/27/97
© 1997 United Feature Syndicate, Inc.

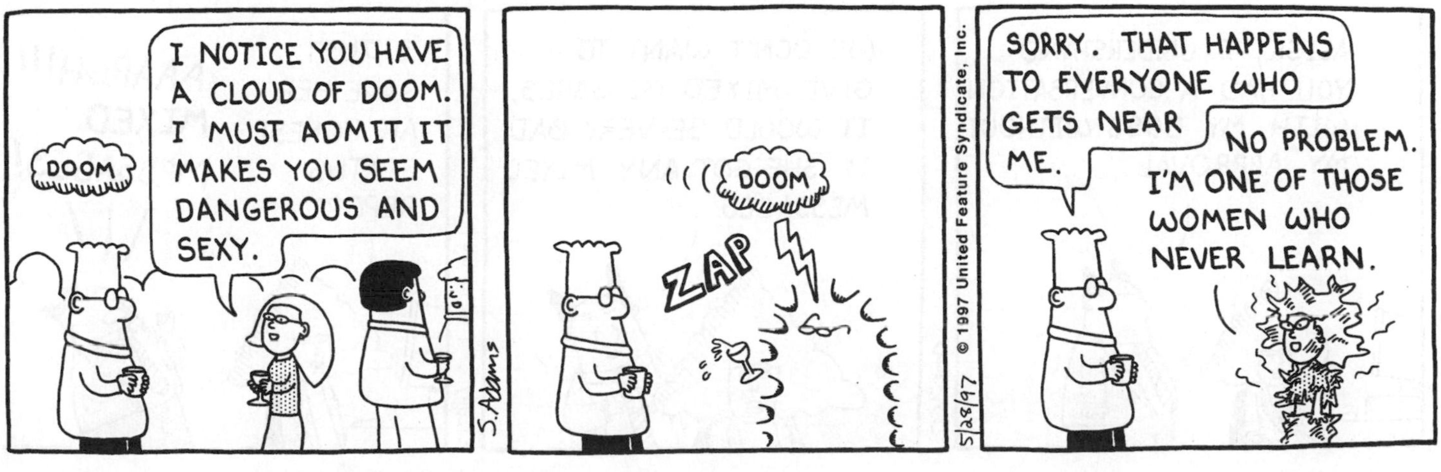

DOOM
I NOTICE YOU HAVE A CLOUD OF DOOM. I MUST ADMIT IT MAKES YOU SEEM DANGEROUS AND SEXY.
DOOM
ZAP
SORRY. THAT HAPPENS TO EVERYONE WHO GETS NEAR ME.
NO PROBLEM. I'M ONE OF THOSE WOMEN WHO NEVER LEARN.
S. Adams
5/28/97
© 1997 United Feature Syndicate, Inc.

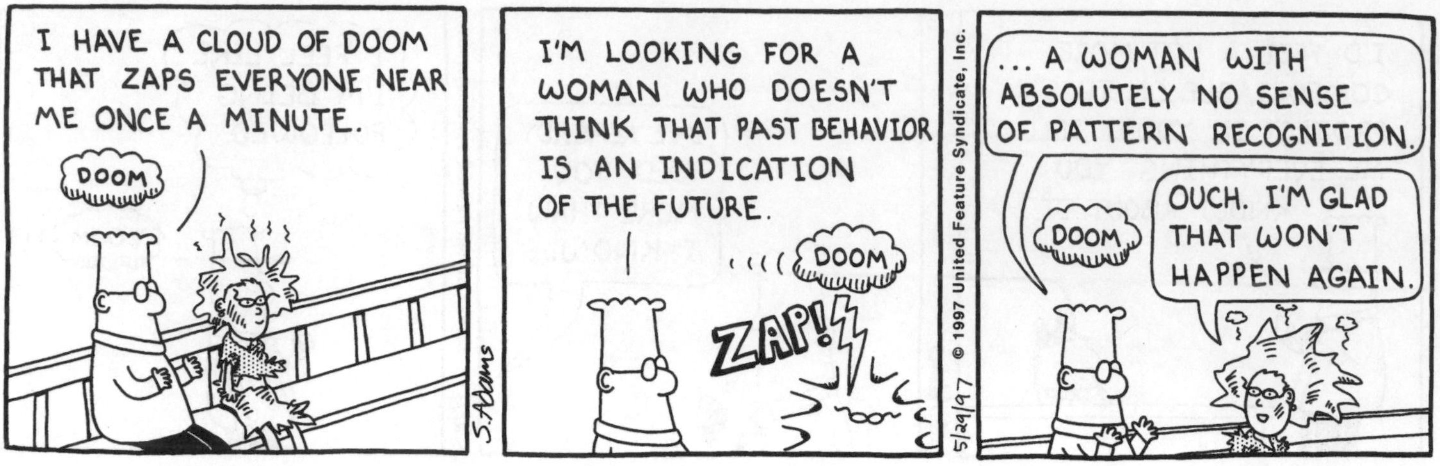
I HAVE A CLOUD OF DOOM THAT ZAPS EVERYONE NEAR ME ONCE A MINUTE.
DOOM
I'M LOOKING FOR A WOMAN WHO DOESN'T THINK THAT PAST BEHAVIOR IS AN INDICATION OF THE FUTURE.
DOOM
ZAP!
... A WOMAN WITH ABSOLUTELY NO SENSE OF PATTERN RECOGNITION.
DOOM
OUCH. I'M GLAD THAT WON'T HAPPEN AGAIN.
S.Adams
5/29/97 © 1997 United Feature Syndicate, Inc.

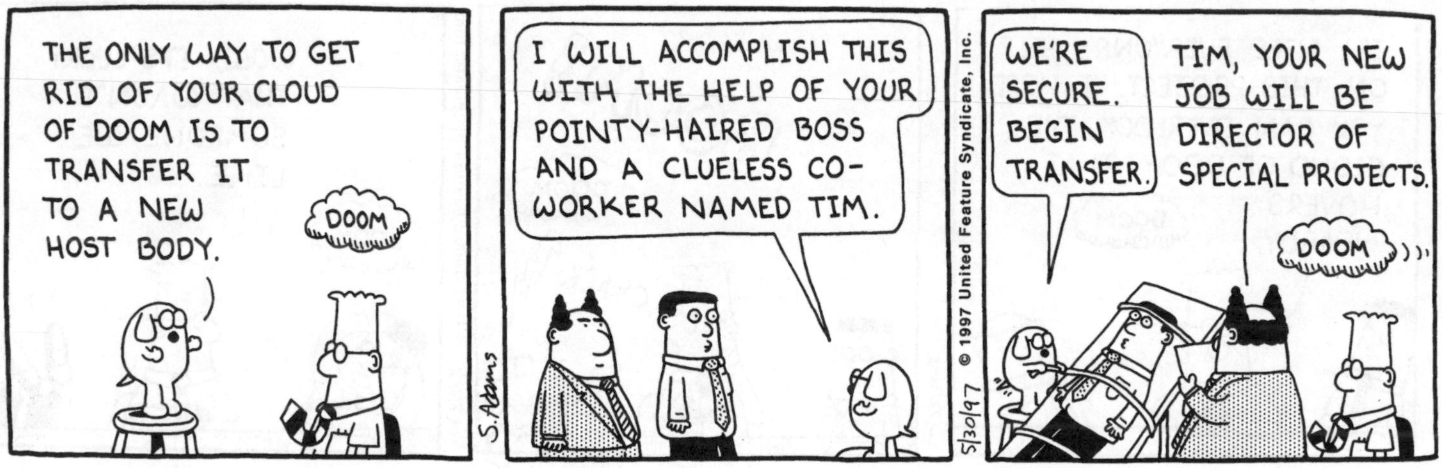
THE ONLY WAY TO GET RID OF YOUR CLOUD OF DOOM IS TO TRANSFER IT TO A NEW HOST BODY.
DOOM
I WILL ACCOMPLISH THIS WITH THE HELP OF YOUR POINTY-HAIRED BOSS AND A CLUELESS CO-WORKER NAMED TIM.
WE'RE SECURE. BEGIN TRANSFER.
TIM, YOUR NEW JOB WILL BE DIRECTOR OF SPECIAL PROJECTS.
DOOM
S.Adams
5/30/97 © 1997 United Feature Syndicate, Inc.

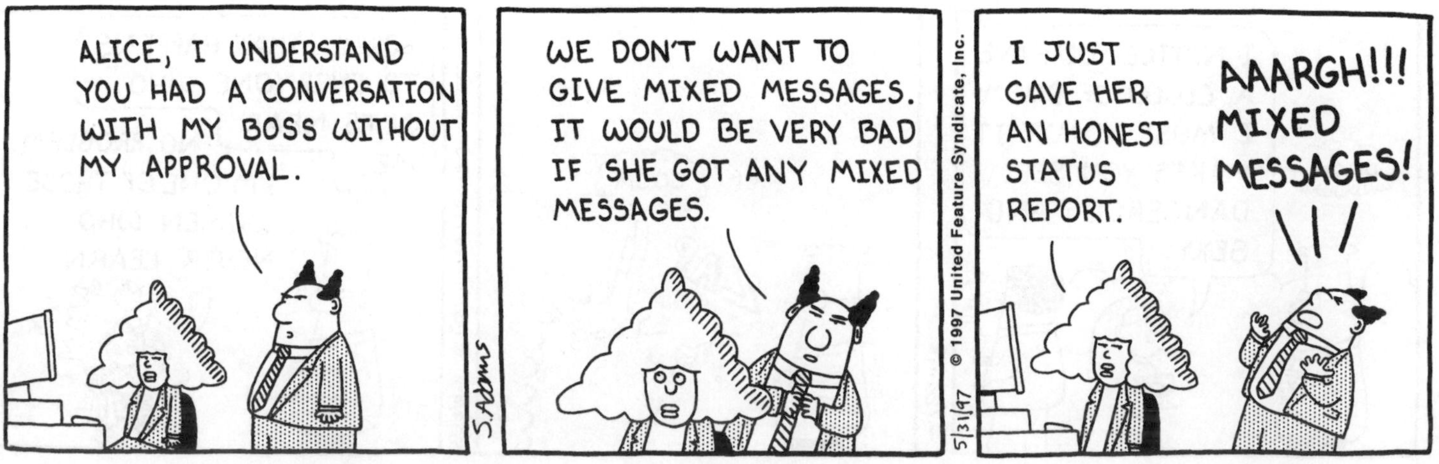
ALICE, I UNDERSTAND YOU HAD A CONVERSATION WITH MY BOSS WITHOUT MY APPROVAL.
WE DON'T WANT TO GIVE MIXED MESSAGES. IT WOULD BE VERY BAD IF SHE GOT ANY MIXED MESSAGES.
I JUST GAVE HER AN HONEST STATUS REPORT.
AAARGH!!!! MIXED MESSAGES!
S.Adams
5/31/97 © 1997 United Feature Syndicate, Inc.

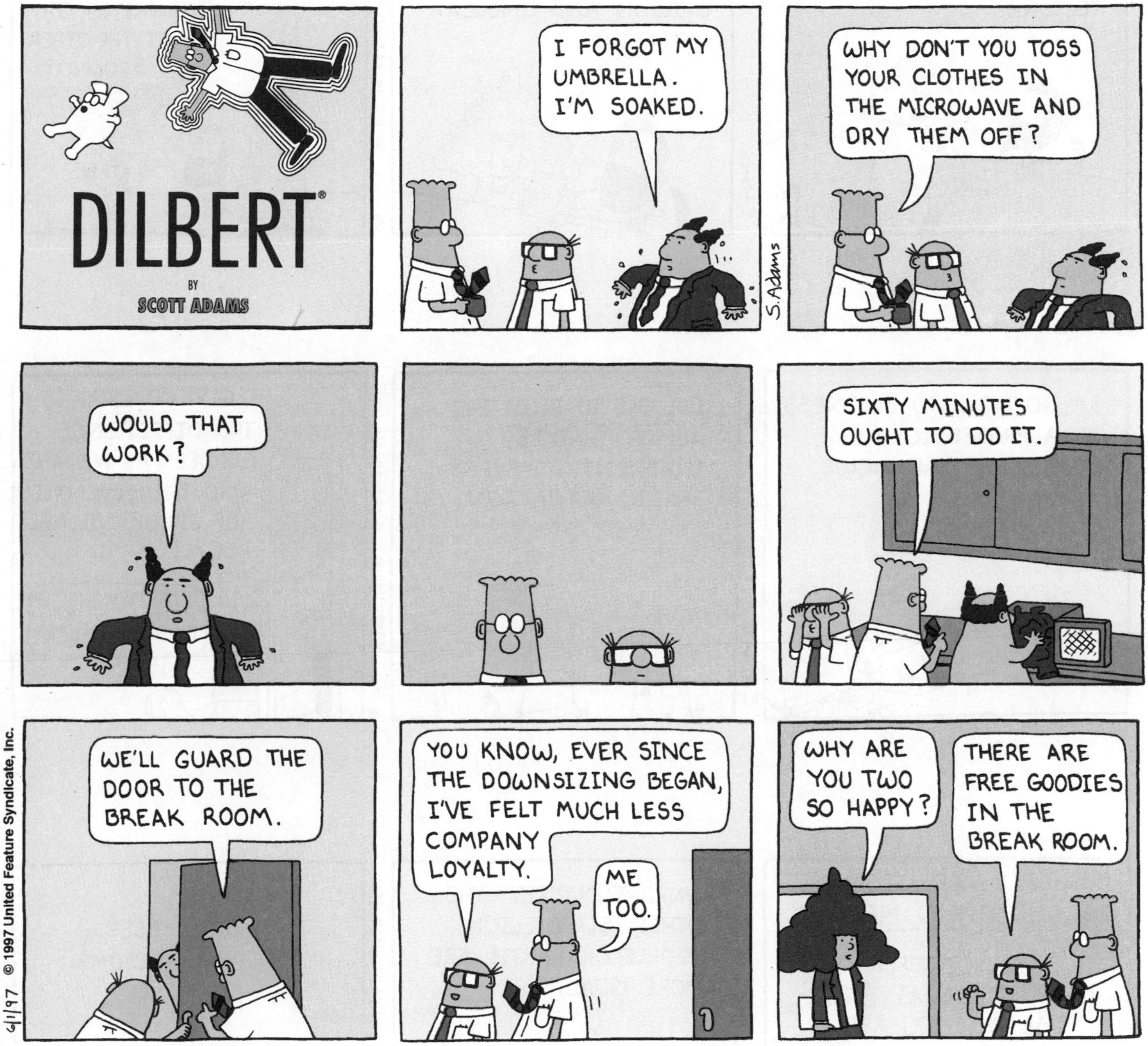
DILBERT®
BY
SCOTT ADAMS
I FORGOT MY UMBRELLA. I'M SOAKED.
S. Adams
WHY DON'T YOU TOSS YOUR CLOTHES IN THE MICROWAVE AND DRY THEM OFF?
WOULD THAT WORK?
SIXTY MINUTES OUGHT TO DO IT.
6/1/97 © 1997 United Feature Syndicate, Inc.
WE'LL GUARD THE DOOR TO THE BREAK ROOM.
YOU KNOW, EVER SINCE THE DOWNSIZING BEGAN, I'VE FELT MUCH LESS COMPANY LOYALTY.
ME TOO.
WHY ARE YOU TWO SO HAPPY?
THERE ARE FREE GOODIES IN THE BREAK ROOM.

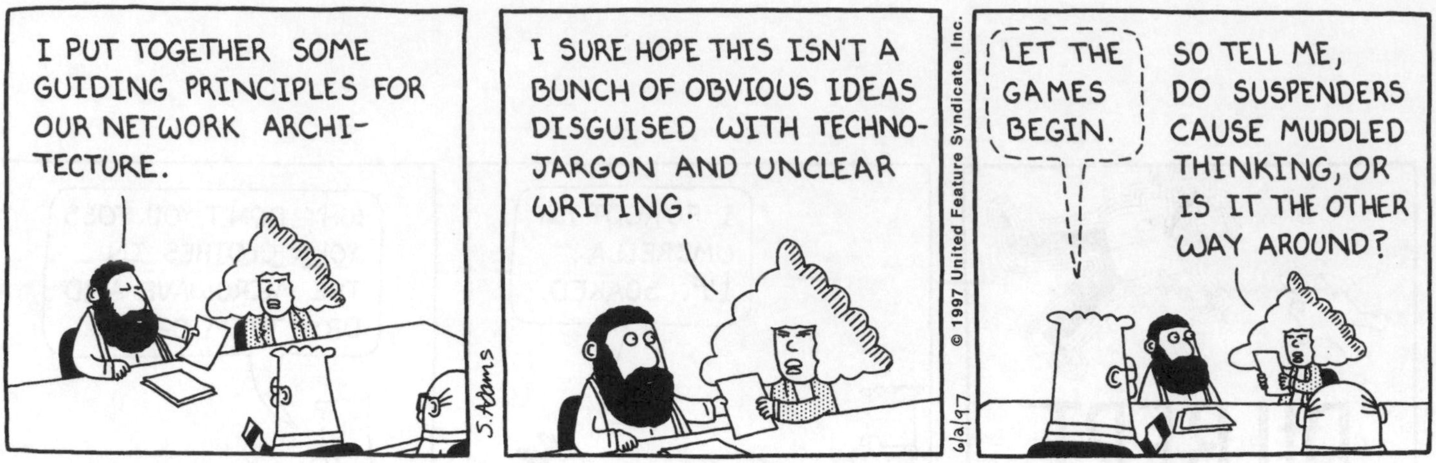
I PUT TOGETHER SOME GUIDING PRINCIPLES FOR OUR NETWORK ARCHITECTURE.
I SURE HOPE THIS ISN'T A BUNCH OF OBVIOUS IDEAS DISGUISED WITH TECHNO-JARGON AND UNCLEAR WRITING.
LET THE GAMES BEGIN.
SO TELL ME, DO SUSPENDERS CAUSE MUDDLED THINKING, OR IS IT THE OTHER WAY AROUND?
S. Adams
6/2/97
© 1997 United Feature Syndicate, Inc.

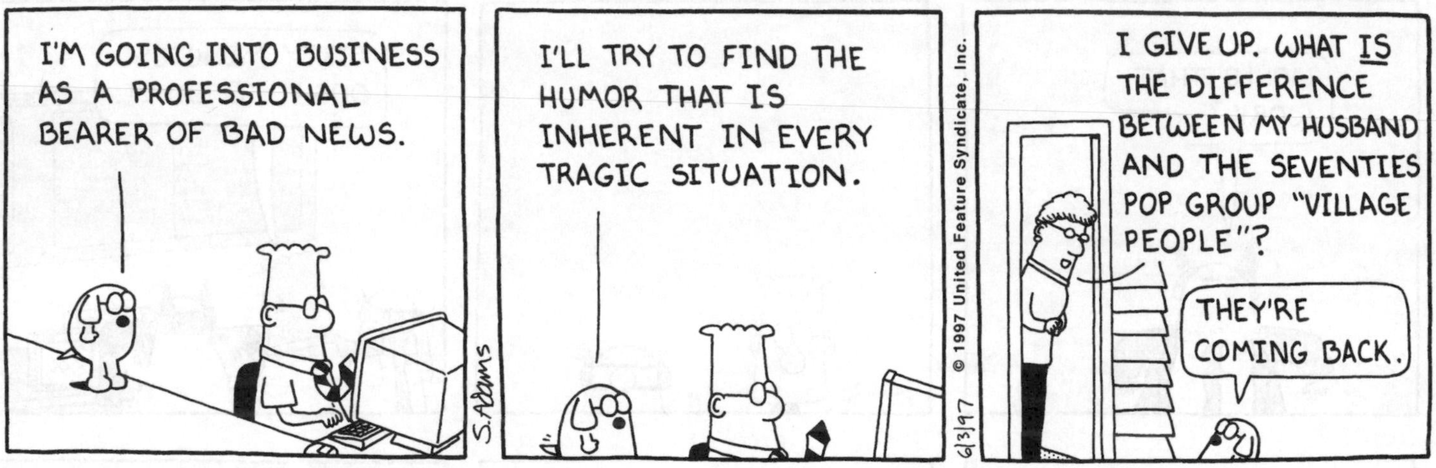
I'M GOING INTO BUSINESS AS A PROFESSIONAL BEARER OF BAD NEWS.
I'LL TRY TO FIND THE HUMOR THAT IS INHERENT IN EVERY TRAGIC SITUATION.
I GIVE UP. WHAT IS THE DIFFERENCE BETWEEN MY HUSBAND AND THE SEVENTIES POP GROUP "VILLAGE PEOPLE"?
THEY'RE COMING BACK.
S. Adams
6/3/97
© 1997 United Feature Syndicate, Inc.

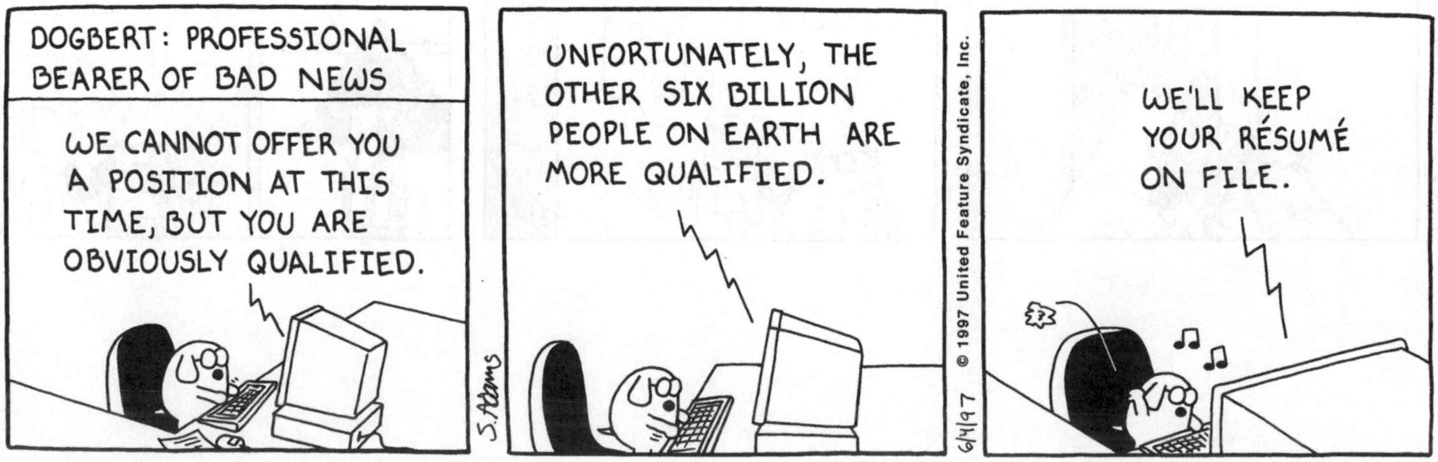
DOGBERT: PROFESSIONAL BEARER OF BAD NEWS
WE CANNOT OFFER YOU A POSITION AT THIS TIME, BUT YOU ARE OBVIOUSLY QUALIFIED.
UNFORTUNATELY, THE OTHER SIX BILLION PEOPLE ON EARTH ARE MORE QUALIFIED.
WE'LL KEEP YOUR RÉSUMÉ ON FILE.
S. Adams
6/4/97
© 1997 United Feature Syndicate, Inc.

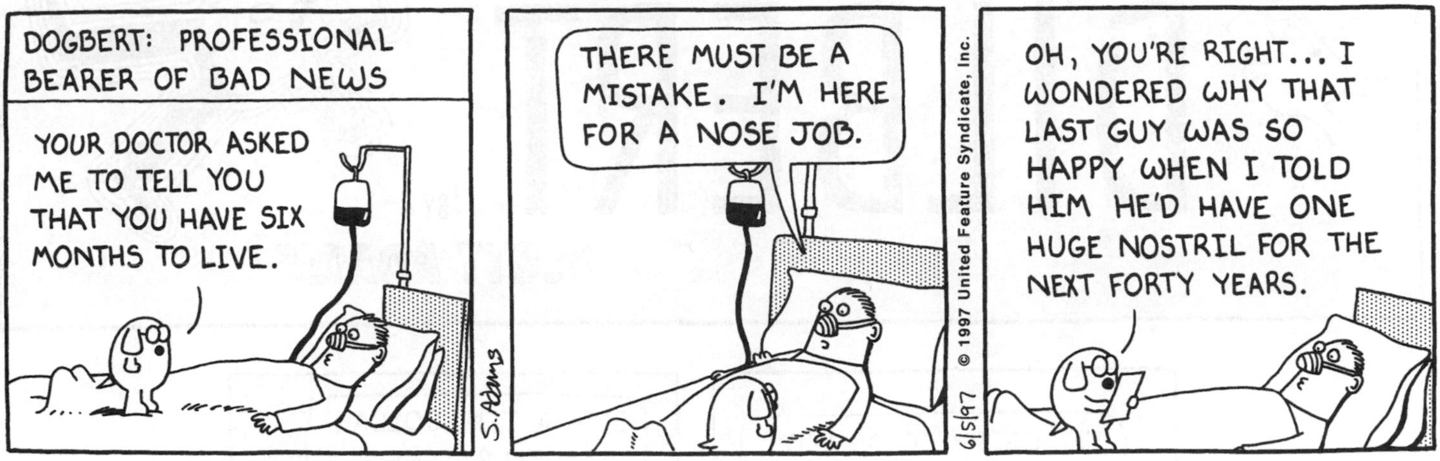
DOGBERT: PROFESSIONAL BEARER OF BAD NEWS
YOUR DOCTOR ASKED ME TO TELL YOU THAT YOU HAVE SIX MONTHS TO LIVE.
THERE MUST BE A MISTAKE. I'M HERE FOR A NOSE JOB.
OH, YOU'RE RIGHT... I WONDERED WHY THAT LAST GUY WAS SO HAPPY WHEN I TOLD HIM HE'D HAVE ONE HUGE NOSTRIL FOR THE NEXT FORTY YEARS.
S. Adams
6/5/97
© 1997 United Feature Syndicate, Inc.

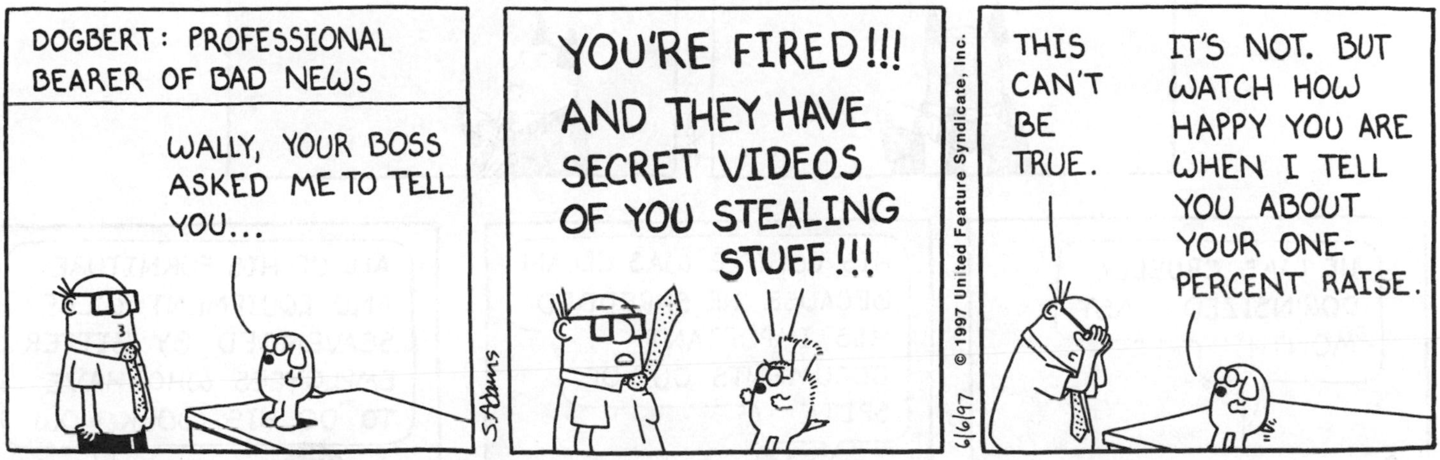
DOGBERT: PROFESSIONAL BEARER OF BAD NEWS
WALLY, YOUR BOSS ASKED ME TO TELL YOU...
YOU'RE FIRED!!! AND THEY HAVE SECRET VIDEOS OF YOU STEALING STUFF!!!
THIS CAN'T BE TRUE.
IT'S NOT. BUT WATCH HOW HAPPY YOU ARE WHEN I TELL YOU ABOUT YOUR ONE-PERCENT RAISE.
S. Adams
6/6/97
© 1997 United Feature Syndicate, Inc.

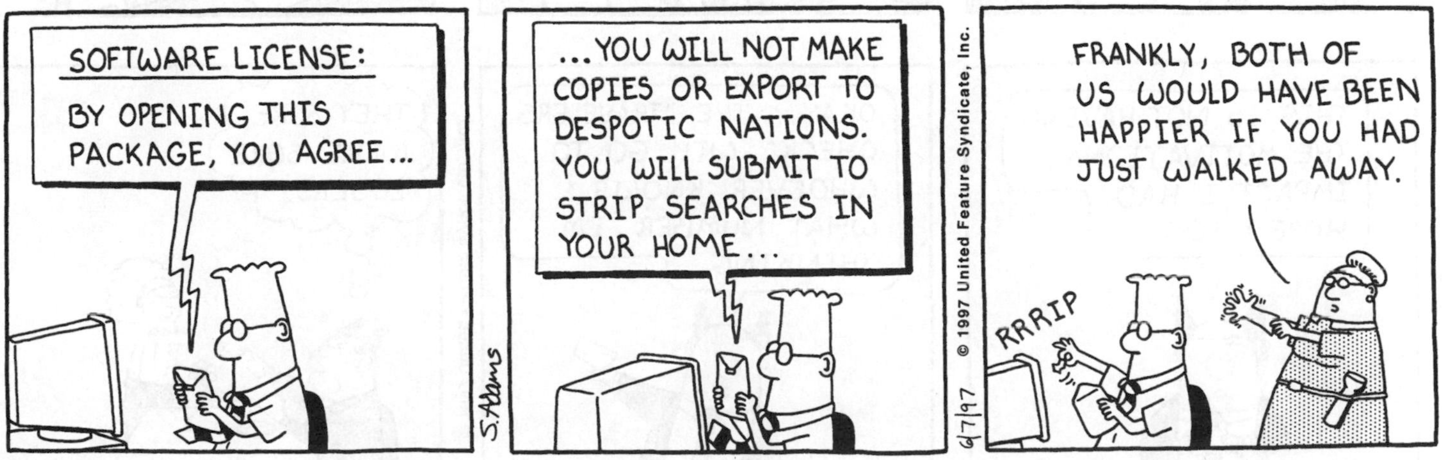
SOFTWARE LICENSE:
BY OPENING THIS PACKAGE, YOU AGREE...
...YOU WILL NOT MAKE COPIES OR EXPORT TO DESPOTIC NATIONS. YOU WILL SUBMIT TO STRIP SEARCHES IN YOUR HOME...
RRRIP
FRANKLY, BOTH OF US WOULD HAVE BEEN HAPPIER IF YOU HAD JUST WALKED AWAY.
S. Adams
6/7/97
© 1997 United Feature Syndicate, Inc.

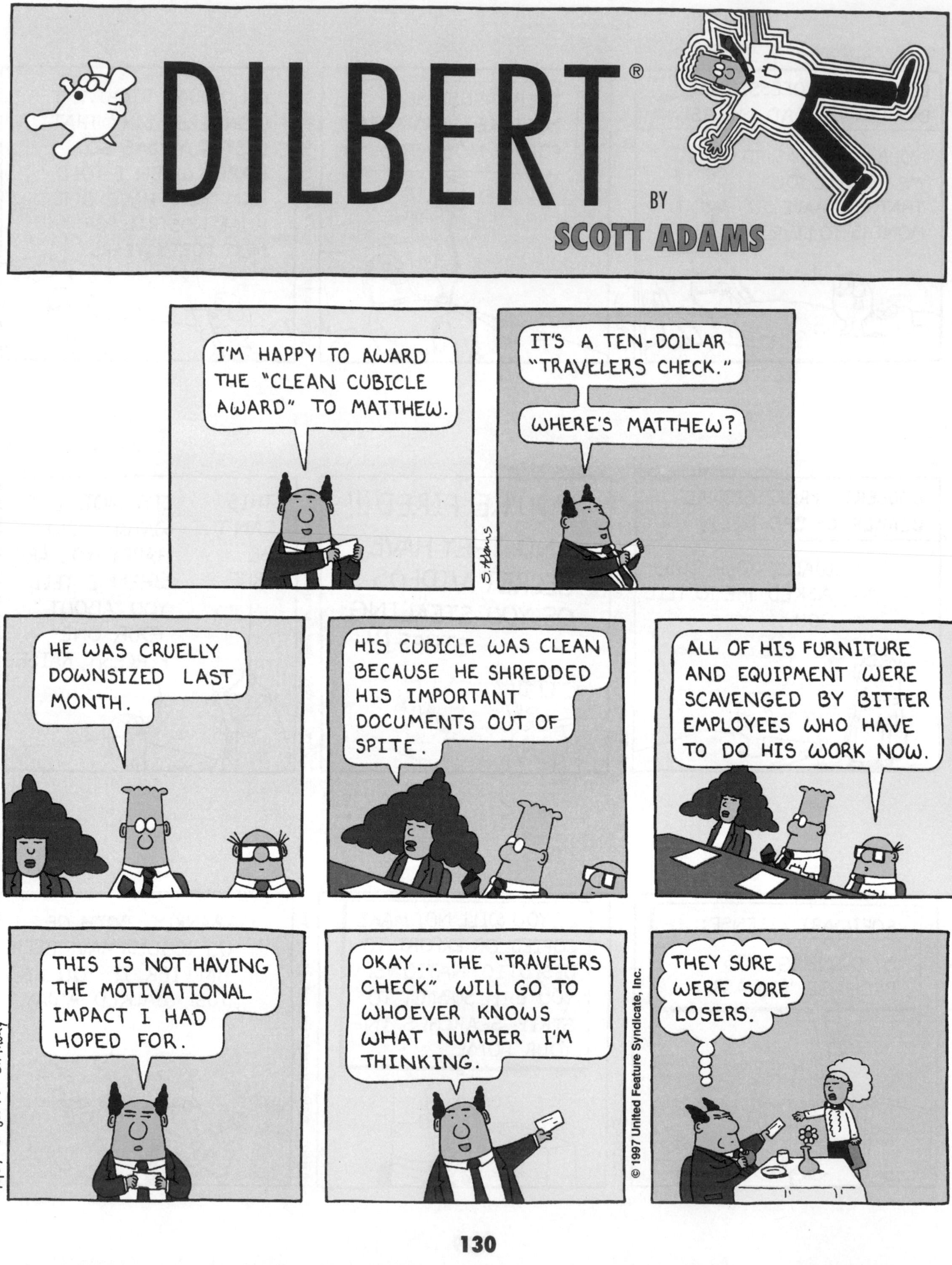
DILBERT®
BY
SCOTT ADAMS
I'M HAPPY TO AWARD THE "CLEAN CUBICLE AWARD" TO MATTHEW.
IT'S A TEN-DOLLAR "TRAVELERS CHECK."
WHERE'S MATTHEW?
S. Adams
HE WAS CRUELLY DOWNSIZED LAST MONTH.
HIS CUBICLE WAS CLEAN BECAUSE HE SHREDDED HIS IMPORTANT DOCUMENTS OUT OF SPITE.
ALL OF HIS FURNITURE AND EQUIPMENT WERE SCAVENGED BY BITTER EMPLOYEES WHO HAVE TO DO HIS WORK NOW.
6/8/57 - Dogbert's Birthday
THIS IS NOT HAVING THE MOTIVATIONAL IMPACT I HAD HOPED FOR.
OKAY... THE "TRAVELERS CHECK" WILL GO TO WHOEVER KNOWS WHAT NUMBER I'M THINKING.
© 1997 United Feature Syndicate, Inc.
THEY SURE WERE SORE LOSERS.

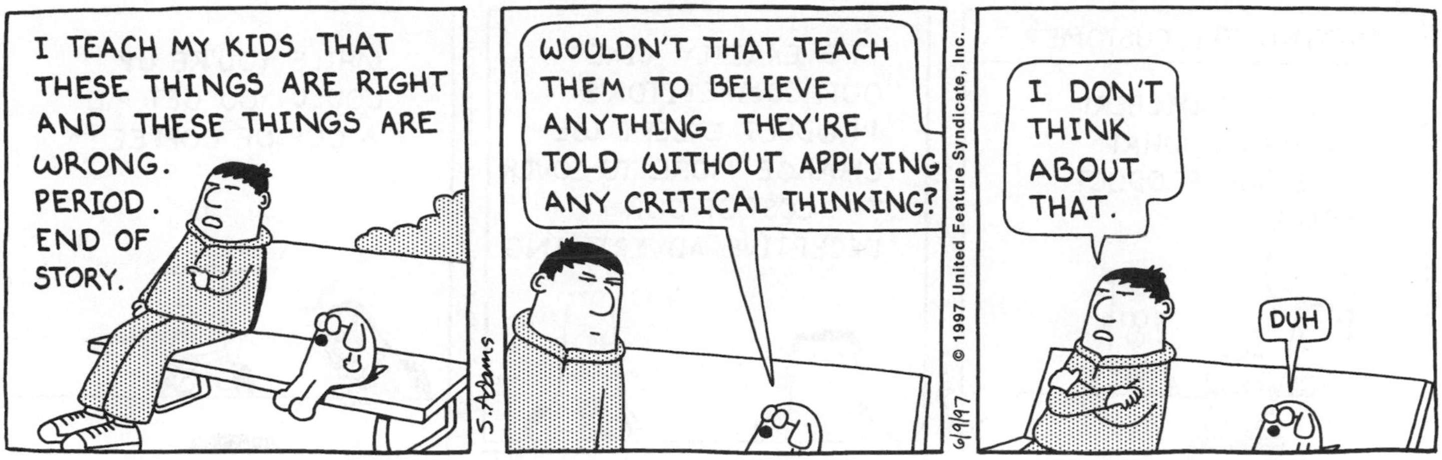
I TEACH MY KIDS THAT THESE THINGS ARE RIGHT AND THESE THINGS ARE WRONG. PERIOD. END OF STORY.
S. Adams
WOULDN'T THAT TEACH THEM TO BELIEVE ANYTHING THEY'RE TOLD WITHOUT APPLYING ANY CRITICAL THINKING?
6/9/97 © 1997 United Feature Syndicate, Inc.
I DON'T THINK ABOUT THAT.
DUH

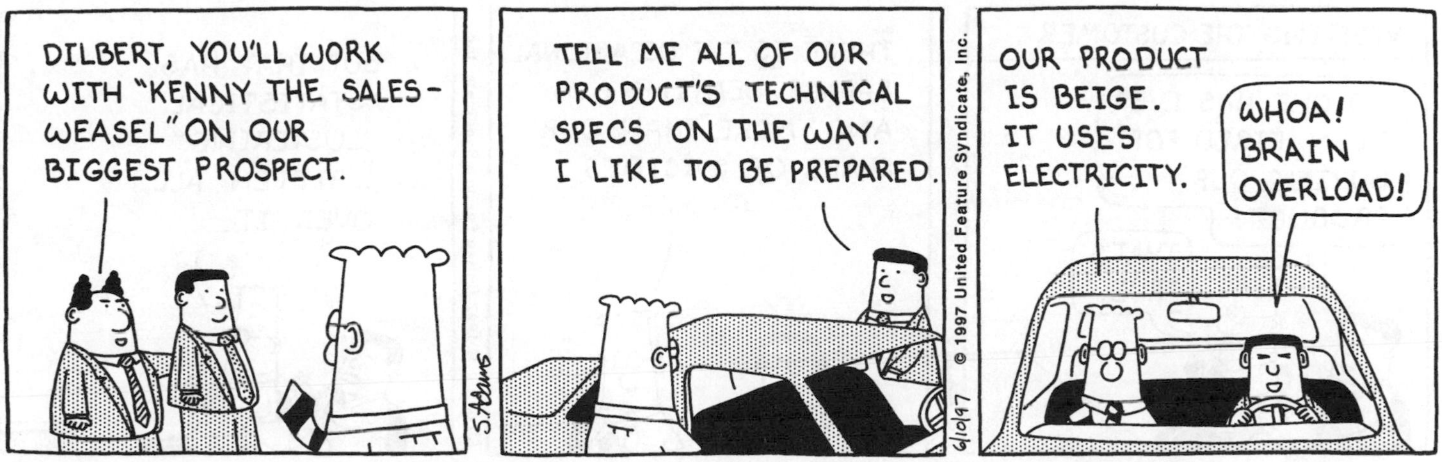
DILBERT, YOU'LL WORK WITH "KENNY THE SALES-WEASEL" ON OUR BIGGEST PROSPECT.
S. Adams
TELL ME ALL OF OUR PRODUCT'S TECHNICAL SPECS ON THE WAY. I LIKE TO BE PREPARED.
6/10/97 © 1997 United Feature Syndicate, Inc.
OUR PRODUCT IS BEIGE. IT USES ELECTRICITY.
WHOA! BRAIN OVERLOAD!

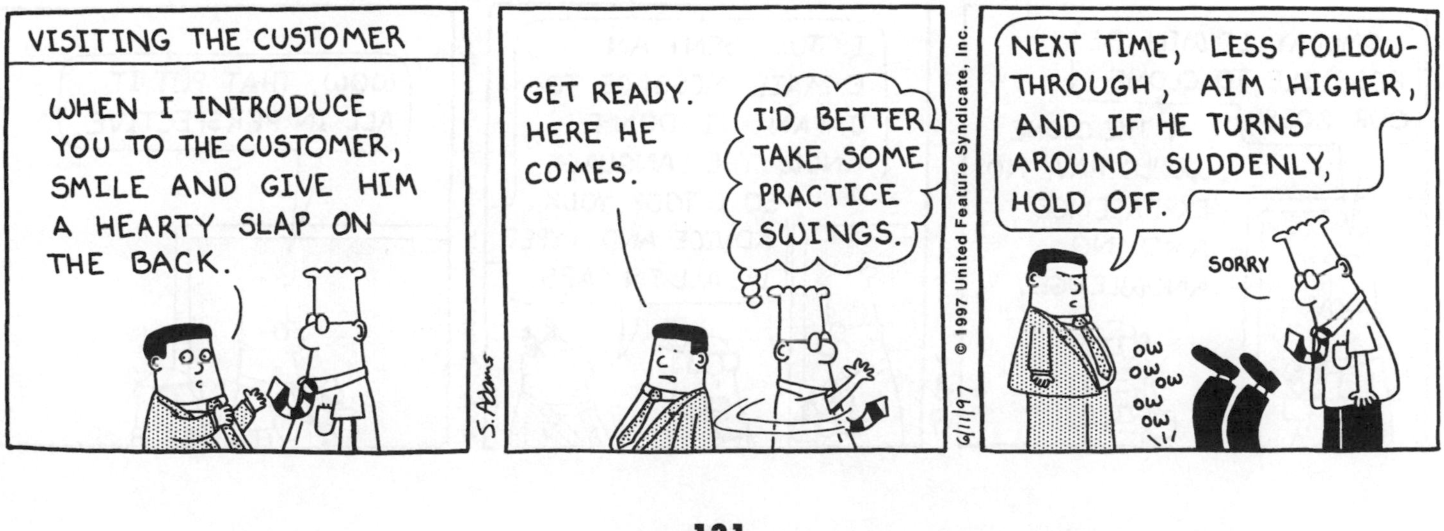
VISITING THE CUSTOMER
WHEN I INTRODUCE YOU TO THE CUSTOMER, SMILE AND GIVE HIM A HEARTY SLAP ON THE BACK.
S. Adams
GET READY. HERE HE COMES.
I'D BETTER TAKE SOME PRACTICE SWINGS.
6/11/97 © 1997 United Feature Syndicate, Inc.
NEXT TIME, LESS FOLLOW-THROUGH, AIM HIGHER, AND IF HE TURNS AROUND SUDDENLY, HOLD OFF.
SORRY
OW OW OW OW OW

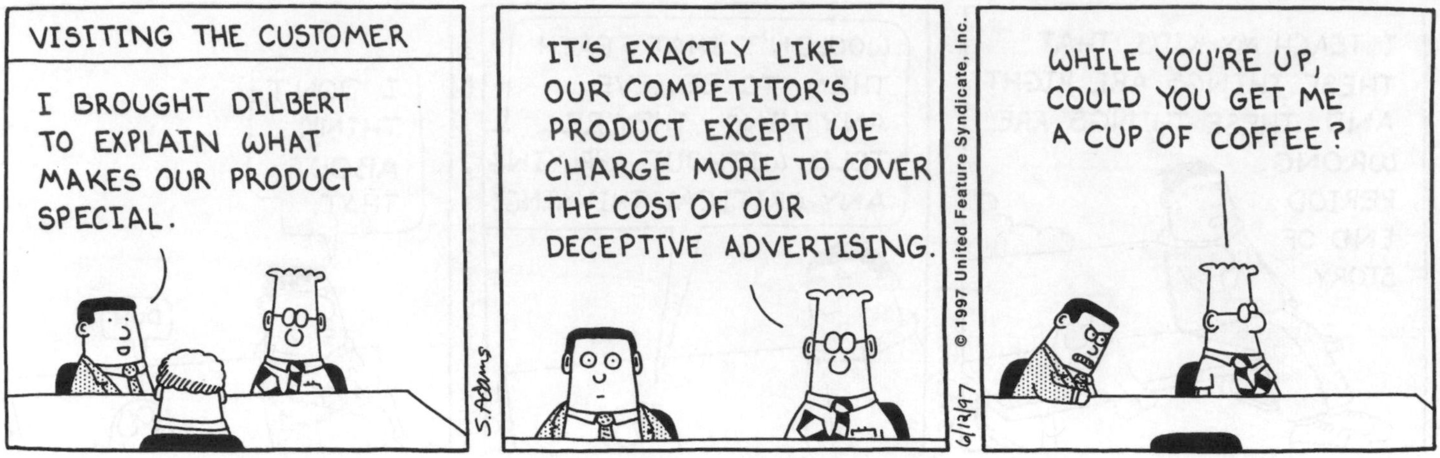
VISITING THE CUSTOMER
I BROUGHT DILBERT TO EXPLAIN WHAT MAKES OUR PRODUCT SPECIAL.
IT'S EXACTLY LIKE OUR COMPETITOR'S PRODUCT EXCEPT WE CHARGE MORE TO COVER THE COST OF OUR DECEPTIVE ADVERTISING.
6/12/97 © 1997 United Feature Syndicate, Inc.
WHILE YOU'RE UP, COULD YOU GET ME A CUP OF COFFEE?

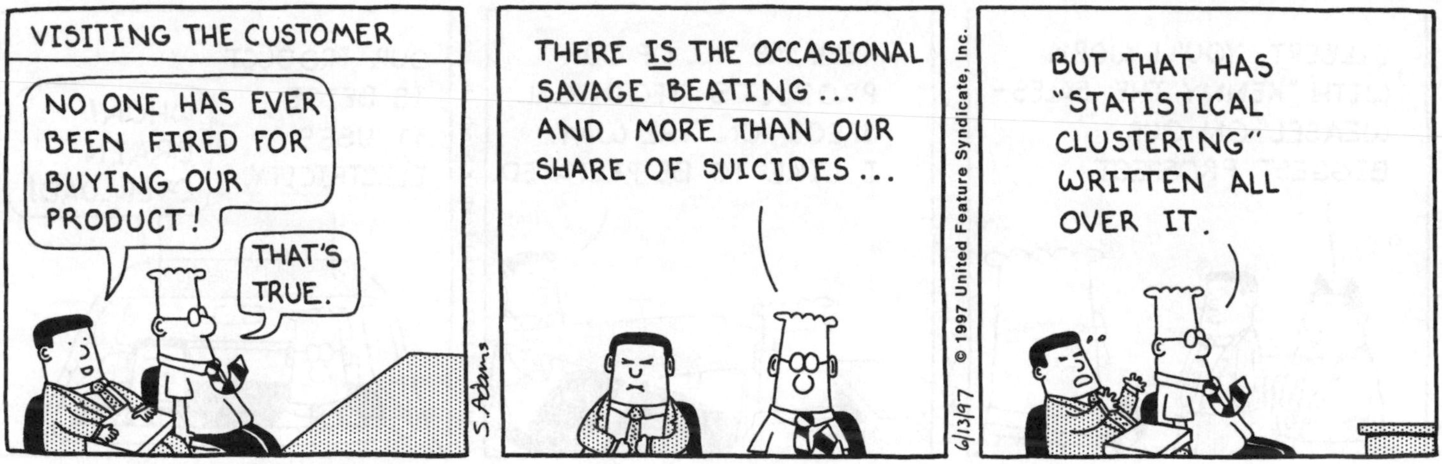
VISITING THE CUSTOMER
NO ONE HAS EVER BEEN FIRED FOR BUYING OUR PRODUCT!
THAT'S TRUE.
THERE IS THE OCCASIONAL SAVAGE BEATING... AND MORE THAN OUR SHARE OF SUICIDES...
6/13/97 © 1997 United Feature Syndicate, Inc.
BUT THAT HAS "STATISTICAL CLUSTERING" WRITTEN ALL OVER IT.

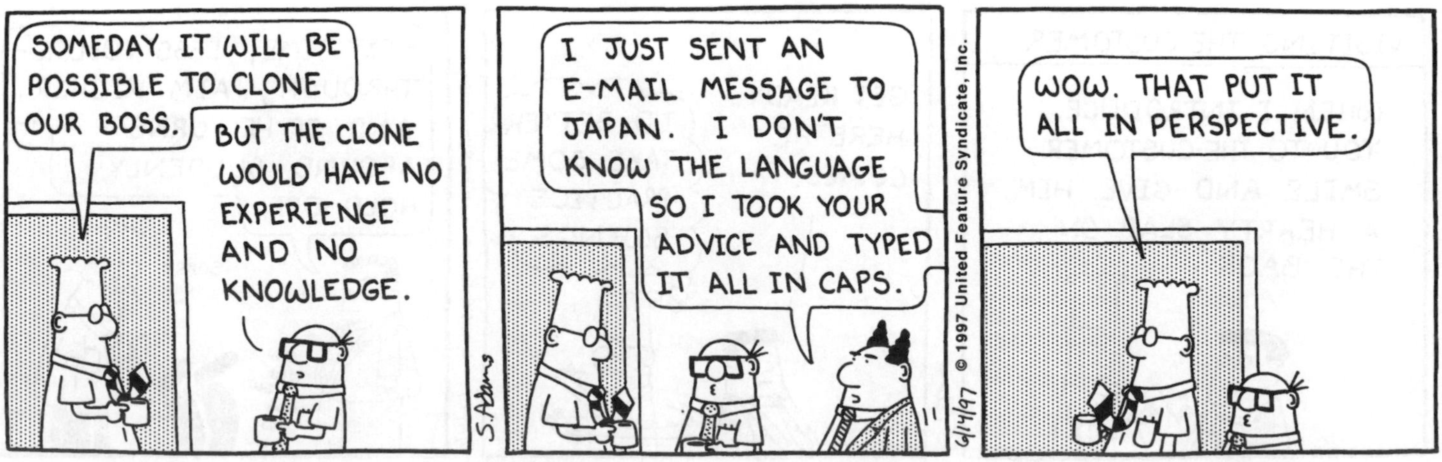
SOMEDAY IT WILL BE POSSIBLE TO CLONE OUR BOSS.
BUT THE CLONE WOULD HAVE NO EXPERIENCE AND NO KNOWLEDGE.
I JUST SENT AN E-MAIL MESSAGE TO JAPAN. I DON'T KNOW THE LANGUAGE SO I TOOK YOUR ADVICE AND TYPED IT ALL IN CAPS.
6/14/97 © 1997 United Feature Syndicate, Inc.
WOW. THAT PUT IT ALL IN PERSPECTIVE.

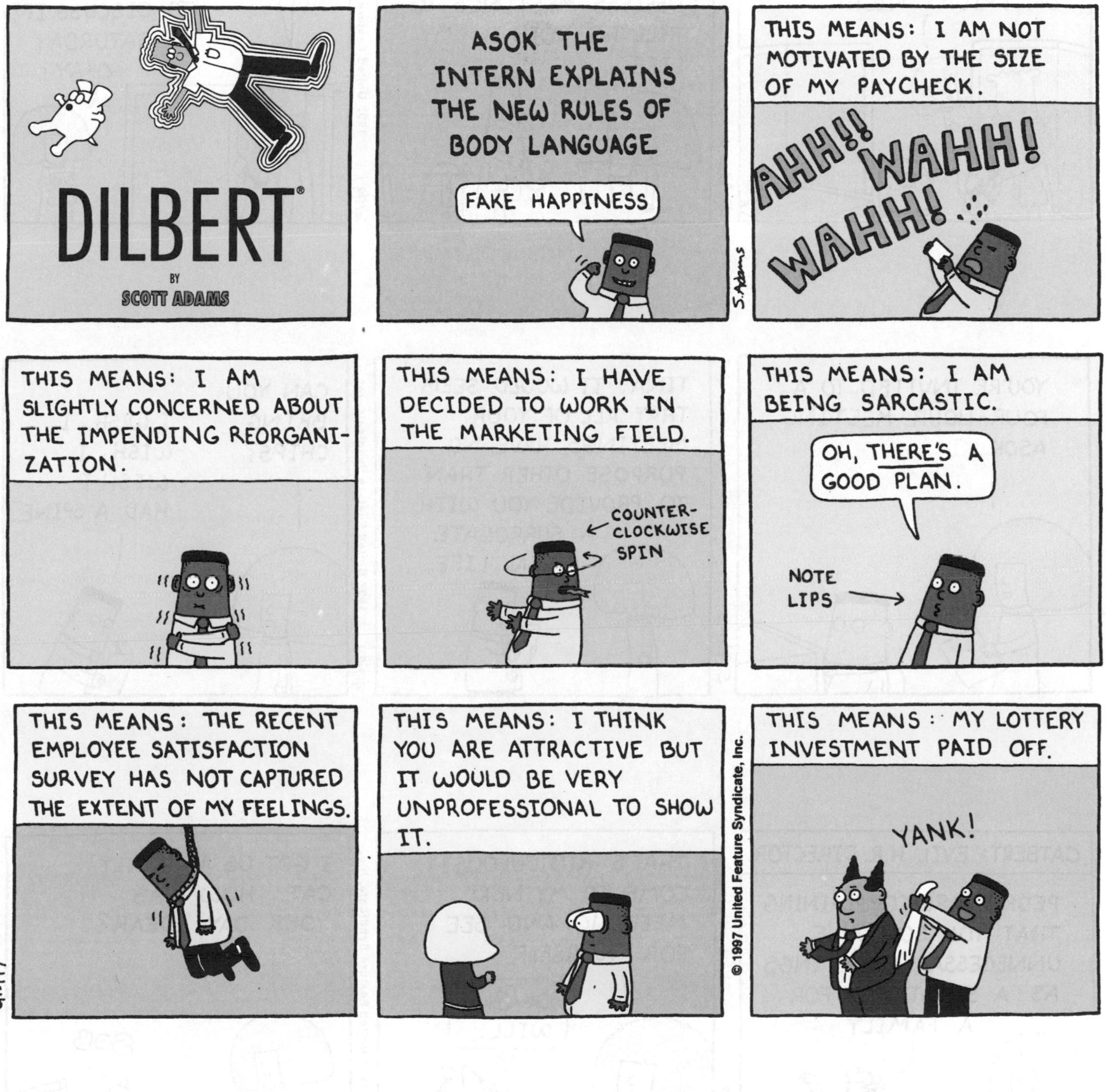
DILBERT®
BY
SCOTT ADAMS
ASOK THE INTERN EXPLAINS THE NEW RULES OF BODY LANGUAGE
FAKE HAPPINESS
THIS MEANS: I AM NOT MOTIVATED BY THE SIZE OF MY PAYCHECK.
AHH!! WAHH! WAHH!
S. Adams
THIS MEANS: I AM SLIGHTLY CONCERNED ABOUT THE IMPENDING REORGANIZATION.
THIS MEANS: I HAVE DECIDED TO WORK IN THE MARKETING FIELD.
COUNTER-CLOCKWISE SPIN
THIS MEANS: I AM BEING SARCASTIC.
OH, THERE'S A GOOD PLAN.
NOTE LIPS
THIS MEANS: THE RECENT EMPLOYEE SATISFACTION SURVEY HAS NOT CAPTURED THE EXTENT OF MY FEELINGS.
6/5/97
THIS MEANS: I THINK YOU ARE ATTRACTIVE BUT IT WOULD BE VERY UNPROFESSIONAL TO SHOW IT.
© 1997 United Feature Syndicate, Inc.
THIS MEANS: MY LOTTERY INVESTMENT PAID OFF.
YANK!

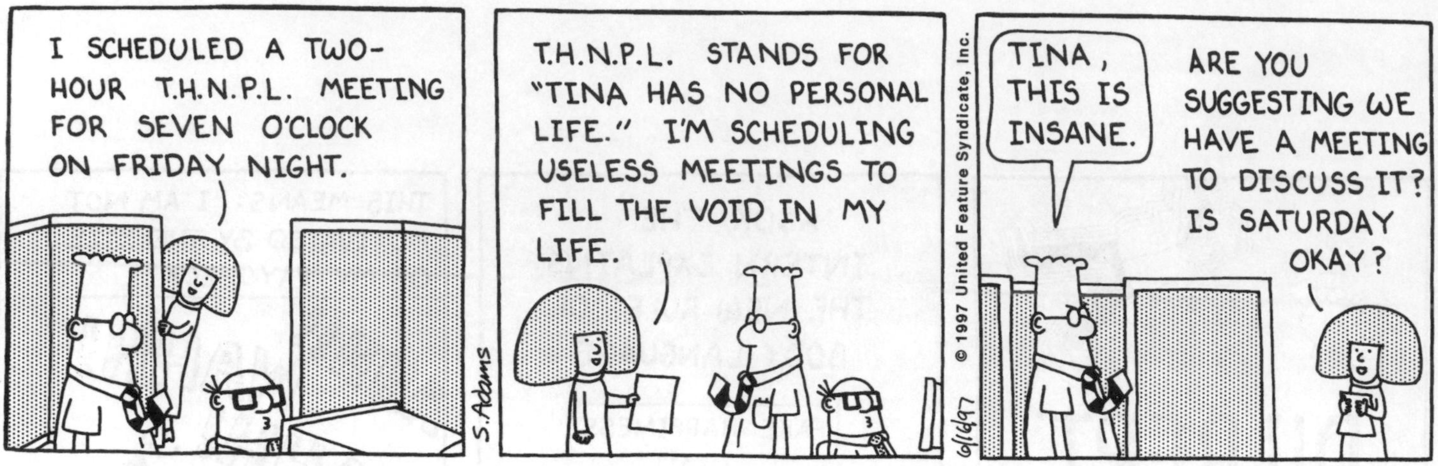
I SCHEDULED A TWO-HOUR T.H.N.P.L. MEETING FOR SEVEN O'CLOCK ON FRIDAY NIGHT.
S. Adams
T.H.N.P.L. STANDS FOR "TINA HAS NO PERSONAL LIFE." I'M SCHEDULING USELESS MEETINGS TO FILL THE VOID IN MY LIFE.
6/16/97
© 1997 United Feature Syndicate, Inc.
TINA, THIS IS INSANE.
ARE YOU SUGGESTING WE HAVE A MEETING TO DISCUSS IT? IS SATURDAY OKAY?

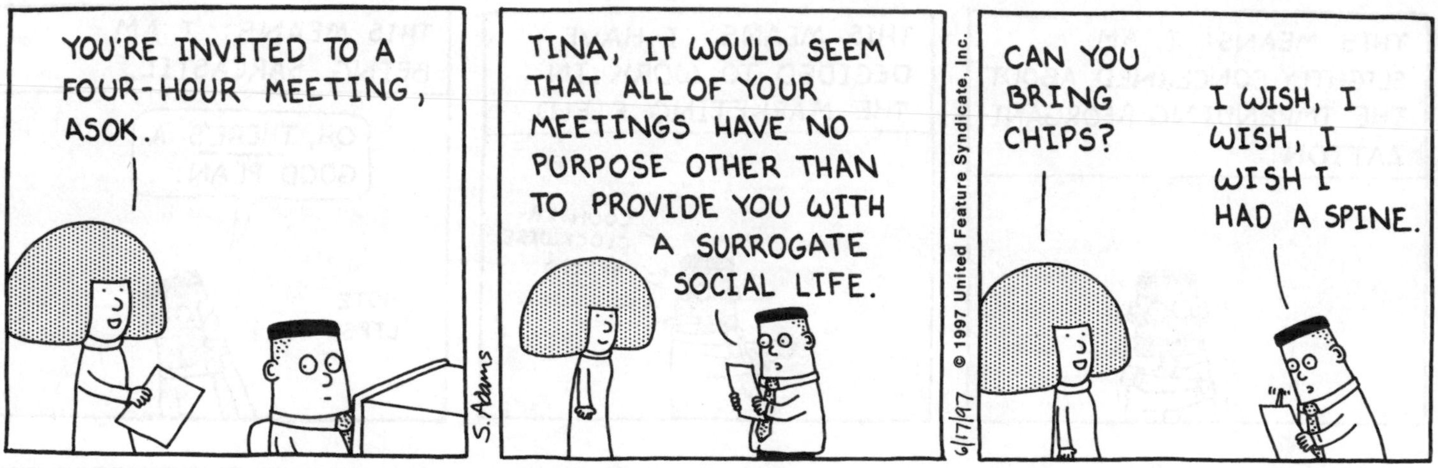
YOU'RE INVITED TO A FOUR-HOUR MEETING, ASOK.
S. Adams
TINA, IT WOULD SEEM THAT ALL OF YOUR MEETINGS HAVE NO PURPOSE OTHER THAN TO PROVIDE YOU WITH A SURROGATE SOCIAL LIFE.
6/17/97
© 1997 United Feature Syndicate, Inc.
CAN YOU BRING CHIPS?
I WISH, I WISH, I WISH I HAD A SPINE.

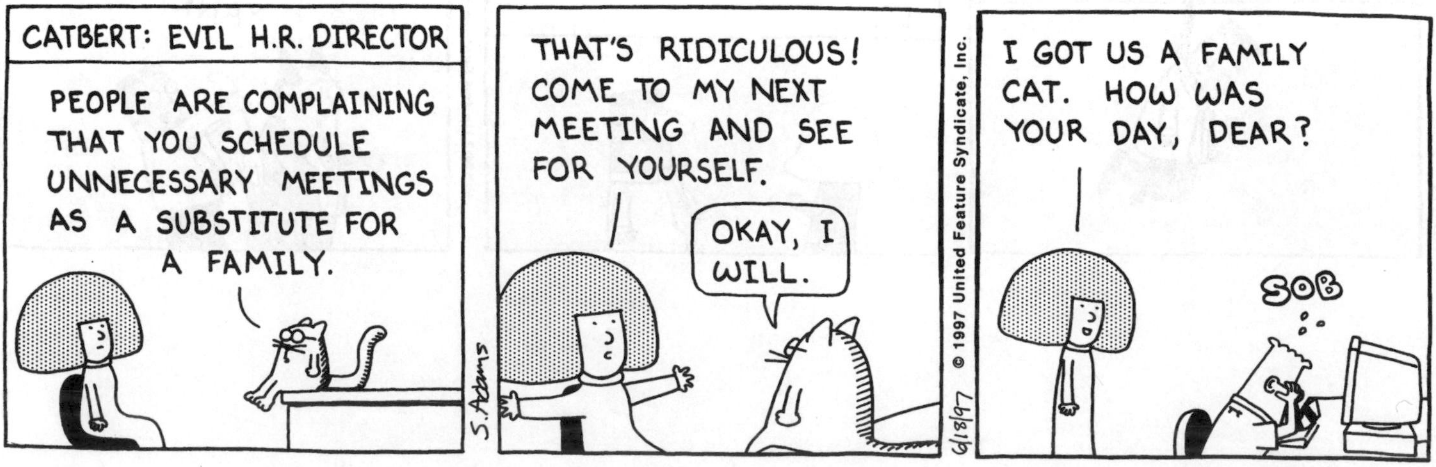
CATBERT: EVIL H.R. DIRECTOR
PEOPLE ARE COMPLAINING THAT YOU SCHEDULE UNNECESSARY MEETINGS AS A SUBSTITUTE FOR A FAMILY.
S. Adams
THAT'S RIDICULOUS! COME TO MY NEXT MEETING AND SEE FOR YOURSELF.
OKAY, I WILL.
6/18/97
© 1997 United Feature Syndicate, Inc.
I GOT US A FAMILY CAT. HOW WAS YOUR DAY, DEAR?
SOB

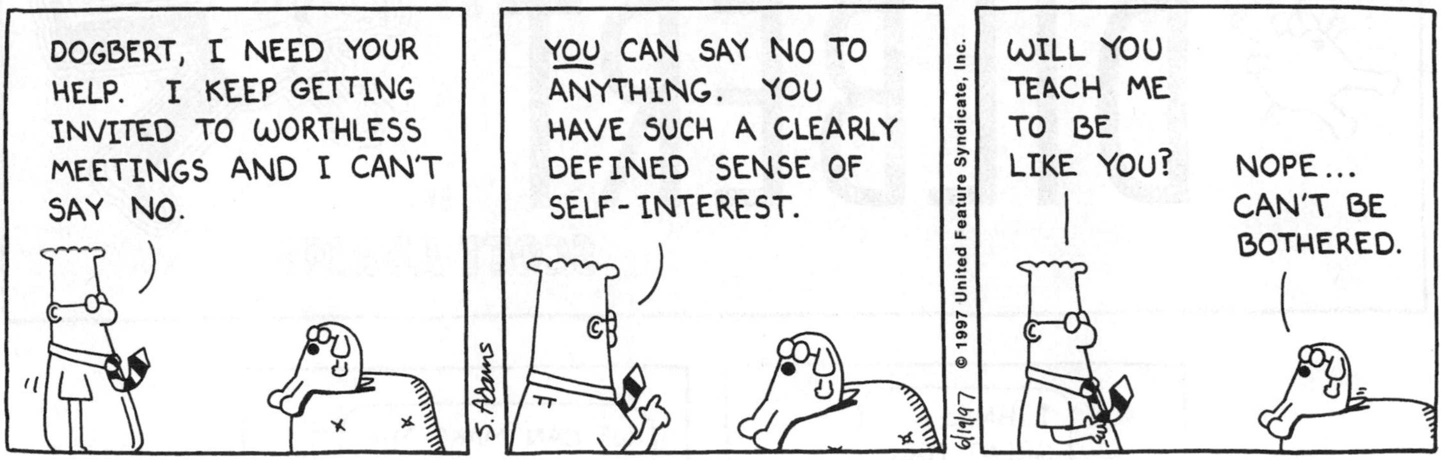
DOGBERT, I NEED YOUR HELP. I KEEP GETTING INVITED TO WORTHLESS MEETINGS AND I CAN'T SAY NO.
YOU CAN SAY NO TO ANYTHING. YOU HAVE SUCH A CLEARLY DEFINED SENSE OF SELF-INTEREST.
S. Adams
© 1997 United Feature Syndicate, Inc.
6/19/97
WILL YOU TEACH ME TO BE LIKE YOU?
NOPE... CAN'T BE BOTHERED.

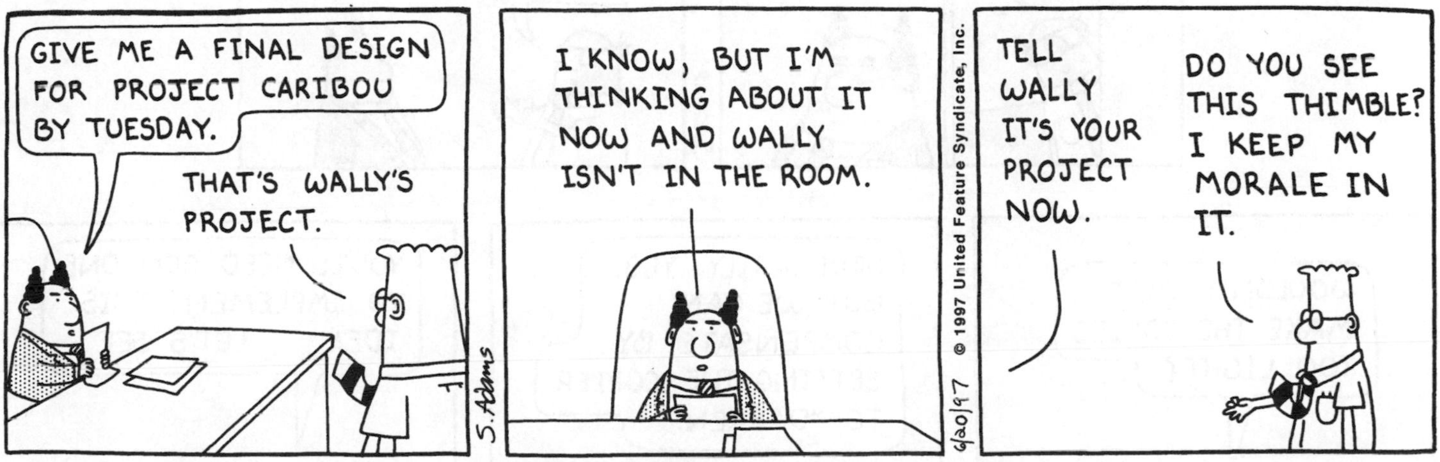
GIVE ME A FINAL DESIGN FOR PROJECT CARIBOU BY TUESDAY.
THAT'S WALLY'S PROJECT.
I KNOW, BUT I'M THINKING ABOUT IT NOW AND WALLY ISN'T IN THE ROOM.
S. Adams
© 1997 United Feature Syndicate, Inc.
6/20/97
TELL WALLY IT'S YOUR PROJECT NOW.
DO YOU SEE THIS THIMBLE? I KEEP MY MORALE IN IT.

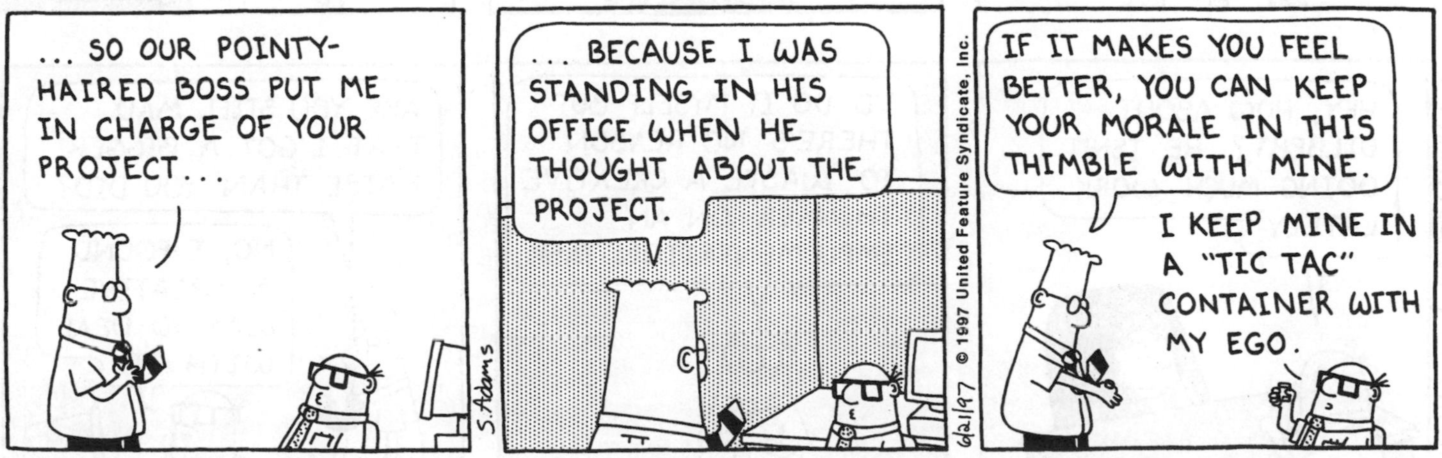
... SO OUR POINTY-HAIRED BOSS PUT ME IN CHARGE OF YOUR PROJECT...
... BECAUSE I WAS STANDING IN HIS OFFICE WHEN HE THOUGHT ABOUT THE PROJECT.
S. Adams
© 1997 United Feature Syndicate, Inc.
6/21/97
IF IT MAKES YOU FEEL BETTER, YOU CAN KEEP YOUR MORALE IN THIS THIMBLE WITH MINE.
I KEEP MINE IN A "TIC TAC" CONTAINER WITH MY EGO.

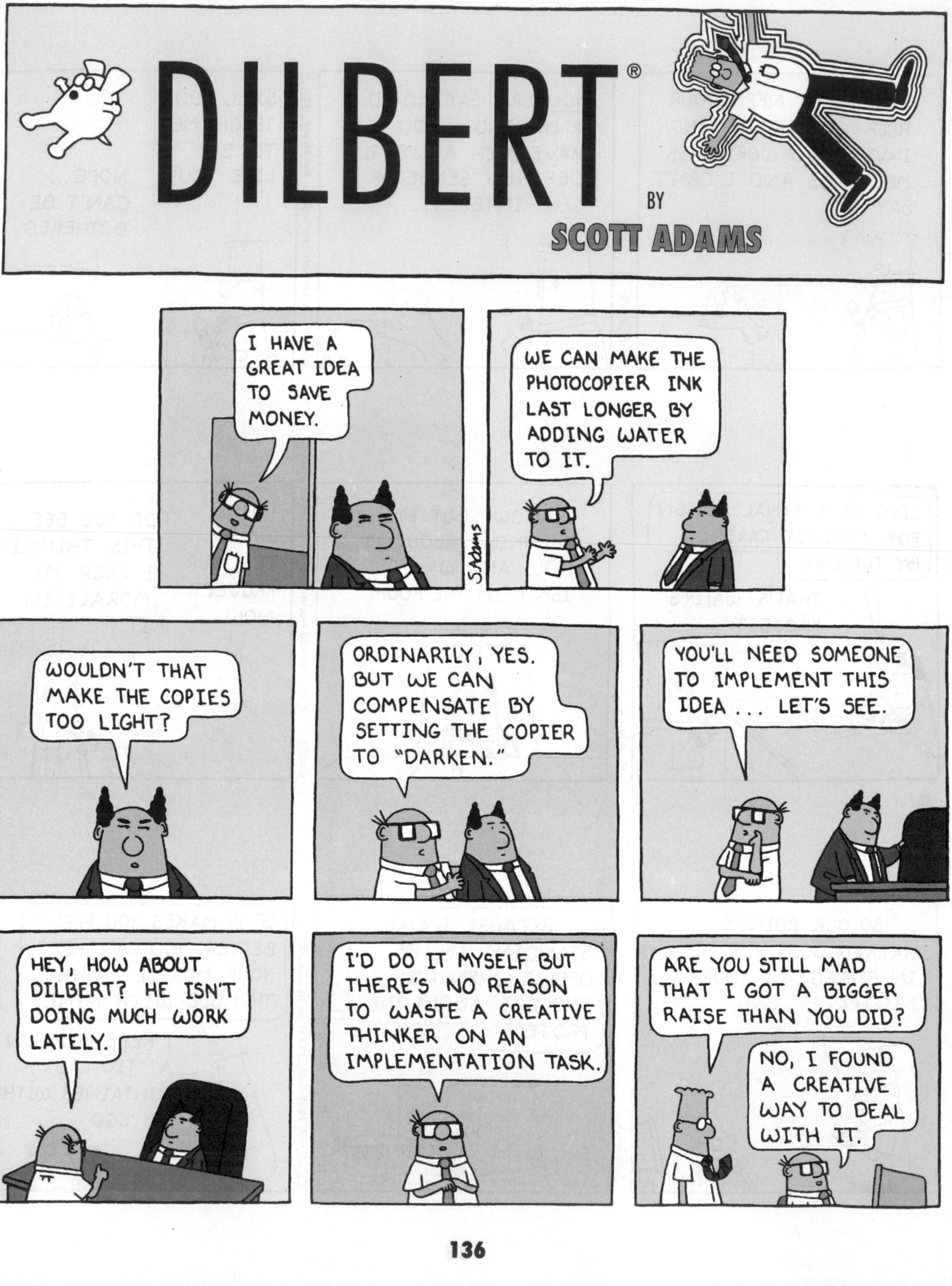
DILBERT®
BY
SCOTT ADAMS
I HAVE A GREAT IDEA TO SAVE MONEY.
WE CAN MAKE THE PHOTOCOPIER INK LAST LONGER BY ADDING WATER TO IT.
S. Adams
WOULDN'T THAT MAKE THE COPIES TOO LIGHT?
ORDINARILY, YES. BUT WE CAN COMPENSATE BY SETTING THE COPIER TO "DARKEN."
YOU'LL NEED SOMEONE TO IMPLEMENT THIS IDEA ... LET'S SEE.
HEY, HOW ABOUT DILBERT? HE ISN'T DOING MUCH WORK LATELY.
I'D DO IT MYSELF BUT THERE'S NO REASON TO WASTE A CREATIVE THINKER ON AN IMPLEMENTATION TASK.
ARE YOU STILL MAD THAT I GOT A BIGGER RAISE THAN YOU DID?
NO, I FOUND A CREATIVE WAY TO DEAL WITH IT.
6/22/97 © 1997 United Feature Syndicate, Inc.

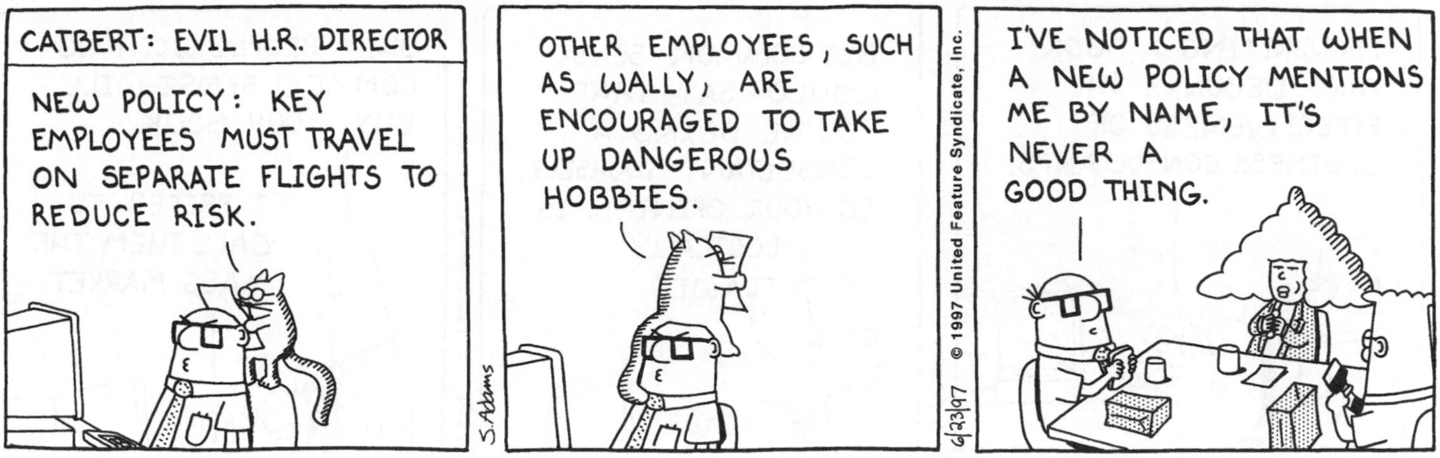
CATBERT: EVIL H.R. DIRECTOR
NEW POLICY: KEY EMPLOYEES MUST TRAVEL ON SEPARATE FLIGHTS TO REDUCE RISK.
OTHER EMPLOYEES, SUCH AS WALLY, ARE ENCOURAGED TO TAKE UP DANGEROUS HOBBIES.
S. Adams
6/23/97
© 1997 United Feature Syndicate, Inc.
I'VE NOTICED THAT WHEN A NEW POLICY MENTIONS ME BY NAME, IT'S NEVER A GOOD THING.

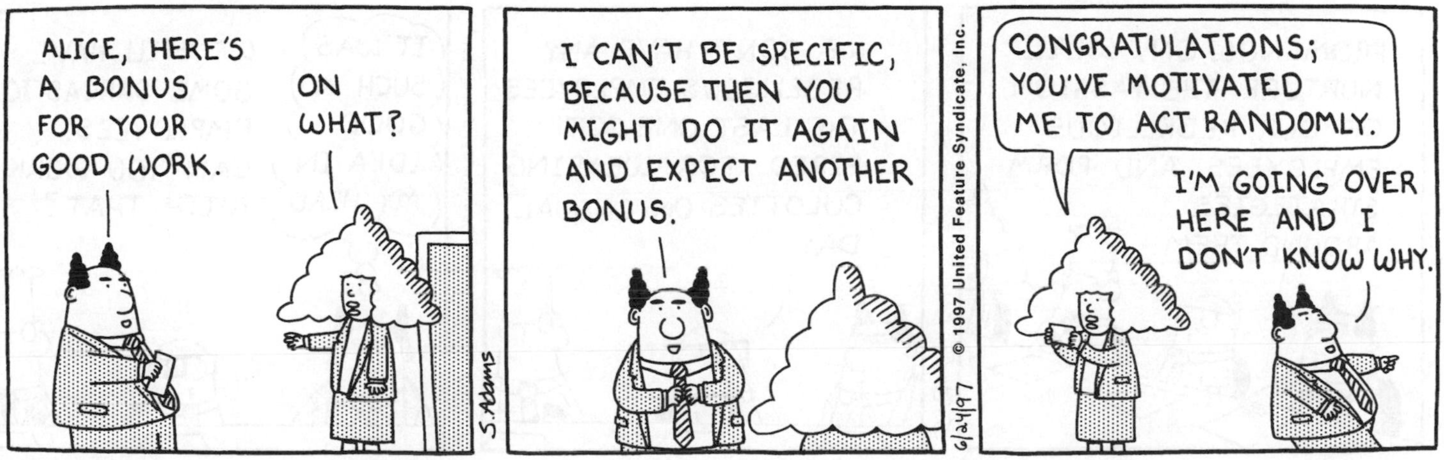
ALICE, HERE'S A BONUS FOR YOUR GOOD WORK.
ON WHAT?
S. Adams
I CAN'T BE SPECIFIC, BECAUSE THEN YOU MIGHT DO IT AGAIN AND EXPECT ANOTHER BONUS.
6/24/97
© 1997 United Feature Syndicate, Inc.
CONGRATULATIONS; YOU'VE MOTIVATED ME TO ACT RANDOMLY.
I'M GOING OVER HERE AND I DON'T KNOW WHY.

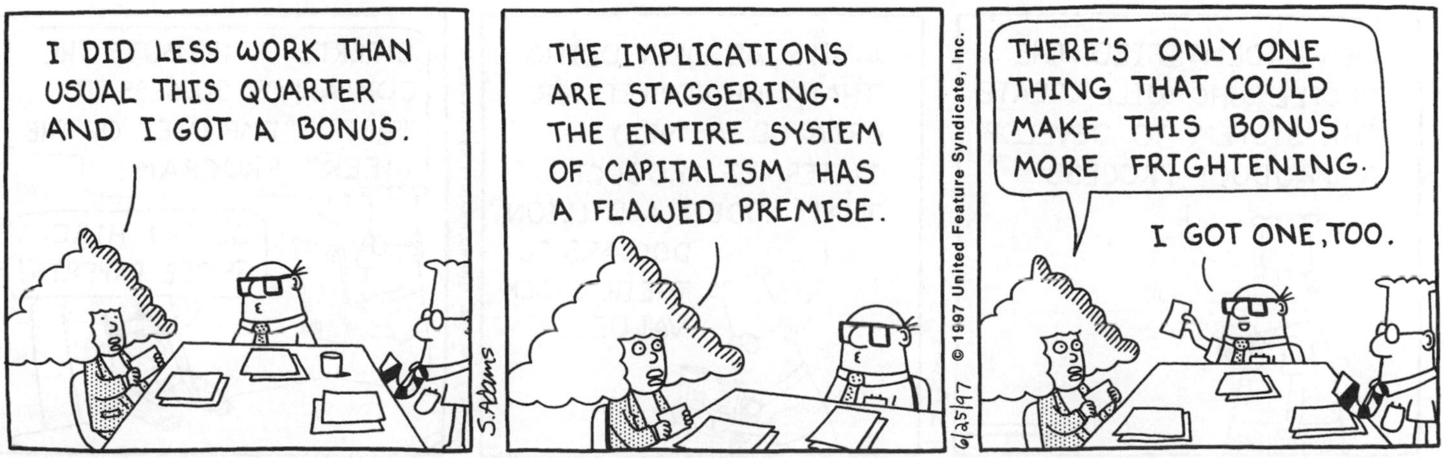
I DID LESS WORK THAN USUAL THIS QUARTER AND I GOT A BONUS.
S. Adams
THE IMPLICATIONS ARE STAGGERING. THE ENTIRE SYSTEM OF CAPITALISM HAS A FLAWED PREMISE.
6/25/97
© 1997 United Feature Syndicate, Inc.
THERE'S ONLY ONE THING THAT COULD MAKE THIS BONUS MORE FRIGHTENING.
I GOT ONE, TOO.

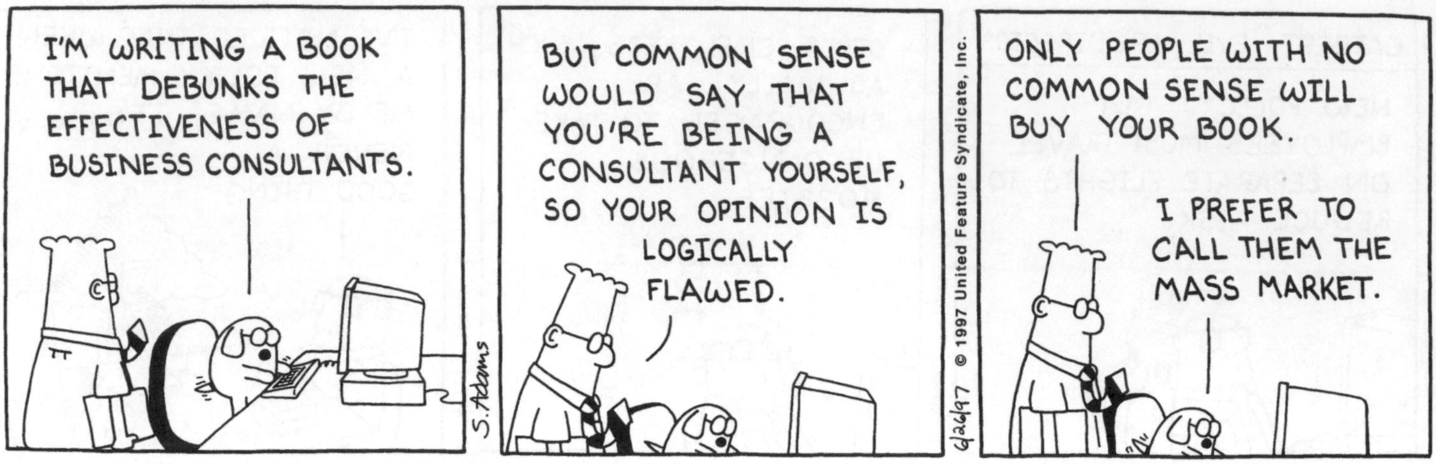
I'M WRITING A BOOK THAT DEBUNKS THE EFFECTIVENESS OF BUSINESS CONSULTANTS.
BUT COMMON SENSE WOULD SAY THAT YOU'RE BEING A CONSULTANT YOURSELF, SO YOUR OPINION IS LOGICALLY FLAWED.
ONLY PEOPLE WITH NO COMMON SENSE WILL BUY YOUR BOOK.
I PREFER TO CALL THEM THE MASS MARKET.
S. Adams
6/26/97 © 1997 United Feature Syndicate, Inc.

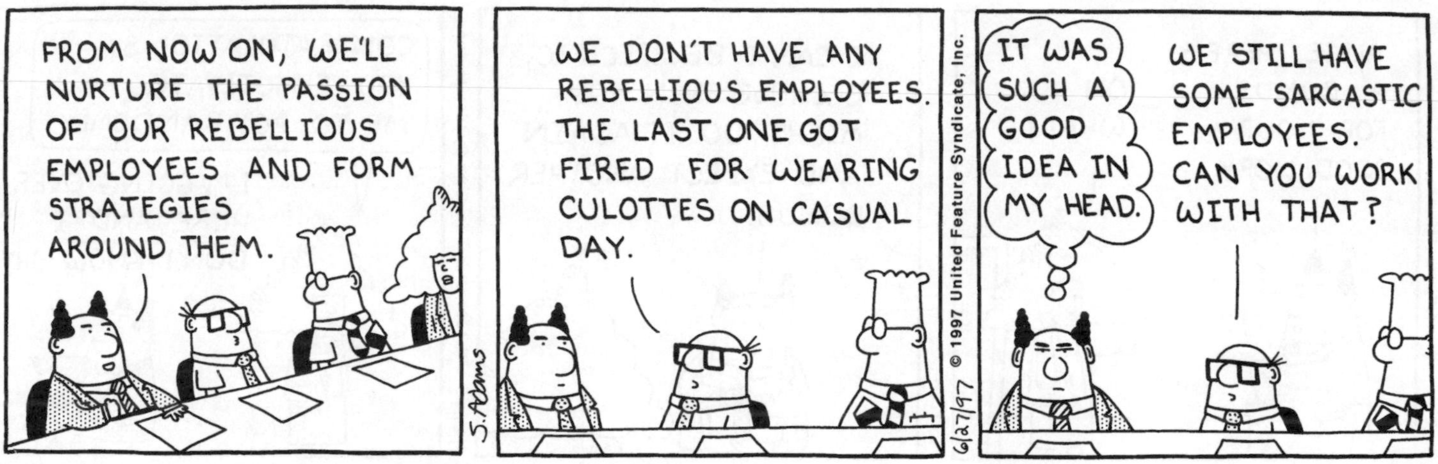
FROM NOW ON, WE'LL NURTURE THE PASSION OF OUR REBELLIOUS EMPLOYEES AND FORM STRATEGIES AROUND THEM.
WE DON'T HAVE ANY REBELLIOUS EMPLOYEES. THE LAST ONE GOT FIRED FOR WEARING CULOTTES ON CASUAL DAY.
IT WAS SUCH A GOOD IDEA IN MY HEAD.
WE STILL HAVE SOME SARCASTIC EMPLOYEES. CAN YOU WORK WITH THAT?
S. Adams
6/27/97 © 1997 United Feature Syndicate, Inc.

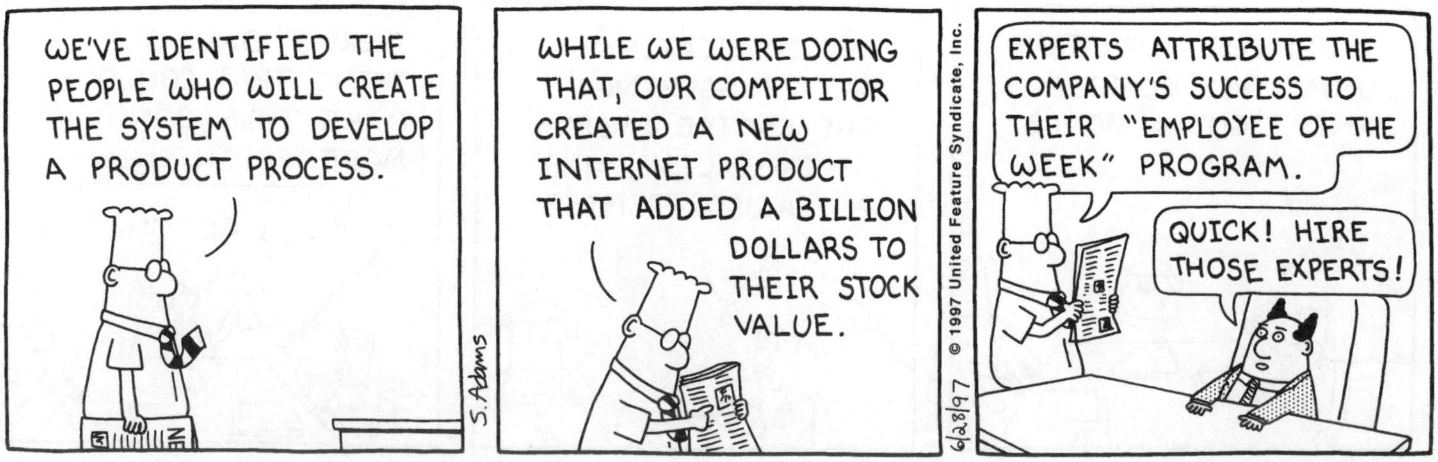
WE'VE IDENTIFIED THE PEOPLE WHO WILL CREATE THE SYSTEM TO DEVELOP A PRODUCT PROCESS.
WHILE WE WERE DOING THAT, OUR COMPETITOR CREATED A NEW INTERNET PRODUCT THAT ADDED A BILLION DOLLARS TO THEIR STOCK VALUE.
EXPERTS ATTRIBUTE THE COMPANY'S SUCCESS TO THEIR "EMPLOYEE OF THE WEEK" PROGRAM.
QUICK! HIRE THOSE EXPERTS!
S. Adams
6/28/97 © 1997 United Feature Syndicate, Inc.

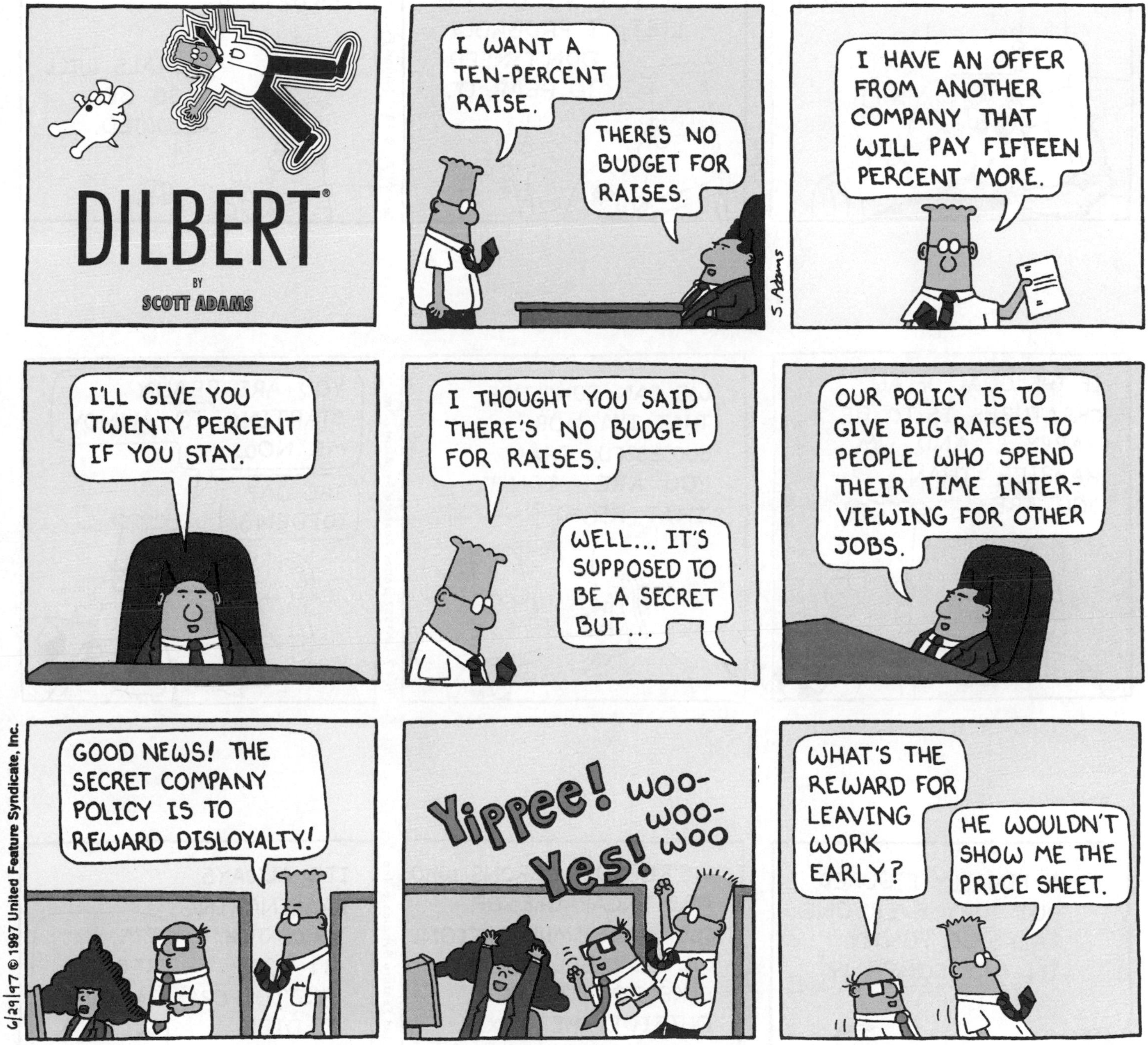
DILBERT®
BY
SCOTT ADAMS
I WANT A TEN-PERCENT RAISE.
THERE'S NO BUDGET FOR RAISES.
S. Adams
I HAVE AN OFFER FROM ANOTHER COMPANY THAT WILL PAY FIFTEEN PERCENT MORE.
I'LL GIVE YOU TWENTY PERCENT IF YOU STAY.
I THOUGHT YOU SAID THERE'S NO BUDGET FOR RAISES.
WELL... IT'S SUPPOSED TO BE A SECRET BUT...
OUR POLICY IS TO GIVE BIG RAISES TO PEOPLE WHO SPEND THEIR TIME INTERVIEWING FOR OTHER JOBS.
6/29/97 © 1997 United Feature Syndicate, Inc.
GOOD NEWS! THE SECRET COMPANY POLICY IS TO REWARD DISLOYALTY!
Yippee! Yes!
WOO-WOO-WOO
WHAT'S THE REWARD FOR LEAVING WORK EARLY?
HE WOULDN'T SHOW ME THE PRICE SHEET.

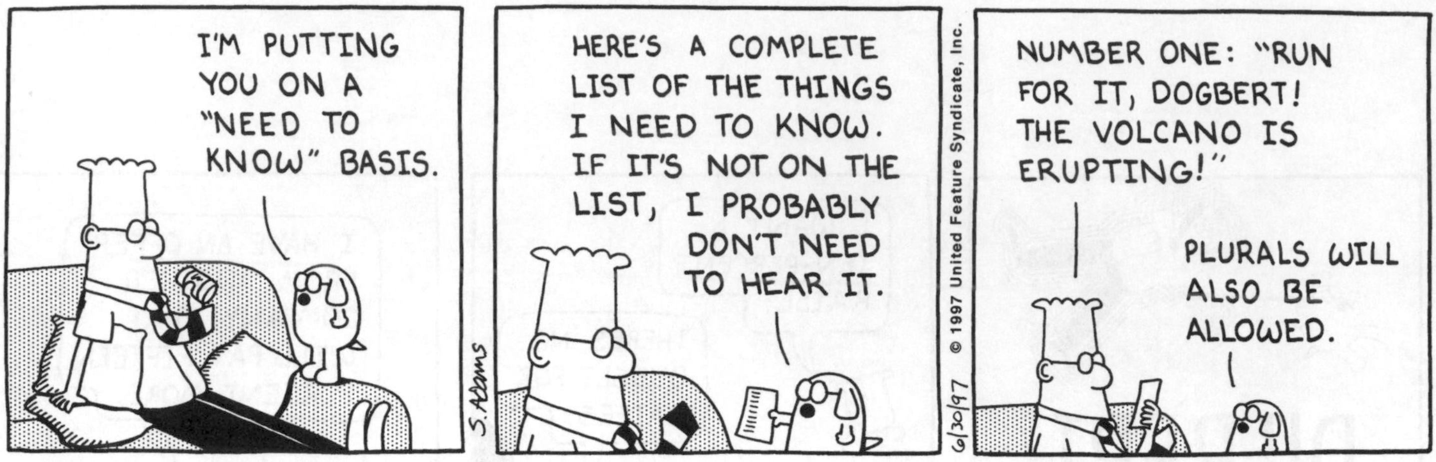
I'M PUTTING YOU ON A "NEED TO KNOW" BASIS.
S. Adams
HERE'S A COMPLETE LIST OF THE THINGS I NEED TO KNOW. IF IT'S NOT ON THE LIST, I PROBABLY DON'T NEED TO HEAR IT.
6/30/97 © 1997 United Feature Syndicate, Inc.
NUMBER ONE: "RUN FOR IT, DOGBERT! THE VOLCANO IS ERUPTING!"
PLURALS WILL ALSO BE ALLOWED.

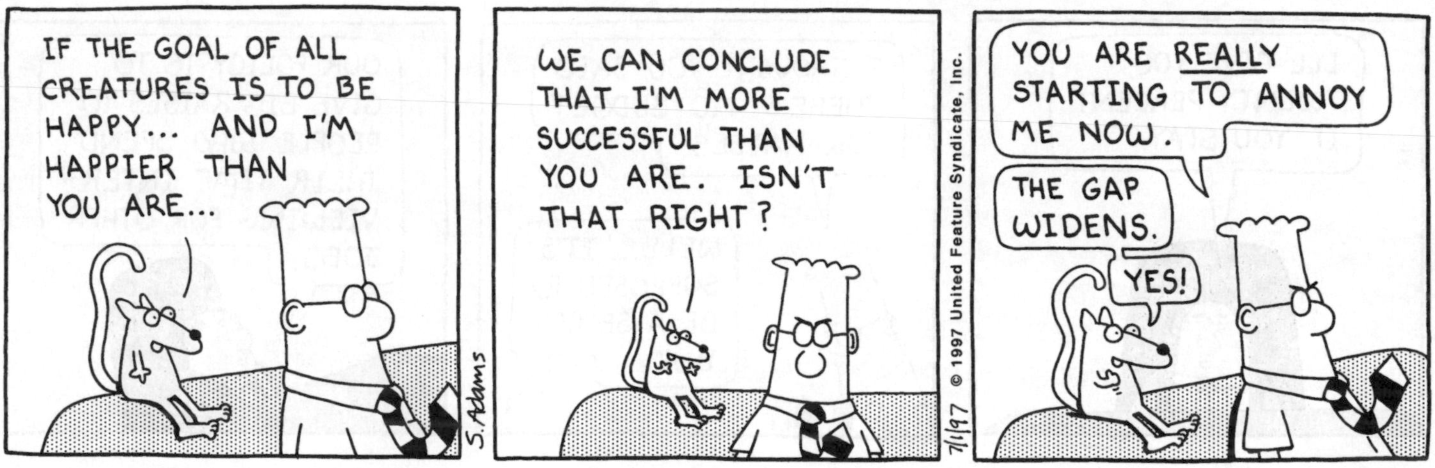
IF THE GOAL OF ALL CREATURES IS TO BE HAPPY... AND I'M HAPPIER THAN YOU ARE...
S. Adams
WE CAN CONCLUDE THAT I'M MORE SUCCESSFUL THAN YOU ARE. ISN'T THAT RIGHT?
7/1/97 © 1997 United Feature Syndicate, Inc.
YOU ARE REALLY STARTING TO ANNOY ME NOW.
THE GAP WIDENS.
YES!

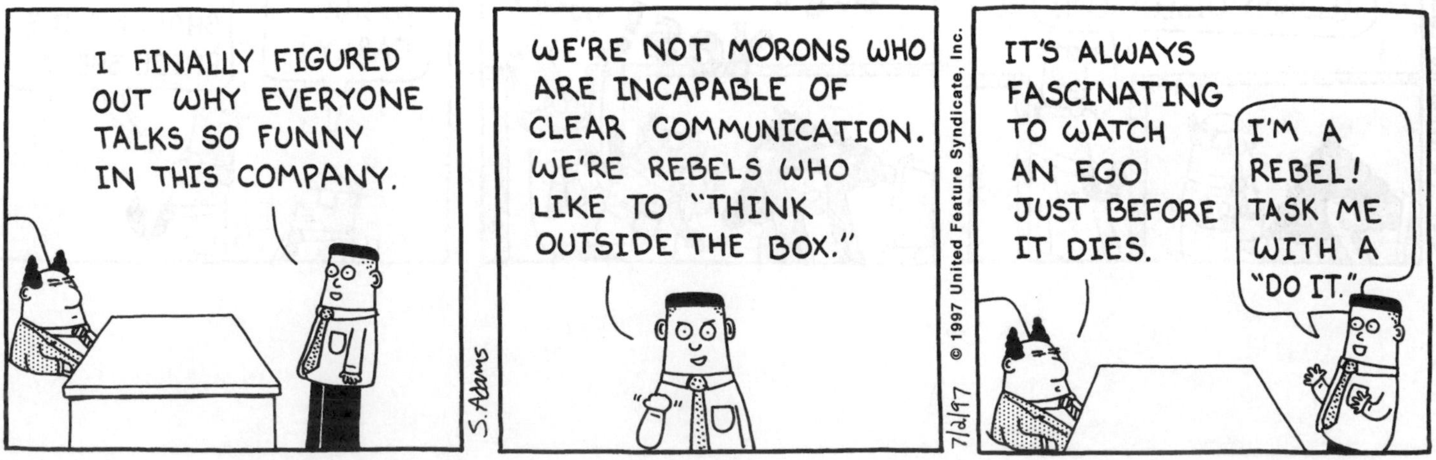
I FINALLY FIGURED OUT WHY EVERYONE TALKS SO FUNNY IN THIS COMPANY.
S. Adams
WE'RE NOT MORONS WHO ARE INCAPABLE OF CLEAR COMMUNICATION. WE'RE REBELS WHO LIKE TO "THINK OUTSIDE THE BOX."
7/2/97 © 1997 United Feature Syndicate, Inc.
IT'S ALWAYS FASCINATING TO WATCH AN EGO JUST BEFORE IT DIES.
I'M A REBEL! TASK ME WITH A "DO IT."

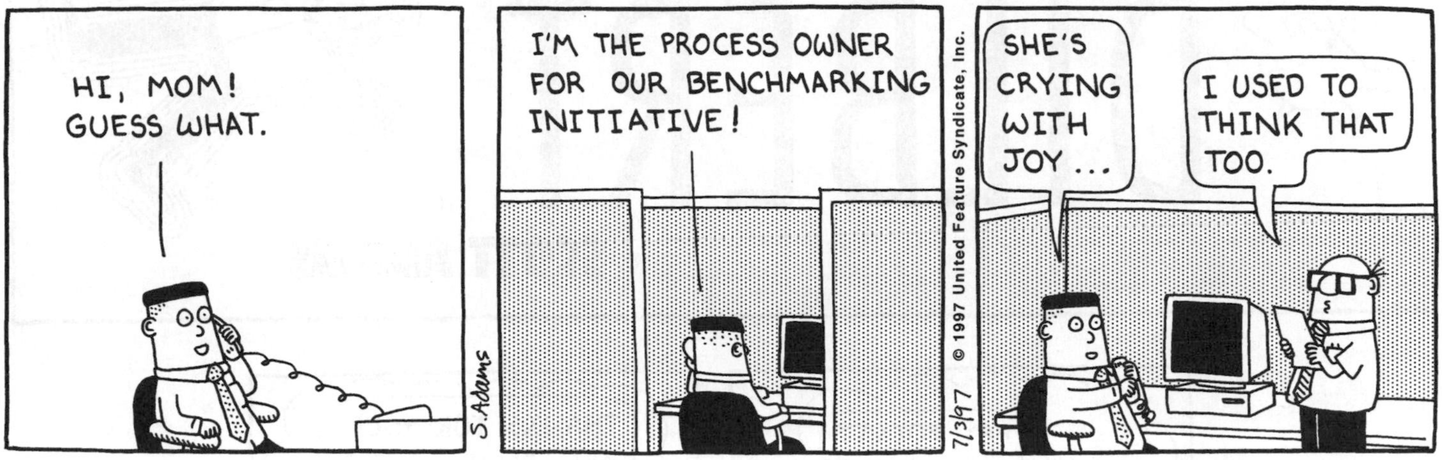
HI, MOM! GUESS WHAT.
I'M THE PROCESS OWNER FOR OUR BENCHMARKING INITIATIVE!
SHE'S CRYING WITH JOY...
I USED TO THINK THAT TOO.
S. Adams
7/3/97
© 1997 United Feature Syndicate, Inc.

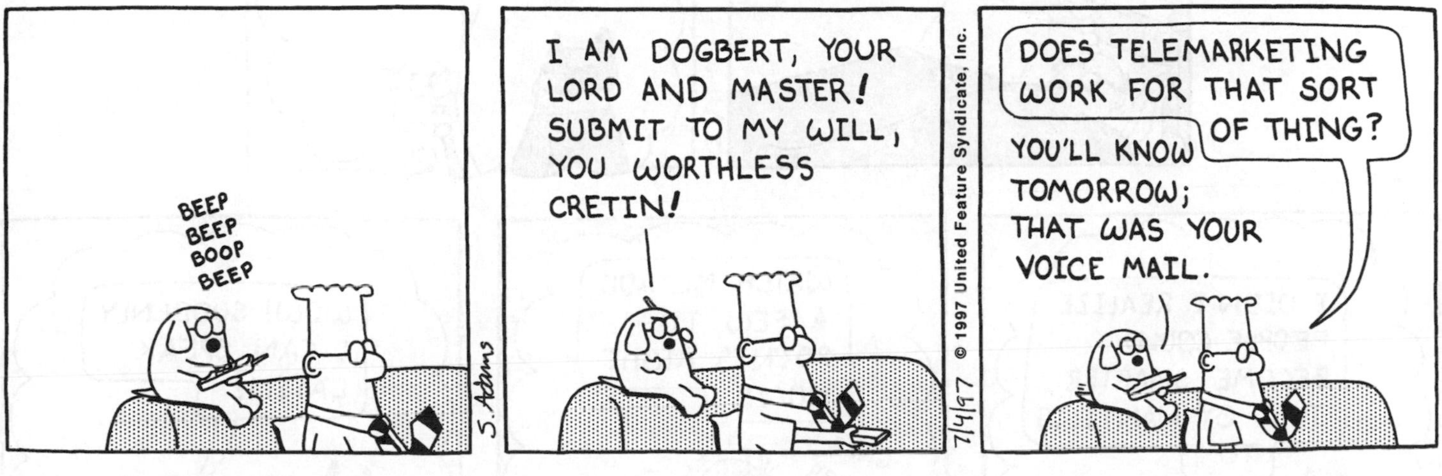
BEEP BEEP BOOP BEEP
I AM DOGBERT, YOUR LORD AND MASTER! SUBMIT TO MY WILL, YOU WORTHLESS CRETIN!
DOES TELEMARKETING WORK FOR THAT SORT OF THING?
YOU'LL KNOW TOMORROW; THAT WAS YOUR VOICE MAIL.
S. Adams
7/4/97
© 1997 United Feature Syndicate, Inc.

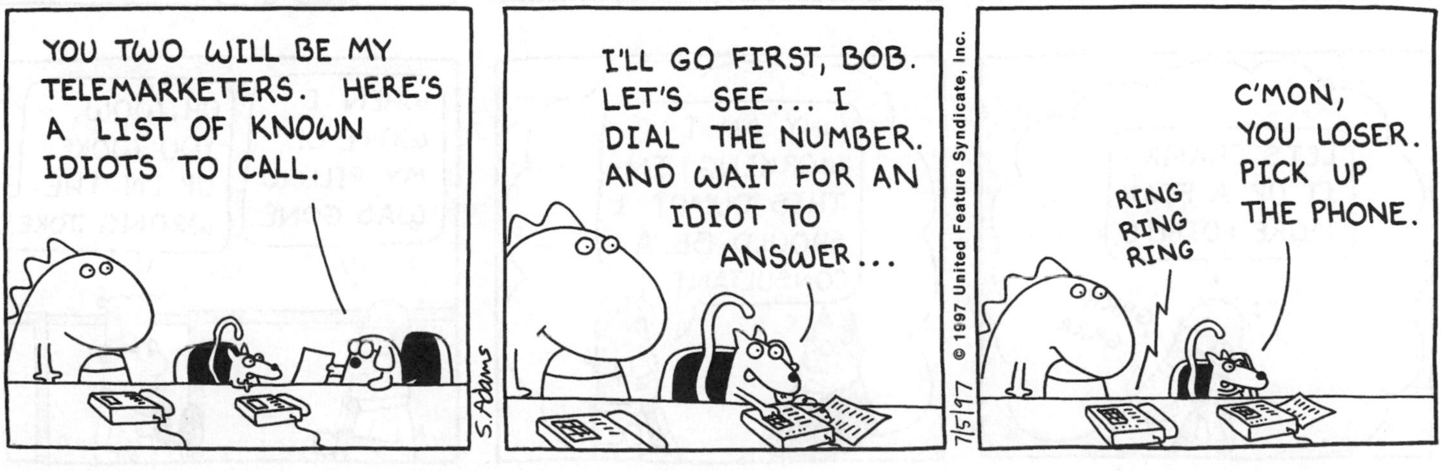
YOU TWO WILL BE MY TELEMARKETERS. HERE'S A LIST OF KNOWN IDIOTS TO CALL.
I'LL GO FIRST, BOB. LET'S SEE... I DIAL THE NUMBER. AND WAIT FOR AN IDIOT TO ANSWER...
RING RING RING
C'MON, YOU LOSER. PICK UP THE PHONE.
S. Adams
7/5/97
© 1997 United Feature Syndicate, Inc.

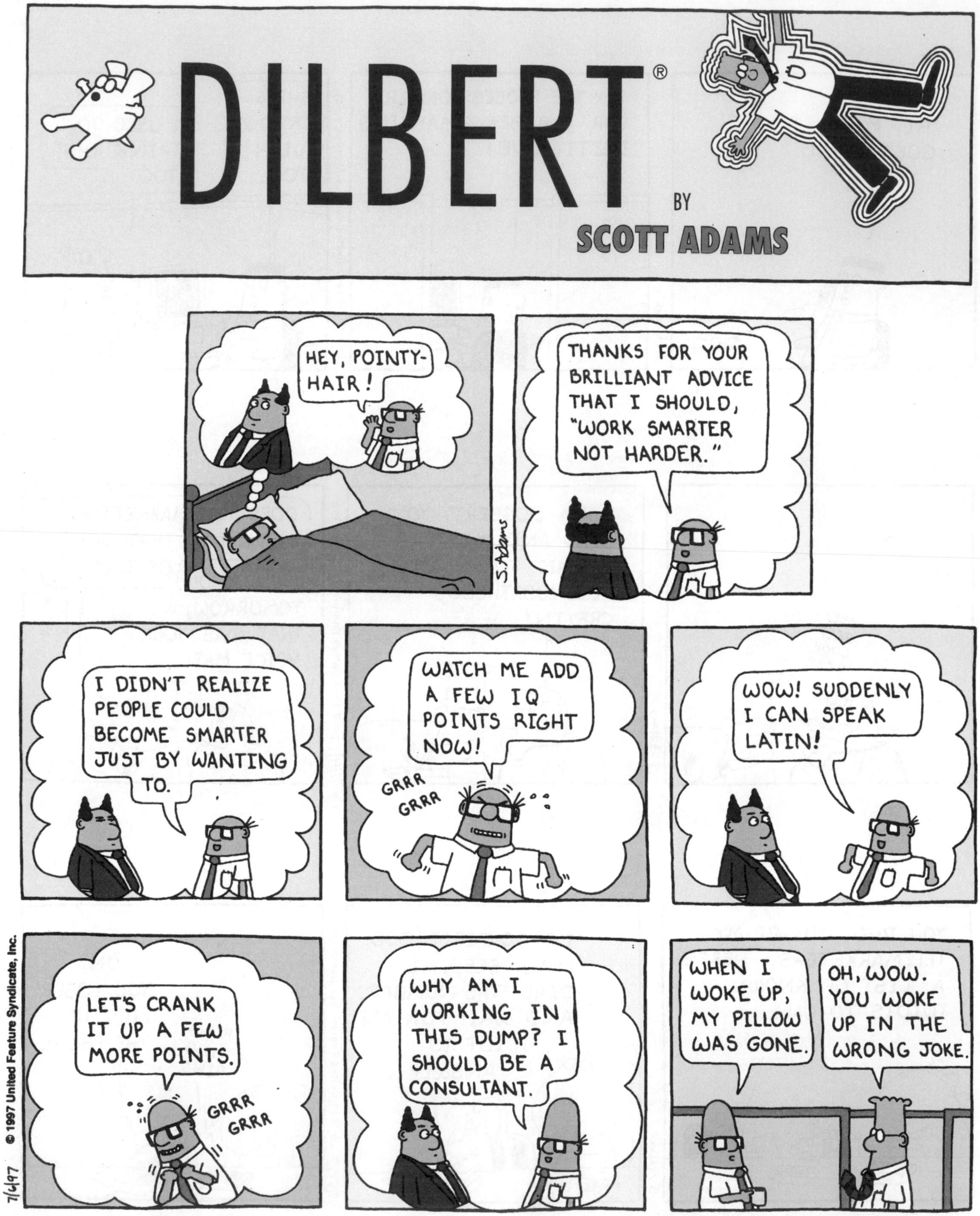
DILBERT®
BY
SCOTT ADAMS
HEY, POINTY-HAIR!
S. Adams
THANKS FOR YOUR BRILLIANT ADVICE THAT I SHOULD, "WORK SMARTER NOT HARDER."
I DIDN'T REALIZE PEOPLE COULD BECOME SMARTER JUST BY WANTING TO.
WATCH ME ADD A FEW IQ POINTS RIGHT NOW!
GRRR GRRR
WOW! SUDDENLY I CAN SPEAK LATIN!
LET'S CRANK IT UP A FEW MORE POINTS.
GRRR GRRR
WHY AM I WORKING IN THIS DUMP? I SHOULD BE A CONSULTANT.
WHEN I WOKE UP, MY PILLOW WAS GONE.
OH, WOW. YOU WOKE UP IN THE WRONG JOKE.
7/6/97
© 1997 United Feature Syndicate, Inc.

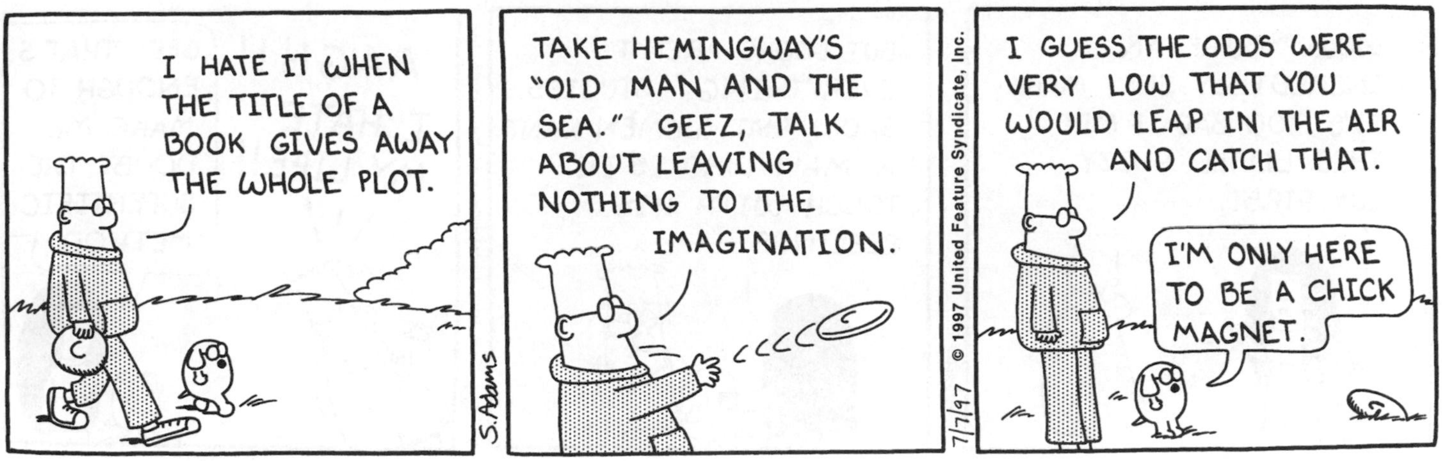
I HATE IT WHEN THE TITLE OF A BOOK GIVES AWAY THE WHOLE PLOT.
S. Adams
TAKE HEMINGWAY'S "OLD MAN AND THE SEA." GEEZ, TALK ABOUT LEAVING NOTHING TO THE IMAGINATION.
7/7/97
© 1997 United Feature Syndicate, Inc.
I GUESS THE ODDS WERE VERY LOW THAT YOU WOULD LEAP IN THE AIR AND CATCH THAT.
I'M ONLY HERE TO BE A CHICK MAGNET.

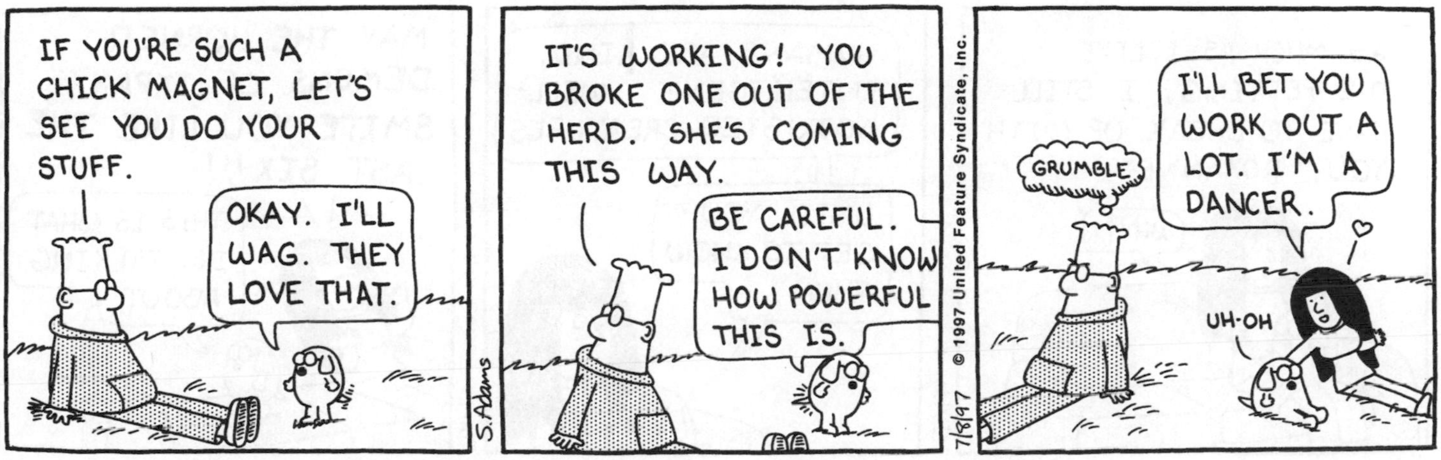
IF YOU'RE SUCH A CHICK MAGNET, LET'S SEE YOU DO YOUR STUFF.
OKAY. I'LL WAG. THEY LOVE THAT.
S. Adams
IT'S WORKING! YOU BROKE ONE OUT OF THE HERD. SHE'S COMING THIS WAY.
BE CAREFUL. I DON'T KNOW HOW POWERFUL THIS IS.
7/8/97
© 1997 United Feature Syndicate, Inc.
GRUMBLE
I'LL BET YOU WORK OUT A LOT. I'M A DANCER.
UH-OH

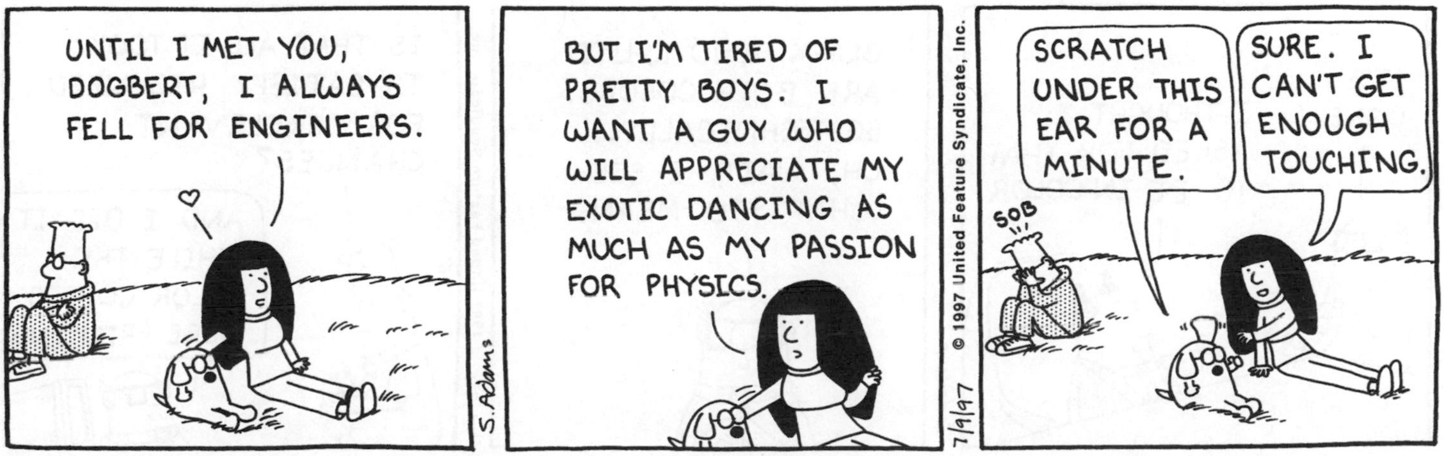
UNTIL I MET YOU, DOGBERT, I ALWAYS FELL FOR ENGINEERS.
S. Adams
BUT I'M TIRED OF PRETTY BOYS. I WANT A GUY WHO WILL APPRECIATE MY EXOTIC DANCING AS MUCH AS MY PASSION FOR PHYSICS.
7/9/97
© 1997 United Feature Syndicate, Inc.
SOB
SCRATCH UNDER THIS EAR FOR A MINUTE.
SURE. I CAN'T GET ENOUGH TOUCHING.

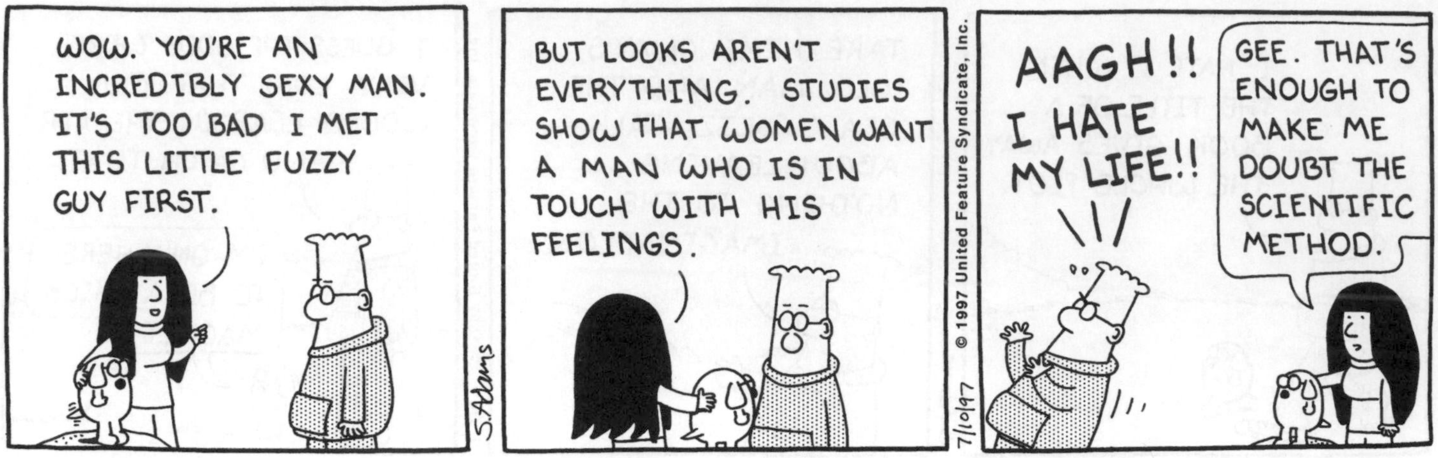
WOW. YOU'RE AN INCREDIBLY SEXY MAN. IT'S TOO BAD I MET THIS LITTLE FUZZY GUY FIRST.
S. Adams
BUT LOOKS AREN'T EVERYTHING. STUDIES SHOW THAT WOMEN WANT A MAN WHO IS IN TOUCH WITH HIS FEELINGS.
7/10/97 © 1997 United Feature Syndicate, Inc.
AAGH!! I HATE MY LIFE!!
GEE. THAT'S ENOUGH TO MAKE ME DOUBT THE SCIENTIFIC METHOD.

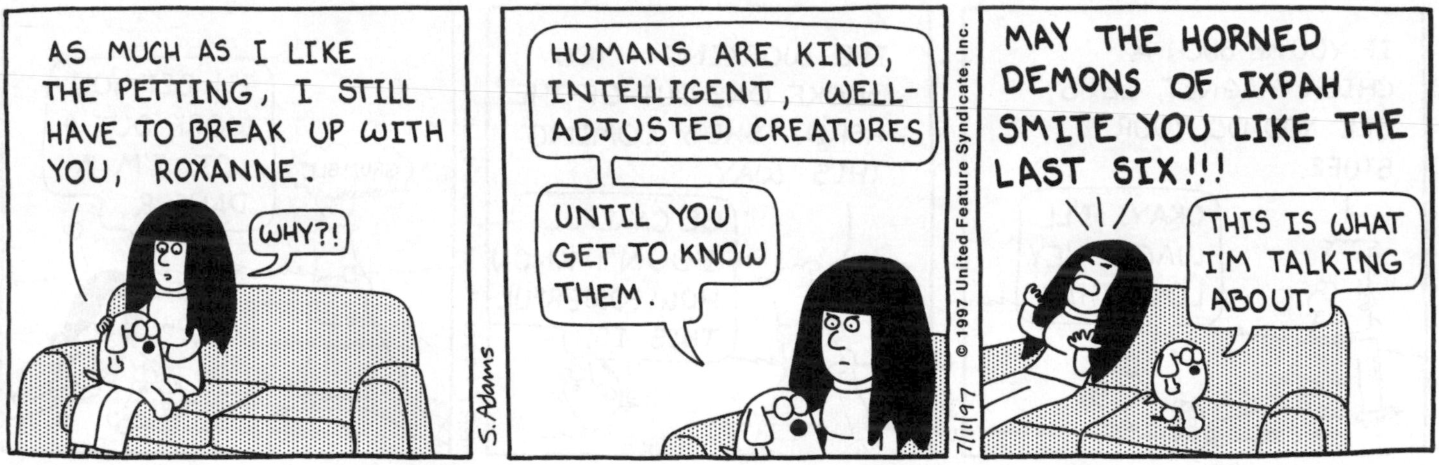
AS MUCH AS I LIKE THE PETTING, I STILL HAVE TO BREAK UP WITH YOU, ROXANNE.
WHY?!
S. Adams
HUMANS ARE KIND, INTELLIGENT, WELL-ADJUSTED CREATURES
UNTIL YOU GET TO KNOW THEM.
7/11/97 © 1997 United Feature Syndicate, Inc.
MAY THE HORNED DEMONS OF IXPAH SMITE YOU LIKE THE LAST SIX!!!
THIS IS WHAT I'M TALKING ABOUT.

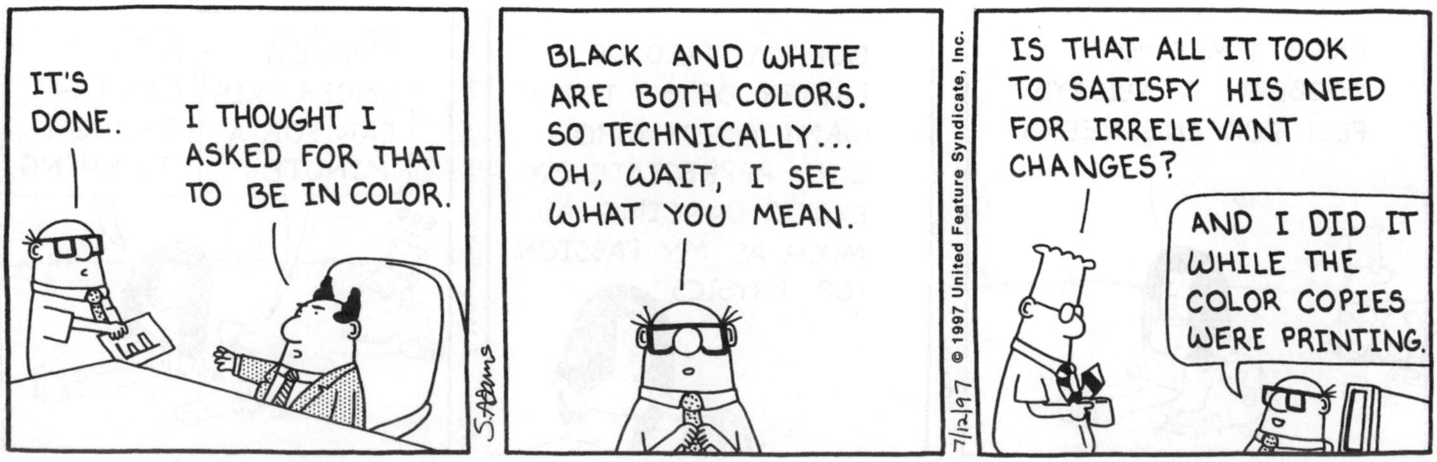
IT'S DONE.
I THOUGHT I ASKED FOR THAT TO BE IN COLOR.
S. Adams
BLACK AND WHITE ARE BOTH COLORS. SO TECHNICALLY... OH, WAIT, I SEE WHAT YOU MEAN.
7/12/97 © 1997 United Feature Syndicate, Inc.
IS THAT ALL IT TOOK TO SATISFY HIS NEED FOR IRRELEVANT CHANGES?
AND I DID IT WHILE THE COLOR COPIES WERE PRINTING.

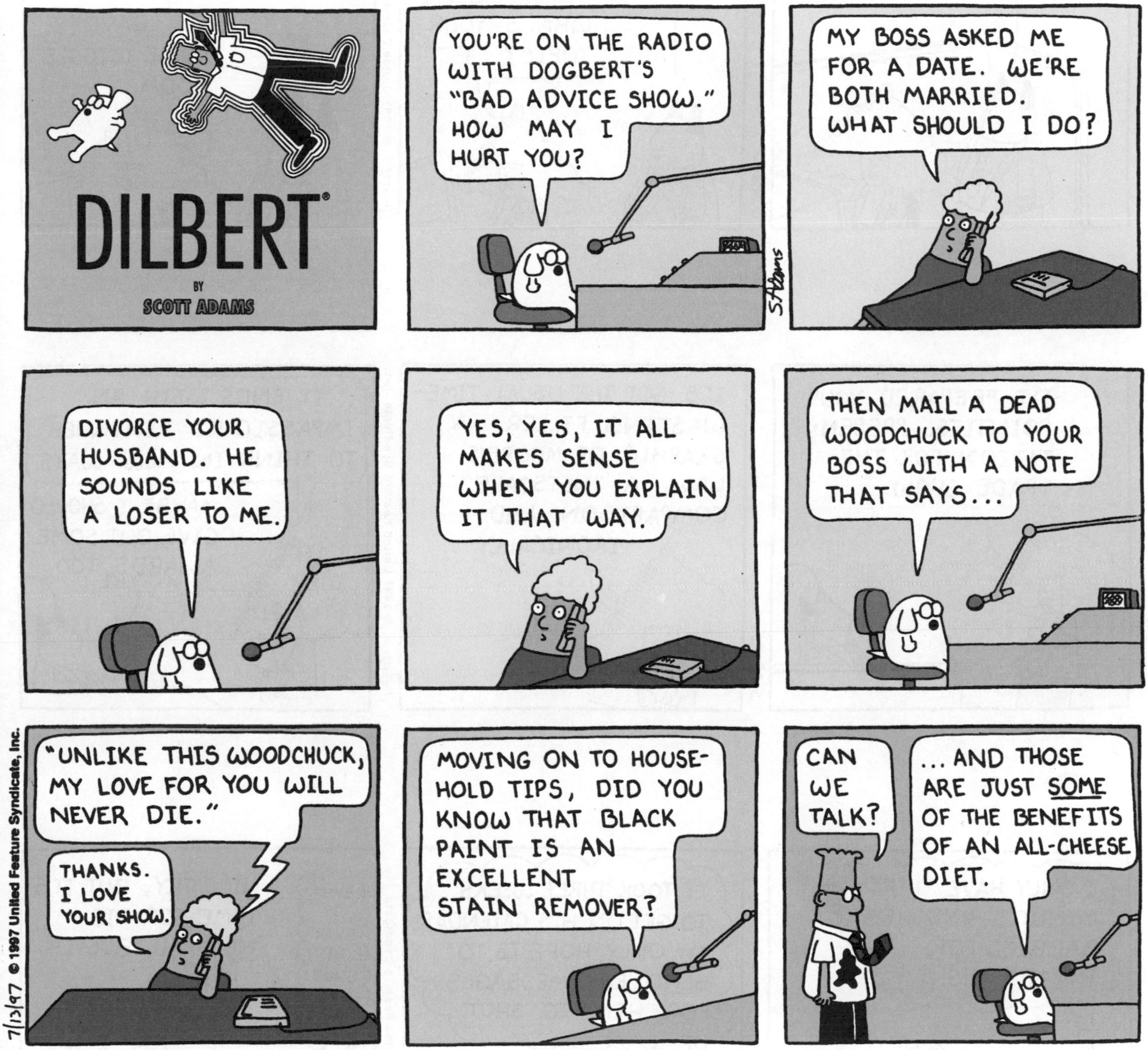
DILBERT®
BY
SCOTT ADAMS
YOU'RE ON THE RADIO WITH DOGBERT'S "BAD ADVICE SHOW." HOW MAY I HURT YOU?
MY BOSS ASKED ME FOR A DATE. WE'RE BOTH MARRIED. WHAT SHOULD I DO?
DIVORCE YOUR HUSBAND. HE SOUNDS LIKE A LOSER TO ME.
YES, YES, IT ALL MAKES SENSE WHEN YOU EXPLAIN IT THAT WAY.
THEN MAIL A DEAD WOODCHUCK TO YOUR BOSS WITH A NOTE THAT SAYS...
"UNLIKE THIS WOODCHUCK, MY LOVE FOR YOU WILL NEVER DIE."
THANKS. I LOVE YOUR SHOW.
MOVING ON TO HOUSE-HOLD TIPS, DID YOU KNOW THAT BLACK PAINT IS AN EXCELLENT STAIN REMOVER?
CAN WE TALK?
... AND THOSE ARE JUST SOME OF THE BENEFITS OF AN ALL-CHEESE DIET.
7/13/97 © 1997 United Feature Syndicate, Inc.

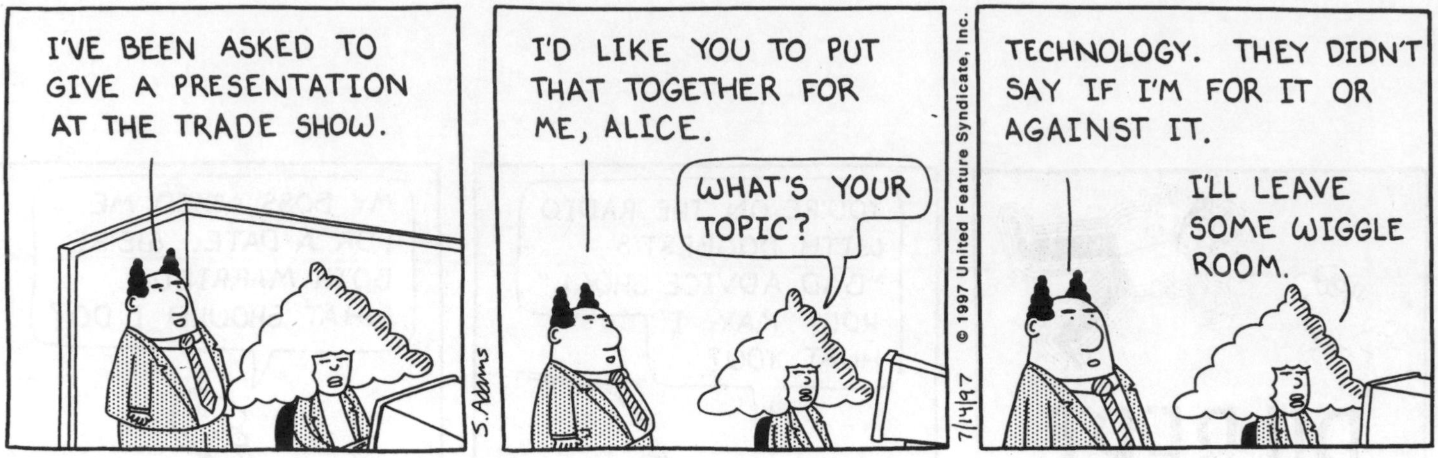
I'VE BEEN ASKED TO GIVE A PRESENTATION AT THE TRADE SHOW.
I'D LIKE YOU TO PUT THAT TOGETHER FOR ME, ALICE.
WHAT'S YOUR TOPIC?
TECHNOLOGY. THEY DIDN'T SAY IF I'M FOR IT OR AGAINST IT.
I'LL LEAVE SOME WIGGLE ROOM.
S. Adams
7/14/97
© 1997 United Feature Syndicate, Inc.

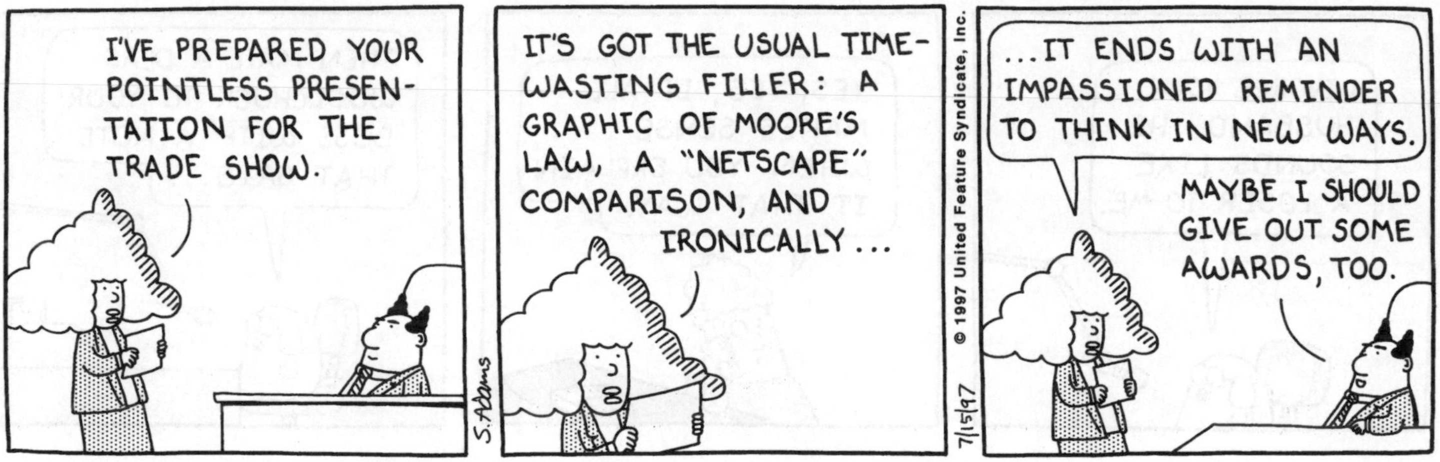
I'VE PREPARED YOUR POINTLESS PRESENTATION FOR THE TRADE SHOW.
IT'S GOT THE USUAL TIME-WASTING FILLER: A GRAPHIC OF MOORE'S LAW, A "NETSCAPE" COMPARISON, AND IRONICALLY ...
...IT ENDS WITH AN IMPASSIONED REMINDER TO THINK IN NEW WAYS.
MAYBE I SHOULD GIVE OUT SOME AWARDS, TOO.
S. Adams
7/15/97
© 1997 United Feature Syndicate, Inc.

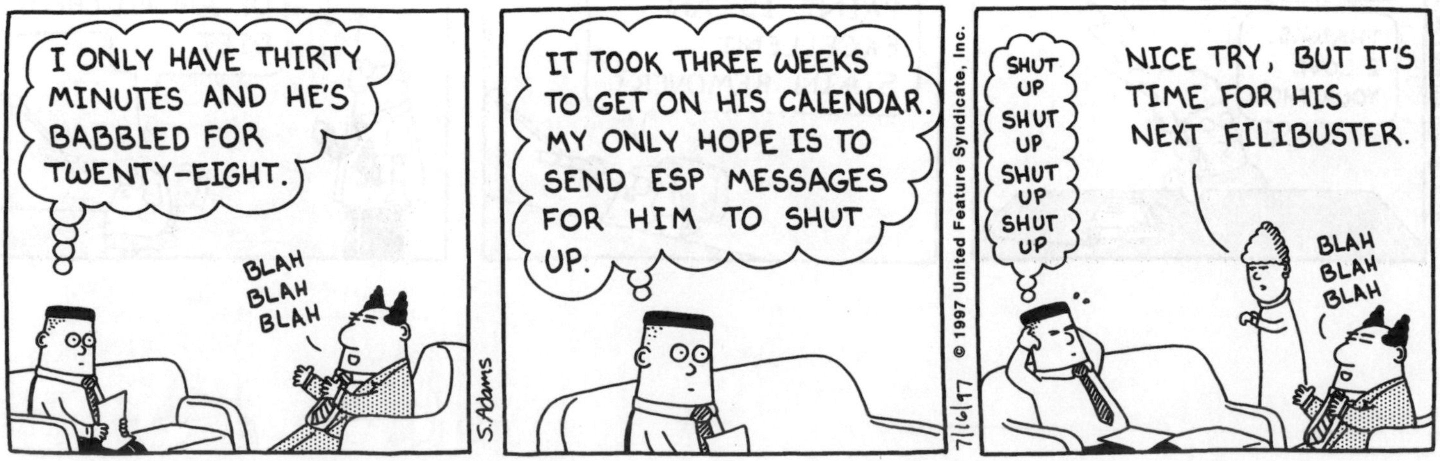
I ONLY HAVE THIRTY MINUTES AND HE'S BABBLED FOR TWENTY-EIGHT.
BLAH BLAH BLAH
IT TOOK THREE WEEKS TO GET ON HIS CALENDAR. MY ONLY HOPE IS TO SEND ESP MESSAGES FOR HIM TO SHUT UP.
SHUT UP SHUT UP SHUT UP SHUT UP
NICE TRY, BUT IT'S TIME FOR HIS NEXT FILIBUSTER.
BLAH BLAH BLAH
S. Adams
7/16/97
© 1997 United Feature Syndicate, Inc.

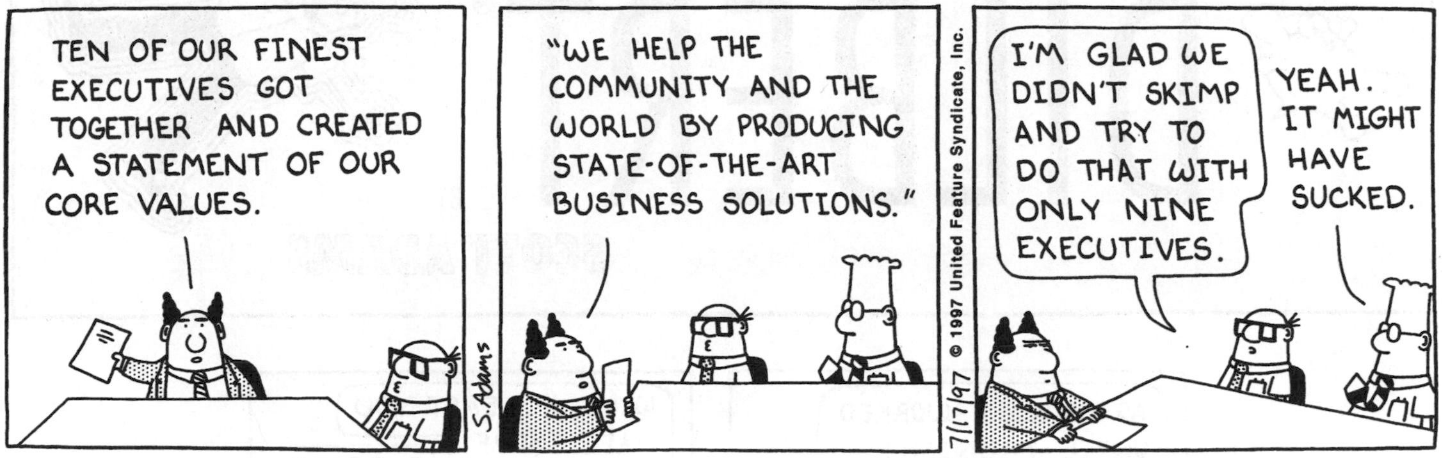
TEN OF OUR FINEST EXECUTIVES GOT TOGETHER AND CREATED A STATEMENT OF OUR CORE VALUES.
"WE HELP THE COMMUNITY AND THE WORLD BY PRODUCING STATE-OF-THE-ART BUSINESS SOLUTIONS."
S. Adams
I'M GLAD WE DIDN'T SKIMP AND TRY TO DO THAT WITH ONLY NINE EXECUTIVES.
YEAH. IT MIGHT HAVE SUCKED.
7/17/97 © 1997 United Feature Syndicate, Inc.

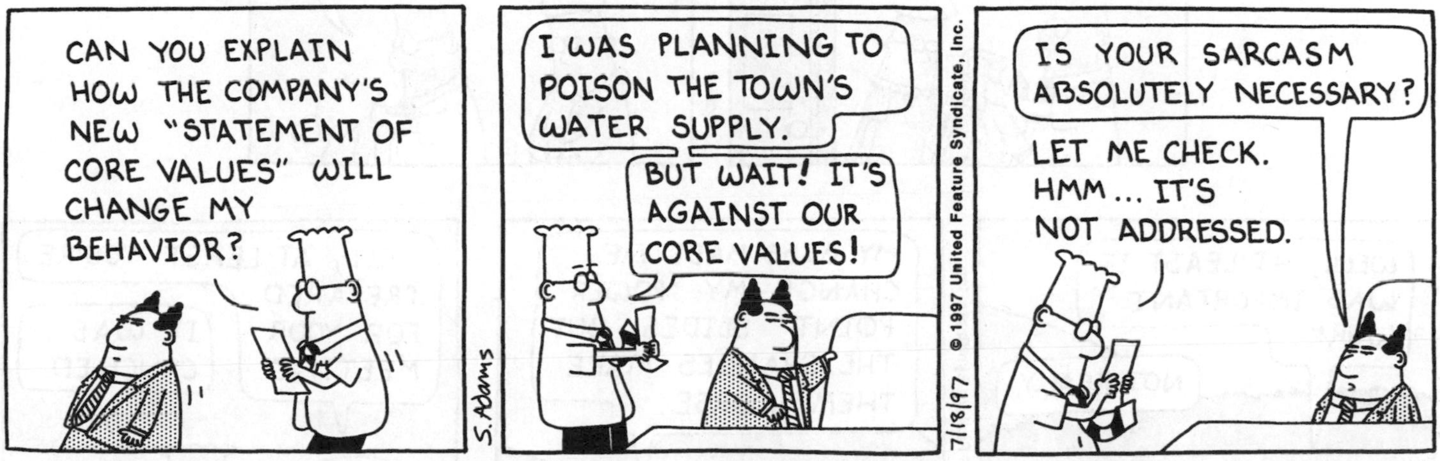
CAN YOU EXPLAIN HOW THE COMPANY'S NEW "STATEMENT OF CORE VALUES" WILL CHANGE MY BEHAVIOR?
I WAS PLANNING TO POISON THE TOWN'S WATER SUPPLY.
BUT WAIT! IT'S AGAINST OUR CORE VALUES!
S. Adams
IS YOUR SARCASM ABSOLUTELY NECESSARY?
LET ME CHECK. HMM ... IT'S NOT ADDRESSED.
7/18/97 © 1997 United Feature Syndicate, Inc.

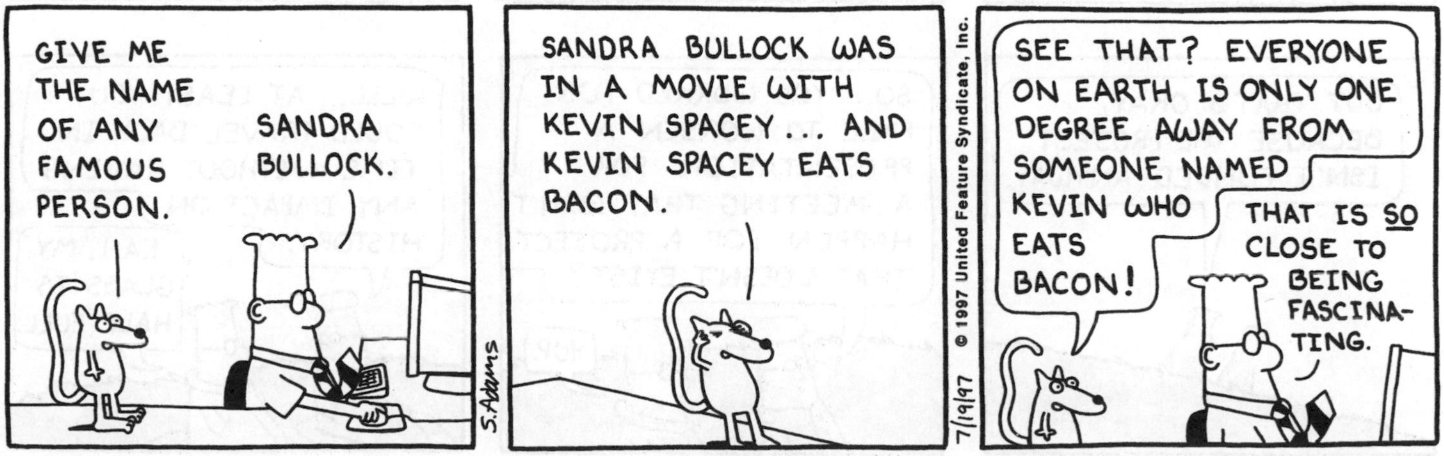
GIVE ME THE NAME OF ANY FAMOUS PERSON.
SANDRA BULLOCK.
SANDRA BULLOCK WAS IN A MOVIE WITH KEVIN SPACEY ... AND KEVIN SPACEY EATS BACON.
S. Adams
SEE THAT? EVERYONE ON EARTH IS ONLY ONE DEGREE AWAY FROM SOMEONE NAMED KEVIN WHO EATS BACON!
THAT IS SO CLOSE TO BEING FASCINA-TING.
7/19/97 © 1997 United Feature Syndicate, Inc.

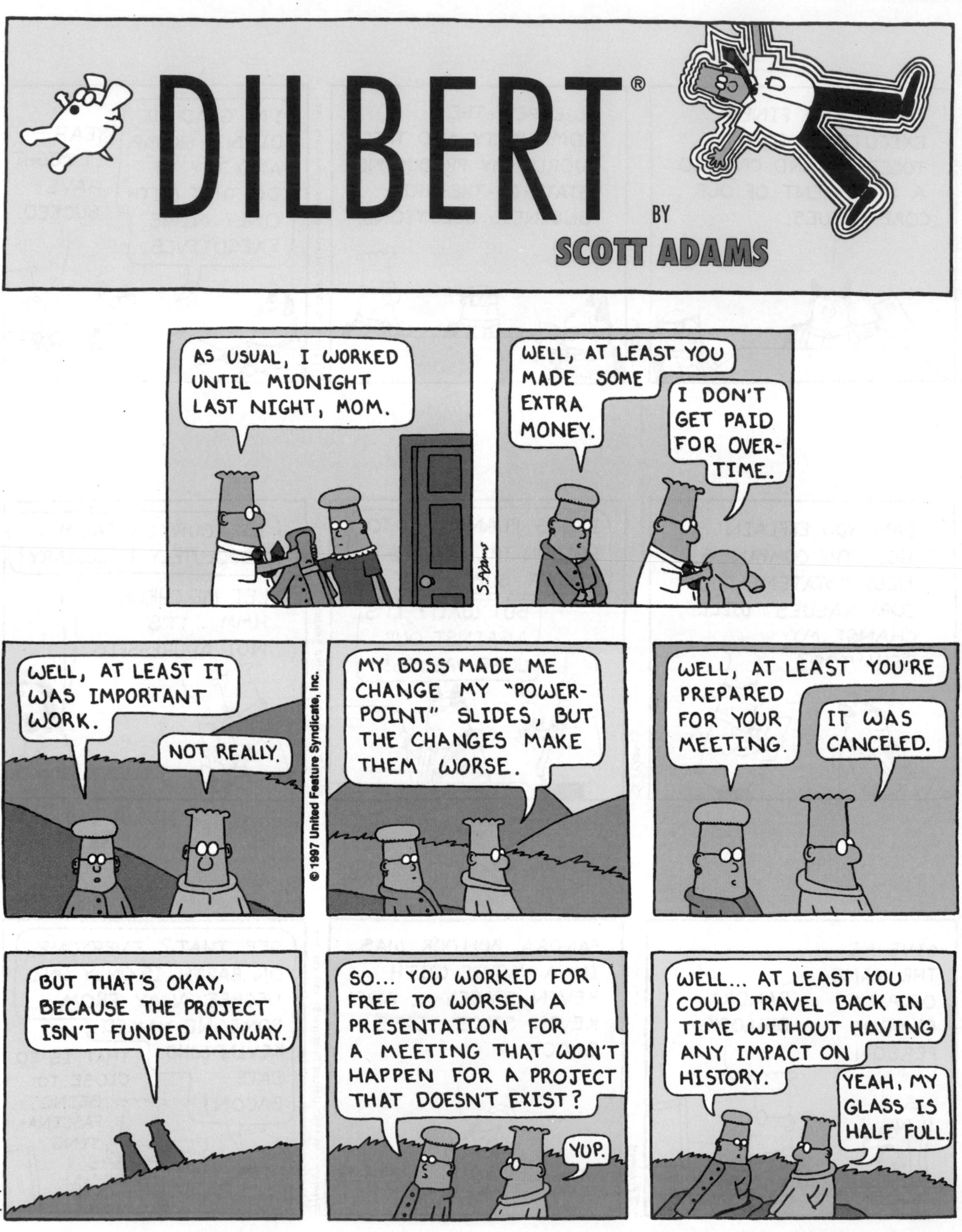

DILBERT®
BY
SCOTT ADAMS
AS USUAL, I WORKED UNTIL MIDNIGHT LAST NIGHT, MOM.
S. Adams
WELL, AT LEAST YOU MADE SOME EXTRA MONEY.
I DON'T GET PAID FOR OVER-TIME.
WELL, AT LEAST IT WAS IMPORTANT WORK.
NOT REALLY.
© 1997 United Feature Syndicate, Inc.
MY BOSS MADE ME CHANGE MY "POWER-POINT" SLIDES, BUT THE CHANGES MAKE THEM WORSE.
WELL, AT LEAST YOU'RE PREPARED FOR YOUR MEETING.
IT WAS CANCELED.
7/20/97
BUT THAT'S OKAY, BECAUSE THE PROJECT ISN'T FUNDED ANYWAY.
SO... YOU WORKED FOR FREE TO WORSEN A PRESENTATION FOR A MEETING THAT WON'T HAPPEN FOR A PROJECT THAT DOESN'T EXIST?
YUP.
WELL... AT LEAST YOU COULD TRAVEL BACK IN TIME WITHOUT HAVING ANY IMPACT ON HISTORY.
YEAH, MY GLASS IS HALF FULL.

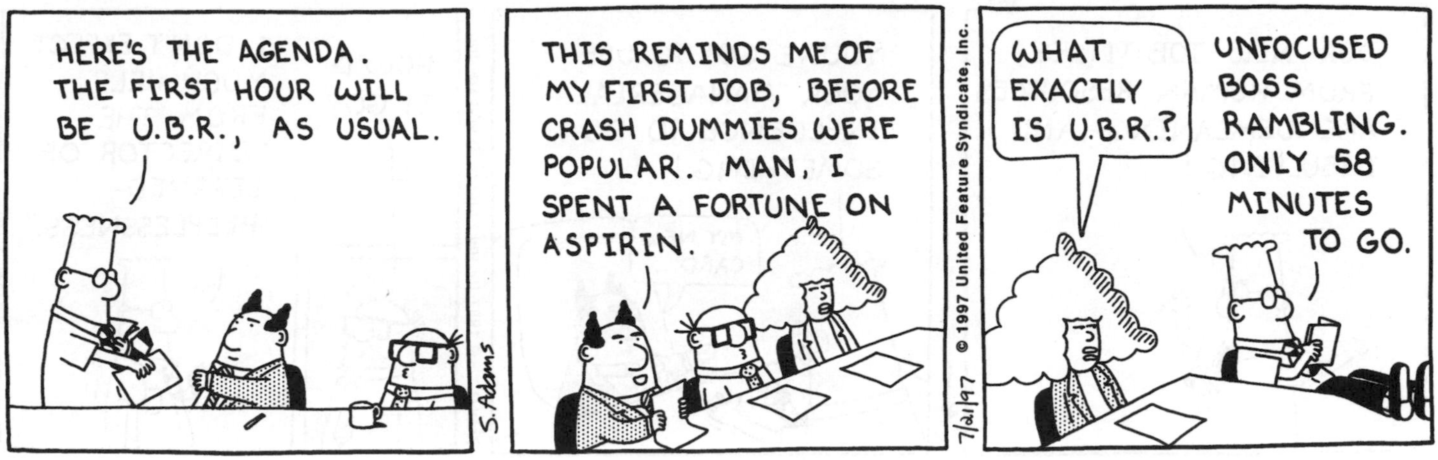
HERE'S THE AGENDA. THE FIRST HOUR WILL BE U.B.R., AS USUAL.
S. Adams
THIS REMINDS ME OF MY FIRST JOB, BEFORE CRASH DUMMIES WERE POPULAR. MAN, I SPENT A FORTUNE ON ASPIRIN.
7/21/97 © 1997 United Feature Syndicate, Inc.
WHAT EXACTLY IS U.B.R.?
UNFOCUSED BOSS RAMBLING. ONLY 58 MINUTES TO GO.

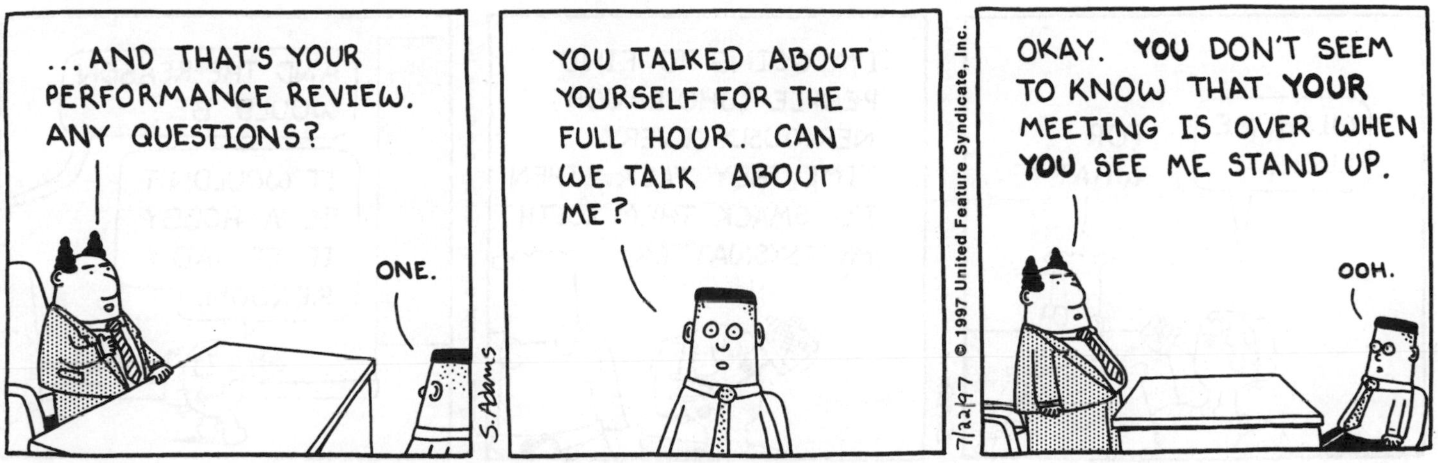
... AND THAT'S YOUR PERFORMANCE REVIEW. ANY QUESTIONS?
ONE.
S. Adams
YOU TALKED ABOUT YOURSELF FOR THE FULL HOUR. CAN WE TALK ABOUT ME?
7/22/97 © 1997 United Feature Syndicate, Inc.
OKAY. YOU DON'T SEEM TO KNOW THAT YOUR MEETING IS OVER WHEN YOU SEE ME STAND UP.
OOH.

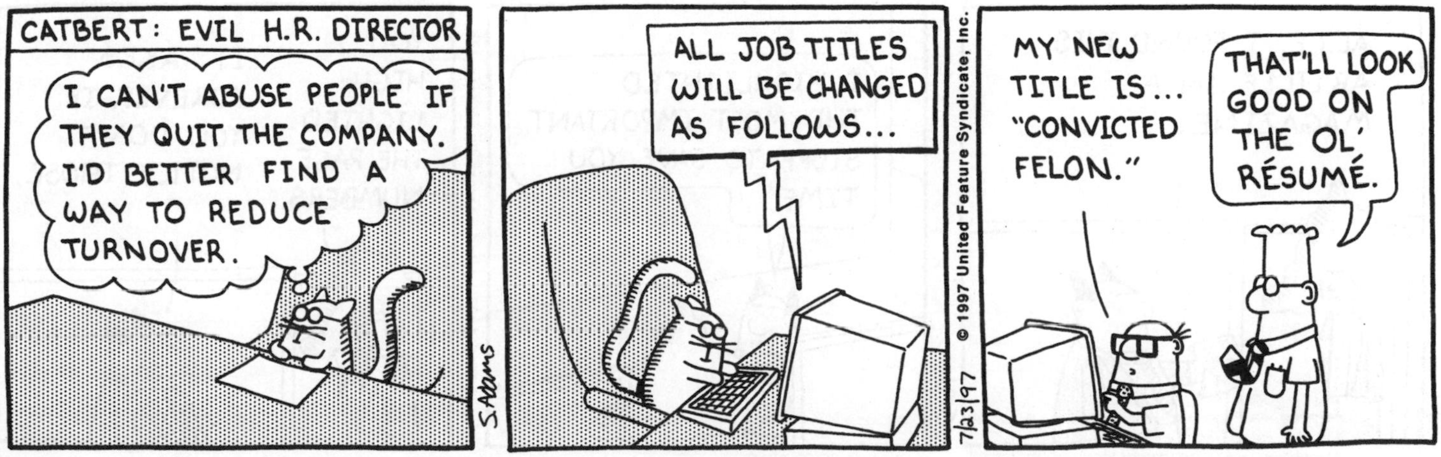
CATBERT: EVIL H.R. DIRECTOR
I CAN'T ABUSE PEOPLE IF THEY QUIT THE COMPANY. I'D BETTER FIND A WAY TO REDUCE TURNOVER.
S. Adams
ALL JOB TITLES WILL BE CHANGED AS FOLLOWS...
7/23/97 © 1997 United Feature Syndicate, Inc.
MY NEW TITLE IS... "CONVICTED FELON."
THAT'LL LOOK GOOD ON THE OL' RÉSUMÉ.

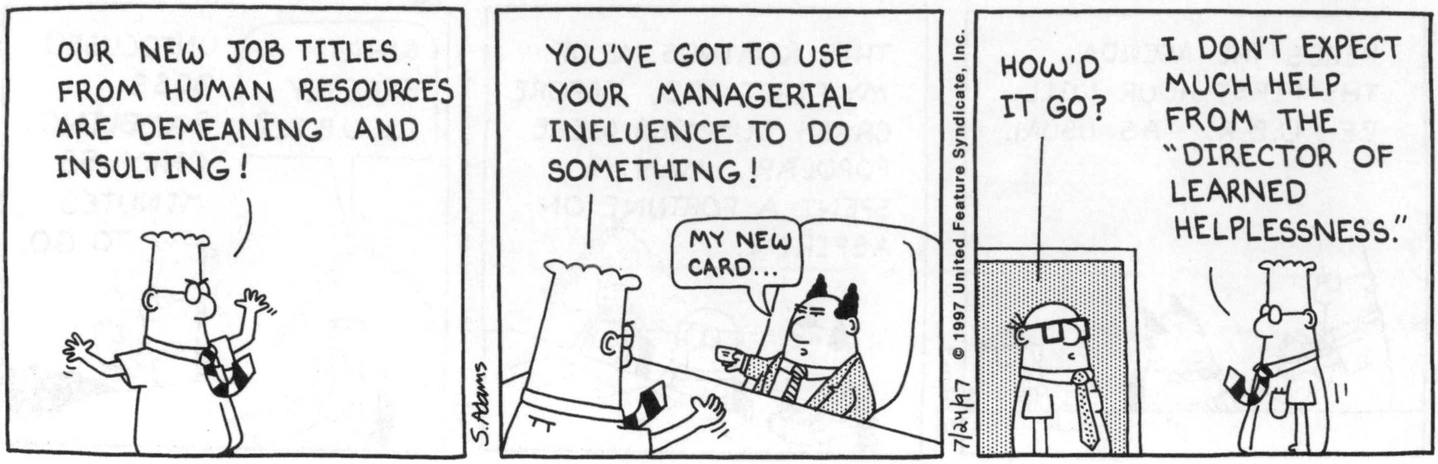
OUR NEW JOB TITLES FROM HUMAN RESOURCES ARE DEMEANING AND INSULTING!
YOU'VE GOT TO USE YOUR MANAGERIAL INFLUENCE TO DO SOMETHING!
MY NEW CARD...
HOW'D IT GO?
I DON'T EXPECT MUCH HELP FROM THE "DIRECTOR OF LEARNED HELPLESSNESS."
S. Adams
7/24/97 © 1997 United Feature Syndicate, Inc.

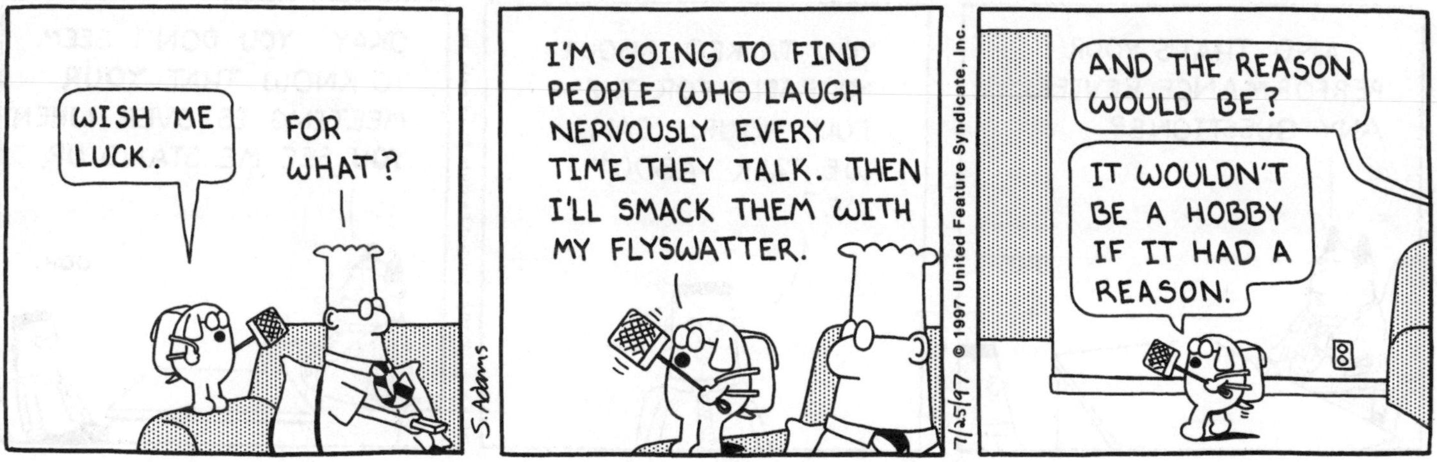
WISH ME LUCK.
FOR WHAT?
I'M GOING TO FIND PEOPLE WHO LAUGH NERVOUSLY EVERY TIME THEY TALK. THEN I'LL SMACK THEM WITH MY FLYSWATTER.
AND THE REASON WOULD BE?
IT WOULDN'T BE A HOBBY IF IT HAD A REASON.
S. Adams
7/25/97 © 1997 United Feature Syndicate, Inc.

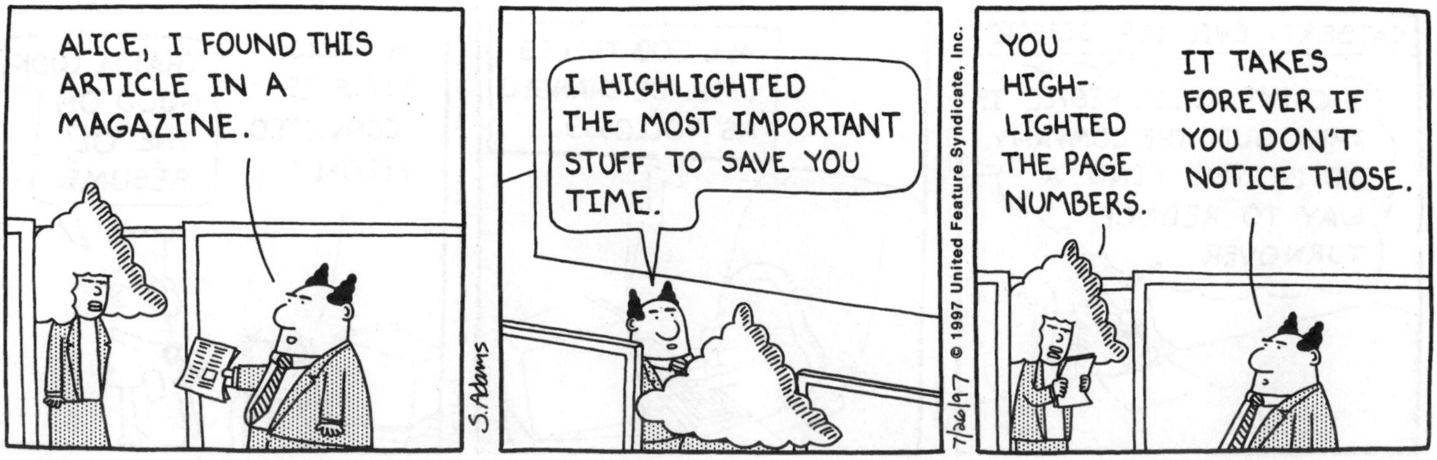
ALICE, I FOUND THIS ARTICLE IN A MAGAZINE.
I HIGHLIGHTED THE MOST IMPORTANT STUFF TO SAVE YOU TIME.
YOU HIGH-LIGHTED THE PAGE NUMBERS.
IT TAKES FOREVER IF YOU DON'T NOTICE THOSE.
S. Adams
7/26/97 © 1997 United Feature Syndicate, Inc.

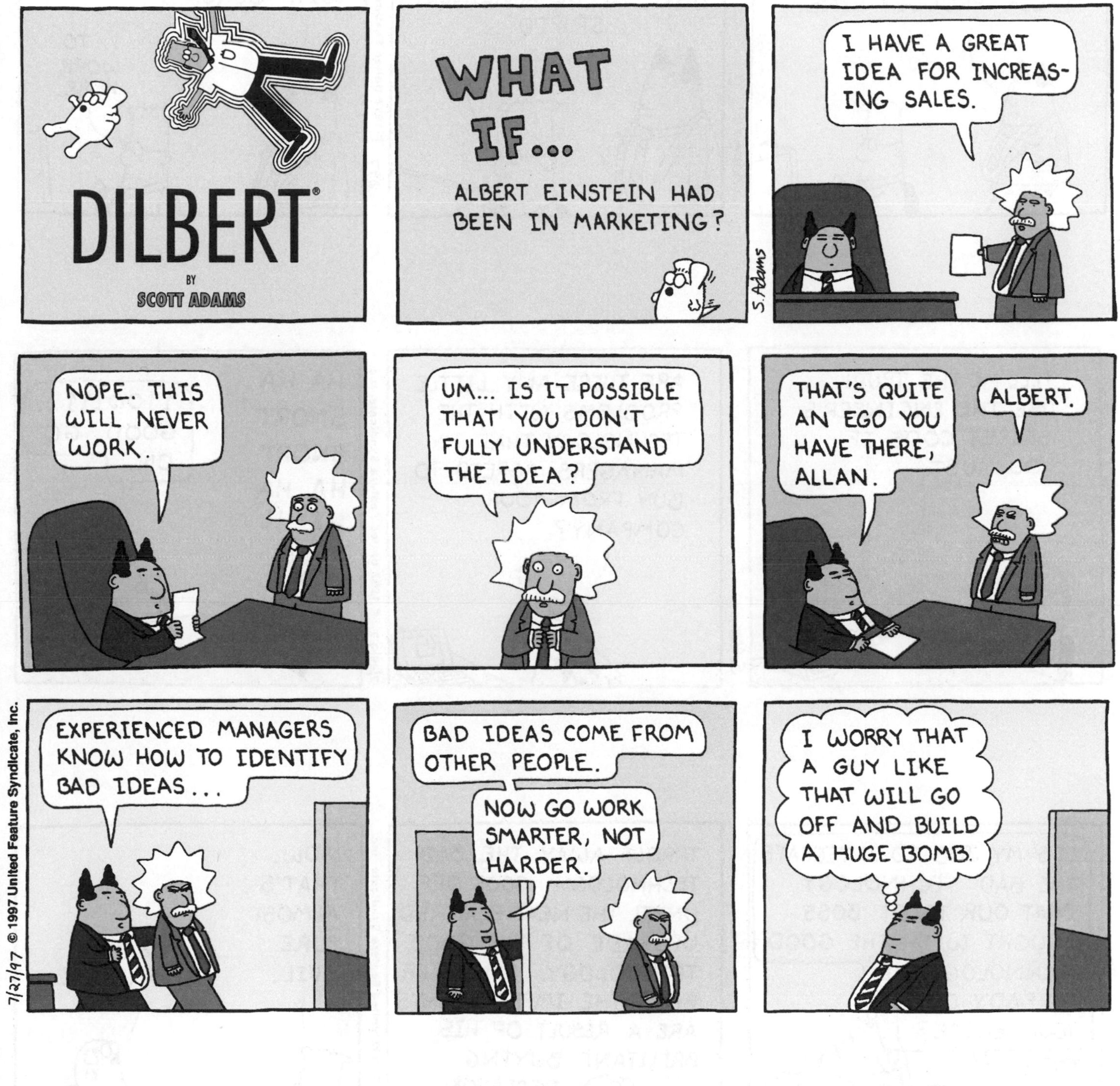

DILBERT®
BY
SCOTT ADAMS
WHAT IF...
ALBERT EINSTEIN HAD BEEN IN MARKETING?
S. Adams
I HAVE A GREAT IDEA FOR INCREASING SALES.
NOPE. THIS WILL NEVER WORK.
UM... IS IT POSSIBLE THAT YOU DON'T FULLY UNDERSTAND THE IDEA?
THAT'S QUITE AN EGO YOU HAVE THERE, ALLAN.
ALBERT.
EXPERIENCED MANAGERS KNOW HOW TO IDENTIFY BAD IDEAS...
BAD IDEAS COME FROM OTHER PEOPLE.
NOW GO WORK SMARTER, NOT HARDER.
I WORRY THAT A GUY LIKE THAT WILL GO OFF AND BUILD A HUGE BOMB.
7/27/97 © 1997 United Feature Syndicate, Inc.

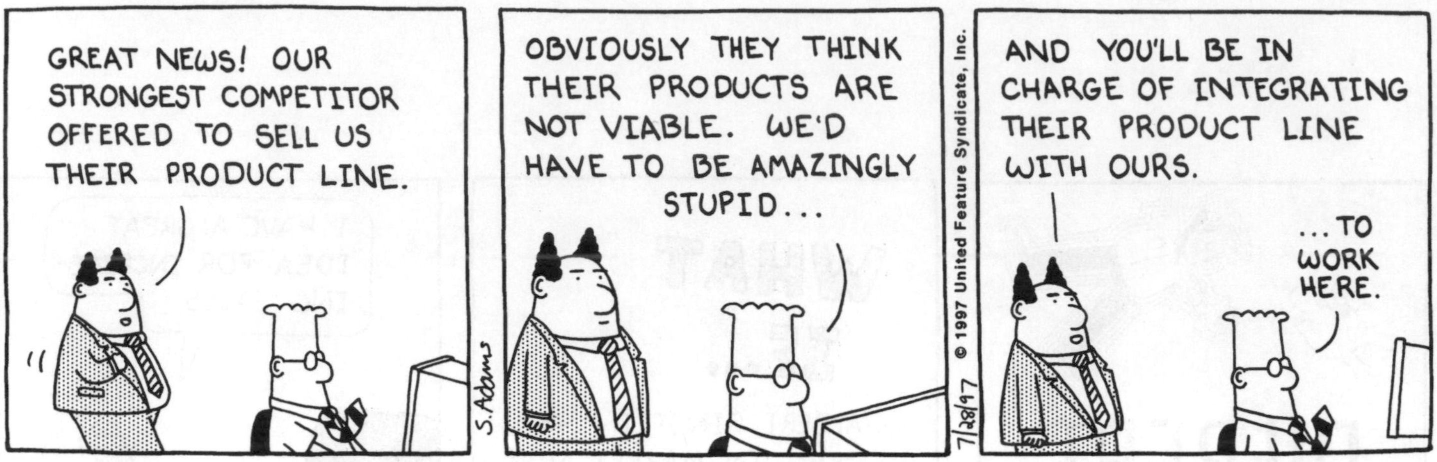
GREAT NEWS! OUR STRONGEST COMPETITOR OFFERED TO SELL US THEIR PRODUCT LINE.
S. Adams
OBVIOUSLY THEY THINK THEIR PRODUCTS ARE NOT VIABLE. WE'D HAVE TO BE AMAZINGLY STUPID...
7/28/97
© 1997 United Feature Syndicate, Inc.
AND YOU'LL BE IN CHARGE OF INTEGRATING THEIR PRODUCT LINE WITH OURS.
...TO WORK HERE.

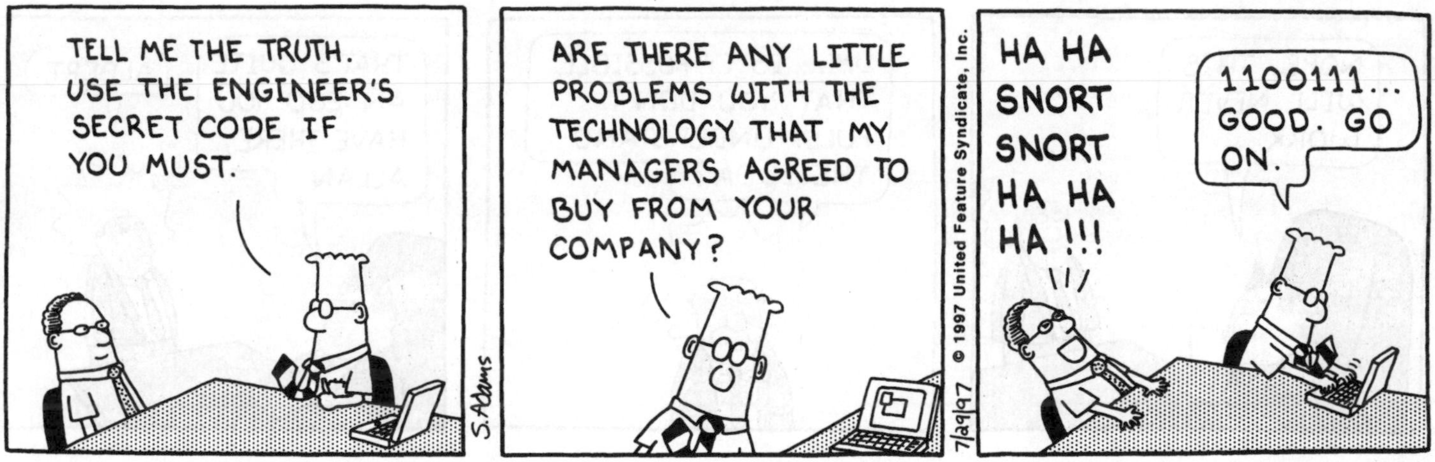
TELL ME THE TRUTH. USE THE ENGINEER'S SECRET CODE IF YOU MUST.
S. Adams
ARE THERE ANY LITTLE PROBLEMS WITH THE TECHNOLOGY THAT MY MANAGERS AGREED TO BUY FROM YOUR COMPANY?
7/29/97
© 1997 United Feature Syndicate, Inc.
HA HA SNORT SNORT HA HA HA !!!
1100111... GOOD. GO ON.

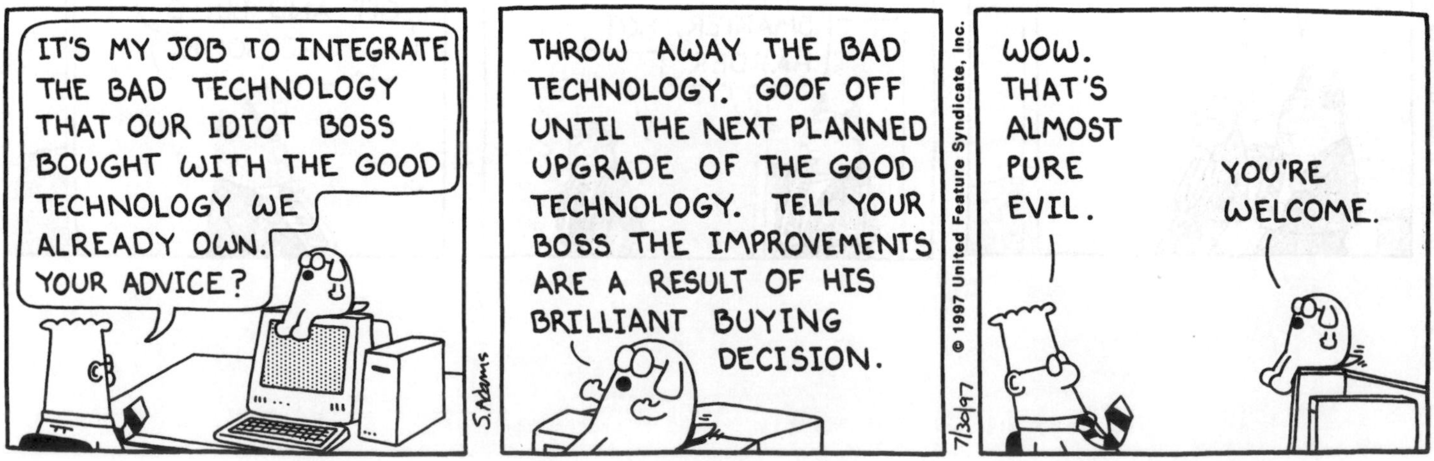
IT'S MY JOB TO INTEGRATE THE BAD TECHNOLOGY THAT OUR IDIOT BOSS BOUGHT WITH THE GOOD TECHNOLOGY WE ALREADY OWN. YOUR ADVICE?
S. Adams
THROW AWAY THE BAD TECHNOLOGY. GOOF OFF UNTIL THE NEXT PLANNED UPGRADE OF THE GOOD TECHNOLOGY. TELL YOUR BOSS THE IMPROVEMENTS ARE A RESULT OF HIS BRILLIANT BUYING DECISION.
7/30/97
© 1997 United Feature Syndicate, Inc.
WOW. THAT'S ALMOST PURE EVIL.
YOU'RE WELCOME.

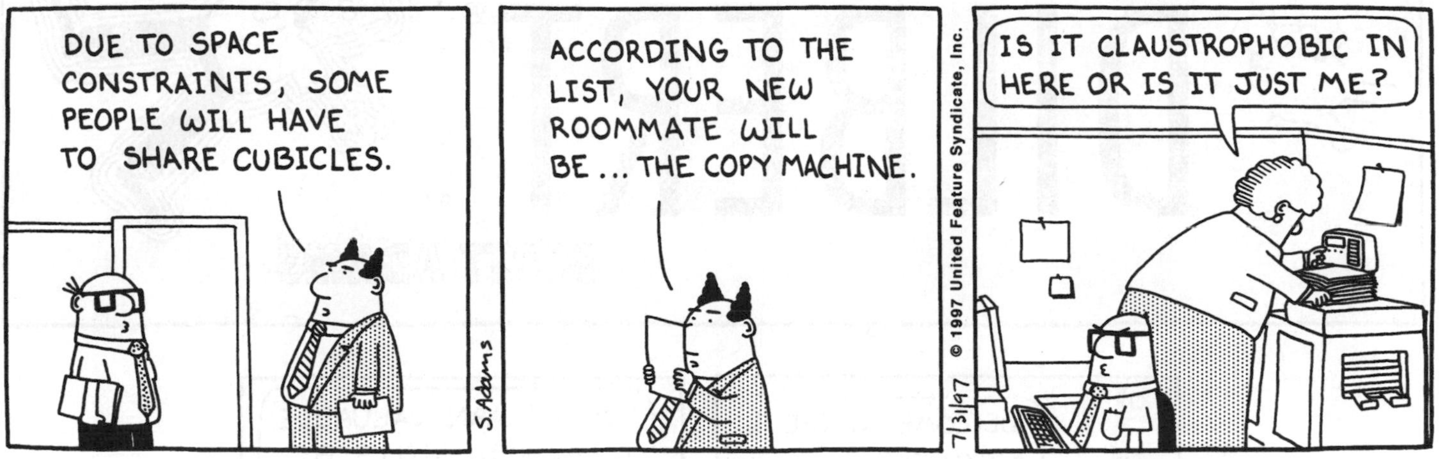
DUE TO SPACE CONSTRAINTS, SOME PEOPLE WILL HAVE TO SHARE CUBICLES.
ACCORDING TO THE LIST, YOUR NEW ROOMMATE WILL BE ... THE COPY MACHINE.
IS IT CLAUSTROPHOBIC IN HERE OR IS IT JUST ME?
S. Adams
7/3/97 © 1997 United Feature Syndicate, Inc.

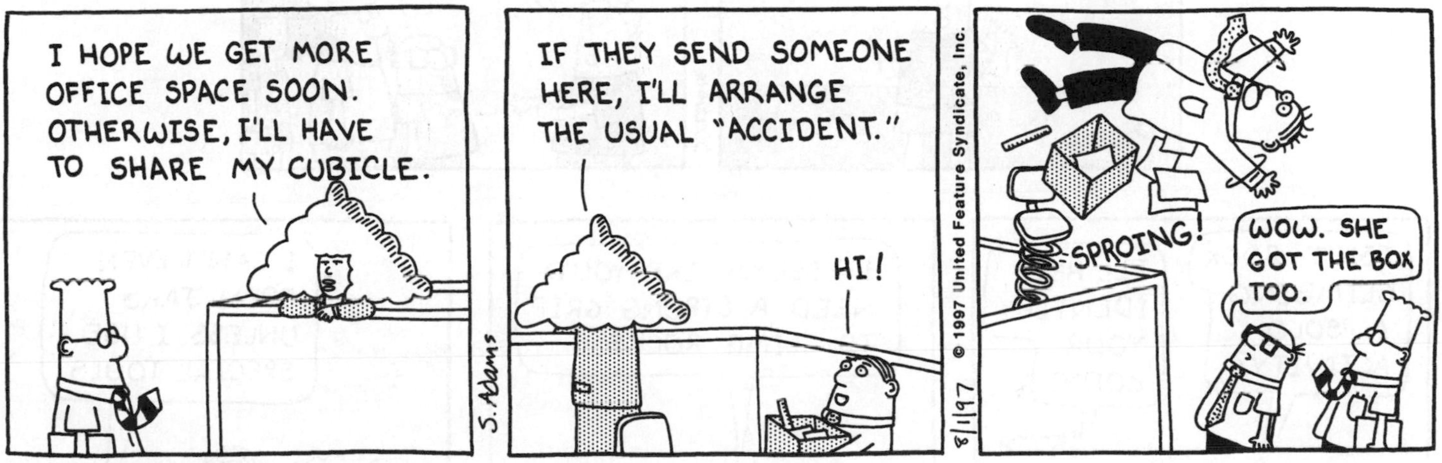
I HOPE WE GET MORE OFFICE SPACE SOON. OTHERWISE, I'LL HAVE TO SHARE MY CUBICLE.
IF THEY SEND SOMEONE HERE, I'LL ARRANGE THE USUAL "ACCIDENT."
HI!
SPROING!
WOW. SHE GOT THE BOX TOO.
S. Adams
8/1/97 © 1997 United Feature Syndicate, Inc.

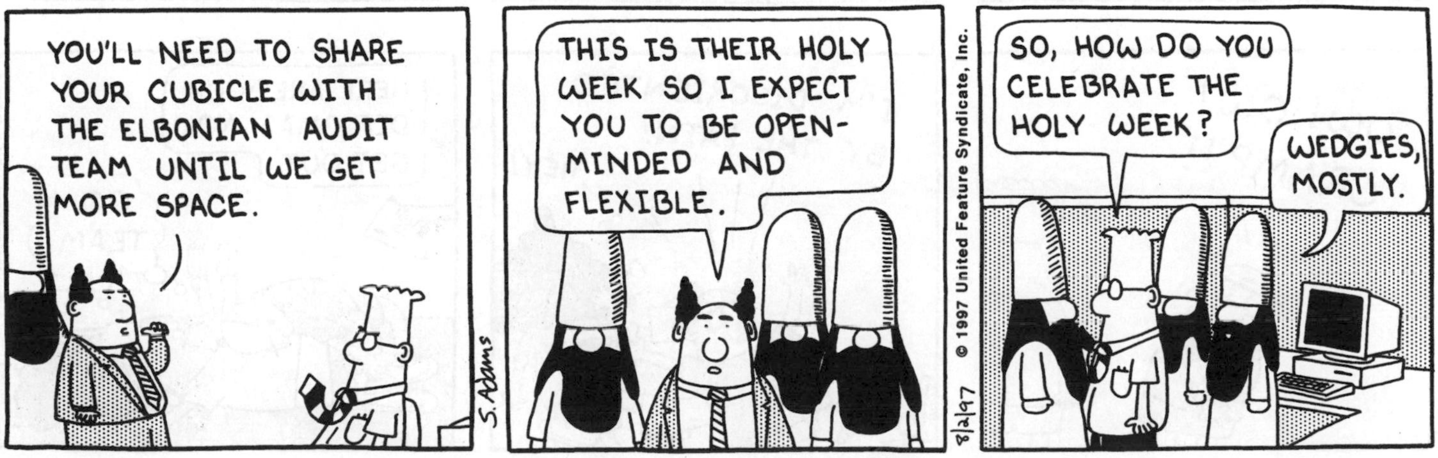
YOU'LL NEED TO SHARE YOUR CUBICLE WITH THE ELBONIAN AUDIT TEAM UNTIL WE GET MORE SPACE.
THIS IS THEIR HOLY WEEK SO I EXPECT YOU TO BE OPEN-MINDED AND FLEXIBLE.
SO, HOW DO YOU CELEBRATE THE HOLY WEEK?
WEDGIES, MOSTLY.
S. Adams
8/2/97 © 1997 United Feature Syndicate, Inc.

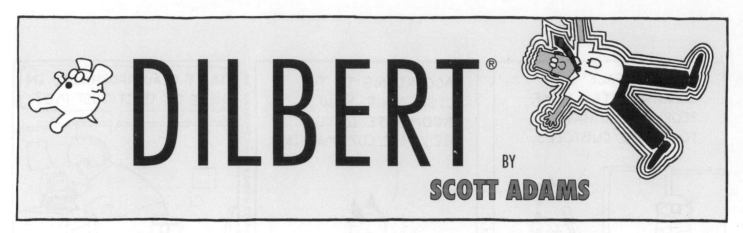

DILBERT

BY **SCOTT ADAMS**

WELCOME TO THE EMPLOYEE ROCK-CLIMBING SEMINAR.

YOU'LL LEARN VALUABLE TEAMWORK SKILLS BY DOING DANGEROUS THINGS UNRELATED TO YOUR JOBS.

S. Adams

ISN'T ROCK CLIMBING A SOLO ACTIVITY?

I'LL HELP IDENTIFY YOUR BODY.

IT SEEMS LIKE YOU'D NEED A STRONG GRIP TO CLIMB ROCKS.

I CAN'T EVEN OPEN JARS UNLESS I USE SPECIAL TOOLS.

OW! OW! CRAMP!!

I'M DISORIENTED BY THE PAIN!

HEY!

HERE ARE YOUR DIPLOMAS. NOW GET OUT.

GO TEAM!

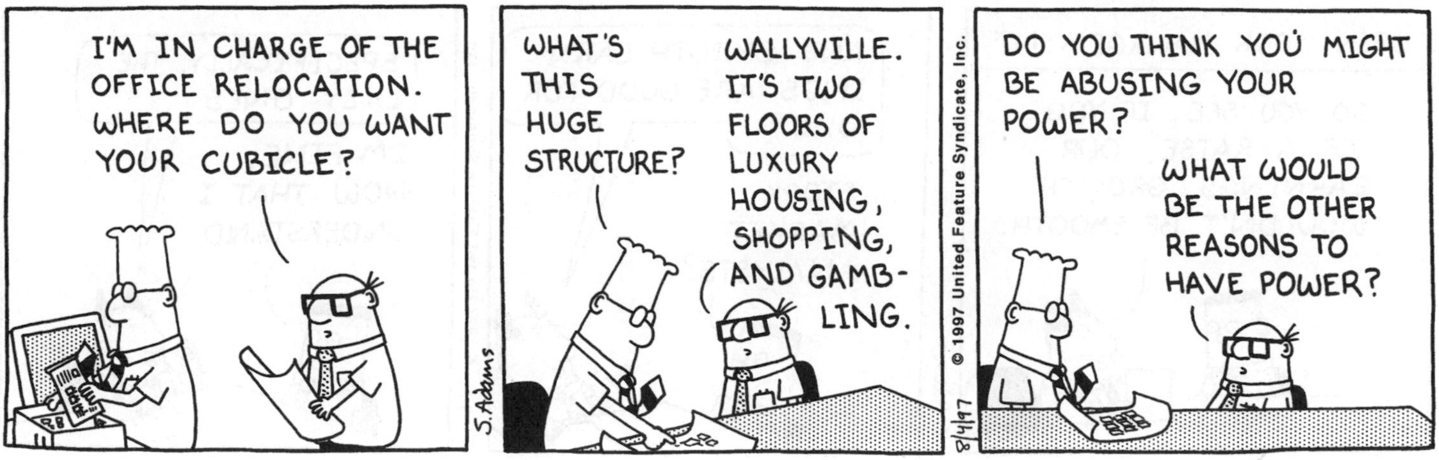
I'M IN CHARGE OF THE OFFICE RELOCATION. WHERE DO YOU WANT YOUR CUBICLE?
WHAT'S THIS HUGE STRUCTURE?
WALLYVILLE. IT'S TWO FLOORS OF LUXURY HOUSING, SHOPPING, AND GAMBLING.
DO YOU THINK YOU MIGHT BE ABUSING YOUR POWER?
WHAT WOULD BE THE OTHER REASONS TO HAVE POWER?
S.Adams
© 1997 United Feature Syndicate, Inc.
8/4/97

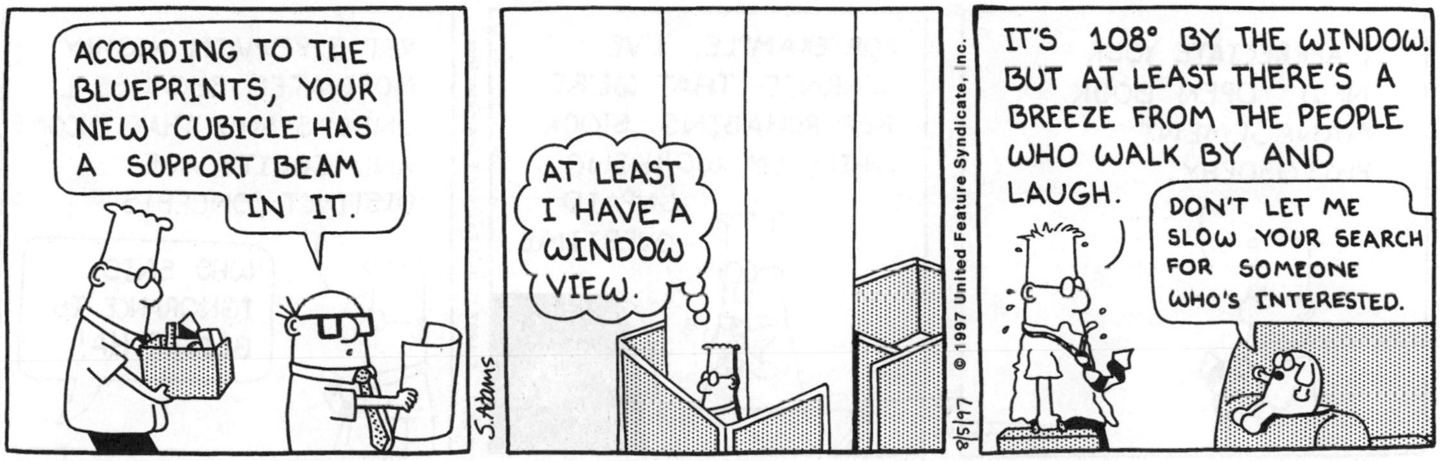
ACCORDING TO THE BLUEPRINTS, YOUR NEW CUBICLE HAS A SUPPORT BEAM IN IT.
AT LEAST I HAVE A WINDOW VIEW.
IT'S 108° BY THE WINDOW. BUT AT LEAST THERE'S A BREEZE FROM THE PEOPLE WHO WALK BY AND LAUGH.
DON'T LET ME SLOW YOUR SEARCH FOR SOMEONE WHO'S INTERESTED.
S.Adams
© 1997 United Feature Syndicate, Inc.
8/5/97

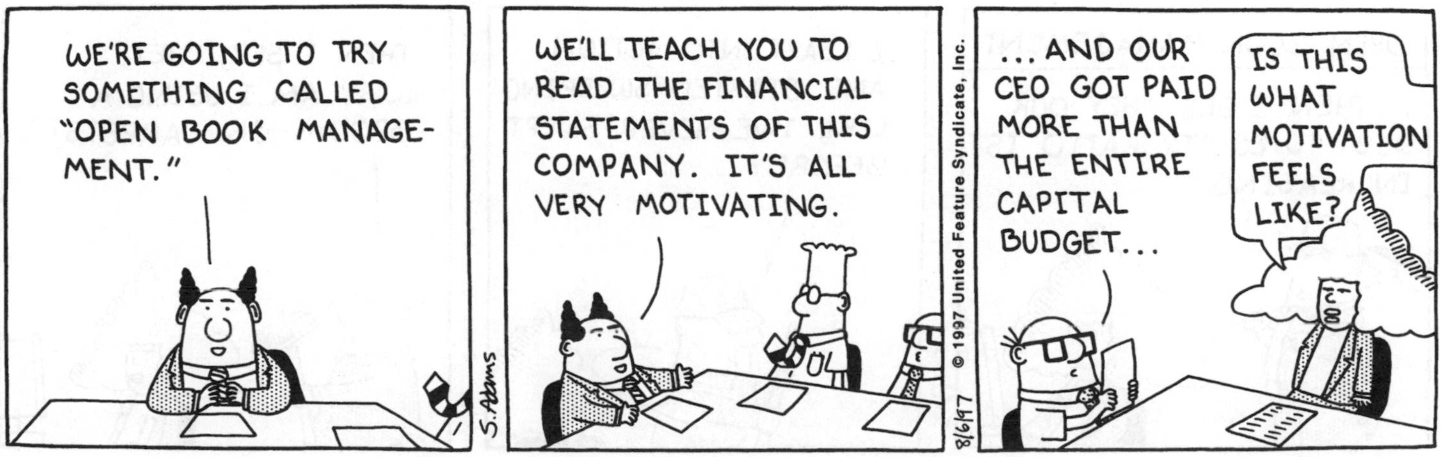
WE'RE GOING TO TRY SOMETHING CALLED "OPEN BOOK MANAGEMENT."
WE'LL TEACH YOU TO READ THE FINANCIAL STATEMENTS OF THIS COMPANY. IT'S ALL VERY MOTIVATING.
... AND OUR CEO GOT PAID MORE THAN THE ENTIRE CAPITAL BUDGET...
IS THIS WHAT MOTIVATION FEELS LIKE?
S.Adams
© 1997 United Feature Syndicate, Inc.
8/6/97

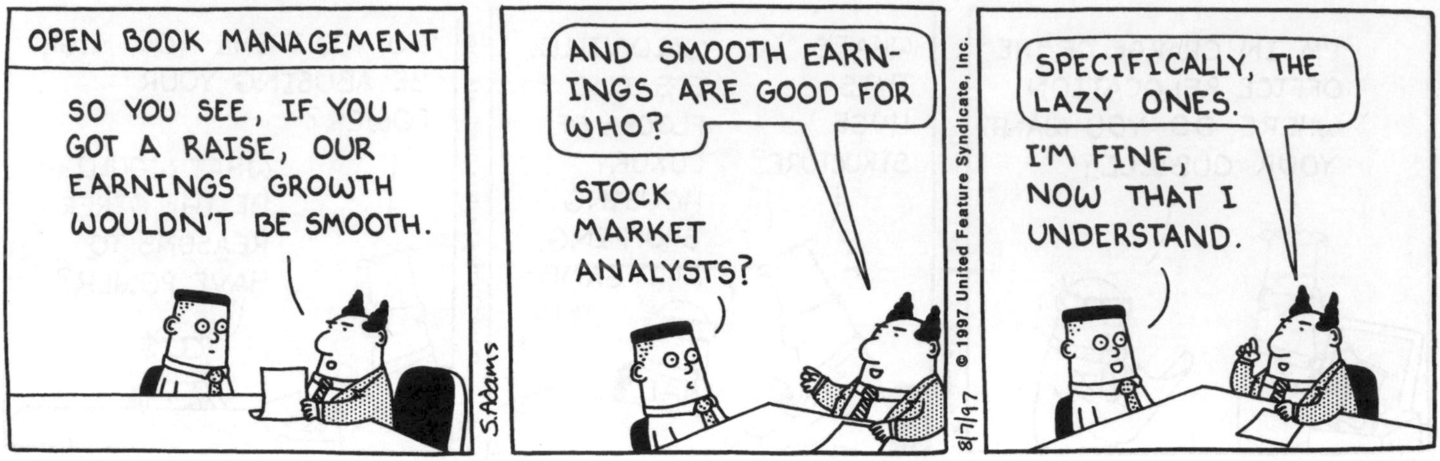
OPEN BOOK MANAGEMENT
SO YOU SEE, IF YOU GOT A RAISE, OUR EARNINGS GROWTH WOULDN'T BE SMOOTH.
AND SMOOTH EARNINGS ARE GOOD FOR WHO?
STOCK MARKET ANALYSTS?
SPECIFICALLY, THE LAZY ONES.
I'M FINE, NOW THAT I UNDERSTAND.
S. Adams
8/7/97
© 1997 United Feature Syndicate, Inc.

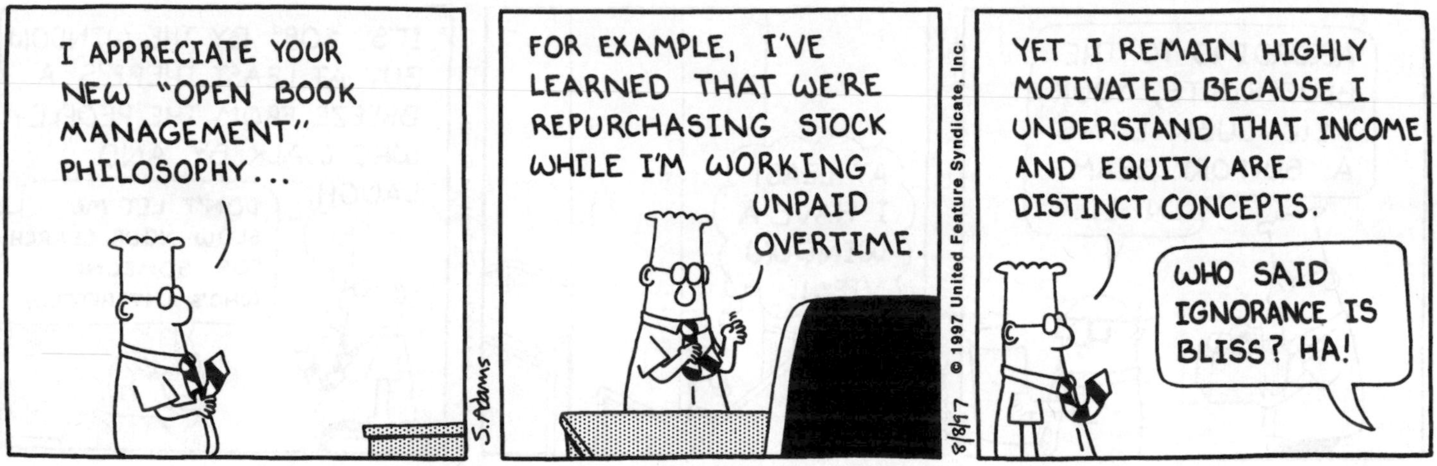
I APPRECIATE YOUR NEW "OPEN BOOK MANAGEMENT" PHILOSOPHY...
FOR EXAMPLE, I'VE LEARNED THAT WE'RE REPURCHASING STOCK WHILE I'M WORKING UNPAID OVERTIME.
YET I REMAIN HIGHLY MOTIVATED BECAUSE I UNDERSTAND THAT INCOME AND EQUITY ARE DISTINCT CONCEPTS.
WHO SAID IGNORANCE IS BLISS? HA!
S. Adams
8/8/97
© 1997 United Feature Syndicate, Inc.

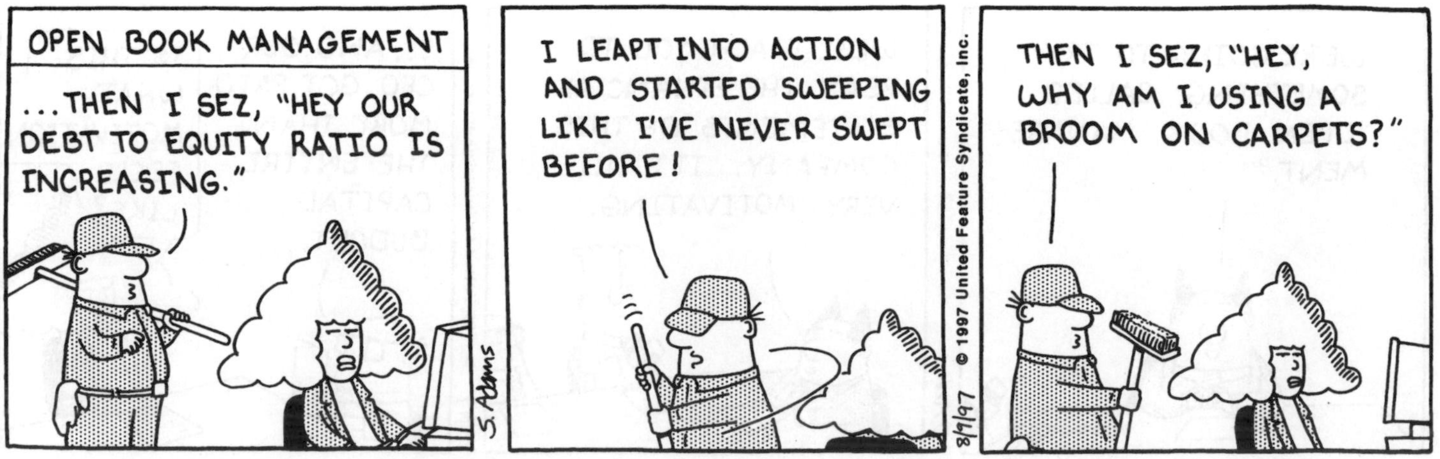
OPEN BOOK MANAGEMENT
...THEN I SEZ, "HEY OUR DEBT TO EQUITY RATIO IS INCREASING."
I LEAPT INTO ACTION AND STARTED SWEEPING LIKE I'VE NEVER SWEPT BEFORE!
THEN I SEZ, "HEY, WHY AM I USING A BROOM ON CARPETS?"
S. Adams
8/9/97
© 1997 United Feature Syndicate, Inc.

DILBERT®
BY
SCOTT ADAMS
ANNOUNCING PROJECT "SPARKLE," THE CLEAN DESK POLICY.
S. Adams
THIS IS A COMPANY-WIDE EFFORT TO KEEP OUR WORK SPACES CLEAN.
TINY QUESTION. I'M CURIOUS ABOUT ONE THING.
I'M PICTURING OUR TOP EXECUTIVES IN THE "WAR ROOM."
THEY TALK ABOUT THE COMPETITIVE THREAT AND OUR LACK OF RESOURCES. SUDDENLY, PANIC SETS IN!!
8/10/97 © 1997 United Feature Syndicate, Inc.
A LONE VOICE OF REASON PENETRATES THE CONFUSION. TWO WORDS: "PAPER TOWELS."
IS THAT PRETTY MUCH HOW IT WENT?
MOVING ALONG, YOU EACH GET A LAMINATED CARD WITH OUR MISSION STATEMENT.
LET ME DO THIS ONE.

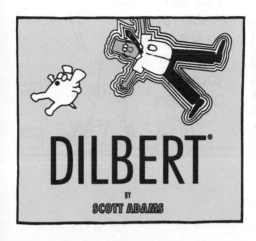

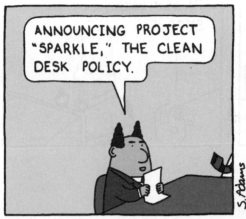

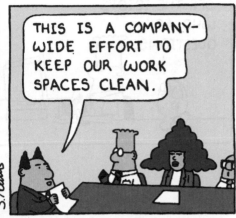

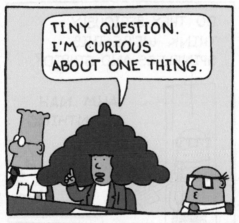

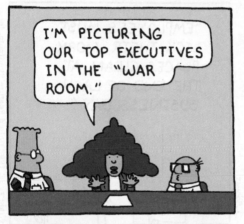

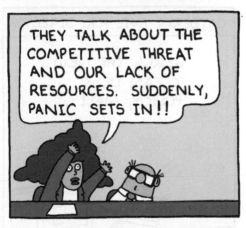

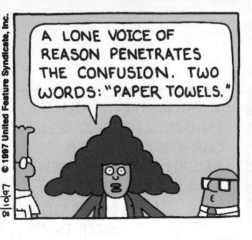

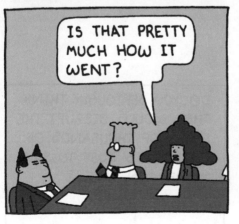

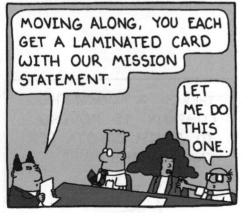

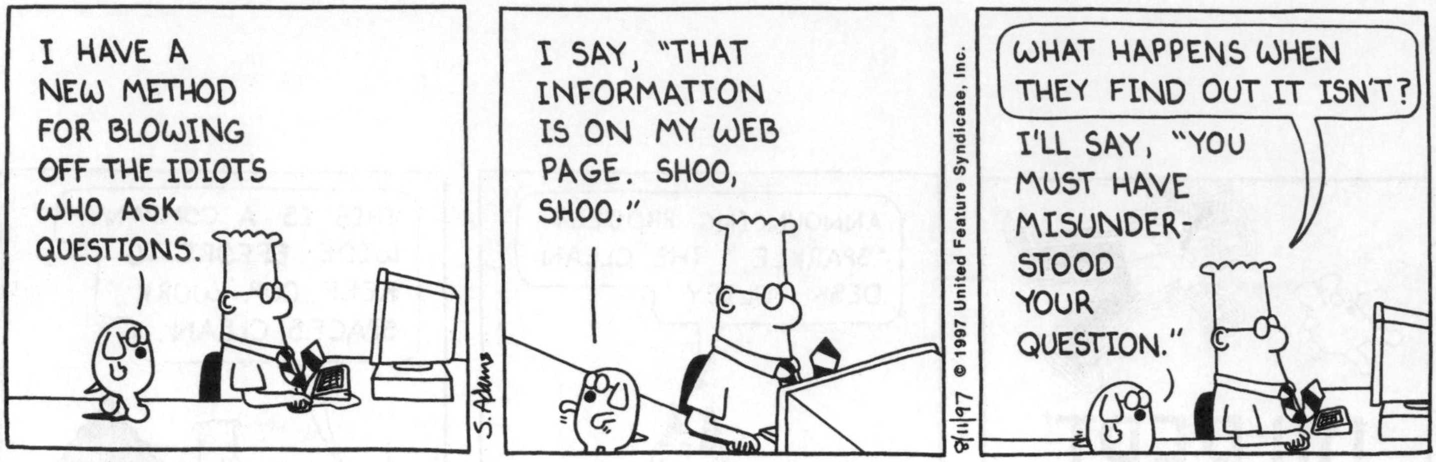
I HAVE A NEW METHOD FOR BLOWING OFF THE IDIOTS WHO ASK QUESTIONS.
S. Adams
I SAY, "THAT INFORMATION IS ON MY WEB PAGE. SHOO, SHOO."
8/11/97 © 1997 United Feature Syndicate, Inc.
WHAT HAPPENS WHEN THEY FIND OUT IT ISN'T?
I'LL SAY, "YOU MUST HAVE MISUNDERSTOOD YOUR QUESTION."

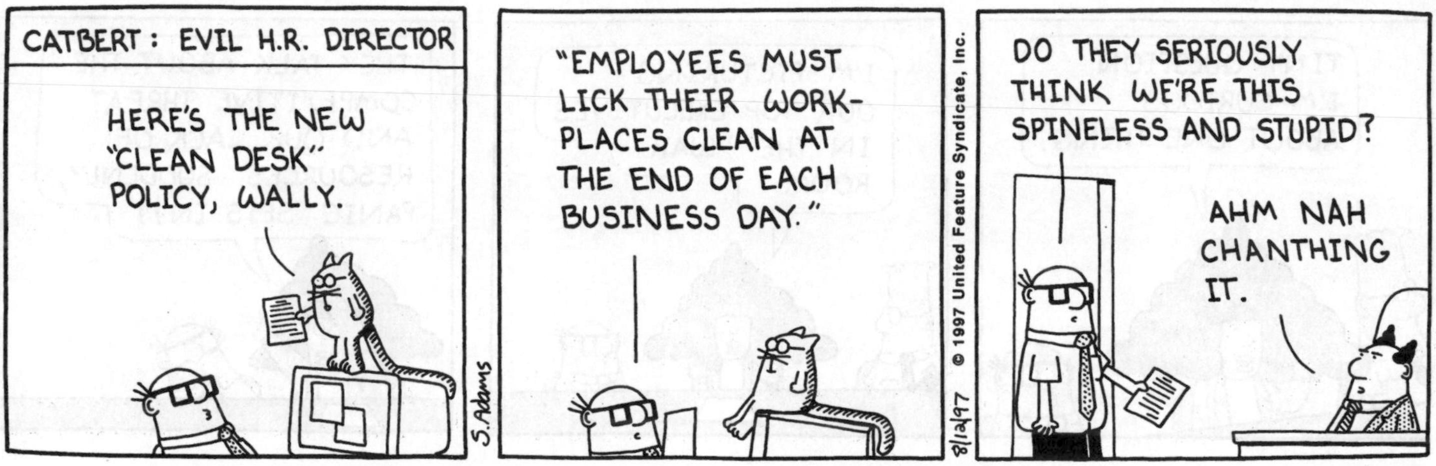
CATBERT: EVIL H.R. DIRECTOR
HERE'S THE NEW "CLEAN DESK" POLICY, WALLY.
S. Adams
"EMPLOYEES MUST LICK THEIR WORKPLACES CLEAN AT THE END OF EACH BUSINESS DAY."
8/12/97 © 1997 United Feature Syndicate, Inc.
DO THEY SERIOUSLY THINK WE'RE THIS SPINELESS AND STUPID?
AHM NAH CHANTHING IT.

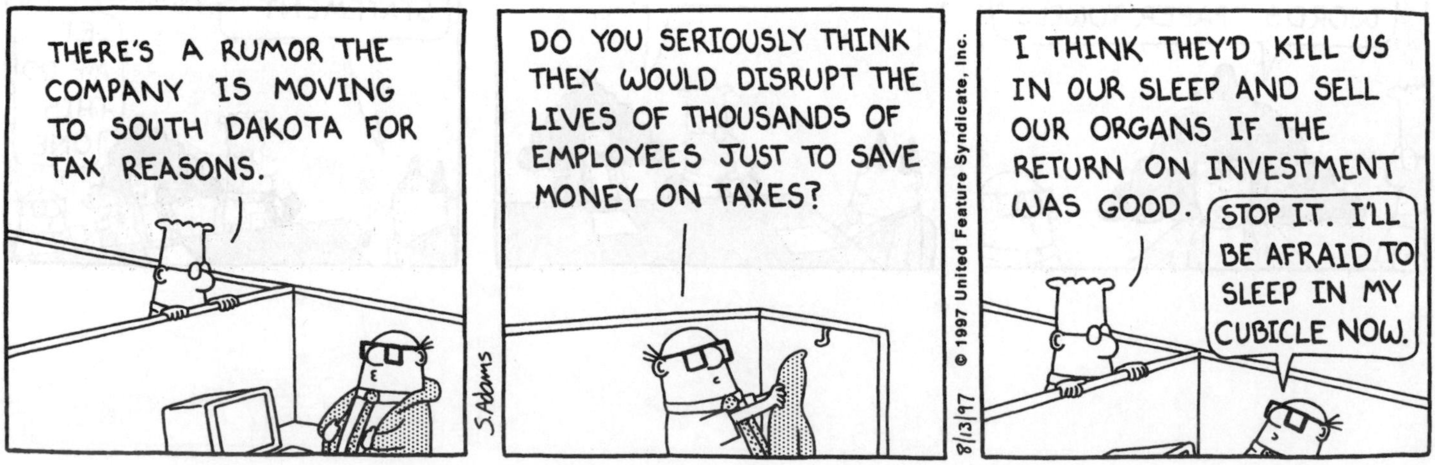
THERE'S A RUMOR THE COMPANY IS MOVING TO SOUTH DAKOTA FOR TAX REASONS.
S. Adams
DO YOU SERIOUSLY THINK THEY WOULD DISRUPT THE LIVES OF THOUSANDS OF EMPLOYEES JUST TO SAVE MONEY ON TAXES?
8/13/97 © 1997 United Feature Syndicate, Inc.
I THINK THEY'D KILL US IN OUR SLEEP AND SELL OUR ORGANS IF THE RETURN ON INVESTMENT WAS GOOD.
STOP IT. I'LL BE AFRAID TO SLEEP IN MY CUBICLE NOW.

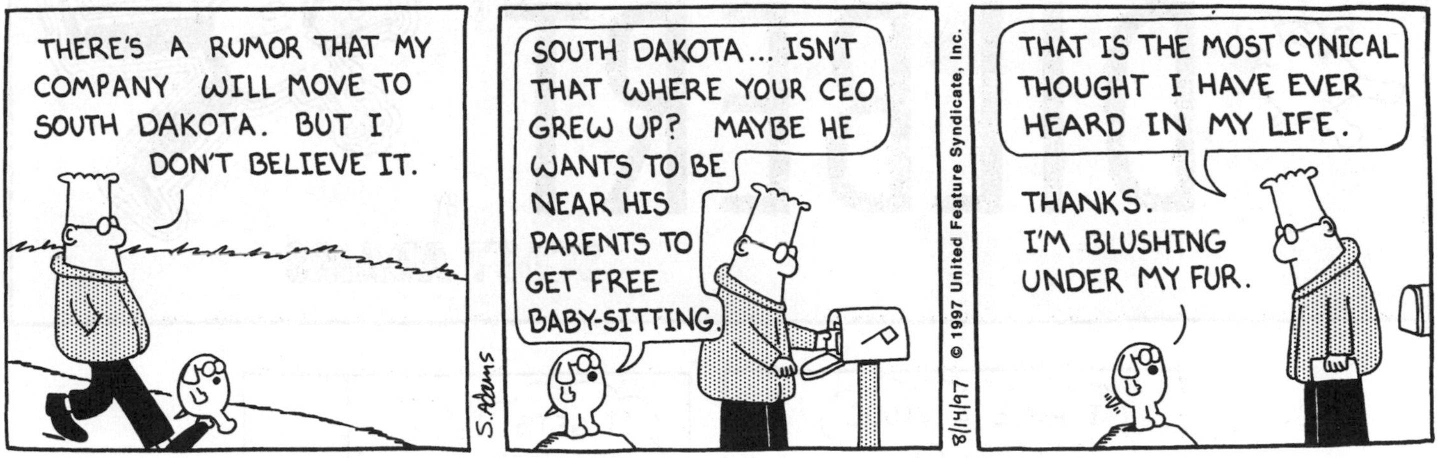
THERE'S A RUMOR THAT MY COMPANY WILL MOVE TO SOUTH DAKOTA. BUT I DON'T BELIEVE IT.
SOUTH DAKOTA... ISN'T THAT WHERE YOUR CEO GREW UP? MAYBE HE WANTS TO BE NEAR HIS PARENTS TO GET FREE BABY-SITTING.
THAT IS THE MOST CYNICAL THOUGHT I HAVE EVER HEARD IN MY LIFE.
THANKS. I'M BLUSHING UNDER MY FUR.
S. Adams
8/14/97 © 1997 United Feature Syndicate, Inc.

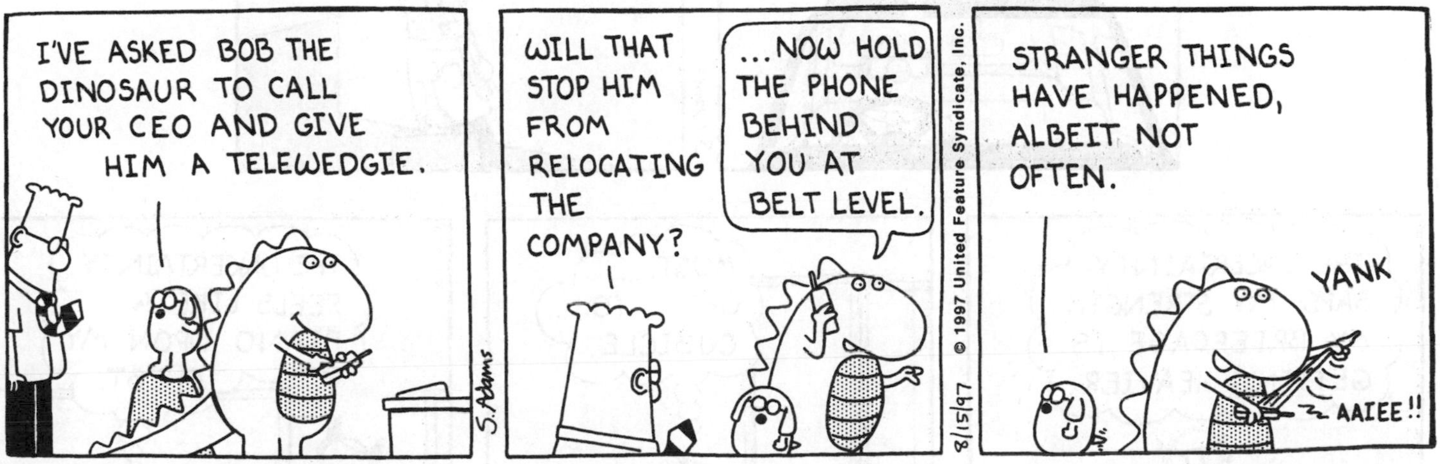
I'VE ASKED BOB THE DINOSAUR TO CALL YOUR CEO AND GIVE HIM A TELEWEDGIE.
WILL THAT STOP HIM FROM RELOCATING THE COMPANY?
...NOW HOLD THE PHONE BEHIND YOU AT BELT LEVEL.
STRANGER THINGS HAVE HAPPENED, ALBEIT NOT OFTEN.
YANK
AAIEE!!
S. Adams
8/15/97 © 1997 United Feature Syndicate, Inc.

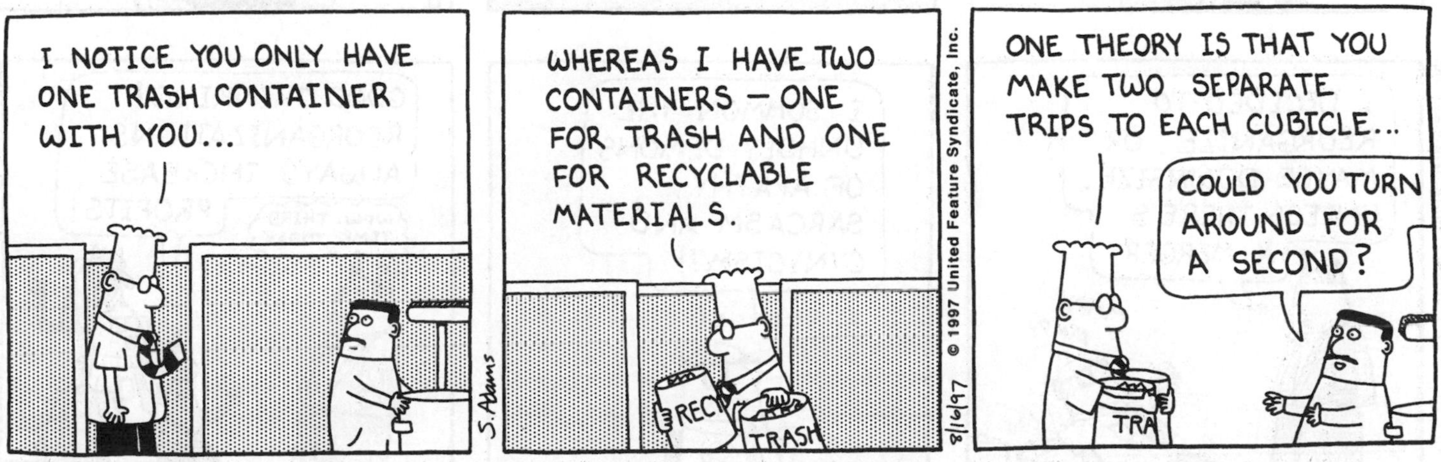
I NOTICE YOU ONLY HAVE ONE TRASH CONTAINER WITH YOU...
WHEREAS I HAVE TWO CONTAINERS — ONE FOR TRASH AND ONE FOR RECYCLABLE MATERIALS.
RECY
TRASH
ONE THEORY IS THAT YOU MAKE TWO SEPARATE TRIPS TO EACH CUBICLE...
COULD YOU TURN AROUND FOR A SECOND?
TRA
S. Adams
8/16/97 © 1997 United Feature Syndicate, Inc.

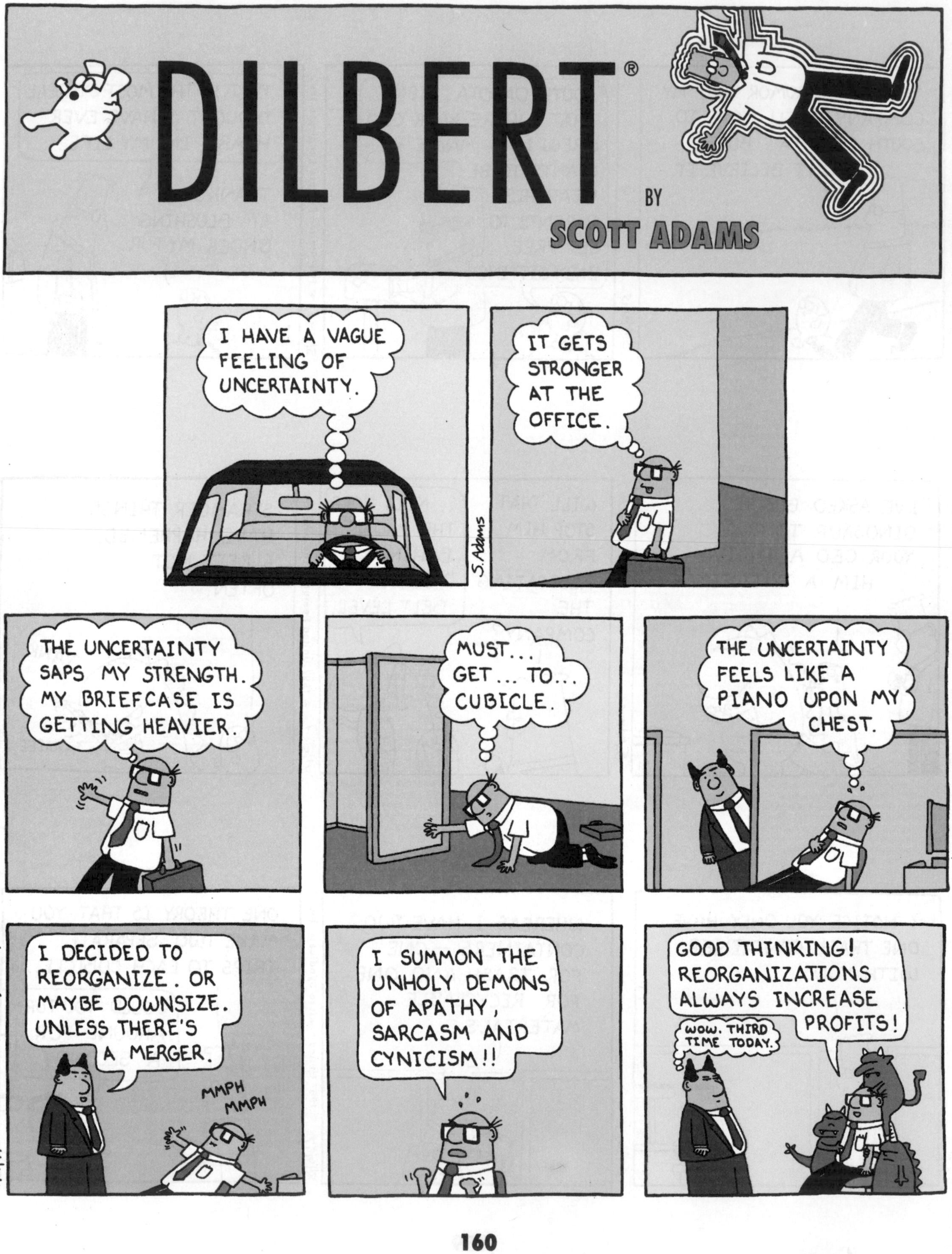
DILBERT®
BY
SCOTT ADAMS
I HAVE A VAGUE FEELING OF UNCERTAINTY.
S. Adams
IT GETS STRONGER AT THE OFFICE.
THE UNCERTAINTY SAPS MY STRENGTH. MY BRIEFCASE IS GETTING HEAVIER.
MUST... GET... TO... CUBICLE.
THE UNCERTAINTY FEELS LIKE A PIANO UPON MY CHEST.
I DECIDED TO REORGANIZE. OR MAYBE DOWNSIZE. UNLESS THERE'S A MERGER.
MMPH MMPH
I SUMMON THE UNHOLY DEMONS OF APATHY, SARCASM AND CYNICISM!!
GOOD THINKING! REORGANIZATIONS ALWAYS INCREASE PROFITS!
WOW. THIRD TIME TODAY.

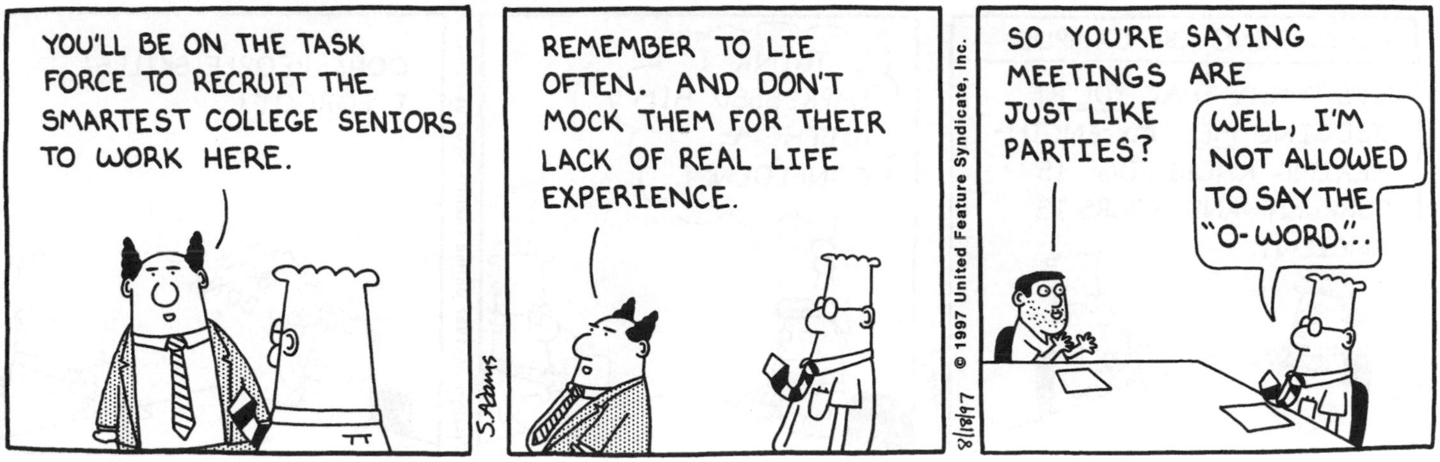
YOU'LL BE ON THE TASK FORCE TO RECRUIT THE SMARTEST COLLEGE SENIORS TO WORK HERE.
REMEMBER TO LIE OFTEN. AND DON'T MOCK THEM FOR THEIR LACK OF REAL LIFE EXPERIENCE.
S. Adams
8/18/97 © 1997 United Feature Syndicate, Inc.
SO YOU'RE SAYING MEETINGS ARE JUST LIKE PARTIES?
WELL, I'M NOT ALLOWED TO SAY THE "O-WORD."..

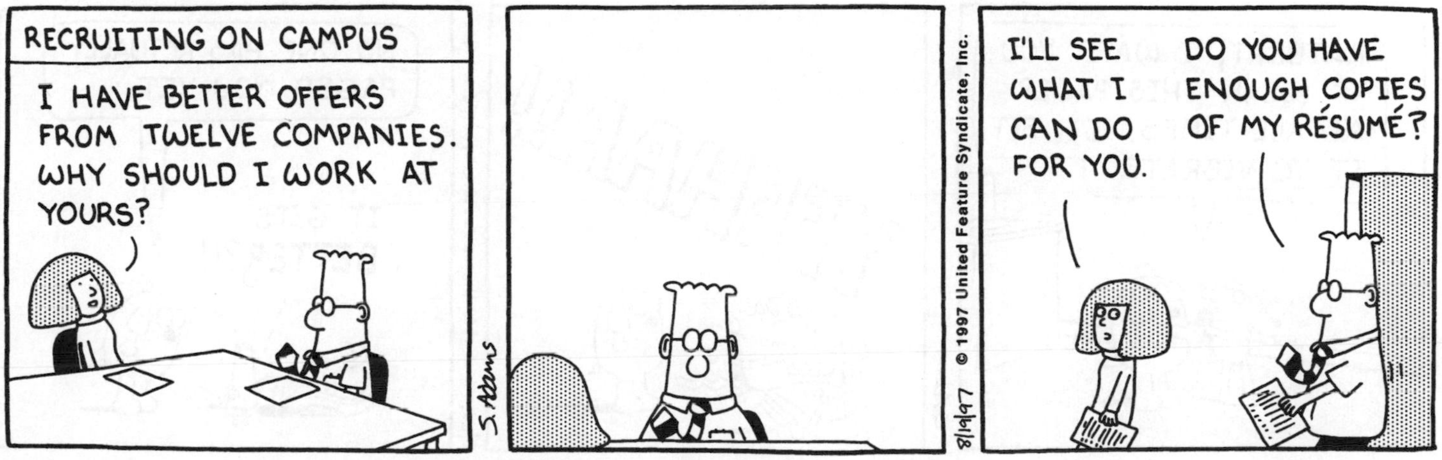
RECRUITING ON CAMPUS
I HAVE BETTER OFFERS FROM TWELVE COMPANIES. WHY SHOULD I WORK AT YOURS?
S. Adams
8/19/97 © 1997 United Feature Syndicate, Inc.
I'LL SEE WHAT I CAN DO FOR YOU.
DO YOU HAVE ENOUGH COPIES OF MY RÉSUMÉ?

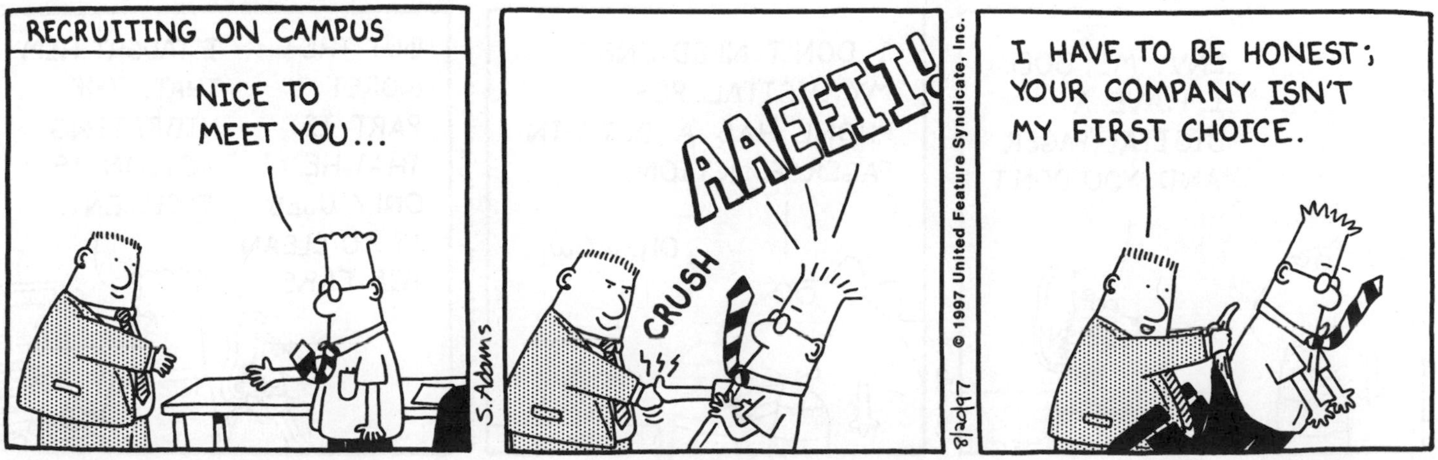
RECRUITING ON CAMPUS
NICE TO MEET YOU...
S. Adams
CRUSH
AAEEII!
8/20/97 © 1997 United Feature Syndicate, Inc.
I HAVE TO BE HONEST; YOUR COMPANY ISN'T MY FIRST CHOICE.

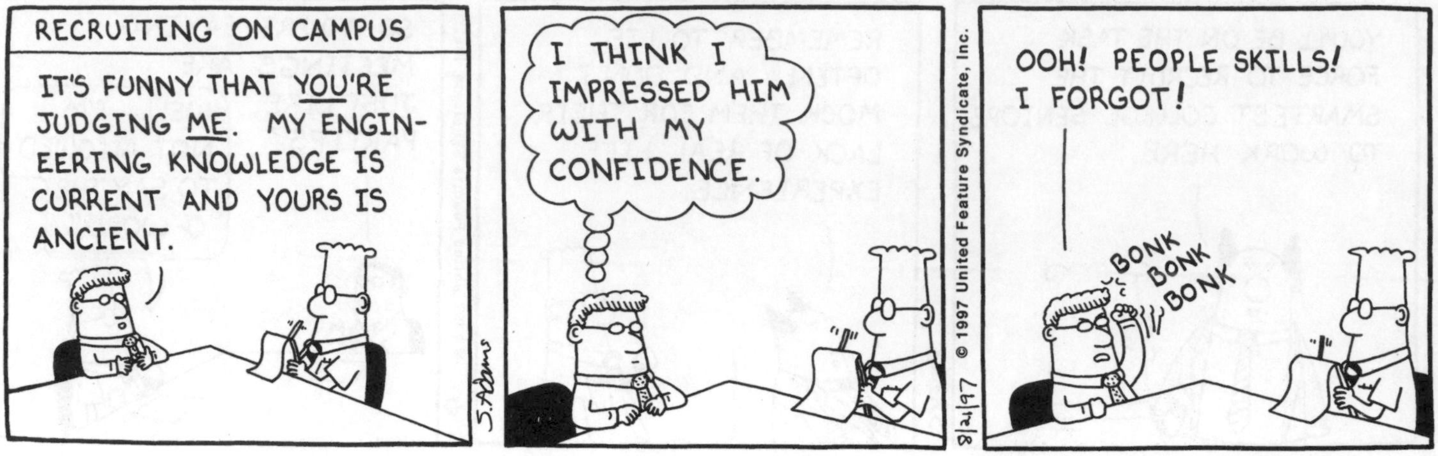
RECRUITING ON CAMPUS
IT'S FUNNY THAT YOU'RE JUDGING ME. MY ENGINEERING KNOWLEDGE IS CURRENT AND YOURS IS ANCIENT.
I THINK I IMPRESSED HIM WITH MY CONFIDENCE.
OOH! PEOPLE SKILLS! I FORGOT!
BONK BONK BONK
S. Adams
8/21/97 © 1997 United Feature Syndicate, Inc.

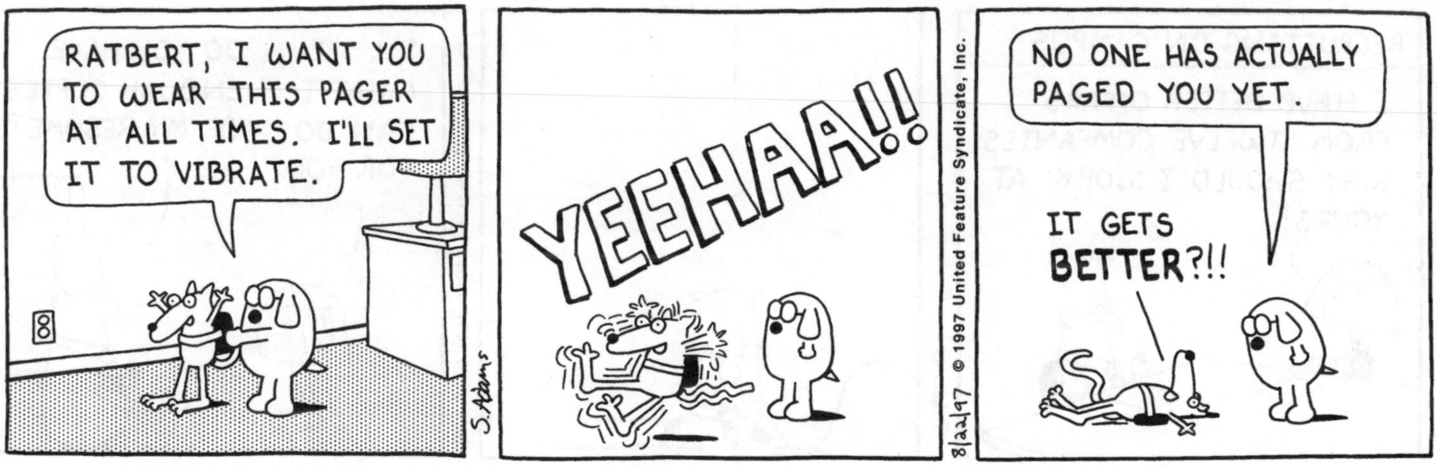
RATBERT, I WANT YOU TO WEAR THIS PAGER AT ALL TIMES. I'LL SET IT TO VIBRATE.
YEEHAA!!
NO ONE HAS ACTUALLY PAGED YOU YET.
IT GETS BETTER?!!
S. Adams
8/22/97 © 1997 United Feature Syndicate, Inc.

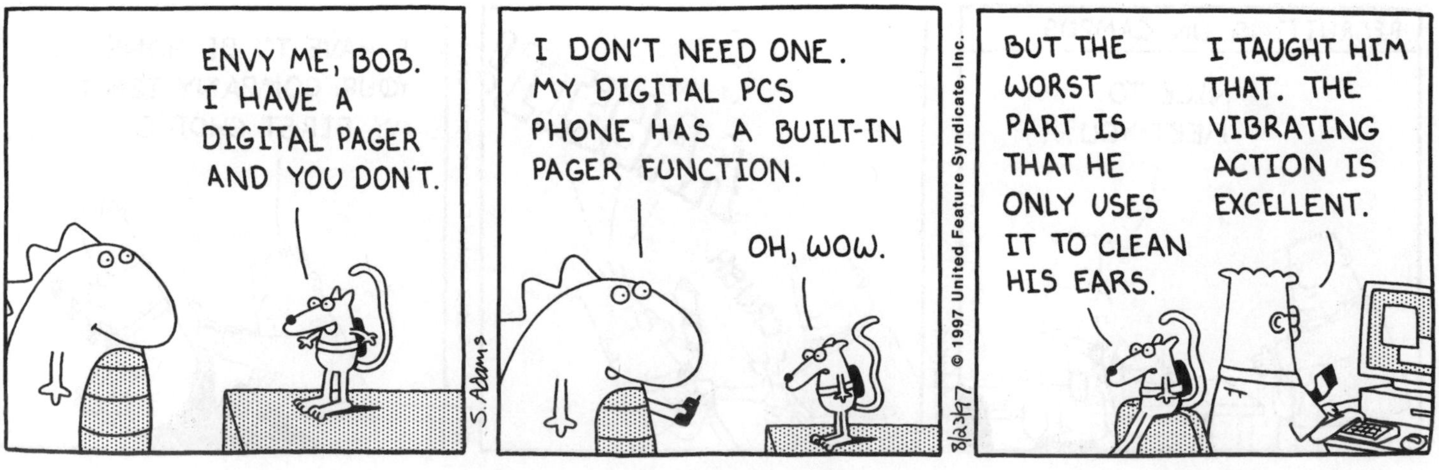
ENVY ME, BOB. I HAVE A DIGITAL PAGER AND YOU DON'T.
I DON'T NEED ONE. MY DIGITAL PCS PHONE HAS A BUILT-IN PAGER FUNCTION.
OH, WOW.
BUT THE WORST PART IS THAT HE ONLY USES IT TO CLEAN HIS EARS.
I TAUGHT HIM THAT. THE VIBRATING ACTION IS EXCELLENT.
S. Adams
8/23/97 © 1997 United Feature Syndicate, Inc.

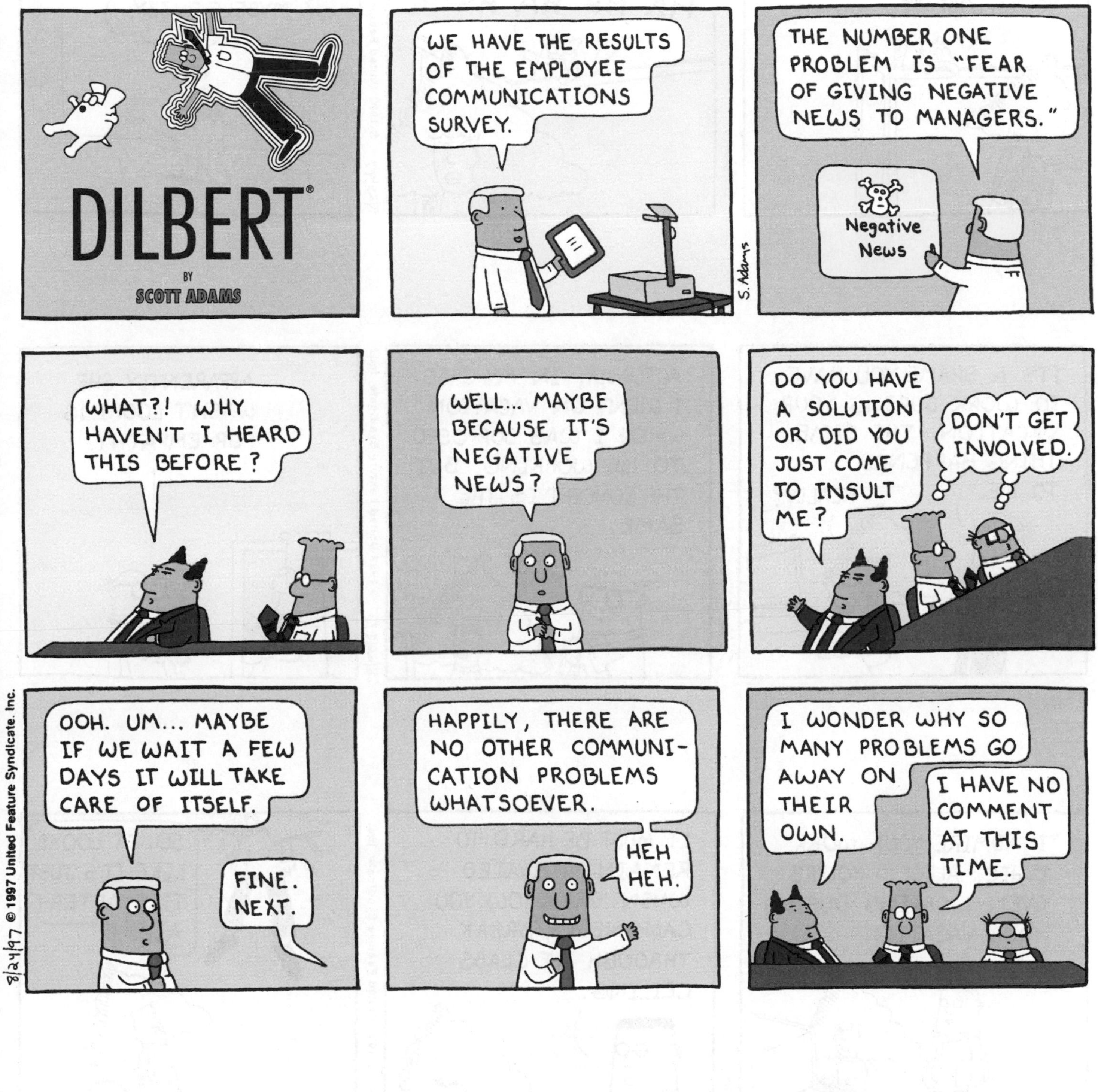
DILBERT®
BY
SCOTT ADAMS
WE HAVE THE RESULTS OF THE EMPLOYEE COMMUNICATIONS SURVEY.
S. Adams
THE NUMBER ONE PROBLEM IS "FEAR OF GIVING NEGATIVE NEWS TO MANAGERS."
Negative News
WHAT?! WHY HAVEN'T I HEARD THIS BEFORE?
WELL... MAYBE BECAUSE IT'S NEGATIVE NEWS?
DO YOU HAVE A SOLUTION OR DID YOU JUST COME TO INSULT ME?
DON'T GET INVOLVED.
OOH. UM... MAYBE IF WE WAIT A FEW DAYS IT WILL TAKE CARE OF ITSELF.
FINE. NEXT.
HAPPILY, THERE ARE NO OTHER COMMUNICATION PROBLEMS WHATSOEVER.
HEH HEH.
I WONDER WHY SO MANY PROBLEMS GO AWAY ON THEIR OWN.
I HAVE NO COMMENT AT THIS TIME.
8/24/97 © 1997 United Feature Syndicate, Inc.

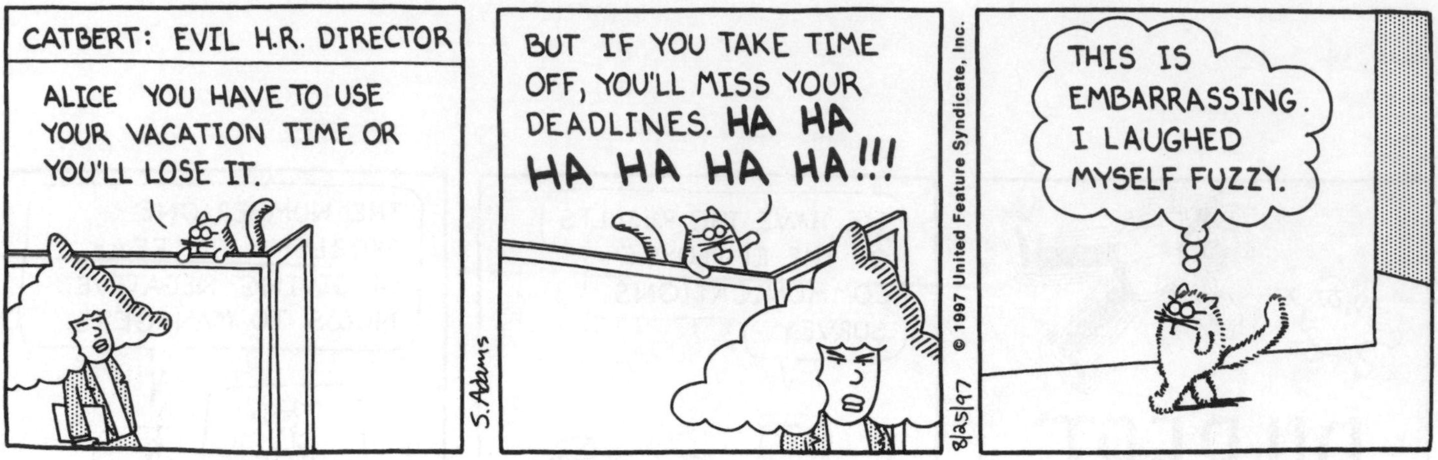
CATBERT: EVIL H.R. DIRECTOR
ALICE YOU HAVE TO USE YOUR VACATION TIME OR YOU'LL LOSE IT.
S. Adams
BUT IF YOU TAKE TIME OFF, YOU'LL MISS YOUR DEADLINES. HA HA HA HA HA HA!!!
8/25/97
© 1997 United Feature Syndicate, Inc.
THIS IS EMBARRASSING. I LAUGHED MYSELF FUZZY.

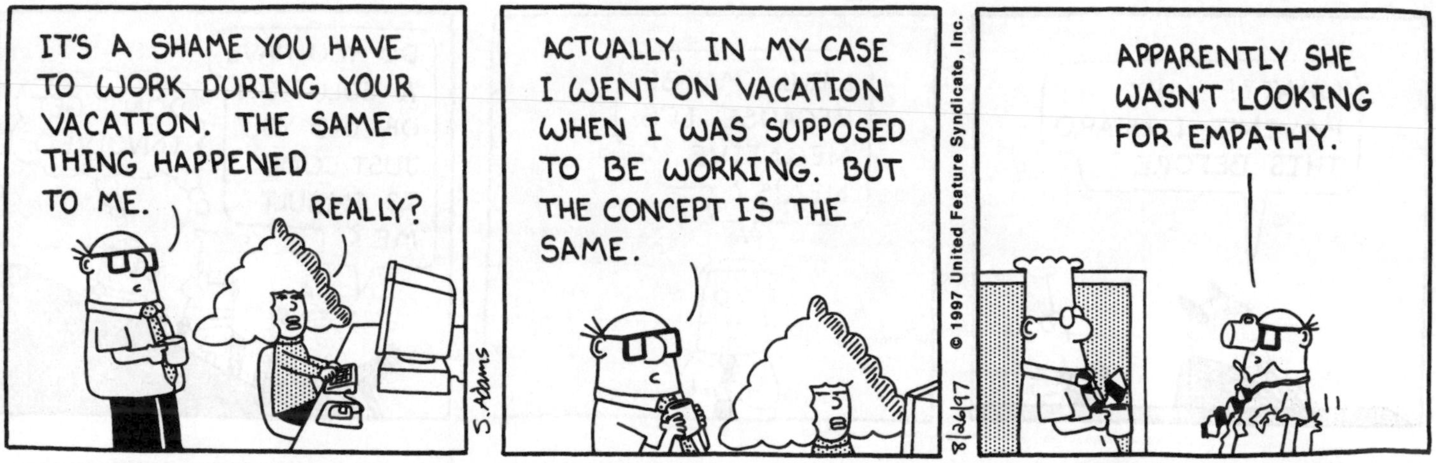
IT'S A SHAME YOU HAVE TO WORK DURING YOUR VACATION. THE SAME THING HAPPENED TO ME.
REALLY?
S. Adams
ACTUALLY, IN MY CASE I WENT ON VACATION WHEN I WAS SUPPOSED TO BE WORKING. BUT THE CONCEPT IS THE SAME.
8/26/97
© 1997 United Feature Syndicate, Inc.
APPARENTLY SHE WASN'T LOOKING FOR EMPATHY.

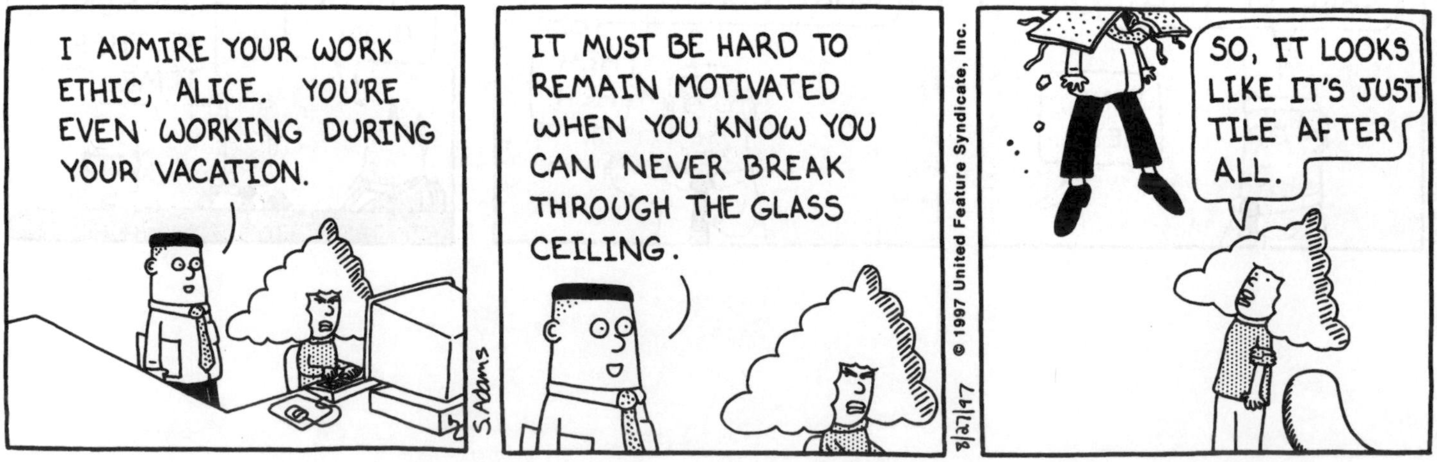
I ADMIRE YOUR WORK ETHIC, ALICE. YOU'RE EVEN WORKING DURING YOUR VACATION.
S. Adams
IT MUST BE HARD TO REMAIN MOTIVATED WHEN YOU KNOW YOU CAN NEVER BREAK THROUGH THE GLASS CEILING.
8/27/97
© 1997 United Feature Syndicate, Inc.
SO, IT LOOKS LIKE IT'S JUST TILE AFTER ALL.

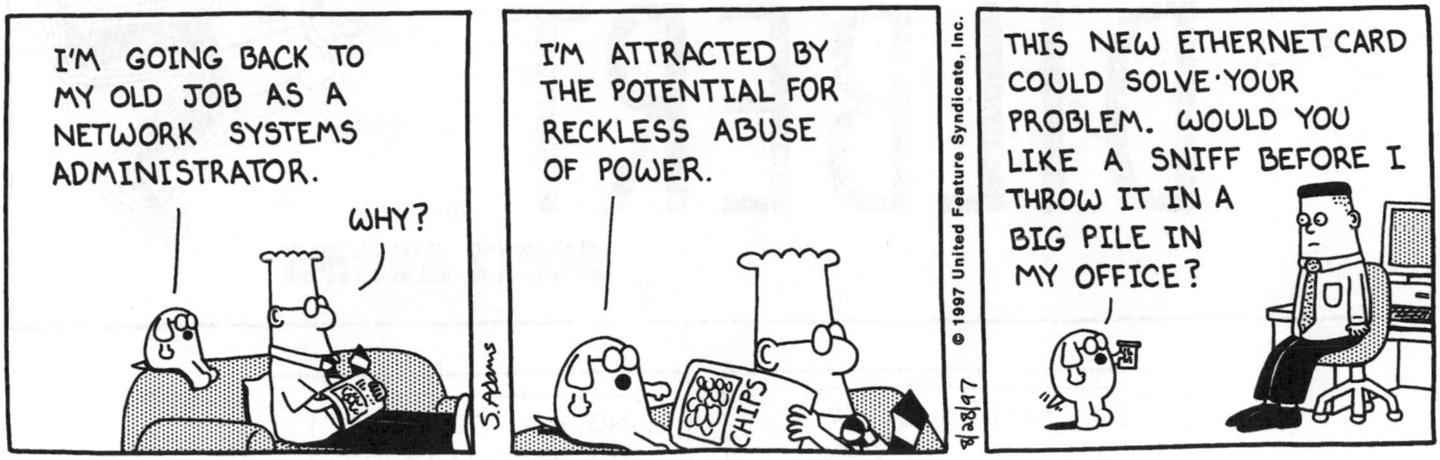
I'M GOING BACK TO MY OLD JOB AS A NETWORK SYSTEMS ADMINISTRATOR.
WHY?
S. Adams
I'M ATTRACTED BY THE POTENTIAL FOR RECKLESS ABUSE OF POWER.
CHIPS
© 1997 United Feature Syndicate, Inc.
8/28/97
THIS NEW ETHERNET CARD COULD SOLVE YOUR PROBLEM. WOULD YOU LIKE A SNIFF BEFORE I THROW IT IN A BIG PILE IN MY OFFICE?

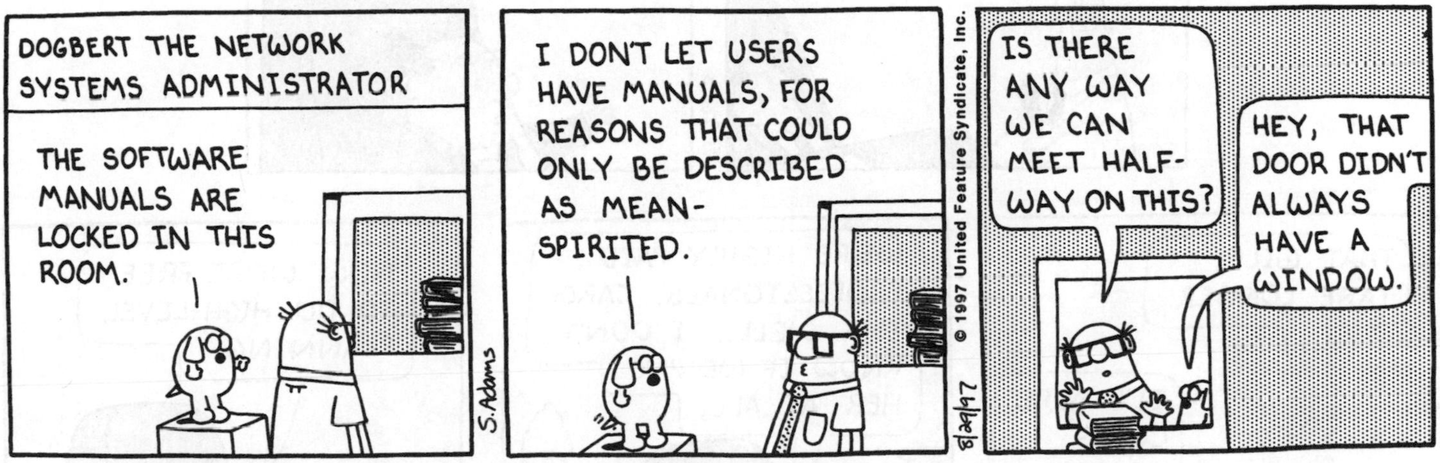
DOGBERT THE NETWORK SYSTEMS ADMINISTRATOR
THE SOFTWARE MANUALS ARE LOCKED IN THIS ROOM.
S. Adams
I DON'T LET USERS HAVE MANUALS, FOR REASONS THAT COULD ONLY BE DESCRIBED AS MEAN-SPIRITED.
© 1997 United Feature Syndicate, Inc.
8/29/97
IS THERE ANY WAY WE CAN MEET HALF-WAY ON THIS?
HEY, THAT DOOR DIDN'T ALWAYS HAVE A WINDOW.

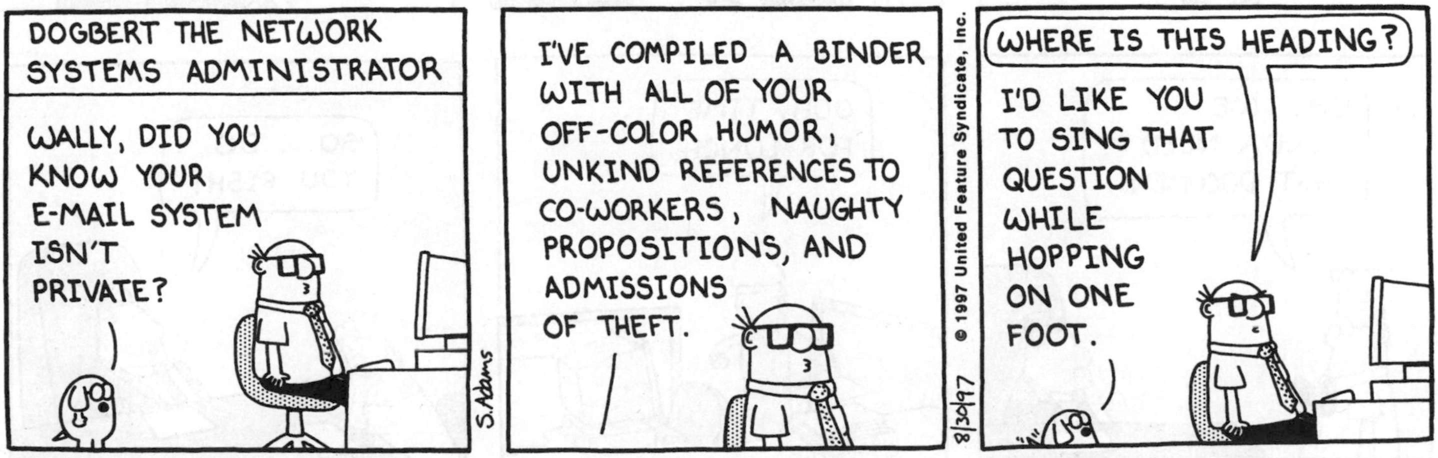
DOGBERT THE NETWORK SYSTEMS ADMINISTRATOR
WALLY, DID YOU KNOW YOUR E-MAIL SYSTEM ISN'T PRIVATE?
S. Adams
I'VE COMPILED A BINDER WITH ALL OF YOUR OFF-COLOR HUMOR, UNKIND REFERENCES TO CO-WORKERS, NAUGHTY PROPOSITIONS, AND ADMISSIONS OF THEFT.
© 1997 United Feature Syndicate, Inc.
8/30/97
WHERE IS THIS HEADING?
I'D LIKE YOU TO SING THAT QUESTION WHILE HOPPING ON ONE FOOT.

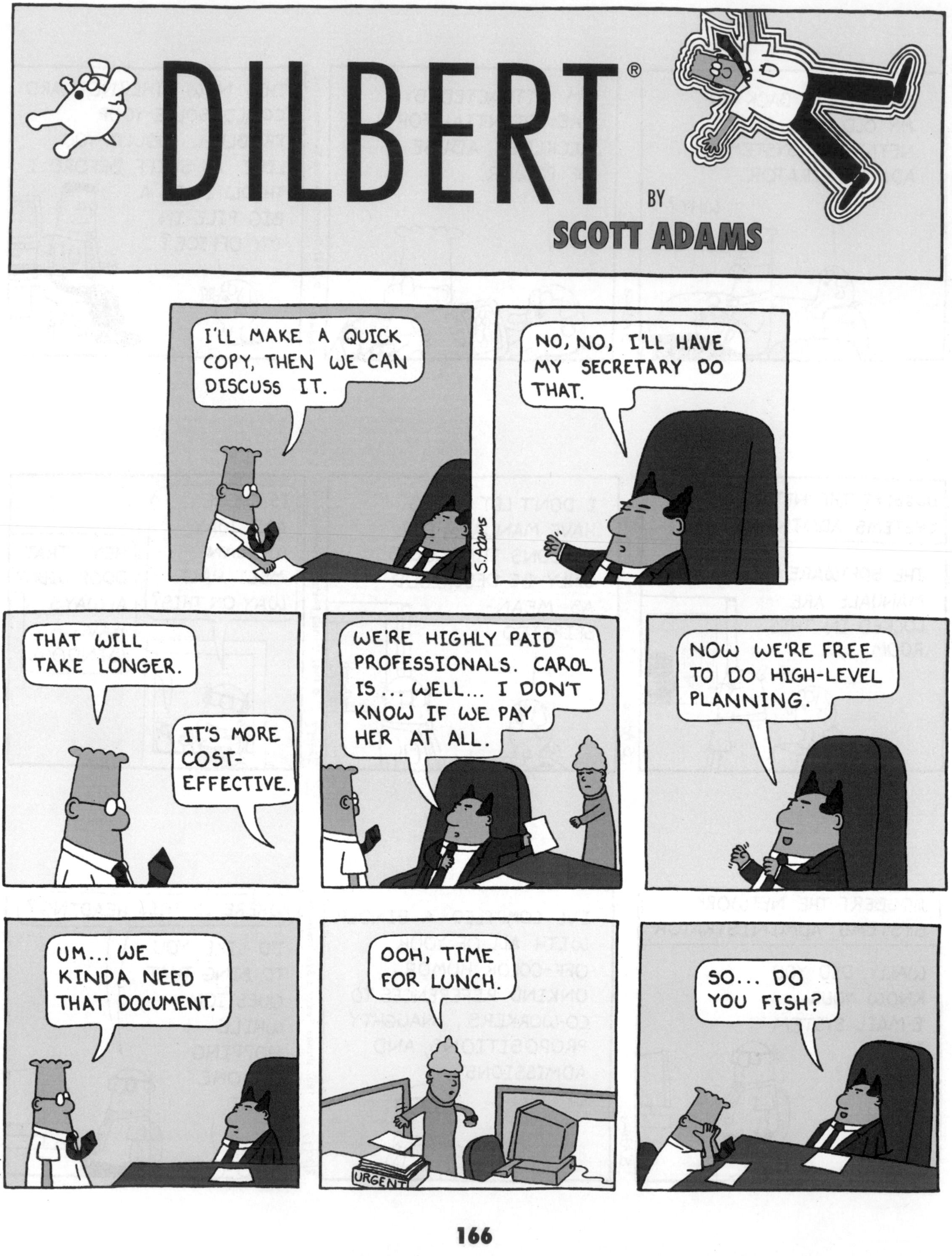
DILBERT®
BY
SCOTT ADAMS
I'LL MAKE A QUICK COPY, THEN WE CAN DISCUSS IT.
S. Adams
NO, NO, I'LL HAVE MY SECRETARY DO THAT.
THAT WILL TAKE LONGER.
IT'S MORE COST-EFFECTIVE.
WE'RE HIGHLY PAID PROFESSIONALS. CAROL IS... WELL... I DON'T KNOW IF WE PAY HER AT ALL.
NOW WE'RE FREE TO DO HIGH-LEVEL PLANNING.
UM... WE KINDA NEED THAT DOCUMENT.
OOH, TIME FOR LUNCH.
URGENT
SO... DO YOU FISH?
8/31/97 © 1997 United Feature Syndicate, Inc.

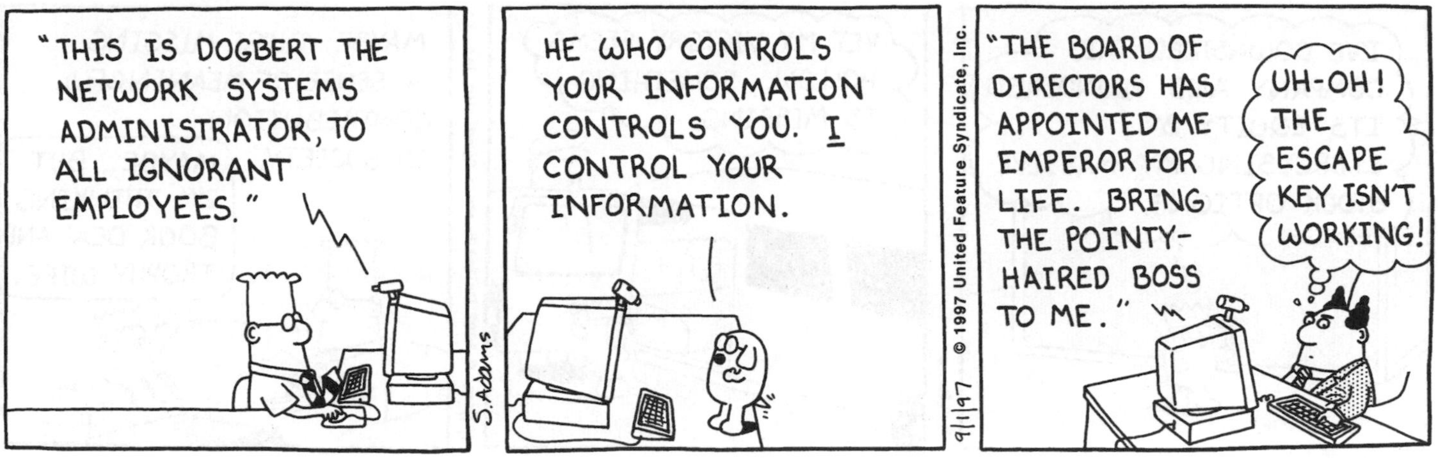
"THIS IS DOGBERT THE NETWORK SYSTEMS ADMINISTRATOR, TO ALL IGNORANT EMPLOYEES."
S. Adams
HE WHO CONTROLS YOUR INFORMATION CONTROLS YOU. I CONTROL YOUR INFORMATION.
9/1/97
© 1997 United Feature Syndicate, Inc.
"THE BOARD OF DIRECTORS HAS APPOINTED ME EMPEROR FOR LIFE. BRING THE POINTY-HAIRED BOSS TO ME."
UH-OH! THE ESCAPE KEY ISN'T WORKING!

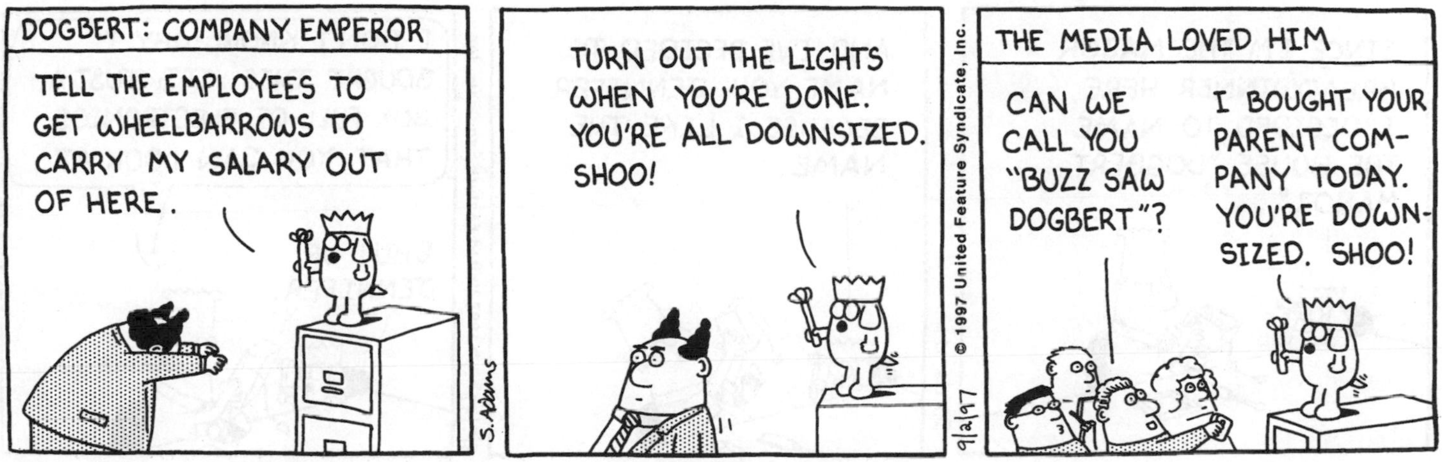
DOGBERT: COMPANY EMPEROR
TELL THE EMPLOYEES TO GET WHEELBARROWS TO CARRY MY SALARY OUT OF HERE.
S. Adams
TURN OUT THE LIGHTS WHEN YOU'RE DONE. YOU'RE ALL DOWNSIZED. SHOO!
9/2/97
© 1997 United Feature Syndicate, Inc.
THE MEDIA LOVED HIM
CAN WE CALL YOU "BUZZ SAW DOGBERT"?
I BOUGHT YOUR PARENT COMPANY TODAY. YOU'RE DOWNSIZED. SHOO!

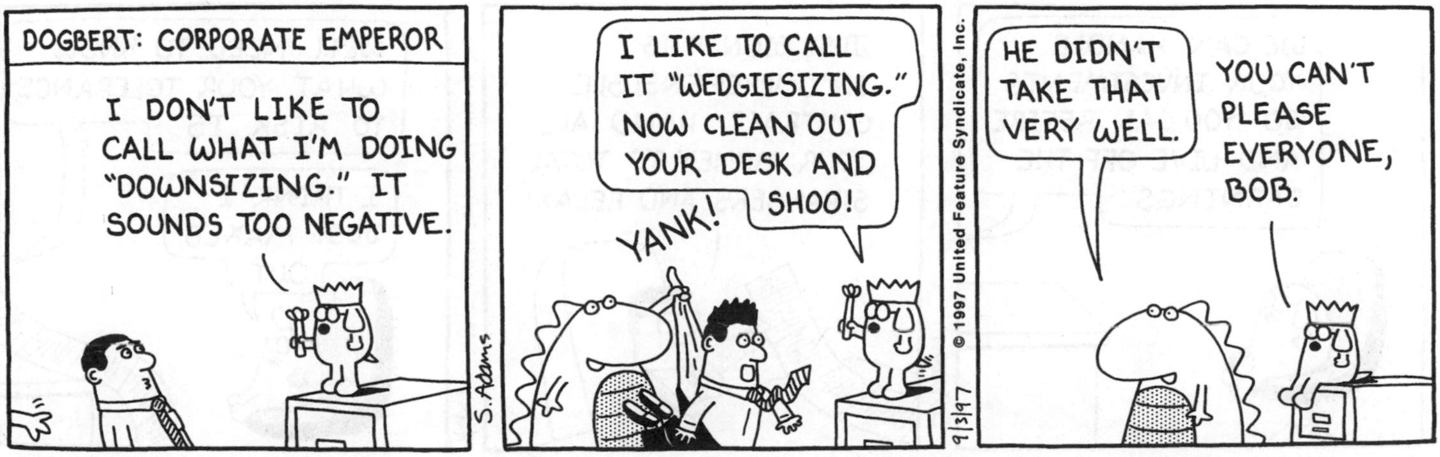
DOGBERT: CORPORATE EMPEROR
I DON'T LIKE TO CALL WHAT I'M DOING "DOWNSIZING." IT SOUNDS TOO NEGATIVE.
S. Adams
I LIKE TO CALL IT "WEDGIESIZING." NOW CLEAN OUT YOUR DESK AND SHOO!
YANK!
9/3/97
© 1997 United Feature Syndicate, Inc.
HE DIDN'T TAKE THAT VERY WELL.
YOU CAN'T PLEASE EVERYONE, BOB.

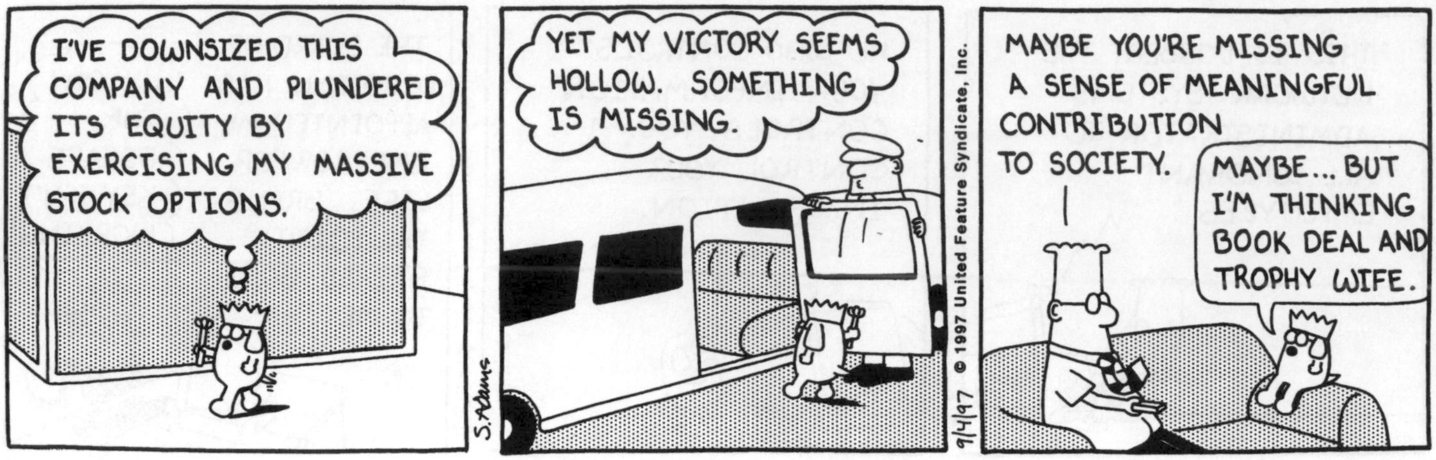
I'VE DOWNSIZED THIS COMPANY AND PLUNDERED ITS EQUITY BY EXERCISING MY MASSIVE STOCK OPTIONS.
YET MY VICTORY SEEMS HOLLOW. SOMETHING IS MISSING.
MAYBE YOU'RE MISSING A SENSE OF MEANINGFUL CONTRIBUTION TO SOCIETY.
MAYBE... BUT I'M THINKING BOOK DEAL AND TROPHY WIFE.
S. Adams
9/4/97
© 1997 United Feature Syndicate, Inc.

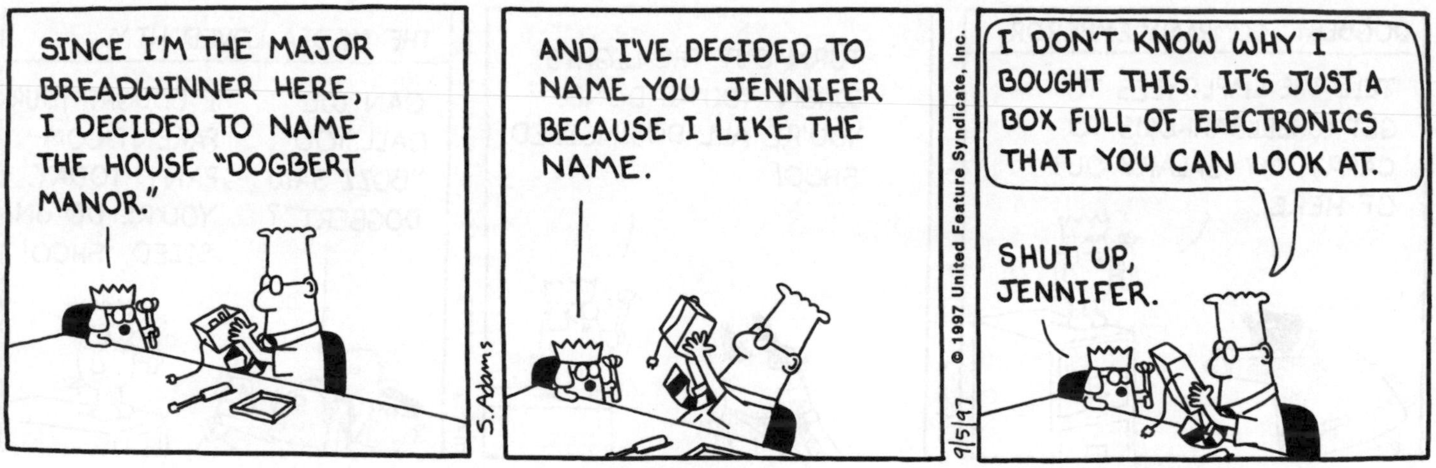
SINCE I'M THE MAJOR BREADWINNER HERE, I DECIDED TO NAME THE HOUSE "DOGBERT MANOR."
AND I'VE DECIDED TO NAME YOU JENNIFER BECAUSE I LIKE THE NAME.
I DON'T KNOW WHY I BOUGHT THIS. IT'S JUST A BOX FULL OF ELECTRONICS THAT YOU CAN LOOK AT.
SHUT UP, JENNIFER.
S. Adams
9/5/97
© 1997 United Feature Syndicate, Inc.

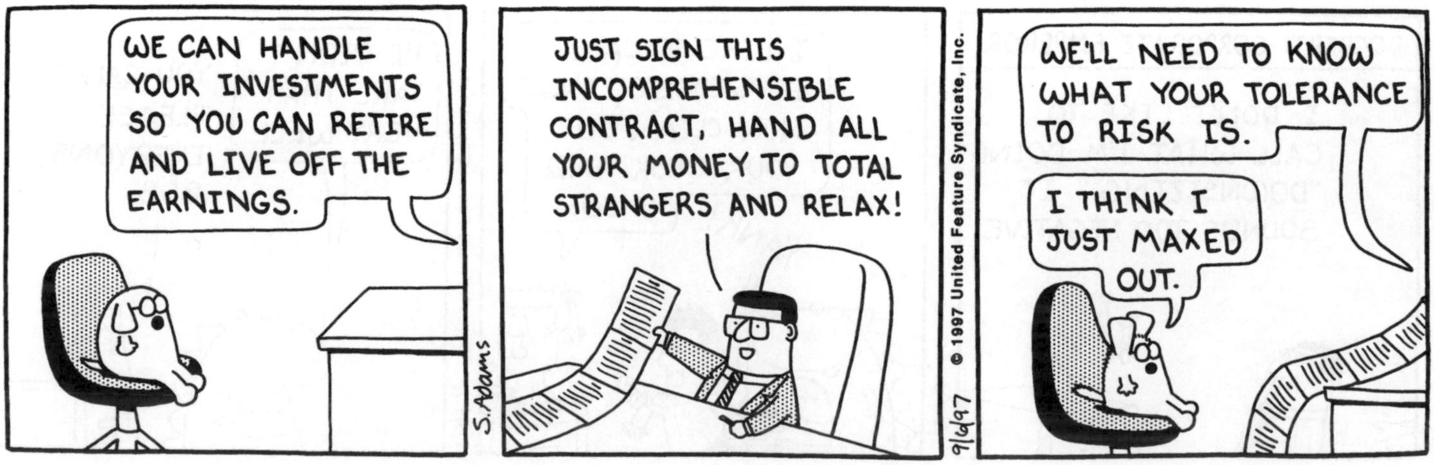
WE CAN HANDLE YOUR INVESTMENTS SO YOU CAN RETIRE AND LIVE OFF THE EARNINGS.
JUST SIGN THIS INCOMPREHENSIBLE CONTRACT, HAND ALL YOUR MONEY TO TOTAL STRANGERS AND RELAX!
WE'LL NEED TO KNOW WHAT YOUR TOLERANCE TO RISK IS.
I THINK I JUST MAXED OUT.
S. Adams
9/6/97
© 1997 United Feature Syndicate, Inc.

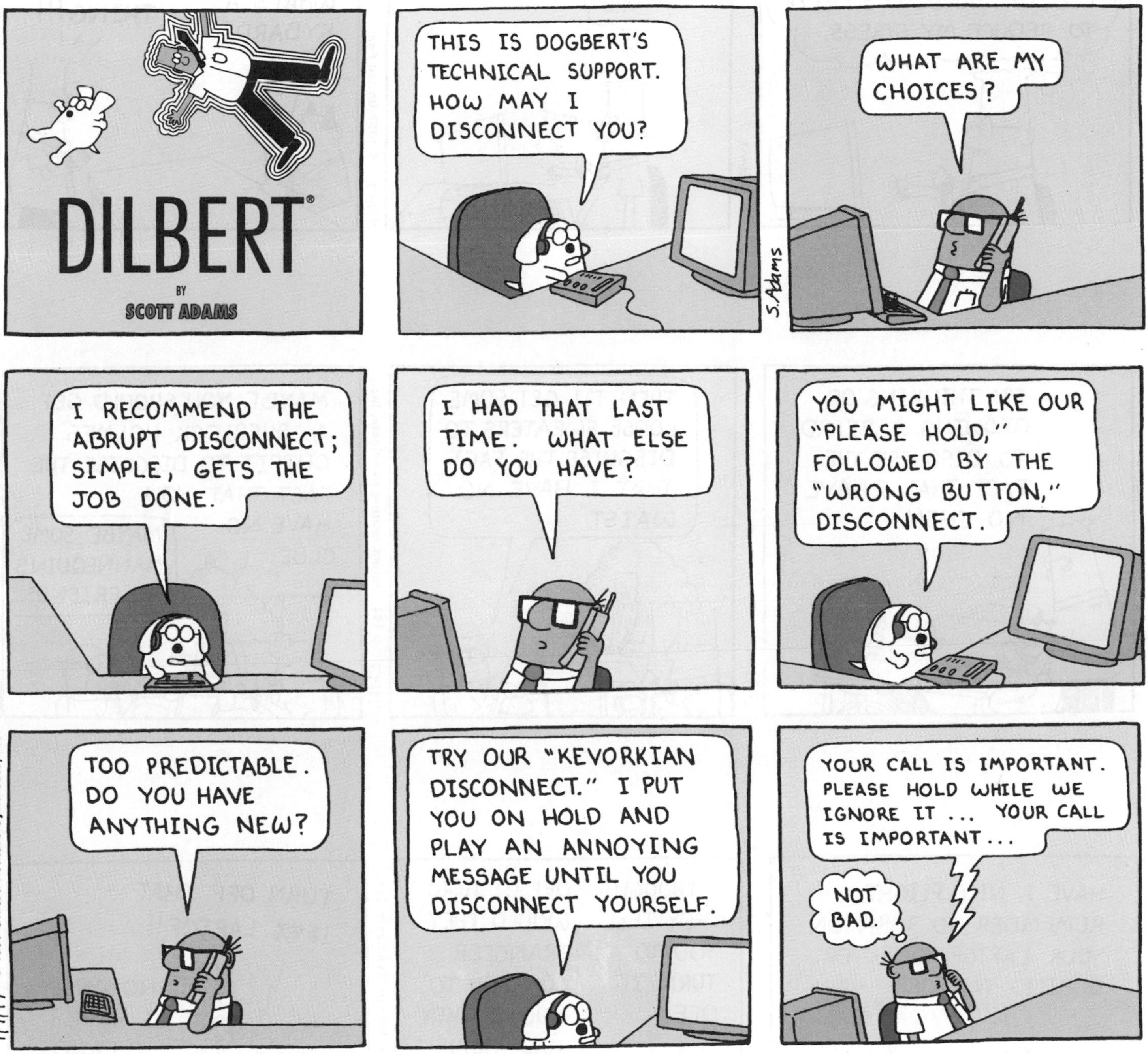
DILBERT
BY
SCOTT ADAMS
THIS IS DOGBERT'S TECHNICAL SUPPORT. HOW MAY I DISCONNECT YOU?
S. Adams
WHAT ARE MY CHOICES?
I RECOMMEND THE ABRUPT DISCONNECT; SIMPLE, GETS THE JOB DONE.
I HAD THAT LAST TIME. WHAT ELSE DO YOU HAVE?
YOU MIGHT LIKE OUR "PLEASE HOLD," FOLLOWED BY THE "WRONG BUTTON," DISCONNECT.
9/7/97 © 1997 United Feature Syndicate, Inc.
TOO PREDICTABLE. DO YOU HAVE ANYTHING NEW?
TRY OUR "KEVORKIAN DISCONNECT." I PUT YOU ON HOLD AND PLAY AN ANNOYING MESSAGE UNTIL YOU DISCONNECT YOURSELF.
YOUR CALL IS IMPORTANT. PLEASE HOLD WHILE WE IGNORE IT ... YOUR CALL IS IMPORTANT ...
NOT BAD.

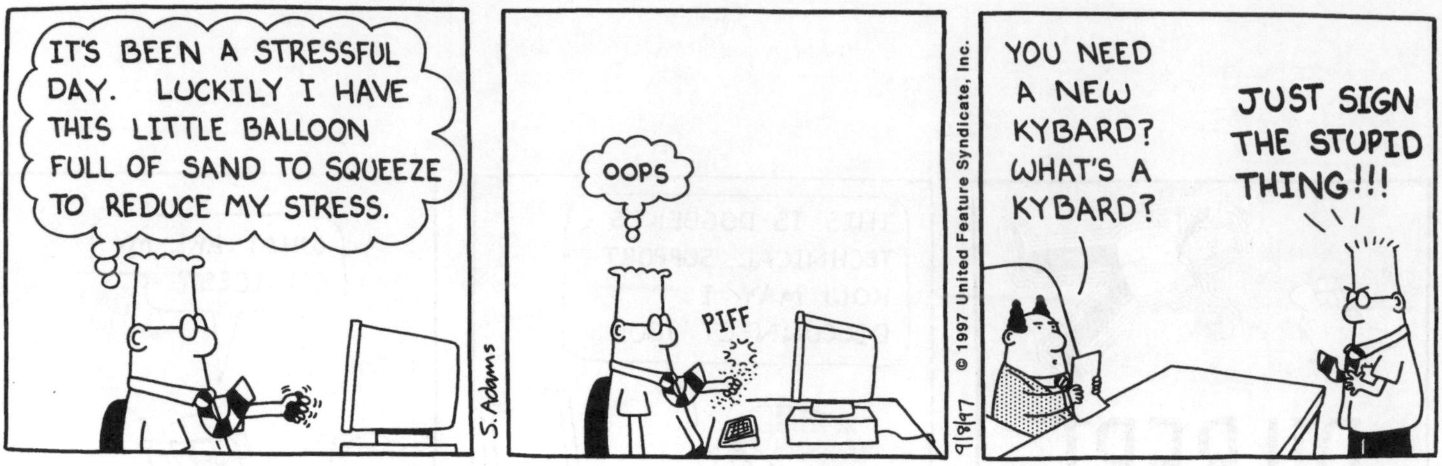
IT'S BEEN A STRESSFUL DAY. LUCKILY I HAVE THIS LITTLE BALLOON FULL OF SAND TO SQUEEZE TO REDUCE MY STRESS.
S. Adams
OOPS
PIFF
9/8/97
© 1997 United Feature Syndicate, Inc.
YOU NEED A NEW KYBARD? WHAT'S A KYBARD?
JUST SIGN THE STUPID THING!!!

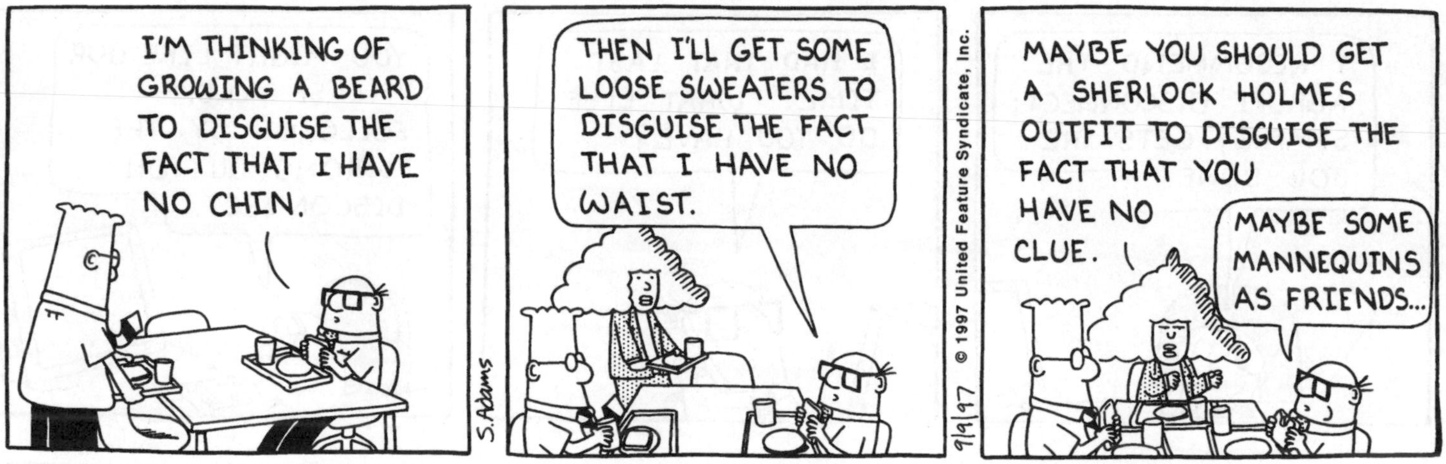
I'M THINKING OF GROWING A BEARD TO DISGUISE THE FACT THAT I HAVE NO CHIN.
S. Adams
THEN I'LL GET SOME LOOSE SWEATERS TO DISGUISE THE FACT THAT I HAVE NO WAIST.
9/9/97
© 1997 United Feature Syndicate, Inc.
MAYBE YOU SHOULD GET A SHERLOCK HOLMES OUTFIT TO DISGUISE THE FACT THAT YOU HAVE NO CLUE.
MAYBE SOME MANNEQUINS AS FRIENDS...

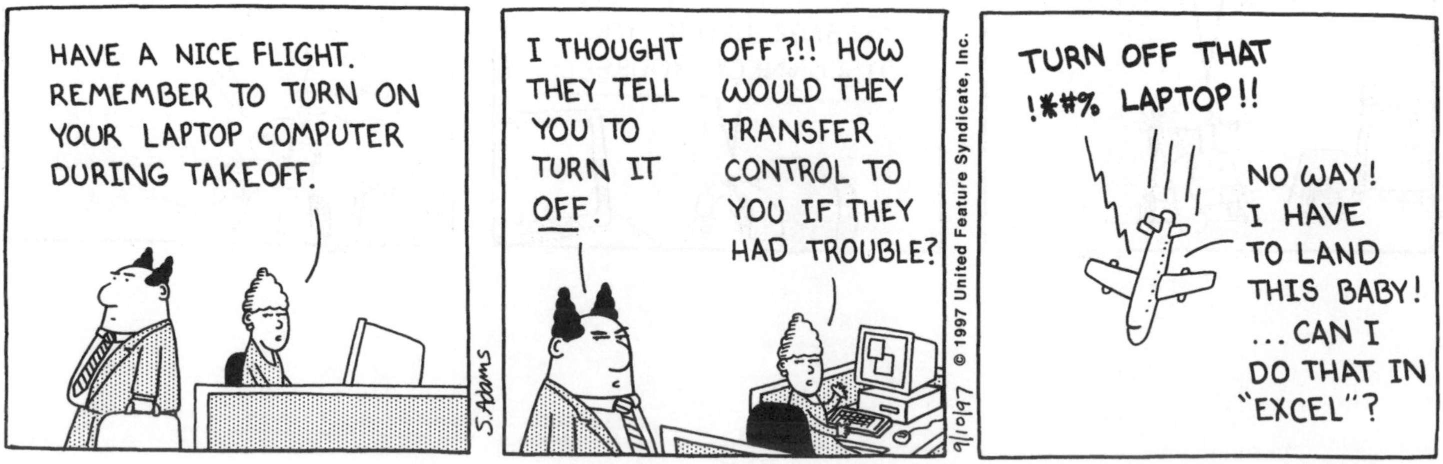
HAVE A NICE FLIGHT. REMEMBER TO TURN ON YOUR LAPTOP COMPUTER DURING TAKEOFF.
S. Adams
I THOUGHT THEY TELL YOU TO TURN IT OFF.
OFF?!! HOW WOULD THEY TRANSFER CONTROL TO YOU IF THEY HAD TROUBLE?
9/10/97
© 1997 United Feature Syndicate, Inc.
TURN OFF THAT !*#% LAPTOP!!
NO WAY! I HAVE TO LAND THIS BABY! ... CAN I DO THAT IN "EXCEL"?

I JUST HEARD THAT OUR POINTY-HAIRED BOSS'S PLANE CRASHED.
I MUST ADMIT I HAVE MIXED FEELINGS.
YOU DON'T KNOW IF YOU SHOULD MOURN OR CELEBRATE, RIGHT?
NO, I MEAN CELEBRATE OR LEAVE EARLY.
HURRY IF YOU WANT SOME CAKE.
S. Adams
9/11/97
© 1997 United Feature Syndicate, Inc.

NOW THAT OUR BOSS IS PRESUMED DEAD, I FOUND OUT I LIKE TO WORK.
I FINISHED THREE PROJECTS TODAY!
I LOST FIVE POUNDS, GAVE UP COFFEE, AND APPLIED FOR SEVEN PATENTS!
GO, ALICE!
LIFE WITHOUT MANAGEMENT IS LIKE PARADISE!
WHO WANTS TO SPOON-HUG?
S. Adams
9/12/97
© 1997 United Feature Syndicate, Inc.

WORK HAS BEEN GREAT SINCE OUR BOSS WENT DOWN ON THE JET!
UH-OH
I SURVIVED WITH ONLY MINOR HAIR INJURIES. I WAS LUCKY TO BE ON A FLIGHT THAT HAD A HUNDRED NUNS ONBOARD!
YOU WERE SAVED BY PRAYER?
NO, PADDING. THEY DON'T DO A LOT OF AEROBICS AT THE NUNNERY.
S. Adams
9/13/97
© 1997 United Feature Syndicate, Inc.

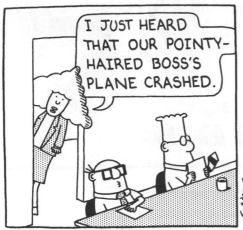

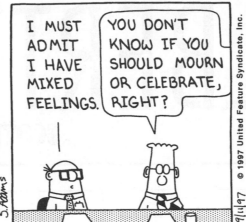

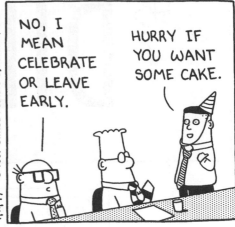

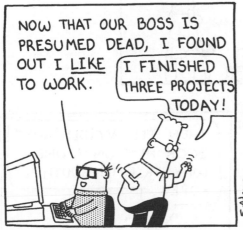

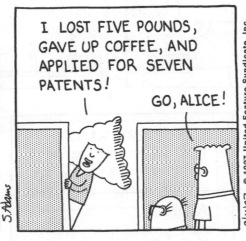

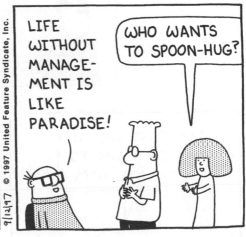

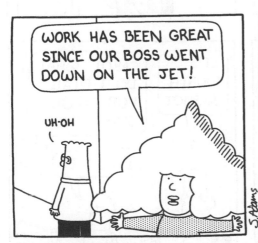

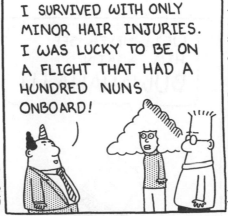

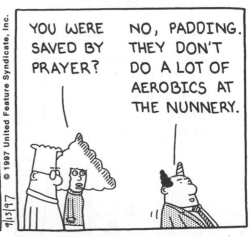

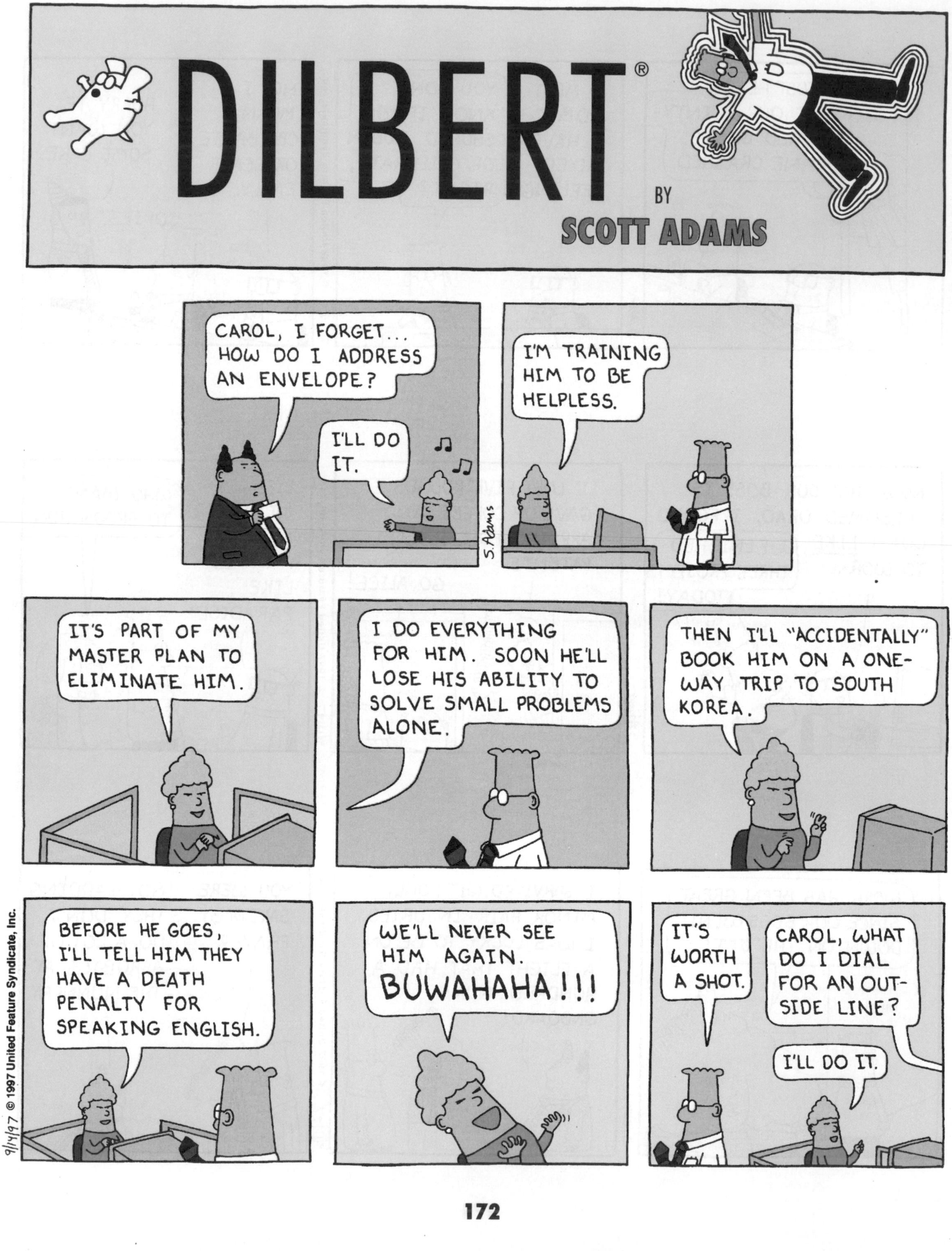
DILBERT®
BY
SCOTT ADAMS
CAROL, I FORGET... HOW DO I ADDRESS AN ENVELOPE?
I'LL DO IT.
S. Adams
I'M TRAINING HIM TO BE HELPLESS.
IT'S PART OF MY MASTER PLAN TO ELIMINATE HIM.
I DO EVERYTHING FOR HIM. SOON HE'LL LOSE HIS ABILITY TO SOLVE SMALL PROBLEMS ALONE.
THEN I'LL "ACCIDENTALLY" BOOK HIM ON A ONE-WAY TRIP TO SOUTH KOREA.
BEFORE HE GOES, I'LL TELL HIM THEY HAVE A DEATH PENALTY FOR SPEAKING ENGLISH.
WE'LL NEVER SEE HIM AGAIN. BUWAHAHA!!!
IT'S WORTH A SHOT.
CAROL, WHAT DO I DIAL FOR AN OUT-SIDE LINE?
I'LL DO IT.
9/14/97 © 1997 United Feature Syndicate, Inc.

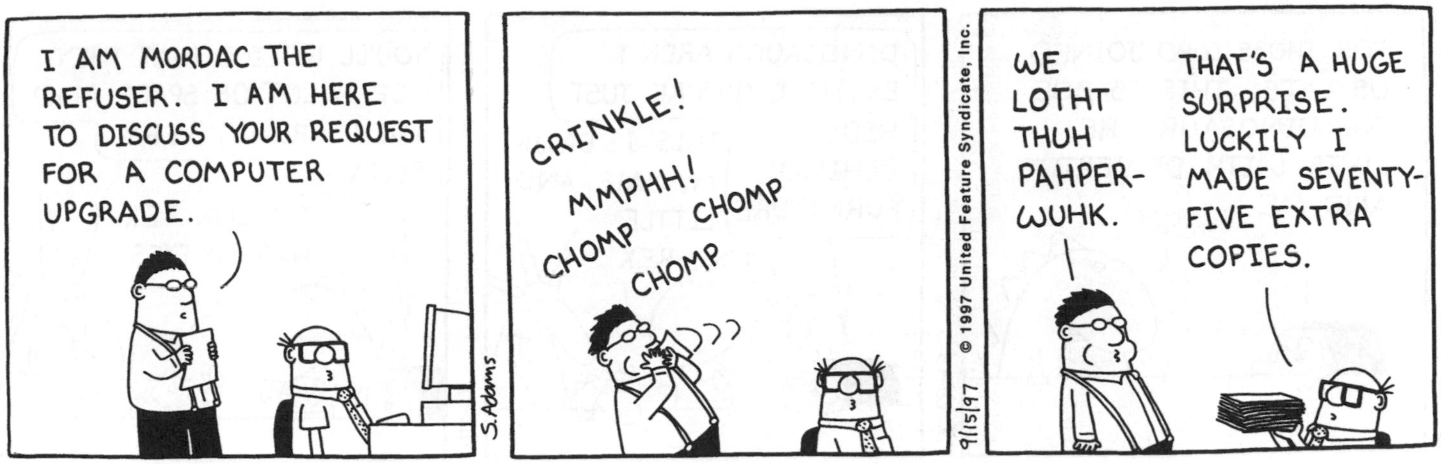
I AM MORDAC THE REFUSER. I AM HERE TO DISCUSS YOUR REQUEST FOR A COMPUTER UPGRADE.
S. Adams
CRINKLE!
MMPHH!
CHOMP CHOMP
CHOMP
9/15/97
© 1997 United Feature Syndicate, Inc.
WE LOTHT THUH PAHPER-WUHK.
THAT'S A HUGE SURPRISE. LUCKILY I MADE SEVENTY-FIVE EXTRA COPIES.

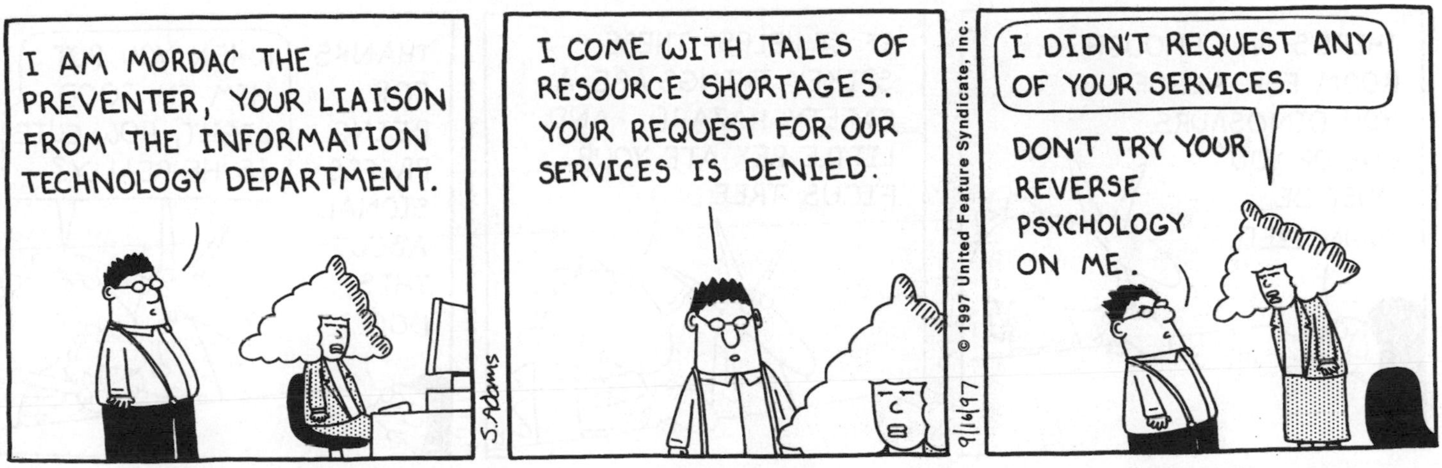
I AM MORDAC THE PREVENTER, YOUR LIAISON FROM THE INFORMATION TECHNOLOGY DEPARTMENT.
S. Adams
I COME WITH TALES OF RESOURCE SHORTAGES. YOUR REQUEST FOR OUR SERVICES IS DENIED.
9/16/97
© 1997 United Feature Syndicate, Inc.
I DIDN'T REQUEST ANY OF YOUR SERVICES.
DON'T TRY YOUR REVERSE PSYCHOLOGY ON ME.

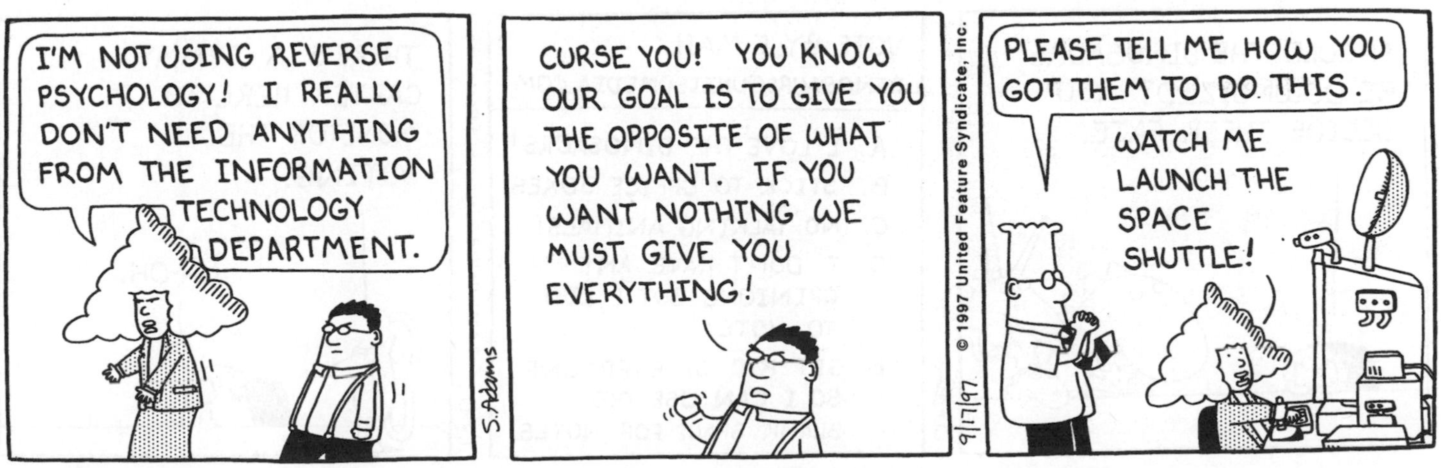
I'M NOT USING REVERSE PSYCHOLOGY! I REALLY DON'T NEED ANYTHING FROM THE INFORMATION TECHNOLOGY DEPARTMENT.
S. Adams
CURSE YOU! YOU KNOW OUR GOAL IS TO GIVE YOU THE OPPOSITE OF WHAT YOU WANT. IF YOU WANT NOTHING WE MUST GIVE YOU EVERYTHING!
9/17/97
© 1997 United Feature Syndicate, Inc.
PLEASE TELL ME HOW YOU GOT THEM TO DO THIS.
WATCH ME LAUNCH THE SPACE SHUTTLE!

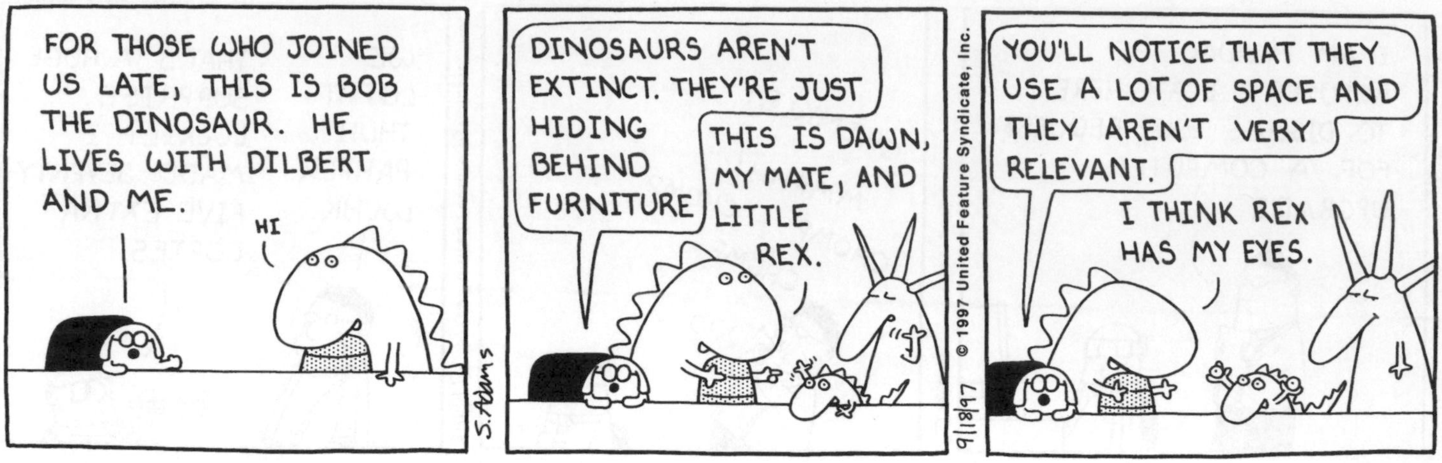
FOR THOSE WHO JOINED US LATE, THIS IS BOB THE DINOSAUR. HE LIVES WITH DILBERT AND ME.
HI
DINOSAURS AREN'T EXTINCT. THEY'RE JUST HIDING BEHIND FURNITURE
THIS IS DAWN, MY MATE, AND LITTLE REX.
YOU'LL NOTICE THAT THEY USE A LOT OF SPACE AND THEY AREN'T VERY RELEVANT.
I THINK REX HAS MY EYES.
S. Adams
9/18/97
© 1997 United Feature Syndicate, Inc.

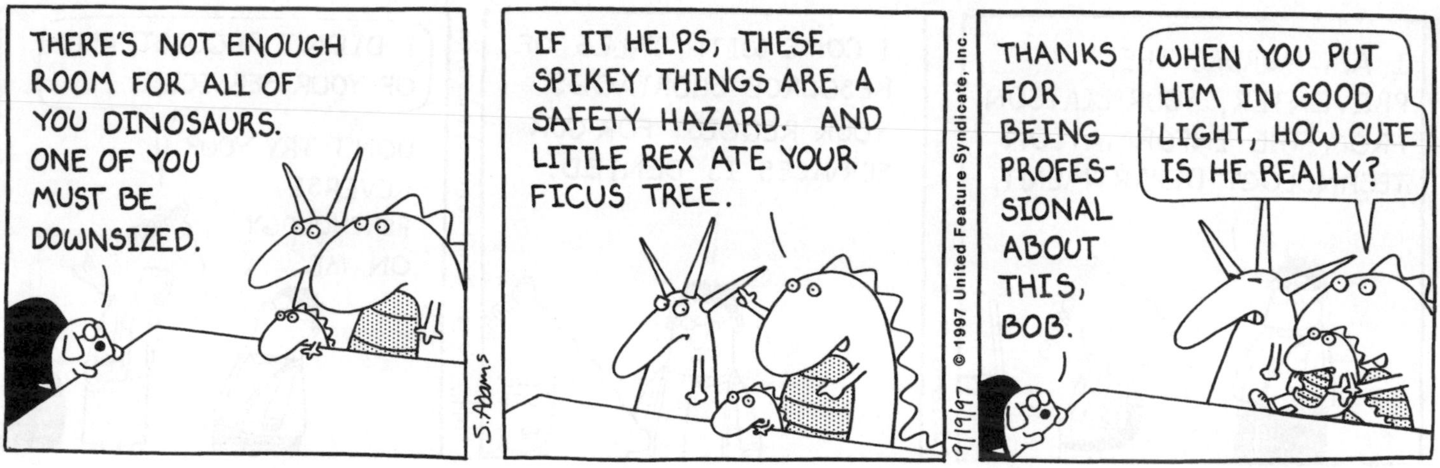
THERE'S NOT ENOUGH ROOM FOR ALL OF YOU DINOSAURS. ONE OF YOU MUST BE DOWNSIZED.
IF IT HELPS, THESE SPIKEY THINGS ARE A SAFETY HAZARD. AND LITTLE REX ATE YOUR FICUS TREE.
THANKS FOR BEING PROFES- SIONAL ABOUT THIS, BOB.
WHEN YOU PUT HIM IN GOOD LIGHT, HOW CUTE IS HE REALLY?
S. Adams
9/19/97
© 1997 United Feature Syndicate, Inc.

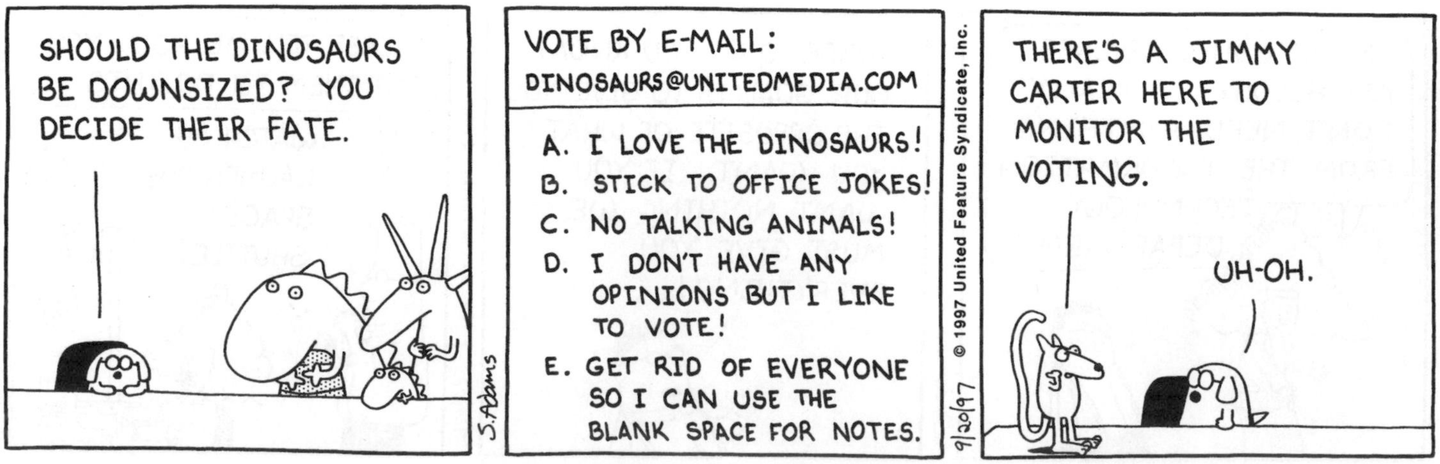
SHOULD THE DINOSAURS BE DOWNSIZED? YOU DECIDE THEIR FATE.
VOTE BY E-MAIL:
DINOSAURS@UNITEDMEDIA.COM
A. I LOVE THE DINOSAURS!
B. STICK TO OFFICE JOKES!
C. NO TALKING ANIMALS!
D. I DON'T HAVE ANY OPINIONS BUT I LIKE TO VOTE!
E. GET RID OF EVERYONE SO I CAN USE THE BLANK SPACE FOR NOTES.
THERE'S A JIMMY CARTER HERE TO MONITOR THE VOTING.
UH-OH.
S. Adams
9/20/97
© 1997 United Feature Syndicate, Inc.

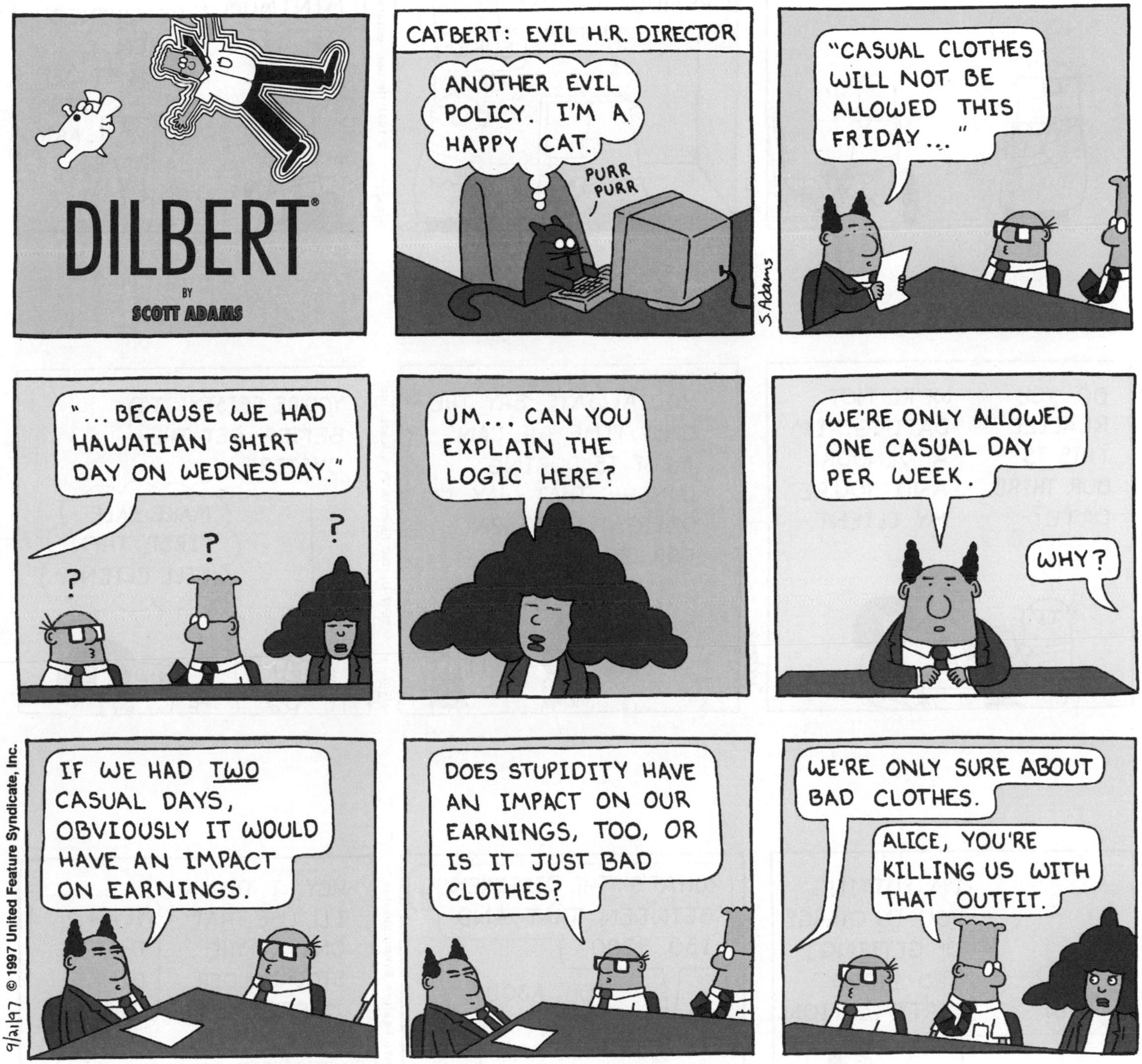
DILBERT®
BY
SCOTT ADAMS
CATBERT: EVIL H.R. DIRECTOR
ANOTHER EVIL POLICY. I'M A HAPPY CAT.
PURR PURR
S. Adams
"CASUAL CLOTHES WILL NOT BE ALLOWED THIS FRIDAY..."
"...BECAUSE WE HAD HAWAIIAN SHIRT DAY ON WEDNESDAY."
?
?
?
UM... CAN YOU EXPLAIN THE LOGIC HERE?
WE'RE ONLY ALLOWED ONE CASUAL DAY PER WEEK.
WHY?
9/21/97 © 1997 United Feature Syndicate, Inc.
IF WE HAD TWO CASUAL DAYS, OBVIOUSLY IT WOULD HAVE AN IMPACT ON EARNINGS.
DOES STUPIDITY HAVE AN IMPACT ON OUR EARNINGS, TOO, OR IS IT JUST BAD CLOTHES?
WE'RE ONLY SURE ABOUT BAD CLOTHES.
ALICE, YOU'RE KILLING US WITH THAT OUTFIT.

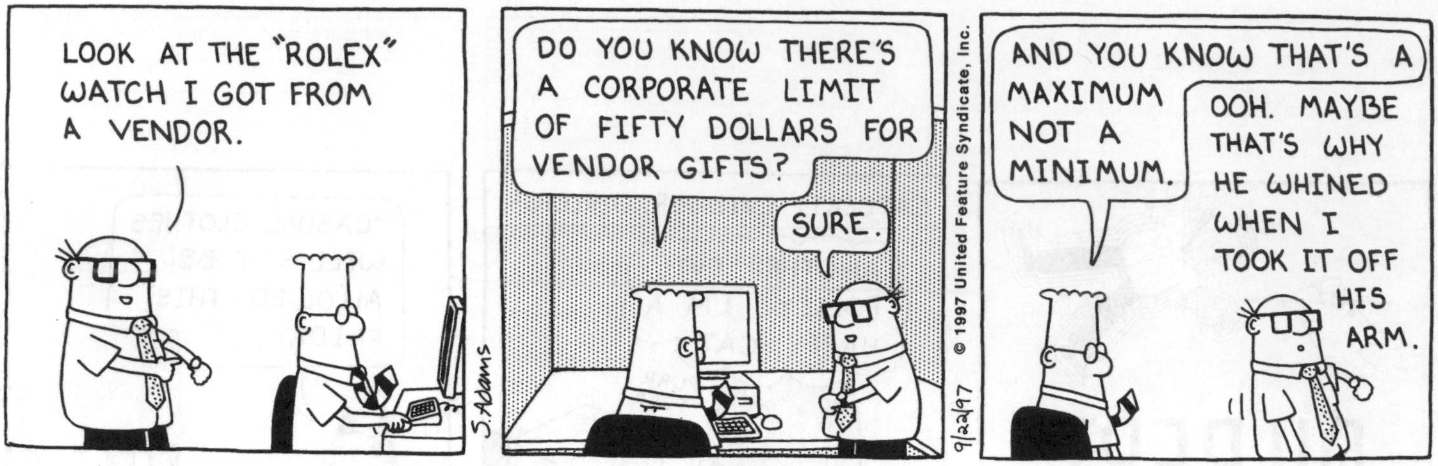
LOOK AT THE "ROLEX" WATCH I GOT FROM A VENDOR.
DO YOU KNOW THERE'S A CORPORATE LIMIT OF FIFTY DOLLARS FOR VENDOR GIFTS?
SURE.
AND YOU KNOW THAT'S A MAXIMUM NOT A MINIMUM.
OOH. MAYBE THAT'S WHY HE WHINED WHEN I TOOK IT OFF HIS ARM.
S. Adams
9/22/97
© 1997 United Feature Syndicate, Inc.

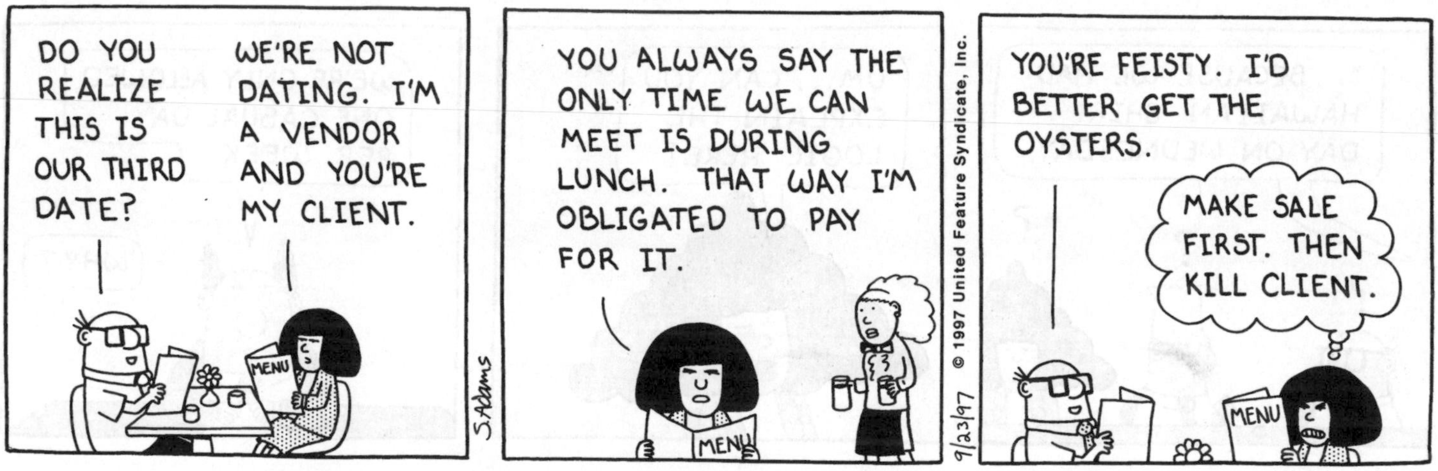
DO YOU REALIZE THIS IS OUR THIRD DATE?
WE'RE NOT DATING. I'M A VENDOR AND YOU'RE MY CLIENT.
MENU
YOU ALWAYS SAY THE ONLY TIME WE CAN MEET IS DURING LUNCH. THAT WAY I'M OBLIGATED TO PAY FOR IT.
MENU
YOU'RE FEISTY. I'D BETTER GET THE OYSTERS.
MAKE SALE FIRST. THEN KILL CLIENT.
MENU
S. Adams
9/23/97
© 1997 United Feature Syndicate, Inc.

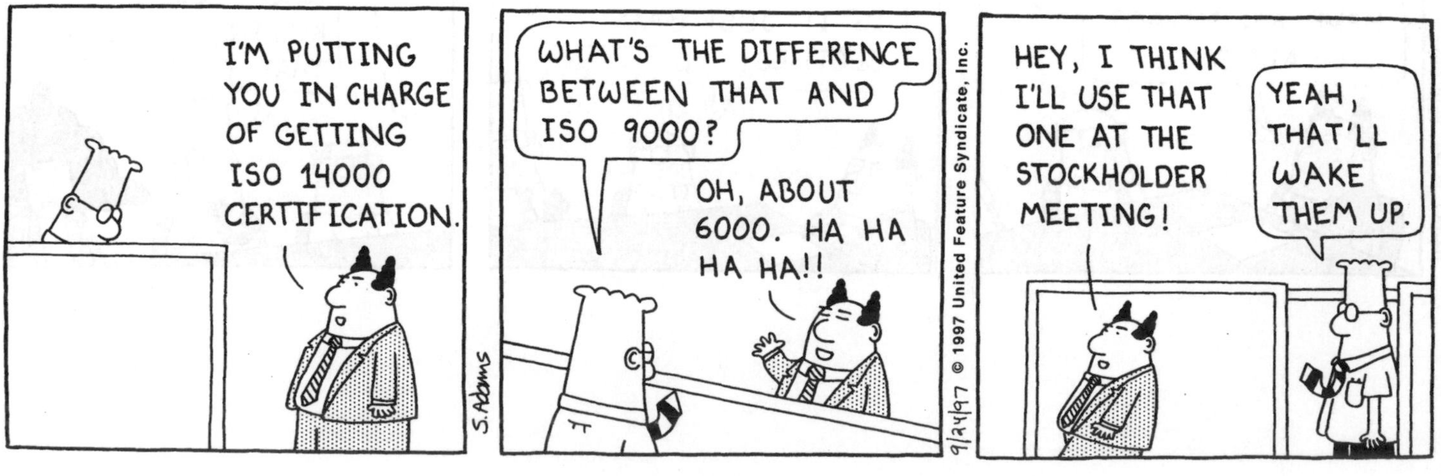
I'M PUTTING YOU IN CHARGE OF GETTING ISO 14000 CERTIFICATION.
WHAT'S THE DIFFERENCE BETWEEN THAT AND ISO 9000?
OH, ABOUT 6000. HA HA HA HA!!
HEY, I THINK I'LL USE THAT ONE AT THE STOCKHOLDER MEETING!
YEAH, THAT'LL WAKE THEM UP.
S. Adams
9/24/97
© 1997 United Feature Syndicate, Inc.

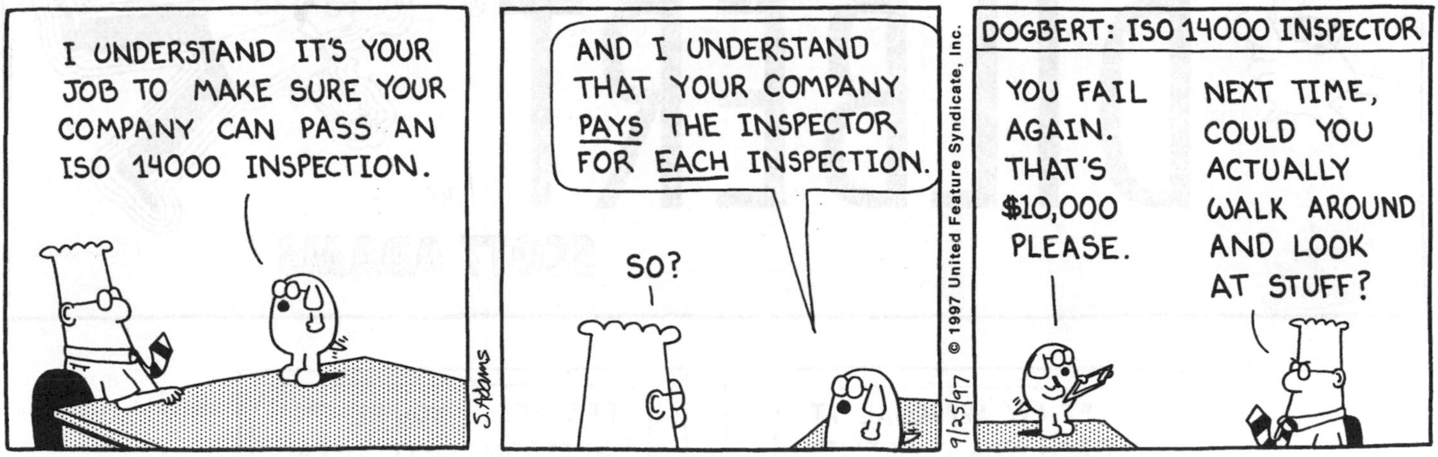
I UNDERSTAND IT'S YOUR JOB TO MAKE SURE YOUR COMPANY CAN PASS AN ISO 14000 INSPECTION.
S. Adams
AND I UNDERSTAND THAT YOUR COMPANY PAYS THE INSPECTOR FOR EACH INSPECTION.
SO?
© 1997 United Feature Syndicate, Inc.
9/25/97
DOGBERT: ISO 14000 INSPECTOR
YOU FAIL AGAIN. THAT'S $10,000 PLEASE.
NEXT TIME, COULD YOU ACTUALLY WALK AROUND AND LOOK AT STUFF?

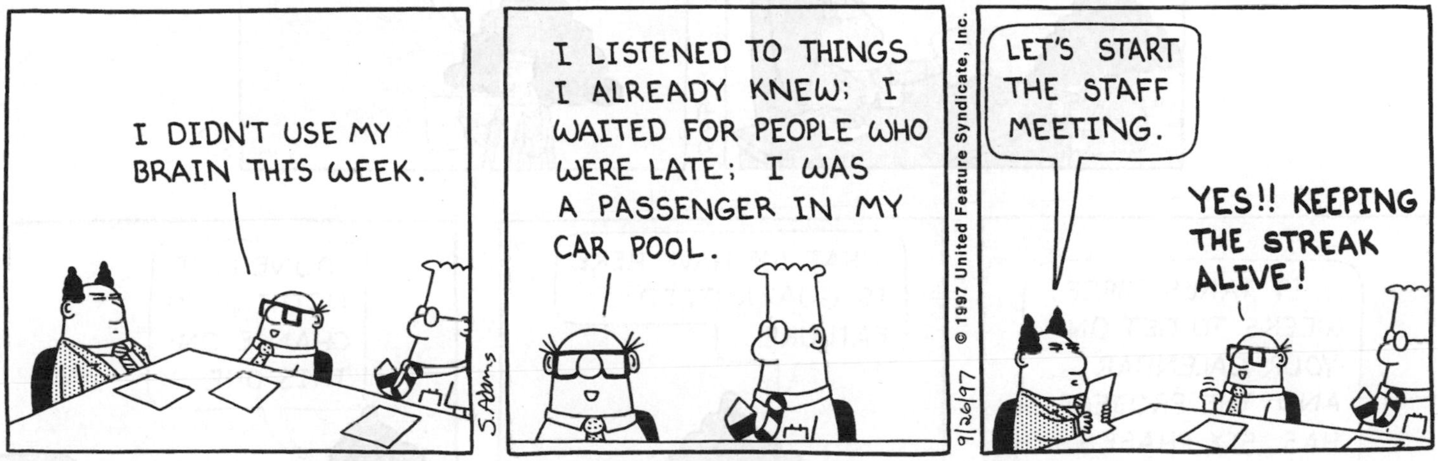
I DIDN'T USE MY BRAIN THIS WEEK.
S. Adams
I LISTENED TO THINGS I ALREADY KNEW; I WAITED FOR PEOPLE WHO WERE LATE; I WAS A PASSENGER IN MY CAR POOL.
© 1997 United Feature Syndicate, Inc.
9/26/97
LET'S START THE STAFF MEETING.
YES!! KEEPING THE STREAK ALIVE!

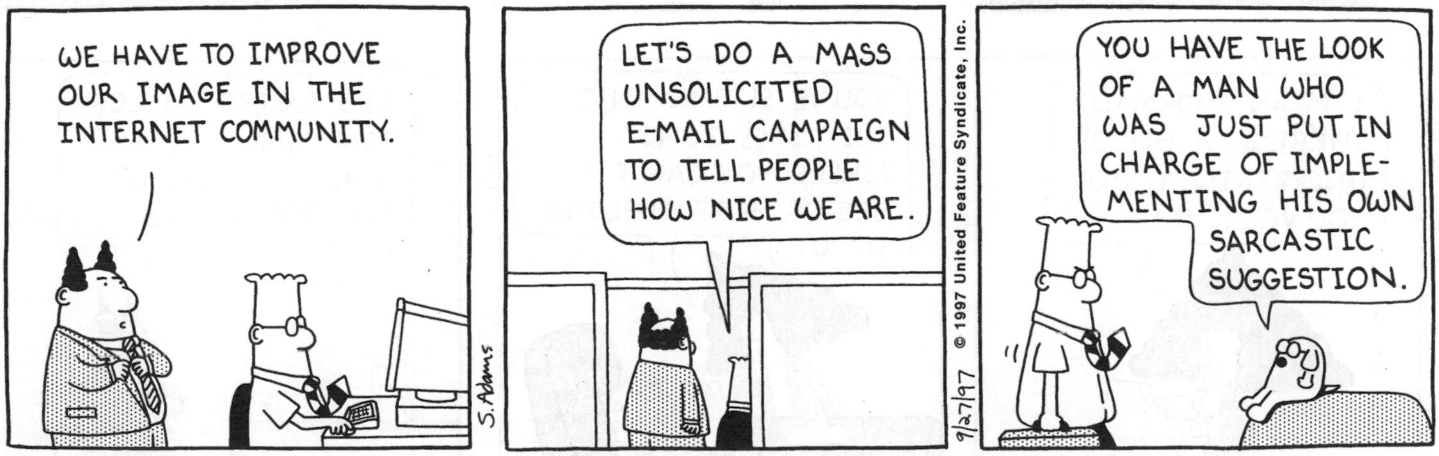
WE HAVE TO IMPROVE OUR IMAGE IN THE INTERNET COMMUNITY.
S. Adams
LET'S DO A MASS UNSOLICITED E-MAIL CAMPAIGN TO TELL PEOPLE HOW NICE WE ARE.
© 1997 United Feature Syndicate, Inc.
9/27/97
YOU HAVE THE LOOK OF A MAN WHO WAS JUST PUT IN CHARGE OF IMPLE-MENTING HIS OWN SARCASTIC SUGGESTION.

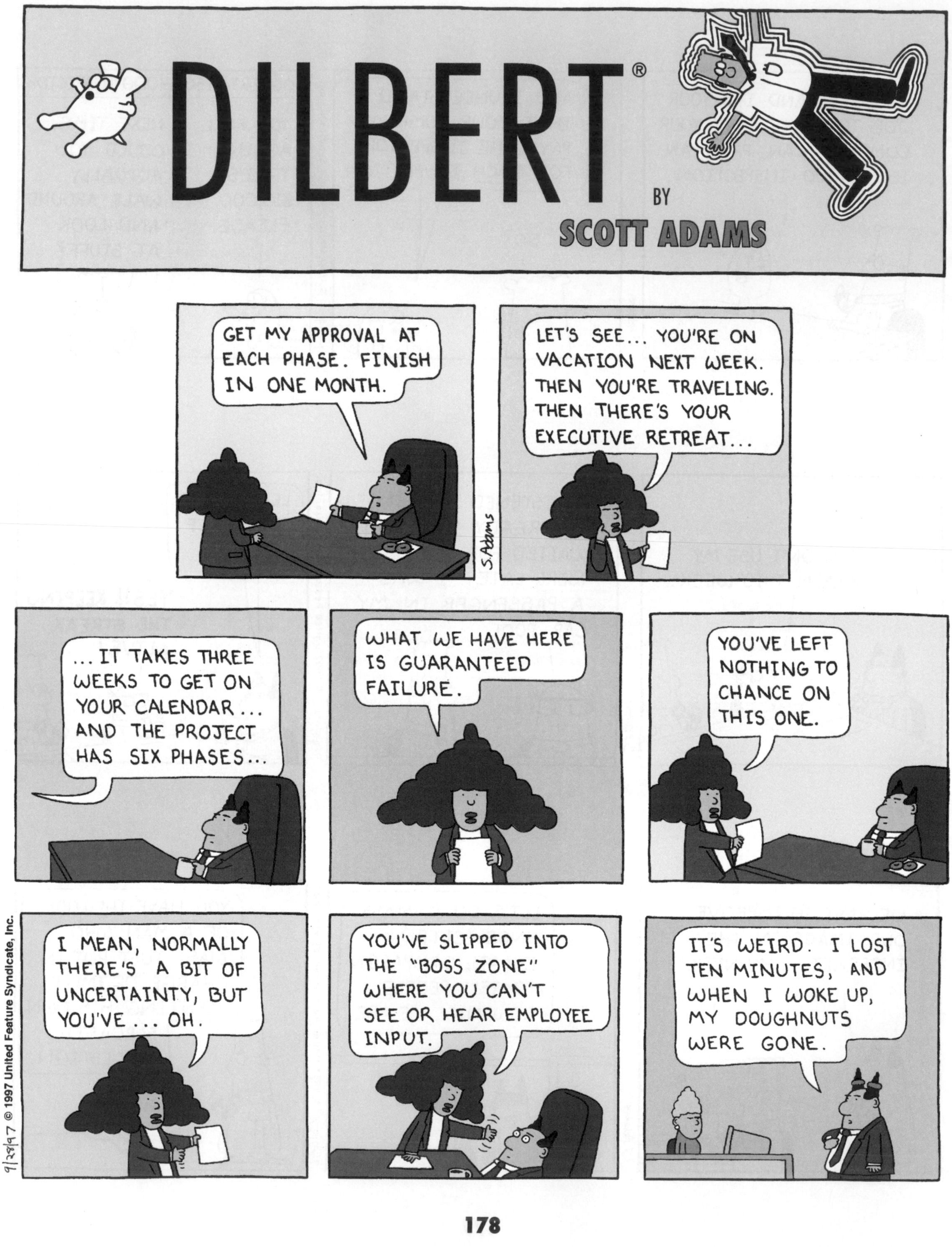
DILBERT®
BY
SCOTT ADAMS
GET MY APPROVAL AT EACH PHASE. FINISH IN ONE MONTH.
S. Adams
LET'S SEE... YOU'RE ON VACATION NEXT WEEK. THEN YOU'RE TRAVELING. THEN THERE'S YOUR EXECUTIVE RETREAT...
... IT TAKES THREE WEEKS TO GET ON YOUR CALENDAR ... AND THE PROJECT HAS SIX PHASES ...
WHAT WE HAVE HERE IS GUARANTEED FAILURE.
YOU'VE LEFT NOTHING TO CHANCE ON THIS ONE.
I MEAN, NORMALLY THERE'S A BIT OF UNCERTAINTY, BUT YOU'VE ... OH.
YOU'VE SLIPPED INTO THE "BOSS ZONE" WHERE YOU CAN'T SEE OR HEAR EMPLOYEE INPUT.
IT'S WEIRD. I LOST TEN MINUTES, AND WHEN I WOKE UP, MY DOUGHNUTS WERE GONE.
9/28/97 © 1997 United Feature Syndicate, Inc.

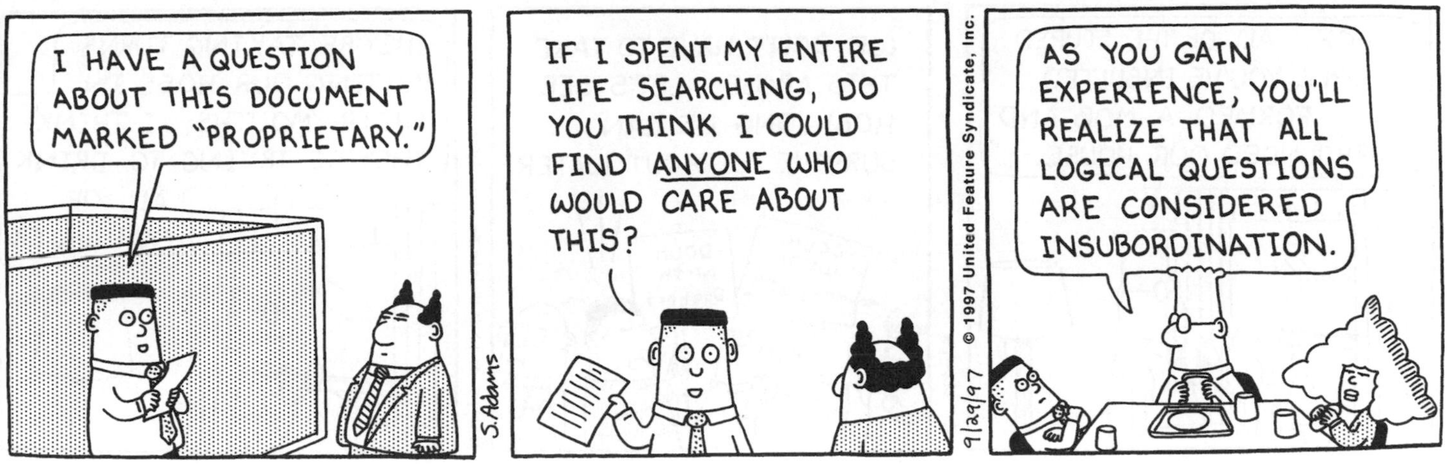
I HAVE A QUESTION ABOUT THIS DOCUMENT MARKED "PROPRIETARY."
IF I SPENT MY ENTIRE LIFE SEARCHING, DO YOU THINK I COULD FIND ANYONE WHO WOULD CARE ABOUT THIS?
AS YOU GAIN EXPERIENCE, YOU'LL REALIZE THAT ALL LOGICAL QUESTIONS ARE CONSIDERED INSUBORDINATION.
© 1997 United Feature Syndicate, Inc.

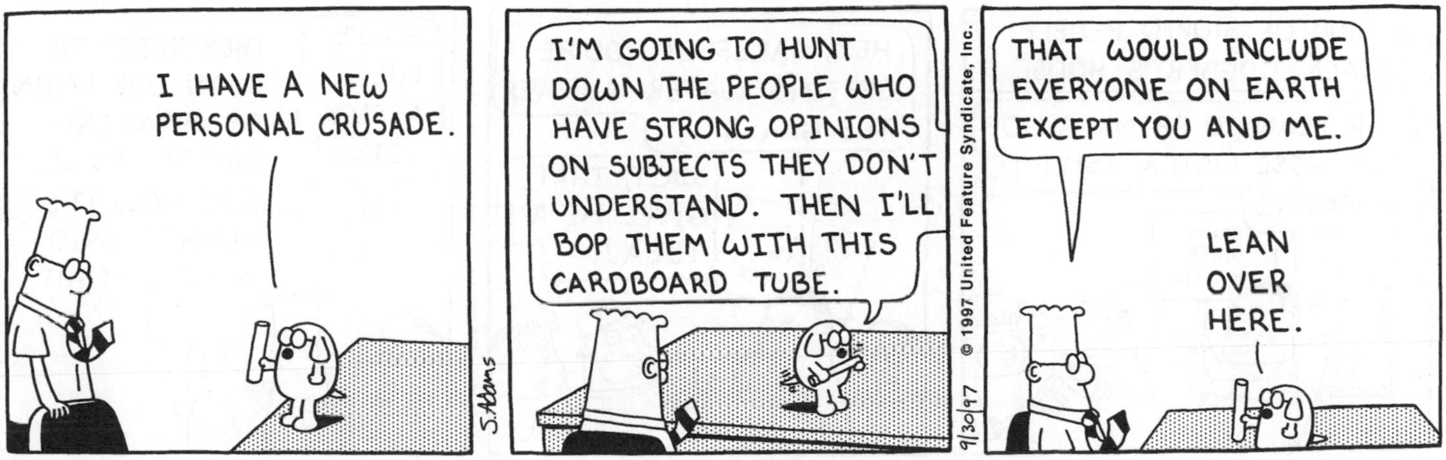
I HAVE A NEW PERSONAL CRUSADE.
I'M GOING TO HUNT DOWN THE PEOPLE WHO HAVE STRONG OPINIONS ON SUBJECTS THEY DON'T UNDERSTAND. THEN I'LL BOP THEM WITH THIS CARDBOARD TUBE.
THAT WOULD INCLUDE EVERYONE ON EARTH EXCEPT YOU AND ME.
LEAN OVER HERE.
© 1997 United Feature Syndicate, Inc.

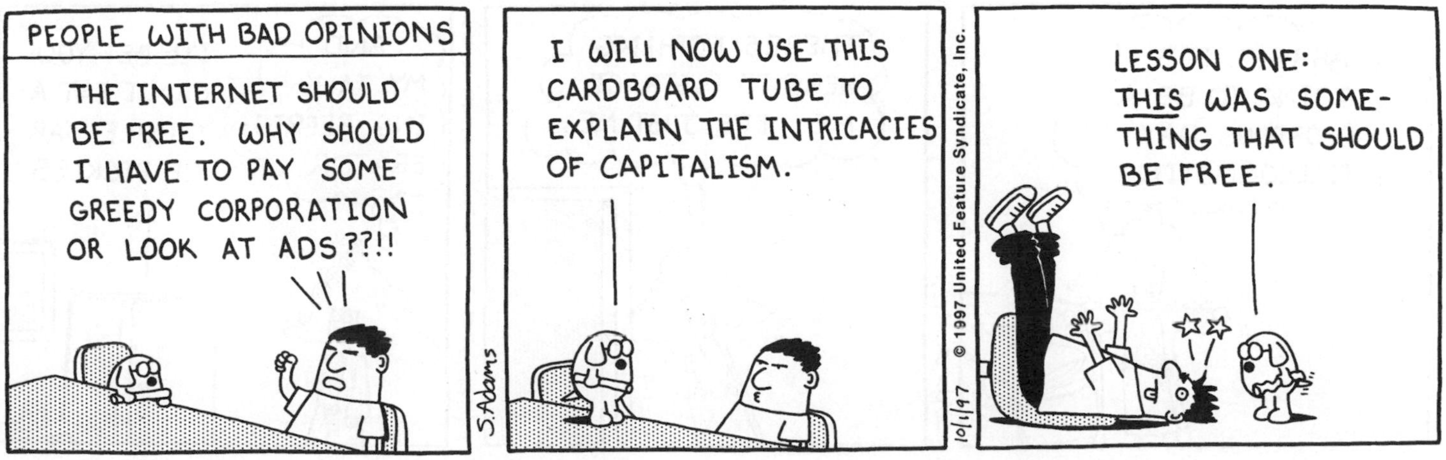
PEOPLE WITH BAD OPINIONS
THE INTERNET SHOULD BE FREE. WHY SHOULD I HAVE TO PAY SOME GREEDY CORPORATION OR LOOK AT ADS??!!
I WILL NOW USE THIS CARDBOARD TUBE TO EXPLAIN THE INTRICACIES OF CAPITALISM.
LESSON ONE: THIS WAS SOMETHING THAT SHOULD BE FREE.
© 1997 United Feature Syndicate, Inc.

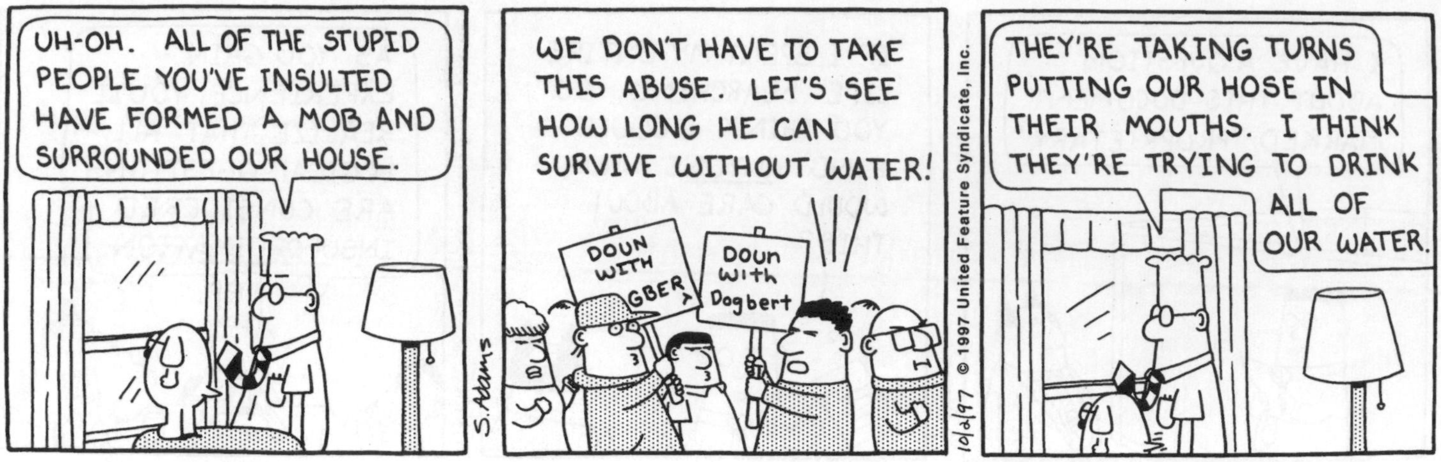
UH-OH. ALL OF THE STUPID PEOPLE YOU'VE INSULTED HAVE FORMED A MOB AND SURROUNDED OUR HOUSE.
S. Adams
WE DON'T HAVE TO TAKE THIS ABUSE. LET'S SEE HOW LONG HE CAN SURVIVE WITHOUT WATER!
DOUN WITH GBER
Doun with Dogbert
10/6/97 © 1997 United Feature Syndicate, Inc.
THEY'RE TAKING TURNS PUTTING OUR HOSE IN THEIR MOUTHS. I THINK THEY'RE TRYING TO DRINK ALL OF OUR WATER.

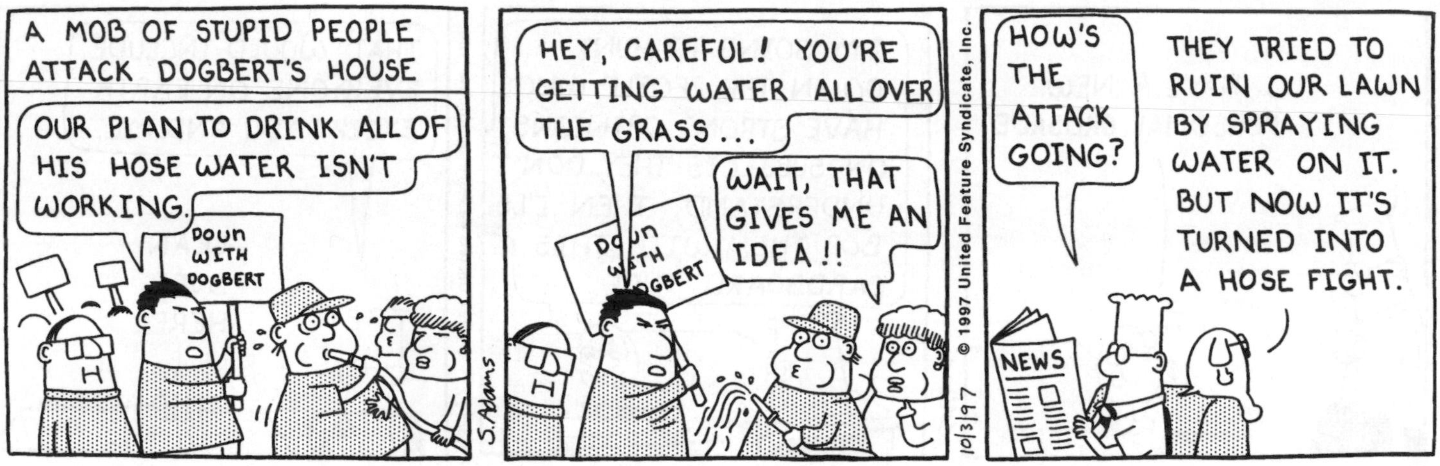
A MOB OF STUPID PEOPLE ATTACK DOGBERT'S HOUSE
OUR PLAN TO DRINK ALL OF HIS HOSE WATER ISN'T WORKING.
DOUN WITH DOGBERT
S. Adams
HEY, CAREFUL! YOU'RE GETTING WATER ALL OVER THE GRASS...
WAIT, THAT GIVES ME AN IDEA!!
DOUN WITH OGBERT
10/3/97 © 1997 United Feature Syndicate, Inc.
HOW'S THE ATTACK GOING?
THEY TRIED TO RUIN OUR LAWN BY SPRAYING WATER ON IT. BUT NOW IT'S TURNED INTO A HOSE FIGHT.
NEWS

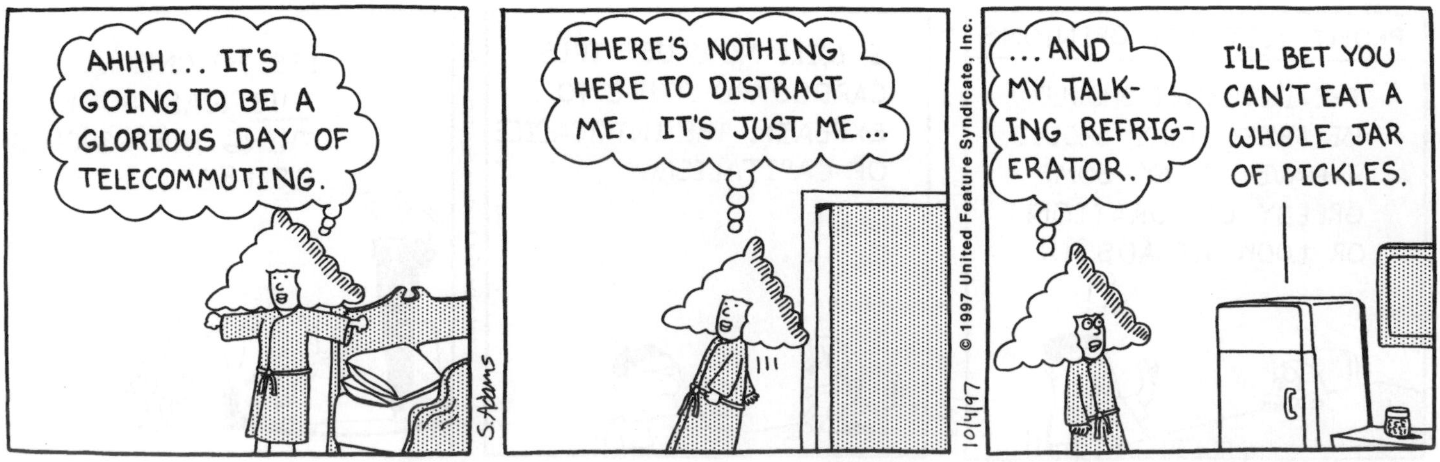
AHHH... IT'S GOING TO BE A GLORIOUS DAY OF TELECOMMUTING.
S. Adams
THERE'S NOTHING HERE TO DISTRACT ME. IT'S JUST ME...
10/4/97 © 1997 United Feature Syndicate, Inc.
...AND MY TALK-ING REFRIG-ERATOR.
I'LL BET YOU CAN'T EAT A WHOLE JAR OF PICKLES.

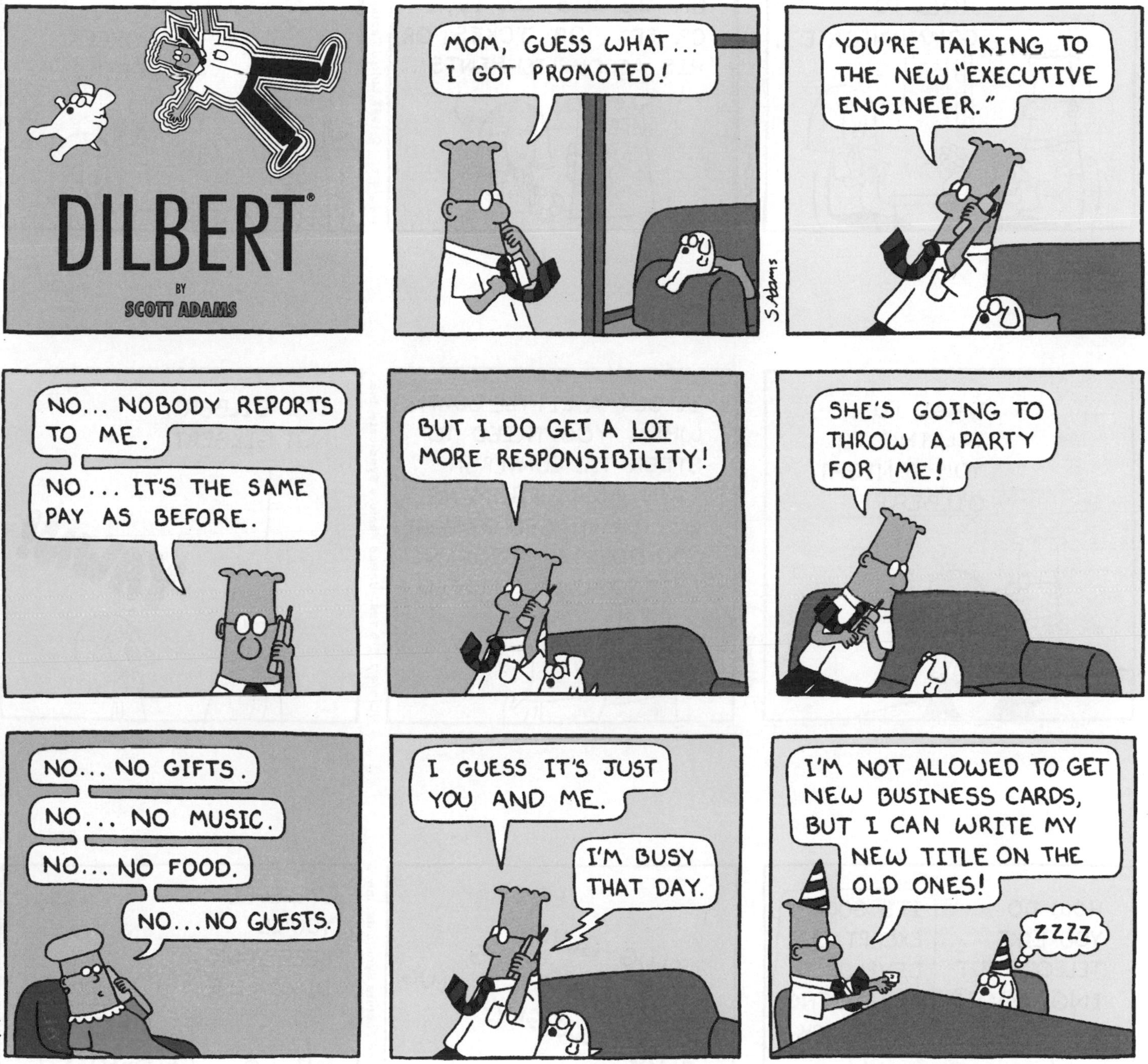
DILBERT®
BY
SCOTT ADAMS
MOM, GUESS WHAT... I GOT PROMOTED!
YOU'RE TALKING TO THE NEW "EXECUTIVE ENGINEER."
S.Adams
NO... NOBODY REPORTS TO ME.
NO... IT'S THE SAME PAY AS BEFORE.
BUT I DO GET A LOT MORE RESPONSIBILITY!
SHE'S GOING TO THROW A PARTY FOR ME!
NO... NO GIFTS.
NO... NO MUSIC.
NO... NO FOOD.
NO... NO GUESTS.
I GUESS IT'S JUST YOU AND ME.
I'M BUSY THAT DAY.
I'M NOT ALLOWED TO GET NEW BUSINESS CARDS, BUT I CAN WRITE MY NEW TITLE ON THE OLD ONES!
ZZZZ

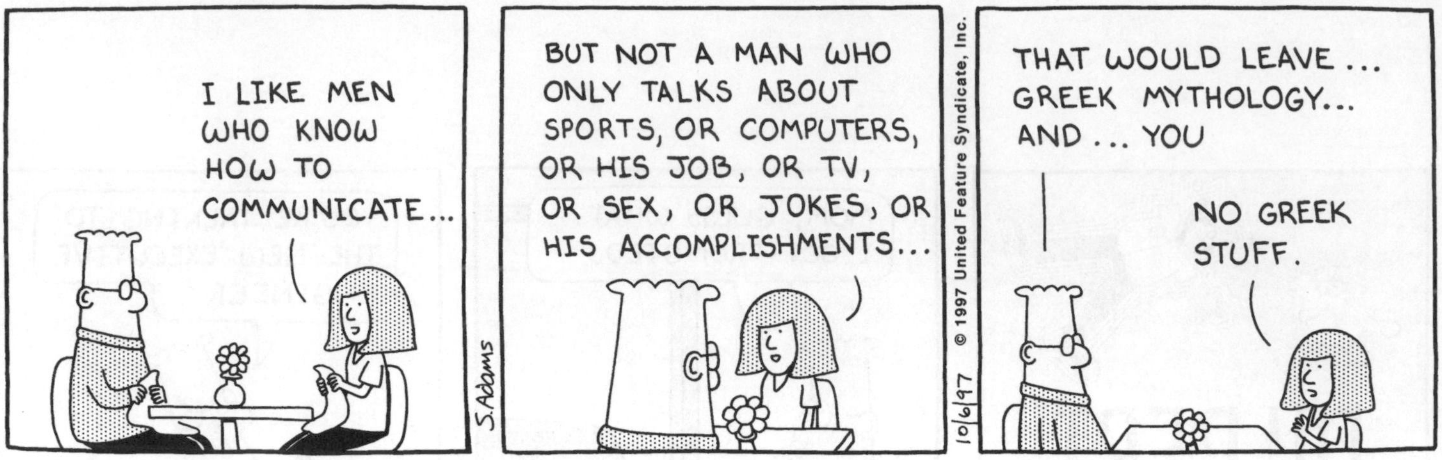
I LIKE MEN WHO KNOW HOW TO COMMUNICATE...
S. Adams
BUT NOT A MAN WHO ONLY TALKS ABOUT SPORTS, OR COMPUTERS, OR HIS JOB, OR TV, OR SEX, OR JOKES, OR HIS ACCOMPLISHMENTS...
10/6/97 © 1997 United Feature Syndicate, Inc.
THAT WOULD LEAVE... GREEK MYTHOLOGY... AND... YOU
NO GREEK STUFF.

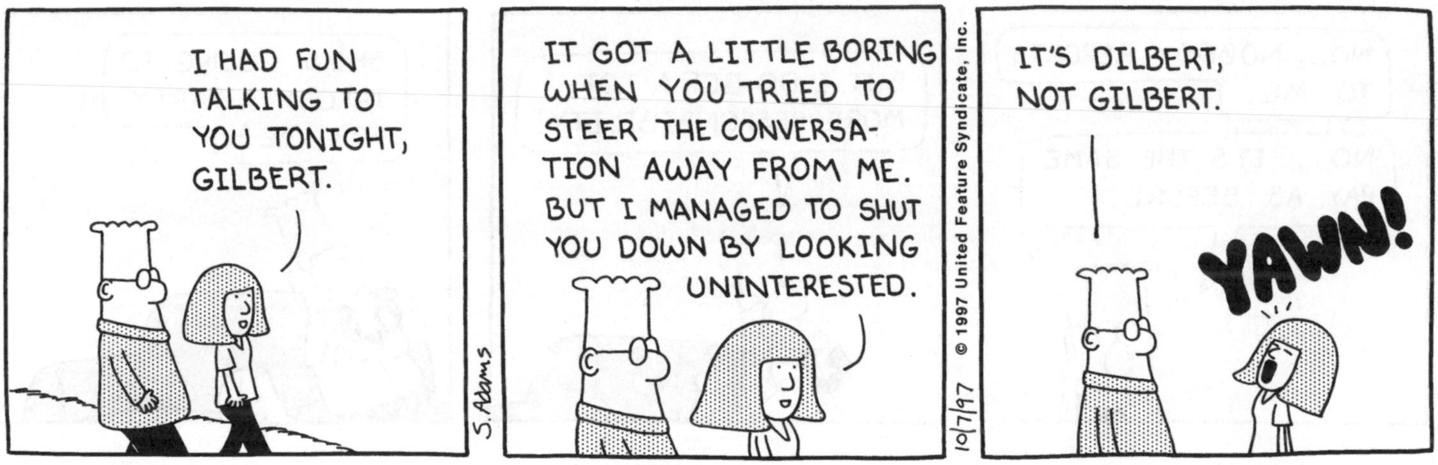
I HAD FUN TALKING TO YOU TONIGHT, GILBERT.
S. Adams
IT GOT A LITTLE BORING WHEN YOU TRIED TO STEER THE CONVERSATION AWAY FROM ME. BUT I MANAGED TO SHUT YOU DOWN BY LOOKING UNINTERESTED.
10/7/97 © 1997 United Feature Syndicate, Inc.
IT'S DILBERT, NOT GILBERT.
YAWN!

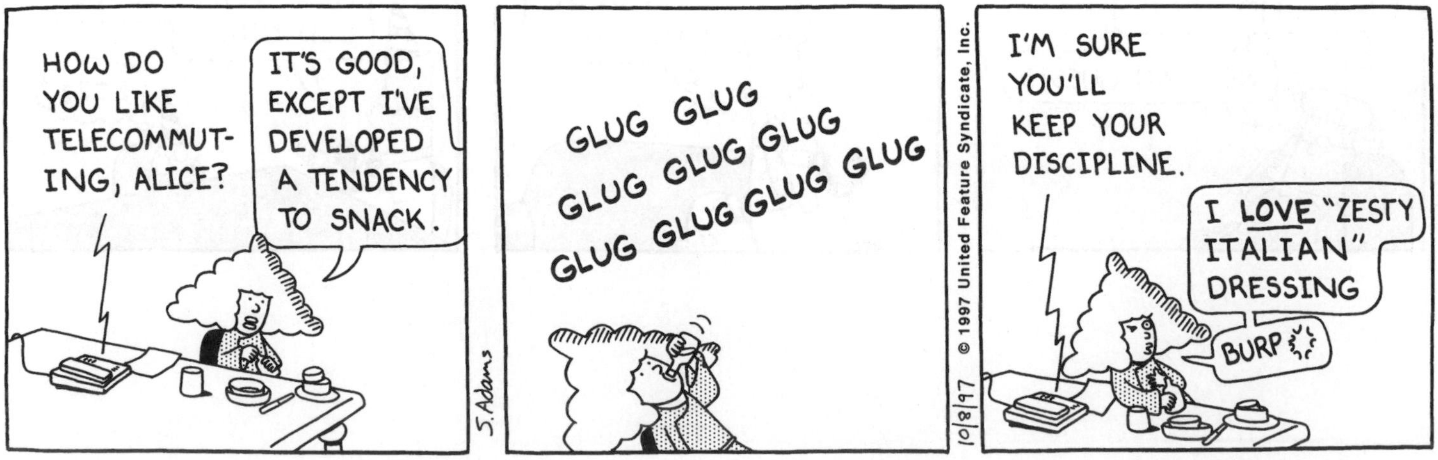
HOW DO YOU LIKE TELECOMMUTING, ALICE?
IT'S GOOD, EXCEPT I'VE DEVELOPED A TENDENCY TO SNACK.
S. Adams
GLUG GLUG
GLUG GLUG GLUG
GLUG GLUG GLUG GLUG
10/8/97 © 1997 United Feature Syndicate, Inc.
I'M SURE YOU'LL KEEP YOUR DISCIPLINE.
I LOVE "ZESTY ITALIAN" DRESSING
BURP

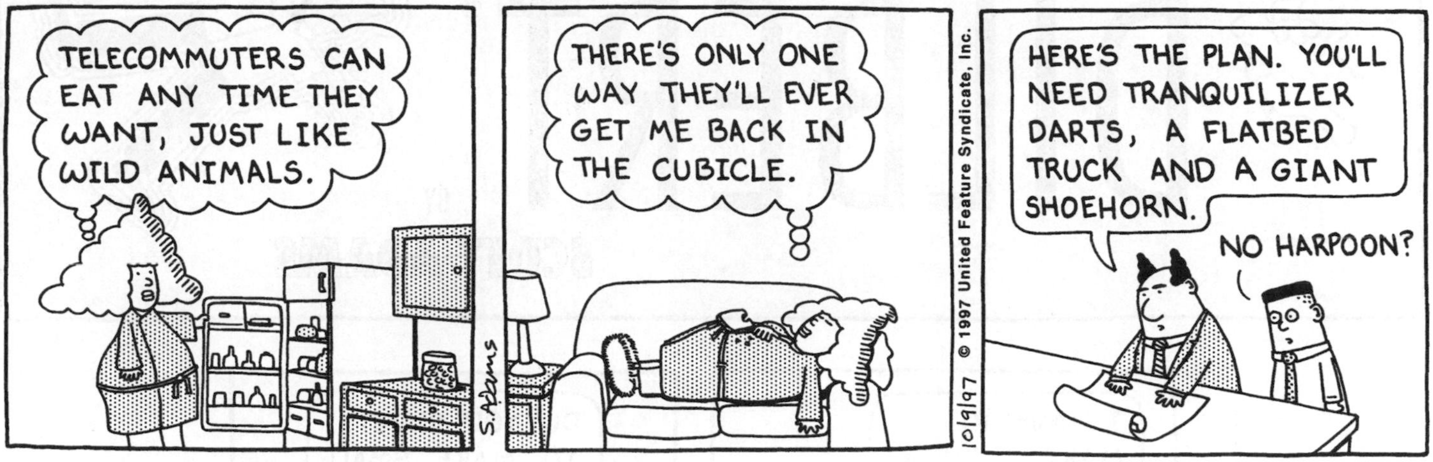
TELECOMMUTERS CAN EAT ANY TIME THEY WANT, JUST LIKE WILD ANIMALS.
THERE'S ONLY ONE WAY THEY'LL EVER GET ME BACK IN THE CUBICLE.
HERE'S THE PLAN. YOU'LL NEED TRANQUILIZER DARTS, A FLATBED TRUCK AND A GIANT SHOEHORN.
NO HARPOON?
S. Adams
10/9/97 © 1997 United Feature Syndicate, Inc.

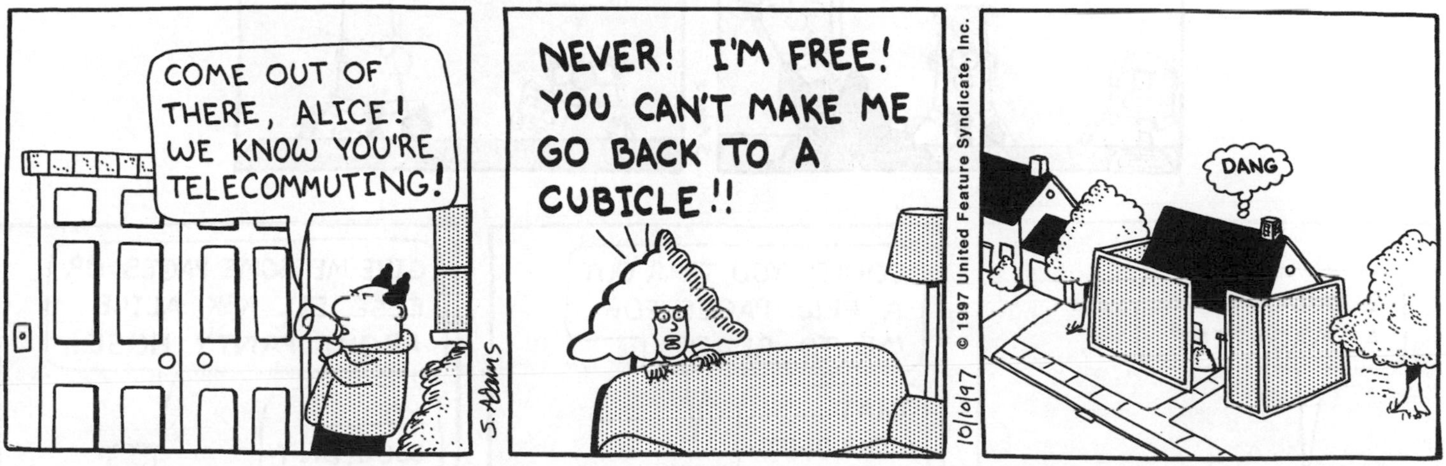
COME OUT OF THERE, ALICE! WE KNOW YOU'RE TELECOMMUTING!
NEVER! I'M FREE! YOU CAN'T MAKE ME GO BACK TO A CUBICLE!!
DANG
S. Adams
10/10/97 © 1997 United Feature Syndicate, Inc.

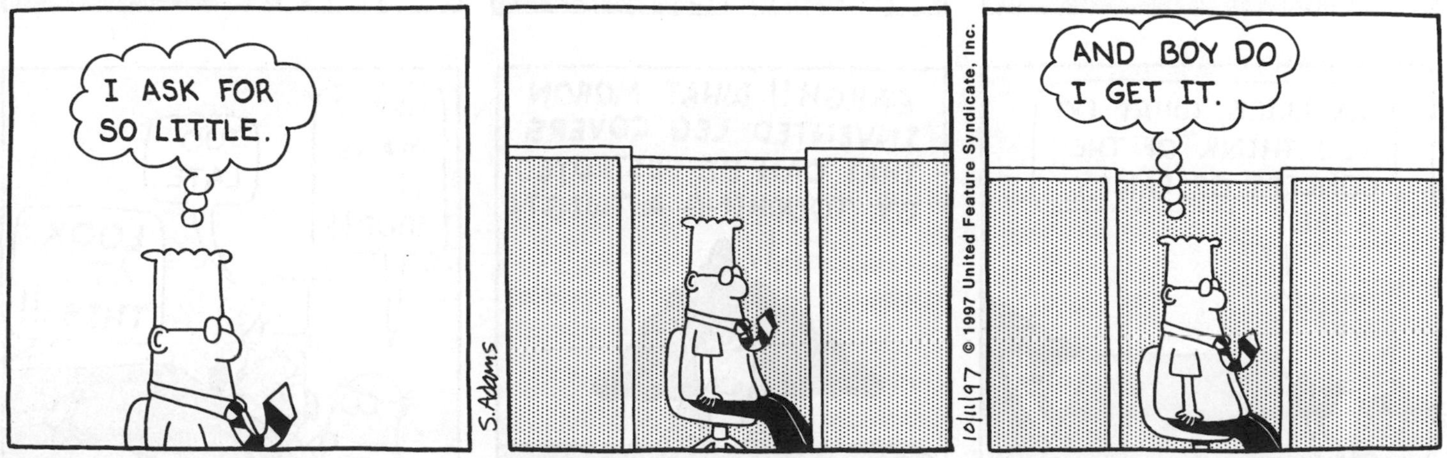
I ASK FOR SO LITTLE.
AND BOY DO I GET IT.
S. Adams
10/11/97 © 1997 United Feature Syndicate, Inc.

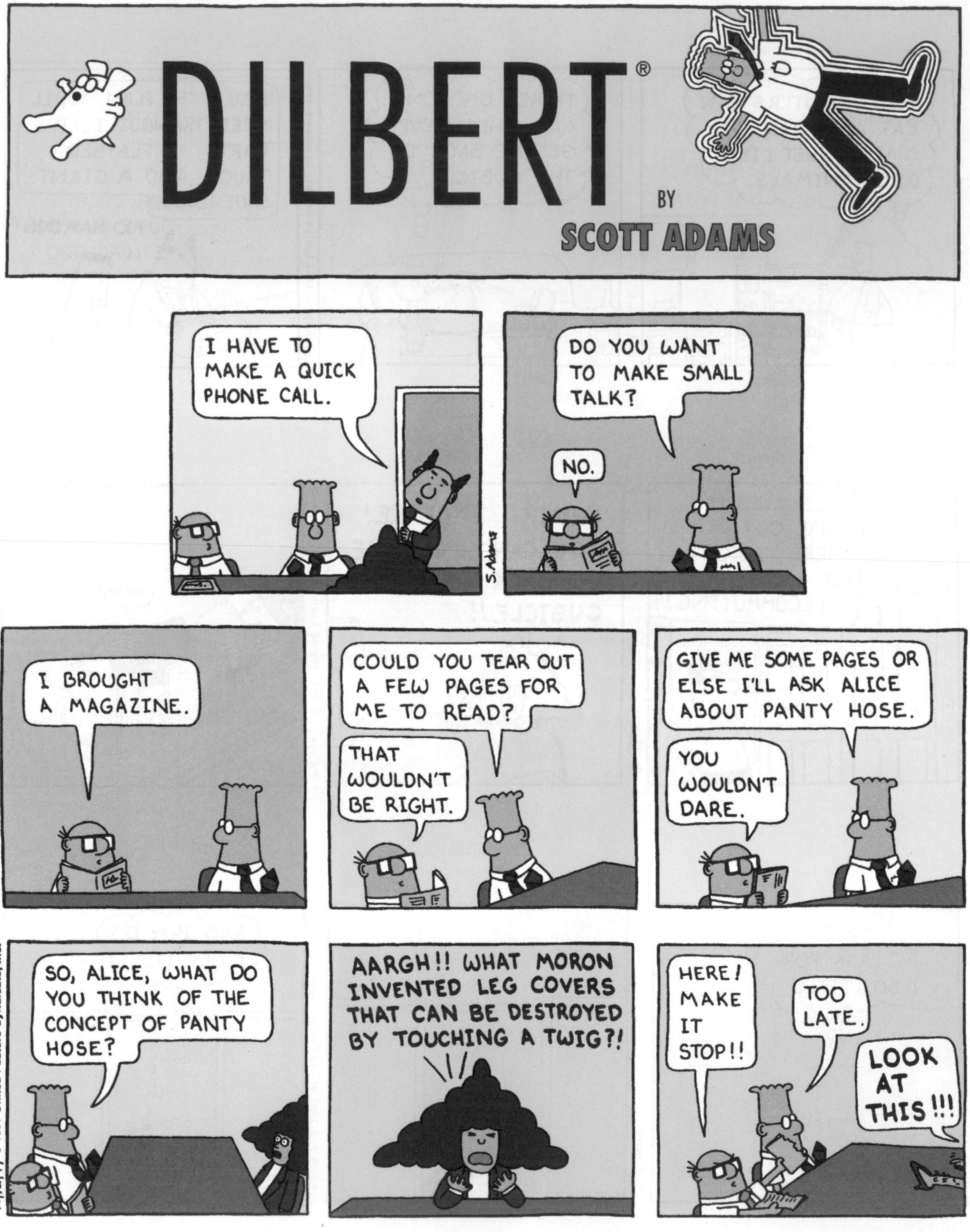
DILBERT®
BY
SCOTT ADAMS
I HAVE TO MAKE A QUICK PHONE CALL.
S. Adams
DO YOU WANT TO MAKE SMALL TALK?
NO.
I BROUGHT A MAGAZINE.
COULD YOU TEAR OUT A FEW PAGES FOR ME TO READ?
THAT WOULDN'T BE RIGHT.
GIVE ME SOME PAGES OR ELSE I'LL ASK ALICE ABOUT PANTY HOSE.
YOU WOULDN'T DARE.
10/12/97 © 1997 United Feature Syndicate, Inc.
SO, ALICE, WHAT DO YOU THINK OF THE CONCEPT OF PANTY HOSE?
AARGH!! WHAT MORON INVENTED LEG COVERS THAT CAN BE DESTROYED BY TOUCHING A TWIG?!
HERE! MAKE IT STOP!!
TOO LATE.
LOOK AT THIS!!!

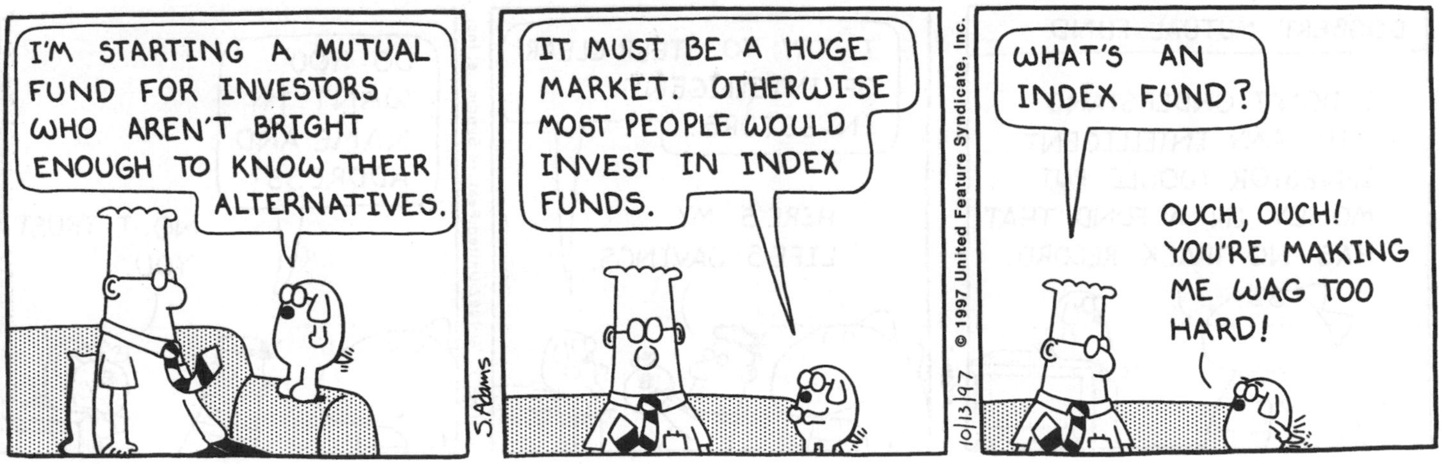
I'M STARTING A MUTUAL FUND FOR INVESTORS WHO AREN'T BRIGHT ENOUGH TO KNOW THEIR ALTERNATIVES.
IT MUST BE A HUGE MARKET. OTHERWISE MOST PEOPLE WOULD INVEST IN INDEX FUNDS.
WHAT'S AN INDEX FUND?
OUCH, OUCH! YOU'RE MAKING ME WAG TOO HARD!
S. Adams
10/13/97
© 1997 United Feature Syndicate, Inc.

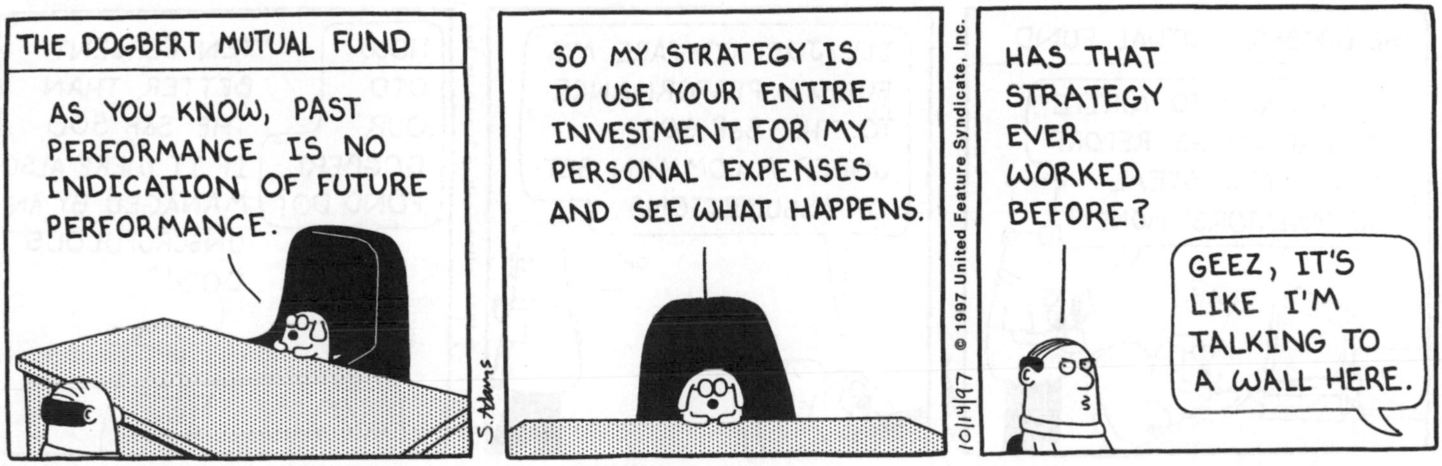
THE DOGBERT MUTUAL FUND
AS YOU KNOW, PAST PERFORMANCE IS NO INDICATION OF FUTURE PERFORMANCE.
SO MY STRATEGY IS TO USE YOUR ENTIRE INVESTMENT FOR MY PERSONAL EXPENSES AND SEE WHAT HAPPENS.
HAS THAT STRATEGY EVER WORKED BEFORE?
GEEZ, IT'S LIKE I'M TALKING TO A WALL HERE.
S. Adams
10/14/97
© 1997 United Feature Syndicate, Inc.

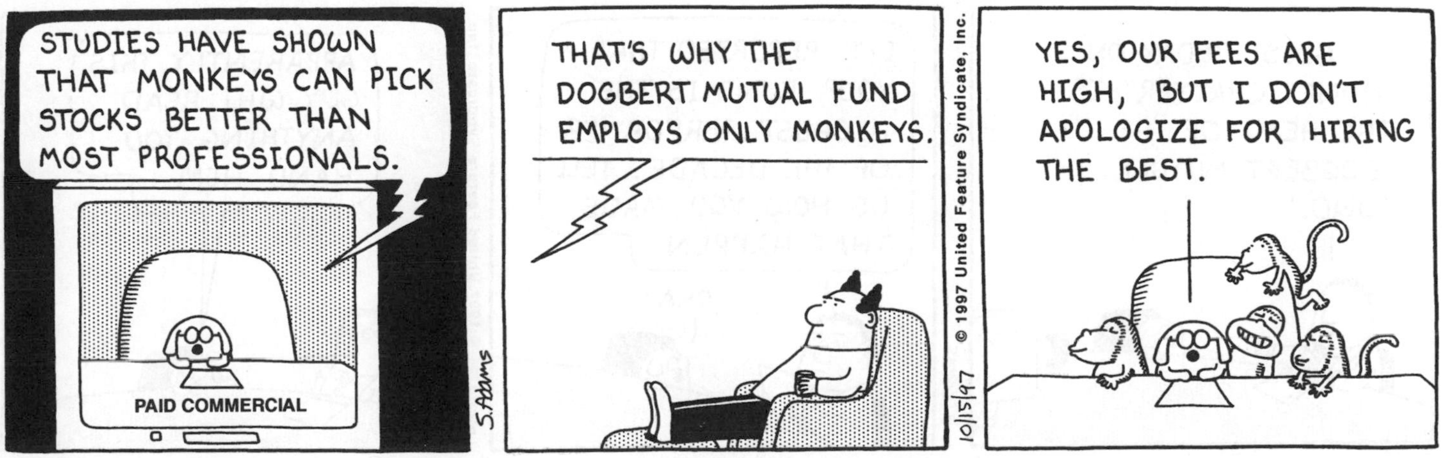
STUDIES HAVE SHOWN THAT MONKEYS CAN PICK STOCKS BETTER THAN MOST PROFESSIONALS.
PAID COMMERCIAL
THAT'S WHY THE DOGBERT MUTUAL FUND EMPLOYS ONLY MONKEYS.
YES, OUR FEES ARE HIGH, BUT I DON'T APOLOGIZE FOR HIRING THE BEST.
S. Adams
10/15/97
© 1997 United Feature Syndicate, Inc.

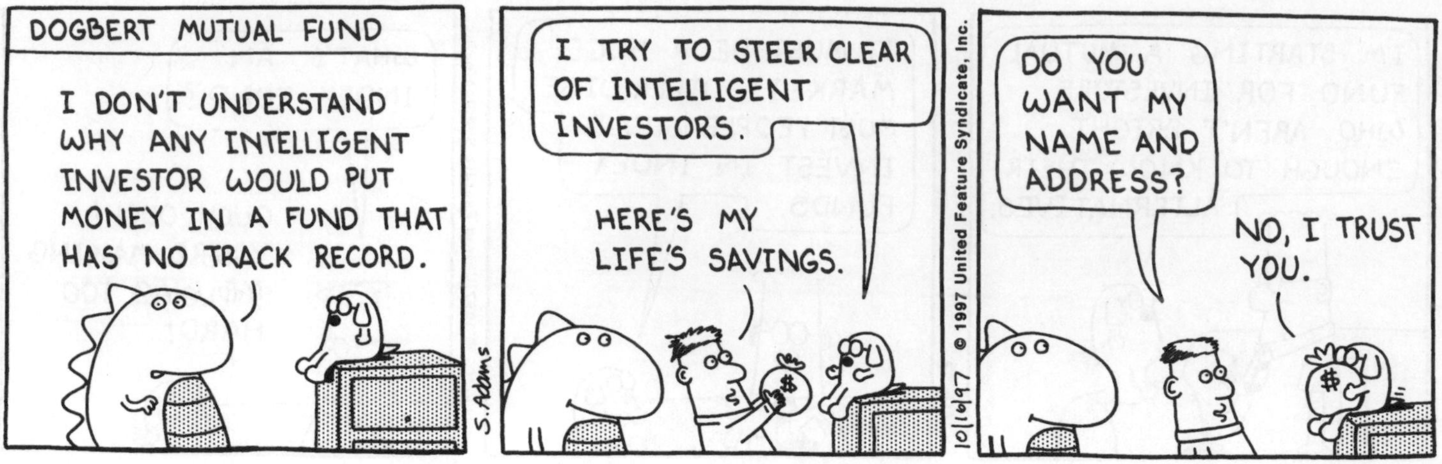
DOGBERT MUTUAL FUND
I DON'T UNDERSTAND WHY ANY INTELLIGENT INVESTOR WOULD PUT MONEY IN A FUND THAT HAS NO TRACK RECORD.
S. Adams
I TRY TO STEER CLEAR OF INTELLIGENT INVESTORS.
HERE'S MY LIFE'S SAVINGS.
10/16/97 © 1997 United Feature Syndicate, Inc.
DO YOU WANT MY NAME AND ADDRESS?
NO, I TRUST YOU.

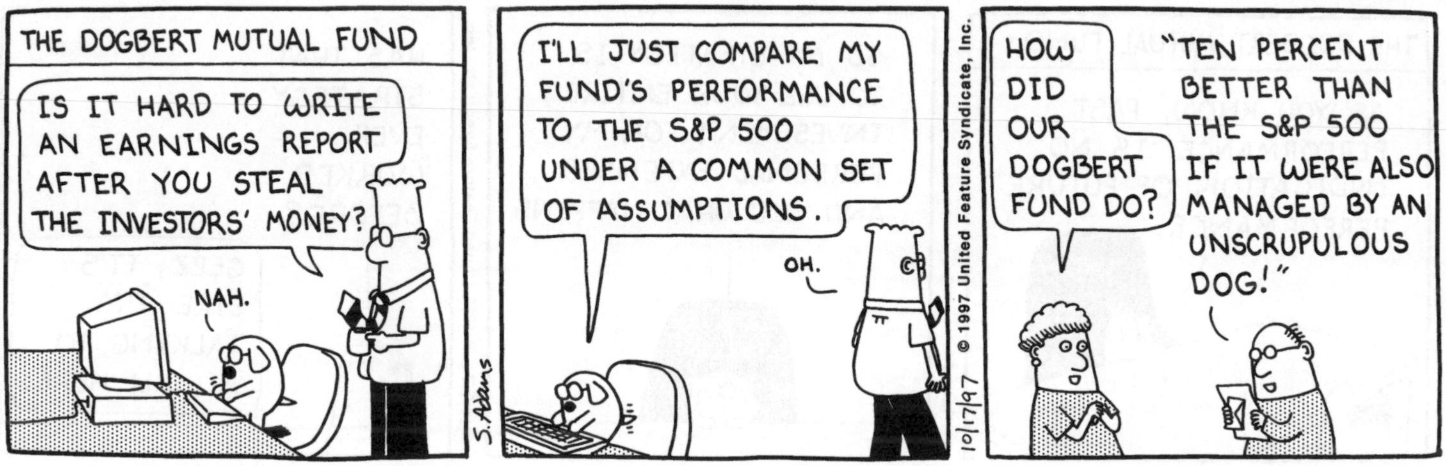
THE DOGBERT MUTUAL FUND
IS IT HARD TO WRITE AN EARNINGS REPORT AFTER YOU STEAL THE INVESTORS' MONEY?
NAH.
S. Adams
I'LL JUST COMPARE MY FUND'S PERFORMANCE TO THE S&P 500 UNDER A COMMON SET OF ASSUMPTIONS.
OH.
10/17/97 © 1997 United Feature Syndicate, Inc.
HOW DID OUR DOGBERT FUND DO?
"TEN PERCENT BETTER THAN THE S&P 500 IF IT WERE ALSO MANAGED BY AN UNSCRUPULOUS DOG!"

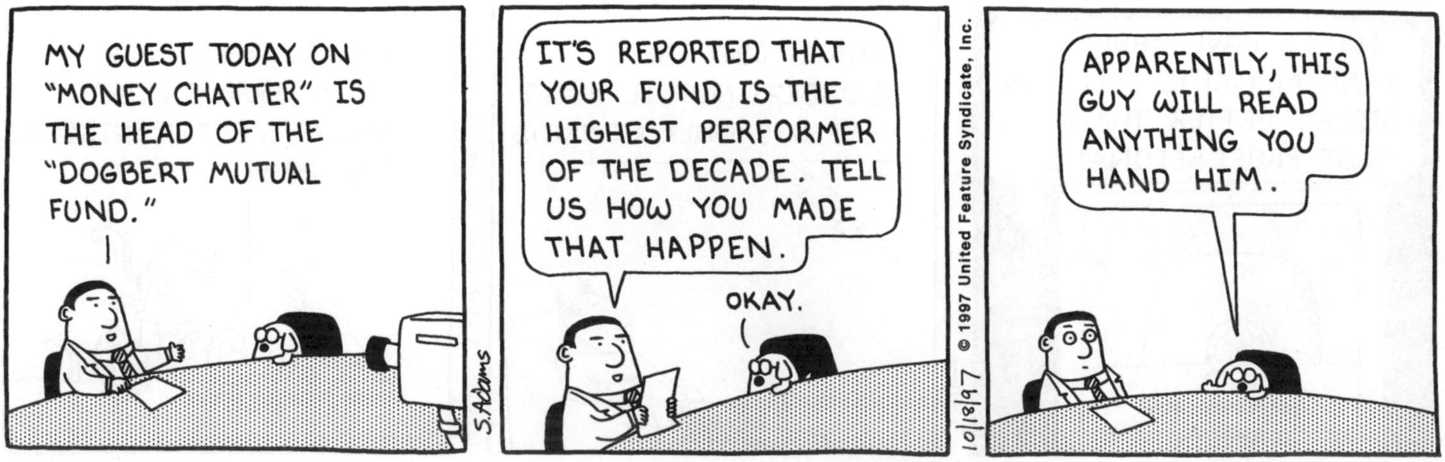
MY GUEST TODAY ON "MONEY CHATTER" IS THE HEAD OF THE "DOGBERT MUTUAL FUND."
S. Adams
IT'S REPORTED THAT YOUR FUND IS THE HIGHEST PERFORMER OF THE DECADE. TELL US HOW YOU MADE THAT HAPPEN.
OKAY.
10/18/97 © 1997 United Feature Syndicate, Inc.
APPARENTLY, THIS GUY WILL READ ANYTHING YOU HAND HIM.

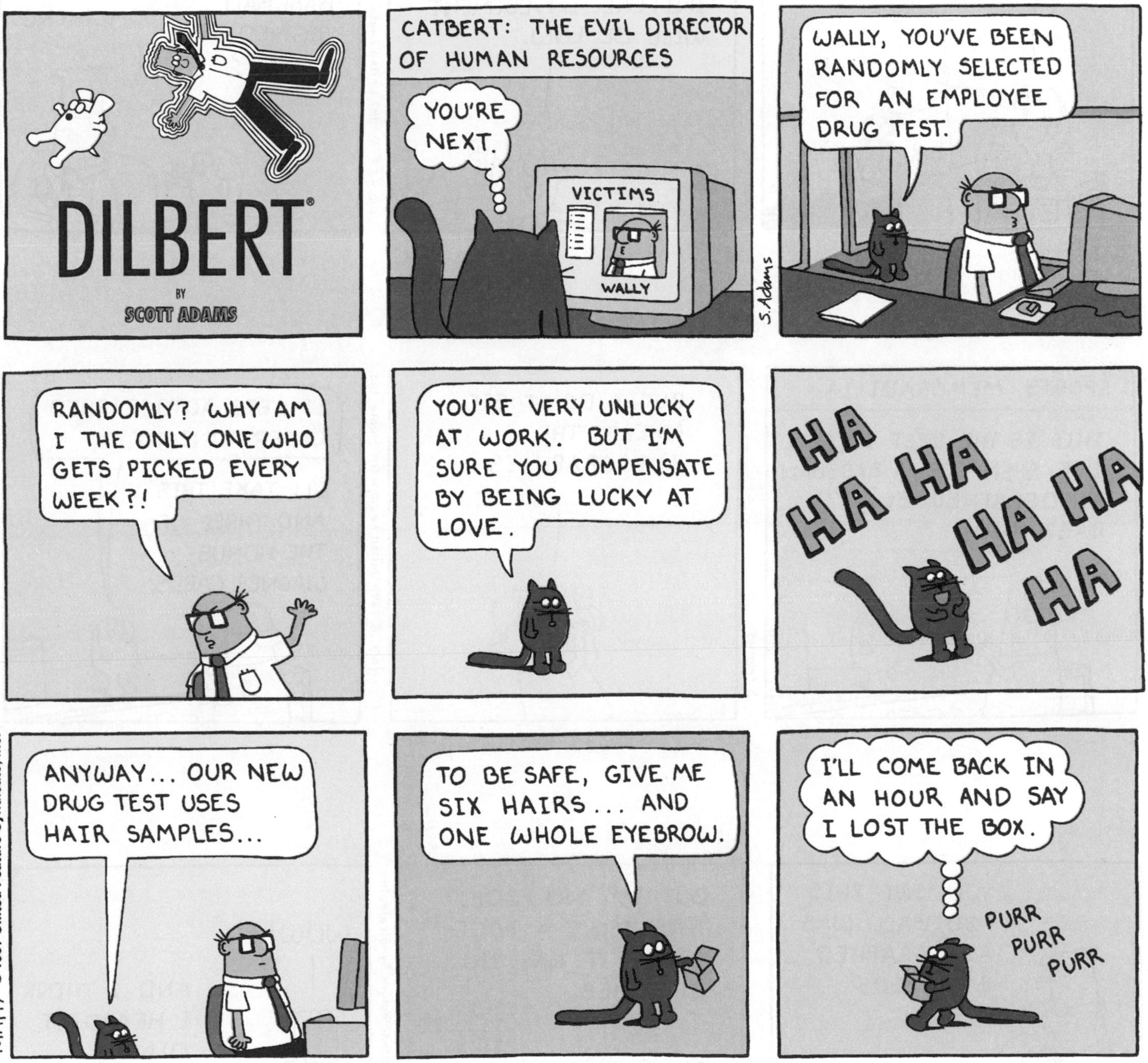
DILBERT®
BY
SCOTT ADAMS
CATBERT: THE EVIL DIRECTOR OF HUMAN RESOURCES
YOU'RE NEXT.
VICTIMS
WALLY
S. Adams
WALLY, YOU'VE BEEN RANDOMLY SELECTED FOR AN EMPLOYEE DRUG TEST.
RANDOMLY? WHY AM I THE ONLY ONE WHO GETS PICKED EVERY WEEK?!
YOU'RE VERY UNLUCKY AT WORK. BUT I'M SURE YOU COMPENSATE BY BEING LUCKY AT LOVE.
HA HA HA HA HA HA HA
ANYWAY... OUR NEW DRUG TEST USES HAIR SAMPLES...
TO BE SAFE, GIVE ME SIX HAIRS... AND ONE WHOLE EYEBROW.
I'LL COME BACK IN AN HOUR AND SAY I LOST THE BOX.
PURR PURR PURR
10/19/97

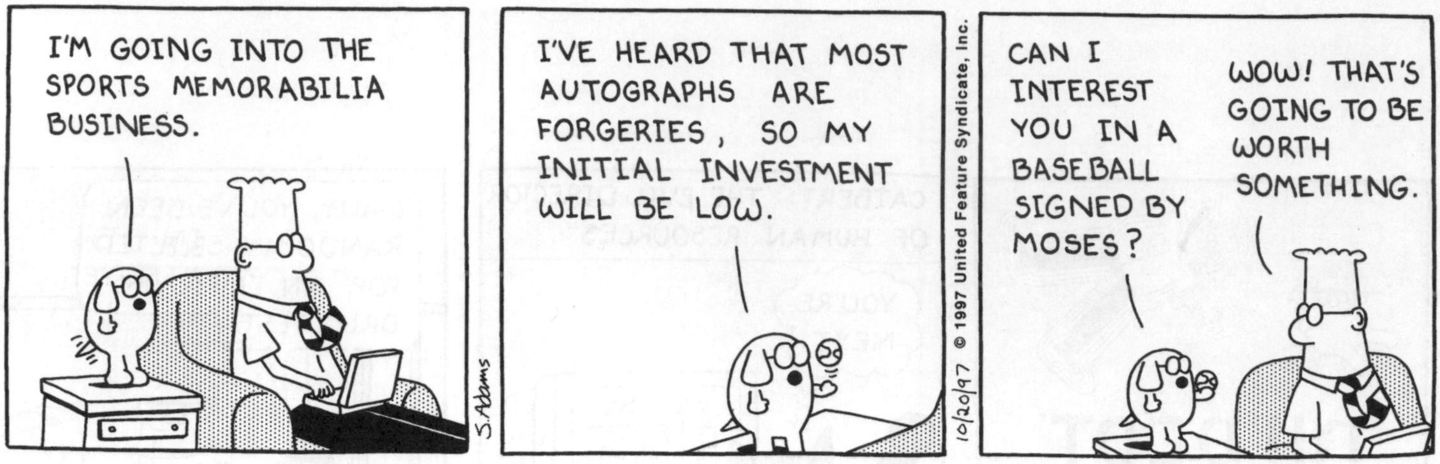
I'M GOING INTO THE SPORTS MEMORABILIA BUSINESS.
S. Adams
I'VE HEARD THAT MOST AUTOGRAPHS ARE FORGERIES, SO MY INITIAL INVESTMENT WILL BE LOW.
10/20/97 © 1997 United Feature Syndicate, Inc.
CAN I INTEREST YOU IN A BASEBALL SIGNED BY MOSES?
WOW! THAT'S GOING TO BE WORTH SOMETHING.

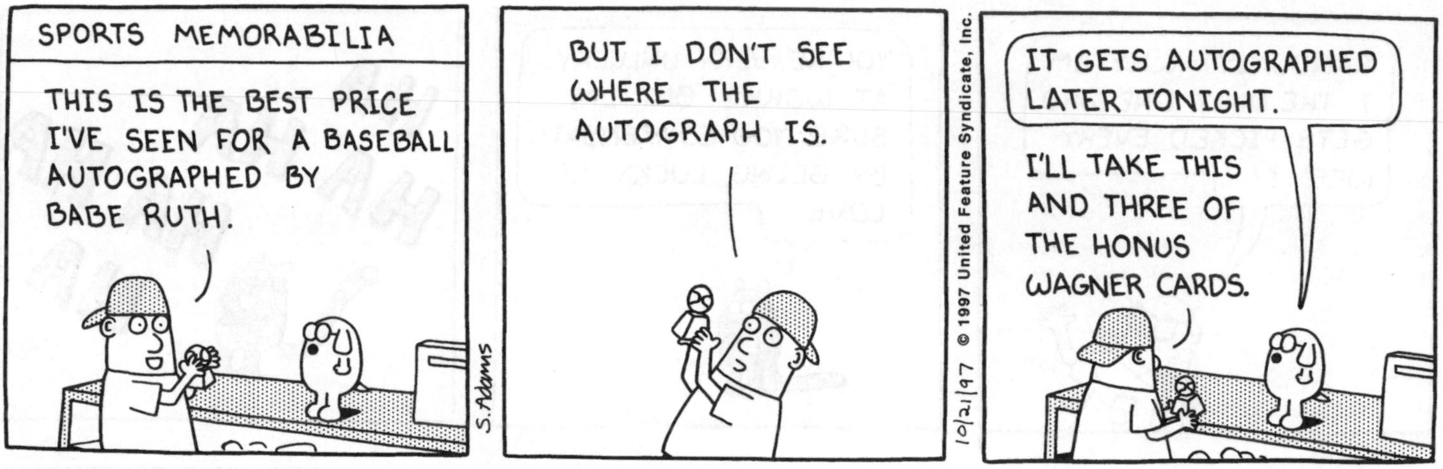
SPORTS MEMORABILIA
THIS IS THE BEST PRICE I'VE SEEN FOR A BASEBALL AUTOGRAPHED BY BABE RUTH.
S. Adams
BUT I DON'T SEE WHERE THE AUTOGRAPH IS.
10/21/97 © 1997 United Feature Syndicate, Inc.
IT GETS AUTOGRAPHED LATER TONIGHT.
I'LL TAKE THIS AND THREE OF THE HONUS WAGNER CARDS.

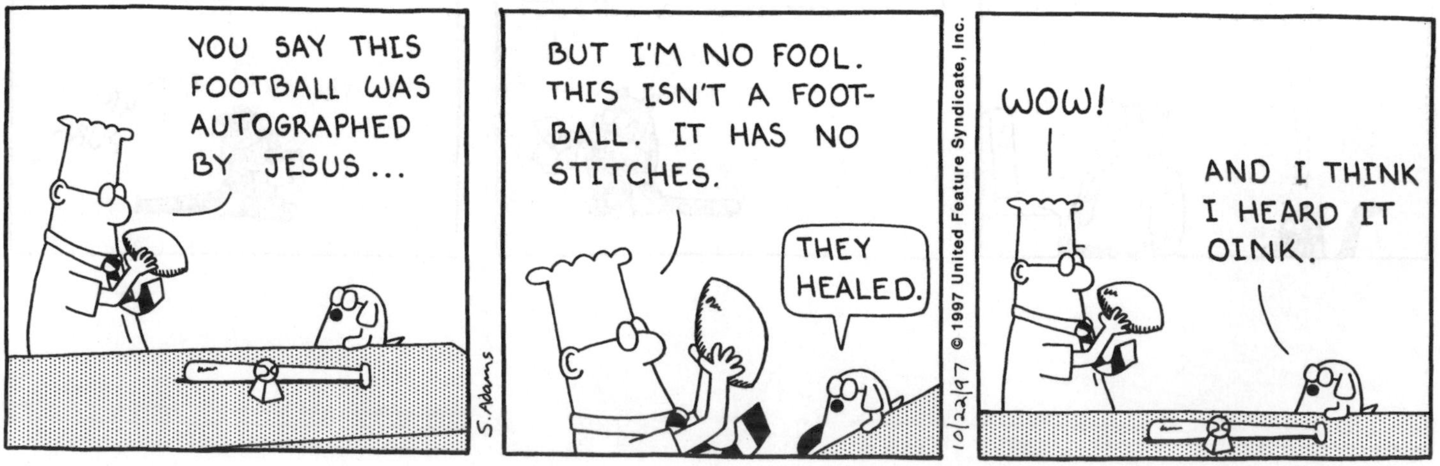
YOU SAY THIS FOOTBALL WAS AUTOGRAPHED BY JESUS...
S. Adams
BUT I'M NO FOOL. THIS ISN'T A FOOT-BALL. IT HAS NO STITCHES.
THEY HEALED.
10/22/97 © 1997 United Feature Syndicate, Inc.
WOW!
AND I THINK I HEARD IT OINK.

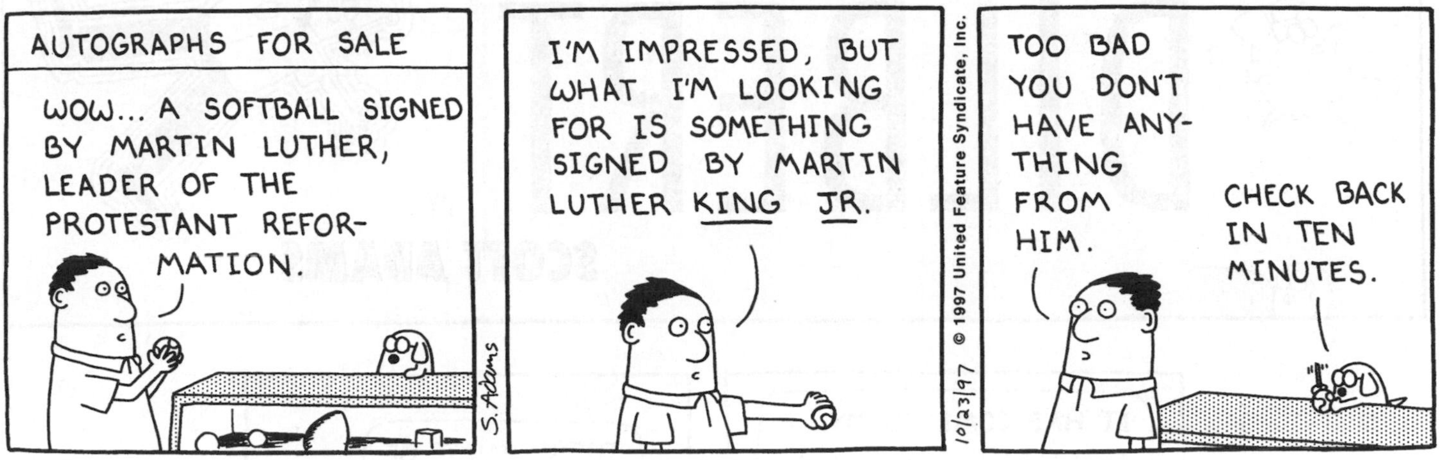
AUTOGRAPHS FOR SALE
WOW... A SOFTBALL SIGNED BY MARTIN LUTHER, LEADER OF THE PROTESTANT REFORMATION.
I'M IMPRESSED, BUT WHAT I'M LOOKING FOR IS SOMETHING SIGNED BY MARTIN LUTHER KING JR.
TOO BAD YOU DON'T HAVE ANYTHING FROM HIM.
CHECK BACK IN TEN MINUTES.
S. Adams
10/23/97
© 1997 United Feature Syndicate, Inc.

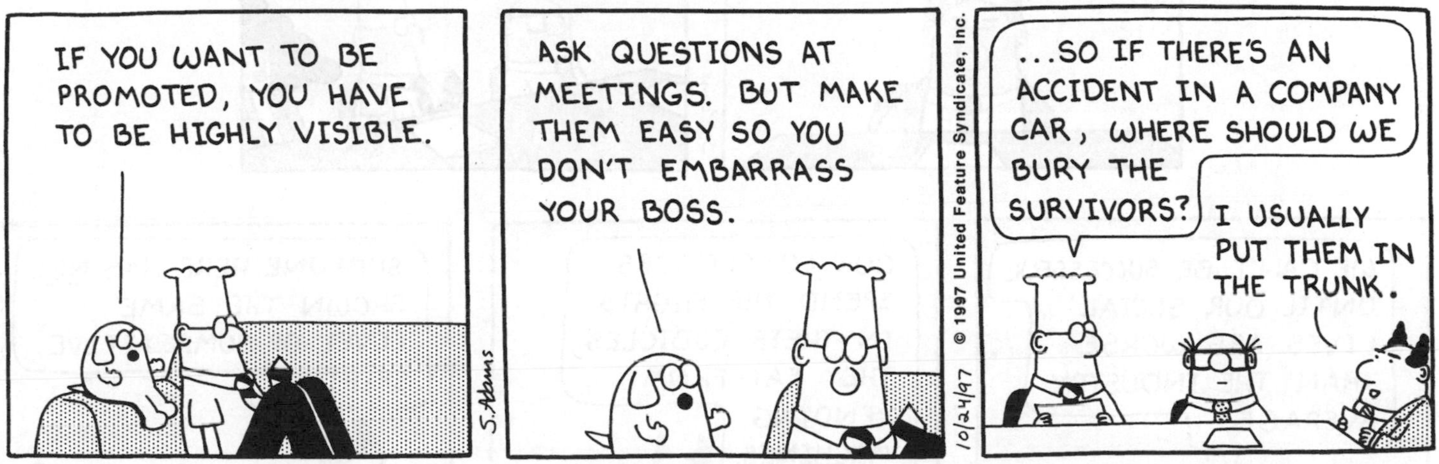
IF YOU WANT TO BE PROMOTED, YOU HAVE TO BE HIGHLY VISIBLE.
ASK QUESTIONS AT MEETINGS. BUT MAKE THEM EASY SO YOU DON'T EMBARRASS YOUR BOSS.
...SO IF THERE'S AN ACCIDENT IN A COMPANY CAR, WHERE SHOULD WE BURY THE SURVIVORS?
I USUALLY PUT THEM IN THE TRUNK.
S. Adams
10/24/97
© 1997 United Feature Syndicate, Inc.

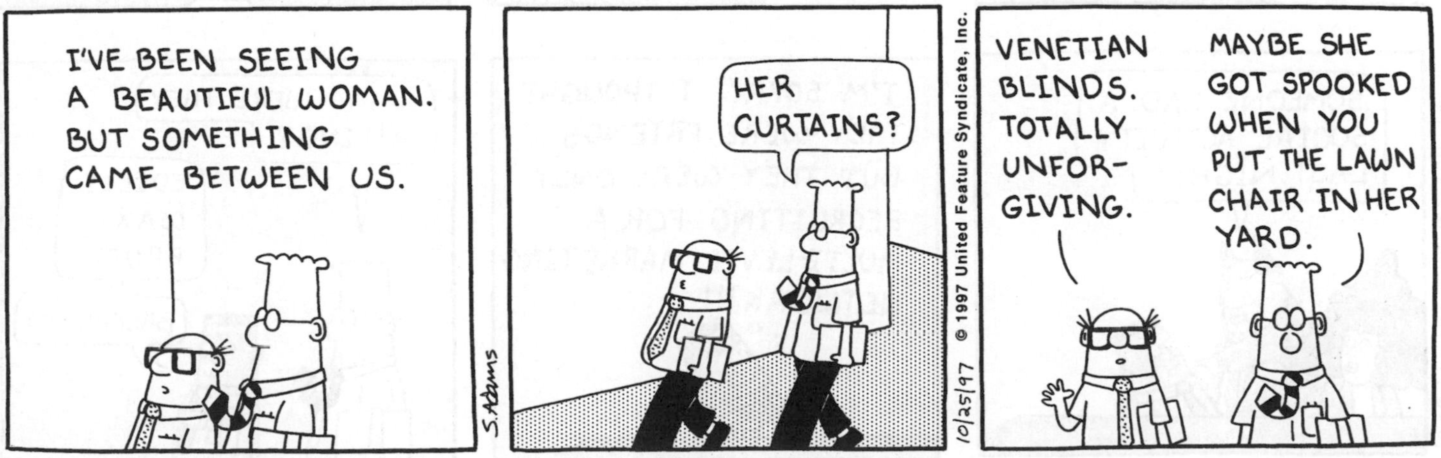
I'VE BEEN SEEING A BEAUTIFUL WOMAN. BUT SOMETHING CAME BETWEEN US.
HER CURTAINS?
VENETIAN BLINDS. TOTALLY UNFORGIVING.
MAYBE SHE GOT SPOOKED WHEN YOU PUT THE LAWN CHAIR IN HER YARD.
S. Adams
10/25/97
© 1997 United Feature Syndicate, Inc.

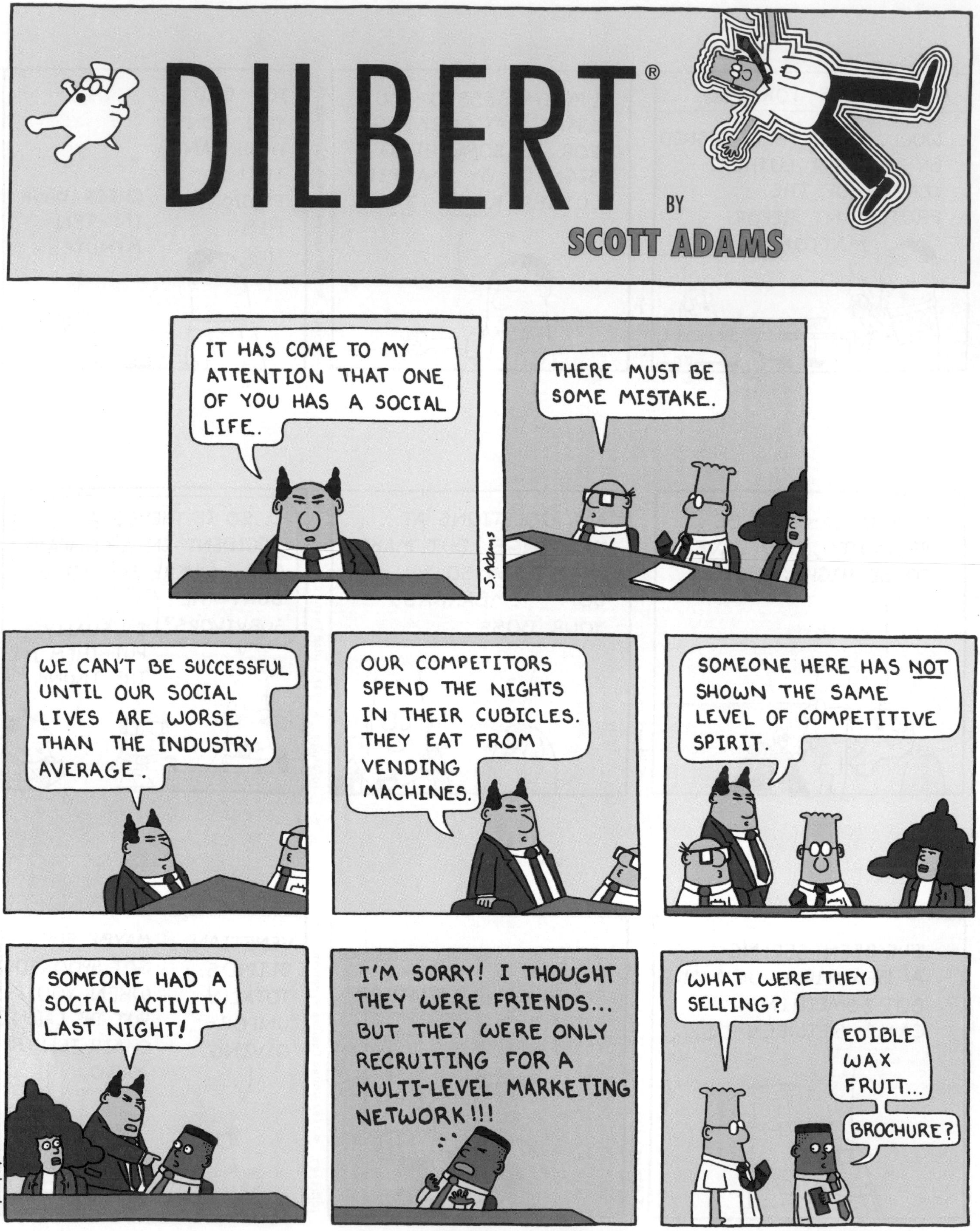
DILBERT®
BY SCOTT ADAMS
IT HAS COME TO MY ATTENTION THAT ONE OF YOU HAS A SOCIAL LIFE.
THERE MUST BE SOME MISTAKE.
S. Adams
WE CAN'T BE SUCCESSFUL UNTIL OUR SOCIAL LIVES ARE WORSE THAN THE INDUSTRY AVERAGE.
OUR COMPETITORS SPEND THE NIGHTS IN THEIR CUBICLES. THEY EAT FROM VENDING MACHINES.
SOMEONE HERE HAS NOT SHOWN THE SAME LEVEL OF COMPETITIVE SPIRIT.
SOMEONE HAD A SOCIAL ACTIVITY LAST NIGHT!
I'M SORRY! I THOUGHT THEY WERE FRIENDS... BUT THEY WERE ONLY RECRUITING FOR A MULTI-LEVEL MARKETING NETWORK!!!
WHAT WERE THEY SELLING?
EDIBLE WAX FRUIT...
BROCHURE?
10/26/97 © 1997 United Feature Syndicate, Inc.

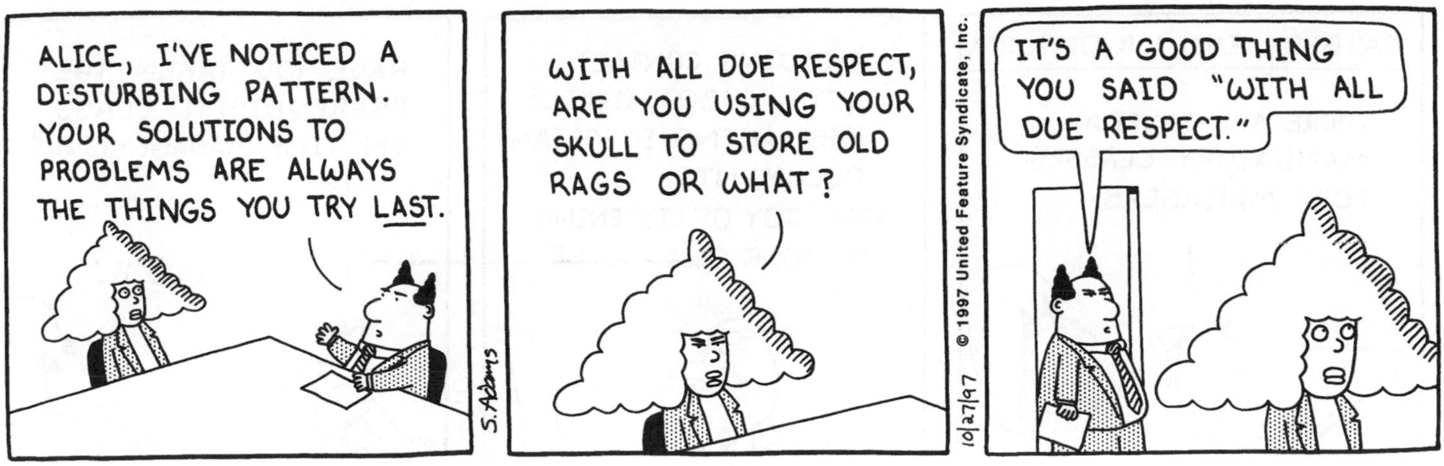
ALICE, I'VE NOTICED A DISTURBING PATTERN. YOUR SOLUTIONS TO PROBLEMS ARE ALWAYS THE THINGS YOU TRY LAST.
WITH ALL DUE RESPECT, ARE YOU USING YOUR SKULL TO STORE OLD RAGS OR WHAT?
IT'S A GOOD THING YOU SAID "WITH ALL DUE RESPECT."
S. Adams
10/27/97 © 1997 United Feature Syndicate, Inc.

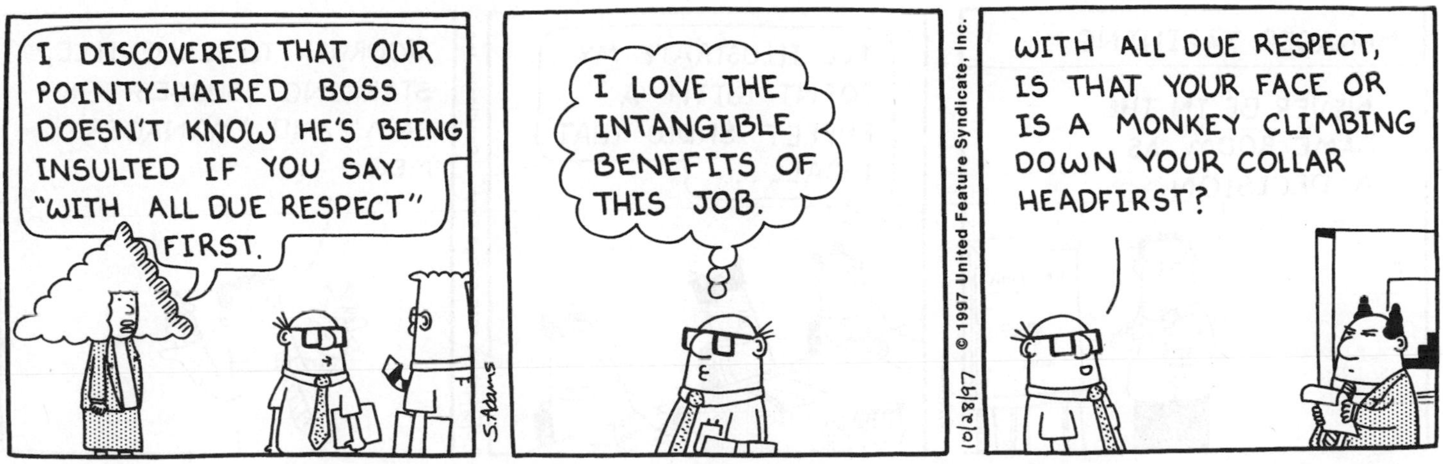
I DISCOVERED THAT OUR POINTY-HAIRED BOSS DOESN'T KNOW HE'S BEING INSULTED IF YOU SAY "WITH ALL DUE RESPECT" FIRST.
I LOVE THE INTANGIBLE BENEFITS OF THIS JOB.
WITH ALL DUE RESPECT, IS THAT YOUR FACE OR IS A MONKEY CLIMBING DOWN YOUR COLLAR HEADFIRST?
S. Adams
10/28/97 © 1997 United Feature Syndicate, Inc.

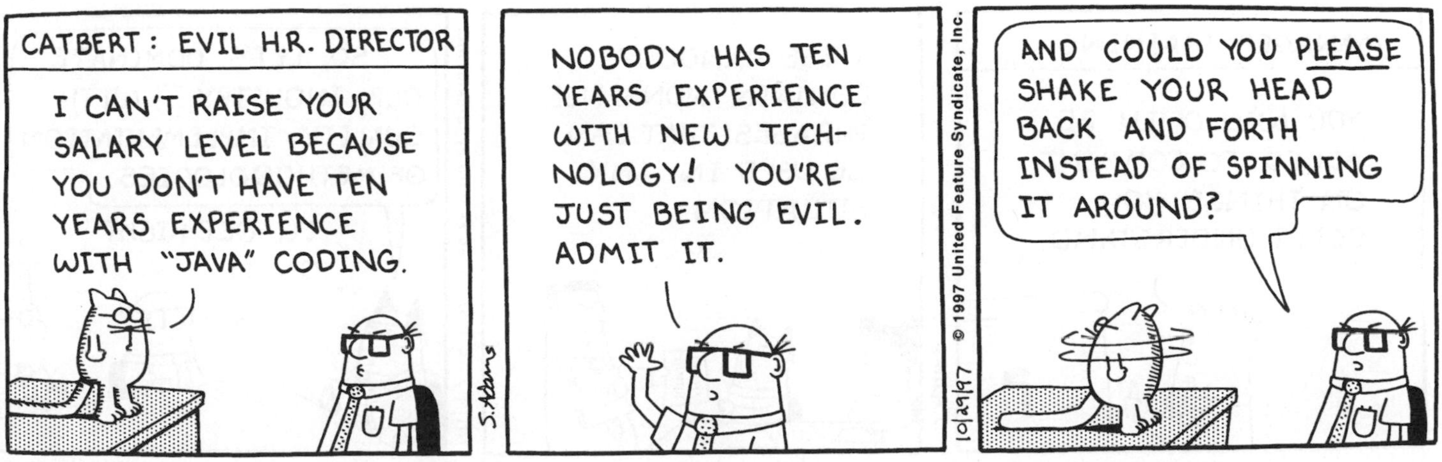
CATBERT: EVIL H.R. DIRECTOR
I CAN'T RAISE YOUR SALARY LEVEL BECAUSE YOU DON'T HAVE TEN YEARS EXPERIENCE WITH "JAVA" CODING.
NOBODY HAS TEN YEARS EXPERIENCE WITH NEW TECHNOLOGY! YOU'RE JUST BEING EVIL. ADMIT IT.
AND COULD YOU PLEASE SHAKE YOUR HEAD BACK AND FORTH INSTEAD OF SPINNING IT AROUND?
S. Adams
10/29/97 © 1997 United Feature Syndicate, Inc.

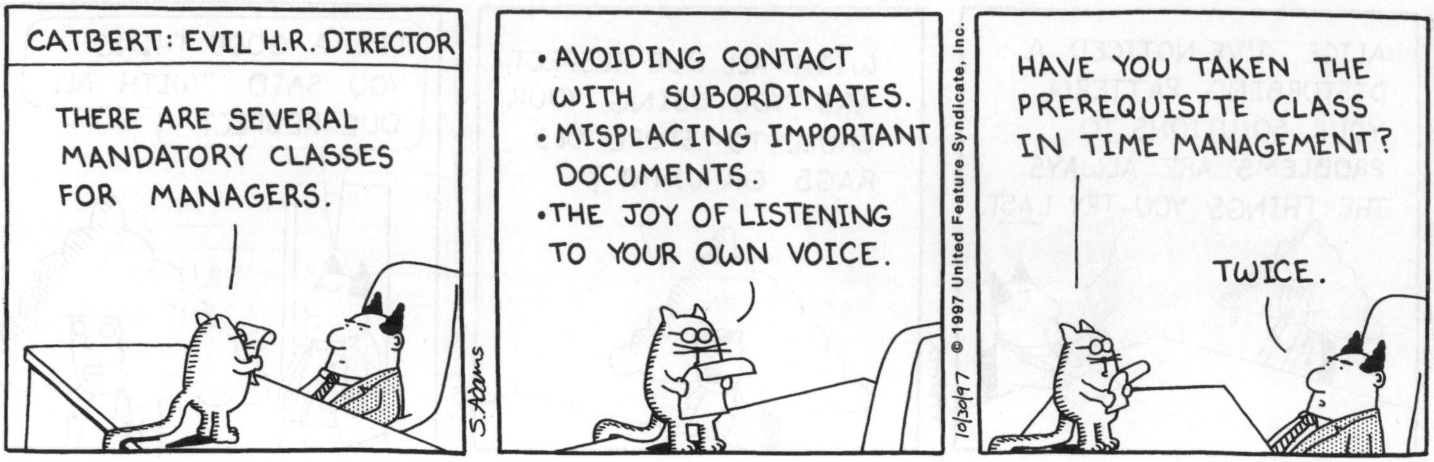
CATBERT: EVIL H.R. DIRECTOR
THERE ARE SEVERAL MANDATORY CLASSES FOR MANAGERS.
• AVOIDING CONTACT WITH SUBORDINATES.
• MISPLACING IMPORTANT DOCUMENTS.
• THE JOY OF LISTENING TO YOUR OWN VOICE.
10/30/97 © 1997 United Feature Syndicate, Inc.
HAVE YOU TAKEN THE PREREQUISITE CLASS IN TIME MANAGEMENT?
TWICE.

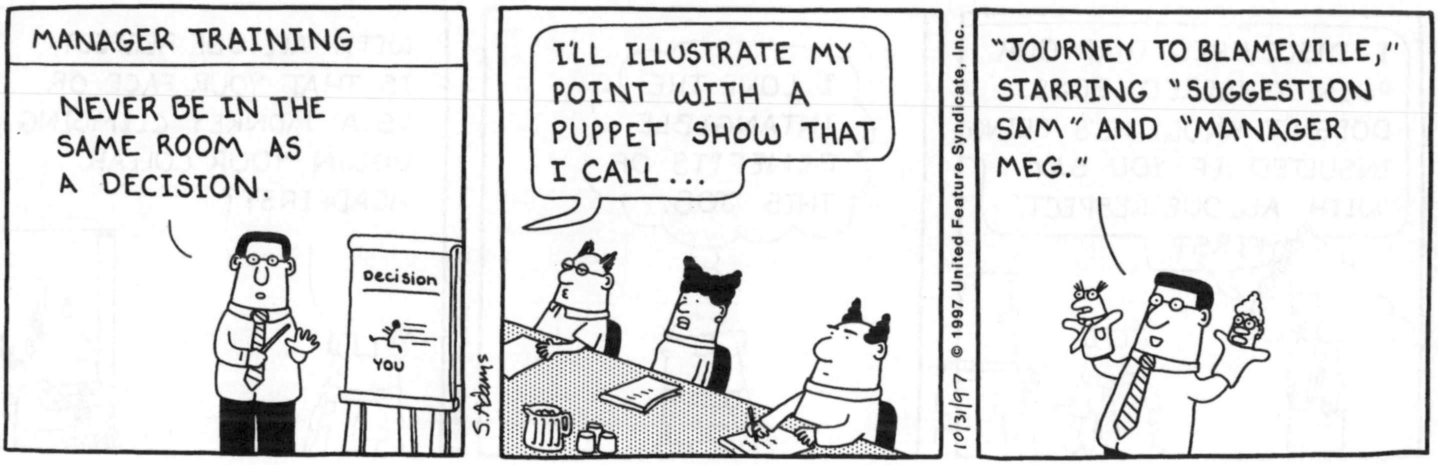
MANAGER TRAINING
NEVER BE IN THE SAME ROOM AS A DECISION.
Decision
YOU
I'LL ILLUSTRATE MY POINT WITH A PUPPET SHOW THAT I CALL...
10/31/97 © 1997 United Feature Syndicate, Inc.
"JOURNEY TO BLAMEVILLE," STARRING "SUGGESTION SAM" AND "MANAGER MEG."

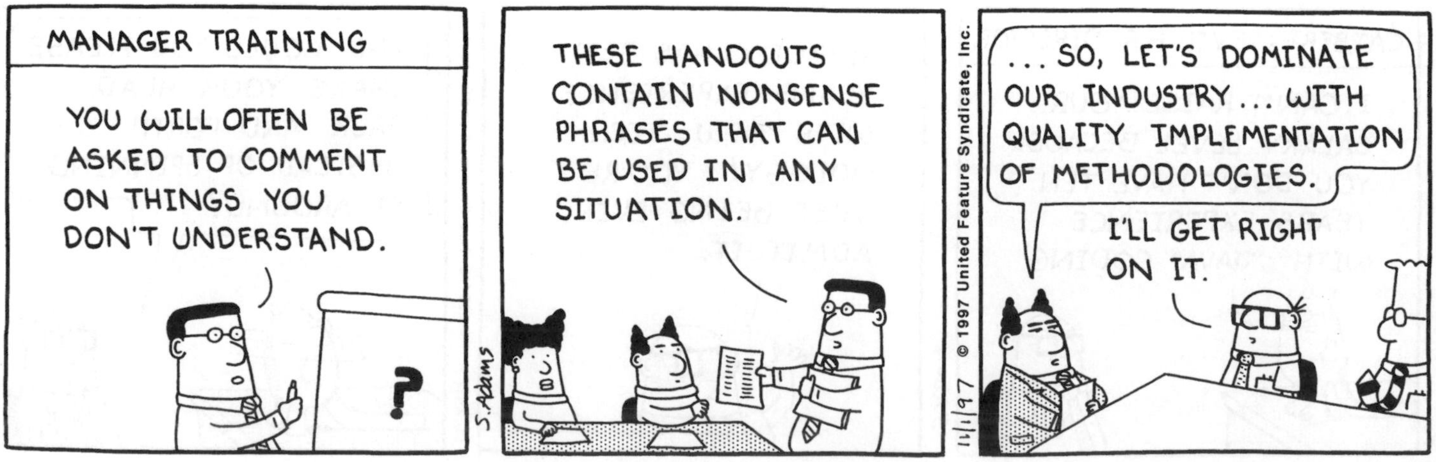
MANAGER TRAINING
YOU WILL OFTEN BE ASKED TO COMMENT ON THINGS YOU DON'T UNDERSTAND.
?
THESE HANDOUTS CONTAIN NONSENSE PHRASES THAT CAN BE USED IN ANY SITUATION.
11/1/97 © 1997 United Feature Syndicate, Inc.
... SO, LET'S DOMINATE OUR INDUSTRY ... WITH QUALITY IMPLEMENTATION OF METHODOLOGIES.
I'LL GET RIGHT ON IT.

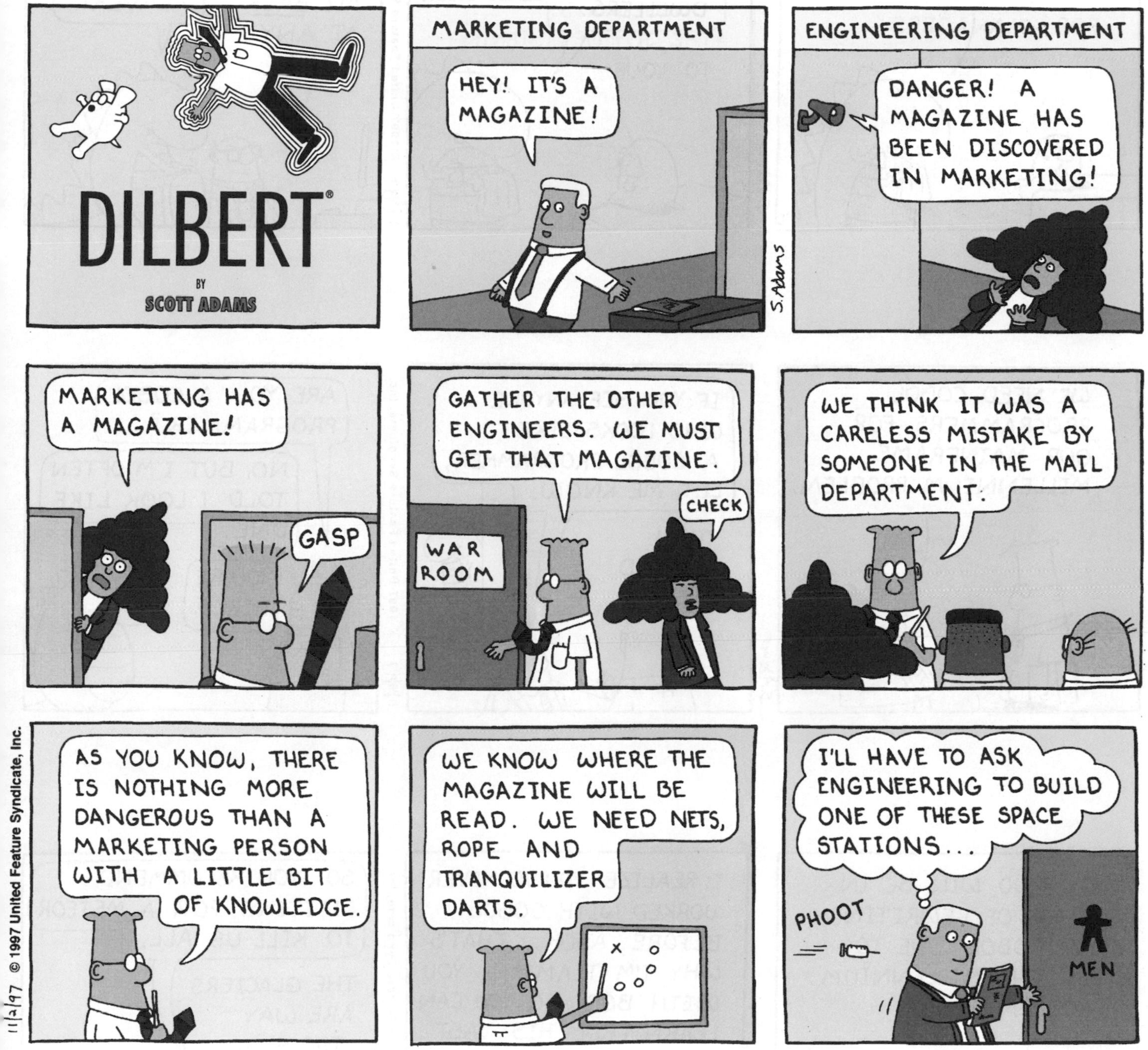
DILBERT
BY
SCOTT ADAMS
MARKETING DEPARTMENT
HEY! IT'S A MAGAZINE!
S. Adams
ENGINEERING DEPARTMENT
DANGER! A MAGAZINE HAS BEEN DISCOVERED IN MARKETING!
MARKETING HAS A MAGAZINE!
GASP
GATHER THE OTHER ENGINEERS. WE MUST GET THAT MAGAZINE.
WAR ROOM
CHECK
WE THINK IT WAS A CARELESS MISTAKE BY SOMEONE IN THE MAIL DEPARTMENT.
AS YOU KNOW, THERE IS NOTHING MORE DANGEROUS THAN A MARKETING PERSON WITH A LITTLE BIT OF KNOWLEDGE.
WE KNOW WHERE THE MAGAZINE WILL BE READ. WE NEED NETS, ROPE AND TRANQUILIZER DARTS.
I'LL HAVE TO ASK ENGINEERING TO BUILD ONE OF THESE SPACE STATIONS...
PHOOT
MEN
11/2/97 © 1997 United Feature Syndicate, Inc.

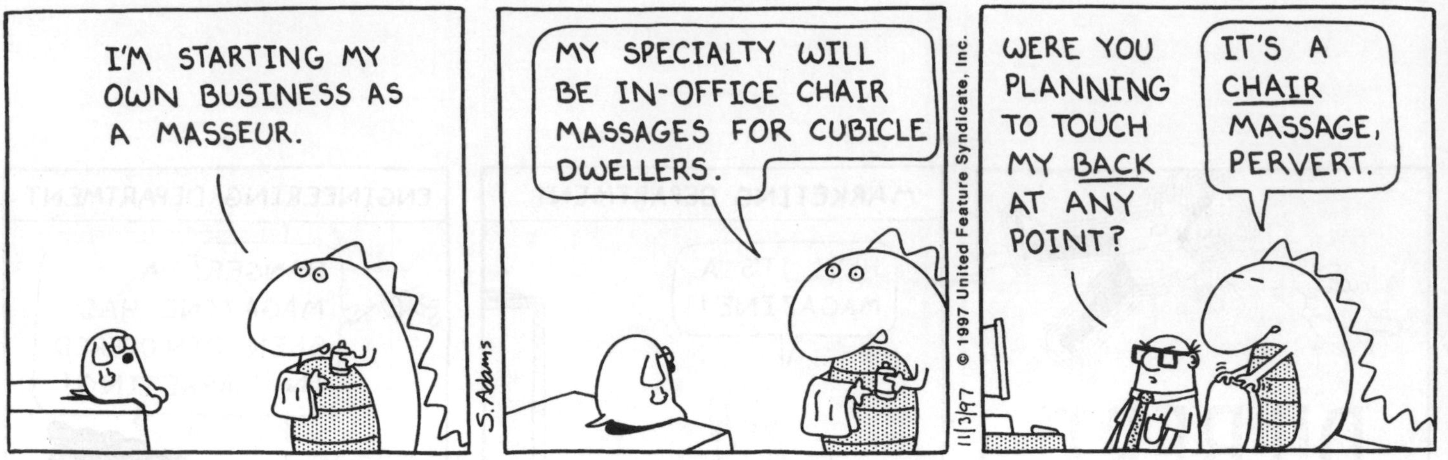
I'M STARTING MY OWN BUSINESS AS A MASSEUR.
S. Adams
MY SPECIALTY WILL BE IN-OFFICE CHAIR MASSAGES FOR CUBICLE DWELLERS.
11/3/97 © 1997 United Feature Syndicate, Inc.
WERE YOU PLANNING TO TOUCH MY BACK AT ANY POINT?
IT'S A CHAIR MASSAGE, PERVERT.

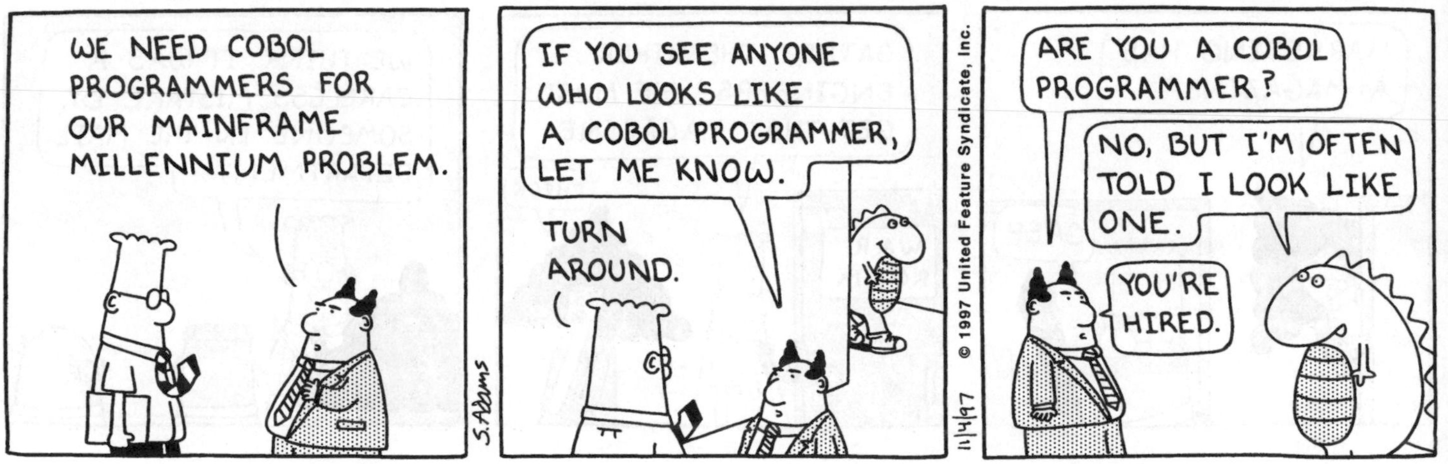
WE NEED COBOL PROGRAMMERS FOR OUR MAINFRAME MILLENNIUM PROBLEM.
S. Adams
IF YOU SEE ANYONE WHO LOOKS LIKE A COBOL PROGRAMMER, LET ME KNOW.
TURN AROUND.
11/4/97 © 1997 United Feature Syndicate, Inc.
ARE YOU A COBOL PROGRAMMER?
NO, BUT I'M OFTEN TOLD I LOOK LIKE ONE.
YOU'RE HIRED.

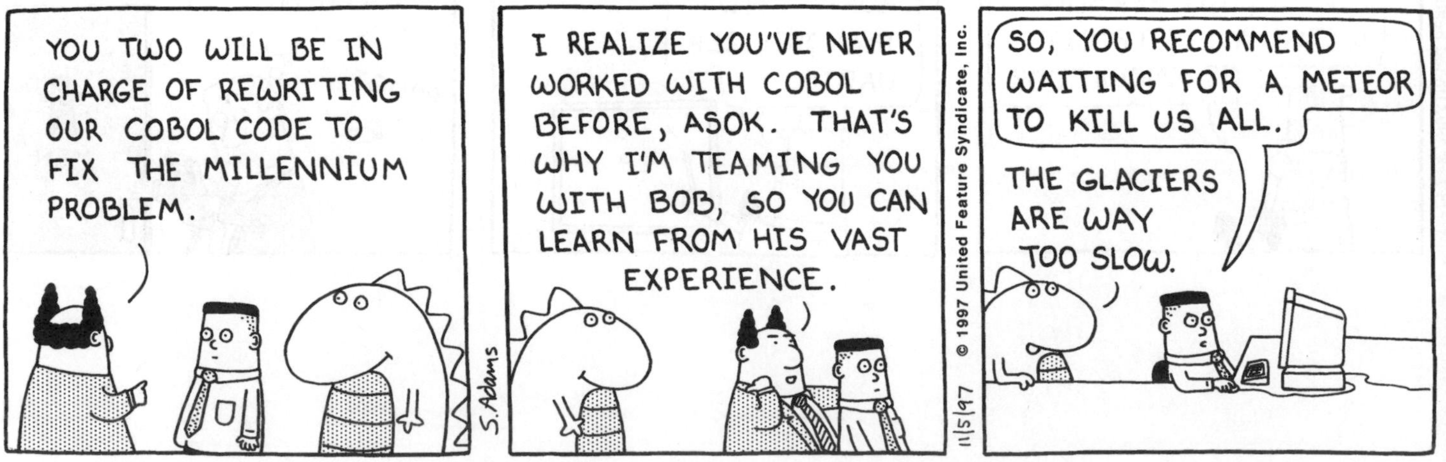
YOU TWO WILL BE IN CHARGE OF REWRITING OUR COBOL CODE TO FIX THE MILLENNIUM PROBLEM.
S. Adams
I REALIZE YOU'VE NEVER WORKED WITH COBOL BEFORE, ASOK. THAT'S WHY I'M TEAMING YOU WITH BOB, SO YOU CAN LEARN FROM HIS VAST EXPERIENCE.
11/5/97 © 1997 United Feature Syndicate, Inc.
SO, YOU RECOMMEND WAITING FOR A METEOR TO KILL US ALL.
THE GLACIERS ARE WAY TOO SLOW.

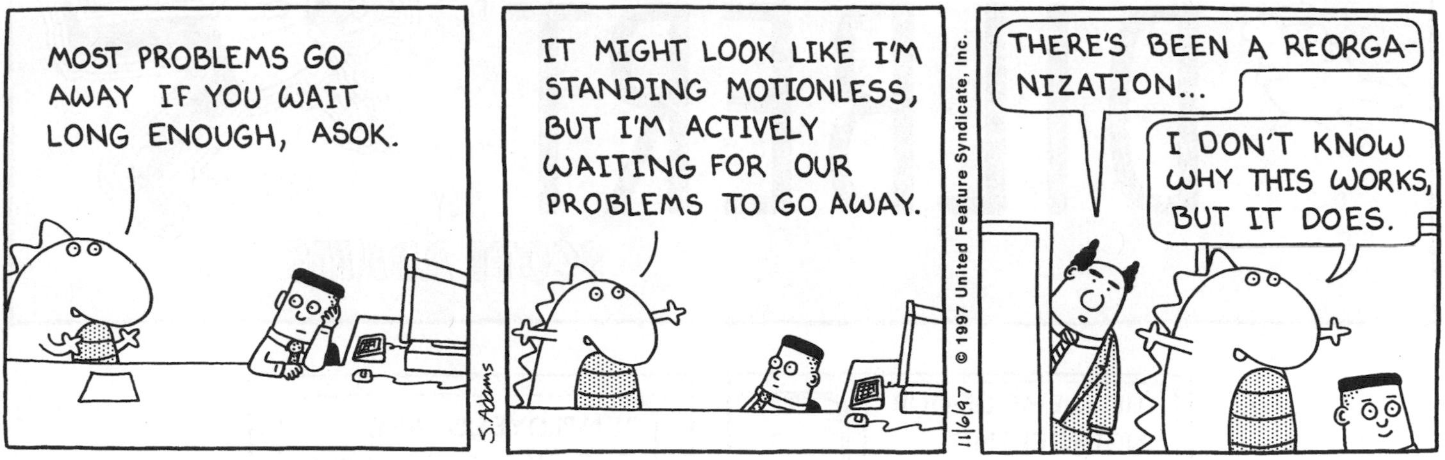
MOST PROBLEMS GO AWAY IF YOU WAIT LONG ENOUGH, ASOK.
S. Adams
IT MIGHT LOOK LIKE I'M STANDING MOTIONLESS, BUT I'M ACTIVELY WAITING FOR OUR PROBLEMS TO GO AWAY.
11/6/97 © 1997 United Feature Syndicate, Inc.
THERE'S BEEN A REORGANIZATION...
I DON'T KNOW WHY THIS WORKS, BUT IT DOES.

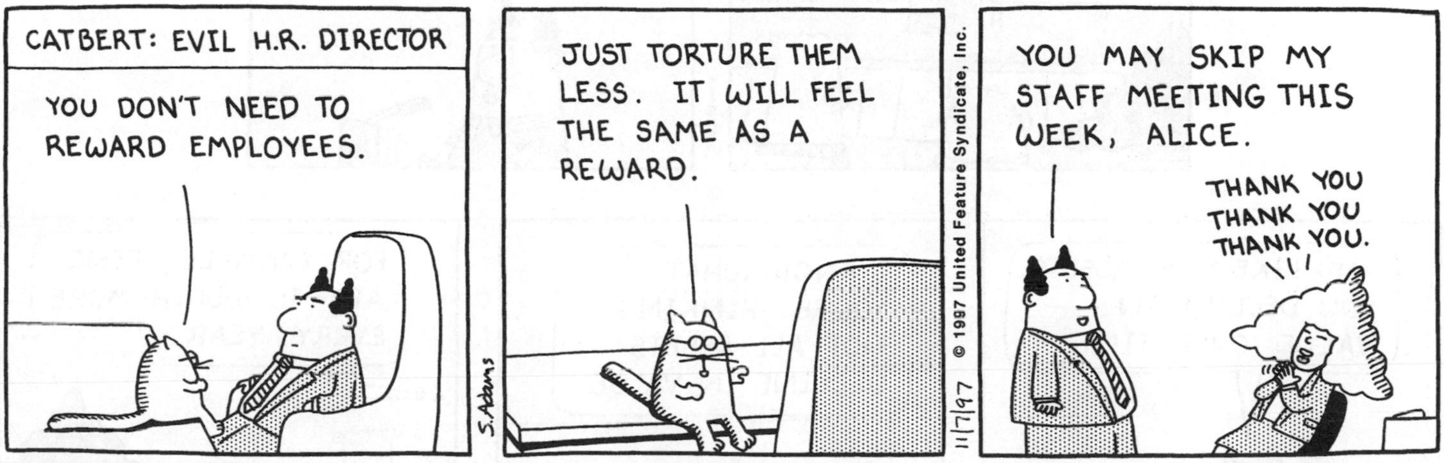
CATBERT: EVIL H.R. DIRECTOR
YOU DON'T NEED TO REWARD EMPLOYEES.
S. Adams
JUST TORTURE THEM LESS. IT WILL FEEL THE SAME AS A REWARD.
11/7/97 © 1997 United Feature Syndicate, Inc.
YOU MAY SKIP MY STAFF MEETING THIS WEEK, ALICE.
THANK YOU THANK YOU THANK YOU.

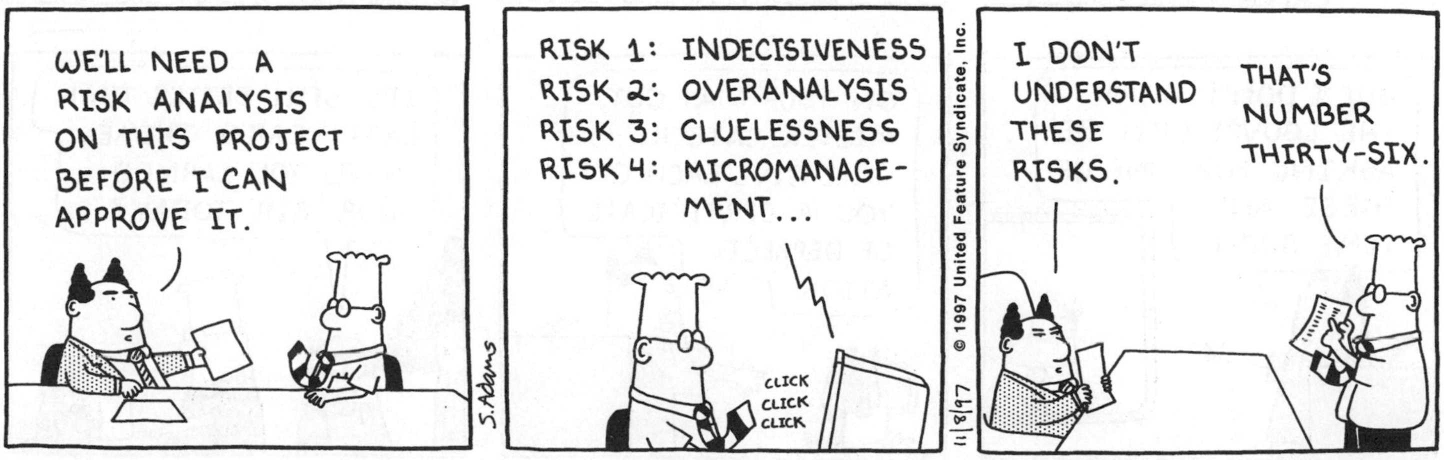
WE'LL NEED A RISK ANALYSIS ON THIS PROJECT BEFORE I CAN APPROVE IT.
S. Adams
RISK 1: INDECISIVENESS
RISK 2: OVERANALYSIS
RISK 3: CLUELESSNESS
RISK 4: MICROMANAGEMENT...
CLICK CLICK CLICK
11/8/97 © 1997 United Feature Syndicate, Inc.
I DON'T UNDERSTAND THESE RISKS.
THAT'S NUMBER THIRTY-SIX.

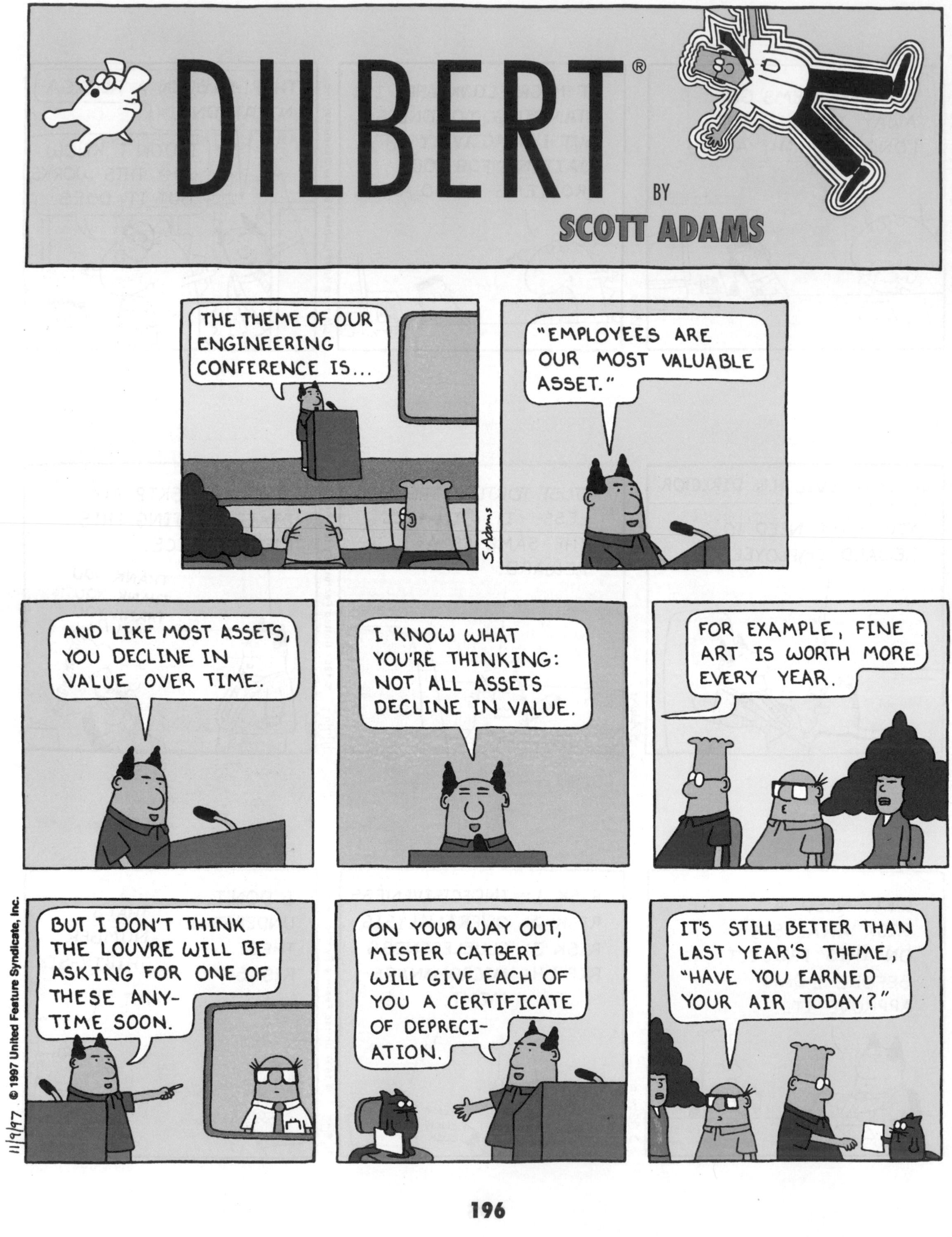
DILBERT®
BY
SCOTT ADAMS
THE THEME OF OUR ENGINEERING CONFERENCE IS...
S. Adams
"EMPLOYEES ARE OUR MOST VALUABLE ASSET."
AND LIKE MOST ASSETS, YOU DECLINE IN VALUE OVER TIME.
I KNOW WHAT YOU'RE THINKING: NOT ALL ASSETS DECLINE IN VALUE.
FOR EXAMPLE, FINE ART IS WORTH MORE EVERY YEAR.
BUT I DON'T THINK THE LOUVRE WILL BE ASKING FOR ONE OF THESE ANY-TIME SOON.
ON YOUR WAY OUT, MISTER CATBERT WILL GIVE EACH OF YOU A CERTIFICATE OF DEPRECI-ATION.
IT'S STILL BETTER THAN LAST YEAR'S THEME, "HAVE YOU EARNED YOUR AIR TODAY?"
11/9/97 © 1997 United Feature Syndicate, Inc.

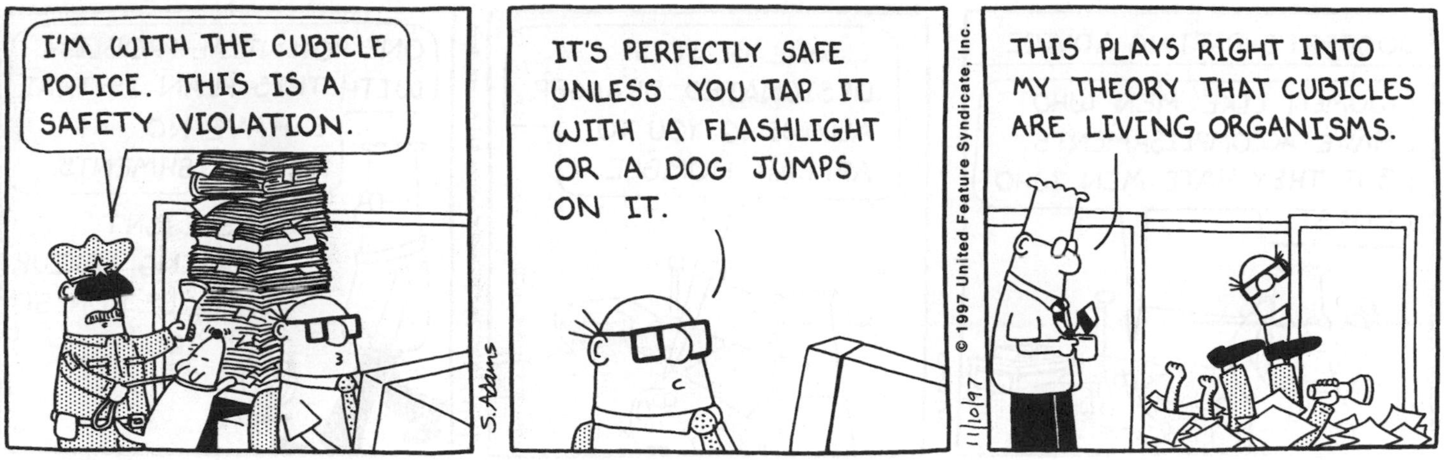
I'M WITH THE CUBICLE POLICE. THIS IS A SAFETY VIOLATION.
S. Adams
IT'S PERFECTLY SAFE UNLESS YOU TAP IT WITH A FLASHLIGHT OR A DOG JUMPS ON IT.
11/10/97
© 1997 United Feature Syndicate, Inc.
THIS PLAYS RIGHT INTO MY THEORY THAT CUBICLES ARE LIVING ORGANISMS.

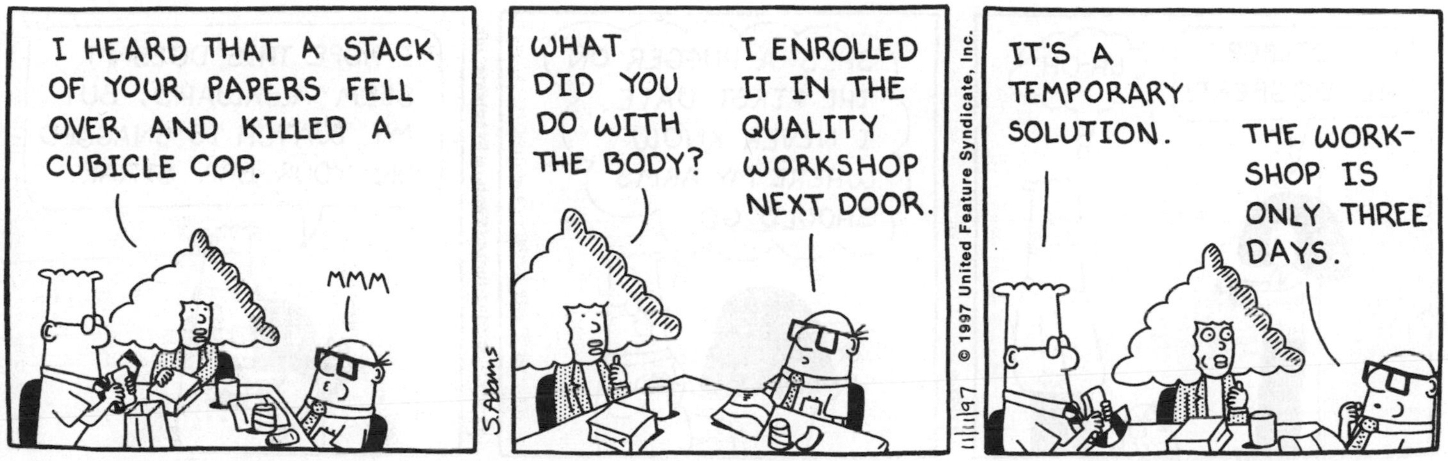
I HEARD THAT A STACK OF YOUR PAPERS FELL OVER AND KILLED A CUBICLE COP.
MMM
S. Adams
WHAT DID YOU DO WITH THE BODY?
I ENROLLED IT IN THE QUALITY WORKSHOP NEXT DOOR.
11/11/97
© 1997 United Feature Syndicate, Inc.
IT'S A TEMPORARY SOLUTION.
THE WORK-SHOP IS ONLY THREE DAYS.

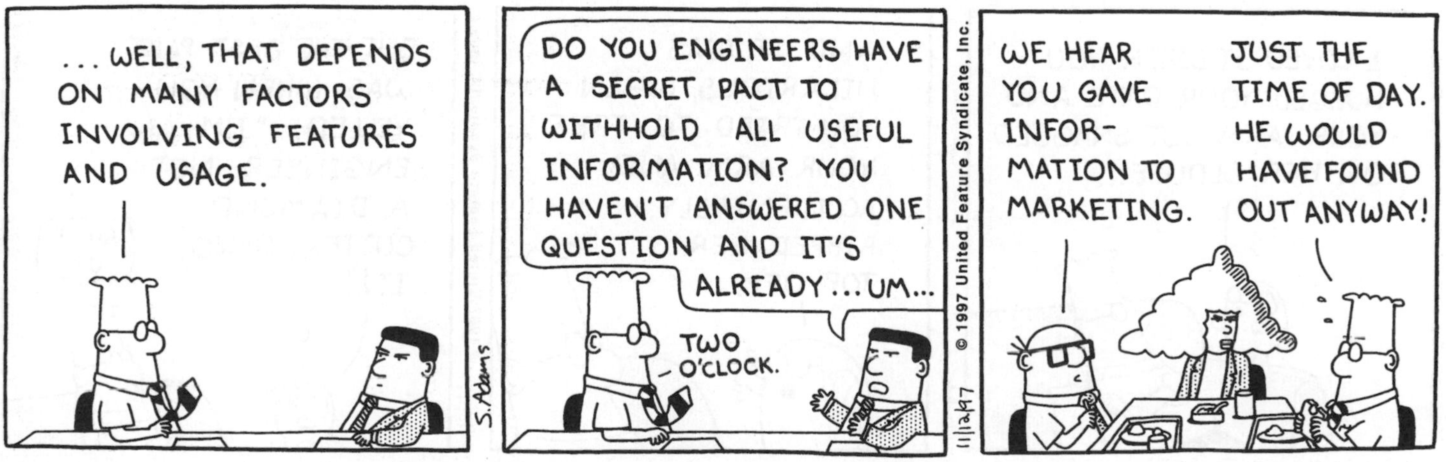
... WELL, THAT DEPENDS ON MANY FACTORS INVOLVING FEATURES AND USAGE.
S. Adams
DO YOU ENGINEERS HAVE A SECRET PACT TO WITHHOLD ALL USEFUL INFORMATION? YOU HAVEN'T ANSWERED ONE QUESTION AND IT'S ALREADY ... UM...
TWO O'CLOCK.
11/12/97
© 1997 United Feature Syndicate, Inc.
WE HEAR YOU GAVE INFOR-MATION TO MARKETING.
JUST THE TIME OF DAY. HE WOULD HAVE FOUND OUT ANYWAY!

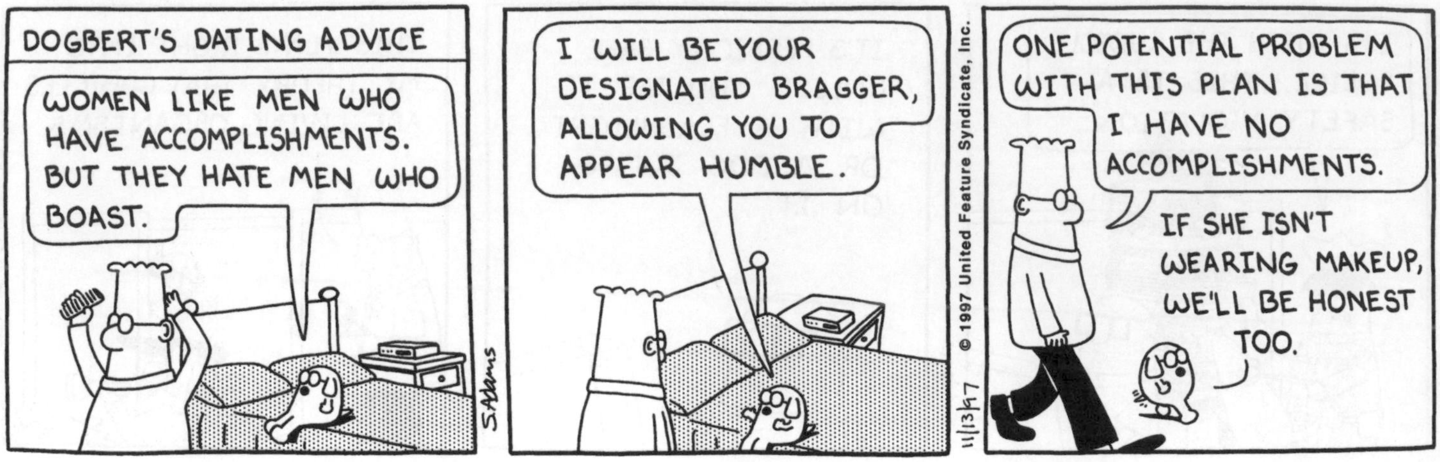
DOGBERT'S DATING ADVICE
WOMEN LIKE MEN WHO HAVE ACCOMPLISHMENTS. BUT THEY HATE MEN WHO BOAST.
I WILL BE YOUR DESIGNATED BRAGGER, ALLOWING YOU TO APPEAR HUMBLE.
ONE POTENTIAL PROBLEM WITH THIS PLAN IS THAT I HAVE NO ACCOMPLISHMENTS.
IF SHE ISN'T WEARING MAKEUP, WE'LL BE HONEST TOO.
S. Adams
11/13/97
© 1997 United Feature Syndicate, Inc.

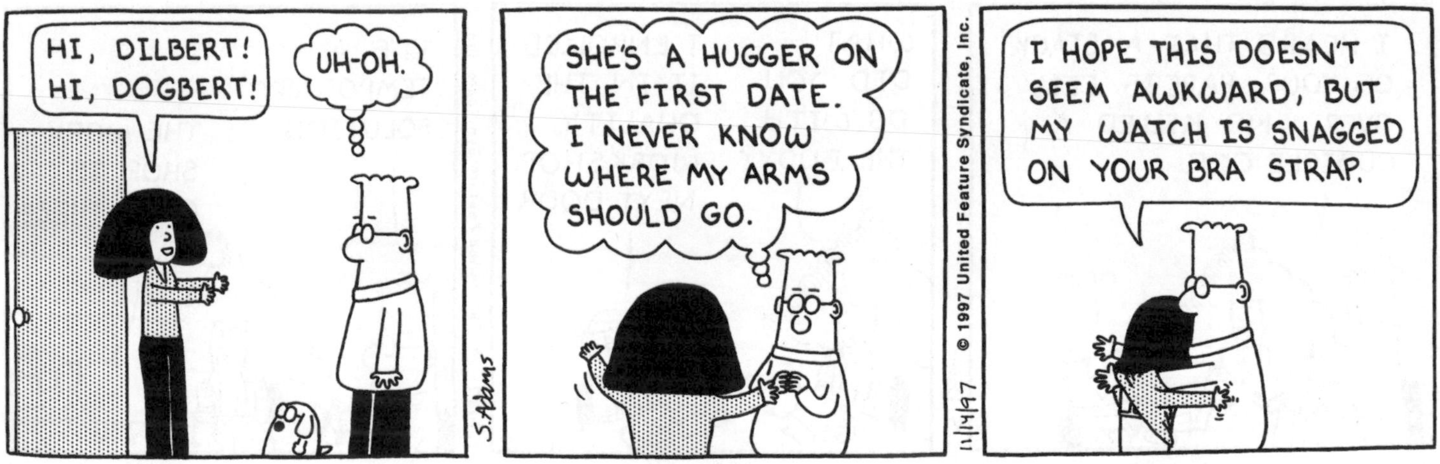
HI, DILBERT! HI, DOGBERT!
UH-OH.
SHE'S A HUGGER ON THE FIRST DATE. I NEVER KNOW WHERE MY ARMS SHOULD GO.
I HOPE THIS DOESN'T SEEM AWKWARD, BUT MY WATCH IS SNAGGED ON YOUR BRA STRAP.
S. Adams
11/14/97
© 1997 United Feature Syndicate, Inc.

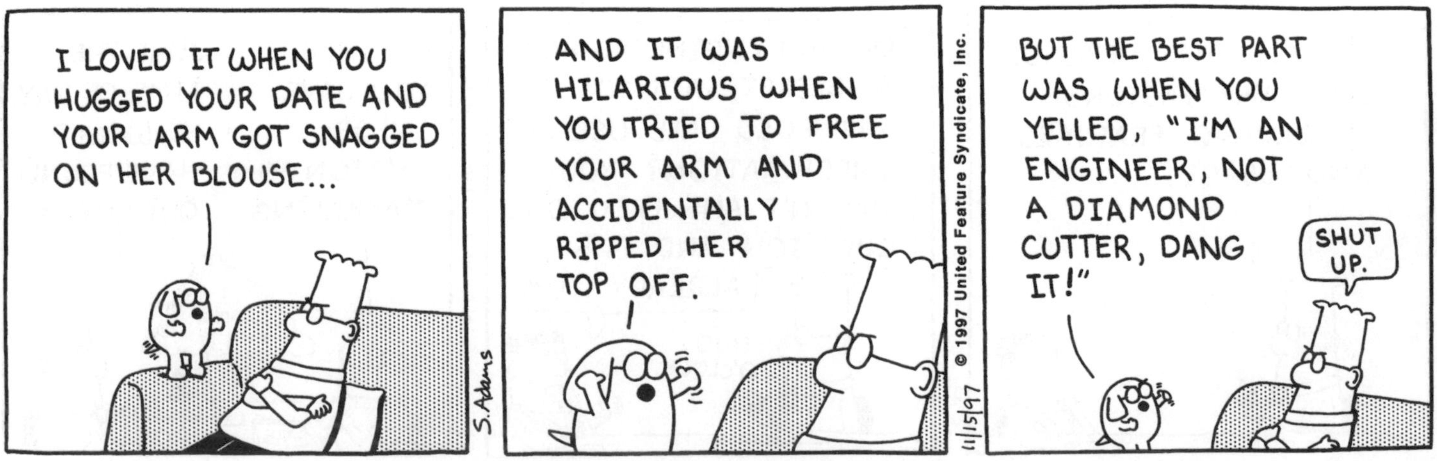
I LOVED IT WHEN YOU HUGGED YOUR DATE AND YOUR ARM GOT SNAGGED ON HER BLOUSE...
AND IT WAS HILARIOUS WHEN YOU TRIED TO FREE YOUR ARM AND ACCIDENTALLY RIPPED HER TOP OFF.
BUT THE BEST PART WAS WHEN YOU YELLED, "I'M AN ENGINEER, NOT A DIAMOND CUTTER, DANG IT!"
SHUT UP.
S. Adams
11/15/97
© 1997 United Feature Syndicate, Inc.

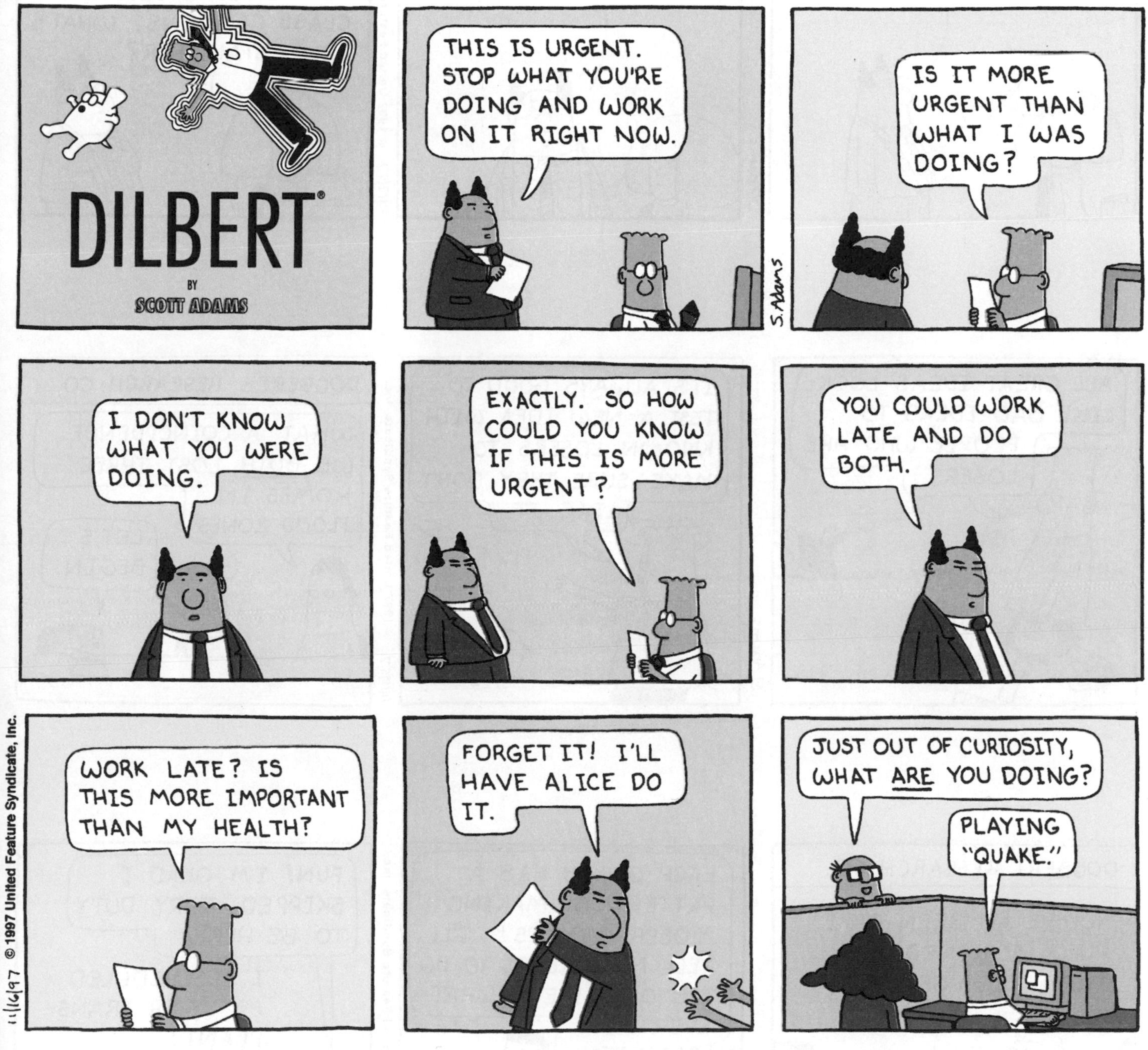
DILBERT®
BY
SCOTT ADAMS
THIS IS URGENT. STOP WHAT YOU'RE DOING AND WORK ON IT RIGHT NOW.
S. Adams
IS IT MORE URGENT THAN WHAT I WAS DOING?
I DON'T KNOW WHAT YOU WERE DOING.
EXACTLY. SO HOW COULD YOU KNOW IF THIS IS MORE URGENT?
YOU COULD WORK LATE AND DO BOTH.
WORK LATE? IS THIS MORE IMPORTANT THAN MY HEALTH?
FORGET IT! I'LL HAVE ALICE DO IT.
JUST OUT OF CURIOSITY, WHAT ARE YOU DOING?
PLAYING "QUAKE."
11/16/97 © 1997 United Feature Syndicate, Inc.

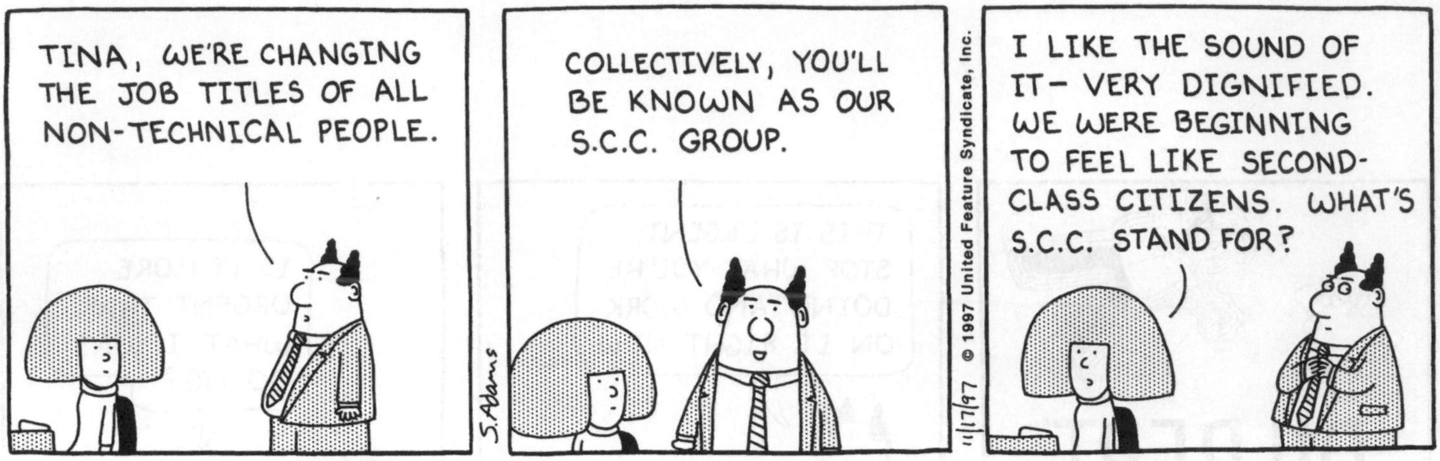
TINA, WE'RE CHANGING THE JOB TITLES OF ALL NON-TECHNICAL PEOPLE.
S. Adams
COLLECTIVELY, YOU'LL BE KNOWN AS OUR S.C.C. GROUP.
11/7/97 © 1997 United Feature Syndicate, Inc.
I LIKE THE SOUND OF IT– VERY DIGNIFIED. WE WERE BEGINNING TO FEEL LIKE SECOND-CLASS CITIZENS. WHAT'S S.C.C. STAND FOR?

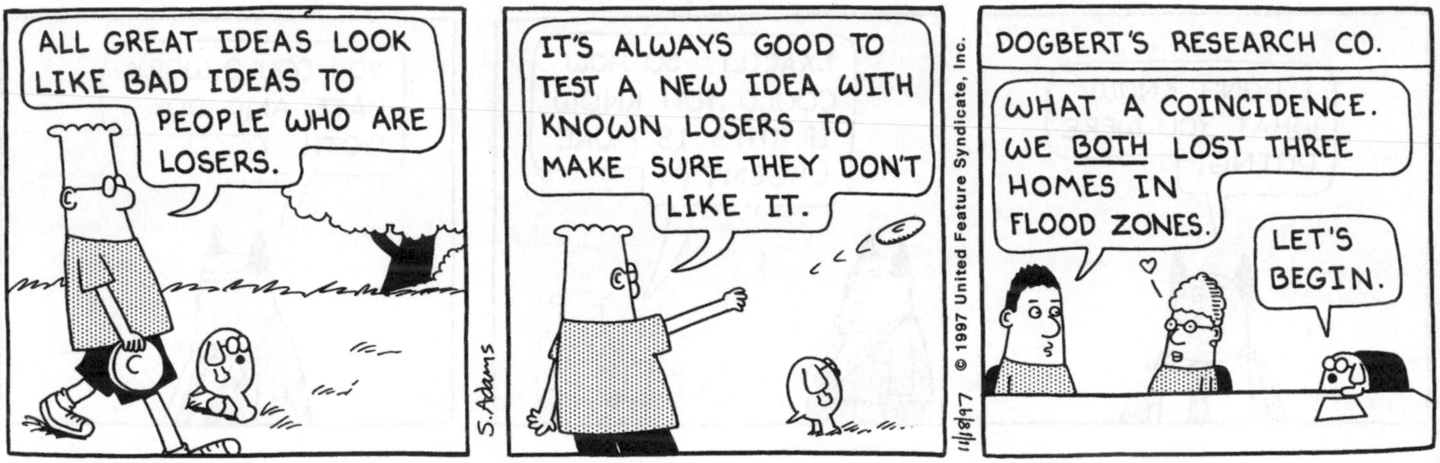
ALL GREAT IDEAS LOOK LIKE BAD IDEAS TO PEOPLE WHO ARE LOSERS.
S. Adams
IT'S ALWAYS GOOD TO TEST A NEW IDEA WITH KNOWN LOSERS TO MAKE SURE THEY DON'T LIKE IT.
11/8/97 © 1997 United Feature Syndicate, Inc.
DOGBERT'S RESEARCH CO.
WHAT A COINCIDENCE. WE BOTH LOST THREE HOMES IN FLOOD ZONES.
LET'S BEGIN.

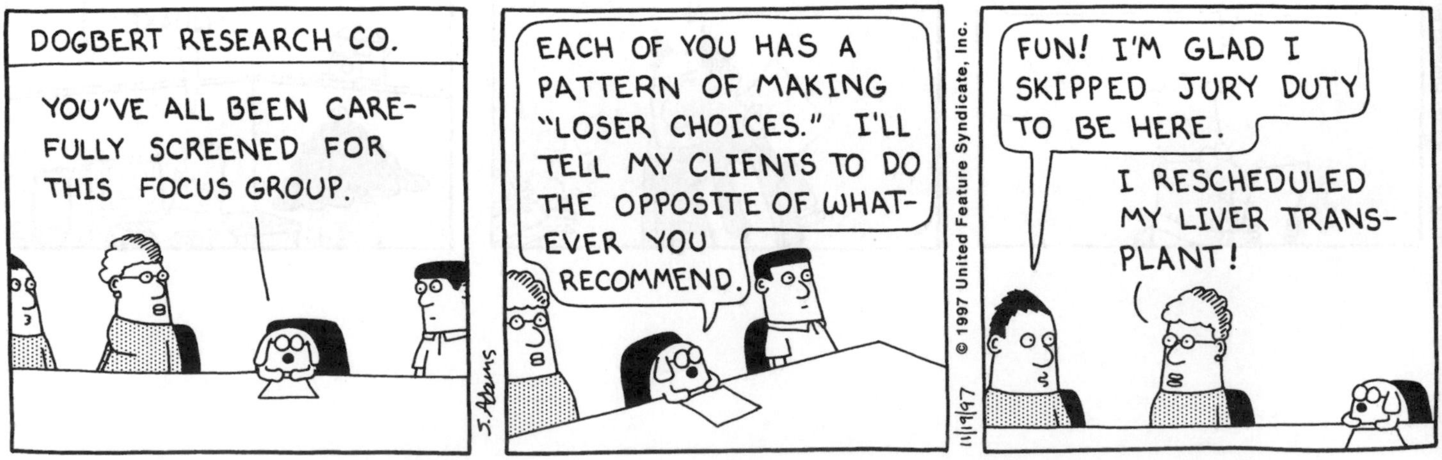
DOGBERT RESEARCH CO.
YOU'VE ALL BEEN CAREFULLY SCREENED FOR THIS FOCUS GROUP.
S. Adams
EACH OF YOU HAS A PATTERN OF MAKING "LOSER CHOICES." I'LL TELL MY CLIENTS TO DO THE OPPOSITE OF WHATEVER YOU RECOMMEND.
11/9/97 © 1997 United Feature Syndicate, Inc.
FUN! I'M GLAD I SKIPPED JURY DUTY TO BE HERE.
I RESCHEDULED MY LIVER TRANSPLANT!

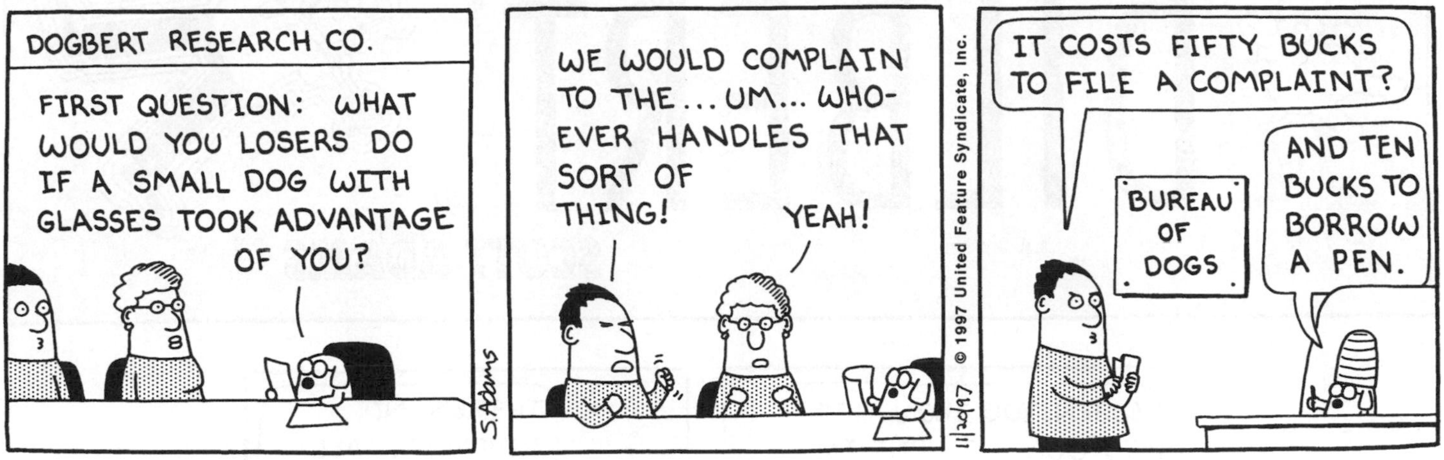
DOGBERT RESEARCH CO.
FIRST QUESTION: WHAT WOULD YOU LOSERS DO IF A SMALL DOG WITH GLASSES TOOK ADVANTAGE OF YOU?
S. Adams
WE WOULD COMPLAIN TO THE... UM... WHO-EVER HANDLES THAT SORT OF THING!
YEAH!
11/20/97 © 1997 United Feature Syndicate, Inc.
IT COSTS FIFTY BUCKS TO FILE A COMPLAINT?
BUREAU OF DOGS
AND TEN BUCKS TO BORROW A PEN.

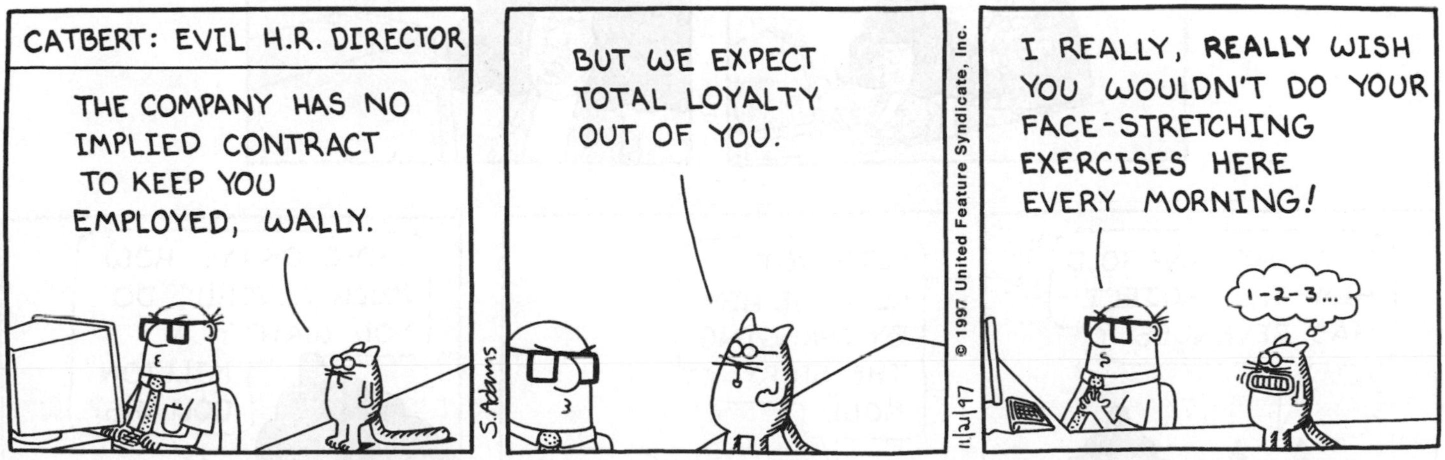
CATBERT: EVIL H.R. DIRECTOR
THE COMPANY HAS NO IMPLIED CONTRACT TO KEEP YOU EMPLOYED, WALLY.
S. Adams
BUT WE EXPECT TOTAL LOYALTY OUT OF YOU.
11/21/97 © 1997 United Feature Syndicate, Inc.
I REALLY, REALLY WISH YOU WOULDN'T DO YOUR FACE-STRETCHING EXERCISES HERE EVERY MORNING!
1-2-3...

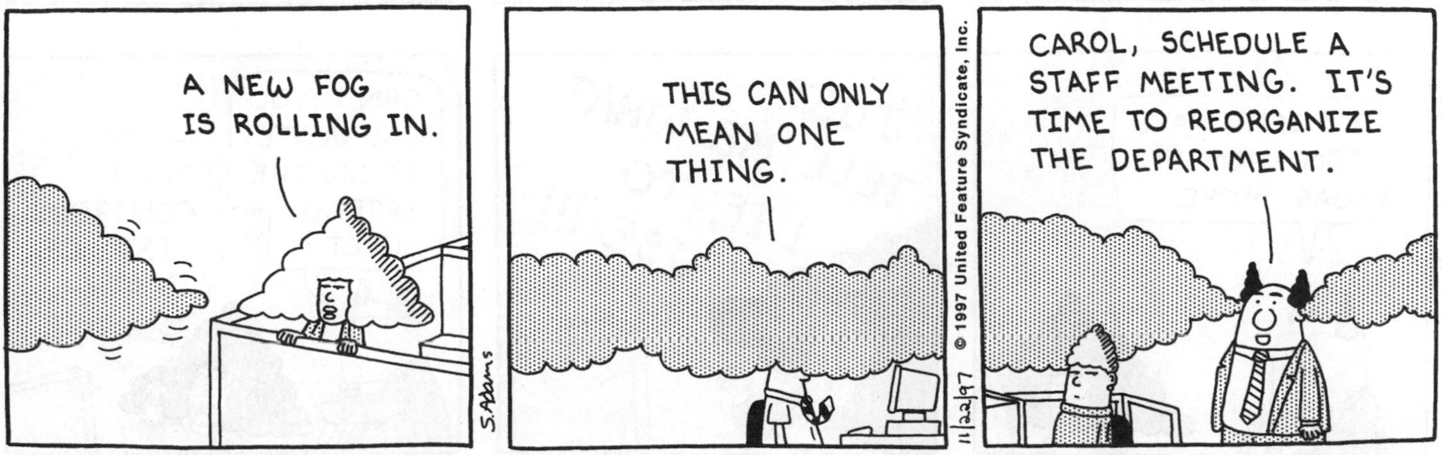
A NEW FOG IS ROLLING IN.
S. Adams
THIS CAN ONLY MEAN ONE THING.
11/22/97 © 1997 United Feature Syndicate, Inc.
CAROL, SCHEDULE A STAFF MEETING. IT'S TIME TO REORGANIZE THE DEPARTMENT.

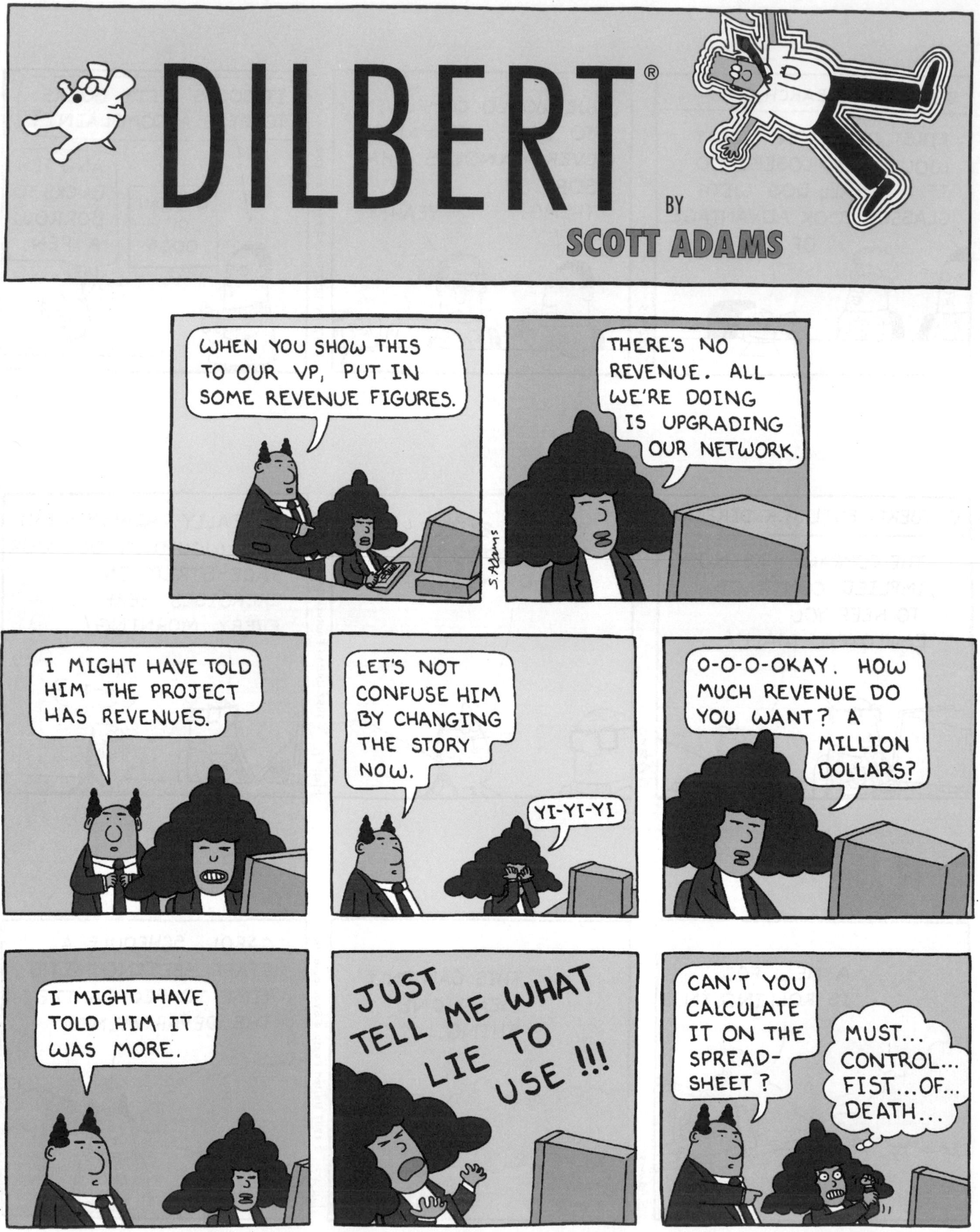
DILBERT®
BY
SCOTT ADAMS
WHEN YOU SHOW THIS TO OUR VP, PUT IN SOME REVENUE FIGURES.
S. Adams
THERE'S NO REVENUE. ALL WE'RE DOING IS UPGRADING OUR NETWORK.
I MIGHT HAVE TOLD HIM THE PROJECT HAS REVENUES.
LET'S NOT CONFUSE HIM BY CHANGING THE STORY NOW.
YI-YI-YI
O-O-O-OKAY. HOW MUCH REVENUE DO YOU WANT? A MILLION DOLLARS?
I MIGHT HAVE TOLD HIM IT WAS MORE.
JUST TELL ME WHAT LIE TO USE !!!
CAN'T YOU CALCULATE IT ON THE SPREAD-SHEET?
MUST... CONTROL... FIST...OF... DEATH...

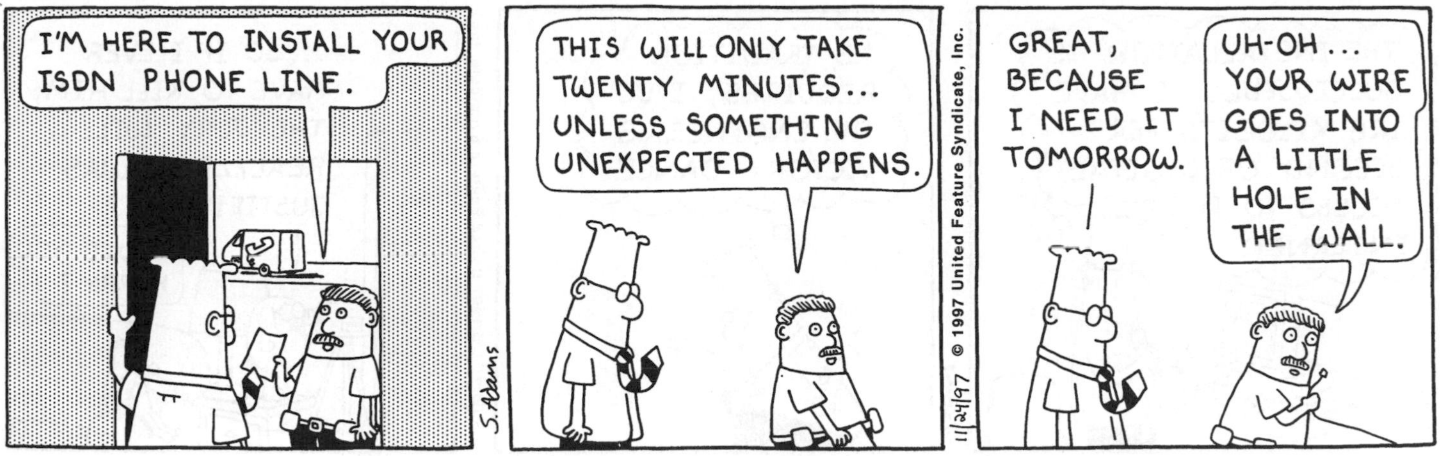
I'M HERE TO INSTALL YOUR ISDN PHONE LINE.
THIS WILL ONLY TAKE TWENTY MINUTES... UNLESS SOMETHING UNEXPECTED HAPPENS.
GREAT, BECAUSE I NEED IT TOMORROW.
UH-OH... YOUR WIRE GOES INTO A LITTLE HOLE IN THE WALL.
© 1997 United Feature Syndicate, Inc.

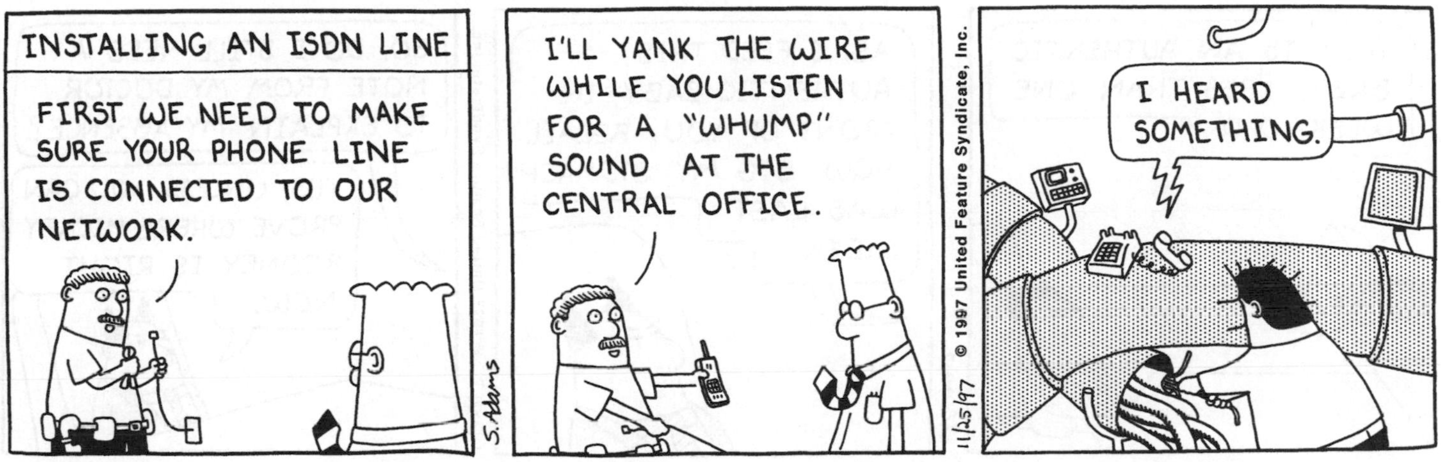
INSTALLING AN ISDN LINE
FIRST WE NEED TO MAKE SURE YOUR PHONE LINE IS CONNECTED TO OUR NETWORK.
I'LL YANK THE WIRE WHILE YOU LISTEN FOR A "WHUMP" SOUND AT THE CENTRAL OFFICE.
I HEARD SOMETHING.
© 1997 United Feature Syndicate, Inc.

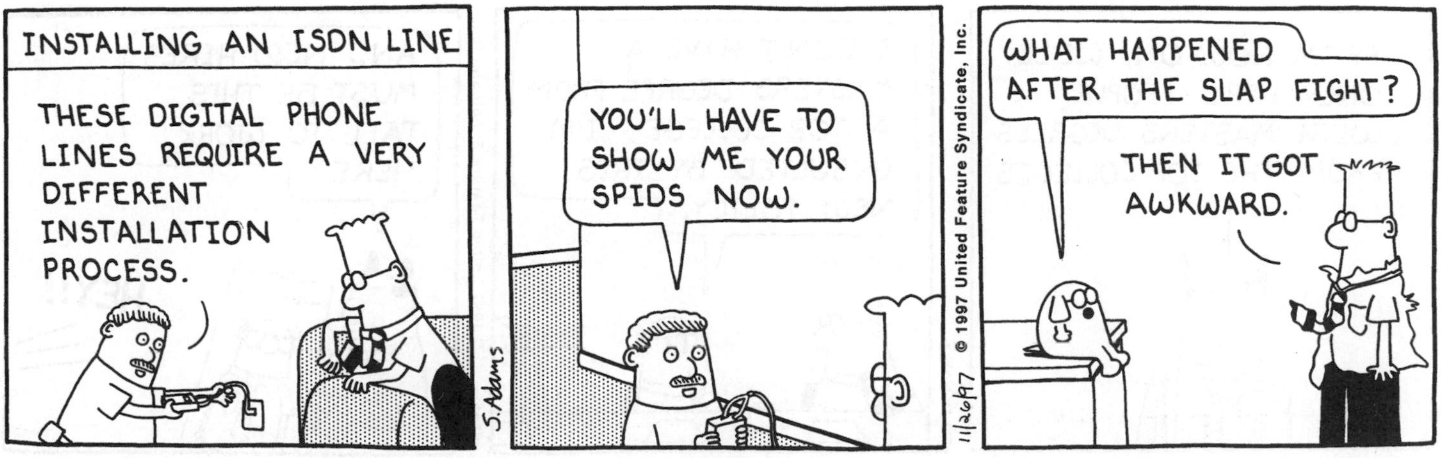
INSTALLING AN ISDN LINE
THESE DIGITAL PHONE LINES REQUIRE A VERY DIFFERENT INSTALLATION PROCESS.
YOU'LL HAVE TO SHOW ME YOUR SPIDS NOW.
WHAT HAPPENED AFTER THE SLAP FIGHT?
THEN IT GOT AWKWARD.
© 1997 United Feature Syndicate, Inc.

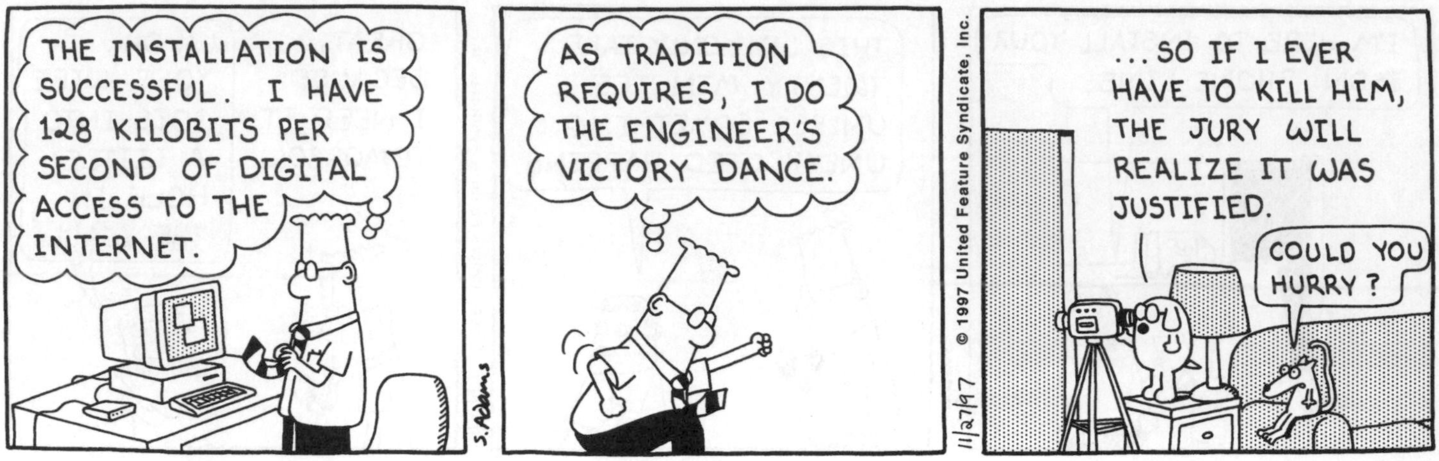
THE INSTALLATION IS SUCCESSFUL. I HAVE 128 KILOBITS PER SECOND OF DIGITAL ACCESS TO THE INTERNET.
AS TRADITION REQUIRES, I DO THE ENGINEER'S VICTORY DANCE.
...SO IF I EVER HAVE TO KILL HIM, THE JURY WILL REALIZE IT WAS JUSTIFIED.
COULD YOU HURRY?
S. Adams
11/27/97
© 1997 United Feature Syndicate, Inc.

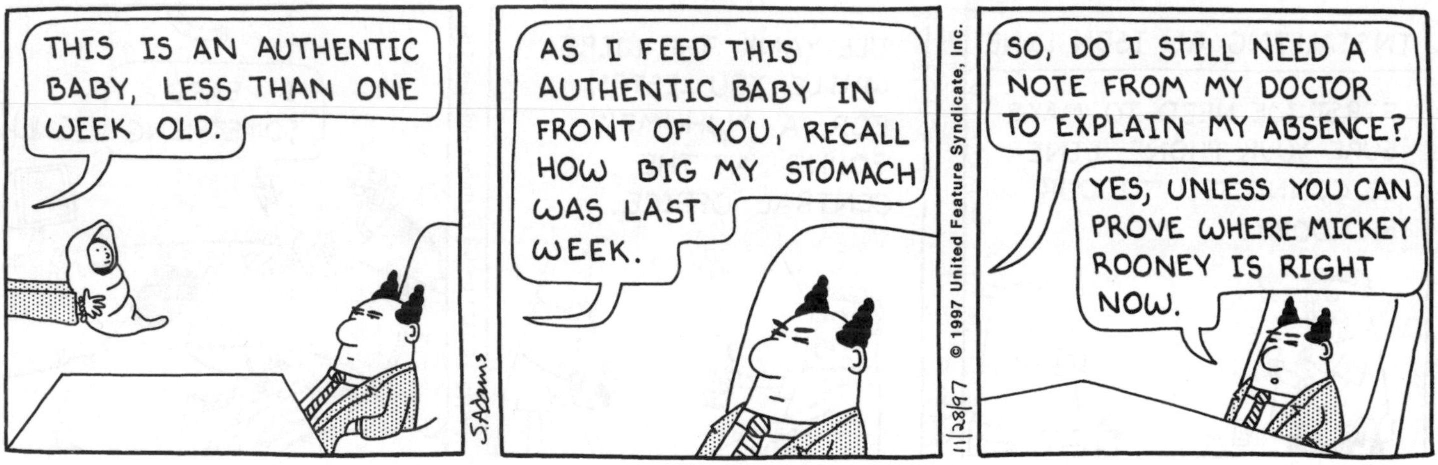
THIS IS AN AUTHENTIC BABY, LESS THAN ONE WEEK OLD.
AS I FEED THIS AUTHENTIC BABY IN FRONT OF YOU, RECALL HOW BIG MY STOMACH WAS LAST WEEK.
SO, DO I STILL NEED A NOTE FROM MY DOCTOR TO EXPLAIN MY ABSENCE?
YES, UNLESS YOU CAN PROVE WHERE MICKEY ROONEY IS RIGHT NOW.
S. Adams
11/28/97
© 1997 United Feature Syndicate, Inc.

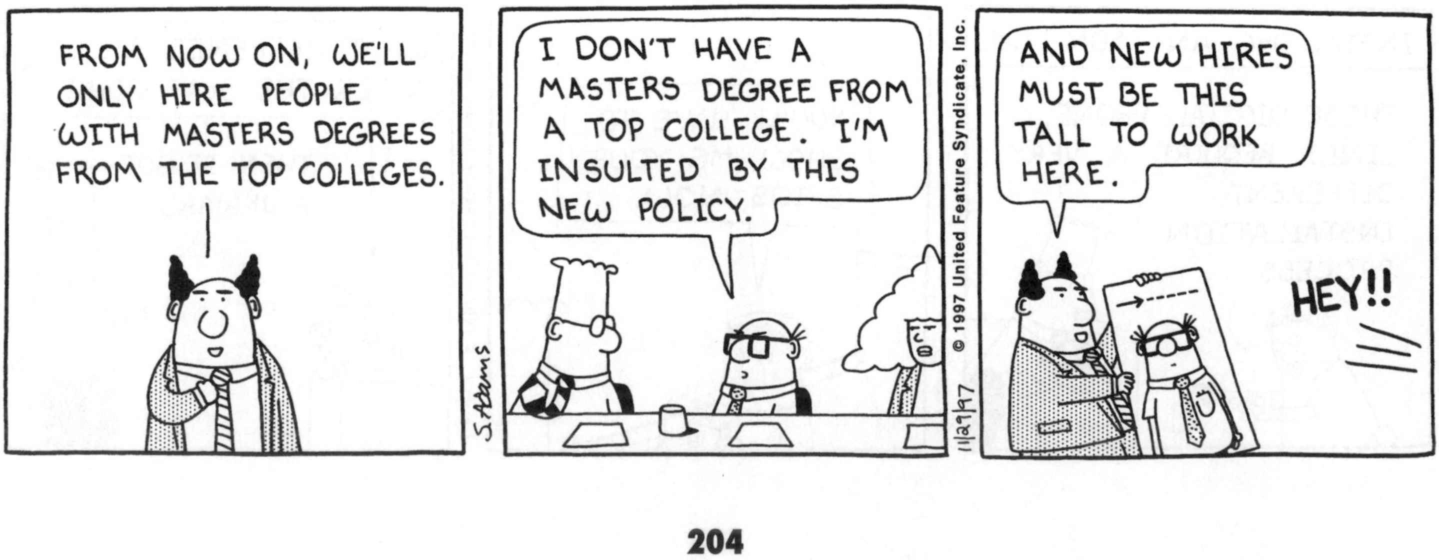
FROM NOW ON, WE'LL ONLY HIRE PEOPLE WITH MASTERS DEGREES FROM THE TOP COLLEGES.
I DON'T HAVE A MASTERS DEGREE FROM A TOP COLLEGE. I'M INSULTED BY THIS NEW POLICY.
AND NEW HIRES MUST BE THIS TALL TO WORK HERE.
HEY!!
S. Adams
11/29/97
© 1997 United Feature Syndicate, Inc.

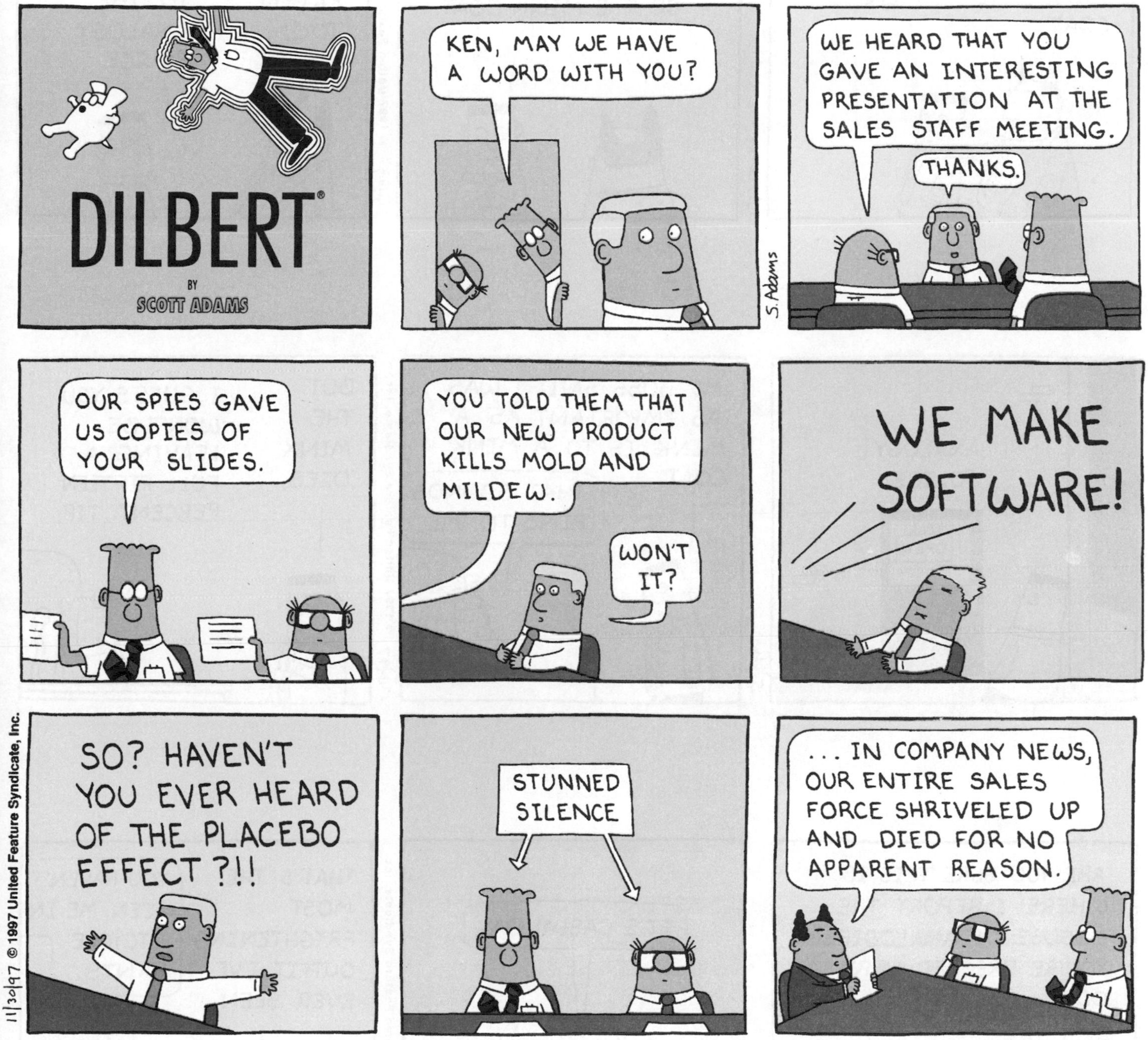
DILBERT®
BY
SCOTT ADAMS
KEN, MAY WE HAVE A WORD WITH YOU?
S. Adams
WE HEARD THAT YOU GAVE AN INTERESTING PRESENTATION AT THE SALES STAFF MEETING.
THANKS.
OUR SPIES GAVE US COPIES OF YOUR SLIDES.
YOU TOLD THEM THAT OUR NEW PRODUCT KILLS MOLD AND MILDEW.
WON'T IT?
WE MAKE SOFTWARE!
SO? HAVEN'T YOU EVER HEARD OF THE PLACEBO EFFECT?!!
STUNNED SILENCE
... IN COMPANY NEWS, OUR ENTIRE SALES FORCE SHRIVELED UP AND DIED FOR NO APPARENT REASON.
11/30/97 © 1997 United Feature Syndicate, Inc.

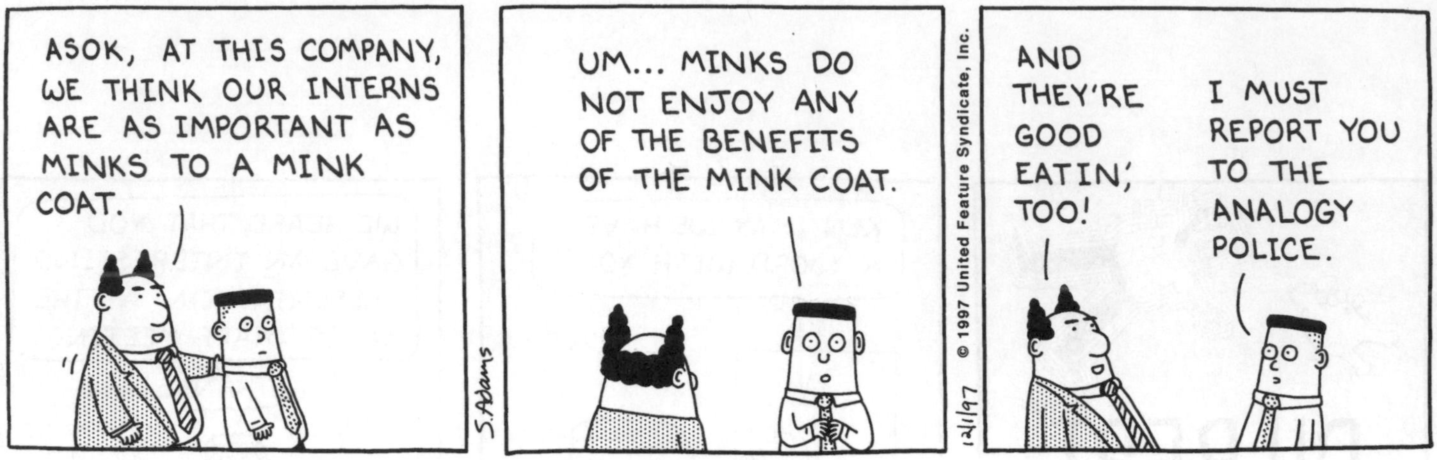
ASOK, AT THIS COMPANY, WE THINK OUR INTERNS ARE AS IMPORTANT AS MINKS TO A MINK COAT.
UM... MINKS DO NOT ENJOY ANY OF THE BENEFITS OF THE MINK COAT.
AND THEY'RE GOOD EATIN', TOO!
I MUST REPORT YOU TO THE ANALOGY POLICE.
S. Adams
12/1/97
© 1997 United Feature Syndicate, Inc.

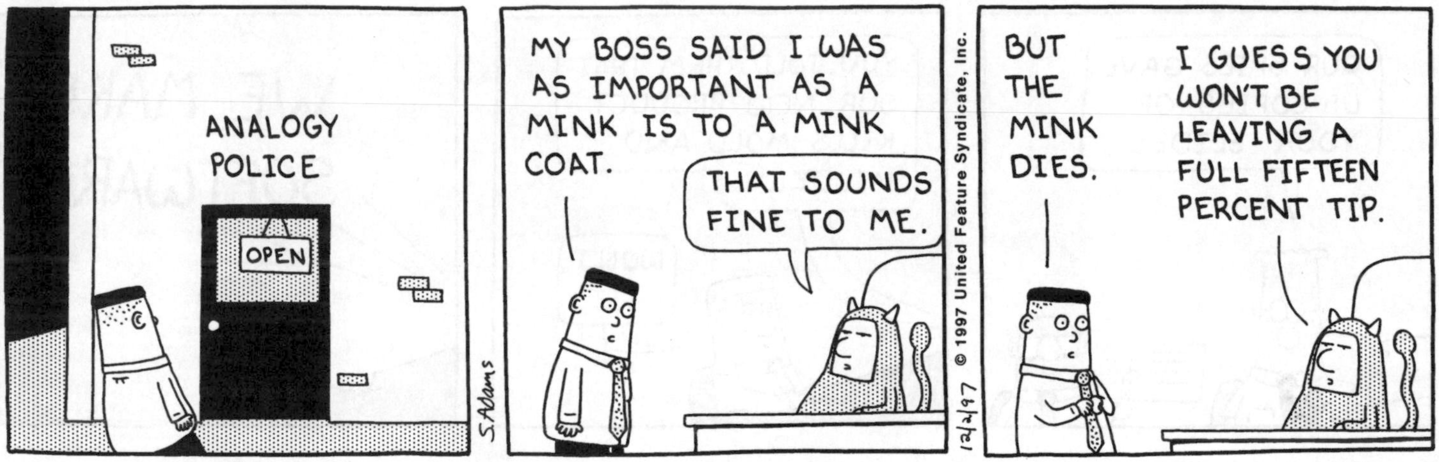
ANALOGY POLICE
OPEN
MY BOSS SAID I WAS AS IMPORTANT AS A MINK IS TO A MINK COAT.
THAT SOUNDS FINE TO ME.
BUT THE MINK DIES.
I GUESS YOU WON'T BE LEAVING A FULL FIFTEEN PERCENT TIP.
S. Adams
12/2/97
© 1997 United Feature Syndicate, Inc.

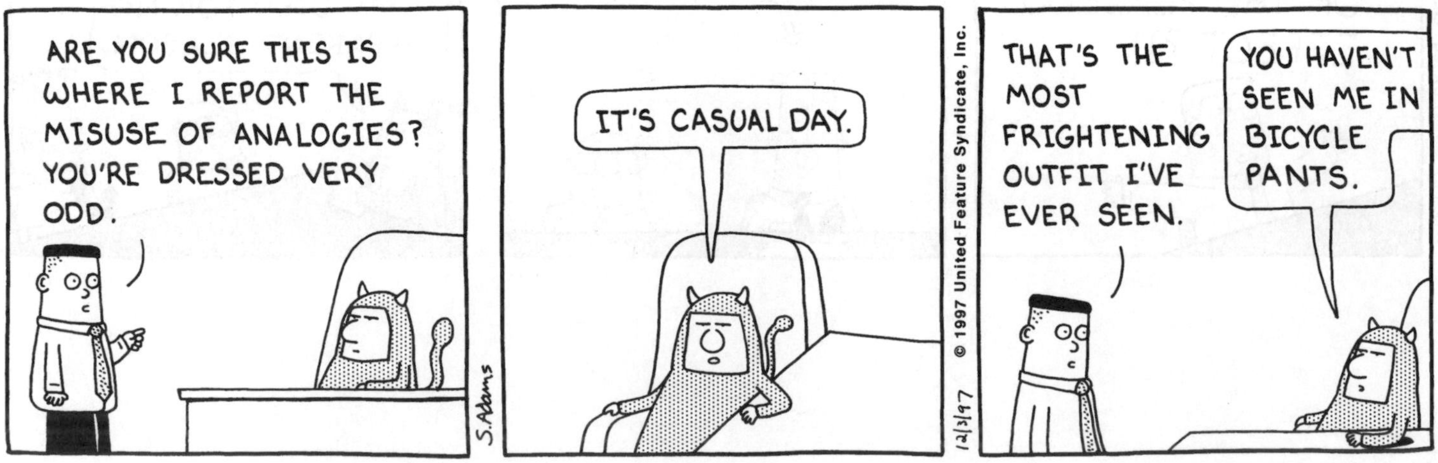
ARE YOU SURE THIS IS WHERE I REPORT THE MISUSE OF ANALOGIES? YOU'RE DRESSED VERY ODD.
IT'S CASUAL DAY.
THAT'S THE MOST FRIGHTENING OUTFIT I'VE EVER SEEN.
YOU HAVEN'T SEEN ME IN BICYCLE PANTS.
S. Adams
12/3/97
© 1997 United Feature Syndicate, Inc.

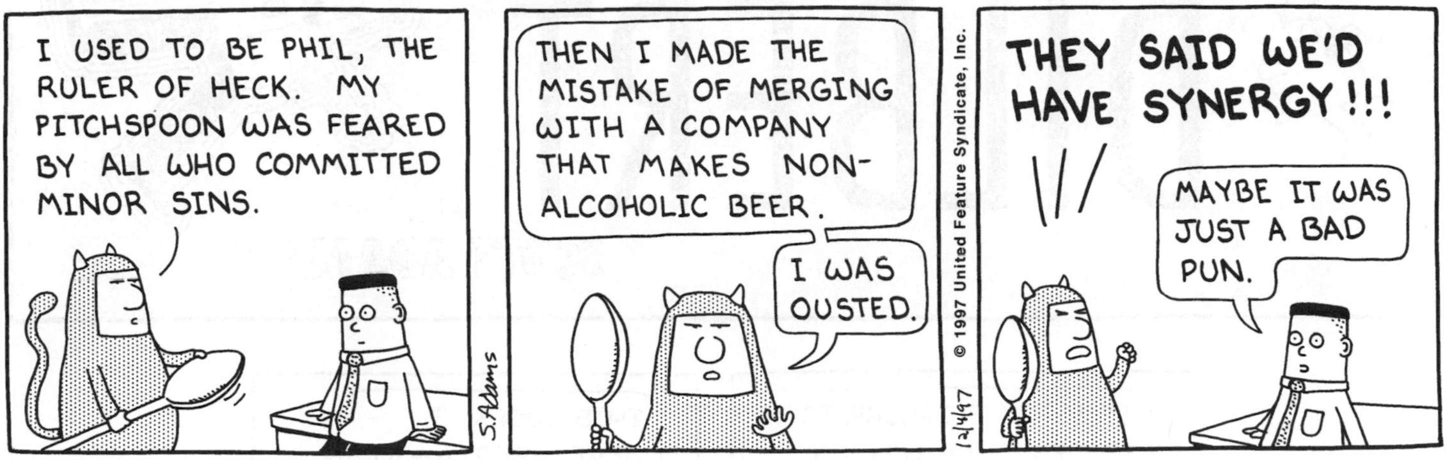
I USED TO BE PHIL, THE RULER OF HECK. MY PITCHSPOON WAS FEARED BY ALL WHO COMMITTED MINOR SINS.
S. Adams
THEN I MADE THE MISTAKE OF MERGING WITH A COMPANY THAT MAKES NON-ALCOHOLIC BEER.
I WAS OUSTED.
12/4/97
© 1997 United Feature Syndicate, Inc.
THEY SAID WE'D HAVE SYNERGY!!!
MAYBE IT WAS JUST A BAD PUN.

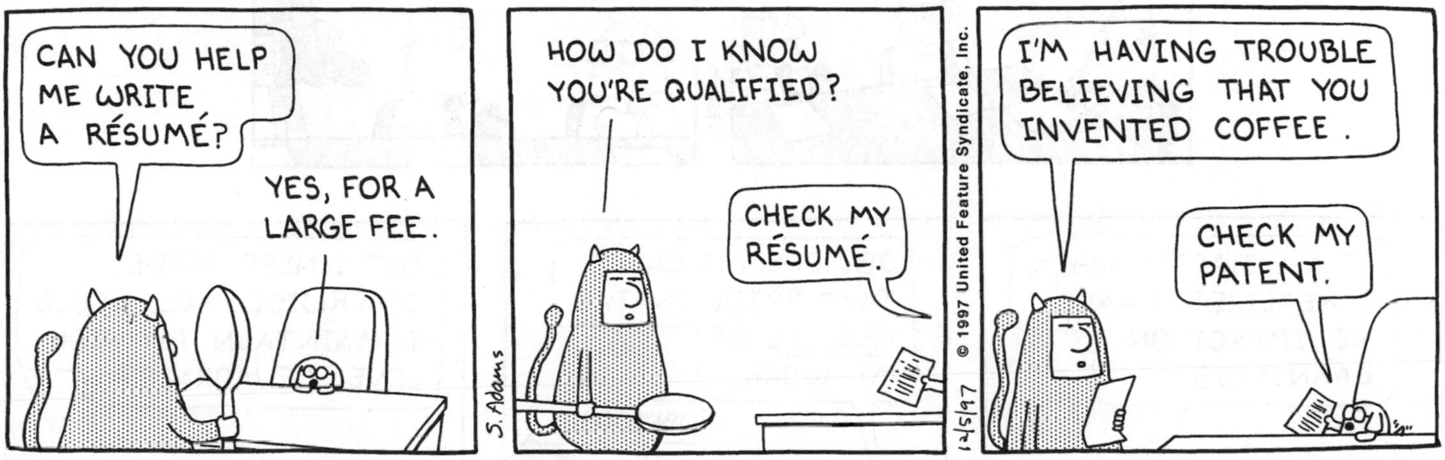
CAN YOU HELP ME WRITE A RÉSUMÉ?
YES, FOR A LARGE FEE.
S. Adams
HOW DO I KNOW YOU'RE QUALIFIED?
CHECK MY RÉSUMÉ.
12/5/97
© 1997 United Feature Syndicate, Inc.
I'M HAVING TROUBLE BELIEVING THAT YOU INVENTED COFFEE.
CHECK MY PATENT.

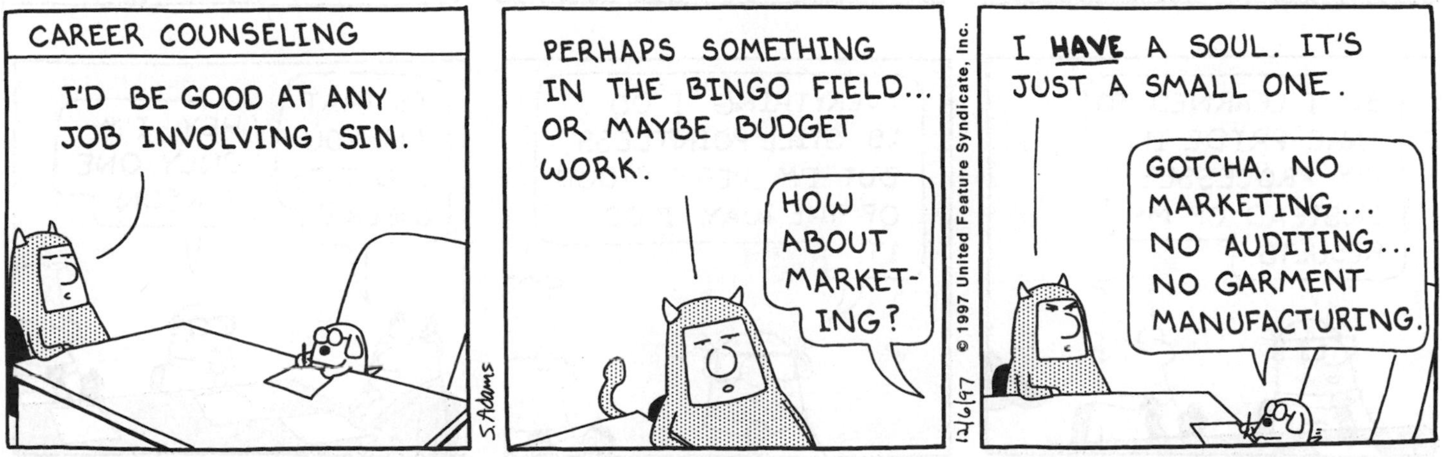
CAREER COUNSELING
I'D BE GOOD AT ANY JOB INVOLVING SIN.
S. Adams
PERHAPS SOMETHING IN THE BINGO FIELD... OR MAYBE BUDGET WORK.
HOW ABOUT MARKETING?
12/6/97
© 1997 United Feature Syndicate, Inc.
I HAVE A SOUL. IT'S JUST A SMALL ONE.
GOTCHA. NO MARKETING... NO AUDITING... NO GARMENT MANUFACTURING.

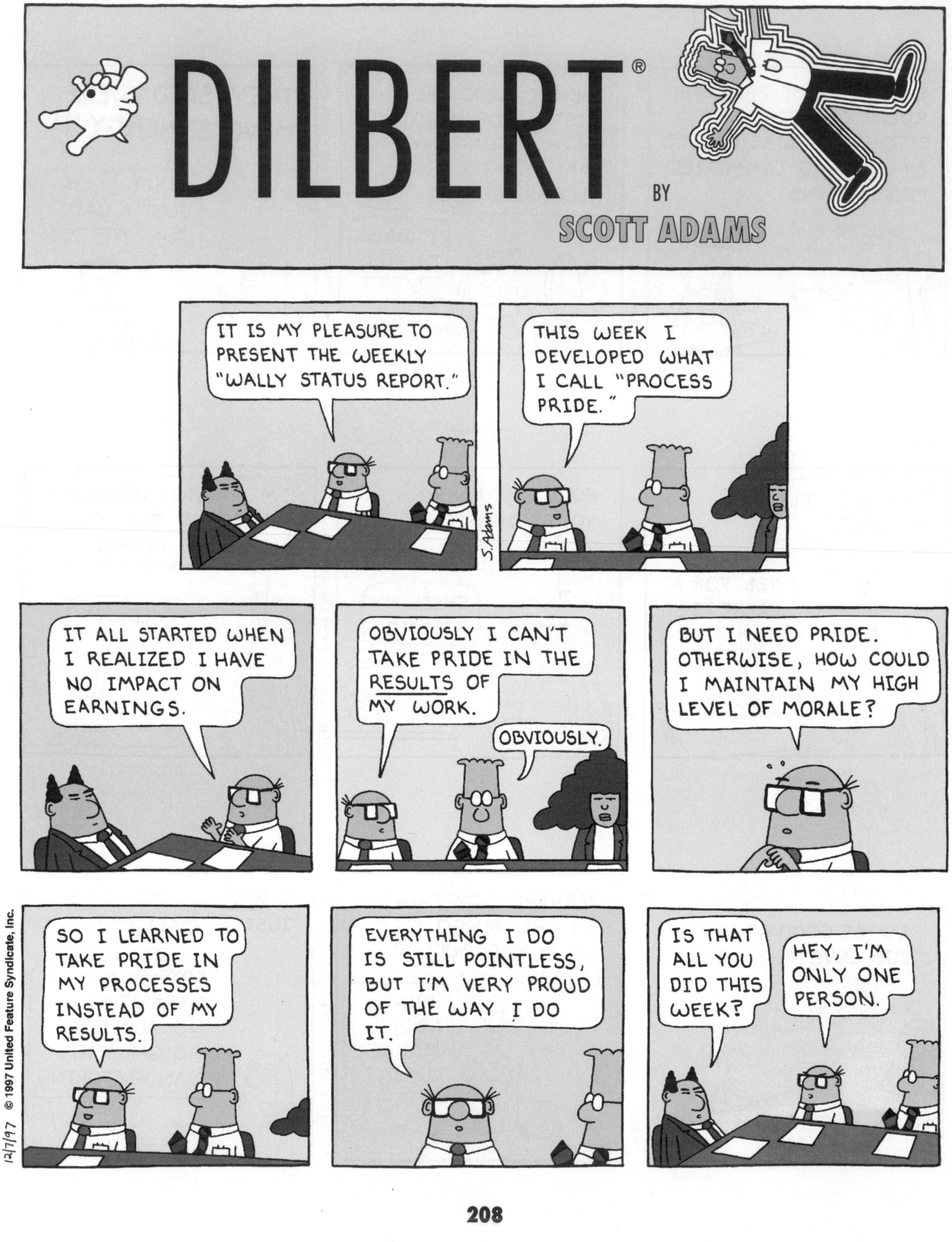
DILBERT®
BY
SCOTT ADAMS
IT IS MY PLEASURE TO PRESENT THE WEEKLY "WALLY STATUS REPORT."
S. Adams
THIS WEEK I DEVELOPED WHAT I CALL "PROCESS PRIDE."
IT ALL STARTED WHEN I REALIZED I HAVE NO IMPACT ON EARNINGS.
OBVIOUSLY I CAN'T TAKE PRIDE IN THE RESULTS OF MY WORK.
OBVIOUSLY.
BUT I NEED PRIDE. OTHERWISE, HOW COULD I MAINTAIN MY HIGH LEVEL OF MORALE?
SO I LEARNED TO TAKE PRIDE IN MY PROCESSES INSTEAD OF MY RESULTS.
EVERYTHING I DO IS STILL POINTLESS, BUT I'M VERY PROUD OF THE WAY I DO IT.
IS THAT ALL YOU DID THIS WEEK?
HEY, I'M ONLY ONE PERSON.
12/7/97 © 1997 United Feature Syndicate, Inc.

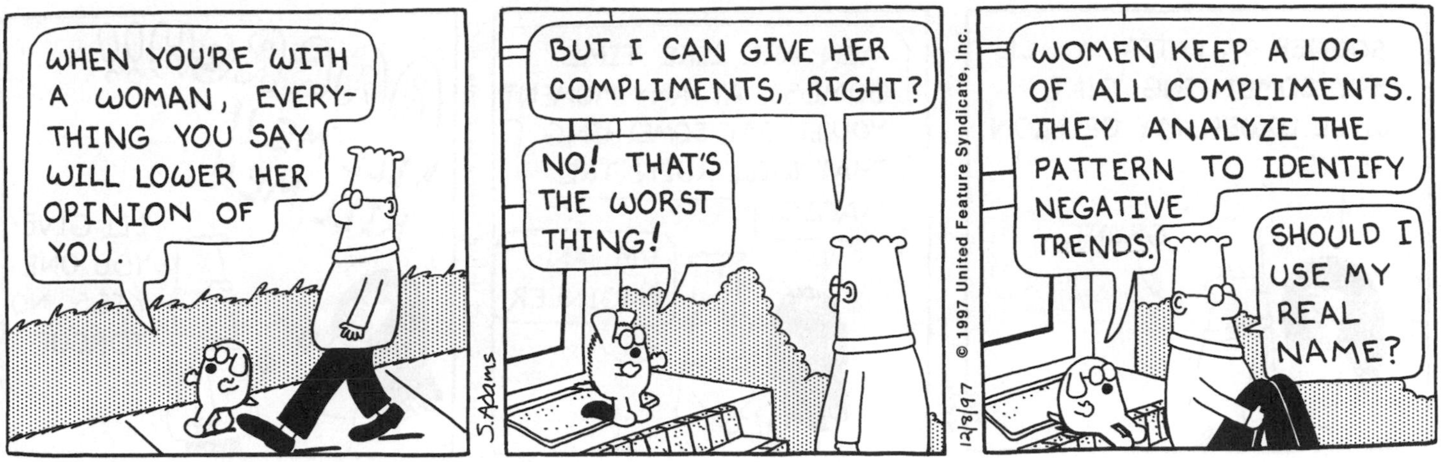
WHEN YOU'RE WITH A WOMAN, EVERYTHING YOU SAY WILL LOWER HER OPINION OF YOU.
BUT I CAN GIVE HER COMPLIMENTS, RIGHT?
NO! THAT'S THE WORST THING!
WOMEN KEEP A LOG OF ALL COMPLIMENTS. THEY ANALYZE THE PATTERN TO IDENTIFY NEGATIVE TRENDS.
SHOULD I USE MY REAL NAME?
S. Adams
12/8/97
© 1997 United Feature Syndicate, Inc.

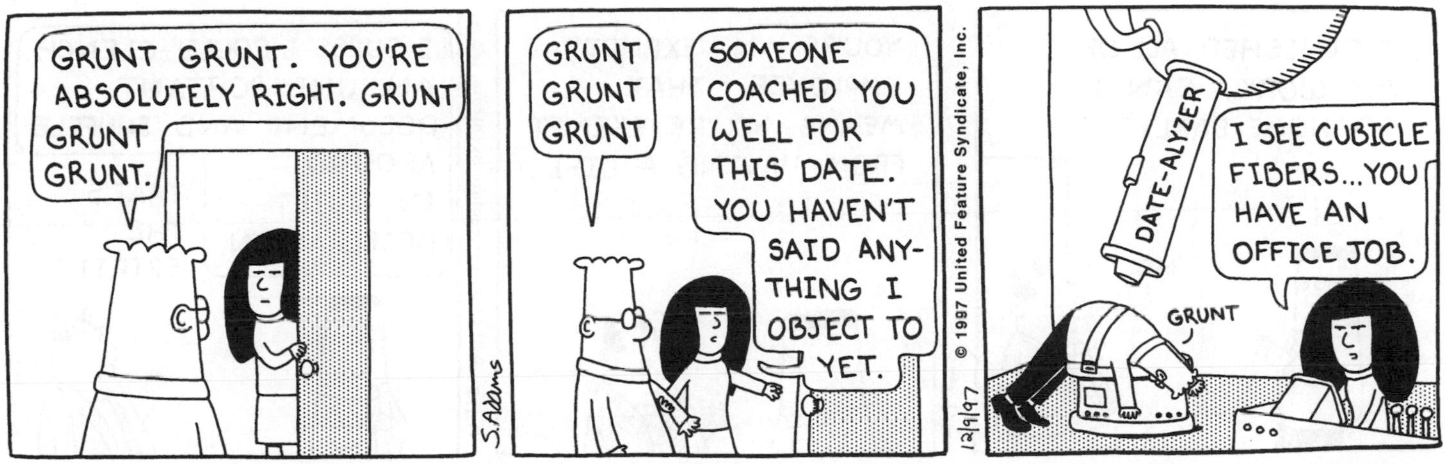
GRUNT GRUNT. YOU'RE ABSOLUTELY RIGHT. GRUNT GRUNT GRUNT.
GRUNT GRUNT GRUNT
SOMEONE COACHED YOU WELL FOR THIS DATE. YOU HAVEN'T SAID ANYTHING I OBJECT TO YET.
DATE-ALYZER
GRUNT
I SEE CUBICLE FIBERS... YOU HAVE AN OFFICE JOB.
S. Adams
12/9/97
© 1997 United Feature Syndicate, Inc.

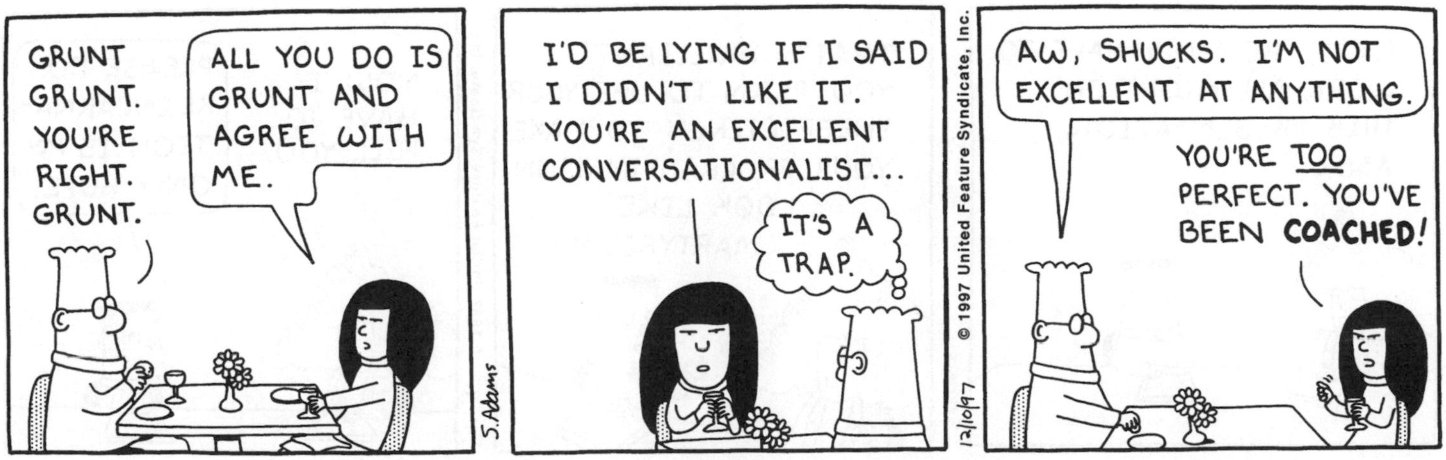
GRUNT GRUNT. YOU'RE RIGHT. GRUNT.
ALL YOU DO IS GRUNT AND AGREE WITH ME.
I'D BE LYING IF I SAID I DIDN'T LIKE IT. YOU'RE AN EXCELLENT CONVERSATIONALIST...
IT'S A TRAP.
AW, SHUCKS. I'M NOT EXCELLENT AT ANYTHING.
YOU'RE TOO PERFECT. YOU'VE BEEN COACHED!
S. Adams
12/10/97
© 1997 United Feature Syndicate, Inc.

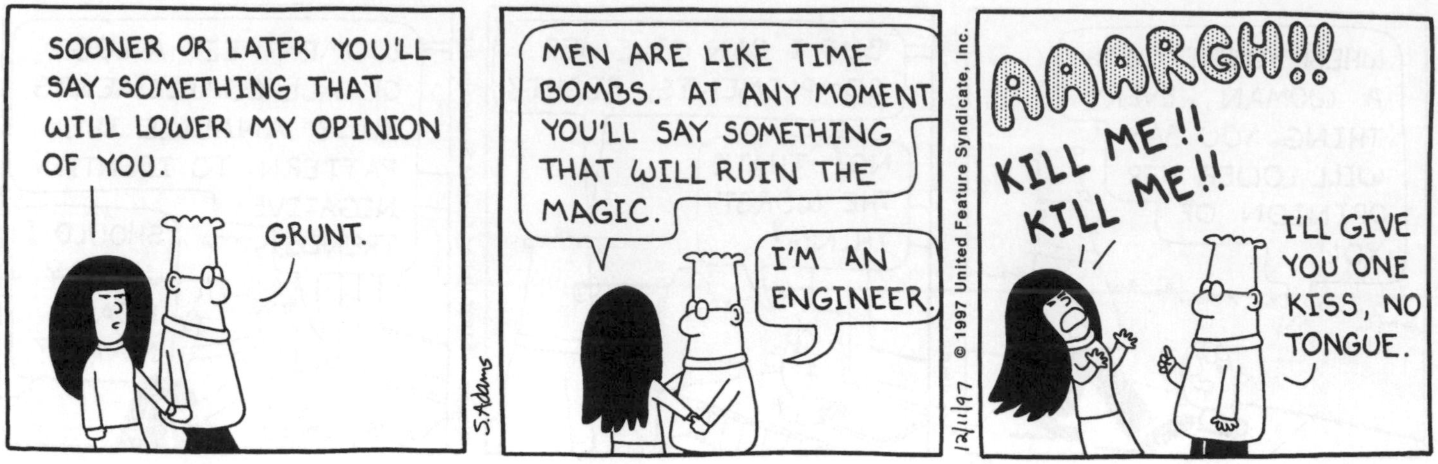
SOONER OR LATER YOU'LL SAY SOMETHING THAT WILL LOWER MY OPINION OF YOU.
GRUNT.
S. Adams
MEN ARE LIKE TIME BOMBS. AT ANY MOMENT YOU'LL SAY SOMETHING THAT WILL RUIN THE MAGIC.
I'M AN ENGINEER.
12/11/97 © 1997 United Feature Syndicate, Inc.
AAARGH!!
KILL ME!! KILL ME!!
I'LL GIVE YOU ONE KISS, NO TONGUE.

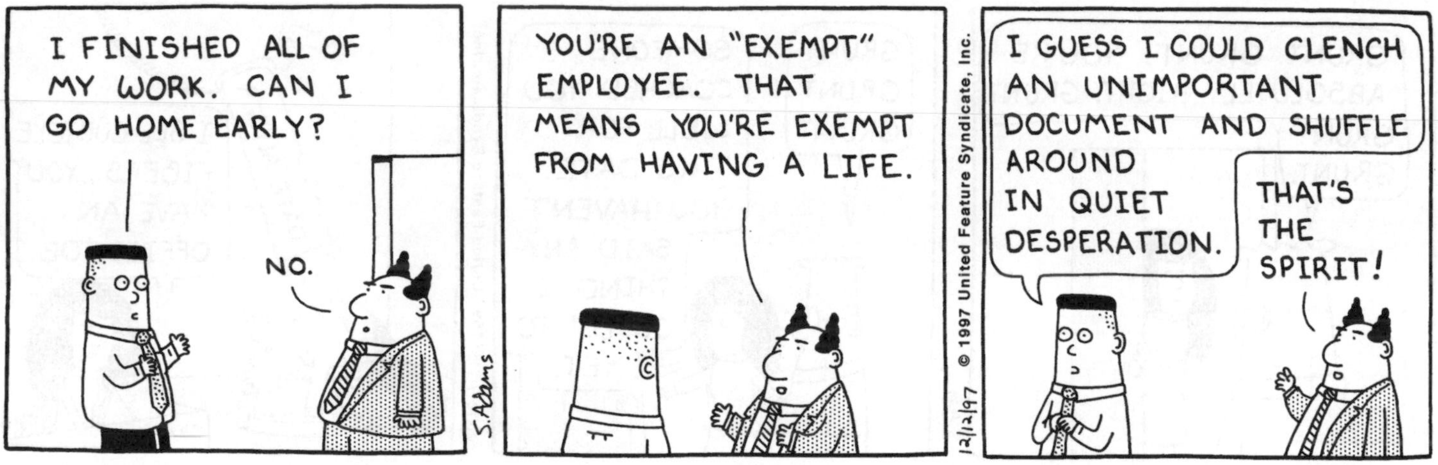
I FINISHED ALL OF MY WORK. CAN I GO HOME EARLY?
NO.
S. Adams
YOU'RE AN "EXEMPT" EMPLOYEE. THAT MEANS YOU'RE EXEMPT FROM HAVING A LIFE.
12/12/97 © 1997 United Feature Syndicate, Inc.
I GUESS I COULD CLENCH AN UNIMPORTANT DOCUMENT AND SHUFFLE AROUND IN QUIET DESPERATION.
THAT'S THE SPIRIT!

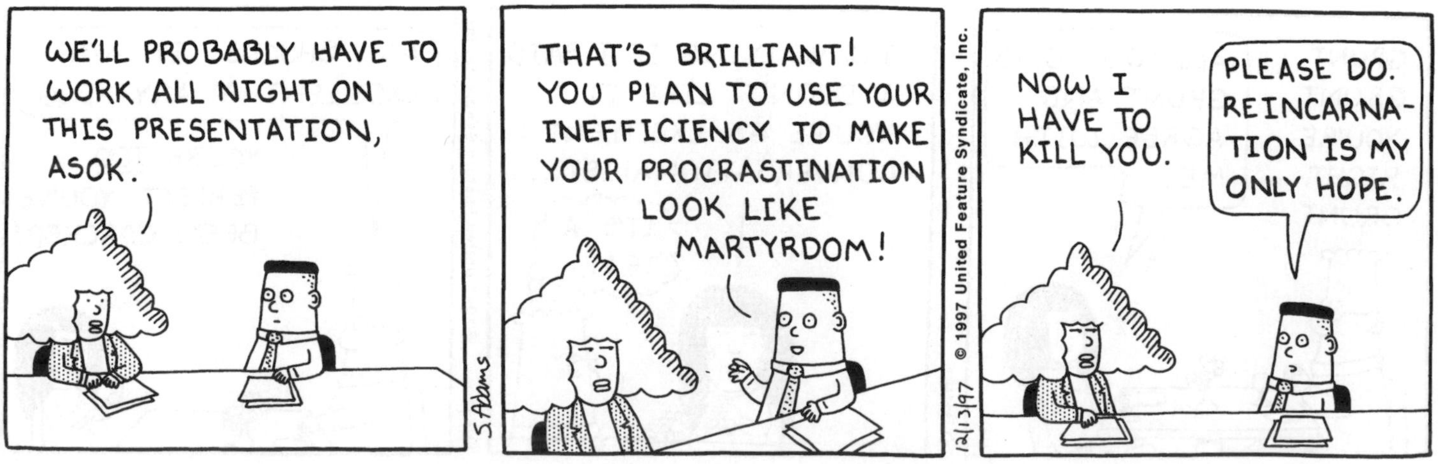
WE'LL PROBABLY HAVE TO WORK ALL NIGHT ON THIS PRESENTATION, ASOK.
S. Adams
THAT'S BRILLIANT! YOU PLAN TO USE YOUR INEFFICIENCY TO MAKE YOUR PROCRASTINATION LOOK LIKE MARTYRDOM!
12/13/97 © 1997 United Feature Syndicate, Inc.
NOW I HAVE TO KILL YOU.
PLEASE DO. REINCARNATION IS MY ONLY HOPE.

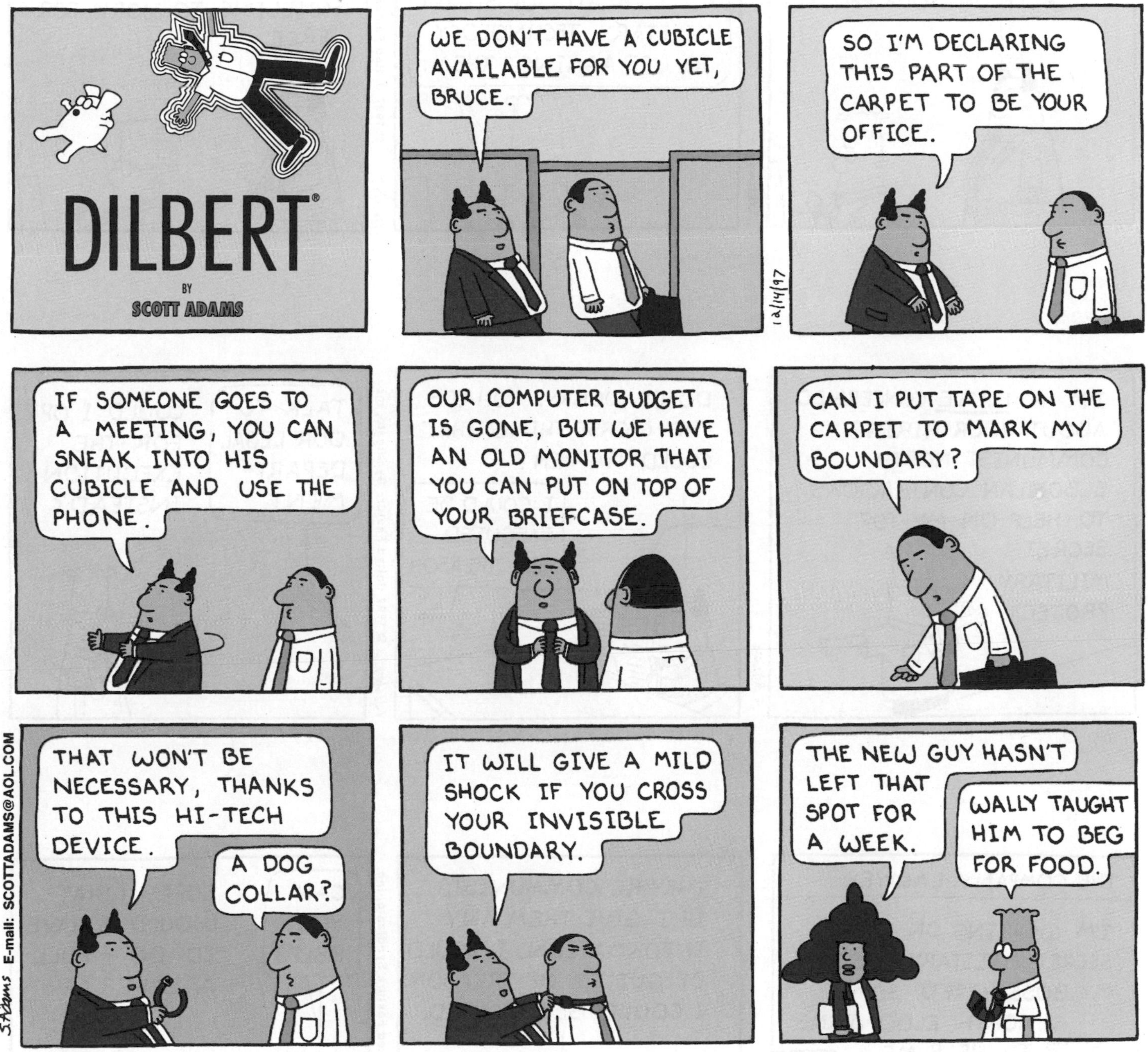
DILBERT®
BY
SCOTT ADAMS
WE DON'T HAVE A CUBICLE AVAILABLE FOR YOU YET, BRUCE.
12/14/97
SO I'M DECLARING THIS PART OF THE CARPET TO BE YOUR OFFICE.
IF SOMEONE GOES TO A MEETING, YOU CAN SNEAK INTO HIS CUBICLE AND USE THE PHONE.
OUR COMPUTER BUDGET IS GONE, BUT WE HAVE AN OLD MONITOR THAT YOU CAN PUT ON TOP OF YOUR BRIEFCASE.
CAN I PUT TAPE ON THE CARPET TO MARK MY BOUNDARY?
S.Adams E-mail: SCOTTADAMS@AOL.COM
THAT WON'T BE NECESSARY, THANKS TO THIS HI-TECH DEVICE.
A DOG COLLAR?
IT WILL GIVE A MILD SHOCK IF YOU CROSS YOUR INVISIBLE BOUNDARY.
THE NEW GUY HASN'T LEFT THAT SPOT FOR A WEEK.
WALLY TAUGHT HIM TO BEG FOR FOOD.

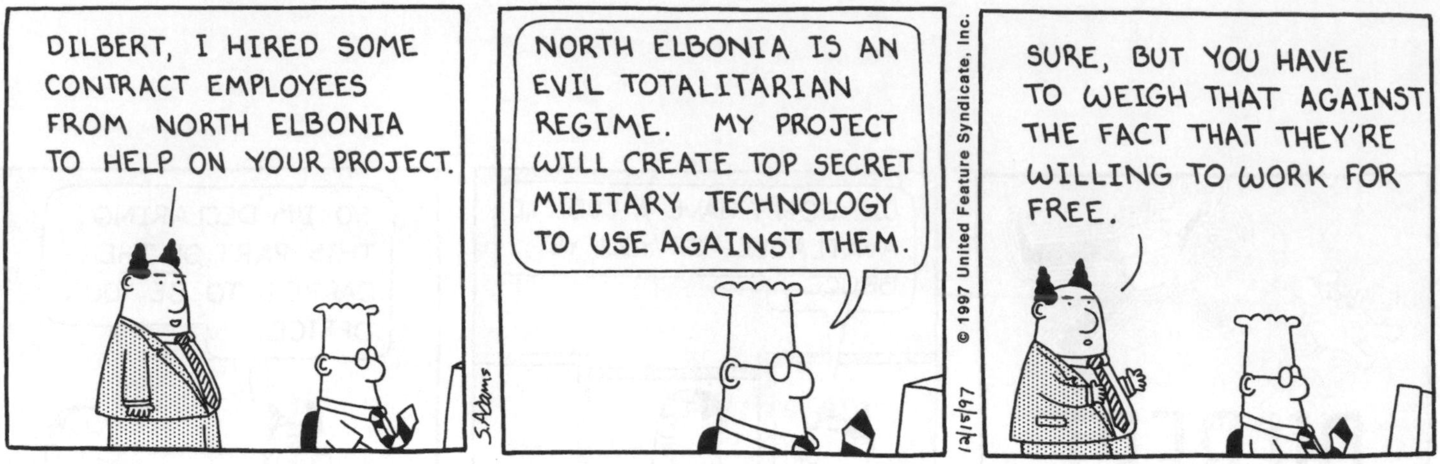
DILBERT, I HIRED SOME CONTRACT EMPLOYEES FROM NORTH ELBONIA TO HELP ON YOUR PROJECT.
NORTH ELBONIA IS AN EVIL TOTALITARIAN REGIME. MY PROJECT WILL CREATE TOP SECRET MILITARY TECHNOLOGY TO USE AGAINST THEM.
SURE, BUT YOU HAVE TO WEIGH THAT AGAINST THE FACT THAT THEY'RE WILLING TO WORK FOR FREE.
S.Adams
12/5/97
© 1997 United Feature Syndicate, Inc.

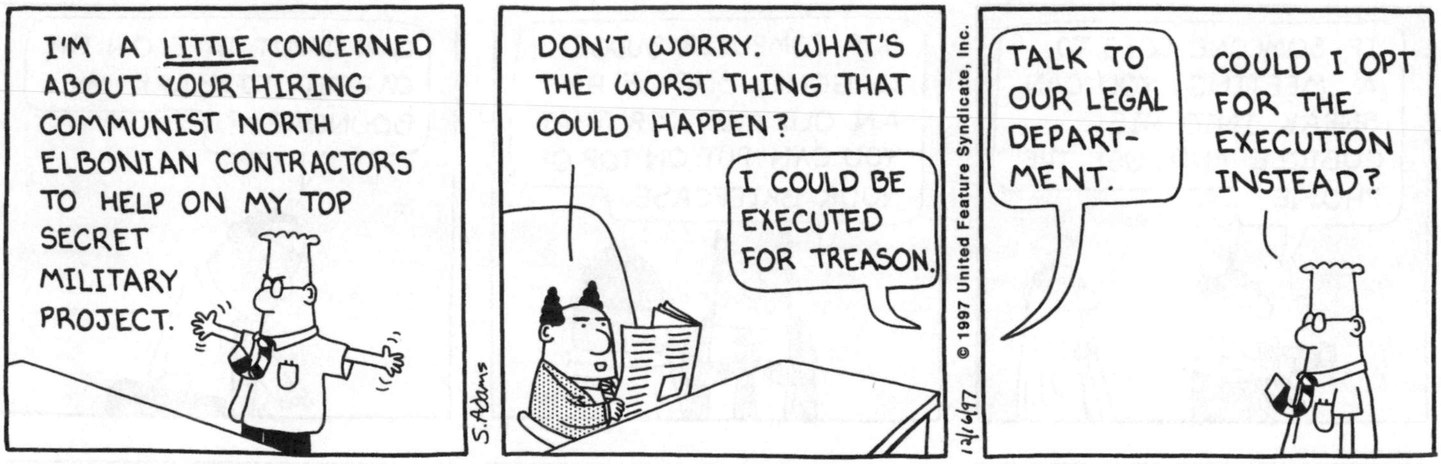
I'M A LITTLE CONCERNED ABOUT YOUR HIRING COMMUNIST NORTH ELBONIAN CONTRACTORS TO HELP ON MY TOP SECRET MILITARY PROJECT.
DON'T WORRY. WHAT'S THE WORST THING THAT COULD HAPPEN?
I COULD BE EXECUTED FOR TREASON.
TALK TO OUR LEGAL DEPART-MENT.
COULD I OPT FOR THE EXECUTION INSTEAD?
S.Adams
12/6/97
© 1997 United Feature Syndicate, Inc.

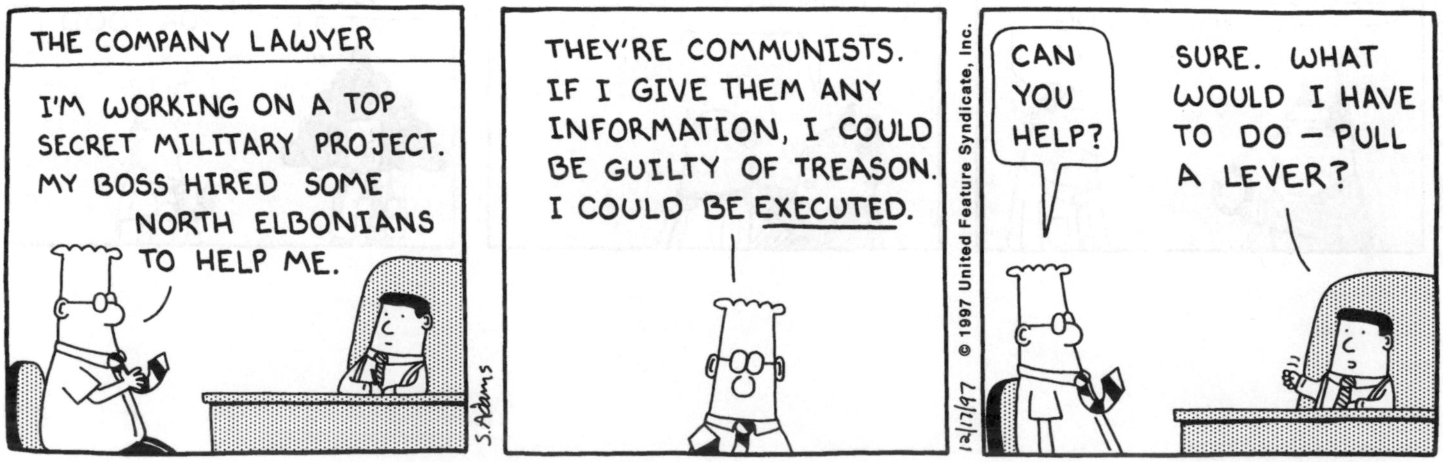
THE COMPANY LAWYER
I'M WORKING ON A TOP SECRET MILITARY PROJECT. MY BOSS HIRED SOME NORTH ELBONIANS TO HELP ME.
THEY'RE COMMUNISTS. IF I GIVE THEM ANY INFORMATION, I COULD BE GUILTY OF TREASON. I COULD BE EXECUTED.
CAN YOU HELP?
SURE. WHAT WOULD I HAVE TO DO – PULL A LEVER?
S.Adams
12/7/97
© 1997 United Feature Syndicate, Inc.

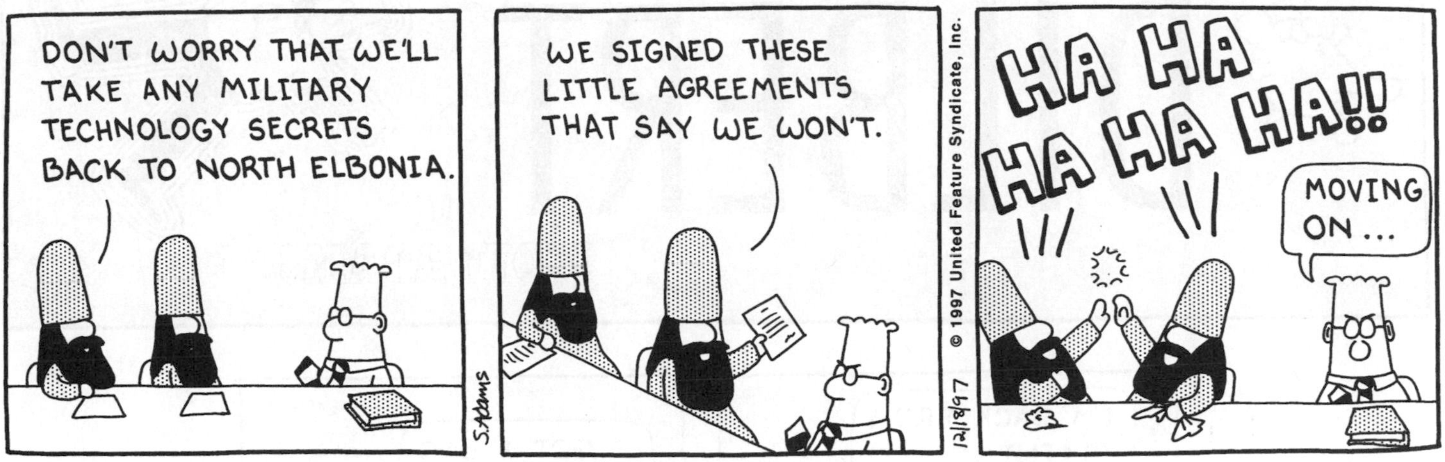
DON'T WORRY THAT WE'LL TAKE ANY MILITARY TECHNOLOGY SECRETS BACK TO NORTH ELBONIA.
WE SIGNED THESE LITTLE AGREEMENTS THAT SAY WE WON'T.
HA HA HA HA HA!!
MOVING ON...
S.Adams
12/18/97
© 1997 United Feature Syndicate, Inc.

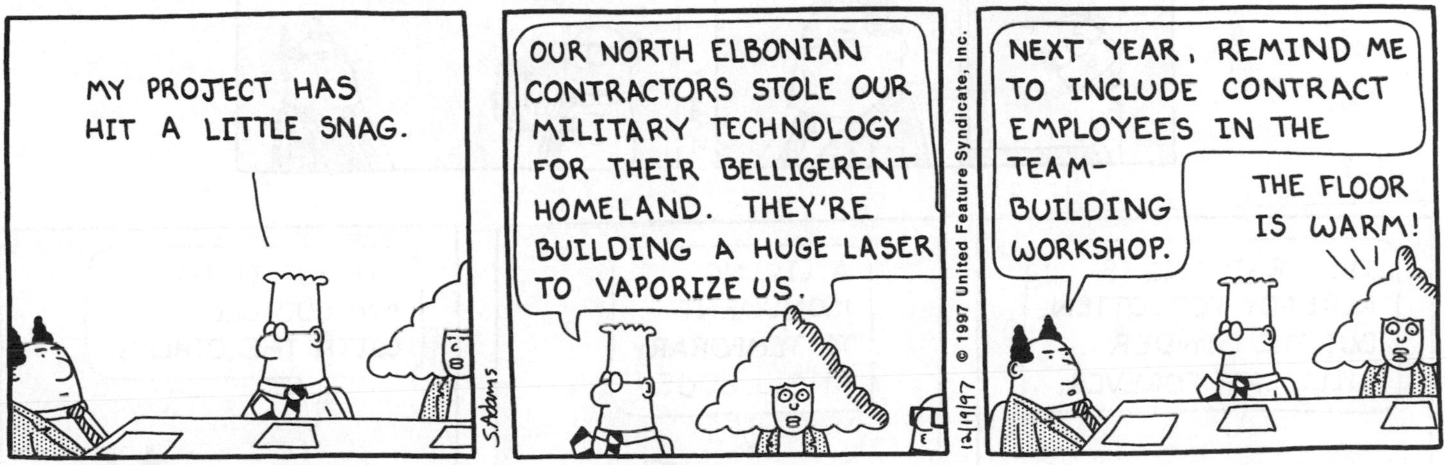
MY PROJECT HAS HIT A LITTLE SNAG.
OUR NORTH ELBONIAN CONTRACTORS STOLE OUR MILITARY TECHNOLOGY FOR THEIR BELLIGERENT HOMELAND. THEY'RE BUILDING A HUGE LASER TO VAPORIZE US.
NEXT YEAR, REMIND ME TO INCLUDE CONTRACT EMPLOYEES IN THE TEAM-BUILDING WORKSHOP.
THE FLOOR IS WARM!
S.Adams
12/19/97
© 1997 United Feature Syndicate, Inc.

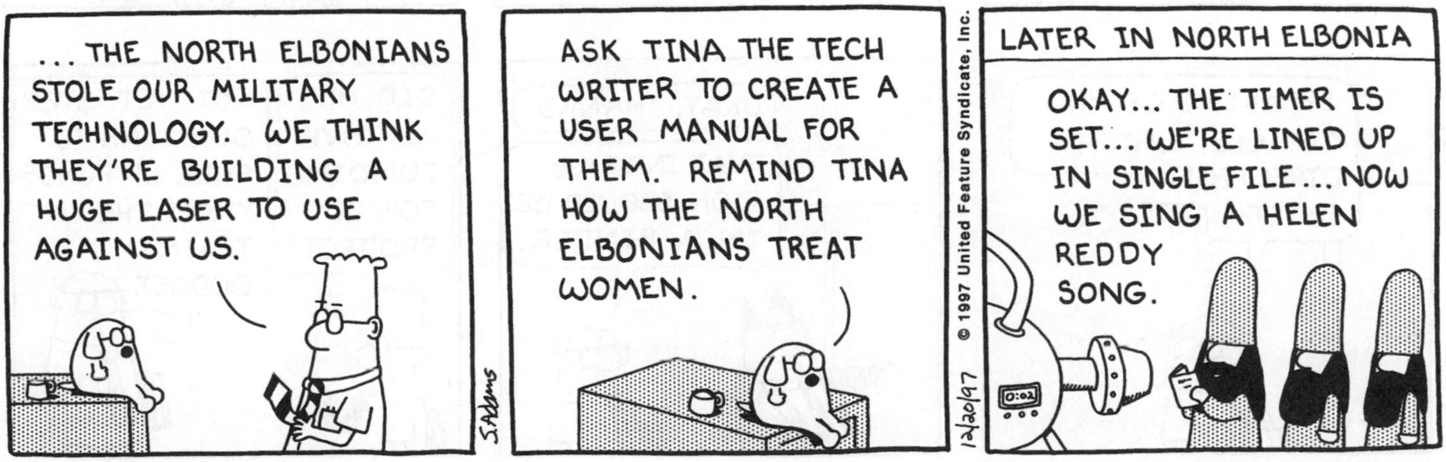
... THE NORTH ELBONIANS STOLE OUR MILITARY TECHNOLOGY. WE THINK THEY'RE BUILDING A HUGE LASER TO USE AGAINST US.
ASK TINA THE TECH WRITER TO CREATE A USER MANUAL FOR THEM. REMIND TINA HOW THE NORTH ELBONIANS TREAT WOMEN.
LATER IN NORTH ELBONIA
OKAY... THE TIMER IS SET... WE'RE LINED UP IN SINGLE FILE... NOW WE SING A HELEN REDDY SONG.
S.Adams
12/20/97
© 1997 United Feature Syndicate, Inc.

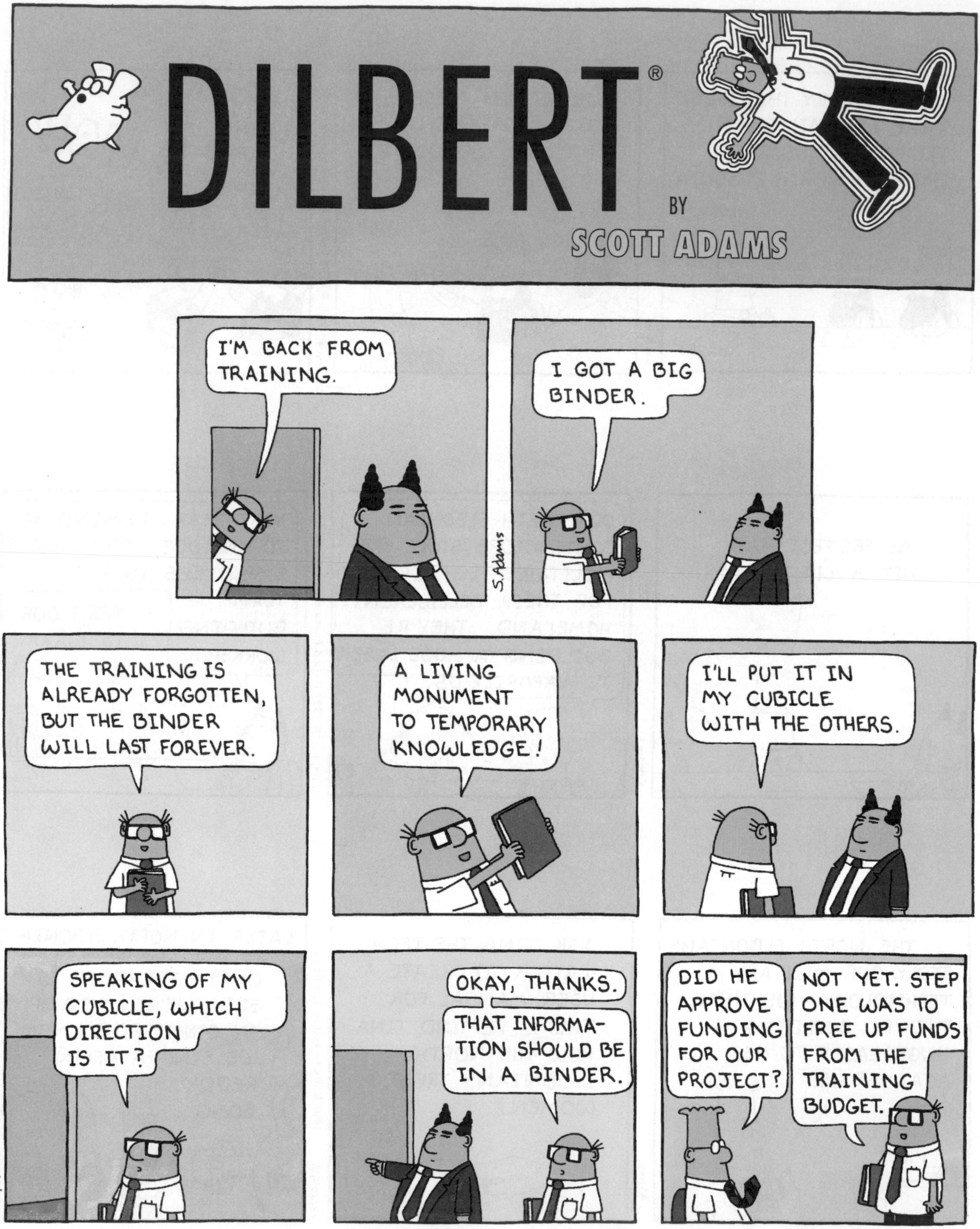
DILBERT®
BY
SCOTT ADAMS
I'M BACK FROM TRAINING.
I GOT A BIG BINDER.
S. Adams
THE TRAINING IS ALREADY FORGOTTEN, BUT THE BINDER WILL LAST FOREVER.
A LIVING MONUMENT TO TEMPORARY KNOWLEDGE!
I'LL PUT IT IN MY CUBICLE WITH THE OTHERS.
SPEAKING OF MY CUBICLE, WHICH DIRECTION IS IT?
OKAY, THANKS.
THAT INFORMATION SHOULD BE IN A BINDER.
DID HE APPROVE FUNDING FOR OUR PROJECT?
NOT YET. STEP ONE WAS TO FREE UP FUNDS FROM THE TRAINING BUDGET.

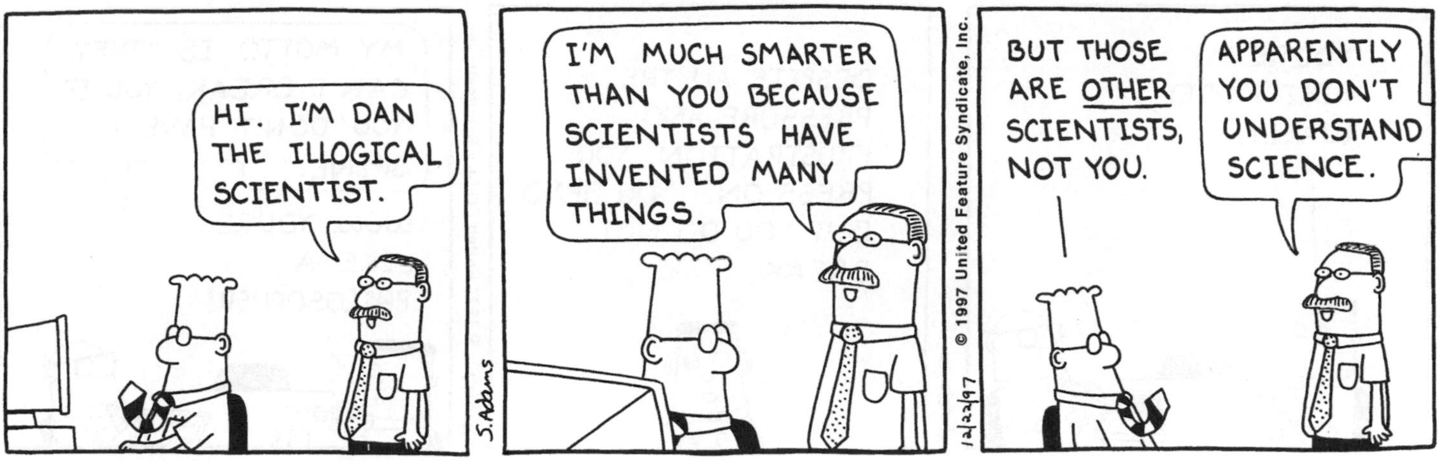
HI. I'M DAN THE ILLOGICAL SCIENTIST.
S. Adams
I'M MUCH SMARTER THAN YOU BECAUSE SCIENTISTS HAVE INVENTED MANY THINGS.
12/22/97
© 1997 United Feature Syndicate, Inc.
BUT THOSE ARE OTHER SCIENTISTS, NOT YOU.
APPARENTLY YOU DON'T UNDERSTAND SCIENCE.

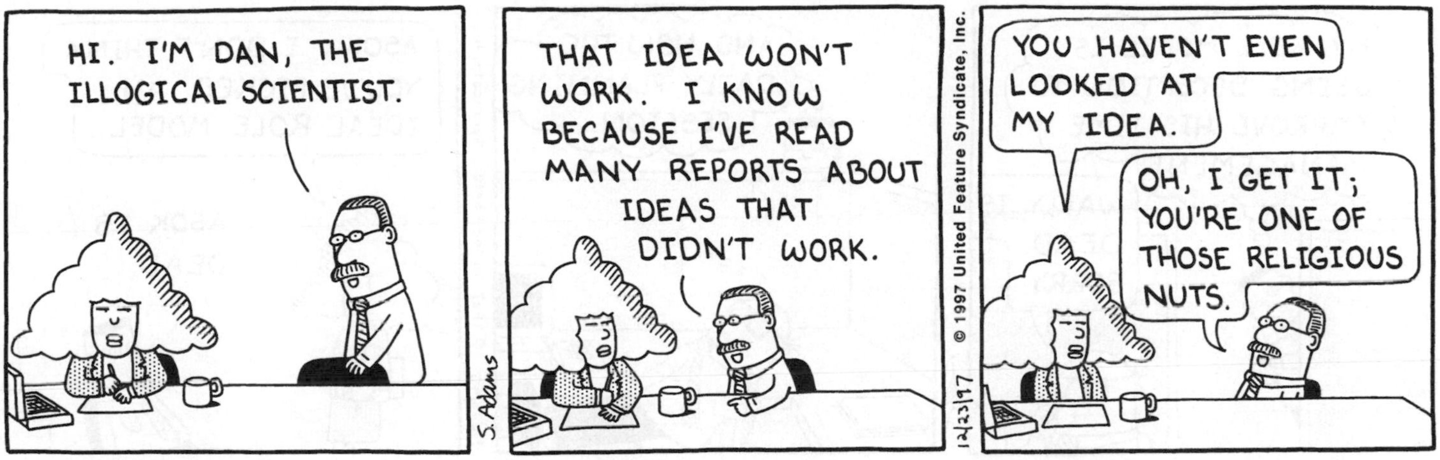
HI. I'M DAN, THE ILLOGICAL SCIENTIST.
S. Adams
THAT IDEA WON'T WORK. I KNOW BECAUSE I'VE READ MANY REPORTS ABOUT IDEAS THAT DIDN'T WORK.
12/23/97
© 1997 United Feature Syndicate, Inc.
YOU HAVEN'T EVEN LOOKED AT MY IDEA.
OH, I GET IT; YOU'RE ONE OF THOSE RELIGIOUS NUTS.

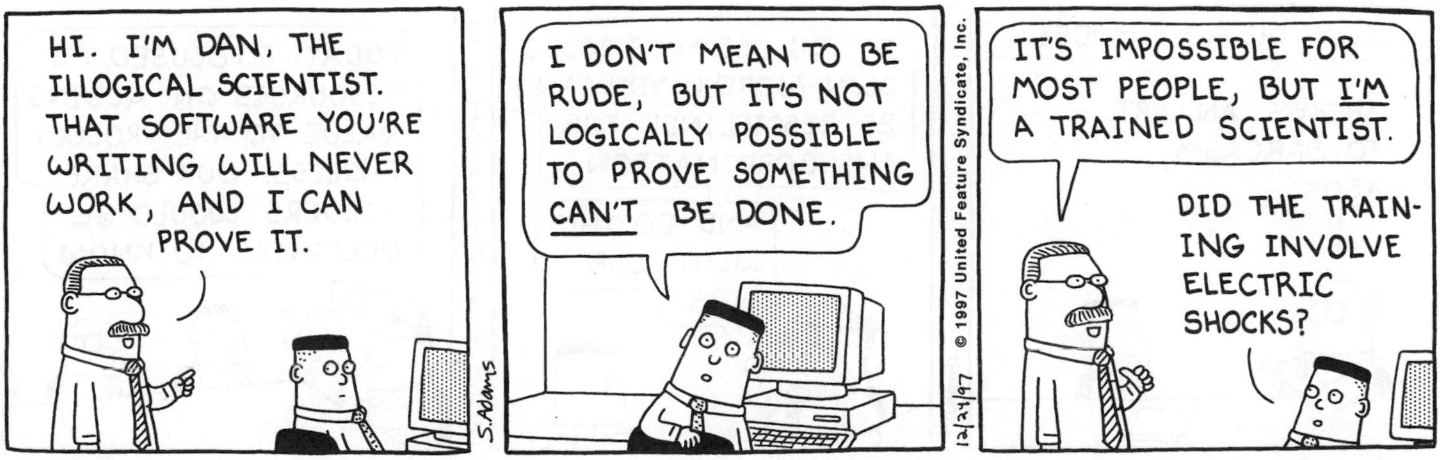
HI. I'M DAN, THE ILLOGICAL SCIENTIST. THAT SOFTWARE YOU'RE WRITING WILL NEVER WORK, AND I CAN PROVE IT.
S. Adams
I DON'T MEAN TO BE RUDE, BUT IT'S NOT LOGICALLY POSSIBLE TO PROVE SOMETHING CAN'T BE DONE.
12/24/97
© 1997 United Feature Syndicate, Inc.
IT'S IMPOSSIBLE FOR MOST PEOPLE, BUT I'M A TRAINED SCIENTIST.
DID THE TRAINING INVOLVE ELECTRIC SHOCKS?

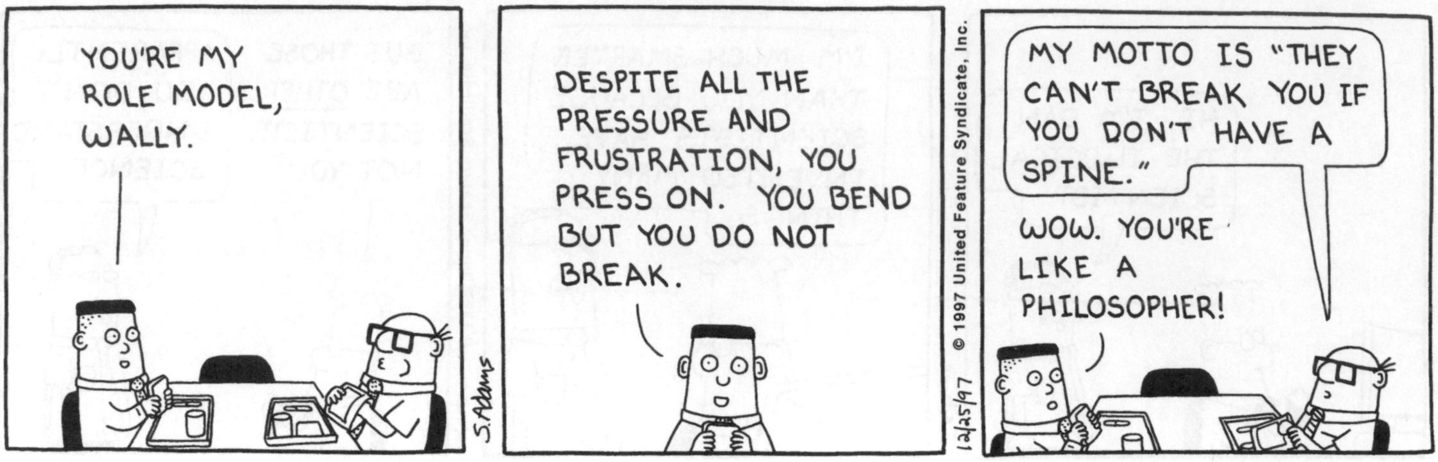
YOU'RE MY ROLE MODEL, WALLY.
DESPITE ALL THE PRESSURE AND FRUSTRATION, YOU PRESS ON. YOU BEND BUT YOU DO NOT BREAK.
MY MOTTO IS "THEY CAN'T BREAK YOU IF YOU DON'T HAVE A SPINE."
WOW. YOU'RE LIKE A PHILOSOPHER!
S. Adams
12/25/97 © 1997 United Feature Syndicate, Inc.

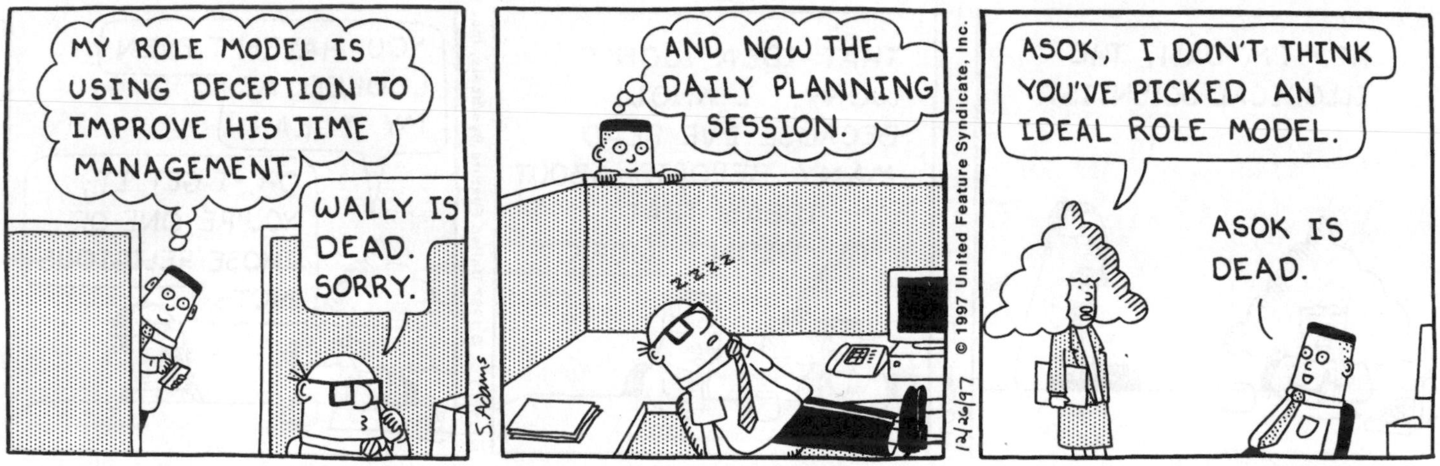
MY ROLE MODEL IS USING DECEPTION TO IMPROVE HIS TIME MANAGEMENT.
WALLY IS DEAD. SORRY.
AND NOW THE DAILY PLANNING SESSION.
Z Z Z Z
ASOK, I DON'T THINK YOU'VE PICKED AN IDEAL ROLE MODEL.
ASOK IS DEAD.
S. Adams
12/26/97 © 1997 United Feature Syndicate, Inc.

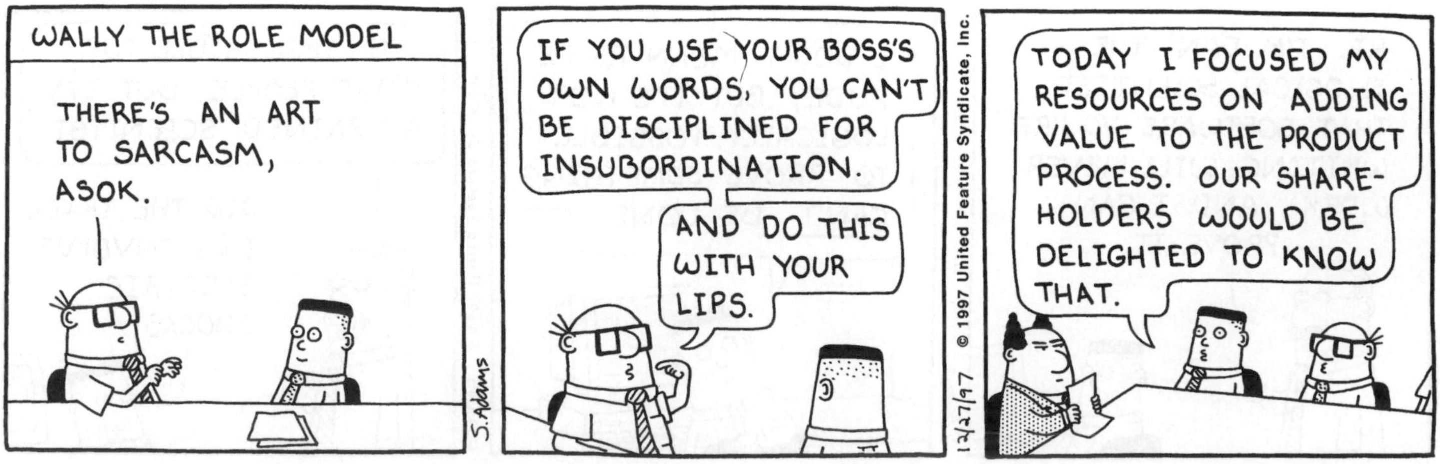
WALLY THE ROLE MODEL
THERE'S AN ART TO SARCASM, ASOK.
IF YOU USE YOUR BOSS'S OWN WORDS, YOU CAN'T BE DISCIPLINED FOR INSUBORDINATION.
AND DO THIS WITH YOUR LIPS.
TODAY I FOCUSED MY RESOURCES ON ADDING VALUE TO THE PRODUCT PROCESS. OUR SHARE-HOLDERS WOULD BE DELIGHTED TO KNOW THAT.
S. Adams
12/27/97 © 1997 United Feature Syndicate, Inc.

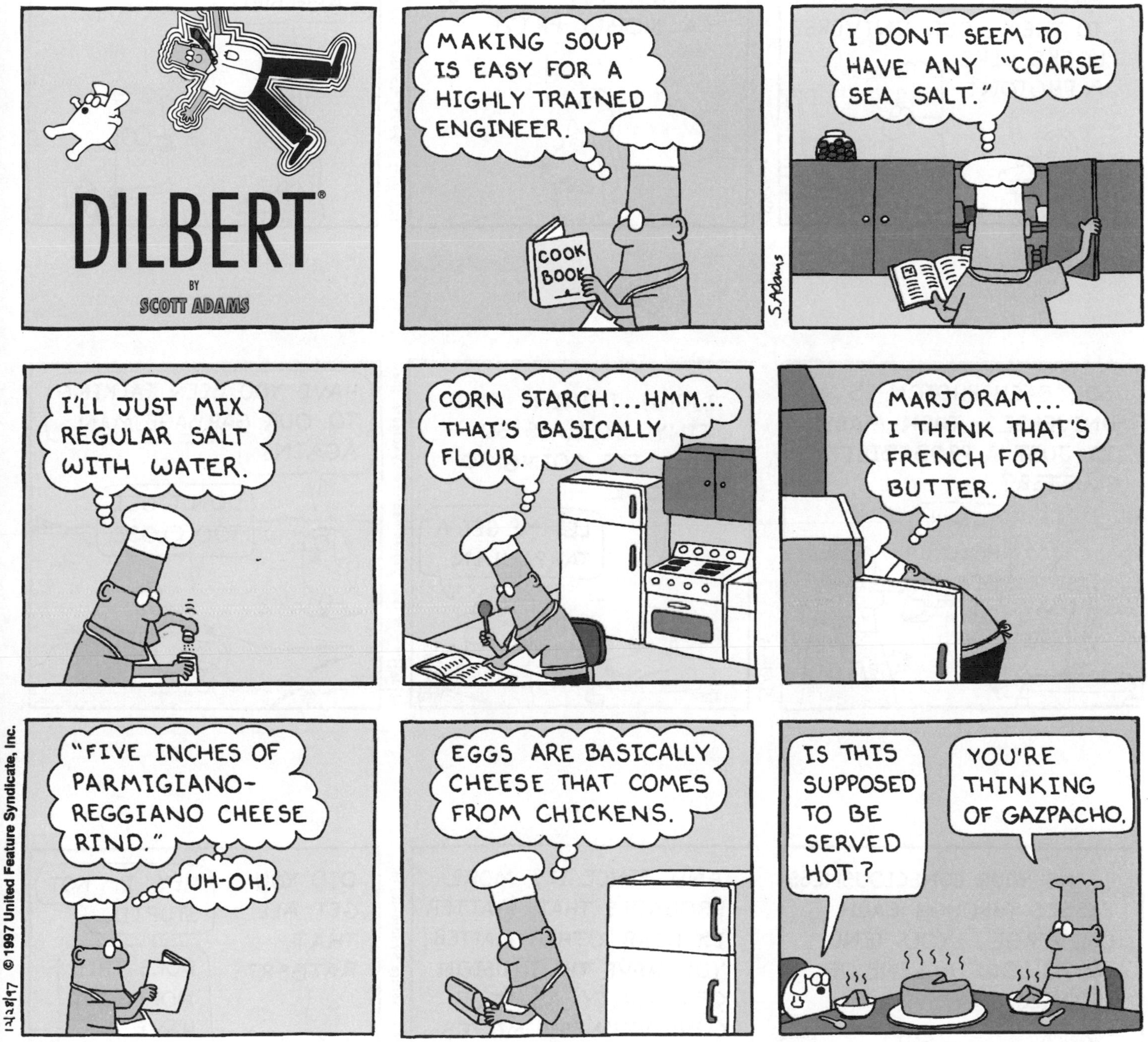
DILBERT®
BY
SCOTT ADAMS
MAKING SOUP IS EASY FOR A HIGHLY TRAINED ENGINEER.
COOK BOOK
I DON'T SEEM TO HAVE ANY "COARSE SEA SALT."
S. Adams
I'LL JUST MIX REGULAR SALT WITH WATER.
CORN STARCH...HMM... THAT'S BASICALLY FLOUR.
MARJORAM... I THINK THAT'S FRENCH FOR BUTTER.
"FIVE INCHES OF PARMIGIANO-REGGIANO CHEESE RIND."
UH-OH.
EGGS ARE BASICALLY CHEESE THAT COMES FROM CHICKENS.
IS THIS SUPPOSED TO BE SERVED HOT?
YOU'RE THINKING OF GAZPACHO.
12/28/97 © 1997 United Feature Syndicate, Inc.

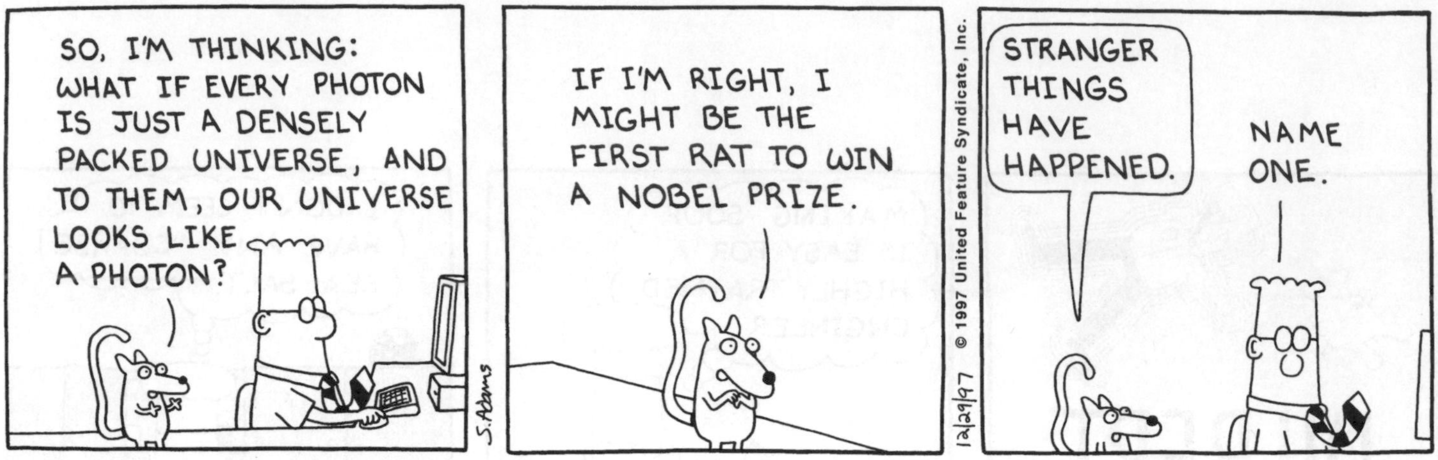
SO, I'M THINKING: WHAT IF EVERY PHOTON IS JUST A DENSELY PACKED UNIVERSE, AND TO THEM, OUR UNIVERSE LOOKS LIKE A PHOTON?
S. Adams
IF I'M RIGHT, I MIGHT BE THE FIRST RAT TO WIN A NOBEL PRIZE.
12/29/97 © 1997 United Feature Syndicate, Inc.
STRANGER THINGS HAVE HAPPENED.
NAME ONE.

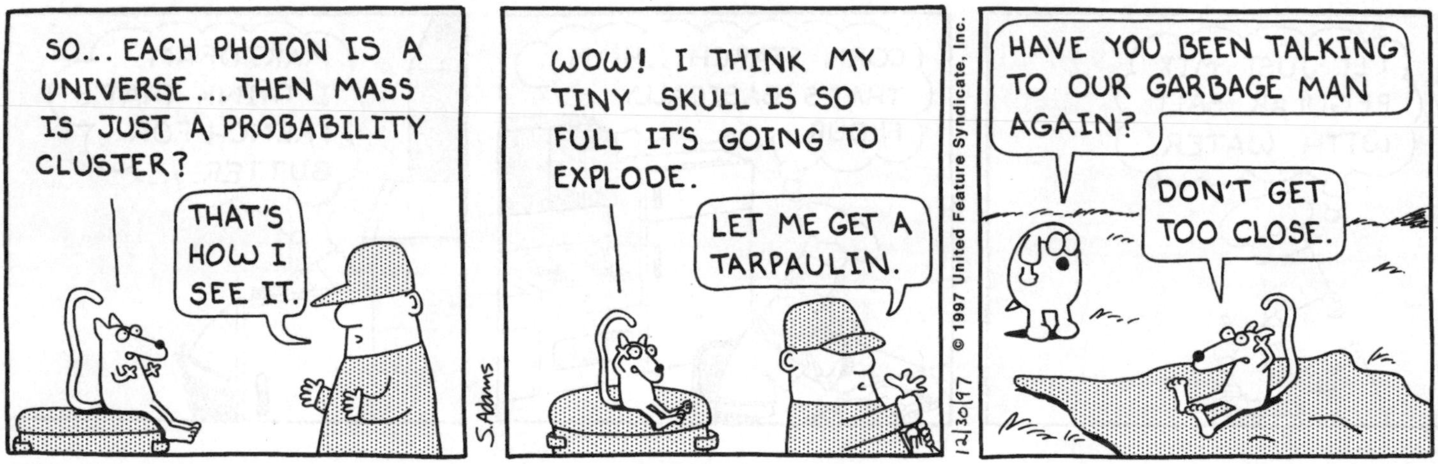
SO... EACH PHOTON IS A UNIVERSE... THEN MASS IS JUST A PROBABILITY CLUSTER?
THAT'S HOW I SEE IT.
S. Adams
WOW! I THINK MY TINY SKULL IS SO FULL IT'S GOING TO EXPLODE.
LET ME GET A TARPAULIN.
12/30/97 © 1997 United Feature Syndicate, Inc.
HAVE YOU BEEN TALKING TO OUR GARBAGE MAN AGAIN?
DON'T GET TOO CLOSE.

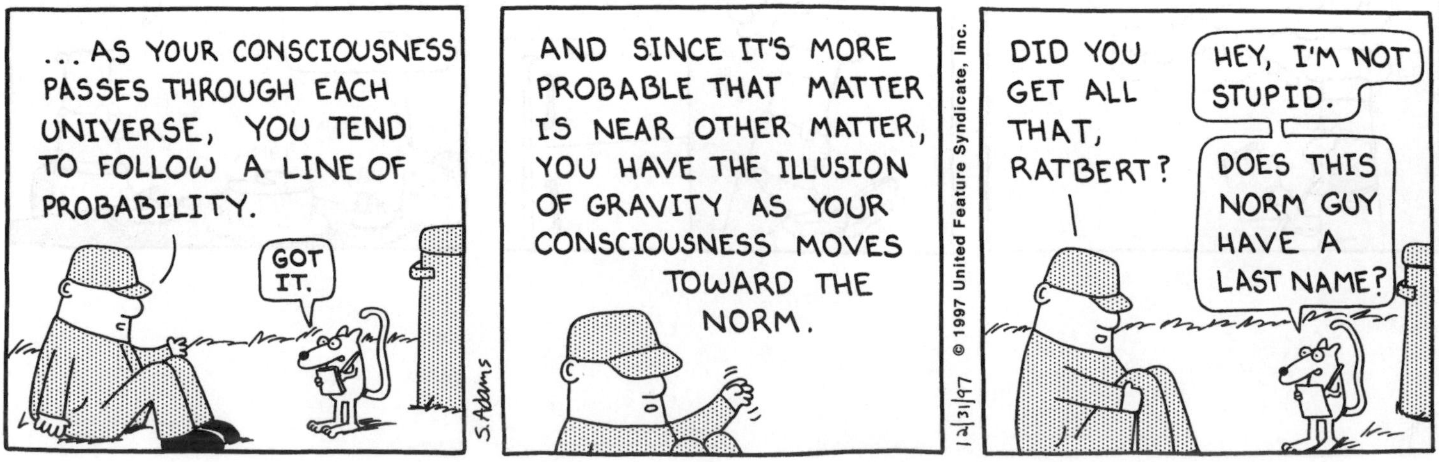
... AS YOUR CONSCIOUSNESS PASSES THROUGH EACH UNIVERSE, YOU TEND TO FOLLOW A LINE OF PROBABILITY.
GOT IT.
S. Adams
AND SINCE IT'S MORE PROBABLE THAT MATTER IS NEAR OTHER MATTER, YOU HAVE THE ILLUSION OF GRAVITY AS YOUR CONSCIOUSNESS MOVES TOWARD THE NORM.
12/31/97 © 1997 United Feature Syndicate, Inc.
DID YOU GET ALL THAT, RATBERT?
HEY, I'M NOT STUPID.
DOES THIS NORM GUY HAVE A LAST NAME?

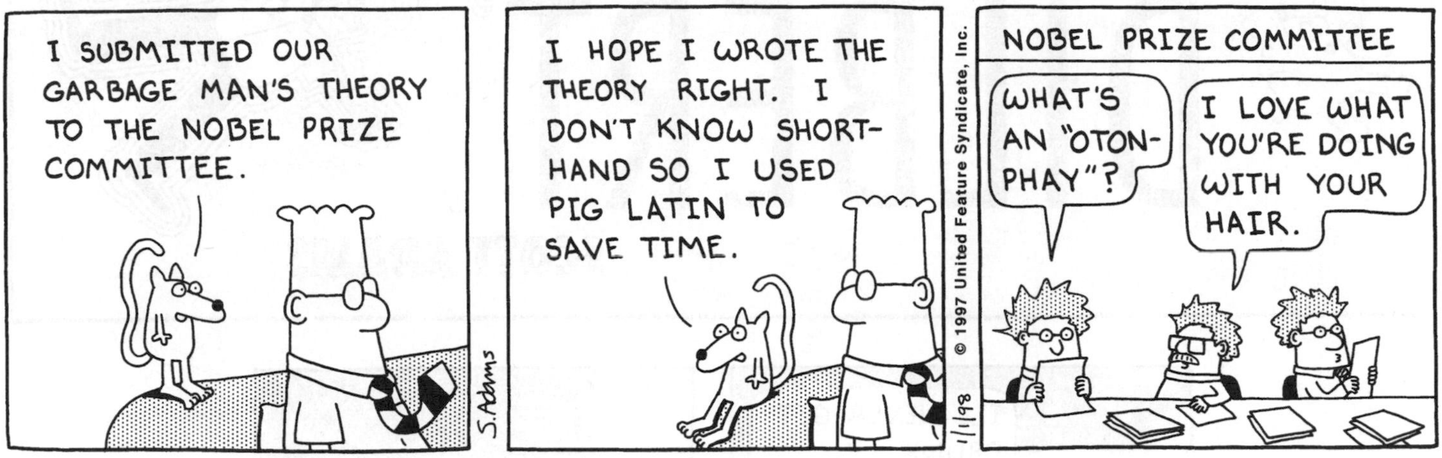
I SUBMITTED OUR GARBAGE MAN'S THEORY TO THE NOBEL PRIZE COMMITTEE.
S. Adams
I HOPE I WROTE THE THEORY RIGHT. I DON'T KNOW SHORT-HAND SO I USED PIG LATIN TO SAVE TIME.
1/1/98 © 1997 United Feature Syndicate, Inc.
NOBEL PRIZE COMMITTEE
WHAT'S AN "OTON-PHAY"?
I LOVE WHAT YOU'RE DOING WITH YOUR HAIR.

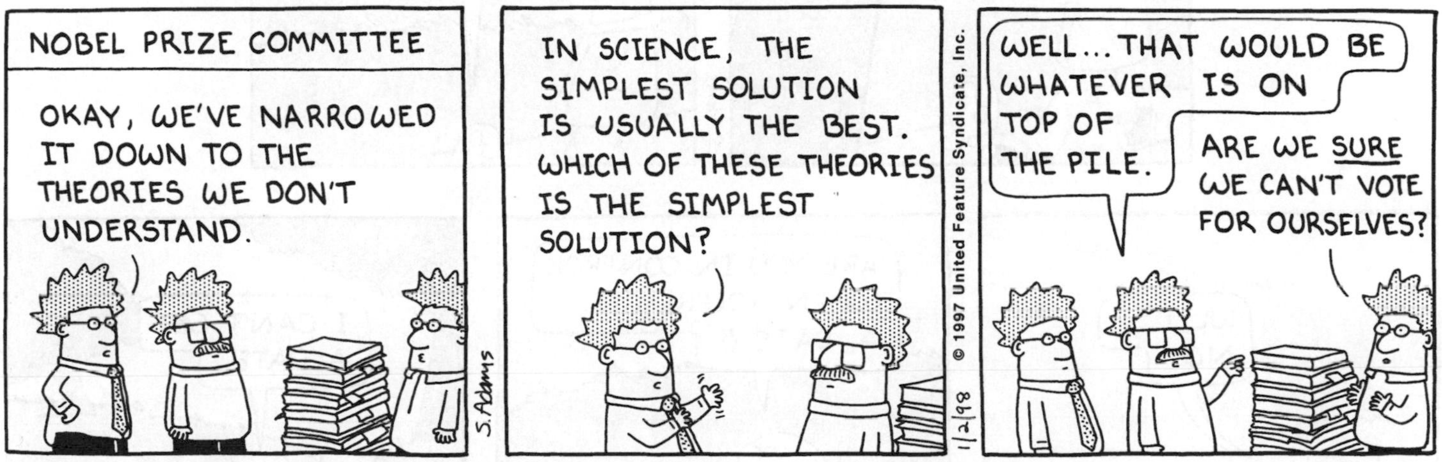
NOBEL PRIZE COMMITTEE
OKAY, WE'VE NARROWED IT DOWN TO THE THEORIES WE DON'T UNDERSTAND.
S. Adams
IN SCIENCE, THE SIMPLEST SOLUTION IS USUALLY THE BEST. WHICH OF THESE THEORIES IS THE SIMPLEST SOLUTION?
1/2/98 © 1997 United Feature Syndicate, Inc.
WELL... THAT WOULD BE WHATEVER IS ON TOP OF THE PILE.
ARE WE SURE WE CAN'T VOTE FOR OURSELVES?

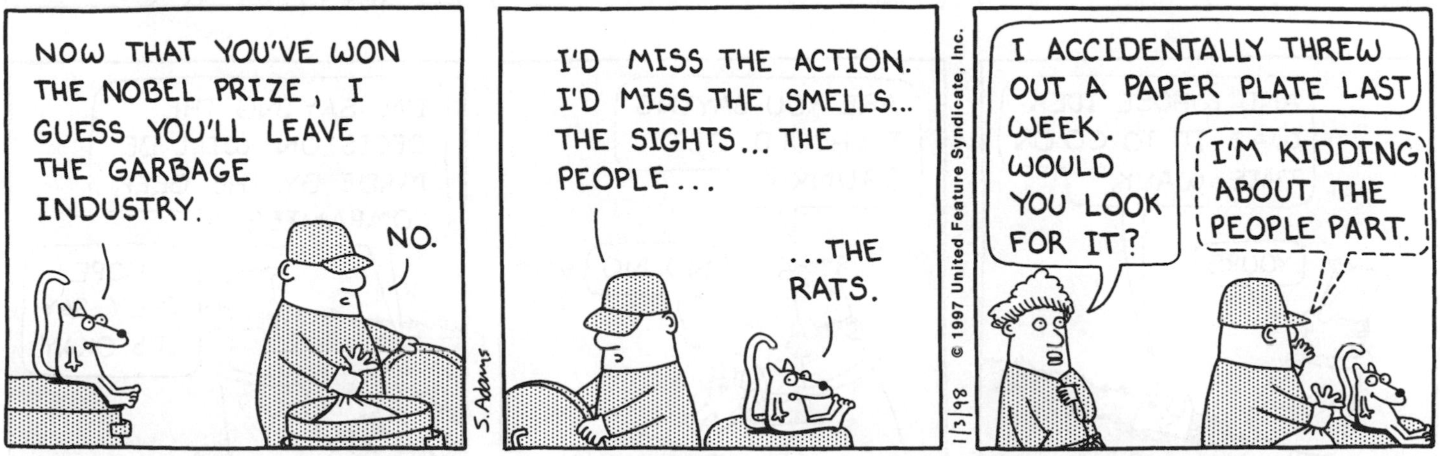
NOW THAT YOU'VE WON THE NOBEL PRIZE, I GUESS YOU'LL LEAVE THE GARBAGE INDUSTRY.
NO.
S. Adams
I'D MISS THE ACTION. I'D MISS THE SMELLS... THE SIGHTS... THE PEOPLE...
...THE RATS.
1/3/98 © 1997 United Feature Syndicate, Inc.
I ACCIDENTALLY THREW OUT A PAPER PLATE LAST WEEK. WOULD YOU LOOK FOR IT?
I'M KIDDING ABOUT THE PEOPLE PART.

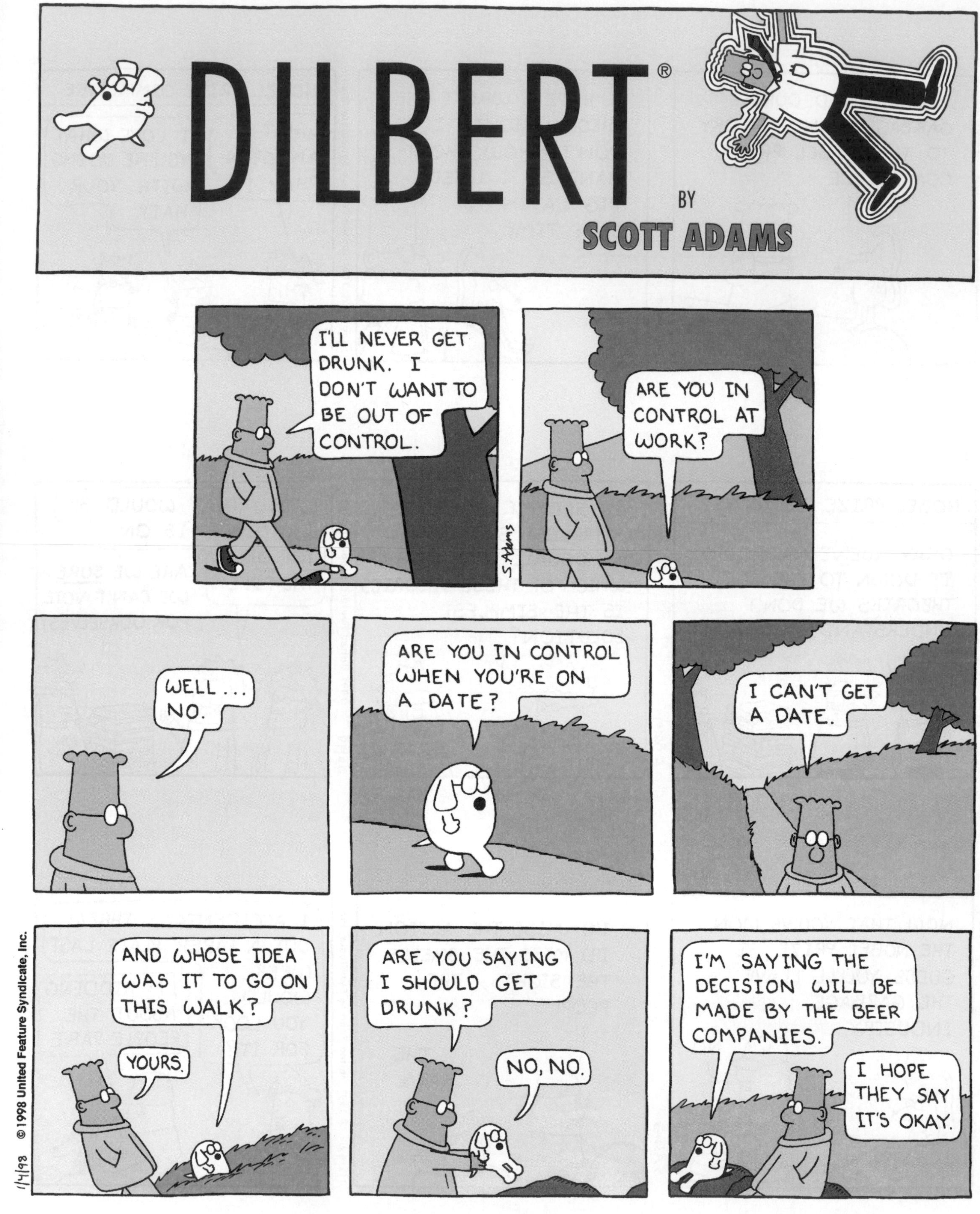
DILBERT®
BY
SCOTT ADAMS
I'LL NEVER GET DRUNK. I DON'T WANT TO BE OUT OF CONTROL.
ARE YOU IN CONTROL AT WORK?
WELL ... NO.
ARE YOU IN CONTROL WHEN YOU'RE ON A DATE?
I CAN'T GET A DATE.
AND WHOSE IDEA WAS IT TO GO ON THIS WALK?
YOURS.
ARE YOU SAYING I SHOULD GET DRUNK?
NO, NO.
I'M SAYING THE DECISION WILL BE MADE BY THE BEER COMPANIES.
I HOPE THEY SAY IT'S OKAY.
S. Adams
1/4/98 © 1998 United Feature Syndicate, Inc.

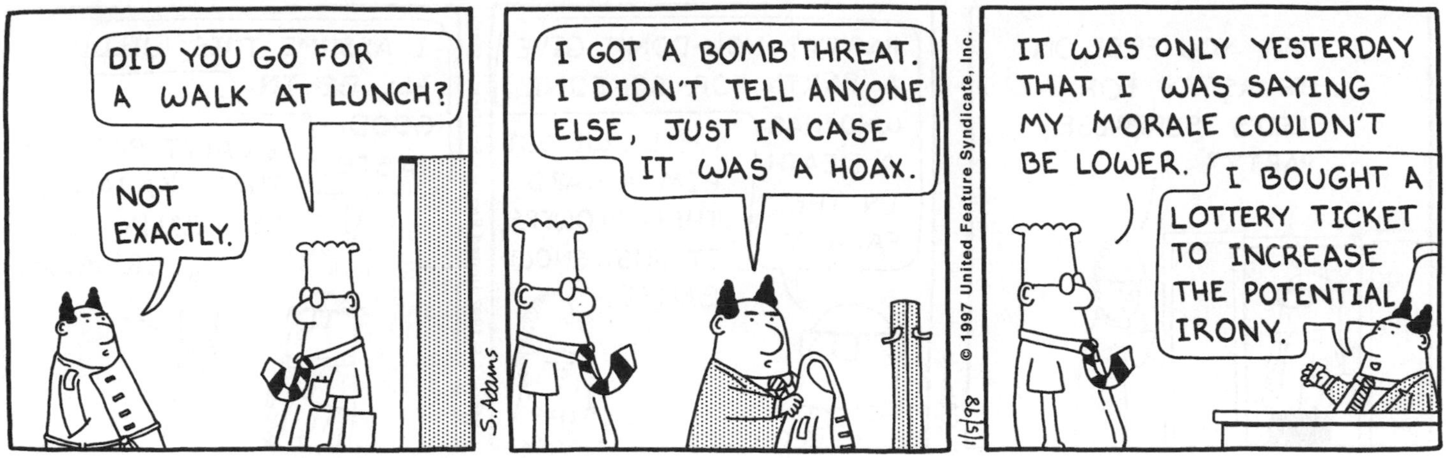
DID YOU GO FOR A WALK AT LUNCH?
NOT EXACTLY.
S. Adams
I GOT A BOMB THREAT. I DIDN'T TELL ANYONE ELSE, JUST IN CASE IT WAS A HOAX.
© 1997 United Feature Syndicate, Inc.
1/5/98
IT WAS ONLY YESTERDAY THAT I WAS SAYING MY MORALE COULDN'T BE LOWER.
I BOUGHT A LOTTERY TICKET TO INCREASE THE POTENTIAL IRONY.

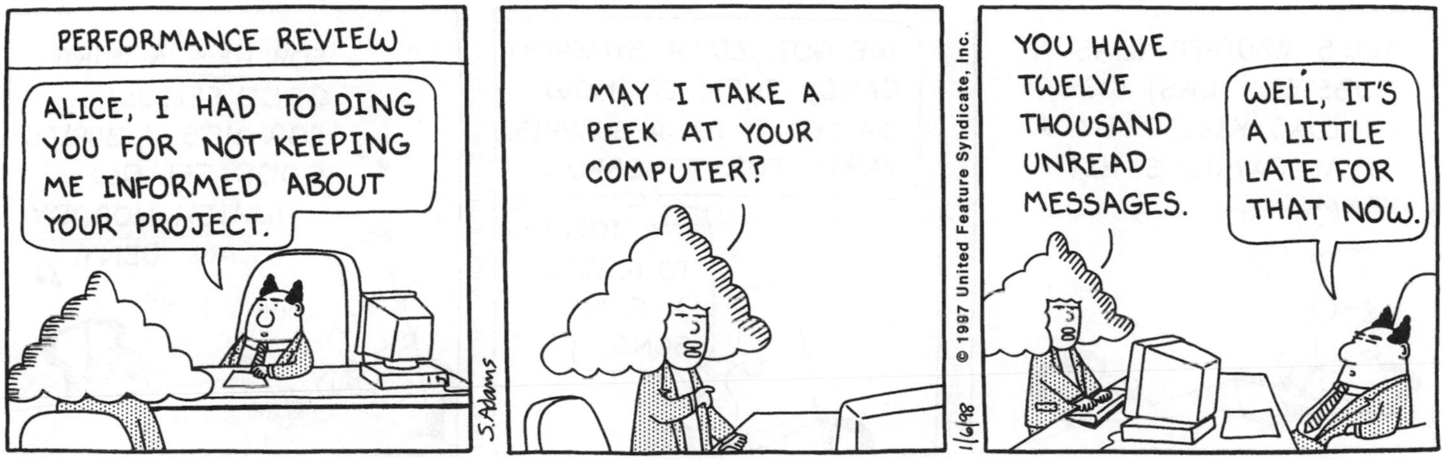
PERFORMANCE REVIEW
ALICE, I HAD TO DING YOU FOR NOT KEEPING ME INFORMED ABOUT YOUR PROJECT.
S. Adams
MAY I TAKE A PEEK AT YOUR COMPUTER?
© 1997 United Feature Syndicate, Inc.
1/6/98
YOU HAVE TWELVE THOUSAND UNREAD MESSAGES.
WELL, IT'S A LITTLE LATE FOR THAT NOW.

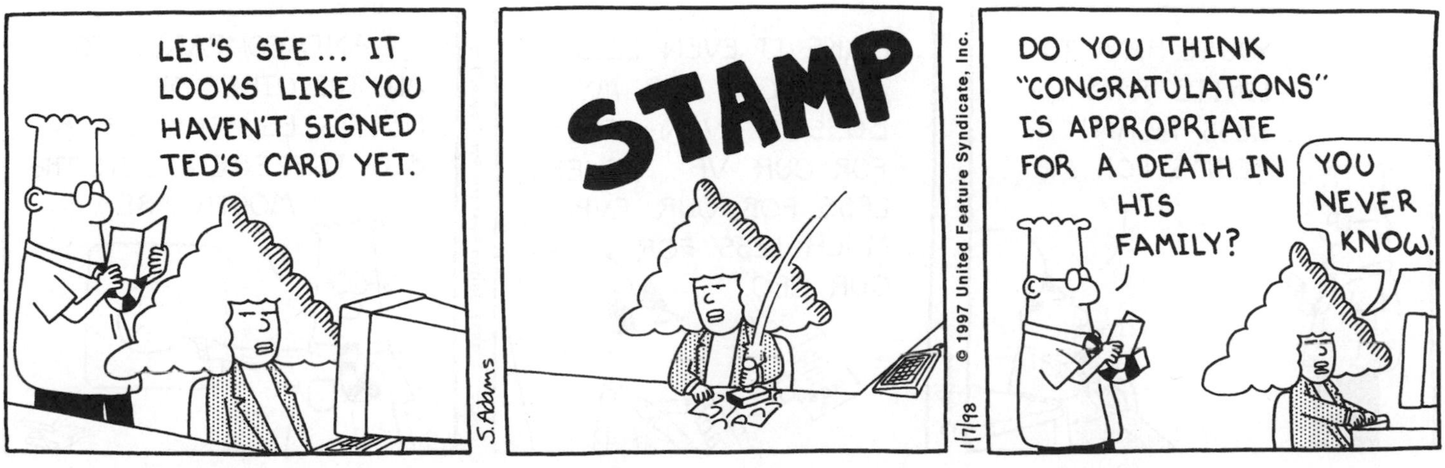
LET'S SEE... IT LOOKS LIKE YOU HAVEN'T SIGNED TED'S CARD YET.
S. Adams
STAMP
© 1997 United Feature Syndicate, Inc.
1/7/98
DO YOU THINK "CONGRATULATIONS" IS APPROPRIATE FOR A DEATH IN HIS FAMILY?
YOU NEVER KNOW.

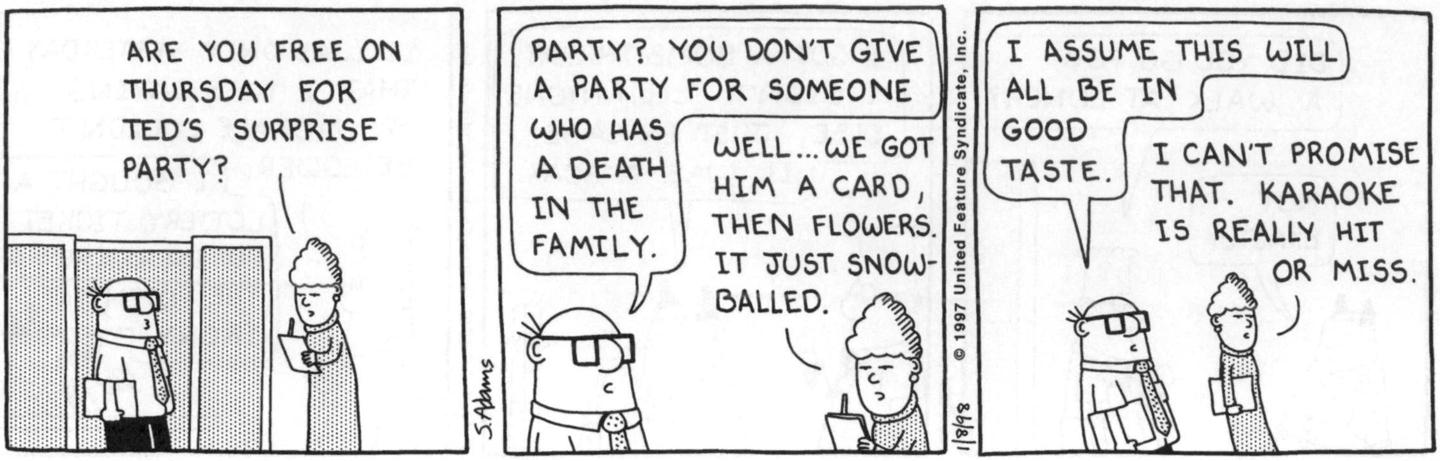
ARE YOU FREE ON THURSDAY FOR TED'S SURPRISE PARTY?
PARTY? YOU DON'T GIVE A PARTY FOR SOMEONE WHO HAS A DEATH IN THE FAMILY.
WELL... WE GOT HIM A CARD, THEN FLOWERS. IT JUST SNOW-BALLED.
I ASSUME THIS WILL ALL BE IN GOOD TASTE.
I CAN'T PROMISE THAT. KARAOKE IS REALLY HIT OR MISS.
S. Adams
1/8/98
© 1997 United Feature Syndicate, Inc.

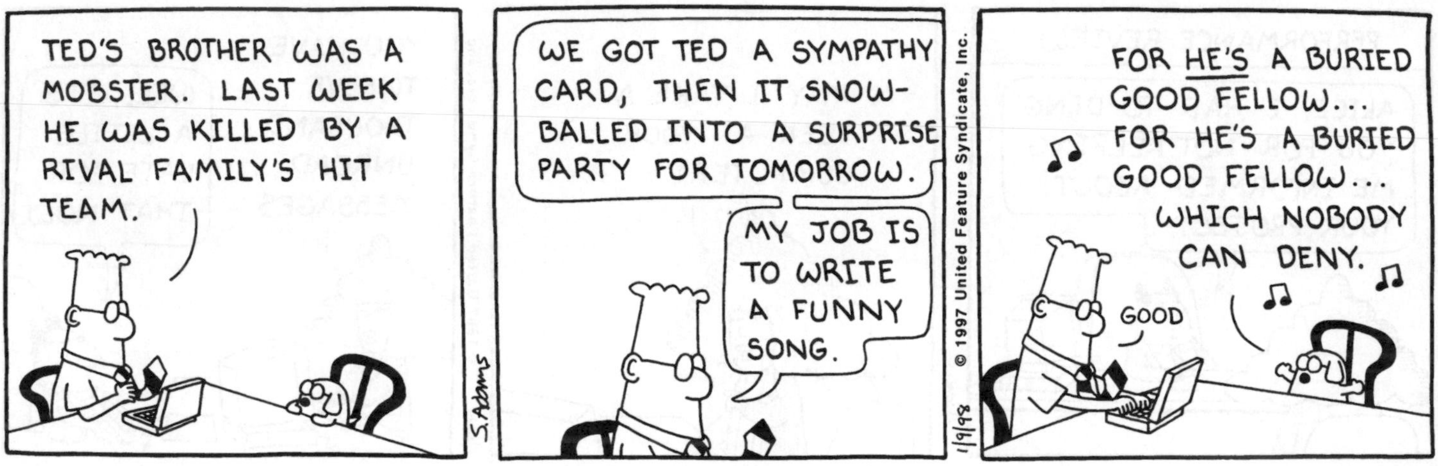
TED'S BROTHER WAS A MOBSTER. LAST WEEK HE WAS KILLED BY A RIVAL FAMILY'S HIT TEAM.
WE GOT TED A SYMPATHY CARD, THEN IT SNOW-BALLED INTO A SURPRISE PARTY FOR TOMORROW.
MY JOB IS TO WRITE A FUNNY SONG.
FOR HE'S A BURIED GOOD FELLOW... FOR HE'S A BURIED GOOD FELLOW... WHICH NOBODY CAN DENY.
GOOD
S. Adams
1/9/98
© 1997 United Feature Syndicate, Inc.

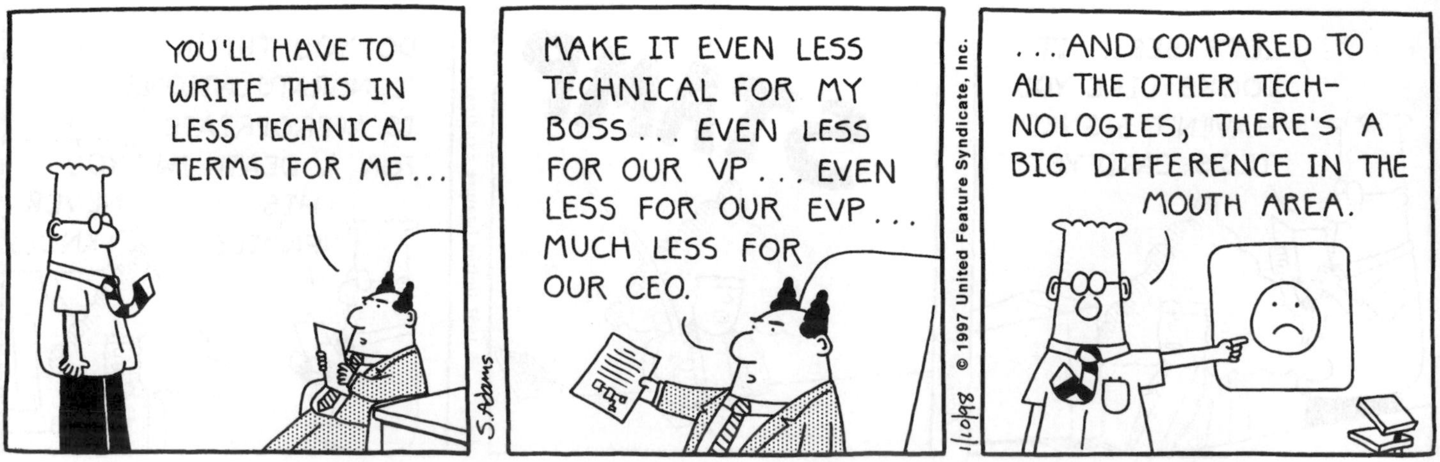
YOU'LL HAVE TO WRITE THIS IN LESS TECHNICAL TERMS FOR ME...
MAKE IT EVEN LESS TECHNICAL FOR MY BOSS... EVEN LESS FOR OUR VP... EVEN LESS FOR OUR EVP... MUCH LESS FOR OUR CEO.
...AND COMPARED TO ALL THE OTHER TECH-NOLOGIES, THERE'S A BIG DIFFERENCE IN THE MOUTH AREA.
S. Adams
1/10/98
© 1997 United Feature Syndicate, Inc.

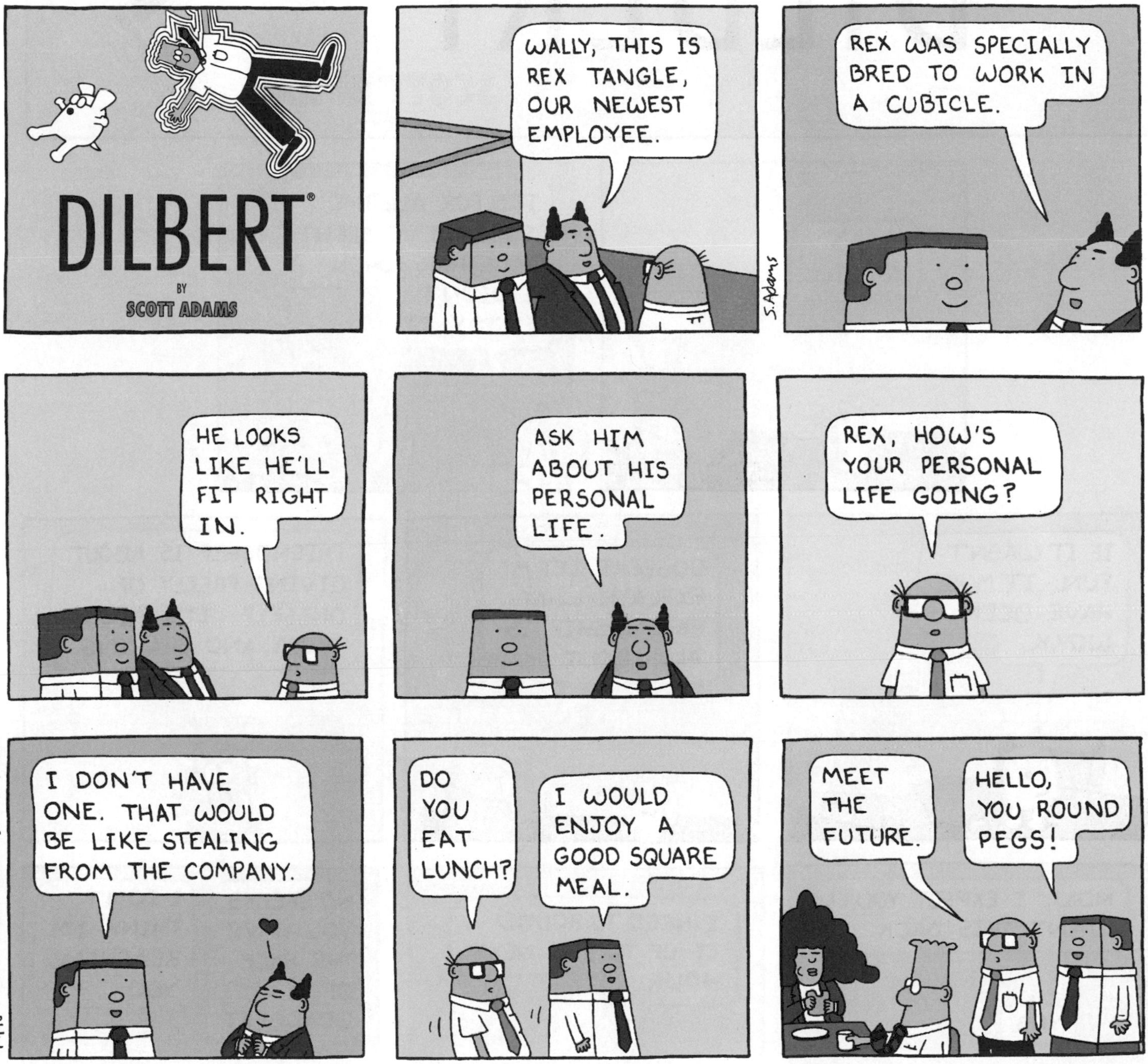
DILBERT®
BY
SCOTT ADAMS
WALLY, THIS IS REX TANGLE, OUR NEWEST EMPLOYEE.
S. Adams
REX WAS SPECIALLY BRED TO WORK IN A CUBICLE.
HE LOOKS LIKE HE'LL FIT RIGHT IN.
ASK HIM ABOUT HIS PERSONAL LIFE.
REX, HOW'S YOUR PERSONAL LIFE GOING?
I DON'T HAVE ONE. THAT WOULD BE LIKE STEALING FROM THE COMPANY.
DO YOU EAT LUNCH?
I WOULD ENJOY A GOOD SQUARE MEAL.
MEET THE FUTURE.
HELLO, YOU ROUND PEGS!

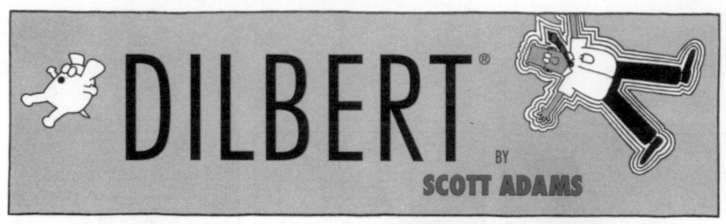

DILBERT®
BY
SCOTT ADAMS
HERE'S MY BILL.
IT'S FOR ALL THE TIME WE'VE SPENT TOGETHER WHEN I DIDN'T ENJOY IT.
S. Adams
IF IT WASN'T FUN, IT MUST HAVE BEEN WORK.
DOGBERT, LET ME EXPLAIN WHAT FRIENDSHIP IS ALL ABOUT.
FRIENDSHIP IS ABOUT GIVING FREELY OF ONESELF. IT'S ABOUT TRUST AND SHARING.
NOW, I EXPECT YOU'LL WANT THIS BACK.
YES.
I NEED TO ROUND IT UP TO THE NEXT HOUR.
NO CHECKS. YOU HAVE THE FACE OF A DEADBEAT.
I DON'T THINK I'M REACHING YOU.
1/18/98 © 1998 United Feature Syndicate, Inc.

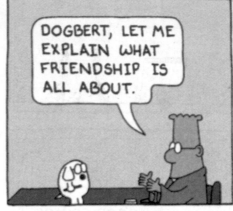

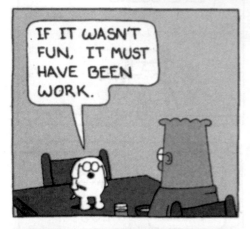

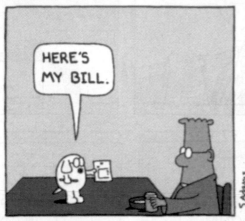

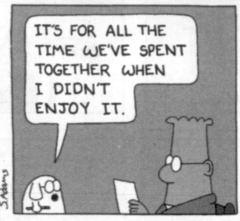

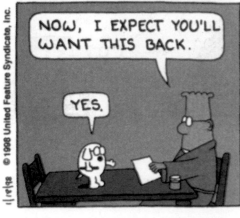

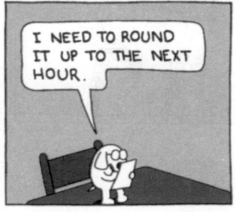

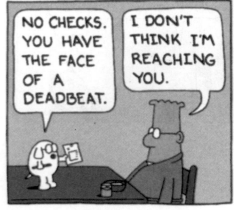